# INTERCONNECTED WORLDS

## Innovation and Technology in the World Economy

MARTIN KENNEY, EDITOR
  University of California, Davis and Berkeley
  Roundtable on the International Economy

# Interconnected Worlds

## GLOBAL ELECTRONICS AND PRODUCTION NETWORKS IN EAST ASIA

Henry Wai-chung Yeung

STANFORD BUSINESS BOOKS
An Imprint of Stanford University Press
Stanford, California

STANFORD UNIVERSITY PRESS
Stanford, California

Special discounts for bulk quantities of Stanford Business Books are available to corporations, professional associations, and other organizations. For details and discount information, contact the special sales department of Stanford University Press. Tel: (650) 725-0820, Fax: (650) 725-3457

Printed in the United States of America on acid-free, archival-quality paper

Library of Congress Cataloging-in-Publication Data

Names: Yeung, Henry Wai-chung, author.
Title: Interconnected worlds : global electronics and production networks in East Asia / Henry Wai-chung Yeung.
Other titles: Innovation and technology in the world economy.
Description: Stanford, California : Stanford Business Books, an Imprint of Stanford University Press, 2022. | Series: Innovation and technology in the world economy | Includes bibliographical references and index.
Identifiers: LCCN 2021043940 (print) | LCCN 2021043941 (ebook) | ISBN 9781503615298 (cloth) | ISBN 9781503632226 (paperback) | ISBN 9781503632233 (ebook)
Subjects: LCSH: Electronic industries—East Asia. | Globalization—Economic aspects—East Asia. | Business networks—East Asia.
Classification: LCC HD9696.A3 Y48 2022 (print) | LCC HD9696.A3 (ebook) | DDC 338.4/7621381095—dc23
LC record available at https://lccn.loc.gov/2021043940
LC ebook record available at https://lccn.loc.gov/2021043941

Cover art: Shutterstock | Eugenius777
Cover design: Tandem Design
Typeset by Newgen in Galliard 10/14

*For Yeung Ching Kwong, my late father*
*and Peter Dicken, my mentor and fatherly figure*

# Contents

# Illustrations

**Tables**

# Preface

The global electronics industry—"global electronics" in short—is certainly one of the most innovation-driven and technology-intensive sectors in the contemporary world economy. The COVID-19 pandemic in 2020 and 2021 made us all deeply aware of the critical importance of various electronic devices in supporting our remote work, learning, and daily life, and their intricate production across the world. Indeed, global electronics is characterized by organizationally fragmented and geographically dispersed production networks. Many devices and products in today's information and communications technology (ICT) sector are developed and manufactured in several macroregions and yet sold worldwide in all end markets. From semiconductor chips powering these devices to end products such as personal computers, smartphones, and televisions, complex transnational production and value-generating activities—coordinated by lead firms through their in-house facilities and/or outsourced partners around the world—have integrated diverse macroregions and national economies worldwide into what might be termed the "interconnected worlds" of global electronics.

Using the motif of "worlds" to describe the predominant model(s) of organizing electronics production, I argue that the current era of interconnected worlds started in the early 1990s when electronics production moved from the multinational worlds of innovation and production systems dominated by domestic lead firms in the US, Western Europe, and Japan toward increasingly globalized and cross-macroregional worlds of electronics manufacturing centered in East Asia—a large region comprising Northeast Asia (e.g., China, Japan, South Korea, and Taiwan) and Southeast Asia (e.g., Indonesia, Malaysia, Singapore, and Vietnam). Over time and as more electronics manufacturing shifted toward key locations in East Asia, lead firms in the US, Western Europe, and Japan remained dominant in technological innovation and product development. By the 2010s, the book's main focus, this coevolution of production network complexity and interconnectedness led to a transformative shift in global electronics through which lead firms from South Korea, Taiwan, and China emerged as key players by integrating their home macroregion—East Asia—into these interconnected worlds of global electronics production comprising predominantly the US, East Asia, and Europe.

This monograph describes and explains this coevolution of globalized electronics production centered in East Asia during the 2010s. To date, a significant body of literature has been written about the historical development of the electronics industry in specific national economies. But very few of these scholarly studies have extended their analytical coverage to the 2010s, the decade in which East Asian economies and lead firms became dominant in electronics manufacturing. In theoretical terms, this work also differs substantively from most earlier academic studies of the electronics industry, as I do not focus on individual national economies and industrial transformation *within* them—I have previously published a monograph taking this international political economy approach to industrial transformation in East Asia (*Strategic Coupling*, Cornell University Press, 2016). Contributing to cutting-edge social science debates on global production networks and global value chains, my theoretical framing in this book is premised on a *network* approach that examines intrafirm and interfirm production activities across different national economies and subnational regions. Understanding the innovative organization of these firm-specific activities in the form of global production networks, in turn, allows us to appreciate better the evolving complexity of the interconnected worlds of global electronics. This conceptual approach extends my earlier theoretical work in *Global Production Networks* (with Neil Coe, Oxford University Press, 2015).

In a nutshell then, this work is meant to be a theory-driven analysis of electronics global production networks. My main goal is to develop the idea of global production networks as innovative organizational platforms that connect different and yet interdependent "worlds" of production (e.g., from technological innovation in Silicon Valley to innovation and production in East Asia) and to demonstrate how the theory of global production networks, known as "GPN 2.0" in Coe and Yeung (2015), can be productively applied to explain these organizational dynamics in global electronics. The book thus offers an industrial-organizational analysis of *where*, *how*, and *why* electronics global production networks operate, from a social science perspective. It is neither a detailed history of the development of any of its four major industry segments (semiconductors, personal computers, mobile handsets, and consumer electronics/TVs), nor a country-level study of these segments and national competitiveness per se. In this sense, it certainly goes beyond an industry analysis or a country study.

The book's main contribution should ideally be read as one that illustrates empirically the geographical configurations ("where"), organizational strategies ("how"), and causal drivers ("why") of electronics global production networks throughout the 2010s. This most contemporary decade can be characterized by much more complex worlds of electronics production—coordinated by lead firms from the US, East Asia, and Western Europe, underpinned by significant US-origin technologies and knowhow, and yet co-constituted by East Asia–based manufacturing facilities and firm-specific capabilities. This main focus on unpacking and explaining the organizational dynamics of electronics production networks in East Asia also means that the book has much less to say about broader economic development issues, such as labor, industrial upgrading, environment, and the state (politics and policies). But my focus on the "network box" and its underlying causal dynamics will be relevant for those development scholars interested in the unequal and contentious consequences for localities and subnational regions that are "plugged" into or strategically coupled with these production networks.

While adopting the global production networks theory, this book primarily takes on an *empirical focus* through its wide-ranging analysis of global electronics throughout the 2010s. This analysis is underpinned by substantial new empirical material based on a custom dataset and personal interviews. First, I have acquired from IHS Markit/Informa Tech comprehensive proprietary data at the firm and component levels in the four major segments of global electronics (covering up to 2019 Q3): semiconductors, personal computers, mobile handsets, and consumer electronics (TVs). This custom material also includes highly detailed quantitative data on key electronics production networks in 2015 and 2018. Acknowledging semiconductors' distinctiveness as critical intermediate goods for ICT end products and their capital-intensive production networks, my empirical discussion in all chapters will follow the same logical order—starting with semiconductors before going into such end products as personal computers, mobile handsets, and TVs. Second, my qualitative dataset is derived from 64 interviews with senior executives of 44 lead firms in these four segments. All interviews were conducted between 2017 and 2018 in various locations in East Asia—Singapore, Taiwan, South Korea, and China. Through the in-depth analysis of this new and complementary material, the book's empirical chapters demonstrate where these electronics production networks operated throughout the 2010s, how they were organized in innovative ways, and why their pivot toward East Asia could be explained by several causal drivers and risk mitigation conceptualized in the GPN 2.0 theory.

The incredible and unexpected world events during the late 2019 to 2021 period, however, have added a major twist to my book's empirical analysis and potential use for future research, education, and policy. While I originally had the ongoing US-China trade conflicts in mind during the manuscript preparation starting in the second half of 2019, empirical events linked to the devastating COVID-19 pandemic since early 2020 have now clearly upended the world's expectations on the future of economic globalization and cross-border production networks in *all* industries and economic sectors. I believe there are very challenging policy implications and academic research agendas arising from these massive disruptions on a global scale during and after the pandemic. Where appropriate, I bring some of these current events and issues to the fore throughout the book and address them more fully in the concluding chapter. To some skeptical readers, though, it might be tempting to dismiss this book's empirical observations on the interconnected worlds of global electronics up to the late 2010s and their relevance for the postpandemic world economy in the 2020s. My sense is that much of the current discussion of global supply chain restructuring and national economic resilience in the public domain remains rather speculative and cursory due to the highly uncertain nature of these latest developments associated with the pandemic and ongoing geopolitical tensions (e.g., the US-China trade war since March 2018 and its likely refashioning in the post-Trump era under the Biden administration). Solid and complete up-to-date empirical data are rare in these media reports and business analyses—they are simply very hard to collect due to the widespread travel and social restrictions in 2020 and 2021!

While I am able to update some empirical material to 2020/2021 based on data releases up to July 2021 (finalization of manuscript), I believe the book's comprehensive analysis of global electronics production networks up to the late 2010s can serve as a definitive benchmark for future academic and policy research into the dynamic transformations in global electronics and, perhaps, other manufacturing industries. My book can also be a standard baseline reference for post-2020 empirical studies of global economic change. Some of these studies can be found in the current research on "COVID-19: what's next in the world economy?" and the "deglobalization/decoupling" literature focusing on the reshoring of manufacturing back to advanced countries and the disintegration of China-centered production networks. Future empirical research in different academic disciplines can certainly take advantage of this book's novel empirical material on intra- and interfirm networks in all major segments of global electronics that "ends" at a relatively high point in the globalization of electronics production in 2018/2019—an all-time high in both shipment and markets of semiconductors and mobile handsets, and near peak in personal computers and televisions. I believe these future comparative studies will very likely appreciate how the interconnected worlds of global electronics in the technology, production, and market domains are rather enduring and cannot be easily replaced by the politically motivated decoupling and reshoring initiatives that might seem fashionable in today's highly contentious world.

# Acknowledgments

This book would not be possible without the extremely generous US$4 million strategic grant (R109000183646) awarded by the National University of Singapore that enabled me, as principal investigator, and my co-PI and codirector Neil Coe to establish the Global Production Networks Centre (GPN@NUS) in October 2014. I am most grateful to our founding team members from departments of Geography (Karen Lai and Godfrey Yeung), Economics (Davin Chor, Albert Hu, and Jang-Sup Shin), Political Science (Soo Yeon Kim), and Sociology (Kurtuluş Gemici and Solee Shin) for their collective wisdom and efforts in making GPN@NUS a successful intellectual hub. Under the Centre's auspices and funding support, I acquired the costly custom dataset to the tune of several hundred thousand dollars and conducted the multilocation empirical research on global electronics that underpins this book's core analysis. In particular, I thank our Centre's former research assistants, Aloysius Chia and Lydia Jiang, for their excellent research support and arrangements for interviews in Singapore and other locations throughout East Asia. Carlo Inverardi-Ferri, postdoctoral fellow in the electronics group, also provided outstanding field support and independent work. Graduate student Tan Xuan Kai conducted additional database research. Many thanks also to Dione Ng, our outstanding Centre manager, for holding us together and making the Centre's activities—both academic and social—highly enjoyable and sustainable! Finally, I appreciate much the intellectual support for this project over the years by several of our International Advisory Committee members—Yuqing Xing, Gary Gereffi, and Stefano Ponte.

While conducting the extensive empirical fieldwork in East Asia during 2017 and 2018, I benefitted enormously from the wonderful hospitality of my great friends, Weidong Liu (Beijing) and Jinn-yuh Hsu (Taipei). Their comradeship over several decades made my many trips to China and Taiwan much less daunting than otherwise. Other colleagues and friends in Seoul (Keun Lee and Bae-Gyoon Park) and Beijing (Mick Dunford, Canfei He, and Shengjun Zhu) also kept me well informed and entertained during these research trips. Among the many senior executives interviewed for this project, I am particularly grateful to several of them for rendering me their utmost support and firm-specific material: Goran Malm, Younghee Lee, and Ben Suh (Samsung Electronics), Keith Miears (Dell), Feng Zhang (Xiaomi), Tien Wu (ASE), and John Waite (Micron). My ex-neighbor, the late Bruno Guilmart (former CEO of Kulicke & Soffa and independent director of Avago/Broadcom) taught me much about the global semiconductor industry leisurely over red wine at his home next door; we also shared a strong penchant for the same Italian marque founded in Bologna (made in its Modena headquarter factory)!

Some chapter material has been presented in various invited lectures, scholarly workshops, and academic conferences just before and during the COVID-19 pandemic. I am very thankful to these scholars for organizing these events and/or commenting on my work: Giulio Buciuni, Dieter Kogler, Gary Gereffi, and Ram Mudambi (Global Value Chains Workshop, Trinity Business School, Ireland, May 2–3, 2019); Jana Maria Kleibert and Oliver Ibert (Berlin Economic Geography Lecture, Humboldt University, Germany, May 20, 2019); Weidong Liu (Renowned Scholars Lecture, Chinese Academy of Sciences, Beijing, China, September 17, 2019); Keun Lee, John Mathews, Tariq Malik, Elizabeth Thurbon, and Linda Weiss (the Laboratory Program for Korean Study Workshop on "Comparative Perspective on Capitalism in East Asia," National University of Singapore, January 19, 2020); Dieter Kogler, Jennifer Clark, Andrés Rodríguez-Pose, Jim Murphy, Eric Sheppard, and Ron Boschma (Regional Studies Annual Lecture 2020, First Regional Studies Association Webinar, April 29, 2020); Anna Giunta, Valentina De Marchi, Rory Horner, and Joonkoo Lee (Global Value Chains session, Annual E-Meeting of the Society for the Advancement of Socio-Economics, August 18, 2020); Karen Lai and

Tom Kemeny (Regional Studies Association Global China Webinar, November 3, 2020); Liu Yi, Canfei He, and Charlotte Yang (Geographical Research Workshop on "Dynamics of Strategic Coupling and Global Production Networks in China," January 9, 2021); Paola Perez-Aleman (Featured Presidential Panel session on "Transformative Innovation and Grand Challenges," Annual E-Meeting of the Society for the Advancement of Socio-Economics, Amsterdam, the Netherlands, July 5, 2021); and Huiwen Gong, Robert Hassink, Christopher Foster, and Martin Hess (virtual session on "Globalisation in Reverse? Reconfiguring the Geographies of Value Chains and Production Networks," Annual Conference of the Royal Geographical Society, London, August 31, 2021).

Two occasions in 2019 deserve special mention and credits for engendering this book project. First, my sincere appreciation goes to Herald Van Der Linde, Head of Asia Equity at HSBC Hong Kong, who organized a special lunchtime talk by the GPN@NUS Centre, entitled "HSBC Local Insights: Global Production Networks in an Era of Trade Uncertainty," at Singapore's Fullerton Hotel on July 31, 2019. I presented some of the key findings in this study of global electronics to over thirty invited fund managers and financial analysts from leading investment banks and financial institutions. Right after the luncheon, Herald brought me and three other GPN@NUS founding members to the Government Investment Corporation of Singapore to meet with five senior vice presidents and several other senior executives and discuss further current issues in global production networks. From these two closed-door events, I gained much insight into the business relevance of my work and the subsequent book writing. The second event made me truly determined that this book was indeed viable and necessary. During the annual meeting of the American Association of Geographers at Washington DC, April 3–7, 2019, I ran into several geographer friends of global production networks research at the conference hotel bar one fateful night. They might not remember much about the session—blame it on the alcohol! But let me thank Martin Hess, Rory Horner, and Adrian Smith for their genuine (dis-)beliefs in this project that spurred me on. Of course, no good deed goes unpunished—they were duly asked to comment on my first full draft!

All these bring me to the most critical part of this book's existence and its global production—my editors, reviewers, and other professionals who collectively made it happen. First and foremost, tremendous credit and thanks should go to my two editors—Martin Kenney and Steve Catalano.

As editor of this Innovation and Technology in the World Economy Series, Martin's incredibly positive and swift response to my initial email in November 2019 made a world of difference! His continual support and insightful comments on the proposals, sample chapters, and full manuscripts throughout this project went well beyond his call of duty. At Stanford University Press, Steve was amazingly supportive and enthusiastic from day one. He was indeed an "author's editor," as I had read about him! I am very grateful for his expert advice and handling of the entire editorial process. Constructive comments and suggestions from two anonymous reviewers of my book proposal and three sample chapters and another three anonymous readers of the full manuscript in its two iterations are most appreciated. They certainly made the book much more streamlined and coherent. The usual disclaimer applies, though.

Among my dear friends of global production networks research, Neil Coe and Jim Murphy clearly stood out for their very close reading of the first full draft. My long-time good friend and GPN "partner in crime," Neil provided unparalleled insights into how the manuscript and my writing could be done better. I thank him especially for all the personal and intellectual support rendered over almost three decades since we first met in Manchester during our PhD days. Parts of Chapter 3 draw on our joint paper published earlier in *Economic Geography* (volume 91, 2015, ©Clark University). Jim Murphy, my fellow coeditor of *Economic Geography*, also offered very detailed chapter-by-chapter comments on the first draft. Taking on board most of his constructive comments made this book much more readable and useful. Further comments from Martin Hess, Rory Horner, and Charlotte Yang were very helpful in my revisions. My home department's retired cartographer, Lee Li Kheng, kindly helped with the maps included in this book, but blame me for their complexity and credit Li Kheng for her excellent professional drawing. Copyright permissions granted by Oxford University Press and Informa UK (Taylor & Francis) for reproducing several figures from my earlier joint work with Neil Coe are gratefully acknowledged.

My final but surely unpayable debt of gratitude goes to my family. Writing this book during a once-in-a-lifetime pandemic (hopefully!) was certainly extraordinary to say the least, and the prolonged period of work / learning-from-home made me much more appreciative of our loved ones! From completing the first draft in the first half of 2020 to its revisions in late 2020 and early 2021 and its finalization in mid-2021, I had unwavering support of my family. Losing my father in April 2020 due to illness unrelated to COVID was painful, though I managed to stay with him until the very end. My English dad and GPN guru in Manchester, Peter Dicken, was always encouraging, and our frequent video chats kept me focused on the project and, hopefully, distracted him from various lockdowns in the UK! I dedicate this book to both of them. To my wife, Weiyu, and children, Kay and Lucas, who witnessed the entire book's writing in the communal living area of our house, thank you for all the love, laughter, and forbearance.

*Henry Wai-chung Yeung*
home, Singapore
July 2021

# Abbreviations

APT—assembly, packaging, and testing
ASEAN—Association of Southeast Asian Nations
ASIC—application-specific integrated circuits
ASP—average selling price
AVAP—assigned vendor assigned price
Capex—capital expenditure
CMOS—complementary metal-oxide-semiconductor
CPU—central processing unit
DARPA—Defense Advanced Research Projects Agency
DRAM—dynamic random access memory
EDA—electronic design automation
EEC—European Economic Community
EMEA—Europe, the Middle East, and Africa
EMS—electronics manufacturing services
EPS—earnings per share
ERSO—Electronic Research Service Organization, Taiwan
ESPRIT—European Strategic Programme for Research and Develop-
         ment in Information Technology
ETRI—Electronic Technology Research Institute, South Korea
EUV—extreme ultraviolet lithography
FDI—foreign direct investment

GPN—global production network
GPU—graphics processing unit
GVC—global value chain
IC—integrated circuit
ICT—information and communications technology
IDM—integrated device manufacturing
ITRI—Industrial Technology Research Institute, Taiwan
JETRO—Japan External Trade Organization
JV—joint ventures
KIST—Korea Institute of Science and Technology
LCD—liquid crystal display
LED—light-emitting diode
M&A—mergers and acquisitions
MITI—Ministry of International Trade and Industry
NAICS—North American Industry Classification System
NAND—non-volatile memory
NIEs—newly industrialized economies
ODM—original design manufacturing
OEM—original equipment manufacturing
PC—personal computer
QLED—quantum light-emitting diode
R&D—research and development
RCEP—Regional Comprehensive Economic Partnership
ROE—return on equity
ROIC—return on invested capital
SCM—supply chain management
SEMATECH—Semiconductor Manufacturing Technology, US
SEMI—Semiconductor Equipment and Materials International
SIC—Standard Industrial Classification
SMIC—Semiconductor Manufacturing International Corporation
SoC—system-on-a-chip
TFT-LCD—thin film transistor-liquid crystal display
TNC—transnational corporation
Triad—East Asia, Western Europe, and North America
TSMC—Taiwan Semiconductor Manufacturing Company
UMC—United Microelectronics Corporation
USPTO—United States Patent and Trademark Office

VAT—value added tax
VCR—video-cassette recorder
VMI—vendor managed inventories
WLAN—wireless local area network
WTO—World Trade Organization

# INTERCONNECTED WORLDS

CHAPTER 1

# Worlds of Electronics: From National Innovations to Global Production

IN EARLY 1971, DON HOEFLER, a writer for *Electronic News*, gave the world a snappy metonym for high-tech electronics by christening a suburban region within Northern California as "Silicon Valley." From his tavern "field office" in Mountain View, Hoefler saw the clustering of a growing number of electronics and semiconductor firms, some of which would dominate the worlds of electronics even five decades later. Silicon Valley was and, today, still is "*the* world" of electronics distinguished by its innovative and technologically dynamic production systems.[1] Its emergence and success by the 1970s and the 1980s was predicated on the techno-nationalism deeply associated with Cold War geopolitics and the military-industrial complex in the United States.[2] In *The Code*, Margaret O'Mara (2019, 260) noted that defense-related spending in the 1980s "remained the big-government engine hidden under the hood of the Valley's shiny new entrepreneurial sports car, flying largely under the radar screen of the saturation [*sic*] media coverage of hackers and capitalists." Together with Boston's Route 128 on the East Coast, Silicon Valley was then the prime world of electronics innovations driven by the national security state.[3]

By 1990, this innovative "national world" of electronics based in Silicon Valley and elsewhere in the US had dominated in semiconductors and computers. To Mazurek (1999, 4–5), "[t]he growth and development of the semiconductor is inextricably linked to a region once known as the

1

prune capital of America. Now called Silicon Valley, this 50-mile stretch of land south of San Francisco houses the highest concentration of semiconductor and electronics companies in the world." And yet, even Silicon Valley began to show signs of decline in the early 1990s. As pointed out succinctly by Florida and Kenney (1990a, 74), while many Silicon Valley firms were highly innovative due to localized agglomeration advantages, "the markets for their high-technology products are shaped by strong market forces that are increasingly global in scope and may in fact ultimately contribute to the demise of U.S. high technology itself." These electronics firms were unable to move from locally embedded innovation to the mass production of end products because of a high degree of intrafirm vertical integration, industrial fragmentation through many smaller firms, and the lack of economies of scale.[4] While some scholars noted the emergence of nascent interfirm production networks in then Silicon Valley, these networks of lead firms and suppliers remained relatively recent and locally oriented.[5]

This industrial-organizational predicament in Silicon Valley and the subsequent globalization of its localized production networks heralded the coevolution of *complex* and *globalized worlds* of electronics production that are indeed much more global in scope and shaped by diverse market forces and the increasing fragmentation of production on a worldwide scale. In these "interconnected worlds" of electronics production underpinned by the emergence of global production networks since the 1990s, the mass production of electronic products and key components has become highly concentrated over time in East Asia comprising Northeast Asia (e.g., China, Japan, South Korea, and Taiwan) and Southeast Asia (e.g., Indonesia, Malaysia, and Singapore), supported by an extensive combination of both intra- and interfirm connections with Silicon Valley and the major technological centers elsewhere in the US and Western Europe, and within East Asia. Some of these interfirm connections are embedded in US-led technologies and knowhow, such as in software (e.g., operating systems and applications) and designs (e.g., from chipsets to end products), whereas others are manifested in the sourcing of core components (e.g., semiconductors) and capital equipment for high-tech manufacturing from US, European, and Japanese lead firms.[6]

Together, these global production networks in the electronics industry have integrated cutting-edge technological innovations developed in the US, Western Europe, and East Asia, with strong manufacturing capabilities located in different East Asian economies.[7] In their pioneering analysis of Asia's computer challenge to US firms during the 1990s, Dedrick and Kraemer (1998, 13; my emphasis) indeed anticipated this shift toward global production networks spearheaded by US firms focusing largely on East Asia:

> This remarkable shift in the computer market also led to a complete restructuring of the industry. The vertically integrated industry structure of the mainframe industry was replaced by a decentralized industry structure based on network economies. Different companies competed in each segment of the production chain, from components to systems to software. The disintegration of the industry into horizontal segments allowed the creation of a *global production network*, with different activities spread around the world. A Taiwanese entrepreneur could produce a cable or connector and sell it to any of the hundreds of PC [personal computer] makers in the world, and each of those PC makers could choose from hundreds of suppliers of cables and connectors. In such an environment, companies looked for the best or cheapest suppliers, subcontractors, or production sites, wherever they might be. The nature of competition changed and some companies and countries thrived while others struggled.

## A Global Shift in Electronics?

Let me briefly illustrate this coevolutionary shift in the global electronics industry (or "global electronics" in short throughout this book) toward more sophisticated and spatially dispersed production networks with some extended examples up to 2020.[8] In 1990, US dominance in semiconductors was much reduced. Only three US firms—Intel, Motorola, and Texas Instruments—were among the top ten producers in an industry segment then ruled by Japanese firms, such as NEC, Toshiba, Hitachi, Fujitsu, Mitsubishi, and so on. But the US still accounted for the lion's share of global sales in mainframe computers (over 60 percent), minicomputers (over 80 percent), personal computers (PCs; over 90 percent), and mobile phones (dominated by Motorola since 1983; Finland's Nokia and Sweden's Ericsson only launched their first mobile handsets in 1987).[9] With total revenue of more than $69 billion in 1990, IBM from New York remained the world's largest computer firm and clearly dominated the entire spectrum of the computer industry.[10] In PCs, most of the world's top ten firms were from the US, and several were based in Silicon Valley (e.g., Apple and Hewlett-Packard) and elsewhere (Packard Bell in Los Angeles, IBM in New York, and Compaq and Dell in Texas). Meanwhile, Motorola cornered the early mobile phones and communications market to achieve a record revenue of $10.9 billion in 1990.[11]

Meanwhile in East Asia, China still was not a major player in the electronics industry, and the four Asian "tigers" of Hong Kong, Singapore, South Korea, and Taiwan were just emerging as offshore production sites of national firms from advanced industrialized economies. Nevertheless, even South Korea remained very dependent on low-cost subcontracting work for leading brand name firms from the US and Japan. In 1990, some 70–80 percent of South Korea's total electronics exports and 60 percent of exports by three largest chaebol or conglomerates in electronics (Samsung, Lucky-Goldstar, and Daewoo) were in this mode of subcontracting arrangement. These percentage shares remained the same up to the mid-1990s.[12] Even as of 1996, a prominent business historian of US and Japanese electronics giants during the 1980s and the 1990s did not think any firm from these East Asian economies nor China would pose a major challenge to US and Japanese domination in semiconductors and computers. In light of Japan's renewed challenge to the US, Alfred Chandler (2001, 212) asked "Would the growing electronic industries in other Asian countries, specifically those of the 'Four Tigers'—namely, Taiwan, Korea, Singapore, and Hong Kong—give rise to another set of challengers? As of 1996 the answer was, not at the moment."

Two decades later by the late 2010s, East Asia became the home base of not only most manufacturing facilities in electronics global production networks but also many of the world's top lead firms in semiconductors, PCs, mobile handsets, and televisions (TVs): the four most important segments in today's global electronics in terms of market revenue and firm numbers.[13] As shown in Table 1.1's comprehensive data up to 2018 (with some updates to 2020), the total revenue of these four segments almost reached $1.2 trillion in 2018.[14] More importantly, most of these top lead firms from East Asia are not from Japan, but rather from South Korea, China, and Taiwan.[15] Industrial concentration also grew significantly between 2010 and 2020 in all four segments, particularly in PCs and mobile handsets, indicating profound organizational consolidation in global production networks throughout the 2010s. The presence of US lead firms is also less visible than in the 1990s or earlier. As will be detailed in later empirical chapters, China, Taiwan, and other Southeast Asian economies (e.g., Malaysia, Singapore, and Thailand) have emerged as the main production sites for virtually all leading US firms in semiconductors (Micron), PCs (Apple, Dell, and Hewlett-Packard), and mobile handsets (Apple). Many East Asian firms, such as Taiwan Semiconductor Manufacturing Company (TSMC), Foxconn, and Quanta from Taiwan, have also emerged to be the key manufacturing partners of lead firms in semiconductor design without their own manufacturing facilities (known as "fabless"), such as Broadcom, Qualcomm, Nvidia, Apple, and Advanced Micro Devices (AMD), and brand-name US lead firms—known as original equipment manufacturing (OEM) firms—in PCs and mobile handsets, such as Apple, Dell, and Hewlett-Packard.

Despite this global shift in electronics manufacturing production networks toward East Asia and much greater industrial concentration among the top ten lead firms throughout the 2010s, the continual domination of US technologies and knowhow in semiconductors (e.g., integrated circuits or "chip" design, software, and manufacturing equipment), PCs (e.g., operating systems, microprocessors, and wireless chipsets), and, more recently, mobile handsets (e.g., operating systems, application processors, and mobile chipsets) should not be underestimated. In turn, almost all East Asian lead firms in Table 1.1 have developed extensive *interfirm* relationships with these US lead firms in technologies, software, and knowhow, ranging from Intel, AMD, Qualcomm, and Broadcom in processors and wireless connectivity chipsets to Microsoft and Google in operating systems.

In semiconductor production, the relative shares of US, European, and Japanese lead firms declined further during the 2010s. In their 2011 preface to an authoritative study at the end of the 2000s, Brown and Linden (2011, xxii) noted that Japan's share had already been eroding slowly to 24 percent in 2010, and that "the shares of the United States and Europe are declining as well. Meanwhile the shares of Korea and Taiwan continue to climb, reaching 20 and 19 percent, respectively, in 2010 as the center of gravity for chip manufacturing shifts inexorably to Asia." This pivot in semiconductor manufacturing or wafer fabrication ("fabs") toward East Asia was indeed relentless throughout the 2010s. By 2020, South Korea's Samsung and SK Hynix and Taiwan's TSMC had emerged as top technology leaders and producers in their respective segments of memory chips and foundry services (contract wafer fabrication for fabless

TABLE 1.1. World's top 10 lead firms in semiconductors, personal computers, mobile handsets, and televisions by revenue/shipment and market share, 2010, 2018, and 2020 (in US$ billions and millions of units)

| Top 10 Lead Firms Semiconductors | 2010 US$ | % | 2018 US$ | % | 2020 US$ | % |
|---|---|---|---|---|---|---|
| Samsung (South Korea) | 27.0 | 8.7 | 74.6 | 15.4 | 57.7 | 12.4 |
| Intel (US) | 42.0 | 13.5 | 69.9 | 14.4 | 72.8 | 15.6 |
| SK Hynix (South Korea) | 9.9 | 3.2 | 36.3 | 7.5 | 25.8 | 5.5 |
| Micron Technology (US) | 8.2 | 2.6 | 29.7 | 6.1 | 22.0 | 4.7 |
| Broadcom (US)[1] | 6.7 | 2.2 | 17.5 | 3.6 | 15.8 | 3.4 |
| Qualcomm (US)[1] | 7.2 | 2.3 | 16.6 | 3.4 | 17.6 | 3.8 |
| Texas Instruments (US) | 11.8 | 3.8 | 15.4 | 3.2 | 13.6 | 2.9 |
| Kioxia/Toshiba (Japan) | 12.4 | 4.0 | 11.4 | 2.4 | 10.4 | 2.2 |
| Nvidia (US)[1] | 3.1 | 1.0 | 10.4 | 2.1 | 10.6 | 2.3 |
| STMicroelec. (Italy/France) | 10.3 | 3.3 | 9.7 | 2.0 | 10.2 | 2.2 |
| Top 10 total (US$) | 139 | 44.6 | 292 | 60.1 | 257 | 55.0 |
| Total revenue (US$) | 311 | 100 | 485 | 100 | 466 | 100 |

| Top 10 Lead Firms Mobile handsets | 2010 Units | % | 2018 Units | % | 2020 Units | % |
|---|---|---|---|---|---|---|
| Samsung (South Korea) | 11.8 | 3.7 | 290 | 20.6 | 263 | 21.0 |
| Huawei (China) | - | - | 206 | 14.6 | 170 | 13.6 |
| Apple (US) | 38.8 | 12.1 | 205 | 14.5 | 199 | 15.9 |
| Xiaomi (China) | - | - | 119 | 8.4 | 146 | 11.7 |
| OPPO (China) | - | - | 115 | 8.2 | 144 | 11.5 |
| Vivo (China) | - | - | 104 | 7.4 | 110 | 9.0 |
| LG (South Korea) | 1.8 | 0.6 | 44.2 | 3.1 | 23.0 | 1.9 |
| Lenovo-Motorola (China) | 15.8 | 4.9 | 39.5 | 2.8 | - | |
| TCL-Alcatel (China) | - | - | 17.1 | 1.2 | - | |
| Microsoft-Nokia (US) | 128 | 40.1 | 15.1 | 1.1 | - | |
| Top 10 total (units) | 197 | 61.4 | 1,155 | 81.9 | - | |
| Total shipment (units) | 320 | 100 | 1,410 | 100 | 1,250 | 100 |
| Total revenue (US$ b) | - | - | 443 | - | - | - |

**Personal computers (desktops & notebooks)**

| | 2010 Units | 2010 % | 2018 Units | 2018 % | 2020 Units | 2020 % |
|---|---|---|---|---|---|---|
| Hewlett-Packard (US) | 62.1 | 19.0 | 59.6 | 23.6 | 58.4 | 21.2 |
| Lenovo (China) | 34.1 | 10.4 | 57.5 | 22.8 | 68.5 | 24.9 |
| Dell (US) | 42.0 | 12.8 | 43.8 | 17.3 | 45.0 | 16.4 |
| Acer (Taiwan) | 41.5 | 12.7 | 17.1 | 6.8 | 16.2 | 5.9 |
| Asus (Taiwan) | 18.0 | 5.5 | 16.2 | 6.4 | 16.4 | 6.0 |
| Apple (US) | 13.7 | 4.2 | 13.0 | 5.1 | 22.5 | 8.2 |
| Samsung (South Korea) | 10.7 | 3.3 | 3.0 | 1.2 | - | - |
| Fujitsu (Japan) | 5.6 | 1.7 | 1.9 | 0.8 | - | - |
| NEC (Japan) | 1.2 | 0.4 | 1.2 | 0.5 | - | - |
| Toshiba (Japan) | 0.4 | 0.1 | 0.4 | 0.2 | - | - |
| **Top 10 total (units)** | 229 | 70.1 | 214 | 84.7 | - | - |
| **Total shipment (units)** | 328 | 100 | 253 | 100 | 275 | 100 |
| Total revenue (US$ b) | - | - | 146 | - | - | - |

**Televisions**

| | 2013[2] Units | 2013[2] % | 2018 Units | 2018 % | 2020 Units | 2020 % |
|---|---|---|---|---|---|---|
| Samsung (South Korea) | 44.2 | 19.1 | 41.4 | 18.7 | 49.3 | 21.9 |
| LG (South Korea) | 31.3 | 13.5 | 27.1 | 12.3 | 26.0 | 11.5 |
| TCL (China) | 14.6 | 6.3 | 17.7 | 8.0 | 24.2 | 10.7 |
| Hisense (China) | 11.5 | 5.0 | 15.9 | 7.2 | 18.2 | 8.1 |
| Sony (Japan) | 13.7 | 5.9 | 11.7 | 5.3 | - | - |
| Xiaomi (China) | - | - | 9.4 | 4.3 | 12.5 | 5.6 |
| Skyworth (China) | 10.2 | 4.4 | 9.2 | 4.2 | - | - |
| TP Vision (China) | 5.2 | 2.2 | 9.0 | 4.1 | - | - |
| Sharp (Japan) | 5.8 | 2.5 | 7.7 | 3.5 | - | - |
| Panasonic (Japan) | 6.9 | 3.0 | 6.2 | 2.8 | - | - |
| **Top 10 total (units)** | 143 | 61.9 | 155 | 70.3 | - | - |
| **Total shipment (units)** | 231 | 100 | 221 | 100 | 225 | 100 |
| Total revenue (US$ b) | 100 | - | 116 | - | - | - |

[1] These are "fabless" semiconductor chip design firms without wafer fabrication facilities.

[2] Data prior to 2013 not available in the same dataset.

Sources: 2010 and 2018 data from IHS Markit/Informa Tech Custom Research for GPN@NUS Centre, July–October 2016 and 2019, and author's interviews; 2020 data on personal computers and semiconductors from Gartner (https://www.gartner.com, released on January 11 and April 12, 2021), mobile handsets from TrendForce (https://www.trendforce.com, released on January 5, 2021), and TVs from Omdia (https://omdia.tech.informa.com, released on February 17, 2021).

chip design firms). Interestingly though, six US firms remained among the top ten semiconductor firms in a global market exceeding $485 billion at its historical peak in 2018 and at $466 billion in 2020 (see Table 1.1). By 2021, the interconnected worlds of globalized semiconductor production clearly became much more complex than what Don Hoefler had observed in Mountain View five decades earlier in 1971. Global production networks among leading semiconductor firms from the US, Western Europe, and East Asia are now tightly interwoven with their software, design, and equipment suppliers (mostly based in Silicon Valley) and their key OEM lead firm customers from the US and East Asia in PCs, mobile handsets, and other electronic devices, and their major manufacturing partners located throughout East Asia.

In PCs, three US OEM giants from the 1980s—Hewlett-Packard, Dell, and Apple—remained among the top ten vendors in 2020 (see Table 1.1). But they relied extensively on the original design manufacturing (ODM) services of Taiwan's top providers, such as Quanta, Compal, Wistron, and Inventec, and contract manufacturers, such as Foxconn.[16] Four PC lead firms in the top ten also emerged from East Asia outside Japan—Lenovo (China), Asus and Acer (Taiwan), and Samsung (South Korea)—in a challenging market that became much more concentrated and dominated by the top five vendors. In 2018 and 2020, the combined share of these top five PC firms was 77 percent, as compared to "only" 60 percent in 2010 and 33 percent in 1990. With the exception of Apple's Macintosh computers operating on its own macOS, the world of PCs remains completely dependent on Microsoft's Windows operating system. As the inventor of the microprocessor not long after its founding in Silicon Valley in 1968, Intel continued to dominate as the largest supplier of microprocessors for almost all PCs, with a 90 percent market share in 2018.[17]

In mobile handsets, Motorola gave way to Finland's Nokia by the late 1990s. In 2010, Nokia dominated the global mobile phone market with a whopping 40 percent share of the almost 320 million units shipped worldwide (Table 1.1). Motorola was still a significant lead firm with 4.9 percent market share, ahead of Samsung's 3.7 percent but behind Apple's 12 percent. Since 2011, however, both Nokia and Motorola have yielded to Samsung and Apple in the huge and expanding global smartphone market—the latter has developed strategic relationships with its manufacturing partners from Taiwan (i.e., Hon Hai Precision or Foxconn, as known in China). By its peak in 2018, four smartphone OEM firms from China—Huawei,

Xiaomi, Oppo, and Vivo—had also joined Samsung and LG from South Korea and Apple as the top seven vendors in the global mobile handset industry, collectively shipping about 77 percent of the total 1.4 billion units worldwide and representing an over fourfold increase from the 2010 total shipment. In 2020, the same top six vendors accounted for 83 percent of total shipment of 1.25 billion units. To be documented in later chapters, the domination of US technologies, software, and core components in this product segment is even more pronounced than in PCs.

Only in large flat panel displays and TVs has the world's center of gravity shifted almost completely toward East Asia (see Table 1.1). South Korea's Samsung and LG had a combined market share of 31 percent in their 2018 shipments and were far ahead of eight other top ten vendors from China (TCL, Hisense, Xiaomi, Skyworth, and TPV) and Japan (Sony, Sharp, and Panasonic) in a global market of more than 221 million units shipped. Their share increased further to 33 percent in 2020. East Asia–based display makers also dominate in the component supply of flat panel displays for PCs and mobile handsets, as will be evident in later chapters.

The above brief illustration at the industry and firm levels points to the much more complex contemporary worlds of electronics production in semiconductors, PCs, and mobile handsets that are coordinated by lead firms from the US and East Asia, underpinned by substantial US- and European/Japanese-origin technologies and knowhow, and yet co-constituted by East Asia-based manufacturing capabilities and facilities. How then do we account for this coevolutionary shift in global electronics from the innovative "national world" of Silicon Valley prior to 1990 to the contemporary worlds of globalized electronics production throughout the 2010s? Building on the earlier literature examining the national worlds of electronics in the US, Western Europe, and Japan, this book focuses on the contemporary worlds of electronics production networks centered in East Asia during the 2010s. In these worlds of production, the competitive success of East Asian firms and economies since the late 1990s has been built on their strategic coupling with global production networks, defined as organizationally fragmented and spatially dispersed configurations of electronics production on a global scale. I call this contemporary phenomenon the *interconnected worlds* of global electronics that bring together multiple worlds—the earlier national worlds of high-tech innovations in advanced economies and the contemporary worlds of highly globalized electronics production.

My primary goal in this book is to describe and explain how these interconnected worlds of electronics production are underpinned by diverse and complex global production networks centered in East Asia during the 2010s.[18] As a dominant feature of today's global economy, these cross-border production networks and value chains represent perhaps *the* most critical industrial-organizational innovation, connecting diverse production sites in East Asia with the technological centers of excellence in North America (e.g., Silicon Valley and Texas), Western Europe (e.g., Cambridge, Eindhoven, and Munich), and East Asia (e.g., Beijing/Shenzhen, Seoul/Suwon, Singapore, Taipei-Hsinchu, and Tokyo-Kyoto-Osaka).[19] Empirically, this book aims to demonstrate how the global electronics industry has coevolved from nationally based production systems in the US, Japan, and Western Europe prior to the 1990s to highly interconnected worlds underpinned by complex global production networks. Based on new proprietary material described in Appendixes A and B, my empirical analysis in Chapters 4 to 6 also provides an important benchmark of globalized electronics production for future comparative work on the massive global restructuring during the early 2020s in light of the devastating COVID-19 pandemic in 2020/2021 and the ensuring economic recovery throughout the world.

Unlike the earlier work on national competition between the US and Japan, however, my main unit of empirical analysis throughout the book's chapters is not at the country level, but rather at the network and firm level (i.e., production networks coordinated by global lead firms). While national political-economic contexts are certainly important for understanding the globalization of these production networks, it is the global lead firm and its strategic partners that co-constitute these networks and spearhead their diverse operations in the interconnected worlds of electronics production. In my earlier work *Strategic Coupling* (Yeung 2016), I have documented at length such national political-economic contexts in relation to the weakened developmental state in South Korea, Taiwan, and Singapore due to political democratization and market liberalization since the late 1980s, and their greater role in promoting industrial upgrading through technological learning, trade, and investment policies. These changing institutional contexts have subsequently enabled domestic firms to work closely with lead firms in global production networks since the 1990s, and their strategic coupling has led to new industrial transformation in East Asia during and beyond the 2000s. As will be evident in later chapters on global electronics centered in East Asia by the late 2010s, such changing national and institutional contexts before 2000 have had enduring influence on electronics lead firms from these East Asian economies (e.g., more internalization of production networks and greater significance of business groups and family or state ownership).

Moreover and despite its firm- and network-centric focus, this book's empirical analysis is less concerned with the business success of individual firms and more with the *different* and *innovative* ways in which their global production networks were organized—where, how, and why—in the four segments of global electronics during the 2010s (e.g., Intel vs. Qualcomm / TSMC in semiconductors and Samsung vs. Apple in smartphones). In fact, the continual US leadership in both software and certain hardware products (e.g., top vendors and processors in both PCs and smartphones) in the late 2010s points to the importance of understanding how these interconnected worlds have provided both competitive production platforms and growing end markets for their success.

Before I outline the book's main arguments, contributions, and organization in the remaining two sections, two important caveats about software and semiconductors are necessary. First, while I recognize the importance of software in information and communications technology (ICT) products in general, I am unable to incorporate it in this work that focuses primarily on the global production networks of electronics hardware (to be defined more explicitly in Chapter 2). My main purpose is to trace the who, where, and what in such production networks and to explain how and why such production networks are organized. While software is crucial to the functionality and manufacturing of these hardware products— as their "invisible engines,"[20] it is often embedded in or bundled with these products through licensing and, due to its "weightless" nature, can be delivered virtually to/from anywhere. The "production" of software in these hardware products is likely located in the design and research and development (R&D) centers of OEM hardware firms whose designers and engineers interact closely with their software vendors in home locations (e.g., Microsoft in Seattle and Google in Menlo Park). But this "invisible" link at the product/component level between hardware firms and software vendors is particularly difficult to identify, and not much data are available from the perspective of global production networks.[21] In most industrial classification and official statistics, software is accounted for as part of ICT services. Software has been well examined in other published studies on ICT services and everyday life.[22] In short, US dominance in software worldwide is taken as an operating context or the wider ICT ecosystem for this book's empirical focus on the global production networks of electronics hardware centered in East Asia.

Second, semiconductors may stand out as a rather unusual segment among end products, such as PCs, mobile handsets, and TVs, in global electronics. While I acknowledge the high human and capital intensity in semiconductor design and production and its crucial role as intermediate inputs into all ICT end products, the segment has a long history of driving technological revolution in modern electronics. As will be documented in Chapter 2, semiconductors are indispensable to the development of complex production networks in ICT devices. Compared to those in PCs and mobile handsets, semiconductor production networks exhibit not only some interesting similarities in organizational innovations, such as outsourcing of wafer fabrication and assembly and testing services to East Asian partners, but also major differences in power and profit asymmetries in favor of large fabless firms and top foundry providers. By 2020/2021, for example, TSMC and Samsung foundry—two East Asian partners of leading US fabless chip design firms—became the top industry leaders in wafer fabrication and overtook Intel in process technology through their collaborative development with network partners and customers in their extensive and globalized ecosystems.

In turn, some of the major OEM firms in ICT end products are also leading semiconductor manufacturers (e.g., Samsung and Toshiba) or fabless firms (e.g., Apple and Huawei). Incorporating semiconductor firms and their global production networks into this book's empirical analysis can offer a more complete understanding of the contemporary global electronics industry, including such contentious public policy issues as the recent May 2020 US export restrictions imposed on the use of US technology by semiconductor suppliers of blacklisted electronics firms in China (e.g., Huawei, ZTE, and Semiconductor Manufacturing International Corporation [SMIC]). To improve clarity and consistency in my empirical analysis in all chapters, I will ensure the following order of discussion—semiconductors, PCs, mobile handsets, and, if relevant, consumer electronics (i.e., TVs). The logic for this order of presentation is premised on the historical evolution and the contemporary significance of each segment/product and the fact that semiconductors are the most critical component in modern ICT devices. This sequence will also enable readers to differentiate better the profound production network characteristics of semiconductors before delving into other end-product segments.

## Main Arguments: Coevolution from Multinational Worlds to Interconnected Worlds of Global Electronics

In a nutshell, this work argues that the transformative shift in global electronics toward today's interconnected worlds of production networks can be understood in relation to three historical periods of coevolution in complexity and interconnectedness over time. First, prior to 1990 electronics used to be embedded in the *multinational worlds* of industrial transformation in advanced countries, and most innovations and production activities were nationally based. Second, while the internationalization of electronics manufacturing had occurred as early as the 1960s, its magnitude, depth, and complexity did not accelerate until the 1990s due to significant deregulation and trade liberalization and the growing capabilities of domestic firms in East Asian economies and, since the 2000s, in China. This was the period of the *emerging worlds* of interconnections. Third, the *interconnected worlds* of global electronics became fully established in the 2010s through broader technological and organizational innovations enabling more diverse and sophisticated global production networks in the different segments of the electronics industry. These innovations were associated with the broad application of production technologies (e.g., modularization and platform specialization) and the maturing of distinct organizational practices (e.g., offshoring, outsourcing, strategic partnership, and foundry production). They required complementary products, technologies, and services among different actors in these cross-macroregional networks who competed successfully in an increasingly fragmented global market. The following three subsections elaborate on each of these historical periods that collectively provide the national and institutional contexts for the book's empirical analysis of lead firms and their production networks in later chapters.

### Multinational Worlds of Innovation and Production Until the Late 1980s

This initial period points to multiple *national worlds* of electronics production embedded in national innovation systems and protectionist regulatory regimes from the 1960s to the late 1980s. In these worlds, national governments in advanced industrialized economies competed fiercely against each other in the race to technological supremacy and market dominance in two key segments of the electronics industry: semiconductors and computers.[23] Governments in the US, Japan, and Western European countries funded and supported national ecosystems of innovation in electronics comprising universities and research institutes, private firms, and industry alliances. Many of the early innovations in semiconductors and large-scale computer systems were related to national defense and other critical military missions (e.g., the defense-related aerospace industry in Southern California, the Scientific City in France, and the M4 corridor in the UK).[24] During this period up to the 1980s, vertical integration was the dominant mode of organizing production among the largest semiconductor and mainframe computer firms in the US (e.g., IBM, Sperry Rand, DEC, Texas Instruments, Motorola, Intel, Fairchild, and National), Western Europe (e.g., ICL, Bull, Olivetti, Philips, Siemens, SGS, and Thomson), and Japan (NEC, Fujitsu, and Hitachi). Until the early 1990s, the global market for electronics had an estimated value of $100 billion, but only about 5 percent was being outsourced.[25]

In semiconductors, domestic firms designed, manufactured, and marketed specialized semiconductor products, such as processor chipsets and memory chips, as core components for computers and other consumer electronics products. Some of these firms also integrated backward to design and manufacture semiconductor equipment (e.g., Fairchild and Texas Instruments in the US). The R&D facilities and manufacturing plants of most of these semiconductor firms were located in home countries. If US firms invested abroad across the Atlantic and/or within Western Europe, their foreign operations were mostly wholly owned subsidiaries. In the US, Japanese and European semiconductor firms were much less involved in greenfield investment and used acquisition as the main mode to establish operations.[26] Outsourcing was limited to nonessential components and services. Still, suppliers were likely to be domestic firms in the respective countries of operations. As noted earlier, most of the East Asian subsidiaries of these US and European semiconductor firms were in the labor-intensive back-end services, such as semiconductor assembly, packaging, and testing.

In short, there was a very limited degree of horizontal or vertical disintegration in semiconductors that might contribute to the formation of cross-border production networks before 1990. Langlois et al.'s (1988, 3) authoritative study of the US semiconductor industry in the late 1980s, for example, focused on the international interrelatedness of the industry and noted that "the model of a battle between distinct and well-defined 'national' industries is an inappropriately unsophisticated one in the case of microelectronics." Still, this study recognized only technological interdependence among US, European, and Japanese firms through foreign direct investment in wholly owned subsidiaries, joint ventures, and cooperative agreements. Much of this international interdependence existed only in the form of "intrafirm international vertical integration," and "American firms have pursued almost exclusively a strategy of *de novo* investment overseas. This should not be entirely surprising, since American firms pioneered semiconductor technology and have remained at the leading edge."[27]

When domestic semiconductor firms were challenged by foreign competitors during the 1980s, national governments engaged in protectionist measures to regulate foreign competition through legal and bureaucratic mechanisms. This irony was not lost on Morgan and Sayer (1988, 65), who examined comprehensively the electronics industry in the UK:

> The American industry began with heavy state support. It quickly progressed to a period of world leadership in the process of internationalization, during which it legitimized itself by appealing to a static conception of comparative advantage and to free markets as a realm of natural justice and order. When such arguments failed to stem the rise of a new state-backed power which refused to accept the static view of comparative advantage, it switched sides. Examples of such opportunism are of course rife in the history of capitalism, but this particular instance is notable in the light of the celebration of the alleged role of free market forces in the development of the industry in the ideology of high tech.

By the early 1980s in the US, the threat of Japanese firms to the dominance of US firms in semiconductors due to the former's better process technology and product quality led to the deployment of such protectionist measures.[28] Voluntary import expansions, such as the US-Japan Semiconductor Trade Agreement of 1986, were imposed on Japanese producers in order to restrict their exports of memory chips to the US for computers and other consumer electronics products (e.g., then video cassette recorders). This restriction would also allow US semiconductor firms, such as Intel and National Semiconductor, to retool their production facilities to compete better in this market segment. The 1986 agreement also guaranteed that the Japanese government would ensure an at least 10 percent share of these US firms in Japan's domestic market. In 1987, the US government led a consortium of fourteen US semiconductor firms, such as Hewlett-Packard, AT&T, IBM, and DEC, to form SEMATECH (Semiconductor Manufacturing Technology) in order to fend off Japanese competition and to regain industrial competitiveness.[29]

In Western Europe, the European Strategic Programme for Research and Development in Information Technology (ESPRIT) was launched in 1983 as a ten-year effort to stimulate R&D cooperation in basic technology in semiconductor, data and knowledge processing, and office and factory automation. Its first five-year phase was funded to the tune of $1.3 billion, half from the European Economic Community and the rest from other stakeholders.[30] Philips and Siemens, then two of Western Europe's largest semiconductor firms, also received some $400 million in state subsidies after the 1985–1987 recession to enter into memory chips markets.[31]

In computers, such multinational worlds of innovation and production also prevailed up to the late 1980s. As noted in Campbell-Kelly and Garcia-Swartz's (2015, 53–54) history of IBM's dominance in the early US computer industry,

> If on the supply side the United States had IBM, on the demand side IBM (and its American competitors) had the United States. The unique strength of both government and civilian demand in the States helped IBM and the other American computer companies pull ahead of their foreign competitors. A large share of the early computer know-how was developed under government contracts. Although the U.S. government did not provide a direct subsidy for computer R&D in private corporations, it did invest heavily in military R&D contracts, and many of the technologies developed for military purposes later found their way into civilian uses. Thus, at a time when there was great uncertainty about the kinds of results that computers could deliver, the government became an important source of demand, both directly through its own military institutions and indirectly through the defense contractors.

Among US and Japanese computer firms, outsourcing of components and peripherals would often be given to other domestic firms in their home countries. IBM famously sourced almost entirely within the US for its mainframe computers. In Japan, NEC, Hitachi, and Fujitsu sourced almost all of their parts and components for PC production from in-house parts operations, affiliated companies, and long-term domestic suppliers in 1990. The only externally sourced component was Intel's microprocessors.[32]

In these multinational worlds of central computing backed by mainframes and minicomputers—before the arrival of personal computers in the early 1980s, Dedrick and Kraemer (1998, 12) noted that "the vast majority of computers were made in the United States, mostly by IBM. 'Big Blue' stood astride the global computer industry like a colossus, controlling nearly half the world market for computers and producing virtually every key component and new technology in its own plants and laboratories. While companies and even governments launched expensive campaigns to unseat IBM from its position atop the computer industry, most competitors struggled to survive."[33] Not surprisingly, OEM lead firms from the US, Western Europe, and Japan mostly developed and manufactured computer systems primarily in and for their home countries. In many cases, "national champions" were favored through public procurement and R&D subsidies to ensure the presence of domestic players in the production of computer systems (e.g., ICL in the UK, Groupe Bull in France, Olivetti in Italy, and Siemens in Germany) and telecommunications equipment (e.g., the nationalization of Thomson, Compagnie Générale d'Electricité, and Bull in France).[34]

### Emerging Worlds of Interconnections: The 1990s and the 2000s

The above landscape of the multinational worlds of innovation and production began to change after 1990 when the internationalization of electronics production toward East Asia gathered pace dramatically. O'Mara (2019, 264–65) observed such *emerging interconnections* between Silicon Valley's high-tech world and production sites in Asian economies in the late 1980s:

> American tech brands expanded beyond Singapore and Taiwan to southern China and India, where economic liberalization and privatization were just starting to create huge new opportunities for foreign companies. The plants themselves were usually owned and operated by an eager and sometimes mercenary cadre of subcontractors, putting the physical work of high-tech production at an even further remove from the Bay Area sunshine. . . . Globalization of production allowed the mythos of a clean, white-collar high-tech world to stay alive and gain velocity.

Within Western Europe, similar internationalization of leading domestic firms and former "national champions" had taken place markedly by the late 1980s. Cawson et al.'s (1990, 350) major study of consumer electronics and telecommunications in Britain, France, and Germany concluded, "National firms serving predominantly national markets have been rapidly changing into international firms addressing increasingly global markets. Firms which have failed to adapt to the internationalization of markets have been forced out or taken over by those that have." In Japan, protectionist responses in the US and Western Europe against Japanese electronics firms during the 1980s and the Plaza Accord in 1985 led to the rapid relocation of Japanese firms to cheaper production sites outside Japan. Between 1985 and 1990, Japan's outward foreign direct investment in the electronics sector grew over tenfold, from $513 million to $5.7 billion, and the share of East Asia increased from 10 percent to 38 percent.[35]

In electronics production, much of this internationalization by US, European, and Japanese firms went to East Asia. By 1988, the four East Asian newly industrialized economies (NIEs) of Hong Kong, Taiwan, Singapore, and South Korea together had exported around $53 billion worth of electronics products, more than the US ($46 billion) and Germany ($26 billion) and nearly 73 percent of Japan ($72 billion). Each of them had already exceeded France and Italy in electronics exports and had been rapidly catching up with the UK ($18 billion).[36] Most of these "East Asian" exports, however, came from local assembly production in the wholly owned subsidiaries of lead firms from Japan, the US, and Western Europe, and their local subcontractors and joint venture partners that still relied extensively on the core components, key technologies, and capital goods from Japan and the US.

In the computer industry, Dedrick and Kraemer (1998, 29) argued that "the rapid growth and technical progress of the computer industry in the United States shaped Asian perceptions of the industry's importance to economic and technological competitiveness. The evolution of the U.S. computer industry also provided the impetus for its Asian expansion, first to Japan, then to the East Asian NIEs, and still later throughout the Asia-Pacific region." In Taiwan, more than one-third of its computer-related exports of $6 billion in 1990 came from these foreign firms and their local joint ventures.[37] In South Korea, even Samsung remained heavily dependent on Japanese lead firms for critical components in PCs and consumer electronics. Samsung was then already the country's leading poster boy for success in producing all kinds of electronics goods. With exports of around $10 billion in 1992, Samsung accounted for 13 percent of South Korea's total exports and 50 percent of its electronics exports! As noted in Hobday's (1995, 87) influential study of East Asian technological catching-up, "Samsung lagged behind the Japanese leaders in consumer electronics in the early 1990s, still dependent for core components and lacking major, internationally successful product innovations. Japanese firms supplied many of the gas plasma displays (used in some advanced TVs), liquid crystal displays (used in laptops and other PCs), charged coupled devices (used in camcorders) and other customized chips."[38]

During the 1990s, nevertheless, the nascent role of these East Asian economies and their domestic firms in emerging and more complex global production networks in the electronics industry began to take shape in response to several *structural changes* and *firm-specific initiatives*. At the global level, significant geopolitical changes took place that in turn facilitated this deepening of internationalization into emerging forms of globalizing production from North America and Western Europe to East Asia. The end of the Cold War in the late 1980s, together with the opening of China a decade earlier in 1979, reduced the geopolitical incentives of the US in supporting state-led development in several East Asian economies, such as South Korea and Taiwan. After dealing with Japan in the late 1980s (e.g., the Plaza Accord in 1985 and the US-Japan Semiconductor Trade Agreement of 1986), the US put pressure on South Korea and Taiwan in the early 1990s to deregulate and liberalize their domestic economies in order to enhance market access and to reduce bilateral trade imbalances with the US.[39]

The emergence of new regimes of global economic governance also ensured continual market liberalization among East Asian economies. The inauguration of the World Trade Organization (WTO) in 1995 (and China's accession in 2001) was a key milestone in the establishment of new international trade rules and enforcement mechanisms that nullified countervailing trade-distorting practices, such as export subsidies and local content requirements.[40] These broader structural changes in the international political economy created a favorable condition for the gradual development of extensive cross-border production networks through both direct investment by major US, European, and Japanese electronics firms and, much more importantly, the increasing international outsourcing arrangements with their East Asian providers of foundry operations in semiconductors and manufacturing services in ICT end products. Indeed, this coevolutionary trend toward the interconnected worlds of electronics production was predicted in Henderson's (1989, 153) earlier study of US semiconductor firms in East Asia in the late 1980s:

> One of the forms the global restructuring of the industry is taking is the emergence of financial and technological alliances between companies spanning national boundaries. If these alliances continue to develop such that entire "national" companies (not merely plants within companies) begin to specialise in the production of particular parts of the semiconductor and/or in particular forms of semiconductor technology, then the conditions for a truly "multi-national" semiconductor industry may have been achieved. . . . [I]t may soon become unlikely that any country will again be capable of developing a fully autonomous semiconductor industry.

Starting in the 1990s, this dynamic shift toward East Asia in the emerging phase of the interconnected worlds of electronics production would not be possible without the simultaneous growth and development in the technological and production capabilities of domestic electronics firms in these East Asian economies. In *semiconductors*, the rise of foundry wafer producers from Taiwan, Singapore, and, to a lesser extent, South Korea presaged the arrival of a new and extremely powerful model of semiconductor manufacturing services prevalent in the subsequent two decades.[41] In particular since the mid-2000s, East Asian foundry providers, such as Taiwan's TSMC and United Microelectronics Corporation (UMC) and Singapore's Chartered Semiconductor (acquired and added to Global-Foundries in 2009), have enabled the emergence of a highly successful and globalized ecosystem of fabless design houses based primarily in the US and, later, in Taiwan, Israel, and other economies. For example, through Taiwan's state-funded Industrial Technology Research Institute, TSMC licensed in 1986 its first semiconductor fabrication technology from Philips of the Netherlands. But by July 2000, TSMC was technologically advanced enough to license its own process technology to National Semiconductor and became the first independent foundry house in Taiwan to license to a top US semiconductor firm.[42] This highly successful fabless-foundry cross-border production network contrasts sharply with the wholly owned model of internationalization common among semiconductor firms from the US, Western Europe, and Japan prior to the 1990s.[43]

In ICT *end products* such as PCs, mobile handsets, and consumer electronics, East Asian firms served US and European lead firm customers through the provision of original design manufacturing (ODM) and electronics manufacturing services (EMS).[44] These two modes of industrial organization were distinctive because ODM firms were more specialized in their product categories (e.g., notebook PCs), whereas EMS providers covered the entire value chain of most consumer electronics (e.g., desktop PCs, mobile handsets, and TVs), from manufacturing to logistics and fulfillment. In an ODM arrangement, East Asian firms were much more involved in product and process design in accordance with a general design layout specified by their OEM customers. In contract manufacturing, leading EMS providers offered large-scale and highly automated manufacturing production systems. Responsible for process innovation, EMS providers also made very large capital investments in production systems in order to secure the entire supply chain, from specialized materials to equipment.

In a more advanced form, an ODM arrangement entailed complete product design by East Asian firms on the basis of their own knowledge of international markets and technical capabilities. This arrangement required ODM firms to internalize system design skills and complex production technologies and component design abilities. The capacity of these East Asian ODM firms to design and integrate different systems while managing large networks of component and modular suppliers became their core capability and value proposition to lead firm customers. It also enabled these ODM firms to achieve enormous economies of scale so that they could rapidly ramp up production volumes. These East Asian ODMs did not just manufacture according to the proprietary specifications of their brand-name OEM customers. Instead, they moved up the value chain and engaged directly in proprietary product design and specifications, and integrated turnkey solutions to secure large orders from their brand-name customers.[45]

More specifically, these East Asian firms built their dynamic capabilities through learning the existing production and management know-how from OEM lead firms in the US, Western Europe, and Japan, and through developing new technological and organizational innovations.[46] By the late 1980s, leading East Asian firms had gained massive manufacturing experience from their earlier phase of subcontracting work for OEM lead firms and developed sophisticated in-house production and management capabilities. They could offer a much wider range of design, technological, and logistical solutions to their lead firm customers. As noted by Hobday (1995, 195), "The form, depth and breadth of East Asian organizational innovations were new to the marketplace and to the world and therefore constitute innovation in the most meaningful sense of the word. Indeed, the manner in which regional development occurred under OEM and subcontracting with foreign firms is a significant departure with no obvious historical parallel. It is a new large-scale feature of economic development only witnessed in the latter part of the 20th century." In one of the earliest studies of the emergence of these cross-border production networks in East Asia by the late 1990s, Borrus, Ernst, and Haggard (2000) noted that these production networks, based on localized technical specialization in Asia, had led to the resurgence of US electronics and enabled US lead firms to establish an alternative supply base in East Asia. These US firms could outcompete large Japanese electronics firms that continued to rely on Japan-centric production systems.

As explained earlier in my *Strategic Coupling* (Yeung 2016, 41–52), this incremental firm-specific learning and capability-development process took place in several East Asian economies through

(1)    learning management, production, and engineering know-how and project execution skills from production for exports— from low-end subcontractors in the 1970s to sophisticated ODM firms (e.g., Compal and Quanta) and EMS providers (e.g., Foxconn and Venture Corp) since the 1990s and beyond,

(2)    acquiring technologies in the international markets by foundry wafer producers (e.g., TSMC and UMC) and domestic firms in semiconductors (e.g., Samsung) since the 1990s,

(3)    building firm-specific local capabilities through reverse "brain drain" by attracting techno-entrepreneurs as returnees, e.g., South Koreans and Taiwanese engineers from Silicon Valley in the 1990s and mainland Chinese from the US since the 2000s,[47]

(4)    support by state-funded research institutes (e.g., South Korea's Electronic Technology Research Institute and Taiwan's Industrial Technology Research Institute) and intensifying in-house R&D activity by domestic lead firms (e.g., Samsung's own

research institute established in 1987 and LG's central research lab), and

(5)    leveraging family or state ownership and cheap global finance to fund capital spending and R&D activities before the 1997/1998 Asian economic crisis and since the 2000s.

As their firm-specific capabilities evolved over time, East Asian firms relied less on domestic sources of technological knowhow because ODM and foundry arrangements provided important technological conduits for them to achieve speedy progress in market access and technology development. Observing these emerging transnational networks of techno-entrepreneurs, Saxenian (2006, 325) noted that by the mid-2000s, "the new Argonauts [transnational techno-entrepreneurs] have initiated a process of reciprocal regional transformation that is shifting the global balance of economic and technological resources. Silicon Valley, once the uncontested technology leader, is now integrated into a dynamic network of specialized and complementary regional economies [East Asia and elsewhere]." While the US and, in particular, Silicon Valley continued to dominate in software, design, and certain core components, lead firms from the US, Western Europe, and Japan increasingly engaged with these East Asian firms not so much as traditional low-tech suppliers or subcontractors for customized parts and components at lower costs, but increasingly as *strategic partners* with their unique specialization in manufacturing and technology-related capabilities (e.g., in memory devices and flat panel displays). While this coevolution of different worlds of electronics production had started well ahead of the 2010s, their extent and intensity became much more apparent during the 2010s.

Table 1.2 summarizes the changing national and institutional contexts for this firm-specific capability building and industrial transformation in four East Asian economies that have come to play a very significant role in global electronics since the 2000s.[48] My empirical analysis of their significance during the 2010s in later Chapters 4 to 6 will refer consistently to this table for national institutional contexts between 1980 and 2021. Succinctly put, the strong developmental state in South Korea and Taiwan pursuing sectoral or target-specific industrial policy during the 1970s and the 1980s became less interventionist since the late 1990s due to the growing capabilities of domestic firms and their strategic coupling with global lead firms and their production networks. The state's elite bureaucracy,

TABLE 1.2. Evolving national and institutional contexts of industry development in selected East Asian economies, 1980–2021

| Historical contexts | South Korea | Taiwan | Singapore | China |
|---|---|---|---|---|
| **1980–2000** | | | | |
| Development strategy | National champions and export firms | Domestic firms for exports and global economy | Foreign firms with limited domestic firms for exports and global economy | State-owned enterprises, fiscal decentralization, and foreign firms for processing exports |
| State policy support | Sectoral industrial policy and high selectivity | Sectoral industrial policy but low selectivity | Horizontal industrial policy and high state ownership | Horizontal industrial policy and high state ownership |
| Capital formation | State and domestic banks; low reliance on FDI before 1997 Asian financial crisis | State and domestic banks; medium reliance on FDI | State financial holdings; high reliance on FDI | State banks; high reliance on FDI |
| Business structure | Dominance of chaebol or conglomerates; high family control | Significant business groups; high family control | High state and foreign ownership; limited family control | High state and foreign ownership |
| Electronics industry | From low-cost subcontracting to emerging domestic lead firms | From low-cost subcontracting to emerging foundry, ODM, and EMS firms | From low-cost assembly by foreign firms to emerging domestic firms in outsourcing | From low-cost assembly by foreign firms to emerging domestic firms in outsourcing |
| **2001–2021** | | | | |
| Development strategy | Corporate restructuring, market liberalization, and financial deregulation | More market liberalization and internationalization of domestic firms | Privatization and promoting domestic firms and their internationalization | Dual tracks of promoting national (state) firms and foreign investment |

| Historical contexts | South Korea | Taiwan | Singapore | China |
|---|---|---|---|---|
| State policy support | Less interventionist industrial policy and lower selectivity; more active free trade arrangements | Horizontal industrial policy promoting firm upgrading; more active free trade arrangements | Horizontal industrial policy promoting firm upgrading; highly active free trade arrangements | Sectoral industrial policy, upgrading, and restructuring of state ownership; WTO entry and export promotion, 2001–; US-China trade war and sanctions, 2018– |
| Capital formation | Restructuring of domestic banks; more FDI and reliance on capital markets | Restructuring of domestic banks; more reliance on capital markets | Continual state financial holdings; high reliance on FDI and capital markets | Large state financial holdings; medium reliance on FDI and capital markets |
| Business structure | Dominance of fewer chaebol; high family control | Family business groups and rise of technology firms | Dominance of government-linked and foreign firms | High state control and medium foreign and family control |
| Electronics industry | From emerging domestic firms to dominant global lead firms in semiconductors, mobile handsets, and consumer electronics | From emerging to dominant foundry, ODM, and EMS firms in semiconductors, PCs, and mobile handsets | From emerging to significant domestic and foreign firms in semiconductors and consumer electronics | From low-cost assembly to some global lead firms in PCs, mobile handsets, and consumer electronics; crippled domestic semiconductor firms due to US sanctions |

Sources: Based on analysis in Yeung (2016, chs. 2–3) and Hamilton-Hart and Yeung (2021b), with further information from Ning (2009); Fuller (2016); Haggard (2018); Lee (2019); Doner, Noble, and Ravenhill (2021); and Xing (2021).

such as South Korea's Economic Planning Board and Taiwan's Council for Economic Planning and Development, was either dismantled or weakened during the 1990s. Meanwhile, the Singaporean state has long been engaging in functional or horizontal industrial policy that promotes trade and investment openness. Since joining the WTO in 2001, China's domestic political economy has been characterized by dual tracks—state promotion of national firms (mostly state-owned) through sectoral industrial policy and continual support for foreign investment through trade liberalization. Within these changing contexts and as will be examined in Chapter 2, domestic firms emerged by the 2010s as lead firms in semiconductors (South Korea and Taiwan), PCs (Taiwan and China), mobile handsets (South Korea and China), and consumer electronics (South Korea and China).

### Interconnected Worlds: The 2010s and Beyond

During the 2010s—the main focus of this book's empirical chapters (4–6), the *interconnected worlds* of global electronics production became fully centered in East Asia. I argue that this maturing of global interconnectedness is underpinned by more diverse and sophisticated global production networks that epitomize the greater magnitude, depth, and complexity of intra- and interfirm relationships in today's global electronics industry. The empirical chapters of this book will explain the organization and co-evolution of these global production networks in relation to several causal drivers conceptualized in Coe and Yeung's (2015) theory of global production networks: (1) optimizing cost-capability ratios, (2) capitalizing on the market imperative, (3) managing financial discipline, and (4) mitigating risks.[49]

Applying this theory to global electronics in the 2010s and its East Asian context in Table 1.2, this book will showcase how these causal drivers can explain complex industrial-organizational dynamics in electronics global production networks. First, lowering cost has been a perennial challenge to lead firms since the beginning of their internationalization in the 1960s (e.g., US semiconductor firms setting up chip assembly and testing facilities in East Asia). However, lower cost in relation to higher production quality and yield were better achieved when the capability development of East Asian manufacturing partners and specialized suppliers became more mature and sophisticated in the 2010s. Second, the rise of China and other East and South Asian economies since the 2000s also created an enormous end market for semiconductors and all ICT end products. Capitalizing on this market imperative became critical to lead firms from the US and Western Europe. Third, decades of financialization, defined as the increasing domination of financial markets in corporate governance, strategy, and activities, led to much greater financial discipline and pressure on lead firms in relation to their stock prices and shareholder value, prompting more of them to outsource and externalize their manufacturing need to East Asian partners during the 2010s. Fourth, global environmental and regulatory constraints became more pronounced in the late 2010s and the early 2020s. The risks associated with these constraints must be better managed and mitigated throughout cross-border production networks.[50]

Driven by these competitive dynamics in the global economy, lead firms from advanced industrialized economies have been compelled to adopt organizational and technological innovations in order to adapt and respond effectively. These industrial-organizational fixes can be implemented primarily through the increasing fragmentation of production and vertical specialization that have defined a new form of industrial organization since the early twenty-first century. This rise of vertical specialization is linked to the vertical (intrafirm) disintegration of value chain activity within lead firms and the subsequent horizontal (interfirm) reintegration of this activity in spatially dispersed production networks and locations throughout the world. This process of vertical disintegration and vertical specialization/reintegration provides a critical *industrial-organizational platform* for East Asian firms to connect with lead firms from North America, Western Europe, and Japan. Strong interfirm partnership has been developed on the basis of mutually beneficial exploitation of firm-specific advantages, such as market access and product development (from global lead firms) and manufacturing capabilities and quality of services (from East Asian firms). This changing industrial organization has been greatly facilitated by the broad application of production technologies (e.g., modularization and platform specialization) and distinct organizational practices (e.g., outsourcing, strategic partnership, and foundry production).[51]

Technological advancement in production facilities through continuous investment is equally significant in the development of firm-specific capability among East Asian firms. Primarily because of their capability, flexibility, response time, and cost competitiveness, East Asian firms have developed strong firm-specific capabilities to serve as "system integrators" that put together different suppliers of technologies and products to serve the strategic imperatives of their global lead firm customers.[52] Through further capability development and enhancement, these East Asian firms have successfully exploited the opportunity arising from global production networks.

Throughout the 2010s, the sophisticated organizational-technological capabilities of leading electronics firms in East Asia ensured their *strategic coupling* with cross-border production networks coordinated by global lead firms. Orchestrating these global production networks in the interconnected worlds of global electronics, lead firms from the US, Western Europe, and Japan worked closely with their East Asian strategic partners in manufacturing to compete effectively through lower production costs and/or faster time-to-market. These firm-specific capabilities were critical to managing the increasing cost and complexity of disruptive technological innovations, the shortening of product cycles, and the rapid shifting of market preferences that could not be addressed only through incremental process innovations.

In semiconductors, established firms from the US, Western Europe, and Japan not only shifted a significant portion of their wafer fabs to East Asian locations to serve their end customers in PCs, mobile handsets, consumer electronics, and other industries (e.g., automotive, aerospace, and medical devices), but also engaged much more extensively East Asian providers in assembly, packaging, and testing services to lower their chipset costs and to ensure product quality and timely delivery. Meanwhile, leading East Asian foundry wafer producers, such as TSMC and Samsung, engaged a strategic coupling mechanism known as "industrial market specialization" by providing highly customized wafer manufacturing and related services to fabless design houses across the world. Their firm-specific capabilities and manufacturing excellence were manifested in new process technology, flexible production and product diversity, and sophisticated organizational knowhow and proprietary access to market information. Supported by an extensive and globalized ecosystem of partners in semiconductor equipment and materials and leading fabless customers, both TSMC and Samsung foundry overtook Intel, the industry's longtime technology leader, in process technology by the end of the 2010s and led with cutting-edge wafer fabrication in their home-based fabs in East Asia (see detailed analysis in Chapter 4).

In ICT end products such as PCs, mobile handsets, and consumer electronics, global lead firms focused on higher-value R&D activities, such as design, engineering, and system integration, and marketing, distribution, and post-sales services. They also developed sophisticated supply chain governance with their East Asian partners and suppliers to optimize the complex production of these electronic products and devices in multiple locations and subregions. This form of coupling with global production networks is known as *strategic partnership*, through which the design, engineering, and manufacturing capabilities of leading East Asian ODM firms and EMS providers are strategically integrated into the product and market development and brand management capabilities of their OEM lead firm customers.[53]

## Contributions and Organization

This book seeks to address both theoretically and empirically this sophisticated and maturing interconnectedness in the worlds of global electronics during the 2010s. By focusing on the cross-macroregional network relations between lead firms from North America, Western Europe, and Japan, and their East Asian partners and other domestic firms, I argue that this emergence and coevolution of more complex global production networks has opened up new opportunities and challenges for understanding economic restructuring in the global economy. Blending a robust theoretical framework of global production networks with in-depth empirical data on global electronics during the 2010s, this book seeks to make three distinct contributions that go beyond the existing empirical literature on the global electronics industry.

First, the book is theory-led but empirically oriented toward explaining how electronics global production networks are actually organized across macroregions and within East Asia, and why they operate in such (innovative) ways that lead firms and strategic partners from different macroregions become mutually dependent and their interfirm partnerships often go well beyond typical OEM-subcontractor relationships identified in the existing literature. My detailed empirical analysis in Chapters 4 to 6 is grounded squarely in Coe and Yeung's (2015) theory of global production networks (GPN 2.0 theory). This GPN 2.0 theory seeks causal explanations of the emergence, organization, and governance of cross-border production networks in an interdependent world economy. While a large body of literature in the social sciences has been developed since the mid-1990s in relation to global production networks and global value chains, there are few in-depth empirical studies closely aligned with this recent GPN 2.0 theory and illustrative of its explanatory efficacy.[54] The earlier theoretical perspectives in this literature between 1994 and 2005 are primarily concerned with developing analytical typologies and organizing frameworks than with conceiving a causal theory to provide the necessary explanatory power in empirical analysis, such as the GPN 2.0 theory.[55]

This work on global electronics represents the first book-length analysis that puts this new GPN 2.0 theory into its full empirical context and goes beyond case studies of specific firms or national economies.[56] Rather than being conceived as a "proof" of the theory, this empirical "stress-testing" represents a modest but necessary step in the further development of a more robust and explanatory theory of global production networks.[57] By opening up the "network box," the book offers not only a clearer focus on the most significant geographical shift in the global electronics industry since the 2000s, but also a theory-led effort in explaining this coevolutionary transformation in geographical configurations and its underlying organizational innovations and competitive dynamics that constitute the interconnected worlds of global electronics.

Second, this book's analytical focus on organizational innovations underpinning electronics global production networks centered in East Asia can motivate a better understanding of industrial and firm-specific changes in today's era of digital ICT. While many existing book-length studies have been published on the electronics industry, they tend to suffer from two general drawbacks. On the one hand, many earlier books focus empirically on the electronics industry in one particular national economy, such as the US, Japan, and Western European or East Asian nations.[58] Their primary aim is to account for the rise, fall, and restructuring of this critical industry within specific national economies. National firms or the entire industry are often the key unit of analysis in these books. We know much less about their production networks, both in the home economies and in the international markets. While this large body of work represents an important contribution to our empirical understanding of the earlier multinational worlds of electronics production, it offers relatively less on how the emergence and coevolution of cross-border production networks has fundamentally reshaped this multinational worldview of electronics production at the firm and industry levels.[59] Set within the changing East Asian national and institutional contexts summarized in Table 1.2, this book aims to fill this empirical gap by illustrating the highly complex ways in which electronics production can be organized across national borders and macroregions.[60]

Third, this book offers comprehensive and up-to-date empirical analysis that covers all major segments of the global electronics industry, from semiconductors to PCs, mobile handsets, and consumer electronics. Earlier influential studies of the industry tend to focus almost exclusively on only one of these segments, but very few cover two or more segments.[61] As explained Appendixes A and B, my study is based on new empirical material derived from a primary dataset built from 64 personal interviews with senior executives of 44 lead firms and their key partners in East Asia during the 2017–2018 period and the proprietary IHS Markit/Informa Tech quantitative datasets on global electronics in all four major segments of semiconductors, PCs, mobile handsets, and consumer electronics in 2015 and 2018. Some 36 of these 44 lead firms are among the top 15–24 global lead firms in the four segments (see details in Table B1 in Appendix B).

The GPN 2.0 theory-led analysis in this book's empirical chapters (4–6) can contribute to a deeper understanding of not only the changing organization and competitive dynamics within each segment of the electronics industry but more importantly also the complex relationships and geographical interconnections across these different segments in today's global electronics. Some of the data to be analyzed and reported in subsequent empirical chapters, such as the key ODM/EMS firms and specialized suppliers of top ten OEM firms in each segment by key components and geographical configurations of production, go substantially beyond standard industry-level or case-study-based data reported in most existing studies. Moreover, few of these earlier studies have obtained primary interview data from senior management in a large number of the top ten lead firms in these four respective segments (see Table B1 in Appendix B and Table 1.1). By combining both sets of primary data from wide-ranging firm interviews and secondary data from proprietary datasets supplied by IHS Markit/Informa Tech, this book aims to serve as a definitive analysis of the interconnected worlds of global electronics throughout the 2010s.

Since 2018, unexpected geopolitical events, US-China trade wars, and the COVID-19 pandemic have clearly created enormous uncertainty in the future organization of globalized production, whether in electronics or in many other industries. While my most recent data in the book's empirical chapters cover up to 2020 (with some forecast data till 2023) and cannot possibly say much about the world economy post-2020, I believe my empirical analysis will be useful as a benchmark for assessing changes in the early 2020s and beyond. The book's empirical material, particularly those proprietary data and interview quotes to be analyzed in Chapters 4 to 6, will be of interest to academic researchers, business analysts, and policy practitioners for their future comparative analysis of the changing organization of global production before and after the 2020/2021 pandemic and associated economic recovery (or crisis). While these ongoing geopolitical and pandemic issues are not central to the book's main narrative focusing on the 2010s, I will bring them to the fore where appropriate in different chapters and revisit them more fully in the concluding chapter.

This brings me to the organization of the book that has six further chapters. Chapter 2 examines in depth the changing fortunes of lead firms in the key segments of global electronics. In particular, I situate the emergence of new lead firms in the historical context of major industrial transformations in semiconductors, personal computers, and mobile handsets. Tracing this historical evolution of key lead firms and major segments in global electronics is important and relevant for illustrating the main arguments on the political economy of global shift at the national scale in Chapter 1 and for setting the crucial industry context for the in-depth analysis of new empirical material in later chapters focusing on the 2010s. Much more than consumer electronics, these three segments constitute the most significant drivers of global electronics today in terms of technological innovation, organizational change, and evolving geographies of global production.

Chapter 3 builds upon Coe and Yeung's (2015) conceptual work to develop a theory of interconnected worlds that will map explicitly onto the subsequent three empirical chapters (4–6). For readers less familiar with the conceptual literature on global production networks and global value chains, this "detour" will offer a quick theoretical guide on how the organizational complexity and interconnectedness of the global economy can be understood. While the GPN 2.0 theory has conceptualized the origin, emergence, causal drivers, and local and regional development outcomes of global production networks, this book's core theoretical concern is with the causal dynamics of organizing and governing electronics production networks on a worldwide basis. Chapter 3 therefore adapts its theoretical framing from the GPN 2.0 theory to conceptualize these complex interactions *within* global production networks through which firm-specific strategies and organizational innovations are causally driven by different competitive dynamics and risk environments that in turn account for the changing geographical configurations of global electronics centered in East Asia during the 2010s. Presented in three main sections, this reworked theory provides the conceptual framing on the geographical configurations ("where" in Chapter 4), causal drivers and competitive dynamics ("why" in Chapter 6), and firm-specific strategies ("how" in Chapter 5) of global production networks that connect diverse worlds of innovation and production.

In the first empirical chapter, I draw upon both primary interview data and secondary IHS Markit/Informa Tech custom data to specify the complex geographical configurations or *where* of global electronics centered in East Asia during the 2010–2018 period. Framed in the changing national contexts of industry development in Table 1.2, this empirical specification is necessary to map out the coevolutionary shift in the worlds of global electronics from the earlier multinational worlds during the late twentieth century to more fully interconnected worlds centered in East Asia during the 2010s. The geographical analysis in this chapter is conducted in two dimensions—industrial-organizational and intrafirm configurations. First, the industrial-organizational geography of global production networks is analyzed on the basis of the worldwide locations of (1) semiconductor production by lead firms and foundry providers between 2000 and 2018, and (2) outsourced manufacturing activities to ODM firms and EMS providers in 2015 and 2018 by their OEM customers in PCs and mobile handsets, and TVs (together with panel display makers). Second, the intrafirm geography of production networks among the forty-four firms interviewed is explored in relation to the worldwide locations of their key corporate functions, from headquarters and manufacturing facilities to R&D, product development, and sales and marketing operations. The empirical evidence in both sections demonstrates conclusively the domination of Northeast Asia, particularly China, as key sites in global electronics manufacturing in all four major segments throughout the 2010s. This geographical consolidation of electronics manufacturing points clearly to its pivotal shift toward East Asia by the late 2010s.

Based on the same custom dataset and interview material, Chapter 5 focuses on *how* firm strategies and organizational innovations have enabled these electronics global production networks to be centered in East Asia. I have taken this analytical step first so that Chapter 6's causal explanations can account for both the *where* and the *how* of these production networks. Mapping directly onto firm strategies theorized in Chapter 3, Chapter 5 sheds light on these strategies and organizational innovations in two ways.

First, I analyze the semiconductor production networks and the top four to five key component suppliers for OEM lead firms in PCs and mobile handsets in 2015 and 2018 to determine their insourcing and outsourcing strategies. This analysis of intrafirm sourcing addresses the most fundamental strategic choice of make/buy decisions (i.e., internalization vs. outsourcing) confronting lead firms and specifies the conditions under which insourcing might be preferred over outsourcing (e.g., innovation and market needs, and risk management). Second, complicated interfirm control and partnership relationships with major customers exist and need to be organized and managed carefully in these different segments. These relationships go beyond OEM lead firm-supplier relationships to include those fabless-foundry, OEM-OEM, ODM-supplier, and ODM-platform leader relationships. The section thus analyzes interfirm network governance dynamics between lead firms and their key customers, suppliers, and strategic partners. My analysis shows that supply chain practices vary substantially across the different segments of global electronics.

The final empirical Chapter 6 provides causal explanations grounded in the GPN 2.0 theory to explain the geographical configurations (where) and firm-specific strategies (how) of global production networks examined respectively in Chapters 4 and 5. Following closely Chapter 3's conceptual framing, I focus on the four sets of causal drivers explaining *why* electronics production networks are driven by specific competitive dynamics at the firm level: optimizing cost-capability ratios, capitalizing on market imperatives, managing financial discipline, and mitigating risks. First, OEM lead firms are particularly concerned with managing cost-capability ratios—the lower the better. Labor cost is still important in assembly production, whereas logistics cost is critical to production network configurations. Second, market imperatives often exert the most influence on a lead firm's geographical organization of production networks because market proximity and customer intimacy are important to locational decisions. New market dynamics in the Asia Pacific can also lead to the greater importance of reaching out to end customers, and large home markets are crucial as testbeds and core business. Third, financial discipline is particularly significant in heavy capital investment by top semiconductor manufacturers and foundry providers and meeting market forecasts by OEM lead firms in end products. Finally, lead firms in these segments also try to source from strategic suppliers with geographically distributed production networks to mitigate environmental risks. Unfavorable government regulation and policies can significantly impact on the geographical diversification of production networks in Asia and elsewhere. The chapter concludes with a comparative analysis of the relative importance of these causal drivers in explaining the key geographical and organizational configurations of production networks in the four segments of global electronics during the 2010s.

In the concluding Chapter 7, I examine the key issues and challenges confronting innovation and development in the interconnected worlds of global electronics characterized by the geographical concentration of production, stringent control and integration within global production networks, and profound uncertainties in market dynamics, technological shifts, and regulatory and geopolitical changes. I begin with some concluding remarks on the book's key findings in relation to globalized electronics production by the late 2010s. I then discuss their major implications for business and public policy in the postpandemic and post-Trump 2020s. For business, I argue that there is a much greater need to be closer to end-market customers and strategic suppliers in East Asia and other macroregions. Supply chain capability and network resilience will remain as the core competitive advantages to future business success, and global lead firms can better compete in the post-COVID-19 world economy through developing strategic partnership with key suppliers. The chapter also addresses the key implications for public policy oriented toward promoting economic development through participation in electronics global production networks. At the end of the chapter, I reflect briefly on some conceptual and methodological lessons from this book's "stress-testing" of the GPN 2.0 theory before (re)turning to the broader academic literature and envisioning some research agendas for advancing future work on global production networks and global value chains in the 2020s and beyond.

## CHAPTER 2

# Changing Fortunes in Global Electronics: A Brief History

ELECTRONICS IS INDISPUTABLY PART of the digital era identified by Zysman and Newman (2006) as the "second great transformation"—after the first great transformation associated with industrial revolution and the development of machines for production in modern capitalism. This book's empirical focus is on the *equipment* or *hardware* part of today's digital era that comprises three fundamental parts: information, networks, and equipment. Underpinned by software and other peripherals, these parts constitute what is commonly known as the information and communications technology (ICT) sector of the global economy in the twenty-first century. The equipment part of this ICT sector not only is one of the leading and fast-growing manufacturing sectors in the global economy, but also is characterized by its immense geographical spread and vital significance for business growth, industrial linkages, and, more broadly, economic development worldwide.

Before we proceed further with a theory-led analysis of new empirical material on electronics global production networks underpinning the interconnected worlds of the 2010s (Chapters 4–6), it is useful to set the global dominance of lead firms in these production networks within the historical context of the emergence of three major segments in the electronics industry from the 1970s/1980s onward: semiconductors, personal computers (PCs), and mobile handsets. Extending Chapter 1's main arguments on the coevolutionary shift in the worlds of electronics at the national scale, this chapter's brief history focuses on leading national firms within their changing industrial-organizational dynamics over time. This historical approach also offers a path-dependent view on the emerging worlds of interconnections in global electronics since the 1990s. Here, we start with the semiconductors segment, without which digitalization and the ICT hardware of PCs and mobile handsets today would look very different. As illustrated in Figure 2.1, technological advancement in semi-conductors maps directly onto leading electronics end products during each historical period, from early day consumer electronics to PCs and mobile handsets during the past three decades and artificial intelligence, fifth-generation (5G) communications, robotics, and cloud computing into the 2020s. In this chapter though, I do not discuss the history of the consumer electronics segment, as it is more mature and relatively less sig-nificant in technological innovation and market size than PCs and mobile handsets in global electronics today (see also Table 1.1).[1]

Over the past thirty years, ICT hardware has been a critical component of expanding world exports, and merchandise exports have become a main driver of development in the global economy. In Figure 2.2, data from

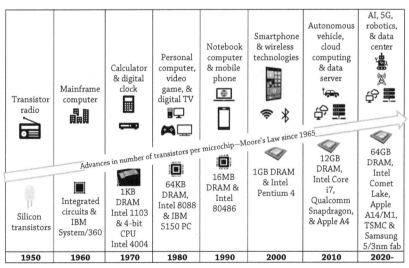

Credits: All icons from Microsoft Word Icons, except transistors from iStock.com/ONYXprj and Intel 4004 CPU from flickr.com/Simon Claessen, with permission.

FIGURE 2.1. Historical evolution of semiconductors and related electronics prod-ucts, 1950–2020s.

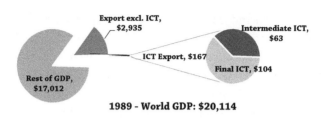

**1989 - World GDP: $20,114**

Export excl. ICT, $2,935
Intermediate ICT, $63
ICT Export, $167
Final ICT, $104
Rest of GDP, $17,012

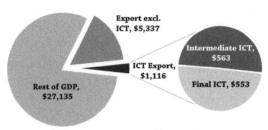

**2000 - World GDP: $33,588**

Export excl. ICT, $5,337
Intermediate ICT, $563
ICT Export, $1,116
Final ICT, $553
Rest of GDP, $27,135

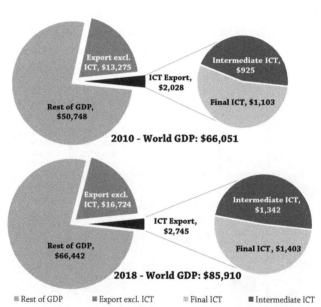

**2010 - World GDP: $66,051**

Export excl. ICT, $13,275
Intermediate ICT, $925
ICT Export, $2,028
Final ICT, $1,103
Rest of GDP, $50,748

**2018 - World GDP: $85,910**

Export excl. ICT, $16,724
Intermediate ICT, $1,342
ICT Export, $2,745
Final ICT, $1,403
Rest of GDP, $66,442

■ Rest of GDP    ■ Export excl. ICT    ▨ Final ICT    ■ Intermediate ICT

Note: In end June 2021, the latest complete data available in the following databases are from 1989 up to 2019. See chapter endnote 2 for my choice of the historical peak year 2018.

FIGURE 2.2. World GDP and merchandise exports of ICT hardware, 1989–2018 (in current US$ billions).

Sources: World GDP data from World Bank World Development Indicators (http://data .worldbank.org/data-catalog/world-development-indicators); World merchandise exports data from UNCTADstat (http://unctadstat.unctad.org/wds); ICT hardware exports data refer to "Intermediate Electronics; Final Electronics" standard product groups from the World Bank's World Integrated Trade Solutions (WITS)-GVC Database (HS 2017 update using a consistent 175 country panel that accounts for 95–98% of world trade) (Advance-Query/GVC via https://wits.worldbank.org/WITS/WITS/Restricted/Login.aspx, accessed on June 17, 2021).

World Bank show that ICT hardware accounted for 14 percent of world merchandise exports in 2018, up from a meagre 5 percent in 1989 when the multinational worlds of electronics began to shift in favor of the emerging interconnected worlds of globalized electronics.[2] In 2000, the share of ICT hardware in world merchandise exports reached the highest point at 17 percent. At its historical peak of $19.5 trillion in 2018, world merchandise exports contributed to some 23 percent or almost one-quarter of world GDP ($85.9 trillion). But world exports declined to $19 trillion in 2019 and $17.6 trillion in 2020. In 1989, total exports were only $3.1 trillion or about 15 percent of world GDP ($20.1 trillion). More importantly, from a modest sum of $167 billion in 1989, ICT hardware exports increased by over 10 percent on a compound annual growth basis to reach a historical high at $2.75 trillion in 2018 (but declined slightly to $2.65 trillion in 2019 and likely lower in 2020). As the key indicator of the worldwide geographical fragmentation of hardware production, the share of intermediate goods, such as parts, components, and modules, in these ICT hardware exports also grew from 38 percent in 1989 to reach its first peak of 51 percent in 2000 and remained at 49 percent in 2018 (see the more detailed analysis of this geographical fragmentation in the 2010s in Chapter 4).

As global electronics production and merchandise exports have expanded massively during the past three decades, the ICT hardware value chain has also become much "longer" and its underlying production networks much more complex, as more intermediate parts and high-value modules are manufactured in countries outside the final assembly of finished products. By 2018 and as shown in Table 1.1, we can observe a very high degree of market concentration among the top ten lead firms in all major segments of global electronics. Figure 2.3 illustrates further the combined revenue of all 55,143 firms worldwide in these four segments at $4.4 trillion in 2018.[3] PCs and mobile handsets are by far two of the largest segments in global electronics. At $2.1 trillion in worldwide revenue, the mobile handset segment was the largest in global electronics, accounting for over 47 percent of total revenue and 61 percent of the total number of firms. With 14,280 firms, the PC segment followed with $1.4 trillion in revenue or 32 percent of total. More significantly, a very small number of publicly listed firms were dominant in each of these segments, with the highest concentration in semiconductors and consumer electronics. In PCs and consumer electronics, the top 15–20 lead firms accounted for

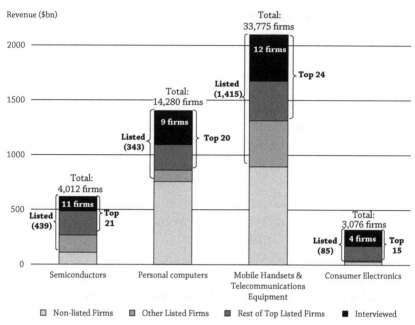

Revenue ($bn)

FIGURE 2.3. Global electronics revenues by major segments, 2018 (in US$ billions).

Sources: Orbis database search (https://www.bvdinfo.com, April–May 2019) and author's interviews.

Note: Firm and revenue data in 2018 are from Orbis database, which contains records of close to 400 million firms worldwide, including over 70,000 public listed firms. Standard NAICS SIC codes were used to identify all firms with revenue data: (1) semiconductors: 3674 (Semiconductors and related devices); (2) personal computers: 3571 (Electronic computers) and 3577 (Computer peripheral equipment); (3) mobile handsets and telecommunications equipment: 3661 (Telephone and telegraph apparatus), 3669 (Communications equipment), and 3679 (Electronic components); and (4) consumer electronics: 3651 (Household audio and video equipment). A few lead firms were moved to the most appropriate segment (e.g., SK Hynix, Infineon, and MediaTek to semiconductors, Dell to personal computers, and Philips and Hitachi to consumer electronics).

84–97 percent of total revenue by all publicly listed firms in 2018. Even in semiconductors and mobile handsets, the top 25 lead firms still contributed to over 65 percent of total revenue by all listed firms. In short, the top 15–25 global lead firms today are extremely powerful in market/revenue share in all segments of global electronics. As indicated in Figure 2.3, some 36 of such global lead firms across all four segments were interviewed for this study during the 2017–2018 period.[4]

The following three sections trace the emergence, key shifts, and drivers of change in semiconductors, PCs, and mobile handsets. This historical analysis provides the necessary industry- and firm-specific contexts for us to appreciate the complex global production networks centered in East Asia during the 2010s that will be analyzed in later empirical Chapters

4–6. As summarized in Table 2.1, this brief history writ large of global electronics since the 1960s witnesses the rise and fall of different national firms and economies in these three major segments and the growing concentration among fewer lead firms and the greater interconnectedness of their production networks and national economies over time. Table 2.1 also provides a quick guide to the detailed analysis in the following three sections.

## Semiconductors

Ever since World War II, the United States has been at the technological forefront of semiconductors, but the dominance of US lead firms has been challenged over time by leading semiconductor firms from Japan, South Korea, Taiwan, and, more recently, China.[5] While the birth of modern semiconductors can be traced back to the invention of the rectifier (AC-DC converter) in 1874, the transistor era for semiconductors and digital computing (Figure 2.1) only began with two key and related inventions— the point-contact transistor by John Bardeen and Walter Brattain at Bell Telephone Laboratories (Bell Labs in short) in New Jersey on December 23, 1947, and the junction transistor by William Shockley in the US in 1948.[6] In February 1959, Jack Kilby from Texas Instruments and, four months later, Robert Noyce from Fairchild almost simultaneously invented silicon-based bipolar integrated circuits or "chips" that heralded the beginning of the "integrated circuits era" until today. By the late 1950s, these semiconductor chips had replaced vacuum tubes as the dominant mode of electronics signal processing and transmission, ushering in the "microelectronics revolution" noted in Table 2.1.[7]

From the late 1950s onward, the integrated circuits era was dominated by the early founders located in Silicon Valley, such as Shockley Laboratories (founded in 1955) and Fairchild Semiconductor (founded in October 1957 by a core group of eight former Shockley employees, including Robert Noyce, the de facto leader, and Gordon Moore, credited for his "Moore's Law" in 1965; see Figure 2.1), and other pioneers such as Texas Instruments (founded in 1951 from Geophysical Service Inc.).[8] By the end of 1961, some 150 to 200 semiconductor operations were spun off from a handful of these firms that had existed in the mid-1950s. Throughout the 1960s, many smaller US firms entered into the semiconductor market as independent producers—commonly known as "integrated device manufacturing" (IDM) firms. By supplying integrated circuits to other

TABLE 2.1. Changing fortunes in global electronics: Key trends and drivers, 1959–2021

| Evolution | Semiconductors | Personal computers | Mobile handsets |
|---|---|---|---|
| Emergence | 1959–late 1970s | 1981–mid-1990s | 1983–1990s |
| Nature | "Microelectronics revolution": invention of integrated circuits and microprocessors | "PC revolution": IBM-compatible desktop PCs | Mobile or feature phones |
| Industrial organization | Vertical integration through integrated device manufacturing | Vertical integration, with limited outsourcing | Vertical integration, with limited outsourcing |
| Leading economies | US | US, Japan | US, Finland, Sweden |
| Lead firms | Fairchild, Texas Instruments, Intel, Motorola, National Semiconductor, AMD | IBM, Apple, Compaq, Packard Bell, Hewlett-Packard, NEC, Fujitsu | Motorola, Nokia, Ericsson |
| Key shifts | Mid-1980s–2010s | Mid-2000s–2010s | 2007–2010s |
| Processes of transition | Changing leadership in memory chips Rise of fabless-foundry model of outsourcing chip production | Rise of East Asian OEMs Market shift to notebook PCs Substantial international outsourcing | Market shift: "smartphone revolution" Substantial international outsourcing |
| Drivers of change | Strong command of process and manufacturing technologies Decoupling of chip design-fabrication with design automation software and intellectual property for design cores High and risky capital investment in new fabs New demand from data centers and wireless communications | Lower cost and higher capability of ODM partners in East Asia Strong ecosystem of suppliers in East Asia | Launch of iPhones and Galaxy S, with powerful operating systems and application processors Lower cost and higher capability of EMS providers in East Asia Strong ecosystem of suppliers in East Asia |

| Evolution | Semiconductors | Personal computers | Mobile handsets |
|---|---|---|---|
| Leading economies | Japan, South Korea, Taiwan, US | US, China, Taiwan, Japan | US, South Korea, China |
| Lead firms | Toshiba & NEC, Samsung & Hynix, TSMC/US fabless (Broadcom, Qualcomm, Nvidia) | Hewlett-Packard, Dell, Lenovo (IBM), Acer, Asus, Toshiba, Fujitsu | Apple, Samsung, Huawei, (with Nokia, Blackberry, Motorola in feature phones) |

| Current status | 2020–2021 | 2020–2021 | 2020–2021 |
|---|---|---|---|
| Nature | Codominance of IDM and fabless/foundry firms High concentration in top 10 Cutting-edge process technology in foundry (5nm) Very high cost of new fabs Dominance of end markets in computer & data storage, wireless communications | Dominance of notebook PCs in revitalized PC market (postpandemic) Very high concentration in top six vendors Very high outsourcing to ODM strategic partners | Dominance of smartphones in maturing market Very high concentration in top six vendors A mix of in-house and outsourced production |
| Lead firms | Intel & Micron, Samsung & Hynix, Broadcom, Qualcomm, Nvidia, Apple, MediaTek | Lenovo, Hewlett-Packard, Dell, Acer, Asus, Apple | Samsung, Apple, Xiaomi, Oppo, Vivo, Huawei/Honor |
| Key manufacturing partners (East Asia) | TSMC, Samsung, UMC, GlobalFoundries | Compal, Quanta, Wistron, Inventec | Foxconn, Pegatron, Flex, BYD |
| Leading economies | US, South Korea, Taiwan, Japan, Germany | US, China, Taiwan | South Korea, US, China |

manufacturers of consumer and industrial electronics products, these IDM firms began to outcompete those large and vertically integrated electronics firms from the transistor era (e.g., the big three of General Electric, RCA, and Westinghouse). By 1966, Texas Instruments led with 17 percent share of the US market, and Fairchild Semiconductor's 13 percent share placed it ahead of Motorola's 12 percent. They were far ahead of the big three electronics firms (at 18 percent collectively).[9]

By the late 1960s, Silicon Valley had become *the* hub of the semiconductor industry in the US and worldwide and was christened as such by Don Hoefler in early 1971. Between 1968 and 1973, the arrival and success of these highly innovative IDM firms, such as Intel, National Semiconductor, Texas Instruments, Motorola, and Advanced Micro Devices (AMD), meant that by the late 1970s, the US had virtually dominated the entire semiconductor industry. As illustrated in Figure 2.1, Intel introduced the world's first 1KB DRAM memory chip Intel 1103 in October 1970 and the 4-bit microprocessor Intel 4004 in November 1971.[10] Between 1947 and 1981, US semiconductor firms produced 48 of the 52 major innovations in semiconductor technology, such as the transistor (Shockley, Bardeen, and Brattain, 1947), the "planar" wafer fabrication process (Jean Hoerni from Fairchild, 1958), the integrated circuit (Kilby from Texas Instrument and Noyce from Fairchild, 1959), and the microprocessor (Ted Hoff from Intel, 1971).[11] As indicated in Table 2.1, these vertically integrated IDM firms designed, manufactured, and marketed specialized semiconductor products, such as microprocessor chipsets and memory devices, as core components for the production of modern electronics products such as computers, consumer, telecommunications, and industrial devices.[12]

From almost nonexistence at the beginning of the 1950s, the worldwide sales of semiconductors reached $115 million in 1956, $750 million in 1960, $1.7 billion in 1965, and $3 billion in 1970.[13] In 1956, US domestic semiconductor sales was only $80 million. Between 1960 and 1970, domestic shipments in US semiconductors increased threefold from $571 million to $1.7 billion. More significantly, the share of integrated circuits in these shipments increased tenfold from only 5.1 percent in 1960 to 51.6 percent in 1970, replacing diodes, rectifiers, and transistors as the dominant semiconductor devices.[14] In 1969, production by US-based firms accounted for 55 percent of world semiconductor consumption at $2.2 billion.[15] Table 2.2 shows that in 1972, two US firms, Texas Instruments and Motorola, had the largest world market shares, followed at a distance by Philips (the

Netherlands), Fairchild (the US), and Toshiba and Hitachi (Japan). In 1980, US firms still accounted for nearly 60 percent of the $10 billion world market in semiconductor devices, as compared to Japan's 15 percent share, and Texas Instruments and Motorola remained as the top two players in Table 2.2, followed by Philips, National Semiconductor, and NEC among the top five.[16] As explained earlier in Chapter 1's main arguments, this was the peak of the multinational worlds of electronics separated territorially by different national systems of innovation and production and governed by protectionist regulatory regimes.

Since the mid-1980s, two major shifts have taken place in semiconductors that presage the rise and eventual dominance of East Asia in global semiconductor production (see Table 2.1):

(1)    changing leadership in memory chips, and
(2)    the rise of fabless-foundry model of international outsourcing and chip production.

First, the decline of the US in semiconductors and, in particular, memory chips began in the 1980s, initially due to major challenges by semiconductor firms from Japan and, later in the 1990s, by firms from South Korea, Taiwan, and elsewhere.[17] By 1982, the US share in the global semiconductor market fell to 51 percent, and Japan more than doubled to 35 percent. In 1984, Japan's NEC, Hitachi, Toshiba, and Fujitsu were ranked among the top ten IDM firms. During the 1980–1990 period (see Table 2.2), semiconductor firms from Japan (e.g., NEC, Toshiba, Hitachi, and others) and Western European countries, such as Italy and France (STMicroelectronics), Germany (Siemens), and the Netherlands (Philips), emerged as major challengers to US dominance in the industry, particularly in analogue, discrete, and memory (DRAM) devices.

The top five market leader Intel exited the DRAM market in 1986 to focus on higher margin microprocessors that subsequently yielded its number one industry position a decade later in 1995. As lamented by its then CEO Andrew Grove, "Intel is a sizable and strong company, but we are located in the wrong country. All of the action in our industry is moving to Japan."[18] Meanwhile, nine of the eleven US-based DRAM producers exited the memory market. At its peak in 1986, Japan's share of world semiconductor market increased to 46 percent and surpassed the 43 percent share held by US firms; some 75 percent of world's DRAM products and 95 percent of the latest generation DRAM devices came from

TABLE 2.2. World's top 15 semiconductor firms by revenue and market share, 1972–2020 (in US$ billions and percent)

| 2018 rank | 1980 rank | Firm | 1972 % | 1980 % | 1990 % | 2000 $ | 2000 % | 2010 $ | 2010 % | 2018 $ | 2018 % | 2019 $ | 2020 $ |
|---|---|---|---|---|---|---|---|---|---|---|---|---|---|
| | | *IDM firms* | | | | | | | | | | | |
| 1 | - | Samsung Electronics | - | - | - | 8.9 | 4.0 | 28.4 | 9.1 | 74.6 | 15.4 | 52.4 | 57.7 |
| 2 | 8 | Intel | 1.3 | 4.1 | 7.0 | 30.2 | 13.7 | 40.4 | 13.0 | 69.9 | 14.4 | 67.8 | 72.8 |
| 3 | - | SK Hynix | - | - | - | 5.1 | 2.3 | 10.4 | 3.3 | 36.3 | 7.5 | 22.3 | 25.8 |
| 4 | - | Micron Technology | - | - | - | 6.3 | 2.9 | 8.9 | 2.9 | 29.7 | 6.1 | 20.3 | 22.0 |
| 7 | 1 | Texas Instruments | 11.8 | 11.2 | 6.0 | 9.2 | 4.2 | 13.0 | 4.2 | 15.4 | 3.2 | 13.4 | 13.6 |
| 8 | 7 | Kioxia (Toshiba) | 4.2 | 4.5 | 7.0 | 10.4 | 4.7 | 13.0 | 4.2 | 11.4 | 2.4 | 7.8 | 10.4 |
| 10 | - | STMicroelectronics | 3.6 | 2.2 | - | 7.9 | 3.6 | 10.3 | 3.3 | 9.7 | 2.0 | 9.6 | 10.2 |
| 11 | 10 | Infineon (Siemens) | 2.3 | 3.0 | - | 4.6 | 2.1 | 6.3 | 2.0 | 9.1 | 1.9 | 9.1 | 9.6 |
| 12 | 3 | NXP (Philips) | 5.1 | 6.6 | 3.0 | 6.3 | 2.9 | 4.0 | 1.3 | 9.0 | 1.9 | 8.9 | 8.6 |
| 14 | 5 | Renesas Elec. (NEC) | - | 5.4 | 8.0 | 8.2 | 3.7 | 11.9 | 3.8 | 6.7 | 1.4 | 6.5 | 6.5 |
| - | 6 | Elpida (Hitachi) | 3.9 | 4.7 | 7.0 | 5.7 | 2.6 | 6.5 | 2.1 | - | - | - | - |
| - | 2 | Freescale (Motorola) | 9.0 | 7.8 | 6.0 | 5.0 | 2.3 | 4.4 | 1.4 | - | - | - | - |
| - | - | Fujitsu | - | - | 5.0 | 5.0 | 2.3 | 3.1 | 1.0 | - | - | - | - |

| | | | | | | | | | | | | |
|---|---|---|---|---|---|---|---|---|---|---|---|---|
| Mitsubishi | - | - | - | 4.0 | 5.8 | 2.6 | 1.6 | 0.5 | - | - | - | - |
| National Semi. | 4 | 2.2 | 5.5 | 4.0 | - | - | 1.4 | 0.4 | - | - | - | - |
| Fairchild Semi. | 9 | 4.8 | 4.0 | - | 1.4 | 0.6 | 1.6 | 0.5 | - | - | - | - |
| *Fablless firms* | | | | | | | | | | | | |
| Broadcom | 5 | - | - | - | 1.1 | 0.5 | 6.7 | 2.2 | 17.5 | 3.6 | 15.3 | 15.8 |
| Qualcomm | 6 | - | - | - | 1.2 | 0.5 | 7.2 | 2.3 | 16.6 | 3.4 | 13.6 | 17.6 |
| Nvidia | 9 | - | - | - | 0.7 | 0.3 | 3.1 | 1.0 | 10.4 | 2.1 | 7.3 | 10.6 |
| MediaTek | 13 | - | - | - | 0.4 | 0.2 | 3.5 | 1.1 | 7.9 | 1.6 | 8.0 | 11.0 |
| AMD | 15 | - | - | - | 3.8 | 1.7 | 6.4 | 2.1 | 6.0 | 1.2 | 6.7 | 9.8 |
| Total fablless revenue | | - | - | - | 16.7 | 7.6 | 65.4 | 18.9 | 97.4 | 20.1 | 126 | 153 |
| Top 10 firms | | 49.7 | 56.8 | 57.0 | 98.9 | 44.8 | 150 | 48.1 | 292 | 60.2 | 232 | 257 |
| Total market ($) | | 3.5 | 10.0 | 50.5 | 221 | - | 312 | - | 485 | - | 422 | 466 |

Note: See full table and notes in Appendix C Table C1.
Sources: Malerba (1985); Brown and Linden (2011); Yeung (2016); IHS Markit/Informa Tech Custom Research for GPN@NUS Centre, July–October 2016 and 2019; Gartner and IC Insights, April–May 2021; and author's interviews.

Japanese firms.[19] By the late 1980s, the US share had dropped further to 37 percent, and Japanese firms had replaced US firms as the dominant market player with almost 50 percent of the entire semiconductor market. As argued by Angel (1994, 66), while Japan's state-sponsored cooperative research program in the late 1970s was instrumental in the catching up of Japanese firms in semiconductor process and manufacturing technologies, "the subsequent competitive success of Japanese firms, however, had less to do with this much publicized form of government intervention than with the internal development efforts of individual firms and the superior manufacturing performance achieved by Japanese semiconductor producers throughout much of the 1980s."[20]

Japan's technological and market leadership in the global semiconductor industry persisted through to the late 1990s when, as was argued in Chapter 1, the multinational worlds of electronics began to shift toward greater internationalization and interdependency. As indicated in Table 2.2, five Japanese firms—NEC (merged with Renesas in 2010), Toshiba, Hitachi, Fujitsu, and Mitsubishi—were still among the top ten semiconductor firms in 2000. Benefitting from its dominant role in microprocessors for PCs, market leader Intel's revenue of $30 billion was far ahead of the next two largest semiconductor firms: Toshiba ($10.4 billion) and Texas Instruments ($9.2 billion). Most importantly, two latecomers from South Korea, Samsung and Hyundai (later renamed to SK Hynix in 2012), began to pose a serious challenge to almost all of these top semiconductor firms from the US and Japan. Their success in the DRAM market owed less to the initial inducement from South Korea's developmental state under President Park Chung Hee, and much more to their subsequent in-house R&D labs, technology agreements with friendly global lead firms, and international industrial associations, particularly in a more liberalized domestic context since the 2000s as described in Chapter 1 and Table 1.2.[21]

To Lee, Lim, and Song (2005, 42), Samsung went beyond second-mover advantages through the successful combination of "technological regimes, the competitive advantages of the innovation outcomes in the market, the foreign and domestic knowledge base, the government policies and firm strategies." Its heavy investments in R&D and production facilities were strategic to its economies of scale that became a formidable barrier to entry to existing competitors from Japan and the US and other latecomers from Taiwan and China. Between 2000 and 2010 in Table 2.2, Samsung's semiconductors revenue more than tripled from $8.9 billion to $28.4 billion. During the same period, most of the top ten Japanese firms and Micron, the only US DRAM competitor, experienced modest increase or even decline in revenue. Throughout the 2010s, Samsung closed its revenue gap with the industry's leader, Intel, and managed to overtake the latter in 2018 with a record revenue of $74.6 billion and a 15.4 percent of the entire semiconductor market. Samsung or Intel's revenue was at least double of the third and fourth largest firms (SK Hynix and Micron). As shown in Table 2.2, the substantial decline in the global semiconductor market in 2019, particularly demand for memory devices, reversed their pole positions.

As remarked in Table 2.1, another extremely important shift in the industrial organization of semiconductor production has taken place since the mid-1980s and thereafter. This refers to the emergence of the fabless-foundry model of chip design and manufacturing that has shaken up the entire industry previously dominated by IDM firms and captive producers (e.g., IBM Microelectronics division), and enabled the massive growth of mobile devices, such as notebooks, smartphones, and Internet of Things products, and data and networking centers during the subsequent two decades—more on these product segments during the 2010s in Chapter 4. To Brown and Linden (2011, 59), this "unforeseen development of semiconductor foundries greatly relieved the pressure on the industry from the rising costs of building fabs."[22] In this new model of semiconductor global production networks, a fabless firm does not need to have manufacturing facilities for wafer fabrication or "fab" in short. Instead, it specializes in developing proprietary technology and designing logic and processor chipsets for ICT products, such as mobile devices, digital TVs, cloud-based servers, and automotive digital display clusters. A fabless firm normally enters into long-term contracts with dedicated or "pureplay" semiconductor foundry service providers, mostly from Taiwan as discussed later, to produce cutting-edge chipsets and other semiconductor devices. Between 1985 and 1994, some 250 fabless start-ups had emerged in Silicon Valley. By 2002, the US hosted 475 of the 640 fabless firms worldwide.[23]

In industrial-organizational terms, the arrival of this innovative pureplay foundry model, defined as foundry fabs dedicated to serving external customers only, means that large capital-intensive foundry providers can meet the cutting-edge wafer fabrication needs based on proprietary designs supplied by their customers such as fabless chip design firms or even those "fab-lite" IDM firms that are unwilling to invest in cutting-edge fabs. Meanwhile, these fabless and fab-lite firms can avoid the heavy capital investment required in building multi-billion-dollar fabs that may go underutilized and depreciate quickly. Outsourcing a portion of their chips to foundry providers, some IDM firms can also hedge the high risk of building new expensive fabs by using foundry capacity during upswings in demand or shorter product life cycles or volume, and by benchmarking in-house fabs against these pureplay foundry providers. By the late 1990s, this fabless-foundry model had enabled the internationalization of semiconductor production beyond simply the assembly, packaging, and testing of chips fabricated in the US, Europe, or Japan. As described by Mazurek (1999, 88), "Whereas design, fabrication, and assembly once took place under a single factory roof, a chip engineered and sold by a Texas firm may now be manufactured by a competitor in Phoenix, New York, or Taiwan, assembled in Singapore, and sold in Los Angeles."

Since the 2000s, this organizational separation of the design and fabrication of semiconductor chipsets has offered both fabless firms and their foundry providers a very significant joint window of opportunity in the rapidly growing global production networks of mobile and networking devices (see my detailed analysis in Chapters 4–6). As argued by Macher, Mowery, and Di Minin (2007, 236), "In contrast to the challenges of the 1980s that threatened the viability and very survival of the U.S. semiconductor industry, the challenges of the early 21st century for U.S. semiconductor firms stem from the need to manage this global division of labor successfully while maintaining leadership in innovation." The enormous success of fabless chip design firms, primarily from the US (and some from Taiwan and elsewhere), is illustrated by their massive growth between 2000 and 2020.[24] As shown in Table 2.2, the top five fabless firms, as market leaders in 2020, had only very modest revenue in 2000 (except AMD when it was still an IDM making microprocessors for PCs). Even Broadcom and Qualcomm, today's two clear market leaders in wireless modem and mobile processor chips shown in Figure 2.1, had just exceeded $1 billion in revenue in 2000 (when Intel's revenue was $30 billion and Toshiba was $10 billion). But their revenue would grow exponentially in the next two decades to respectively $15.8 billion and $17.6 billion and ranked fifth and sixth largest semiconductor firms in 2020.[25] This sharply upward growth trend also occurs to two other market leaders in graphics processors (Nvidia), and system-on-a-chip solutions (MediaTek). From a relatively small total global semiconductor market share of about 7.6

percent in 2000, the revenue share of all fabless firms more than doubled to 18.9 percent in 2010 and reached 32.8 percent in 2020. The total fabless revenue also grew from $16.7 billion in 2000 to peak at $153 billion in 2020.

Table 2.3 offers further details on the world's top fabless firms during the 2000–2020 period. Not surprisingly, the US has been a dominant player in this fabless market. US firms took the top three positions and seven of the top ten positions in 2018, and this trend continued in 2019 and 2020. The market share of the top five fabless firms grew significantly from 40.7 percent in 2000 to 42.1 percent in 2010 and peaked at 61.4 percent in 2018. Similar to the pecking order of IDM firms, this group of fabless firms also experienced tremendous change during this period. Several market leaders in 2000 (e.g., Avago and Altera) were acquired by or merged with other fabless firms (e.g., Broadcom). Other market leaders in 2000, such as Xilinx and PMC-Sierra, experienced stagnation in their revenue and relative decline in market positions.

More crucially, the incredible success of all top five US fabless market leaders is premised on the fabless-foundry model of organizing chip design and manufacturing that simultaneously requires the state-of-the-art production capability and capacity of leading foundry wafer manufacturers mostly based in East Asia, such as those in Table 2.4. Founded respectively in 1980 and 1987 as spin-offs of Taiwan's state-sponsored Industrial Technology Research Institute (ITRI), United Microelectronics Corporation (UMC) and Taiwan Semiconductor Manufacturing Company (TSMC) have been the top three market leaders in semiconductor foundry services since the early 1990s.[26] At the peak of Taiwan's developmental state and sectoral industrial policy (see Table 1.2), ITRI obtained the initial, and often obsolete, technologies in chip fabrication (7-micron node) from the US firm RCA in 1976 and 2-micron technology node from Philips a decade later. These technologies were transferred to UMC and TSMC at the time of their spin-offs in 1980 and 1987. While state-funded R&D institutes were important to the early founding of these foundry providers, their efficacy significantly diminished by the mid-1990s when TSMC and UMC had developed world-class technologies and grown massively to become market leaders in their own right.[27]

The most significant growth period for both TSMC and UMC, however, came from the semiconductor booms in the mid-1990s and the mid-2000s.[28] Their rise to global prominence occurred only at least ten to

TABLE 2.3. World's top fabless semiconductor firms by revenue and market share, 2000–2020 (in US$ billions and percent)

| 2018 rank | 2000 rank | Firm | HQ | 2000 $ | 2010 $ | 2010 % | 2015 $ | 2015 % | 2018 $ | 2018 % | 2019 $ | 2020 $ |
|---|---|---|---|---|---|---|---|---|---|---|---|---|
| 1 | 5 | Broadcom | US | 1.1 | 6.7 | 10.2 | 8.4 | 9.7 | 17.5 | 18.0 | 15.3 | 15.8 |
| 2 | 4 | Qualcomm | US | 1.2 | 7.2 | 11.0 | 16.5 | 19.0 | 16.6 | 17.0 | 13.6 | 17.6 |
| 3 | 6 | Nvidia | US | 0.7 | 3.2 | 4.9 | 4.4 | 5.1 | 10.4 | 10.7 | 7.3 | 10.6 |
| 4 | 8 | MediaTek | Taiwan | 0.4 | 3.6 | 5.5 | 6.7 | 7.7 | 7.9 | 8.1 | 8.0 | 11.0 |
| 5 | - | Apple | US | - | - | - | 6.1 | 7.0 | 6.2 | 6.4 | 8.0 | 10.0 |
| 6 | - | AMD[1] | US | 3.7 | 6.4 | 9.8 | 3.9 | 4.5 | 6.0 | 6.2 | 6.7 | 9.8 |
| 7 | - | HiSilicon | China | - | 0.3 | 0.5 | 3.1 | 3.6 | 5.5 | 5.7 | 7.7 | 5.2[4] |
| 8 | 12 | Marvell | US | 0.1 | 3.6 | 5.5 | 2.7 | 3.1 | 3.1 | 3.2 | 2.7 | 2.9 |
| 9 | 1 | Xilinx | US | 1.6 | 2.3 | 3.5 | 2.2 | 2.5 | 2.9 | 3.0 | 3.2 | 3.1 |
| 10 | 13 | Novatek | Taiwan | 0.1 | 1.2 | 1.8 | 1.6 | 1.9 | 1.8 | 1.9 | 2.1 | 2.7 |
| 11 | - | Tsinghua Unigroup | China | - | - | - | - | - | 1.7 | 1.8 | - | - |

| | | | | | | | | | | | | |
|---|---|---|---|---|---|---|---|---|---|---|---|---|
| 12 | 9 | Realtek | Taiwan | 0.2 | 0.7 | 1.1 | 1.0 | 1.2 | 1.5 | 1.5 | 2.0 | 2.6 |
| - | 7 | PMC-Sierra | Canada | 0.7 | 0.7 | 1.1 | 0.5 | 0.6 | - | - | - | - |
| - | 10 | Semtech | US | 0.2 | 0.5 | 0.8 | 0.5 | 0.6 | - | - | - | - |
| - | 2 | Avago[2] | US/SG | 1.5 | 2.2 | 3.4 | 6.9 | 7.9 | - | - | - | - |
| - | 3 | Altera[3] | US | 1.4 | 2.0 | 3.1 | - | - | - | - | - | - |
| - | 11 | SMSC[3] | US | 0.2 | 0.4 | 0.6 | - | - | - | - | - | - |
| | | Top 5 fabless | | 6.8 | 27.5 | 42.1 | 44.6 | 51.3 | 59.8 | 61.4 | 52.2 | 65.0 |
| | | **Total fabless revenue** | | **16.7** | **65.4** | **100.0** | **87.5** | **100.0** | **97.4** | **100.0** | **126** | **153** |

[1] AMD became fabless after spinning off its wafer fabrication facilities to form GlobalFoundries in 2009. Its IDM revenue in 2000 is not included in the top 5 and total fabless revenue for 2000.

[2] Avago acquired LSI in 2014 and then Broadcom in 2015 to become Broadcom Inc. Its 2015 revenue is incorporated into Broadcom.

[3] Acquired by other entities before 2015.

[4] Data up to June 2020. Full year data unavailable due to US sanctions on foundry suppliers to HiSilicon.

Sources: 2000 data from Breznitz (2007, Table 3.3; 121); 2010–2018 data from IHS Markit/Informa Tech Custom Research for GPN@NUS Centre, July–October 2016 and 2019; and 2019–2020 data from various company reports, Gartner (http://www.gartner.com, released on April 12, 2021), TrendForce (https://www.trendforce.com, released on March 25, 2021), and IC Insights (https://www.icinsights.com, released on August 11, 2020).

TABLE 2.4. World's top 10 semiconductor foundry providers by revenue and market share, 1992–2021 (in US$ billions and percent)

| 2018 rank | 2000 rank | Firm | HQ[1] | 1992 $ | 2000 $ | 2000 % | 2010 $ | 2010 % | 2015 $ | 2015 % | 2018 $ | 2018 % | 2020 $ | 2021 $ |
|---|---|---|---|---|---|---|---|---|---|---|---|---|---|---|
| 1 | 1 | TSMC | TW | 0.26 | 5.1 | 38.1 | 13.0 | 39.3 | 26.5 | 53.1 | 31.1 | 50.6 | 46.0 | 52.0 |
| 2 | 4 | GlobalFoundries[2] | US | - | 0.5 | 3.7 | 3.5 | 10.7 | 4.8 | 9.6 | 6.2 | 10.1 | 5.7 | 6.3 |
| 3 | 2 | UMC | TW | 0.25 | 3.1 | 23.1 | 3.8 | 11.6 | 4.4 | 8.8 | 5.0 | 8.1 | 6.0 | 6.6 |
| 4 | - | Samsung (foundry) | SK | - | - | - | 0.8 | 2.4 | 3.9 | 7.8 | 3.4 | 5.5 | 14.5 | 16.1 |
| 5 | - | SMIC | CN | - | - | - | 1.6 | 4.9 | 2.1 | 4.2 | 3.0 | 4.9 | 4.2 | 3.8 |
| 6 | - | Powerchip (PSMC)[3] | TW | - | - | - | 0.2 | 0.6 | 0.9 | 1.8 | 1.7 | 2.8 | 0.9 | 1.0 |
| 7 | 7 | TowerJazz | IS | - | 0.1 | 0.7 | 0.5 | 1.5 | 1.0 | 2.0 | 1.3 | 2.1 | 0.9 | 1.0 |
| 8 | 6 | Vanguard (VIS) | TW | - | 0.2 | 1.4 | 0.5 | 1.5 | 0.7 | 1.4 | 1.0 | 1.6 | 0.9 | 1.0 |
| 9 | - | HHGrace | CN | - | - | - | 0.5 | 1.5 | 0.7 | 1.4 | 0.9 | 1.5 | 0.9 | 1.0 |
| - | 4 | Dongbu HiTek | SK | - | 0.5 | 3.7 | 0.5 | 1.5 | 0.6 | 1.2 | 0.6 | 1.0 | 0.9 | 1.0 |

| | | Firm | | | | | | | | | | | |
|---|---|---|---|---|---|---|---|---|---|---|---|---|---|
| 10 | - | Micron (foundry) | US | - | - | 0.9 | 2.7 | 0.7 | 1.4 | 0.8 | 1.3 | - | - |
| - | 3 | IBM Microelectronics[2] | US | 0.6 | 4.5 | 0.5 | 1.5 | - | - | - | - | - | - |
| | | Top 5 pureplay[4] | | 9.4 | 70.1 | 22.7 | 69.2 | 41.7 | 83.1 | 48.7 | 79.2 | 76.4 | 80.5 |
| | | Total pureplay revenue | | 10.2 | 76.1 | 25.8 | 78.7 | 45.1 | 89.8 | 55.0 | 89.4 | 81.3 | 90.5 |
| | | **Total foundry revenue[5]** | - | **13.4** | **100.0** | **32.8** | **100.0** | **50.2** | **100.0** | **61.5** | **100.0** | **85.1** | **94.6** |

[1] TW = Taiwan; CN = China; IS = Israel; SK = South Korea.

[2] GlobalFoundries' revenues in 2000 refer to Chartered Semiconductor (Singapore) that its parent firm from Abu Dhabi acquired in September 2009. GlobalFoundries was formerly AMD's semiconductor fabs spun off in March 2009. It was fully acquired by Abu Dhabi's state-owned Advanced Technology Investment Company in 2012. In 2015, GlobalFoundries acquired IBM Microelectronics' three US fabs in Burlington (Vermont) and East Fishkill (New York).

[3] Powerchip Technology was a memory IDM until 2008 when it became a pureplay foundry provider. It was renamed to PSMC in 2018.

[4] Pureplay refers to foundry fabs dedicated to serving external customers only (including Samsung foundry).

[5] Total foundry revenue includes revenue from both foundry by pureplay and foundry by IDM firms (e.g., IBM Microelectronics and Micron). Revenues by these foundry firms are typically attributed as cost of revenue to fabless firms (40–45% of total revenue) and fab-lite IDM customers (e.g., Infineon and NXP), and therefore do not add to the total semiconductor market revenue in Tables 1.1 and 2.2.

Sources: 1992 data from Mathews and Cho (2000, Tables 1.3, 1.8; 38, 49); 2000–2018 data from IHS Markit/Informa Tech Custom Research for GPN@NUS Centre, July–October 2016 and 2019; and 2020–2021 (forecast) data from TrendForce (https://www.trendforce.com, released on April 15, 2021).

fifteen years after they had been spun off from ITRI, an indication of the much stronger role of firm-specific initiatives, particularly their symbiotic relationship with leading US fabless firms and an extensive and collaborative ecosystem of leading equipment and materials suppliers from the US, Europe, and Japan.[29] TSMC was an early pioneer of pureplay foundry manufacturing in the late 1980s as an innovative way of organizing semiconductor production. In the early 1990s, TSMC took advantage of the decoupling of the design and fabrication stages of chip production. As noted in Table 2.1, this technological innovation was made possible by the use of computer-aided design technology and electronic design automation (EDA) software to codify knowledge of device characteristics in computer models. While the complete computer modelling was possible by 1993–1994, TSMC had actually anticipated this trend and begun using the computer model as early as the late 1980s, thus creating a first-mover advantage. But TSMC took tremendous risk with this move toward pureplay, as it was not clear if the digital interface between the fabrication and design of integrated circuits would work in large-scale commercial production.[30]

Today, all major foundry providers have developed strategic relationships with US-based specialized equipment suppliers (e.g., Applied Materials, KLA, and Lam Research) and EDA software firms, such as Cadence, Synopsys, and Mentor Graphics (part of Siemens since 2017), for chip design, implementation, and verification software and intellectual property for design cores. A few European and Japanese suppliers of specialized equipment (e.g., ASML from the Netherlands and Nikon from Japan) and materials (e.g., Siltronic from Germany) are also critical in this complex and globalized ecosystem of cutting-edge wafer fabrication. Another important building block of chip design is access to standard cell libraries and memories, known as intellectual property, because these proprietary designs used to be specific to each IDM firm or foundry provider. Their design and maintenance have taken a huge amount of work due to the continuous revisions needed in relation to changes in fabrication process. By the late 1990s, both IDM and fabless firms realized the importance of timely and cost-effective availability of these design cores from specialized providers such as ARM from the UK and Synopsys and Cadence from the US.[31]

Starting at a very low base of $0.5 billion in 1992, the share of pureplay foundry providers in total foundry revenue had increased massively to 76.1 percent or $10.2 billion in 2000 and, two decades later, 95.5 percent or $81.3 billion in 2020 (Table 2.4). Since the early 1990s, TSMC's leadership in semiconductor foundry has been unparalleled. By the early 2000s, continuous technological innovations at TSMC and UMC had paid off. Taiwan's leading pureplay foundries were well placed at the technological frontiers of wafer fabrication, alongside with Samsung's foundry and other leading IDM firms from the US and Japan. The total foundry revenue share of these three leading foundry providers from East Asia increased very substantially from 53.3 percent in 2010 to 78.1 percent in 2020, indicating their tremendous success and technological leadership vis-à-vis foundry service by IDM firms over the same period. In 2007, TSMC alone had almost $10 billion revenue and over one-third of the total foundry market share.[32] By the end of the 2010s, TSMC maintained its unrivalled market leadership, and its revenue gap with the next two largest foundry providers, GlobalFoundries and UMC, widened even further. Only Samsung foundry was relatively closer in revenue and process technology by 2020/2021. At $31.1 billion, TSMC's revenue in 2018 would already place it above Micron as the fourth largest semiconductor firm in the world.[33] Increasing demand for logic chips by its top fabless customers, such as Apple, HiSilicon (for Huawei), and Nvidia, led to very substantial growth in TSMC's revenue to $34.7 billion in 2019 and a whopping $46 billion in 2020 (third after Intel and Samsung, if included in Table 2.2) and, by forecast, $55 billion in 2021.

After significant capital investment and collaborative ecosystem development during the second half of the 2010s, TSMC's cutting-edge process node at 5 nanometers (nm) in wafer fabrication was more advanced than Intel by 2020. As indicated in Figure 2.1, only Samsung's most advanced 5 nm fabs in South Korea were on par with TSMC's megafabs in Taiwan, and this trend will likely persist in the 2020s. This changing technological leadership in chip making pivoting toward top foundry fabs in East Asia has profound implications for the industrial organization of semiconductor production networks. My empirical Chapters 4–6 will analyze in depth TSMC's central role in the global production networks of the most advanced chipsets in the late 2010s and several cases of leading fabs up to 2020 and beyond by TSMC, Samsung foundry, and Intel in their respective global production networks. As observed in Table 2.1, the late 2010s witnessed this codominance of both IDM and fabless-foundry models of semiconductor global production networks.

From $311 billion in 2010, the global semiconductor industry expanded much further to reach a new historical high of $485 billion in 2018 before it declined to $422 billion in 2019 due to major geopolitical uncertainties and trade wars since March 2018. But because of massive demand for chips during and after the COVID-19 pandemic, the industry's total revenue grew over 10 percent to $466 billion in 2020 and likely further 12 percent to a new record at $525 billion in 2021.[34] Intel's dominant market position, since overtaking Japan's NEC in 1995, was replaced by Samsung in 2018, but it recovered in 2019–2020 (Table 2.2). But in terms of product category, these top semiconductor firms had markedly different specialization in 2018: top three in logic chips (Broadcom, Intel, and Qualcomm), memory devices (Samsung, SK Hynix, and Micron), microprocessors and microcomponent devices (Intel, NXP, and AMD), analogue devices (Texas Instruments, Analog Devices, and Qualcomm), and discrete components (Infineon, ON Semiconductor, and STM). As will be detailed in Chapter 4, each of these product categories is associated with particular segments of global electronics, e.g., PCs and smartphones (logic, microprocessors, memory devices, and optical semiconductors), flat panel displays and TVs (logic and microcomponent devices and optical semiconductors), and automobiles and medical and industrial equipment (microcomponent, analogue, and discrete devices).

Table 2.5 lists the relative importance of these product categories in total semiconductor production and their applications in specific products or industrial sectors. In 1984, some $21 billion of the $26 billion world market for semiconductors was in integrated circuits, with the remaining $5 billion in discrete devices.[35] In 1996, integrated circuits still accounted for 74 percent of the global semiconductor market, followed by discrete devices (13 percent), analogue devices (12 percent), and optical semiconductors (1 percent).[36] Within the different product categories of integrated circuits, the demand for "custom" or application-specific integrated circuits (ASICs) in logic and analogue devices has grown substantially during the 2010s. But the largest growth comes from the rapidly growing demand for memory devices in PCs, smartphones, and other mobile devices (e.g., Internet of Things products) and data storage facilities (e.g., cloud computing). The total revenue of both DRAM and flash memory devices almost doubled between 2008 and 2015 and again between 2015 and 2018.

From a modest size of $45.8 billion or 17.5 percent share of the total semiconductor market in 2008, memory chips overtook the biggest segment, logic chips, in 2018 with revenue of $165 billion or 22 percent share of the total semiconductor market. This dramatic emergence of memory

TABLE 2.5. World's total semiconductor market revenue by product categories and industrial applications, 2008–2021 (in US$ billions)

| | 2008 | 2010 | 2015 | 2018 | 2019 | 2020 | 2021[F] |
|---|---|---|---|---|---|---|---|
| **Revenue by product categories** | | | | | | | |
| **Integrated circuits (ICs)** | **218** | **258** | **286** | **413** | **333** | **361** | **436** |
| Logic ICs | 73.1 | 78.9 | 89.1 | 107 | 107 | 118 | 139 |
| General purpose logic | 12.5 | 12.9 | 11.9 | 14.2 | - | - | - |
| Logic ASICs | 60.6 | 65.9 | 77.3 | 93.0 | - | - | - |
| Memory ICs | 45.8 | 69.8 | 80.8 | 165 | 106 | 117 | 155 |
| DRAM | 23.7 | 39.7 | 45.1 | 98.9 | - | - | - |
| Flash memory | 18.0 | 26.3 | 33.9 | 63.4 | - | - | - |
| Micro-component ICs | 55.6 | 61.0 | 63.1 | 80.1 | 66.4 | 70.0 | 75.3 |
| Microprocessor (MPU) | 34.3 | 39.6 | 44.7 | 58.0 | - | - | - |
| Microcontroller (MCU) | 15.5 | 15.8 | 15.8 | 19.0 | - | - | - |
| Analogue ICs | 43.9 | 47.7 | 52.3 | 61.0 | 53.9 | 55.7 | 67.7 |
| General purpose | 16.2 | 19.1 | 17.9 | 21.1 | - | - | - |
| Analogue ASICs | 27.8 | 28.7 | 34.4 | 39.8 | - | - | - |
| **Discretes** | **18.7** | **21.4** | **20.1** | **25.4** | **23.8** | **23.8** | **28.2** |
| **Optical semiconductor** | 19.2 | 27.3 | 33.6 | 36.9 | 41.6 | 40.4 | 44.4 |
| **Sensors & actuators** | 4.4 | 5.3 | 8.1 | 9.9 | 13.5 | 15.0 | 18.3 |
| **Total semiconductor[1]** | **261** | **311** | **346** | **485** | **412** | **440** | **527** |
| **Revenue by industrial applications** | | | | | | | |
| Computer & data storage | 94.2 | 111 | 111 | 177 | 136 | 160 | 173 |
| Wireless communications | 51.5 | 66.7 | 106 | 146 | 109 | 119 | 147 |
| Wired communications | 16.5 | 20.1 | 20.1 | 26.4 | - | - | - |
| Consumer electronics | 53.1 | 59.3 | 37.6 | 41.7 | 55.7 | 60.0 | 65.3 |
| Industrial electronics | 24.3 | 31.4 | 41.7 | 52.2 | - | - | - |
| Automotive electronics | 20.3 | 23.1 | 29.2 | 41.6 | 42.1 | 38.0 | 43.2 |
| **Total semiconductor[1]** | **261** | **311** | **346** | **485** | **419** | **464** | **522** |

Note: See full table and notes in Appendix C Table C2.
[1] Revenue data for total semiconductor market in 2019–2021 (forecast) are slightly different from Tables 1.1 and 2.2 due to different data sources.
Sources: IHS Markit/Informa Tech Custom Research for GPN@NUS Centre, July–October 2016 and 2019; IHS Markit, November 2020; and World Semiconductor Trade Statistics Forecast and IDC, May–June 2021.

chips in turn explains the historical peak in revenue of top three memory chip producers—Samsung, SK Hynix, and Micron—in 2018. During the COVID-19 pandemic period in 2020 and 2021, the market for memory and logic chips and optical semiconductors (panel displays) remained robust due to greater demand from PCs, home ICT products, servers and data centers, automotive, and the adoption of new technologies, such as 5G communications and artificial intelligence. Still, the US continues to lead in several crucial semiconductor components for ICT products, such as microprocessors for PCs (Intel, AMD, and Apple), application processors for mobile devices (Qualcomm and Apple), wireless communications chips (Qualcomm and Broadcom), graphics chips (Nvidia, AMD, and Intel), and memory (Micron). In terms of industrial applications, while computer and data storage has been the largest category since 2008, the demand for chips in the wireless communications category doubled from $51.5 billion in 2008 to $106 billion in 2015 and increased further by 27 percent to $146 billion in 2018. As mentioned in Table 2.1, this incessant demand is clearly driven by the "smartphone revolution" initiated by two leading vendors—Apple after launching the iPhone in 2007 and Samsung after launching the Galaxy series in 2009 (more detail on these chipsets and smartphone production networks in Chapter 5).

Taken together, the fortunes of leading semiconductor firms are intimately linked with their downstream system or end-product customers that incorporate their chipsets into high-tech ICT products for corporate users and final consumers—the key empirical phenomenon in the 2010s for detailed analysis in this book. Their value capture is primarily achieved through proprietary technologies and standards and strong customer relationships. In the next two sections, I will examine the historical development of two major industrial applications of semiconductors in PCs and mobile handsets that have come to dominate the global electronics industry today (see also Figure 2.3 and Table 2.1).

## Personal Computers

Before IBM launched its first personal computer (PC), IBM 5150, on August 12, 1981, the world of computing and computers was primarily dominated by, and limited to, mainframe systems and minicomputers for institutional and corporate users (see Figure 2.1). The commercialization of computer systems started in the US in the early 1950s, led by IBM and five other domestic firms known as BUNCH (Burroughs, the Univac division of Sperry Rand, NCR, Control Data Corporation, and Honeywell).[37] Overtaking the lead from Remington Rand in 1956, IBM's market share in the US market for mainframe computers hovered around 70 to 80 percent till the mid-1960s. IBM's overwhelming dominance in mainframe computers in the decades to come was further sealed by its introduction of market-leading System/360 in April 1964 and System/370 in June 1970. By 1970, more than 74,000 mainframe computers were installed in the US, and the US corporate world's total investment in computing alone represented some 10 percent of the country's total annual expenditure on capital equipment.[38]

As shown in Table 2.6, by 1971, these US firms specializing in the original equipment manufacturing (OEM) of computers had captured some 92 percent of the world market in large-scale computer systems, with IBM taking a whopping 62 percent share. IBM's R&D expenditure of $500 million was more than the next seven competitors combined.[39] In 1980, the US still had 82 percent of the world market, whereas Japan held about 10 percent.[40] By the early 1980s, IBM was also the world's largest producer of integrated circuits for in-house "captive" use and a major innovator in semiconductor process and product technologies.[41] Its market dominance in large-scale computer systems remained unchallenged by other US computer firms, such as Unisys,[42] DEC, and NCR, as well as the "Big Four" national champions from Western Europe (ICL from Britain, Groupe Bull from France, Siemens from Germany, and Olivetti from Italy) and Japan (Fujitsu, Hitachi, and NEC). By the mid-1980s, Morgan and Sayer (1988, 81) bemoaned the dominance of IBM as the "operating environment" for all other leading computer firms worldwide:

> The degree of monopoly or size of market share possessed by IBM in the computer industry is without parallel. It is the market leader (and often the profit leader) in every capitalist country except Japan. It is eight to ten times the size of its nearest rivals, the "BUNCH" (Burroughs, Univac, NCR, Control Data and Honeywell, also all US-owned), 16 times the size of the largest European producer, Siemens, and over 40 times the size of ICL, the largest British-owned company. IBM's research budget alone is greater than the total annual revenue of Bull, the leading French computer firm. In view of its dominance it is scarcely an exaggeration to say that IBM is not so much a competitor to other firms as the environment in which they operate.

TABLE 2.6. World's top OEM firms in computer systems by market share, 1971–1995 (in percent and US$ billions)

| 1995 rank | 1985 rank | OEM firms | 1971 | 1985 | 1990 | 1995 |
|---|---|---|---|---|---|---|
| | | **Large-scale computer systems (mainframes) (%)** | | | | |
| 1 | 1 | IBM | 62.1 | 49.0 | 40.6 | 32.4 |
| 6 | 2 | Unisys (formerly Sperry Rand) | 5.0 | 8.0 | - | 3.0 |
| 2 | 2 | Fujitsu | 1.1 | 8.0 | - | 25.0 |
| 4 | 4 | NEC | 0.9 | 5.0 | - | 10.0 |
| - | 4 | Control Data | 3.4 | 5.0 | - | - |
| 3 | 6 | Hitachi | 0.8 | 4.0 | - | 12.0 |
| 8 | 6 | Groupe Bull | - | 4.0 | - | 2.0 |
| - | 8 | ICL | 2.6 | 3.0 | - | - |
| 6 | 9 | Amdahl | - | 2.0 | - | 3.0 |
| 5 | - | Siemens-Nixdorf | 0.8 | - | - | 4.0 |
| - | - | Honeywell[1] | 8.5 | - | - | - |
| - | - | Burroughs[1] | 4.0 | - | - | - |
| - | - | NCR[1] | 1.9 | - | - | - |
| | | Japan share (Fujitsu, NEC, Hitachi) | 2.8 | 17.0 | 32.6 | 47.2 |
| | | Total market ($) | - | 21 | 28 | 19 |
| | | **Midrange computer systems (minicomputers and servers)** | | | | |
| 5 | 1 | DEC[2] | - | 14.4 | - | 5.5 |
| 1 | 2 | IBM[3] | - | 10.5 | - | 21.5 |
| 2 | 3 | Hewlett-Packard[2] | - | 5.6 | - | 11.7 |
| 7 | 6 | NCR | - | 3.9 | - | 4.5 |
| 3 | - | Compaq[2] | - | - | - | 9.4 |
| 4 | 8 | Fujitsu | - | 3.1 | - | 8.3 |
| 6 | - | NEC | - | - | - | 5.1 |
| 8 | - | Toshiba | - | - | - | 4.0 |
| 10 | 9 | Siemens-Nixdorf | - | 3.1 | - | 2.9 |
| | | Europe total share | - | 3.1 | - | 2.9 |

| 1995 rank | 1985 rank | OEM firms | 1971 | 1985 | 1990 | 1995 |
|---|---|---|---|---|---|---|
| | | Japan total share | - | 3.3 | - | 17.4 |
| | | Total market ($) | - | 18 | 27 | 30 |
| | | **Personal computers (PCs)** | | | | |
| 2 | 1 | IBM[3] | - | 25.0 | 13.0 | 8.0 |
| - | 2 | Commodore[1] | - | 14.0 | 5.0 | - |
| 2 | 2 | Apple | - | 14.0 | 7.0 | 8.0 |
| - | 4 | Tandy[1] | - | 8.0 | 1.8 | - |
| 1 | 5 | Compaq[2] | - | 3.0 | 4.0 | 10.0 |
| - | 5 | Atari[1] | - | 3.0 | 1.7 | - |
| 5 | 7 | Hewlett-Packard[2] | - | 2.0 | 1.0 | 4.0 |
| 4 | - | Packard Bell[4] | - | - | 2.0 | 7.0 |
| 5 | - | NEC | - | - | 6.0 | 4.0 |
| 7 | - | Dell | - | - | 0.9 | 3.0 |
| 7 | - | Acer | - | - | 1.0 | 3.0 |
| 7 | - | Fujitsu/ICL | - | - | 1.0 | 3.0 |
| 7 | - | Toshiba | - | - | 3.0 | 3.0 |
| | | Japan total share | - | - | 10.0 | 10.0 |
| | | Top 5 share | - | 64.0 | 33.0 | 37.0 |
| | | Total PCs market ($) | - | 16 | 55 | 108 |
| | | Share in world computer market (%) | - | 29.1 | 50.0 | 68.8 |
| | | **Worldwide total computer sales ($)** | - | **55** | **110** | **157** |

[1] Out of top 10 since 1985. Burroughs merged with Sperry Rand to become Unisys in 1986. The rest were bankrupt (Commodore), acquired (NCR by AT&T in 1991), or spun off (Honeywell, Tandy, and Atari) by 1995.
[2] DEC was acquired by Compaq in 1998. Compaq was acquired by Hewlett-Packard in 2002.
[3] IBM sold its PC division and server business to China's Lenovo respectively in 2005 and 2014.
[4] Packard Bell was acquired by NEC in 1996.
Sources: 1971 data from Anchordoguy (1989, Table 16; 107); 1990 data from Steffens (1994, Table 7.17; 340); and 1990 and 1995 data from Dedrick and Kraemer (1998, Figure 1.2, Tables 1.3, 2.2–2.3, 2.7).

As examined in Chapter 1, this was the peak of the multinational worlds of electronics innovation and production in the US, Western Europe, and Japan. Dedrick and Kraemer (1998, 41) further noted that "Europe's efforts to create competitors to IBM turned out to be expensive failures for the most part."[43] By 1989, US share in large-scale computers declined to 57 percent, and Japan's share increased to 28 percent, with Fujitsu, NEC, and Hitachi leading the competition. But even these Japanese computer giants of the 1980s failed to recognize the significance of the coming PC revolution in the subsequent decades.[44]

The IBM 5150 was an instant success and heralded the "PC revolution" noted in Table 2.1. To Steffens (1994, 143), IBM's entrance into the PC market for the corporate sector was so significant that "it dramatically altered the structure of the industry and changed the rules of competition. In so doing, through the market power of IBM, the personal computer was legitimized as a serious and important product within the broader computer requirements of corporate customers." Prior to its 1981 launch and from less than 50,000 personal computers in use in the US in 1977, the United States bought over 724,000 PCs from a couple of dozen computer manufacturers in 1980.[45] And yet according to Chandler (2001, 138–40), "the industry was still in an embryonic stage," with three major domestic players led by Apple (27 percent share), Tandy (21 percent), and Commodore (20 percent), and followed by Hewlett-Packard (5 percent) and Japan's NEC (9 percent).[46] From a meagre $50 million in 1982, IBM's PC revenue rose exponentially to $5 billion in 1984 and levelled off at $5.5 billion in 1985 in a total PC market of $16 billion (Table 2.6). By then, total PC shipments had risen to 3.3 million units, and more than 200 clone PC makers existed worldwide.

After IBM's first PC launched in 1981 and its subsequent standardization into IBM-compatible desktop PCs through Microsoft's MS-DOS operating system (OS) in the early 1980s, the share of PCs in all computer systems worldwide grew massively from 29 percent of $55 billion in 1985 to almost 69 percent of $157 billion in 1995 (see Table 2.6). As mentioned in Table 2.1, much of this early production of PCs during the 1980s was vertically integrated within IBM and other OEM firms. Even if outsourcing took place, it was limited and mostly confined to domestic suppliers in the US and other home countries (e.g., Japan). When IBM first shipped its 5150 PC in 1981, its suppliers and production locations were primarily US-based. IBM signed on Seattle-based Microsoft as the sole supplier of its

MS-DOS operating system and California-based Intel as the supplier of its 8088 microprocessor, culminating in the subsequent era of the "Wintel" model of PCs till today.[47] Other suppliers of electronics components to IBM were Tandon in California (disk drives), Zenith in Michigan (power supplies), SCI Systems (contract manufacturing of circuit boards in its Silicon Valley division), and Seiko Epson (printers from Japan). IBM's own plants assembled circuit boards in Charlotte, North Carolina, and keyboards in Lexington, Kentucky.[48]

As the "PC revolution" progressed into the 1990s, the open and nonproprietary standards of the IBM PC architecture enabled the rise of hundreds of competitors making IBM "clones" or IBM-compatible PCs (e.g., Compaq, Corona, and Eagle in the early 1980s) and thousands of suppliers in computer peripherals and components worldwide. This in turn led to the emergence of many new lead firms in the global computer industry and the corresponding demise of major OEM lead firms in large-scale computers in the 1990s. For example, IBM's worldwide market share in all computer hardware sales was reduced from 37 percent in 1975 to "only" 14 percent in 1995. In 1993, IBM announced the biggest loss in its corporate history to the tune of $6.9 billion on the back of $64.5 billion in revenue.[49] In the minicomputer market, a similar story unfolds in Table 2.6. Originating in Massachusetts' Route 128, DEC led the market segment with 14.4 percent share in 1985. By 1995, IBM regained its leadership in minicomputers, and DEC's share declined to only 5.5 percent.[50]

Against this backdrop of shrinking sales in large-scale computers and minicomputers worldwide by the mid-1990s, the PC market grew rapidly as the dominant segment (almost 69 percent) in the global computer market of $157 billion in 1995. By 1989, the worldwide PC market reached 21 million units in shipment, 94 million units in installation, and $55.7 billion in value.[51] In 1992, IBM still led with 12 percent of the global PC market of $64 billion and 29 million units shipped, of which about one-third was in the US ($24 billion and 11 million units).[52] But by 1995, Compaq had unseated IBM as the top vendor in PCs, commanding 10 percent of worldwide market share (Table 2.6). From shipment of about 71 million units in 1996, the worldwide market of PCs grew to 129 million units in 2001 and peaked in 2011, with about 364 million units of desktops and notebooks sold globally.[53]

Table 2.7 illustrates the historical peak of desktop PC shipment in 2007 at 157 million units and notebook PC shipment in 2012 at 212 million units.

TABLE 2.7. World's top 10 PC OEM firms by shipment and market share, 2001–2018 (in millions of units and percent)

| 2018 rank | 2007 rank | Desktops | 2001[1] units | 2001 % | 2007 units | 2007 % | 2010 units | 2015 units | 2015 % | 2018 units | 2018 % |
|---|---|---|---|---|---|---|---|---|---|---|---|
| 1 | 3 | Lenovo[2] | 8.3 | 6.4 | 11.6 | 7.4 | 14.4 | 18.1 | 19.1 | 21.0 | 23.6 |
| 2 | 1 | Hewlett-Packard | 23.7 | 18.4 | 24.4 | 15.5 | 24.4 | 18.9 | 20.0 | 19.3 | 21.7 |
| 3 | 2 | Dell | 17.0 | 13.2 | 22.4 | 14.2 | 18.8 | 16.4 | 17.4 | 17.1 | 19.2 |
| 4 | 4 | Acer | - | - | 5.6 | 3.5 | 8.4 | 4.7 | 4.9 | 5.1 | 5.7 |
| 5 | 6 | Apple | - | - | 2.6 | 1.6 | 3.9 | 4.4 | 4.6 | 2.6 | 2.9 |
| 6 | - | Asus | - | - | - | - | 1.1 | 1.5 | 1.6 | 2.6 | 2.9 |
| 7 | 7 | Tongfang | - | - | 1.7 | 1.1 | 1.6 | 1.3 | 1.3 | 1.1 | 1.2 |
| 8 | - | Haier | - | - | - | - | 0.8 | 1.0 | 1.0 | 0.8 | 0.9 |
| 9 | - | Samsung | - | - | - | - | 1.0 | 0.3 | 0.3 | 0.3 | 0.3 |
| - | 5 | Fujitsu | - | - | 3.7 | 2.3 | 2.5 | 2.2 | 2.3 | - | - |
| | | Others | 71.4 | 55.4 | 85.5 | 54.3 | 56.4 | 25.7 | 26.8 | 19.2 | 21.5 |
| | | Top 5 | 57.5 | 44.6 | 67.7 | 43.0 | 69.9 | 62.5 | 66.4 | 65.1 | 73.1 |
| | | **Total** | **129** | **100** | **157** | **100** | **133** | **94.1** | **100** | **89.1** | **100** |
| | | Yearly growth (%) | - | - | - | - | 3.4 | -13.2 | - | -3.3 | - |

**Notebooks**

| | | | | | | | | | | | |
|---|---|---|---|---|---|---|---|---|---|---|---|
| 1 | 1 | Hewlett-Packard[3] | - | - | 22.0 | 21.3 | 37.7 | 35.0 | 20.0 | 40.3 | 24.7 |
| 2 | 5 | Lenovo[2] | - | - | 8.5 | 8.2 | 19.7 | 36.3 | 20.5 | 36.5 | 22.3 |
| 3 | 2 | Dell | - | - | 15.2 | 14.7 | 23.2 | 22.0 | 12.4 | 26.7 | 16.3 |
| 4 | 8 | Asus | - | - | 4.4 | 4.3 | 16.9 | 15.4 | 8.7 | 13.6 | 8.3 |
| 5 | 3 | Acer | - | - | 14.6 | 14.1 | 33.1 | 13.7 | 7.7 | 12.0 | 7.3 |
| 6 | 6 | Apple | - | - | 4.7 | 4.5 | 9.8 | 18.0 | 10.1 | 10.4 | 6.4 |
| 7 | 9 | Samsung | - | - | 1.4 | 1.4 | 9.7 | 2.9 | 1.7 | 2.7 | 1.7 |
| 8 | 7 | Fujitsu | - | - | 4.4 | 4.3 | 3.1 | 1.9 | 1.1 | 1.9 | 1.2 |
| 9 | - | NEC | 4.9 | 3.8 | - | - | - | 1.2 | 0.7 | 1.2 | 0.7 |
| 10 | 4 | Toshiba | 3.6 | 2.8 | 11.1 | 10.7 | 19.0 | 6.8 | 3.8 | 0.4 | 0.2 |
| | | Others | - | - | 16.2 | 15.7 | 22.2 | 24.0 | 13.6 | 17.7 | 10.8 |
| | | Top 5 | 57.5 | 44.6 | 71.4 | 69.0 | 133 | 127 | 71.6 | 129 | 79.0 |
| | | **Total** | **129** | **100** | **104** | **100** | **194** | **177** | **100** | **163** | **100** |
| | | Yearly growth (%) | - | - | - | - | 16.4 | -5.8 | - | -3.2 | - |

[1] 2001 data refer to PC desktops, notebooks, and servers.

[2] Lenovo's data for 2001 refer to IBM. Lenovo acquired IBM's PC division and "ThinkPad" line of notebooks and tablets in 2005.

[3] Hewlett-Packard data for 2001 include those for Compaq, which was acquired by Hewlett-Packard in 2002.

Sources: 2001 data from Paprzycki (2005, Table 7.1; 119) and 2007–2018 data from IHS Markit/Informa Tech Custom Research for GPN@NUS Centre, July–October 2016 and 2019.

From its record 364 million units in 2011, total PC shipment declined significantly to 271 million units by 2015. In 2018, this figure decreased further to 253 million units, in tandem with the rapid growth in the worldwide shipment of smartphones that replicate many PC functions, though it recovered slightly to 275 million units in 2020. Due to high demand for home PCs during and after the COVID-19 pandemic, total shipment has been projected to reach about 357 million units in 2021, still lower than its historical record in 2011.[54] In this context of declining sales throughout the 2010s (but revitalized in the early 2020s due to massive remote work/learning–related demand), the entire PC market became much more concentrated in favor of the top five vendors that accounted for between 66 and 72 percent of total market shares in desktops and notebooks in 2015 and 73 and 77 percent in 2018/2020. While Chapters 4–6 will analyze in depth the global production networks of these leading PC vendors in 2015 and 2018, several important industrial shifts in the PC segment since the mid-2000s need further contextualization here (see summary in Table 2.1):

(1)    the shift of PC production toward East Asia and greater market concentration,

(2)    the market shift from desktops to notebooks, and

(3)    the critical role of original design manufacturing (ODM) firms from Taiwan.

First, the most significant change to the pecking order of PC OEM lead firms before 2007 was the acquisition of IBM's PC division by China-based Lenovo in 2005 and Hewlett-Packard's 2002 acquisition of Compaq, the first PC firm that launched IBM-compatible desktop PCs in 1982 and acquired DEC in 1998. Both IBM and Compaq were top PC vendors during the 1990s (Table 2.6), and DEC was a formidable competitor to IBM and others in minicomputers before its acquisition by Compaq. But the shift in PC production toward East Asia was already evident with the rise of Taiwan's Acer during the same period. As one of the approved IBM-compatible PC manufacturers in the 1980s, Acer was heavily dependent on IBM for technology and market access. Its supplier relationship with IBM was mostly captive in nature. Its major customers also exercised a high degree of monitoring and control, and Acer had little control over product specifications and design blueprints in computer manufacturing.

Acer's switching costs during the 1980s were very high due to the market dominance of IBM in the PC industry.

Learning this important lesson from its captive supplier relationship with IBM and, later, Dell, Acer's founder Stan Shih decided to start original brand manufacturing (Acer) in order to exercise market control and product definition and to capture greater value from upstream design and R&D and downstream activities (e.g., marketing and distribution). While keeping its outsourced work under subcontracting arrangements for AT&T, Unisys, and Siemens, Acer eschewed its captive supplier relationship with IBM and others in the 1990s and, as noted in Table 2.6, emerged as a top ten vendor by 1995.[55] By 2007, Acer became a top five OEM lead firm in both desktops and notebooks (Table 2.7). In 2015 and 2018, it remained a top five vendor in both product segments. During the same period, the market share of top five desktop vendors grew rapidly from 33–37 percent in the 1990s (Table 2.6) to 43 percent in 2007 and 73 percent in 2018 (Table 2.7). This phenomenon of high market concentration is much more apparent in notebook PCs, growing from a high base of 69 percent in 2007 to 79 percent in 2018.

Second, the market shift toward notebook PCs has been most pronounced since the late 2000s. In 2007, desktop sales still outstripped notebook sales by almost 50 percent. By 2009, notebook shipment of 167 million units exceeded desktop shipment of 129 million units for the first time, and the trend has persisted since then. More importantly, this market shift has enabled the rise of several OEM lead firms from East Asia, including Lenovo, Acer, and Asus. This functional upgrading of domestic firms to become OEM vendors was well supported by home government's sectoral industrial policies contextualized in Table 1.2. Not long after its acquisition of IBM's PC division in 2005, Lenovo was still a relatively small player, trailing market leaders of Hewlett-Packard, Dell, Acer, and Toshiba in 2007 (Table 2.7).[56] A decade later in 2015, Lenovo overtook Hewlett-Packard, a longstanding market leader, to become the world's top vendor in notebook PC shipment for the first time. It remained a close second to Hewlett-Packard and far ahead of Dell in 2018. In 2020 (Table 1.1), Lenovo became the world's top PC vendor, with over 10 million units more in sales than the second-ranked Hewlett-Packard. Meanwhile, Taiwan's Asus also emerged from its niche role in 2007 to become a top five vendor in notebook PCs in 2015 and 2018/2020. During this period, major Japanese notebook vendors, such as Fujitsu, Sony, and Toshiba, lost much of their market share. From its fourth position in 2007, Toshiba became the tenth-ranked vendor in 2018, capping a decade-long decline for the former world leader in notebook PCs during the 1990s.[57]

Third, the role of ODM firms from Taiwan in the international production of notebook PCs is indispensable (see also supportive national context in Table 1.2). In the late 1980s, the adolescent nature of notebook PCs provided a favorable window of opportunity for ODM firms from Taiwan, allowing them to avoid a captive mode of OEM-supplier relationship commonly found in desktop PC manufacturing.[58] Table 2.8 identifies these leading notebook ODM firms from Taiwan. Many of them were established at the time when product and process technologies for

TABLE 2.8. World's top 6 notebook ODMs from Taiwan by shipment and market share, 1999–2018 (in millions of units and percent)

| ODM | 1999 units | 2004 units | 2010 units | 2015 units | 2015 % | 2018 units | 2018 % | Largest clients in 2018 (ranked by ODM shipment) |
|---|---|---|---|---|---|---|---|---|
| Compal | 1.1 | 7.7 | 48.1 | 31.7 | 17.8 | 40.9 | 30.4 | Dell, HP, Lenovo, Acer |
| Quanta | 2.2 | 11.6 | 52.1 | 40.8 | 22.9 | 36.1 | 26.8 | HP, Apple, Acer, Lenovo |
| Wistron | 1.5 | - | 27.5 | 24.4 | 13.7 | 17.3 | 12.9 | Dell, HP, Lenovo |
| Inventec | 1.2 | - | 16.2 | 14.2 | 10.3 | 11.5 | 8.5 | HP, Toshiba, others |
| Pegatron | - | - | 15.5 | 11.7 | 8.5 | 8.4 | 6.5 | Asus, Acer, Lenovo |
| Hon Hai | - | - | 10.0 | 8.1 | 5.9 | 2.7 | 2.0 | Apple, HP, Dell |
| Others | - | 26.8 | 18.2 | 6.6 | 4.8 | 17.7 | 13.2 | - |
| **Total outsourced** | - | **46.1** | **187.6** | **137.5** | **100.0** | **134.5** | **100.0** | HP, Dell, Lenovo |
| Taiwan share (%) | 39.0 | 72.0 | 95.0 | 95.2 | - | 86.8 | - | 100.0 |

Note: See full table and notes in Appendix C Table C3. Figures include notebooks assembled in China by Taiwanese-owned production facilities.
Sources: Amsden and Chu (2003); Yeung (2016); and IHS Markit/Informa Tech Custom Research for GPN@NUS Centre, July–October 2016 and 2019.

notebook PCs were still emerging, and no dominant industrial player was established. Unlike IBM-compatible desktop PCs, no industrial standards for notebook computers were firmly in place during the 1980s.[59] By the late 1980s, the basic technology for flat panel displays or optical semiconductors in Table 2.5 was also quite mature, and these displays were crucial to the portability of notebook PCs.[60] While Sony from Japan and Compaq from the US had already established their notebook PC divisions by the late 1980s, others OEM lead firms, such as Apple, IBM, Fujitsu, and Siemens, also had strong engineering knowhow and were ready to enter into this new niche business.[61]

This was the time when Taiwan's Quanta was established in 1988 and Inventec and Compal began their notebook PC ODM business in 1988 and 1989, followed much later by others such as Wistron (spun off from Acer in 2001) and Pegatron (in 2008). Their ODM strategy achieved early success that paved way for Taiwan's domination in the notebook PC ODM market throughout the 2010s (see a full analysis in Chapters 4–6). During the late 1980s, however, the notebook PC industry was still evolving, and the niche market remained highly volatile. The lack of industry-wide standardization in notebook PCs gave ambitious firms, particularly those from Taiwan, the initial window of opportunity to break into the ODM business as a strategic partner, rather than as a captive supplier, of OEM lead firms in the 1990s and beyond. Because a notebook PC was, and still is, an all-in-one device rather than a set such as a desktop PC and its necessary peripherals, the internal layout and key components are highly variable, and thus design and engineering always play a decisive role in the miniaturization, functionality, and market success of each generation of notebook PCs.[62]

Before 1995, most top PC OEM lead firms from the US and Japan produced their notebook PCs in-house by leveraging their overall systems knowledge necessary for product development and manufacturing, e.g., design for heat management and power consumption to work with processor chipsets. Most Taiwanese ODM firms had little experience and knowhow in this core design function. But Intel's decision in 1993 to switch strategy toward platform leadership by providing both microprocessors and their chipsets (previously supplied by specialized firms such as Chips and Technologies) in single platforms based on the same technology roadmap created a new opportunity for these ODM firms.[63] By 1995, Intel supplied not only the chipset platform but also a turnkey solution comprising the chipset, evaluation kit, materials list, reference design, and design knowhow. ODM firms from Taiwan could now resolve some of those challenging design issues by using Intel chipsets and compete in notebook PC manufacturing for OEM lead firms.

By 1993, Taiwan had already produced 1.3 million units of notebook PCs and achieved a market share of 22 percent. This compares favorably with its much smaller role in desktop PCs then, with 2.3 million units produced and a market share of only 8 percent.[64] Its share in notebook PCs increased further to 27 percent in 1995, far more than Singapore (12 percent), South Korea (1 percent) and Hong Kong (0 percent).[65] By 1999, these ODM firms from Taiwan had already captured a substantial share of up to 39 percent of the worldwide notebook PC market (Table 2.8). From a modest size of 24.2 million units outsourced in 2000, the outsourcing of notebook PCs by OEM lead firms peaked at 188 million out of 194 million units shipped in 2010 (97 percent). Taiwan's ODM firms held a commanding 95 percent share of this notebook PC outsourcing market.

In 2015 and 2018 of Tables 2.7 and 2.8, this outsourcing to ODM firms was respectively reduced to 138 million out of 177 million units shipped (78 percent) and 135 million out of 163 million units (83 percent) because top OEM Lenovo manufactured in-house about 53–57 percent of its 36 million units in 2015 and 2018.[66] Among the top five ODM firms in Table 2.8, the three largest OEM customers remained broadly similar between 2010 and 2018. In 2010, Hewlett-Packard, Dell, and Asus were respectively the largest OEM customers of Quanta, Wistron, and Pegatron, and they remained so in 2018. Acer was Compal's largest OEM customer in 2010, but it was replaced by Dell in 2018. Similarly, Hewlett-Packard replaced Toshiba as Inventec's largest OEM customer in 2018. Compal and Wistron were Lenovo's major ODM partners.

Dominant by the late 2000s, Quanta, Compal, and other ODM firms from Taiwan have since become the de facto product designers and manufacturers of notebook PCs for major OEM lead firms (see Table 2.1), taking advantage of highly complex and supportive electronics ecosystems in their home base.[67] In turn, these OEM lead firms in PCs can restructure their businesses and leverage the design and manufacturing excellence of leading ODM firms from Taiwan to sustain or improve their market positions in the rapidly evolving global PC industry increasingly challenged by the arrival of smartphones, the more advanced category of mobile handsets, since the late 2000s. During this entire period of PC revolution, the dominance of Wintelism, i.e., Microsoft in operating systems and Intel in microprocessors, remains unchallenged. As will be detailed in Chapter 5, US leadership in PC's operating systems, application software, and micro-processors would still be clearly visible in the global production networks of any top PC vendor from the US and East Asia through to the late 2010s. But in other high-value components for PCs, such as memory chips, flat panel displays, and metal casings, East Asian producers from South Korea, Taiwan, Japan, and China have become the dominant suppliers.

## Mobile Handsets

Just like the world's first microprocessor (Intel 4004) launched by Intel on November 15, 1971 and the world's first open-system PC, IBM 5150, a decade later, another US firm, Motorola, became the first in the world to launch a workable mobile phone or cellphone, DynaTAC 8000x, in 1983. Similar to its counterpart IBM in the PC market, Motorola dominated the mobile phone market for the next fifteen years until Finland's Nokia overtook it to become the largest vendor in 1998.[68] The top four vendors in 1998 were Nokia (24 percent), Motorola (23 percent), Ericsson (14 percent), and Samsung (4 percent).[69] Other leading mobile phone OEM firms were Japan's Sharp, Fujitsu, NEC, and so on; Canada's Research In Motion (RIM's Blackberry); and South Korea's LG.[70] As noted in Table 2.1, much production in this pre-smartphone era was vertically integrated and based mostly in the home countries of OEM lead firms. In 1999, for example, Nokia still accounted for more than 50 percent of the total value of the Helsinki stock market and retained 55 percent of production in Finland, coordinating an industrial cluster of some 300 first-tiered Finnish suppliers and 4,000 ICT-based firms.[71]

Throughout the entire 2000s, Nokia was the dominant market leader with 30 to 38 percent of market share, whereas Motorola's share decreased from 15 percent in 2000 to 5 percent in 2010. In 2005, the mobile phone market was worth around $110 billion. In 2007, Samsung became the world's second largest vendor of mobile phones after overtaking Motorola at about 14 percent market share each, followed by Sony-Ericsson and LG.[72] As indicated in Table 2.9, the worldwide mobile phone market grew rapidly to 161 million units in 2008. In 2010, Nokia's dominance peaked at 40 percent share of a global market of 320 million units shipped. But just one year later in 2011, two of these three market leaders in mobile phones, Nokia and Motorola, would be overtaken by a new breed of OEM lead

TABLE 2.9. World's top mobile handset OEM firms by shipment, market share, and outsourcing, 2008–2021 (in millions of units and percent)

| OEM firms | Samsung | Huawei | Apple | Xiaomi | Oppo | Lenovo-Motorola | Nokia | Blackberry | World Total |
|---|---|---|---|---|---|---|---|---|---|
| 2008 shipment (m) | 5.3 | 0.0 | 13.7 | 0.0 | 0.0 | 9.2 | 60.5 | 22.6 | 161 |
| Market share (%) | 3.3 | - | 8.5 | - | - | 5.7 | 37.6 | 14.0 | 100.0 |
| 2010 shipment (m) | 11.8 | 0.0 | 38.8 | 0.0 | 0.0 | 15.8 | 128 | 56.6 | 320 |
| Market share (%) | 3.7 | - | 12.1 | - | - | 4.9 | 40.1 | 17.7 | 100.0 |
| 2015 shipment (m) | 320 | 109 | 232 | 73.1 | 45.7 | 73.9 | 27.3 | 3.9 | 1,377 |
| Market share (%) | 23.2 | 7.9 | 16.8 | 5.3 | 3.8 | 5.4 | 2.0 | 0.3 | 100.0 |
| 2018 shipment (m) | 290 | 206 | 205 | 119 | 115 | 41.8 | 15.1 | 1.1 | 1,410 |
| Market share (%) | 20.6 | 14.6 | 14.5 | 8.4 | 8.2 | 3.0 | 1.1 | 0.1 | 100.0 |
| 2020 shipment (m) | 263 | 170 | 199 | 146 | 144 | - | - | - | 1,250 |
| Market share (%) | 21.0 | 13.6 | 15.9 | 11.7 | 11.5 | - | - | - | 100.0 |
| 2021F shipment (m) | 267 | 45 | 229 | 198 | 185 | - | - | - | 1,360 |
| **2018 production** | | | | | | | | | |
| In-house (%) | 100 | 13.5 | 0.0 | 5.0 | 70.0 | 61.5 | 0.0 | - | 43.7 |
| Hon Hai/Foxconn | - | 26.5 | 70.0 | 69.0 | 30.0 | - | 100 | - | 28.5 |
| Flex (Singapore) | - | 46.0 | - | - | - | 25.4 | - | - | 7.5 |
| Pegatron (Taiwan) | - | - | 25.7 | - | - | - | - | - | 3.7 |
| BYD (China) | - | 14.0 | - | - | - | - | - | - | 2.0 |
| Wistron (Taiwan) | - | - | 4.3 | 6.1 | - | - | - | - | 1.1 |
| Top 5 share (%) | - | 86.5 | 100 | 75.1 | 30.0 | 25.4 | 100 | - | 42.8 |

Note: See full table and notes in Appendix C Table C4.
Sources: IHS Markit/Informa Tech Custom Research for GPN@NUS Centre, July–October 2016 and 2019; and TrendForce, January 5, 2021.

firms launching smartphones that incorporated both telecommunications and mobile computing through a mobile OS and application software programs (apps). By 2014, both Nokia and Motorola's handset divisions were acquired respectively by Microsoft and Lenovo, ending an earlier era of mobile phones (known as "feature phones" now).[73] As cautioned by Woyke (2014, 9), a prominent pundit of the smartphone industry, "Change is a constant in smartphone history. A company and geographic region will lead innovation for some years, but a challenger always emerges to overtake them."

The dominance of Nokia/Ericsson and the Nordic region in the 1990s and the 2000s was indeed challenged during the 2010s by the resurgence of Silicon Valley (Apple's iPhone) and the emergence of East Asia (South Korea's Samsung and China's Huawei, Xiaomi, Oppo/Vivo, and Lenovo). As stated in Table 2.1, this dramatic transformation in the mobile handset segment of global electronics can be termed the "smartphone revolution" that took place since Apple launched its first iPhone in June 2007. In June 2009, Samsung entered into the emerging smartphone market and launched the Galaxy series smartphones when Nokia and RIM (Blackberry) were still the largest vendors in mobile phones, with a combined market share of over 57.8 percent (Table 2.9). The global market for mobile handsets, however, began to shift decisively in favor of smartphones from 2011 onward, and the three earlier leaders in mobile phones, Nokia, Motorola, and RIM, inadvertently underestimated this revolutionary smartphone market opportunity.[74] Their collective decline in the 2010s had as much, if not more, to do with their operating systems (e.g., Nokia on Symbian and Motorola on Windows Mobile[75]) as with their limited hardware models.

Indeed, this "OS war" won by Apple's in-house iOS launched in 2007 and Google's Android launched in 2008 has underscored the great importance of technological leadership through software platforms in the global smartphone industry.[76] As noted by my interviewee from one of the world's top smartphone OEM firms,[77]

when the iPhone first came out, you have to remember this was the time when Nokia was number one. But they abandoned their simpler OS, and they said they were moving to this totally unproven and not popular Microsoft OS. Why would anybody buy a Nokia product when the future was not accepted? So, the iPhone was not a very good product. But it got into the market at the same time when Nokia was in decline. For the first few years, the iPhone forecast was always far too low. They sold many more than they thought as the iPhone was popular and Nokia was going down. And then Samsung came up with Galaxy, like one year after the iPhone, and that really took off too. Samsung's forecast was also very low.

By 2011, Android already controlled 45 percent of the global OS market. In 2014, Apple and Google together accounted for some 94 percent of the global smartphone OS market, much like Microsoft in the PC OS market. By the first quarter of 2021, Android's share reached 83.8 percent, whereas iOS increased to 16.2 percent; their duopoly market share is expected to be held through to at least 2025.[78] While Apple has been able to extract much value capture from having its own iOS, all Android-based smartphone OEM vendors are embedded in Google's self-reinforcing software ecosystem based around productivity apps for these devices. Once established, these two OS ecosystems (iOS and Android) became formidable barriers for smartphone vendors and their end-user customers to switch to different operating (eco)systems.

Through licensing agreements with Google, Android-based smartphone vendors can save tremendous investment in developing their own OS that can hardly compete against Android's ecosystem of apps (e.g., China's Huawei in 2019[79]). For example, as the first mobile phone vendor adopting Android at the very beginning,[80] Samsung tried to develop its own OS Bada in 2009. But it eventually gave up in 2014 when it signed a ten-year patent cross-licensing agreement with Google and switched back to Android OS for all its smartphones. Under this agreement, Samsung and Google are entitled to use technologies covered by each other's patents. Xiaomi, another top five smartphone vendor in 2018–2021 (Table 2.9), has developed its in-house platform, known as MIUI (MI User Interface)—a customized version of Android, that offers users in China access to a wider range of paid apps. Overall, the availability of Google's Android OS "for free" to smartphone OEM vendors has clearly lowered the entry barriers and allowed more vendors from China and elsewhere (e.g., India's Micromax and Brazil's Positivo) to enter the rapidly expanding global market.

Throughout the 2010s, this smartphone revolution perhaps became the most significant technology and market driver in global electronics. Contrasting global production networks orchestrated by OEM lead firms in smartphones, such as Apple and Samsung, and their platform partners spearheaded major advancement in semiconductor design and manufacturing and much more complex interconnections in the worlds of electronics production centered in East Asia (see empirical Chapters 4–6). In Table 1.1, the total revenue of mobile handsets reached $443 billion in 2018, far larger than PCs ($146 billion) and TVs ($116 billion). From their respective shipments of 11.8 million units and 38.8 million units of smartphones in 2010 (see Table 2.9), Samsung's shipment in 2011 increased almost eightfold to 106 million units and Apple's increased by 140 percent to 93.5 million units. Meanwhile, Nokia's shipment decreased massively from 128 million units in 2010 to 34.7 million in 2012. Between 2008 and 2018, total mobile handset shipment worldwide increased by 755 percent from 161 million to 1.41 billion units, having first crossed the 1 billion units threshold in 2013. Due to ongoing US-China trade wars and the COVID-19 pandemic (human movement restrictions), smartphone shipments in 2019 and 2020 declined respectively to 1.37 billion and 1.25 billion units, but are forecasted to reach 1.36 billion units in 2021 and over 1.4 billion in 2022 (Table 2.9).

In 2015, Nokia's market share in this market plummeted to only 2 percent, whereas market leaders of Samsung and Apple commanded respectively 23.2 percent and 16.8 percent. In 2018, Samsung remained the market leader with 20.6 percent market share, followed by Apple and China's Huawei each with 14.5 percent share. Between 2015 and 2018, the smartphone business contributed to about 50–55 percent of total group revenue of Samsung Electronics ($175 billion to $220 billion) and 55–65 percent of Apple Inc.'s total revenue ($215 billion to $265 billion), underscoring the tremendous importance of these mobile devices in their corporate prowess. These two market leaders were also joined by other competing brands from China (e.g., Huawei, Xiaomi, Oppo, and Vivo) and South Korea (LG).[81] As noted in Table 1.1, however, the relative market shares of Samsung, Apple, and three Chinese brands increased further in 2020 because of Huawei's troubles in sourcing chipsets for its smartphones under export restrictions imposed by the former Trump administration (see further discussion in Chapter 5).

The enormous success of both Apple's iPhones and Samsung's Galaxy smartphones has much to do with their unique innovations in organizing their very contrasting global production networks during the 2010s—a key theme for full analysis in Chapters 4–6 based on new empirical material.

But some early discussion is useful here (see also Table 2.1). Similar to its Macintosh line of desktop and notebook PCs codesigned with and manufactured by Taiwan's Quanta (and Foxconn for desktops), Apple does not manufacture its iPhones and prefers to specialize in the design, engineering, marketing, and distribution of its iPhone products. Instead, Apple relies heavily on key strategic partners from East Asia to manufacture various application processors (Samsung and, since 2017, TSMC), baseband and modem processors (Qualcomm-TSMC), wireless chips (Broadcom-TSMC), memory devices (Samsung and SK Hynix), image sensors (Sony), and flat panel displays (Samsung and Japan Display) that are assembled into successive generations of iPhones by Taiwan's top provider of electronics manufacturing services (EMS), Hon Hai Precision, in their China-based factories under the trade name Foxconn.[82]

This tight coupling of Apple's iPhone R&D in California and its device and component manufacturing in East Asia explains why when the former US president Barack Obama asked the late Steve Jobs, cofounder and former CEO of Apple Inc., in 2012, "What would it take to make iPhones in the United States?," Jobs's reply was that "Those jobs aren't coming back"![83] By the late 2010s, much of the task of assembling over 2 billion successive models of iPhones had gone to Foxconn's industrial clusters located in the cities of Shenzhen and Zhengzhou in China and elsewhere in Asia (e.g., India). Because of Foxconn's immense scale of manufacturing operations and supply chain flexibility, Apple's own executives conceded that switching from Foxconn to other contract manufacturers would be very time consuming, costly, and risky. Since its strategic partnership as *the* EMS provider for assembling Apple's iPhones and iPads, Hon Hai also saw its revenues more than doubling between 2007 and 2010 (from $38.1 billion to $79.4 billion) and growing much further during the 2010s to peak at $179 billion in 2020. Its net profit also grew from $1.3 billion in 2007 and $2.3 billion in 2010 to $3.5–4.9 billion between 2016 and 2020.[84]

This EMS model of independent contract manufacturers and spinning-offs of former manufacturing facilities owned by OEM firms (e.g., Apple and IBM) was first developed in the US and Canada in the late 1980s.[85] But the dominance of these US- and Canada-origin EMS providers in the late 1990s was challenged by the world-leading EMS provider (Hon Hai) and ODM firms from Taiwan (Quanta, Compal, Inventec, and Wistron) during the 2000s. By 2004, Hon Hai's revenue of $17.2 billion and net income of $0.9 billion were ahead of all five EMS providers from the US and Canada. The four largest ODM firms from Taiwan, Quanta, Compal, Inventec, and Wistron, had revenues comparable to or exceeding these US/Canada-origin EMS providers. More importantly, they were much more profitable throughout the 2000s than the four North American EMS giants—Flextronics, Solectron, Celestica, and Sanmina-SCI. These four "first movers" of EMS suffered from record losses when East Asian latecomer EMS providers and ODM firms grew their revenues and market share. By 2008, Hon Hai's revenue of $65.4 billion had already eclipsed the combined total of all other EMS providers in the world's top ten. Its market leadership in EMS production extended further throughout the 2010s.

As indicated in Table 2.9, the key to Hon Hai's successful partnership with Apple and other OEM customers in mobile handsets (e.g., Huawei, Xiaomi, Oppo, and Vivo) during the 2015–2018 period is premised on its firm-specific capability in organizing and managing the entire value chain of an electronic product, from component sourcing to manufacturing and fulfilment. Before its partnership with Apple since 2007, Hon Hai had extensive experience in providing EMS work to the world's leading mobile phone OEM firms, such as Motorola and Nokia. By 2005, its mobile handset-related revenue had already reached $6.3 billion or about 20 percent of total revenue. Since the mid-2000s, a top EMS provider such as Hon Hai and others is no longer a low-end subcontractor to OEM lead firms that govern in a form of captive relationship. Rather, it provides the entire manufacturing solution on a "turnkey" and global basis to strategic customers worldwide. This mutually constitutive relationship between OEM lead firms and their EMS providers resembles a mode of strategic partnership that benefits both parties on a complementary and sustained basis. The success of an EMS provider is critically dependent on its ability to organize and manage the ever-more-challenging task of handling multiple and often complex relationships with their lead firm customers and major suppliers in different markets and global locations (see a full analysis of the 2015–2018 data in Chapters 4–6).

Data in Table 2.9 also show that not all top OEM firms in smartphones rely on the organizational and manufacturing excellence of EMS providers such as Foxconn and others, if these lead firms have developed strong in-house production capabilities. Having accumulated decades of experience and technologies in electronics manufacturing, Samsung and, to a lesser extent, Oppo and Lenovo clearly prefer in-house production of their smartphones. In Samsung's case, its close strategic relationship with US fabless firm Qualcomm, becoming the early adopter of Qualcomm's CDMA-based technologies and chipsets MSM6250 in 2003, has been instrumental in the success of its feature phones during the 2000s and, later, Galaxy smartphones throughout the 2010s and beyond.[86]

Equally important has been Samsung's intrachaebol organization of production networks that enables faster decision and better supply chain management for high quality materials and functionality of its key products at competitive prices over time.[87] This intragroup synergy in R&D capability, information and material flows, and joint branding has given its mobile handset division a much stronger position vis-à-vis major competitors, such as Apple, Nokia, and Motorola. Between 2007 and 2016, Samsung's Device Solutions (semiconductors) division also served as Apple's top foundry supplier of application processor chips for its iPhones. Even though Apple eventually switched its foundry requirement to TSMC's cutting-edge fabs in Taiwan from the A10 chips onward in September 2016 (see a full case study in Chapter 5), Samsung's mobile handset division has been able to tap into this intrachaebol capability in fabricating crucial chipsets and semiconductor devices for smartphone OEM firms. Chapter 5 will offer a detailed analysis of these key components in smartphones and their complex production networks among top OEM lead firms in 2015 and 2018.

**Toward the Interconnected Worlds of Global Electronics**

By 2010, the emerging interconnected worlds of global electronics—led by three major segments of semiconductors, PCs, and mobile handsets—had evolved from the previously multinational worlds of innovation and production (e.g., in Silicon Valley) to more globalized networks of technological innovations and software and design leadership based in the US and manufacturing production centered in East Asia, particularly in China, Taiwan, South Korea, and Singapore. While this coevolution in the worlds of electronics production started in the late 1980s, it gained force significantly throughout the 2000s, as summarized in the changing national contexts in Table 1.2 and the key industrial shifts in Table 2.1. In all three segments, state-of-the-art design and R&D activities were conducted in *both* traditional centers of technological excellence in California, Texas, Western Europe, and Japan, and new centers of excellence in East Asia around Seoul-Suwon, Hsinchu-Taipei, Singapore, and Shenzhen/Shanghai/Beijing. Manufacturing production, long a key stronghold of the US electronics industry, had shifted almost wholesale to East Asian locations. Some important exceptions were in semiconductors, such as the US-based fabs of Intel, Micron, Texas Instruments, and GlobalFoundries.

In all segments of global electronics, US, Japanese, and European OEM lead firms worked closely with their East Asian partners to compete against each other in different markets and product categories worldwide. By the late 2010s and as observed in Table 2.1, the wheels of fortune in global electronics had turned further in favor of East Asian economies. In semiconductors, East Asian locations in South Korea, Taiwan, Singapore, and China now host the vast majority of world's leading wafer fabs among the top ten IDM firms (except Intel) and the top five foundry providers. This is in addition to Japan's continual role as the home base for the trailing wafer fabs of remaining Japanese IDM firms (except Kioxia/Toshiba). Still, Silicon Valley remains as the top spot for a large number of the world's leading fabless chip design firms that rely mostly on the cutting-edge fabs located in East Asia. As noted earlier in this chapter, a very significant chunk of these semiconductor products (up to two-thirds in 2018/2020), such as microprocessors, memory devices, and logic chips, has been earmarked for ICT end products, such as notebook PCs, smartphones, and other mobile devices.

In PCs, the shipment of notebooks had surpassed desktops by 2009 and, since 2013, has almost doubled desktops. With the exception of Lenovo (53 percent in-house), almost 100 percent of all notebooks by top five PC OEM firms in 2018 were outsourced to four Taiwanese ODM firms in their factories mostly located in China. The same outsourcing pattern was also applicable to desktop PCs by OEM firms from the US, Taiwan, and Japan that engaged EMS providers from Taiwan (Foxconn and Pegatron) and Singapore (Flex) to assemble desktops in their factories in China, Southeast Asia, eastern Europe, and Latin America. In mobile handsets, an overwhelming share of smartphone assembly production took place in East Asian locations, particularly in China (Apple, Xiaomi, and Vivo via Foxconn, and Chinese OEM firms), Vietnam (Samsung), and elsewhere (e.g., Foxconn, Wistron, Samsung, and Vivo in India). A number of leading East Asian firms worked closely with OEM lead firms in different global production networks. Some of them also repositioned as global lead firms in their own right.

By 2020/2021, the complex worlds of electronics became highly interconnected through diverse global production networks comprising OEM lead firms from the US, Western Europe, and East Asia, platform and technology leaders in key modules and components (e.g., semiconductors and flat panel displays) and software (e.g., operating systems), manufacturing partners from East Asia (e.g., ODM and EMS providers), and specialized local suppliers in East Asia (e.g., metal casings, electronic devices and modules). These interconnected worlds of global electronics are now vastly different in scale, scope, and complexity from the localized world of semiconductor and electronics firms in California's Mountain View first observed by Don Hoefler in 1971, as was described in Chapter 1's opening.

Since the early internationalization of the electronics industry during the 1970s and the 1980s, the subsequent emergence and dominance of Wintelism, modular production, and contract and foundry manufacturing have consolidated the significant role of East Asia in these interconnected worlds of global electronics. Together with Chapter 1's discussion of the national and institutional context of coevolution in the emerging worlds of electronics production since the 1980s, this chapter's historical analysis of industry- and firm-level dynamics provides further contexts for unpacking and explaining the geography and organizational innovations of these interconnected worlds centered in East Asia by the late 2010s—the focus of this book's empirical Chapters (4–6). But before we embark on such a major undertaking at the analytical level of networks, it is necessary in the next chapter to identify and construct a robust theoretical framework for analyzing such competitive drivers of global electronics in terms of technological innovation, organizational change, and the evolving geographies of global production networks.

CHAPTER 3

# Global Production Networks: A Theory of Interconnected Worlds

IN ITS *WORLD INVESTMENT REPORT 2013*, UNCTAD (2013) estimated that some 80 percent of international merchandise trade was already organized through global production networks coordinated by lead firms investing in cross-border productive assets and trading inputs and outputs with partners, suppliers, and customers worldwide. Many international organizations and research consultancies have recognized these global production networks as the new long-term structural feature of an ever-more interdependent world economy.[1] By the end of the 2010s, global production networks remained as the main conduit for more than two-thirds of world trade, particularly in high-tech industries such as electronics and automotive—two increasingly intertwined industries implicated in the 2020/2021 global chip shortage. As documented in the World Trade Organization's (2019) *Global Value Chain Development Report 2019*, the value added share of "Factory Asia" in cross-macroregional production networks involving North America and Western Europe increased significantly between 2000 and 2017. Meanwhile, intraregional production activities within both North America and Western Europe declined relative to this increasing shift of manufacturing toward East and South Asia. In the highly interconnected worlds of electronics, global production networks are clearly the most critical industrial-organizational platform for the worldwide manufacturing activities coordinated by global lead firms in relation to their main customers, strategic partners, and key suppliers.

Since the late 2000s, theoretical advancement and empirical studies of global production networks and global value chains have also emerged as an influential research foci in the social sciences. This large and rapidly expanding literature develops close connections with the initial conceptual development in the cognate social science fields of development studies, economic geography, economic sociology, international political economy, and regional studies.[2] Grounded in this conceptual literature, the chapter theorizes why and how firm-specific organizational and geographical configurations of production networks can connect disparate "dots" and "hot spots"—places, subnational regions, and economies—in different worlds of innovation and production. To readers not yet familiar with the theoretical literature on global production networks, the chapter also serves as a concise introduction to several key concepts and explanatory variables. Though relatively brief, this conceptual framing will map onto, and enable a better understanding of, the detailed empirical analysis of global electronics in the next three chapters.

Based on Coe and Yeung's (2015) theory of global production networks (the GPN 2.0 theory)[3], this chapter conceptualizes production networks as the key industrial-organizational platform bringing together the strategic activities and developmental trajectories of firms and nonfirm actors in different places and subnational regions across the world economy. Explaining the nature and emergence of the interconnected worlds of innovation and production requires both an understanding of changing national-institutional and industry contexts, as was done in the previous two chapters and summarized in Tables 1.2 and 2.1, and an elucidation of why and how this industrial-organizational platform has come about. This network-based theory of interconnected worlds therefore not only provides an analytical window to examine global production networks as the core backbone of today's world economy. It also eschews the limited focus on endogeneity and national-territorial dynamics in much of the earlier literature on the development and restructuring of the electronics industry within specific multinational worlds.[4]

More specifically, this GPN 2.0-based theory explains why and how three causal drivers—optimizing cost-capability ratios, sustaining market development, and working with financial discipline—interact with firms and nonfirm actors under different risk conditions to produce four different firm-specific strategies for organizing global production networks: intrafirm coordination, interfirm control, interfirm partnership, and extrafirm bargaining. Each of these firm-level strategies is dependent on a unique combination of causal drivers and competitive dynamics.[5] In reality, a lead firm may adopt multiple strategies at any time, as will be evident in later empirical chapters. For analytical purpose though, we can generalize at a "higher" level of abstraction to specify the conditions (or causal dynamics) under which a lead firm chooses a specific strategy for a particular product line and/or production network activity. This in turn enables a useful comparison of different lead firms in terms of their most dominant network configurations and firm-specific strategies.

As will be analyzed in later empirical chapters on global electronics in the 2010s, such contrasting configurations and strategies can be found among different groups of lead firms, such as Intel versus Qualcomm-TSMC in semiconductors, Hewlett-Packard versus Lenovo in PCs, Apple versus Samsung in mobile handsets, and LG versus Xiaomi in TVs. In short, causal dynamics are the independent variables driving firm-specific strategies, which then lead to differential organizational innovations and geographical configurations of production networks. As these causal dynamics are themselves geographically variegated within and across different national economies and industrial/product segments—a historical consequence of industrial restructuring and coevolutionary transformations described in Chapter 2—their causal outcomes on firm-specific strategies and network configurations are likely to be geographically specific and yet uneven.[6]

Taking on the above key themes, the following three sections conceptualize respectively:

(1) the role of production networks in connecting multiple worlds of innovation and production through different geographical configurations (the "where" question),

(2) competitive dynamics and risk environments as causal drivers shaping lead firms and their network members (the "why" of production networks), and

(3) their firm-specific strategies and organizational innovations in production networks (the "how" issue).

Where possible in these sections, I will outline general theoretical arguments before offering some illustrative examples from the different segments of global electronics. Later empirical Chapters 4–6 will develop a much more comprehensive analysis of electronics global production networks during the 2010s that maps directly onto this chapter's theory in relation to the geographical configurations (Chapter 4), firm strategies (Chapter 5), and causal dynamics (Chapter 6) of global production networks. This sequence in empirical analysis allows for both the where and the how of electronics production networks to be explained collectively by specific causal dynamics in Chapter 6, where it all comes together in analytical terms.

## Production Networks: Connecting Multiple Worlds through Geographical Configurations

In general, a production network necessarily involves more than one actor. These actors can be capitalist firms of different sizes, ownership structures, industrial specialization, and national origins; they can also be non-firm entities, such as the state, international organizations, labor groups, business/industry associations, consumers and civil society organizations, and so on. A firm is responsible for the creation of economic value through production, a process of transforming material and intangible inputs into outputs, such as intermediate or finished goods and/or services. Production is therefore a value-transformative process incorporating all economic sectors, from extractive industries in the primary sector to manufacturing activities in the secondary sector and service industries in the tertiary sector. OECD-WTO-UNCTAD (2013, 16) estimated that as intermediate inputs to global production, services contribute directly and indirectly to over 30 percent of the total value added in manufactured goods. In turn, several of these service activities are themselves organized and delivered through global production networks, e.g., software and information and communications technology (ICT) services, finance, advertising, logistics, and retailing.

In its linear form, this process of transformation is commonly understood as taking place along the value chain.[7] If a firm internalizes much of this value chain activity through vertical integration, value transformation is deemed intrafirm in nature. If a firm engages with other firms in the production of value through outsourcing, subcontracting, or strategic alliances, interfirm organizational relations are developed.[8] In this book, however, I advocate a *network* understanding of this economic-geographic process of value transformation in the global mosaic of subnational regions and national worlds of production. In this approach informed by GPN 2.0, value transformation is conceptualized as taking place not only through the interfirm movement of materials (e.g., components, modules, or full sets) and/or intangibles (e.g., software, design, specifications, and proprietary technology) along the value chain in a particular industry; it can also occur simultaneously through innovative organizational relationships within the same firm (intrafirm) or between firms in interconnected production processes and nonfirm actors (extrafirm) in different local or national economies.

In interfirm relations, a lead firm can engage with a variety of other firms, such as platform leaders, strategic partners, specialized suppliers, and generic suppliers, in its value transformation.[9] While a lead firm takes charge of product or market definition based on its firm-specific competitive advantage and capabilities, its network members provide the partial or complete materials supplies (e.g., the manufacture of intermediate or finished goods) and business solutions (e.g., the provision of critical software or advanced business services).[10] In each segment of these interfirm organizational relations (e.g., lead firm-supplier or strategic partner-supplier), a firm can be subject to extrafirm influences from "above" (e.g., the state and the wider regulatory or industry context) and from other actors (e.g., labor unions, industry associations, or consumer organizations). In this network organizational form, coordinating geographically dispersed production is conceptually much more complex than the interfirm governance of value chain activity. Production networks invariably bring together both firms and nonfirm actors and create economic value through a combination of intra-, inter-, and extrafirm relations.

Geographically, the integration of these intra-, inter-, and extrafirm relationships takes place across the world at different spatial scales, from the local and the subregional to the national, the macroregional, and the global scale. The upper box in Figure 3.1 illustrates this cross-macroregional integration of production networks that in turn connects diverse worlds of local and national economies in North America and East Asia. For the purpose of simplicity, the figure depicts only two stylized national worlds of electronics production based in the United States and Taiwan. In both worlds bounded within national economies "N," there are subnational regions "R" (e.g., California) and localities "L" (e.g., Palo Alto/ San Francisco and Hsinchu/Taipei) that host the location of firm-specific functions, such as headquarters (HQ), research and development (R&D),

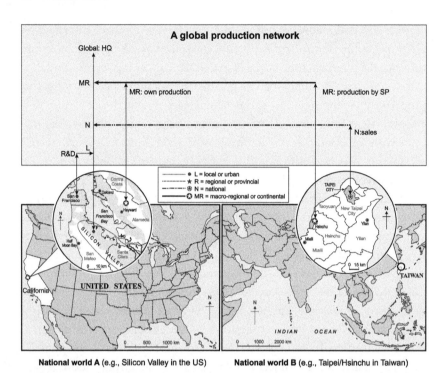

FIGURE 3.1. Production networks: Integrating national worlds of electronics production.

Source: Adapted from Yeung (2021a, Figure 2; 1001). Copyright ©2021, Henry Wai-chung Yeung, Creative Commons Attribution-NonCommercial-NoDerivatives License, CC BY-NC-ND 4.0.

manufacturing production, and distribution and sales. These functional activities within a lead firm and among other firms in the same production network can be organized in various territorial configurations—some are highly localized (e.g., R&D in software and process and product technologies in specific clusters), while others are macroregional and global in nature (e.g., headquarters functions and production activity).

The organization and flow of value activity can be conceived in multiple spatial scales from the local to the global. Each of these organizational relationships, however, must be embedded within a national territorial formation, aggregating from localities such as Santa Clara and Hsinchu to subregional ensembles and from these regions to the national economy (i.e., the US or Taiwan). This geographical conception incorporates both complex organizational relationships of network actors and their territorial embedding. The two are mirror images of each other because, irrespective of their functional scales (e.g., global or macroregional), firms in global production networks must eventually "touch down" or locate in specific territorial ensembles within national economies—be they local or subregional. Once this touching down takes place, value activity tends to spread across different localities and subregions within national economies. Such processes can include geographical spillover in technological innovation, the spatial diffusion of management and marketing practices, and the geographical integration of production activity.

Let me illustrate Figure 3.1 with a stylized example of notebook personal computers (PCs) described in detail in Chapter 2 and followed up more fully in Chapter 4. Within a specific locality such as Silicon Valley, a lead firm can locate its global headquarters function (e.g., Hewlett-Packard Inc. in Palo Alto, California). Another locality nearby within the same home country (i.e., the US) hosts the local R&D activity of this particular global production network, e.g., in-house component design services for its manufacturing plant nearby in Santa Clara County (California) or external proprietary software vendors for its core products, such as Microsoft in Seattle, Washington. Thinking territorially, we can envisage the diffusion and spillover of value activity to adjacent localities and clusters within California. This intra- and interfirm expansion of value activity within the same national economy can serve as an important possibility for industrial upgrading within national world A (e.g., the US).

Over time and as an original equipment manufacturing (OEM) lead firm, Hewlett-Packard develops new interfirm production relationships at the macroregional scale with its strategic partner (SP in Figure 3.1) that engages in original design manufacturing (ODM) activity elsewhere in national world B (e.g., Compal or Quanta in Taiwan). In this cross-regional outsourcing relationship coordinated by Hewlett-Packard, its ODM strategic partner in Taiwan begins production of Hewlett-Packard notebook PCs in a home locality (e.g., Taipei or Hsinchu) for sales within Taiwan or nearby markets in East Asia (e.g., Japan, China, and Malaysia). By now, we begin to witness the cross-regional/continental integration of value activity associated with the interfirm global expansion of Hewlett-Packard's production network in notebook PCs.

Production activity within this OEM-ODM interfirm network is now located in the high-growth subnational regions in two different continents—one performed by the lead firm's own manufacturing facility (e.g., in California, US) and another by its strategic partner (e.g., in Taiwan's Taipei/Hsinchu). Both regional economies are drawn into an intricate set of competitive and cooperative relations—competitive between these in-house and outsourced manufacturing plants and cooperative between the lead firm Hewlett-Packard and its strategic partner (e.g., Taiwan's Compal or Quanta). What were previously "distant" and distinct national worlds of electronics are now interconnected through cooperative interfirm relationships specific to Hewlett-Packard and its "global" production network spanning Silicon Valley in North America and Taipei/Hsinchu in East Asia.

In reality, such interconnections and global integration in the worlds of electronics production are far more complex than depicted in Figure 3.1 (see more empirical details on these geographical configurations in Chapter 4). The same OEM lead firm, Hewlett-Packard, can have multiple network partners in Taiwan and elsewhere in East Asia even in the same product category (e.g., its notebook PCs made by Taiwan's Quanta, Compal, or Inventec). Its design and engineering interactions with platform leaders in PCs, such as Intel in microprocessors and Microsoft in operating system and application software, are likely to be located in its home country (the US). The location of its corporate decision-making centers also varies according to the global mandate of each product, e.g., servers and PCs in the US, but printers and peripherals in Singapore. All of these organizational arrangements complicate much further the simple two-world map in Figure 3.1.

Though rather complex, this intersection of industrial-organizational relationships and territorial embeddedness is precisely the reality of today's global production networks through which different worlds of electronics innovation and production can be "stitched together" to form a global mosaic of interconnected worlds. In this GPN 2.0 thinking, the territoriality of production networks should not be construed exclusively at just one spatial scale (e.g., country-level). A value chain analysis focusing only on the global scale for assessing value capture and industrial upgrading may not inform us sufficiently about how the reconfiguration and changing governance of value activity can impact differentially on localities and subnational regions with diverse resource endowments, institutional settings, and growth trajectories. Equally, a value chain analysis specific to the local scale may be limited because it tends to take for grant extralocal/national processes and competitive dynamics that operate at the wider spatial scales.

More significantly in the interconnected worlds of global electronics, we need to explore how and why production relations become internationalized or even globalized over time. In the GPN 2.0 theory, network embeddedness is the main conduit through which firms and institutions become articulated into global production networks. This network embeddedness can take place through both outward and inward flows of direct investment and international trade in any of the following four forms of geographical configurations (more on these empirically in Chapter 4):

(1)    The internationalization of a domestic firm to other localities outside its home economy (e.g., Taiwan's Wistron or Foxconn setting up assembly factories in China and India): This inside-out process of foreign investment enables a domestic firm to embed into global production networks coordinated by lead firms based elsewhere (e.g., Hewlett-Packard in California) or to develop into a global lead firm in itself by incorporating other firms and nonfirm actors into its expanding production network (e.g., Samsung in Vietnam or Xiaomi in India).

(2)    The export of intermediate goods or services by a domestic firm to other firms outside its home economy (e.g., a semiconductor foundry in Singapore exporting chipsets to assembly factories in Malaysia and China or US firms exporting software products to be installed on PCs and smartphones assembled in China and Mexico): This inside-out form of international trade in industrial goods and software services allows a domestic firm to remain in situ geographically and yet embed in global production networks coordinated by lead firms and their network partners based elsewhere.

(3)    The inward investment of foreign firms in the home locality of a domestic firm (e.g., Hewlett-Packard or Qualcomm setting up regional headquarters and/or R&D operations in Taiwan in order to be close to their strategic partners there): This outside-in process by either lead firms or platform/technology leaders from elsewhere facilitates the embedding of domestic firms into global networks mediated through these foreign

firms. With the participation of these foreign firms, domestic firms and production networks become progressively globalized over time through outsourcing or strategic partnership arrangements with the local subsidiaries of lead firms and/or technology leaders.

(4)    The import of intermediate goods or services by a domestic firm from dedicated suppliers outside its home economy (e.g., Qualcomm and Broadcom supplying wireless chipsets to Huawei's in-house smartphone factories in China or the dependence of Chinese PC and smartphone OEM firms on operating systems from Microsoft and Google in the US): This outside-in mode of network embeddedness takes place when foreign suppliers and platform or technology leaders become articulated into the globalizing production network governed by a locally embedded domestic lead firm.

In the GPN 2.0 theory, strategic coupling is arguably the most widely known concept deployed to explain these complex geographical configurations of production networks that connect diverse worlds of innovation and production.[11] In its essence, strategic coupling with global production networks refers to the intentional convergence and articulation of actors in both local/national economies and global production networks for mutual gains and benefits. It should not be viewed as a static concept resulting in an end-state articulation of local economies and national worlds into global production networks. The strategic nature of these interconnections, mediated through different actors such as firms and non-firm institutions, necessitates continual interactions among these actors at different spatial scales, depicted in Figure 3.1. The concept of strategic coupling allows us to connect and bridge two critical and yet relatively independent sets of competitive dynamics—territorial dynamics at the local or national scale and network dynamics at the global scale. As Chapters 1 and 2 have described empirically, territorial dynamics are the preexisting political and social institutions and economically productive assets that give rise to the unique character and composition of the multinational worlds of innovation and production, such as Silicon Valley in California and Taipei/Hsinchu in Taiwan. In East Asia, these territorial dynamics are strongly embedded in evolving national and institutional contexts summarized in Table 1.2.

Meanwhile, network dynamics are much less governed by preexisting institutions at the local or even the national level. Instead, they are constituted primarily by a wider range of economic actors, such as global lead firms, strategic partners, specialized suppliers, industrial users and final customers, and so on. Some of these are large transnational corporations, whereas others are national or domestic firms. While embedded in specific national worlds of production, these economic actors are mostly driven by the competitive network logics of seeking cost efficiency, market access and development, financial and capital gain, and risk mitigation through the innovative (re-)configuring of their production networks—key topics for the next two sections. These network logics are therefore firm and industry specific, and do not necessarily align with those political and institutional logics in their home origins, i.e., specific local or national economies. In short, global production network dynamics are qualitatively different from localized territorial dynamics.

Strategic coupling with global production networks is therefore a mutually dependent and constitutive process involving shared interests and cooperation between two or more groups of network actors who otherwise might not act in tandem for a common strategic objective. It is a dynamic process through which local actors in subregional or national economies coordinate, mediate, and arbitrage strategic interests with "global" actors—their counterparts in various global production networks. Connecting diverse worlds of global electronics, these translocal processes involve both material flows in transactional terms (e.g., equity investment and movement of production inputs, intermediate or final goods) and nonmaterial flows (e.g., technologies and knowhow, software and IT services, market information and intelligence, and organizational practices) among firms within specific geographical configurations of global production networks. The following two sections will theorize further the key causal drivers and firm-specific strategies that help explain these diverse geographical network configurations constitutive of the interconnected worlds of production.

## Causal Drivers: Competitive Dynamics and Risk Environments

What then drives value activity in global production networks? In the GPN 2.0 theory, competitive dynamics are the raison d'être of global production networks, prompting firm-specific strategies in different worlds of innovation and production.[12] This section identifies several such causal dynamics rather than prioritizing any single one; the latter is necessarily an empirical issue to be determined in the subsequent chapters (see in particular Chapter 6). Three causal drivers exist in the form of optimizing cost-capability ratios (e.g., labor, technology, knowhow, and equipment), sustaining market development (e.g., reach and access, dominance, time-to-market, and customer preferences), and working with financial discipline (e.g., access to finance, and investor and shareholder pressure).[13] Couched in different combinations within specific risk environments, these causal drivers are necessary for explaining why global production networks are organized by lead firms in certain ways, with multifarious consequences for organizational change, technological innovation, and industry development—the diverse empirical outcomes to be documented in Chapters 4–5.

### Optimizing Cost-Capability Ratios

Decades of empirical research have clearly confirmed the importance of cost-based competition in driving the globalization of production organized around spatially dispersed networks of lead firms and their global suppliers. The incessant competitive pressure in advanced capitalist economies to lower the prices of goods and services in end markets has led many lead firms, mostly vertically integrated through to the late 1980s (see Table 2.1), to reconsider their cost structures. These structures are reflected in both direct and indirect costs: direct costs comprising material inputs, labor wages, asset depreciation, and other production-related payments; and indirect costs relating to transaction costs with customers and suppliers, licensing of software, patents, and payments for goodwill and trademarks, investment in proprietary knowhow, and costs associated with raising finance.[14] Direct costs associated with manufacturing activity, particularly wages, become the most obvious arena for optimization. Internationalization to lower wage cost locations, through establishing wholly owned subsidiaries (offshoring) or subcontracting to third-party suppliers (international outsourcing), has opened an entirely new window of locational opportunity for vertically integrated lead firms from advanced industrialized economies and their subcontractors and suppliers in developing economies.[15]

This focus on wage costs as the fundamental driver of global production, however, overlooks the other side of the same coin—the capabilities of the offshored or outsourced firm. Any firm necessarily incurs costs in acquiring and mobilizing resources to complete its productive activity. A resource-based view of the firm appreciates its inherent role as a capable and strategic organizer of productive assets and value activities.[16] In short, cost alone does not offer sufficient analytical purchase to define the firm as the key actor in a production network; cost must be theorized along-side capability to form a complete and actor-oriented view of the firm. A firm can therefore be thought of as a managerial device to optimize the accumulation and deployment of its available resources, defined as its core capability, at the lowest possible cost. These cost and capabilities at the firm level are also shaped by changing national-institutional and industry contexts examined briefly in Chapters 1 and 2 (see summaries in Tables 1.2 and 2.1).[17]

In the GPN 2.0 theory, a dynamic concept of cost-capability ratios has been developed to describe this optimization process that allows different firms in global production networks to achieve greater value creation and capture over time. While cost reduction is clearly an important competitive driver compelling lead firms to engage in offshoring and/or outsourcing to independent suppliers both at home and abroad, cost is ultimately a relative concept. It must be conceptualized in combination with the firm-specific capabilities of these lead firms and their in-house facilities or external suppliers in order to arrive at a complete picture of its causal influence on the formation and evolution of global production networks. The causal dynamics of optimizing cost-capability ratios can explain why certain value activities by global lead firms are offshored through in-house facilities and/or outsourced to independent suppliers, and why the mix of these activities changes over time in specific global production networks. This optimization process is highly contingent on a firm's existing re-source endowment and strategic direction in current and/or new markets. The optimal cost-capability ratio also varies from one firm to another. Some firms can achieve optimal ratios through either cost reduction or building new capabilities, whereas others can accomplish improvements in both dimensions.

In theoretical terms, Table 3.1 presents four stylized scenarios of cost-capability ratios confronting both OEM lead firms and their partners/suppliers (domestic and international), with illustrative examples from global electronics (see the in-depth empirical analysis in Chapter 6). In general, a lead firm or a partner/supplier is most competitive if it enjoys a low cost-capability ratio, achieved through combining low costs with

TABLE 3.1. A matrix of cost-capability ratios in global production networks

| Lead firm (OEM) | Cost | |
|---|---|---|
| *Capability* | *Low* | *High* |
| Low | **LF3**: Market follower with weak long-term survival prospect (e.g., ZTE in mobile handsets) ↓ | **LF4**: Market follower facing immediate exit (e.g., Blackberry and HTC in mobile handsets) |
| High | **LF1**: Highly competitive industrial leader (e.g., Lenovo, Dell, Apple, and Acer in PCs; Apple, Samsung, and Xiaomi in mobile handsets) ←— | **LF2**: Industrial leader but subject to serious cost pressures (e.g., IBM, Compaq, Fujitsu, and Toshiba in PCs; Nokia and LG in mobile handsets) |

| Partner/supplier (domestic or international) | Cost | |
|---|---|---|
| *Capability* | *Low* | *High* |
| Low | **PS3**: A clear price taker with no or little bargaining power (e.g., InfoVision in display, ATL in lithium battery, and SMIC and Vanguard in chip foundry) ↓ | **PS4**: No prospect of securing value activity in global production networks |
| High | **PS1**: Highly competitive and likely a strategic partner of LF1 or LF2 (e.g., TSMC, AMD, Apple, MediaTek, Samsung, and ASE in semiconductors; Compal, Quanta, and Foxconn in ODM/EMS; and Murata and Catcher in components) ←— | **PS2**: Lower prospect of securing value activity in global production networks, except those supplying highly specialized modules and components (e.g., technology leaders such as Intel, Qualcomm, and Kioxia) and proprietary software and platform services (e.g., Microsoft and Google in operating systems) |

Source: Reworked from Yeung and Coe (2015, Table 1; 36). Copyright ©2015, Clark University, reproduced with permission from Informa UK Ltd., trading as Taylor & Francis Group, on behalf of Clark University.

high capabilities (i.e., lead firm LF1 or partner/supplier PS1). High firm-specific capabilities in productivity, technology and knowhow, and/or organizational routines require very substantial investments that tend to drive up overall costs. Market leaders in most globalized industries invest heavily in R&D, human resources, and marketing to sustain their cutting-edge products and/or services. A low cost-capability ratio is much harder to achieve when all value activity, including manufacturing production, takes place in the home economy because labor-related direct production costs in advanced economies tend to be high (e.g., LF2 and PS2). More recently, emerging lead firms from newly industrialized economies have begun to experience higher cost-capability ratios due to growing domestic costs and the inherent limits placed on their firm-specific capabilities (e.g., weaker or truncated national innovation systems).

The successful establishment of a lead firm–specific global production network through the international outsourcing or relocation of value activity (e.g., manufacturing and R&D) will allow a global lead firm, such as Apple, Dell, Samsung, or Lenovo, to reduce production costs. Sustained investment in R&D and product innovation at home or through international acquisitions will also increase the capabilities of these lead firms. Over time, both initiatives enable a lead firm to move from high cost–high capability (Apple and Dell previously as LF2) or low cost–low capability (Lenovo, Samsung, and Xiaomi previously as LF3) toward a more optimal ratio, characterized by lower overall costs and higher capabilities, which enables it to become a highly competitive industrial leader (LF1). A highly competitive strategic partner (e.g., Samsung or Acer in their earlier days as low-cost subcontractors PS3 to OEM lead firms) may emerge as a global lead firm when it ventures successfully into market definition through own brand development and product innovation.

The same competitive dynamic also applies to a high cost–high capability partner/supplier (PS2) or a low cost–low capability partner/supplier (PS3) that seeks to reduce cost and/or increase capability through international outsourcing and firm-specific innovation. With lower production costs achieved through economies of scale and stringent cost controls and higher yields and capabilities through continuous investment and innovation in process technologies and supply chain management, a partner/supplier PS1 can become highly competitive over time, such as TSMC and Foxconn (formerly PS3). Their outsourcing customers can also benefit from overall cost reduction and capability enhancement and thus move from formerly PS2/LF2 (AMD and Apple in chipsets; Dell in PCs) or PS3/LF3 (MediaTek in chipsets and Xiaomi in mobile handsets) to PS1 or LF1. Other partners/suppliers in PS3 place strong emphasis in capability building while exercising stringent control over production costs to become PS1, such as Samsung and ASE in semiconductors and Murata and Catcher in components.

Overall, this dynamic concept of optimizing cost-capability ratios illuminates an important coevolutionary process in competitive electronics global production networks in which OEM lead firms and their partners and suppliers collectively manage to reduce their cost-capability ratios over time—moving in Table 3.1 from LF3/LF2 in the past to LF1 (e.g., Samsung and Lenovo from LF3 and Apple and Dell from LF2) or from PS3/PS2 to PS1 (e.g., TSMC, MediaTek, Samsung, and Foxconn from PS3 and AMD and Apple from PS2). By reducing their cost-capability ratios through international production and outsourcing arrangements, lead firms are able to maintain or regain their industrial leadership in the end markets of global electronics (see examples discussed in Chapter 2). Through strategic coupling with lead firms in specific global production networks, independent partners/suppliers can also enhance their firm-specific capabilities and optimize their ratios over time. Over time, these interfirm learning and deepened transactional relationships evolve further to enable some suppliers to become the strategic partners of global lead firms over time (e.g., the Apple-TSMC and Apple-Foxconn network in iPhone production to be examined further in Chapters 4–5).[18] Cost reduction alone, therefore, cannot be the only driver of evolving global production networks. Rather, both costs and firm-specific capabilities are relative and subject to change over time within the competitive dynamics of global production networks and national institutional contexts. Only by continuously optimizing cost-capability ratios can lead firms and their partners and suppliers engage in a recursive process of sustaining or improving their competitive positions in global electronics.

### Sustaining Market Development

In the GPN 2.0 theory, the causal dynamics of market development are not just about large buyers or producers bringing durable goods or services to mass consumers for their final consumption in preexisting or externally defined end markets.[19] The market is not an externally imposed structure in which producers and customers react and behave passively.

Rather, through their actor-specific practices, these economic agents create and shape market structures.[20] The GPN 2.0 theory thus focuses on both producers and customers in their making of global production networks. In general, a market for a product or service is measured in terms of the volume or size of demand, the rate of growth, and the nature of demand with respect to quality, standards, innovation, differentiation, and so on.

Developing and sustaining market reach imposes strong competitive pressures on global lead firms, irrespective of their cost-capability ratios and functional roles in global production networks (e.g., buyers or manufacturers of goods or providers of services). Lead firms with high cost-capability ratios (e.g., LF2 in Table 3.1) are much more compelled to reconfigure their production networks to maintain and/or redefine their market positions. As market makers, lead firms with low cost-capability ratios (LF1) continue to develop access to new markets and benefit from their first-mover advantages in terms of market creation and value capture. Meanwhile, international partners and suppliers of intermediate or finished goods/services are subject to the same competitive pressure because access to markets in advanced economies through their lead firm "customers" brings potentially larger orders, upgrading opportunities, and, ultimately, better value capture.

Once a new market is created through firm-specific innovations and/or entrepreneurial activities (e.g., new or recombinant technologies, products, or services), lead firms tend to seek *market domination* in order to capture as much value as possible from their proprietary products or services. This is clearly evident among early OEM firms and platform leaders in modern capitalism (see also Chapter 2's history of such early US leaders as Intel, IBM, and Motorola). Lead firms that succeed in optimizing their cost-capability ratios through reconfiguring their global production networks are likely to be dominant players with respect to market creation and control in globalized industries, such as automotive, electronics, aerospace, pharmaceuticals, and so on. As was evident in Chapter 2 (also Tables 1.1 and 2.1), several key segments in global electronics by the late 2010s were characterized by very high market concentration among a few platform or technology leaders in semiconductors (Intel in microprocessors, Qualcomm in wireless chipsets, and Samsung in memory chips) and operating systems/software (Microsoft, Google, and Apple) and top five OEM vendors in PCs, smartphones, and TVs. Meanwhile, increasing supplier capabilities may contribute to greater market concentration in the global supply base, such as top five ODM firms, top three electronics manufacturing service (EMS) providers, and top three semiconductor foundry providers. From the perspective of both lead firms and their major international partners and suppliers, the dynamics of market dominance clearly provide a strong incentive to (re-)configure their global production networks.

The market imperative of global production networks, nevertheless, should not be defined entirely from the perspective of these producers of final goods or services (lead firms, platform and technology leaders, specialized suppliers, and so on). End customers can be just as critical in defining this market imperative. Here, *customer* refers to corporate users in intermediate markets and individual consumers of goods and services in end markets. This simple distinction between intermediate and end markets points to substantially different customer pressures confronting producers. In intermediate markets (e.g., semiconductor chip producers serving OEM lead firms in PCs and smartphones), corporate customers tend to possess more specialized knowhow and generate firm-specific demands for finished goods or services (e.g., intertwined market relationships between major telecommunications carriers and mobile handset vendors).

End markets, however, are fiercely competitive and fast moving precisely because of the extremely diverse nature of consumer demand and preferences. Compared to corporate buyers/intermediate markets, final consumers and their end markets are much more fragmented and sensitive to price and trends. This market impulse is transmitted to producers through their end-product corporate and noncorporate clients and increasingly shapes how producers develop and organize their production networks because of shorter product cycles and greater business risks.[21] The rise of new end markets in developing economies and the partial shift of end markets to the "Global South" in the 2010s has unleashed a new market imperative different from the home markets of most global lead firms. It also creates a unique basis for the emergence of new lead firms from these large developing markets that can capitalize on their home advantages of favorable market access (see further analysis of PC and smartphone OEM firms from China in later chapters).[22]

### Working with Financial Discipline
From being a relatively obscure consideration in the innovation studies and industrial organization literature, financial discipline has come to the

forefront of our understanding of the evolutionary dynamics of industrial actors and production networks in the 2010s. Originating from the US and the UK, the transformative imperative of financialization has been defined by Davis (2009, 93) as a powerful process through which "financial considerations—market valuation—would drive choices about the boundaries and strategies of the firm. Firms would focus on doing one thing well, and that one thing was often determined by the stock market."[23] A complete theory of interconnected worlds must take into account the causal role of finance in driving the complex organization of global production networks.

In particular, the pressures and opportunities associated with financialization impinge on lead firms and compel their strategic shift toward developing and expanding their global production networks. The causal dynamics of financial discipline work through firm-specific strategies and responses that in turn produce different spatial and organizational configurations of these networks. Lead firms that succeed in meeting the demands of financial discipline through globalizing production and establishing strong market presence tend to perform well in the financial markets in terms of rapidly rising stock prices, higher market capitalization, and large executive rewards, prompting a further shift in their strategic orientation toward a finance-driven approach to corporate growth and governance of production networks.

In this iterative sense, financialization works hand-in-hand with the formation and ongoing reconfiguration of global production networks spearheaded by lead firms to sustain higher returns to investment and shareholder funds. As more savings and credit are channeled into financial markets and investment products through mutual funds and financial asset management, lead firms do not need to depend exclusively on retained earnings, banks, and other lending institutions to finance their new investments in capital expenditure, production, and R&D. They can now turn to global capital markets to meet their investment requirements and to access finance on favorable terms, but they have to fulfil the financial objectives of their investors and shareholders who are singularly interested in higher and, often, short-term stock prices. This growing alignment of interests between nonfinancial lead firms—such as those in global electronics—and their demanding shareholders is increasingly underpinned by corporate reengineering focusing on lead firms' "core competences" (e.g., in product development and marketing), the globalization of their production relations (e.g., offshoring and/or outsourcing of manufacturing activity), and changing corporate governance norms (e.g., greater decision-making power among top finance executives).

Since the 2000s, this financialization of nonfinancial lead firms has produced profound incentives for, and pressures on, corporate strategies and decisions. In terms of incentives, lead firms have begun to realize that more profits can be generated through short-term financial reengineering of their existing operations and portfolios than through longer-term capital investment in new plants, equipment, technology, and products. Encouraged by their bankers, venture capitalists, and financial consultants, corporate financial officers find more profit sources in portfolio income from their intangible assets such as patents and goodwill rather than through fixed assets (e.g., factories and equipment). This financial transformation has put immense pressures on nonfinancial lead firms to optimize cost-capability ratios and to engage in global production (offshoring and/or outsourcing). In the realm of global electronics, divestment of high-cost manufacturing operations to increasingly capable international suppliers has allowed OEM lead firms, particularly those from the US, to be "asset-lite" and semiconductor firms to be "fab-lite" or fabless that in turn increases their shareholder values and yet maintains their dominant market positions. In semiconductors, fabless lead firms such as Qualcomm and Nvidia can also capitalize on their intangible assets by licensing patents and goodwill to extract much portfolio income from their technological innovation.

Based primarily in East Asia and benefitting from more patient domestic sources of state and private capital (see Table 1.2), the strategic partners and key suppliers of OEM lead firms and technology leaders in the US have often shouldered the capital investment necessary to supply to these lead firms such that the latter can focus on the maximum extraction of financial value from their proprietary assets (e.g., patents, branding, technology, design, software, and knowhow) and financial assets (e.g., newly acquired or merged businesses). As these East Asian partners and suppliers, such as TSMC and Samsung foundry in semiconductors and Foxconn in final assembly, strive to reduce their cost-capability ratios and take on more value activity in lead firms' global production over time, they are inadvertently subject to the same ruthless financial discipline as their lead firm customers. Under the disguise of supply chain rationalization, most US lead firms source from fewer, but larger, suppliers in East

Asia to achieve greater economies of scale, lower unit purchase prices, and ultimately higher return to investment. These lead firms also bargain for more aggressive price reduction with these suppliers. All of these financial pressures and greater supplier concentration in East Asia can significantly increase the risks of supply chain disruptions on a worldwide scale, as evident during the COVID-19 pandemic in 2020 and beyond.

### Managing Risks

In the interconnected worlds of global production in many industries characterized by rapid technological shifts, massive production fragmentation and cross-regional outsourcing, and the rise of new markets and competitors, OEM lead firms and their international suppliers are confronted with a far greater sense of uncertainty and unpredictability. Managing these challenges successfully requires the entire spectrum of firms and nonfirm actors in global production networks to develop a fuller understanding of changing risk conditions and to create corresponding coping strategies and organizational platforms. Global production networks are fundamentally an industrial-organizational platform wherein economic actors can mitigate and manage different forms of risk accentuated by the above three sets of causal drivers.

As illustrated in Table 3.2 with examples in global electronics, at least five forms of risks exist and shape global production networks. These different risk forms can present disastrous consequences for firms in global production networks and national economies (e.g., the devastating supply chain disruptions during the COVID-19 pandemic in 2020/2021). First, risk is generally produced well beyond the control or confines of individual firms and refers therefore to a common environment confronting firms collectively. While a lead firm can actively participate in the creation of the initial condition underpinning a particular form of risk (e.g., innovating a new technology or product), the translation of this initial condition into an actual risk requires the enrolment of other firms into the same global production network. For a lead firm's new technology to be market-transformative and "risky" to other lead firms in the same industry (e.g., notebooks overtaking desktops in PCs and smartphones cannibalizing feature phones in mobile handsets, as was documented in Chapter 2 and Table 2.1), it must be well supported by strategic partners (e.g., fabless semiconductor firms and manufacturing service providers) and key customers (e.g., telecommunications service providers). Similarly,

TABLE 3.2. Different risk forms in global production networks, 2010–2021

| Form | Nature | Causal effects on firms | Examples in global electronics |
|---|---|---|---|
| Economic risk | Systemic shifts in markets—new technologies and innovations, changing demand, financial disruptions, exchange rate fluctuations, border closure and national lockdowns, and so on | Loss of production capacity and competitive position in cost and/or market leadership; reduction in financial returns and profitability; lower income and structural volatility to localities and regions | Decline of Canada's RIM (BlackBerry), Finland's Nokia, and South Korea's LG in smartphones since 2013; demand shift and supply disruptions due to the COVID-19 pandemic in 2020 and beyond; worldwide shortage of semiconductor chips for automotive production in 2021 |
| Product risk | Quality, safety, branding, and efficiency considerations | Negative views of goods or services by consumers and customers; greater demand for corporate social responsibility | Samsung Galaxy Note 7 faulty battery and fire risks in August–September 2016 |
| Regulatory and geopolitical risk | Political, public-to-private governance, changing standards and norms, and big power conflicts | Disruption or termination of global production, existing industrial practices, and organizational arrangements | US trade sanctions on China's ZTE, Huawei, and SMIC, 2018–2021; Japan's restriction on exports of chemicals for chip making to South Korea, 2019; massive lockdowns worldwide and highly politicized push for domestic production and reshoring during the COVID-19 pandemic in 2020–2021 |

| Form | Nature | Causal effects on firms | Examples in global electronics |
|---|---|---|---|
| Labor risk | Struggles over working conditions, payment delays, and employment practices | Resistance and industrial action by employees; worker rampage and violence; disruptions to global production and employment prospects; and potentially greater reputational risk | Strikes in Foxconn's plants in China, maker of Apple's iPhones, due to workers demanding for better terms and working conditions, 2012–2013; temporary shutdown of Wistron's India factory due to contract worker rampage in December 2020; labor supply crunch due to travel restrictions during the COVID-19 pandemic in 2020–2021 |
| Environmental risk | Natural hazards, public health crisis, or human-made disasters | Accentuating the above four forms of risk and their causal effects | Japan's 2011 Fukushima earthquake and production stoppage at Japanese semiconductor fabs; distortions to global chip markets from SK Hynix's Wuxi (China) plant fire in 2013; winter storm–induced shutdown of Samsung and NXP fabs in Austin (Texas) in February 2021; Renesas's Naka (Japan) fab fire in March 2021; the COVID-19 pandemic in 2020–2021 and unprecedented global production disruptions thereafter |

Source: Reworked from Yeung and Coe (2015, Table 2; 41).

for a regulatory risk to be efficacious, the initial condition (e.g., trade deficits or geopolitical conflicts) must be identified and taken up by nonfirm actors (e.g., US, Chinese, or Japanese governments) with agendas going well beyond free market competition.[24] Identifying the causal effects of risk in shaping global production networks thus requires both firm- and structural-level analyses.

Second, the qualitative nature and causal effects of risk play out differently in the context of global production networks such that it can be termed the "GPN risk." While all five risk forms existed in the multinational worlds of innovation and production (e.g., US/Western Europe versus Japan in semiconductors during the 1980s in Chapter 1), the nature and effects of these risks in the 2010s and beyond have a far broader geographical scope and faster temporal transmission in the interconnected worlds of widely distributed global production networks. Most recently, the COVID-19 pandemic in 2020/2021 has thrown into sharp relief such extensive geographical reach and rapid effects of global supply chain disruptions. To Gereffi and Luo (2014, 6), participation in these global production networks necessarily entails "higher risk because international standards for price, quality, standards and delivery schedules are much less forgiving." Geographically, these risks can spread across the entire range of geographically dispersed actors articulated into different global production networks.[25] Mitigating this kind of GPN risk can have profound causal impact on lead firm strategies and network configurations in the post-COVID world economy—a theme I will return to in the concluding Chapter 7.

Third, risk mitigation is not necessarily a zero-sum process whereby the gain by one lead firm and its partners in the same production networks must entail a loss to another lead firm and its network partners. In many cases (e.g., a major financial crisis or pandemic), most, if not all, economic actors can suffer from the negative consequences of such risk. But in some circumstances (e.g., trade restrictions or natural hazards), exposure to risks may be substantially increased for lead firms or their suppliers from specific countries of origin (e.g., China, South Korea, or Japan) or product segments (e.g., semiconductors). This differential effect of risk under varying circumstances explains why some risks are more causally efficacious in shaping firm-specific strategies because more value can be captured or losses minimized through the appropriate mitigation of these risks. Chapters 5 and 6 will examine these risks as they unfold in the different segments of global electronics.

Taken together, the above causal drivers collectively explain why global production networks emerge and evolve to constitute the interconnected worlds of global electronics (see detailed mapping out of these drivers in Chapter 6's empirical analysis). This GPN 2.0 theory also necessitates a nuanced consideration of the diverse and substantial risks associated with global production. As lead firms engage in more international production/outsourcing and as their foreign partners and suppliers actively develop their own firm-specific capabilities, these economic actors from drastically different national contexts are confronted with an international operating environment that is much less certain and predictable than their home markets. They must develop appropriate firm strategies and organizational innovations so that, in the words of Intel's founding employee and former chairman and CEO Andrew Grove (1996), "Only the paranoid survive."

## Firm Strategies and Organizational Innovations

This section completes my theory development by conceptualizing how economic and noneconomic actors develop, organize, and govern their global production networks in order to respond effectively to the causal challenges inherent in the above competitive dynamics and risk environment. The firm-specific strategies and organizational innovations theorized here serve as the corresponding mechanisms for configuring production networks (see a full empirical analysis in Chapter 5). Together with the causal drivers in the previous section, firm strategies co-constitute the causal mechanisms of global production networks, in turn explaining empirical outcomes such as geographical configurations, firm growth, technological innovation, and industrial upgrading.

The key challenge for the GPN 2.0 theory is to incorporate a full consideration of firm-specific strategies.[26] Focusing on diverse firm actors, this theory analyzes the diversity of interests and strategies in the various functional segments associated with the same or different production networks in globalized industries. Table 3.3 thus identifies a range of firm types in these production networks, with illustrative examples from the electronics industry. This approach to defining diverse firm roles in the same or different networks and product segments can overcome the

TABLE 3.3. A typology of firms in global production networks

| Firms in GPNs | Role | Value activity | Examples in global electronics |
|---|---|---|---|
| Lead firms | Coordination and control | Product and market definition | Lenovo, Dell, and Hewlett-Packard in PCs; Apple, Samsung, and Xiaomi in smartphones; Samsung, LG, and TCL in consumer electronics and TVs |
| Strategic partners | Partial or complete solutions to lead firms | Codesign and development in product, manufacturing, and/or advanced services | Intel, Qualcomm, and Samsung as platform or technology leaders in semiconductors; TSMC in foundry; Microsoft and Google in operating systems; Compal or Quanta (ODM) in notebook PCs; Hon Hai or Flextronics (EMS) in desktop PCs and smartphones |
| Specialized suppliers (industry-specific) | Dedicated supplies to support lead firms and/or their partners | High-value modules, components, or products | Japan Display (displays) and ASE (semiconductor services); Murata and Sharp (modules); Catcher (metal casings); Merry (speakers) |
| Specialized suppliers (multi-industrial) | Critical supplies to lead firms or partners | Cross-industrial intermediate goods or services | Nvidia and NXP (graphics and sensor chipsets for automotive, aerospace, medical, and other equipment); LG Chem (lithium batteries) |
| Generic suppliers | Arm's-length providers of supplies | Standardized and low-value products or services | Plastics and packaging materials |
| Key customers | Transfer of value to lead firms | Intermediate or final consumption | OEM lead firms, corporate and institutional buyers, and final consumers |

Source: Reworked from Yeung and Coe (2015, Table 3; 45).

limitations in the existing models of global value chain governance and explain how dyadic interfirm exchange can translate beyond the interfirm nexus or even within the same value chain.[27] In short, the same lead firm or strategic partner may play different roles in intrafirm and interfirm relationships across different global production networks that may crisscross several global industries.

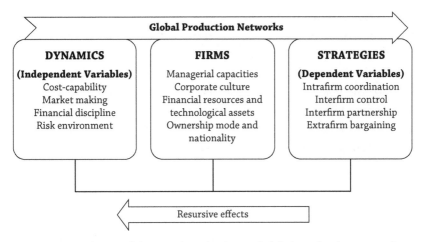

FIGURE 3.2. A theory of the causal mechanisms of global production networks.

Source: Coe and Yeung (2015, Figure 4.1; 124). Copyright ©2015, Oxford University Press, https://global.oup.com/academic/product/global-production-networks-9780198703914, reproduced with permission.

More specifically in Figure 3.2, four firm-specific strategies are theorized in relation to the earlier three causal drivers and risk environment as the causal mechanisms of global production networks. These strategies are an indispensable part of the GPN 2.0 theory because they "translate" the causal power of these drivers in specific risk environment into differential value activities and network configurations. This translation of causal dynamics through firm strategies is recursive in nature such that over time, these industrial-organizational outcomes can feedback into, and influence, both causal dynamics and firm strategies. At the intrafirm level, coordination through internalization and consolidation serves as a firm-specific strategy in organizing global production networks driven by a particular set of causal dynamics.

At the interfirm level, two strategies are prominent—control and partnership. The firm-specific choice of these strategies is determined by different combinations of causal dynamics in favor of external suppliers and strategic partners. As argued by Cassia (2010, 30), this organizational choice has become more strategic: "Nowadays, outsourcing has acquired a strategic position, being a tool for the optimization of the organizational structure, able to make it more flexible and agile." Extrafirm bargaining refers to the strategic interface through which firms interact with nonfirm actors, such as state and nonstate institutions, in diverse ways that can lead to institutional capture or cooperation, and even major breakdowns in production networks (e.g., US export restrictions on US technology to China's Huawei, ZTE, and SMIC since May 2020). This firm-specific approach thus improves on the existing governance models because it allows for the possibility of firms in the same networks exercising all four types of strategy or lead firms exercising multiple strategies in different networks. The precise combination of these strategies can only be ascertained through detailed empirical investigations, as will be documented fully in Chapter 5. The following subsections elaborate conceptually on these four key strategies, with illustrative examples from global electronics.

### Intrafirm Coordination

This strategy is highly important because the existing literature on global value chains and international outsourcing tends to focus exclusively on interfirm relationships. Despite rich interdisciplinary literature on transnational corporations and international business, we know surprisingly little about how different firms in global production networks reorganize their internal value activity to meet the challenges posed by the three causal drivers examined earlier.[28] In general, intrafirm coordination can be defined as the internalization and consolidation of value activity within the lead firm, the strategic partner, and/or the supplier firm within and across national borders in order to achieve greater firm-specific efficiencies, such as lower inventories and cost control, greater market responsiveness, and higher-quality products or services. This coordination goes beyond the firm's strategic repositioning in a global production network to incorporate its management and logistics of production, integration of design and R&D into supply chains, and monitoring of quality standards and production outcomes. Through greater attention to intrafirm coordination, a firm can identify and capture more value from its current bundles of firm-specific resources and organizational capabilities.

Table 3.4 summarizes the likely causal interaction between the three competitive dynamics and risk environments and the adoption of intrafirm coordination strategy by lead firms, and their implications for the organizational configurations of global production networks. Firms with efficient internal cost control and high proprietary capabilities are likely to engage in intrafirm coordination to capitalize on their lower cost-capability ratios (e.g., Samsung in semiconductors, Lenovo in PCs, and Samsung and Huawei in mobile handsets). Outsourcing to third-party foundry

TABLE 3.4. Firm-specific strategies and organizational innovations in global production networks

| | Competitive dynamics | | | | Organizational innovations | Examples in global electronics |
|---|---|---|---|---|---|---|
| Strategy | Cost-capability ratio | Market imperative | Financial discipline | Risks | | |
| Intrafirm coordination | Low to medium | High | Low | High | Domestic expansion and/or FDI and M&As; high level of network integration | Integrated device manufacturing firms in semiconductors and lead firms in desktop PCs, mobile handsets, and TVs |
| Interfirm control | High | Low | High | Medium | Outsourcing but dependent integration of suppliers | Suppliers of modules and parts to lead firms in PCs, mobile handsets, and TVs |
| Interfirm partnership | High | High | High | High | Outsourcing, joint development with strategic partners and platform or technology leaders | Fabless-foundry in semiconductors, OEM-ODM in notebook PCs, and OEM-EMS in mobile handsets |
| Extrafirm bargaining | Medium | High | High | High | Differential (dis)integration in/ from global production systems | Capital/technology-intensive fabrication in semiconductors, and labor-intensive assembly work in PCs, mobile handsets, and TVs |

Source: Reworked from Yeung and Coe (2015, Table 4; 46).

providers or manufacturing service providers is less necessary because it may not significantly lower the costs of producing their end products, but instead may increase the lead firm's risk of capability reduction due to the potential leakage of highly proprietary knowledge or tacit technology to those independent suppliers. Too much reliance on manufacturing service providers may also slow down their in-house technological innovation and new product development, both of which are significant to enhancing the capability of lead firms, particularly those in mobile handsets as will be detailed in Chapter 5's empirical examples.

In adopting intrafirm coordination, these lead firms in global electronics are also more driven by the higher market imperative since product cycles in mobile handsets can be highly dynamic (e.g., quarterly or semi-annually), the industry remains unsaturated (e.g., new semiconductor applications), and new market segments continue to emerge (e.g., cheaper handsets for developing economies). Internalization through domestic expansion and/or internationalization provides an optimal organizational platform to create and capture value in this dynamic market condition. As some of these lead firms do not originate from the US and thus are not subject to intense financial discipline (e.g., more patient capital markets in China and South Korea and the greater role of family/state ownership and control, as summarized in Table 1.2), they are not yet compelled by shareholder pressures to externalize much of their value activity to third-party suppliers or to generate large short-term financial returns for their relatively more patient controlling shareholders (e.g., family control in Samsung and institutional control in TSMC, Lenovo, and Huawei).

In terms of risk, intrafirm coordination can be effective in helping firms navigate risky technological and/or market environments (e.g., Samsung's in-house supply of semiconductors and flat panel displays and Intel's long-standing reliance on own fabs). It allows a lead firm to gain greater control of critical components and technological or marketing resources in the face of such volatile environments. This strategy of intrafirm coordination is likely to produce highly integrated global production networks in which corporate headquarters exercise tight control over their subsidiaries and affiliates worldwide.

## Interfirm Control

This strategy represents a highly managed externalization strategy through which a lead firm outsources a very significant portion of its value activity to independent suppliers and subcontractors, and yet exercises tight control over their production processes and product/service quality. In most globalized industries, this outsourcing applies to key components or services, complete modules or service packages, and systems and subsystems. The high levels of explicit control of suppliers and subcontractors are deemed necessary by a lead firm to gain collective competitiveness in its entire global production network. The literature on global value chains terms this a "captive" form of chain governance, but it tends to generalize at the level of the entire industry (e.g., automotive or apparel). While equity investment by a lead firm in its external suppliers is generally not necessary for such organizational control to be effective, a lead firm may choose to invest in suppliers to shore up their financial strength and/or to secure long-term supply of key materials or services. To account for this strategic choice, we need to revisit the peculiar combination of competitive dynamics and risk environments that drive a lead firm's strategic choices.

As noted in Table 3.4, high cost-capability ratios tend to drive lead firms to engage external suppliers in order to regain cost advantage. In some cases, this process of externalization entails exiting lower value-added activities so that a lead firm can focus on building and sustaining its higher-order and more costly dynamic capabilities (e.g., Apple sold all manufacturing facilities to Sanmina-SCI in 1996, and AMD became "fabless" after spinning off its fabs to form GlobalFoundries in 2009). In general, external sourcing makes sense only when a lead firm suffers from high costs in relation to its existing capabilities (i.e., LF2 in Table 3.1), *and* its manufacturing partners/suppliers enjoy substantial cost advantage through access to cheaper production inputs (e.g., labor, land, and material costs), less stringent regulatory regimes and institutional frameworks (e.g., labor standards and environmental constraints), and strong logistical and ecosystem supports (e.g., favorable transport systems and local industrial linkages). These partners and suppliers are known as PS1 in Table 3.1.

Moreover, externalization may be preferred if the market for a product is generally mature and saturated. The lack of significant new market opportunities hinders a lead firm's desire to engage in intrafirm coordination to compete solely on the basis of new products with far greater capital investment in production capacity and marketing. In addition, financial discipline tends to be high and induces lead firms to focus only on their core competence. This discipline imposes serious pressure on firms to extract greater financial returns from their current assets or investments in order to satisfy their impatient shareholders. Finally, the risks associated with technological change and market shifts cannot be too high for outsourcing to take place because suppliers and subcontractors are less likely or willing to take on this risk. Without these external actors, a lead firm's outsourcing strategy will not work (see brief examples below).

As in Table 3.4, this theorization of the causal role of market, financial discipline, and risk in engendering interfirm control strategy provides a more nuanced conceptualization of the role of different firms, such as lead firms, strategic partners, suppliers, and so on, and their power relations in evolving global production networks. It goes beyond identifying the "captive" form of governance and provides a crucial explanation of why these actors are causally shaped by dynamic imperatives beyond industry-level transactional and technological conditions. Despite its explicit desire to control and lock in suppliers, for example, a lead firm may also be keen in developing supplier capabilities because of the potential for improving collective efficiency at the level of the entire global production network. In the PC and mobile handset segments, the strategy of interfirm control is frequently deployed by OEM lead firms to ensure cost competitiveness, rapid time-to-market, and quality consistency. Lead firms not only outsource significant quantity of components, modules, and subsystem manufacturing to independent suppliers, but also increasingly pressure them to establish production and supply facilities near the final assembly plants of their end products in different locations (e.g., ODM firms' facilities for Dell in China's Chengdu and Samsung's own plants in northern Vietnam). These first-tier suppliers (e.g., printed circuit boards and electric connectors), in turn, compel second- or third-tier suppliers to follow suit or to make the appropriate locational adjustments.

Figure 3.3 describes two dominant interfirm organizational configurations of global production networks, each with a distinctive lead firm and encompassing a wide range of other firm and nonfirm actors. The first configuration is a lead firm-centric model in which the lead firm controls and drives the entire network. This model is aligned mostly with OEM lead firms exercising a tight interfirm control strategy. In semiconductors and telecommunications equipment, for example, a lead firm may bring together material inputs from specialized suppliers (e.g., fabrication equipment, key modules, and core components) and generic suppliers (e.g., chemicals and packaging materials) to produce finished or

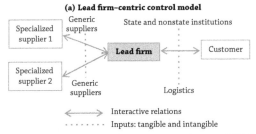

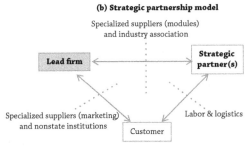

FIGURE 3.3. Organizational configurations of global production networks.

Source: Reworked from Coe and Yeung (2015, Figure 2.2; 60). Copyright ©2015, Oxford University Press, https://global.oup.com/academic/product/global-production-networks -9780198703914, reproduced with permission.

intermediate goods (e.g., semiconductors or telecommunications base stations). As noted earlier, while software and other services are important in production networks, their specific role in influencing interfirm control by lead firms is often implicit and indirect.

Because of their firm-specific choices (e.g., technological and strategic concerns), these lead firms prefer to internalize much of the production process in order to exercise greater control over the quality and delivery of their products to customers (e.g., proprietary chipsets to downstream end-product customers or digital base stations to telecommunications service providers). This delivery and distribution may involve other firms such as logistics, construction, and retail service providers. As the manufacturers of these products, lead firms are also subject to lobbying and other interventions from state and nonstate actors (e.g., restrictions on technology exports, telecommunications standards, and data protection issues). In this lead firm-centric model, our analytical focus tends to fall primarily on the lead firm and its forward and backward linkages with specialized suppliers and key customers. Other inter- and extrafirm actors may mediate these linkages such that the governance power of the lead firm in this network is partially constrained (see more empirical analysis in Chapter 5).

### Interfirm Partnership

Not all interfirm relationships are characterized by lead firms tightly controlling their suppliers and subcontractors. In some cases, cooperative relationships can be formed between lead firms and their strategic partners and highly specialized suppliers. In the global value chain literature, this cooperative form of governance is known as "relational" and "modular" chains at the industry level. Taking a dynamic network rather than a linear chain approach, the GPN 2.0 theory describes this cooperative strategy as interfirm partnership, defined as the collaboration, coevolution, and joint development of a lead firm with its strategic partner(s) or key suppliers in the *same* global production network to compete against other lead firms and their network partners. In this strategic partnership model (Figure 3.3b), a global lead firm engages with another firm as a strategic partner to provide partial or complete solutions for its product or service delivery to key customers. This interfirm partnership crisscrosses with tangible and intangible inputs from specialized suppliers and platform leaders and intersects with broader structural initiatives intermediated by industrial associations such as standardization and modularization.[29]

As described in Table 3.4, while differential cost-capability ratios can partially account for the externalization of production of goods or services from a lead firm (high ratio) to its strategic partner (low ratio) and independent suppliers (low ratios), it is the simultaneous presence of the other two causal drivers—high market imperative and high financial discipline—in a high-risk environment that turns this externalization strategy from strong interfirm control into cooperative partnership. In general, the market imperative is clearly very significant for all firms in a cooperative global production network. The prospect of an expanding and unsaturated market assures a lead firm and its strategies partners and key suppliers that they can collectively benefit from this cooperative value creation process. Even though the capture of this value is unlikely to be evenly distributed among these network actors (e.g., the Apple-TSMC-Foxconn network for iPhones), partnership on a longer-term basis provides a more mutually beneficial competitive strategy for them to thrive in the highly competitive global marketplace. The risk environment in which all cooperative partners operate also tends to be high. These risks range from market volatility to rapid technological shifts and supply chain disruptions, identified in Table 3.2. To reduce their exposure to these risks and to capitalize quickly on rapid market changes, a lead firm and its partners enter into cooperative arrangements underpinned by finely organized divisions of labor and mutual dependency.

In the interconnected worlds of global electronics, while a lead firm in an interfirm partnership retains its effective control over market and product definition (e.g., through its intellectual property, marketing, and R&D capabilities), it cannot fulfil market demand without the cost-effective and on-time production support from its strategic partners and the provision of leading components, modules, or software by its specialized suppliers, e.g., Intel, AMD, Qualcomm, and Broadcom in processor and connectivity chips, and Microsoft or Google in operating systems. These interconnected worlds are increasingly characterized by a high degree of geographical separation between the design and manufacturing of cutting-edge electronics products due to immense competitive pressures from the above-mentioned causal dynamics. Firm-level specialization in the electronics global division of labor is rendered particularly effective by this strategy of interfirm partnership.

To be elaborated more fully in Chapter 5, the case of Apple's iconic iPhone brings together several intersecting global production networks comprising one of the world's leading OEM lead firms (Apple in R&D, design, software, and marketing/sales), its manufacturing partner and the world's largest EMS provider (Hon Hai or Foxconn), and highly specialized suppliers of memory devices and flat panel displays (Samsung in semiconductors) and wireless baseband chips (Qualcomm in fabless design and TSMC and Samsung in semiconductor foundry). In this intersection of multiple production networks across two major segments of global electronics—semiconductors and mobile handsets—we witness the tremendous significance of interfirm partnerships in creating the unprecedented market success of one major consumer product that, as noted in Table 2.1 and Chapter 2, led the "smartphone revolution" in global electronics throughout the 2010s.

Taken together, these two dominant configurations of global production networks in Figure 3.3 are premised on the organizational innovations by diverse actors such as lead firms, strategic partners, suppliers, and extrafirm actors. While each configuration tends to resonate more strongly in particular product segments in global electronics, both configurations can be found in the same segment (e.g., semiconductors, PCs, mobile handsets, and consumer electronics). These configurations may also evolve in a dynamic fashion over time. As was described in Chapter 2, the semiconductors segment has been generally characterized by the lead firm–centric model and vertical integration up to the late 1980s. A specialized provider of foundry production (e.g., TSMC), however, may evolve to become a strategic partner through its firm-specific initiatives (e.g., investing in process innovations and upscaling of production facilities) or industry-wide transformations (e.g., new chip design protocols and standards). This dynamic coevolution can lead to a profound reconfiguration of some semiconductor global production networks from a lead firm-centric model (e.g., Intel and Samsung) to a strategic partnership model (e.g., Apple/Qualcomm-TSMC).

### Extrafirm Bargaining

The role of nonfirm actors such as the state, international organizations, labor groups, business and industry associations, and consumer and civil society organizations has so far been taken as generally supportive and cooperative. The existing frameworks on global value chain governance also offer little explanatory power to these nonfirm actors in shaping interfirm governance; they are often seen as outside the analytical parameters of industry-specific value chains. A growing body of empirical research, however, suggests that these nonfirm actors have significant influence on global production network dynamics. For example, ethical and fair trade initiatives in developed countries, strongly advocated by the state and civil society organizations, are generally seen as effective in influencing sourcing strategies of certain kinds of lead firms, such as major retailers and their domestic and foreign suppliers in the agro-food and apparel industries and some public services such as health care and transport.[30] In high-tech industries such as electronics and automobiles, however, these initiatives have less purchase in shaping how lead firms configure their global production networks. Rather, the state can influence these production networks through direct regulations on trade and technology exports (e.g., the US in 2020/2021) and/or facilitation initiatives, such as free trade agreements, domestic economic liberalization (e.g., South Korea and Taiwan during the 2000s; see Table 1.2), or massive financial support (e.g., China since the mid-2010s).[31]

Meanwhile, we witness the growing importance of what Büthe and Mattli (2011) term the "new global rulers" through the privatization of regulation. These nonstate setters of standards and norms in global industries play an increasingly vital role in the governance of inter- and extrafirm relations. For example, the influence of credit rating agencies extends far beyond that of financial institutions such as banks, affecting global lead firms and their strategic partners seeking funding in different capital markets. Private business associations and industrial consortiums in high-tech industries (e.g., semiconductors) are also crucial in setting new industrial standards and technological parameters and lobbying state support or regulation that profoundly influence the value activities of lead firms, their strategic partners, and customers.

In practice, this highly diverse group of nonfirm actors is often driven by a wide range of institutional logics and rationalities that go beyond any simple classification. In this theory section, the strategy of extrafirm bargaining is critical for understanding how economic processes, embodied in firms, intersect with national development and other noneconomic issues (e.g., political pressures, national security, environmental sustainability, social justice and security, public health concerns, and so on). The strategy works through a contested two-way process of negotiation and accommodation between firms and nonfirm actors to reach a mutually satisfactory outcome in the creation and capture of value through global production networks. This conception of extrafirm bargaining enriches the GPN 2.0 theory because actor-specific interaction in these networks represents far more than a narrow set of power relations along interfirm value chains in the same industry or sector.

As were noted in the previous two chapters, diverse firm- and nonfirm actors in global electronics pursue extrafirm bargaining strategies to achieve strategic objectives in relation to market power, proprietary rights, and even geopolitical advantages. These broader objectives are over and above the cost-specific gains derived from bargaining with state and nonstate institutions, e.g., maximizing financial returns through tax concessions, externalizing the costs of labor training to state agencies, avoiding environmental costs through locations with lower regulatory enforcement, and so on. The market power objective stipulates that lead firms shaped by a strong market imperative are likely to gain from extrafirm bargaining relations with state actors who, for the most part, remain the key regulator of uneven market access (e.g., the US-Japan Semiconductor Trade Agreement of 1986 discussed in Chapter 1).

In Table 3.4, the tensions confronting global lead firms and nation-states should be understood as differentiated integration into and/or decoupling from global production networks. For lead firms, high pressures from causal dynamics may generate dual tendencies, namely, globalizing production networks to achieve greater cost efficiencies, while also localizing or regionalizing operations to ensure a certain degree of autonomy and responsiveness to changing market conditions. For state institutions, conditions of accelerating globalization have been associated with far-reaching forms of political and functional reorganization (e.g., the decentralization of state authority and greater local and regional initiatives). The bargaining relationships between lead firms and domestic state institutions for market access are situated within these complex global-local tensions. These intense bargaining relationships are particularly evident in certain segments of global electronics subject to strong state regulation, such as semiconductors (e.g., the US federal government's efforts in re-shoring wafer fabs in the post-COVID-19 world) and telecommunications (e.g., Huawei and the fifth-generation/5G wireless networks debacle in 2019–2021).

The quest for proprietary rights is another critical motive prompting lead firms to engage in extrafirm bargaining in the context of radical technological and market shifts and host country regulation. Foreign lead firms with extensive local partners in their production networks are more likely able to protect their property rights against host government misappropriation.[32] This bargaining process is prominent in industrial segments characterized by high levels of financial discipline and high risk of technological or market shifts (e.g., semiconductors and high-performance computing/ artificial intelligence). In this competitive environment, domestic firms tend to seek strong regulatory regimes and codification of standards in order to protect their firm-specific R&D investments and intangible assets (e.g., brand names, software, patents, and trademarks). These lead firms may also enter into robust negotiations with relevant domestic nonfirm actors such as state authorities, standards organizations, and industry associations. As domestic firms acquire or develop greater technological and market capabilities, they may bargain with home institutions for preferential access to resources and fiscal incentives given to foreign lead firms and through international trade agreements.[33] Over time, successful technological and market innovations are underpinned by strong extrafirm bargaining between lead firms and nonfirm actors in different geographical locations. The rapid growth of industrial and technological capabilities in Taiwan's ICT sector is a clear example of the positive outcomes from such extrafirm bargaining between global lead firms and nonfirm actors, such as state institutions and business associations (see also Table 1.2).[34]

Not all extrafirm bargaining initiatives are positive, though. Since the second half of the 2010s, geopolitical conflicts between global powers such as the US and China have manifested in greater political influence and extrafirm bargaining in global production networks. During the former Trump administration (2017–2021), major trade restrictions on imports from China and other countries and on exports of US technology to Chinese firms were implemented. In electronics, these restrictive trade practices were launched to curb the ambition and advancement of Chinese high-tech firms in semiconductors (e.g., HiSilicon and SMIC) and mobile handsets and telecommunications equipment (e.g., Huawei and ZTE). As will be analyzed further in Chapters 5 and 6, these severe trade-related restrictions can have profound impact on the (re)organization of global production networks in all four segments of global electronics, in particular semiconductors and mobile handsets. Indeed, many firms in these segments, including US lead firms in semiconductors and ICT devices; specialized suppliers of semiconductor equipment, materials, and software; and industry associations (e.g., SEMI, Semiconductor Equipment and Materials International, based in California), have lobbied hard to delay or exempt from these trade restrictions that impact negatively on their strategic partners (e.g., foundry providers in Taiwan and China) and key customers (e.g., Chinese firms). In short, the complex extrafirm bargaining relations between firms and state actors are significantly dependent on firm-specific interests and pressures as well as the institutional capacity and political priorities of these state actors—an important theme for further analysis in the concluding Chapter 7.

## Conclusion
This chapter's theory of interconnected worlds focuses on the geographical configurations, causal dynamics, and firm-specific strategies of global production networks that crisscross and integrate different territories and macroregions in today's global economy. The key competitive drivers of

global production networks, such as optimizing cost-capability ratios, sustaining market access and development, working with financial discipline, and managing risks, are theorized as the causal dynamics of empirical outcomes to be analyzed in the next three chapters. In theoretical terms (Figure 3.2), these causal dynamics are independent variables that explain the different strategies adopted by lead firms and their partners in global production networks. Conceptualizing these firm-specific strategies is an indispensable part of the theory because they translate the causal power of competitive dynamics and risk environment into differential geographical configurations of value activities that in turn produce diverse coevolutionary outcomes in global electronics described in Chapter 2.

While this theorization of causal dynamics can provide robust explanations to address the question of *why* global production networks are formed, the conceptual exposition on firm-level strategies should offer compelling answers to the question of *how* these networks work and operate in the different segments of global electronics. In this theoretical sense, various causal dynamics provide the structural properties of network causality and emergence, whereas firm-specific strategies serve as the corresponding mechanisms for organizing these networks. Taken together in this GPN 2.0–inspired theory, causal drivers and firm-specific strategies co-constitute the causal mechanisms of global production networks that integrate cross-regional worlds of global electronics.

Mapped explicitly onto this chapter's three conceptual sections and premised on substantial new material, the next three empirical chapters will illustrate these industrial-organizational outcomes in global electronics during the 2010s through a detailed analysis of the complex geographical configurations or "where" of electronics production networks centered in East Asia (Chapter 4), the diverse firm strategies or "how" underpinning these network configurations (Chapter 5), and the key causal dynamics or "why" driving and explaining these global production networks (Chapter 6).

## CHAPTER 4

# Geographical Configurations of Global Electronics Centered in East Asia

BY THE LATE 2010S, the interconnected worlds of global electronics had fully emerged in tandem with the development of sophisticated global production networks underpinned by complex interfirm and intrafirm organizational relationships that were situated in the wider (geo-)political-economic context of more contested extrafirm bargaining. Through these firm-specific networks conceptualized in the previous chapter, electronics production sites in East Asian economies have become highly interdependent with advanced manufacturing and research and development (R&D) centers and end markets in North America and Western Europe and within East Asia. Most global electronics lead firms in original equipment manufacturing (OEM) from these "Triad" macroregions have also engaged their manufacturing partners in East Asia to achieve greater competitive advantages on the basis of lower cost-capability ratios, faster time-to-market, better financial returns and market valuations, and risk mitigation. These extensive interdependencies in the geographical divisions of labor between and within firms in global production networks can be found in all major hardware segments of the global information and communications technology (ICT) sector, ranging from intermediate goods, such as semiconductors, to end products or final goods, such as personal computers (PCs), mobile handsets, and consumer electronics (e.g., TVs).

Recent data on world merchandise trade in ICT intermediate and final goods in Figure 4.1 provide some useful insights into the geographical

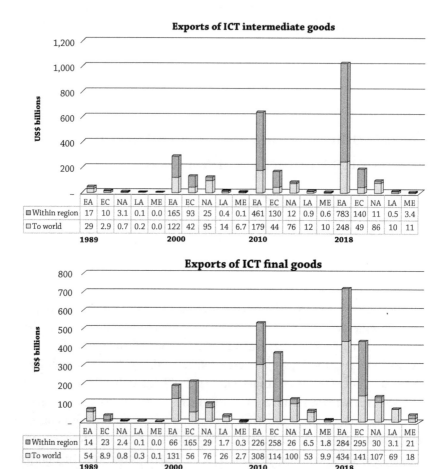

**Exports of ICT intermediate goods**

|  | EA | EC | NA | LA | ME | EA | EC | NA | LA | ME | EA | EC | NA | LA | ME | EA | EC | NA | LA | ME |
|---|---|---|---|---|---|---|---|---|---|---|---|---|---|---|---|---|---|---|---|---|
| ▣ Within region | 17 | 10 | 3.1 | 0.1 | 0.0 | 165 | 93 | 25 | 0.4 | 0.1 | 461 | 130 | 12 | 0.9 | 0.6 | 783 | 140 | 11 | 0.5 | 3.4 |
| ▫ To world | 29 | 2.9 | 0.7 | 0.2 | 0.0 | 122 | 42 | 95 | 14 | 6.7 | 179 | 44 | 76 | 12 | 10 | 248 | 49 | 86 | 10 | 11 |
|  | **1989** | | | | | **2000** | | | | | **2010** | | | | | **2018** | | | | |

**Exports of ICT final goods**

|  | EA | EC | NA | LA | ME | EA | EC | NA | LA | ME | EA | EC | NA | LA | ME | EA | EC | NA | LA | ME |
|---|---|---|---|---|---|---|---|---|---|---|---|---|---|---|---|---|---|---|---|---|
| ▣ Within region | 14 | 23 | 2.4 | 0.1 | 0.0 | 66 | 165 | 29 | 1.7 | 0.3 | 226 | 258 | 26 | 6.5 | 1.8 | 284 | 295 | 30 | 3.1 | 21 |
| ▫ To world | 54 | 8.9 | 0.8 | 0.3 | 0.1 | 131 | 56 | 76 | 26 | 2.7 | 308 | 114 | 100 | 53 | 9.9 | 434 | 141 | 107 | 69 | 18 |
|  | **1989** | | | | | **2000** | | | | | **2010** | | | | | **2018** | | | | |

Note: EA = East Asia & Pacific; EC = Europe & Central Asia; NA = North America; LA = Latin America & Caribbean; and ME = Middle East, Africa, and South Asia.

FIGURE 4.1. World exports of ICT intermediate and final goods by major regions, 1989–2018 (in US$ billions).

Source: Same as Figure 2.2; World Bank's World Integrated Trade Solutions (WITS)-GVC Database (https://wits.worldbank.org/WITS/WITS/Restricted/Login.aspx, accessed on June 17, 2021).

configurations of these extensive *macroregional interdependencies* emerging since the late 1980s.[1] Between 1989 and 2018, exports in both categories of ICT goods from East Asia grew rapidly, initially much more destined for extraregional markets in North America and Europe (at least two-thirds "to world" in 1989). But since the late 1990s, ICT production in all major segments has shifted much more extensively toward East Asia in the evolving contexts of several structural and institutional changes discussed in Chapter 1's subsection on the emerging worlds of interconnections (e.g., market liberalization among East Asian economies and China's WTO accession in 2001; see Table 1.2). By the 2010s, East Asia became the dominant macroregion (or "within region") for both the production and consumption of these goods. Meanwhile, Europe remained as a major market for intermediate goods from East Asia and a major producer of final goods for intraregional consumption. North America was still a relatively significant exporter of both final and intermediate goods to East Asia and Europe.

By 2018, the world's production of, and trade in, ICT goods had become much greater in value and far more globalized. The most significant transformation occurred in the exports of intermediate goods—a crucial indication of the much more sophisticated organization of global production networks centered in East Asia. On the one hand, the share of intermediate goods in total ICT hardware exports worldwide increased substantially from 38 percent of $167 billion in 1989 to 49 percent of $2.7 trillion in 2018 (see also Figure 2.2). With a 73 percent share of the relatively modest total exports of intermediate goods valued at $63 billion in 1989, East Asia's significance in evolving global production networks was already visible. In 2018, its share of the far larger total exports of intermediate goods valued at $1.3 trillion increased further to 77 percent. On the other hand, the share of intraregional exports in intermediate goods within East Asia increased massively from 37 percent of $46 billion in 1989 to 76 percent of $1 trillion in 2018, confirming the macroregion's predominant role in ICT global production networks. In terms of exports of final goods reaching $1.4 trillion in 2018 or almost 14 times of the 1989 value, East Asia (51 percent) and Europe (31 percent) remained by far the largest exporters. As an important end market for these ICT products, East Asia's share of intraregional exports of final goods also reached 40 percent at $284 billion, doubling from 20.6 percent in 1989.

The above broad-brush historical analysis by major macroregions points to the highly globalized geographical configurations of ICT production by the 2010s during which East Asia emerged as both the *leading producer* of intermediate and final goods and a *major market* for both types of ICT exports. This empirical chapter probes much further into this coevolutionary geographical shift at the industrial-organizational level (i.e., within four specific product segments, starting with semiconductors and followed by PCs, mobile handsets, and TVs) and the intrafirm level (i.e., lead firm production networks). It draws upon primary interview data and custom data from IHS Markit/Informa Tech to specify these complex geographical configurations of global electronics production centered in East Asia during the 2010–2018 period.[2] This fairly detailed and extensive mapping illustrates the interconnected worlds of global electronics underpinned by diverse and cross-regional production networks theorized in Chapter 3. It is analytically necessary before the next two chapters that take turn to explain *how* lead firms pursue specific strategies to organize these production networks and *why* their strategies are driven by a combination of causal dynamics in the GPN 2.0 theory. I will therefore defer most of the explanatory work to these later chapters where "it all comes together."

In the context of empirical observations on the coevolutionary worlds of electronics production since the 1990s (Chapters 1 and 2; Tables 1.1 and 2.1), this chapter points to two prominent trends throughout the 2010s:

(1)    the much greater geographical "stretch" or distancing of global production networks, and yet

(2)    a very high degree of geographical consolidation in production in relation to far higher market concentration in each segment of global electronics.

First, as electronics technologies and innovation processes become much more sophisticated and yet production capabilities and capacities in East Asia are located far away from major R&D centers in North America and Western Europe, production networks in global electronics have stretched out further geographically. Through this greater distancing of production networks, more R&D activities are hosted, and intermediate parts and modules manufactured, in national economies and macroregions outside the final assembly of end products. In short, value chains in global electronics have become much "longer" and their underlying production networks far more complex. Second, some global lead firms have successfully capitalized on the benefits of developing production networks at both inter- and intrafirm levels. In many cases discussed in Chapter 2, their competitive success is predicated on strategic partnerships with key design and manufacturing service providers in East Asia. By the late 2010s, this relatively small number of top ten global lead firms became much more dominant in their respective market segments in global electronics (see Table 1.1). Working closely with fewer but much larger manufacturing partners based in East Asia, their production of semiconductors and ICT end products also became highly consolidated geographically within East Asia.

To substantiate these important empirical observations, the next section analyzes the industrial-organizational geography of production networks during the 2010s on the basis of the worldwide locations of all wafer fabrication facilities (fabs) in semiconductors and all outsourced manufacturing activities in ICT end products by original design manufacturing (ODM) and electronics manufacturing service (EMS) providers for their OEM customers. In semiconductors, most US, European, and Japanese firms have substantially reduced their domestic fabs since the early 2010s. Much new capacity in dedicated foundry and memory devices has been added in East Asian locations outside Japan. In ICT end products, outsourced assembly by OEM lead firms is most visible in PCs and mobile handsets, but less so in TVs. East Asia, in particular China, has emerged as the most dominant location for assembly production in these segments. A summary table on these key geographical configurations will be offered at the end of the section.

The penultimate section examines the geographical configurations of intrafirm production networks among forty-four firms in relation to the worldwide locations of their key corporate functions, ranging from control and coordination in corporate and regional headquarters and manufacturing facilities to R&D, product development, and sales and marketing operations. Similar to the earlier analysis of industry-level organizational relationships, this section also points to an obvious presence of Northeast Asia, particularly China, as the key site in global electronics manufacturing in all major segments among these 44 firms that comprise 36 global lead firms and 8 foundry, ODM, and key component suppliers (see firm details in Appendix B).

## Industrial-Organizational Geography of Production Networks

Couched in the coevolutionary national-institutional and industry contexts described in Chapters 1 and 2 (see summary Tables 1.2 and 2.1), this section maps in detail the geographical configurations of wafer fabrication or chip making in semiconductors and final assembly in the three major segments of global electronics (PCs, mobile handsets, and TVs/flat panel displays) in 2015 and 2018. At the industrial-organizational level, these evolving geographies of production in wafer fabrication and end product assembly demonstrate both heavy geographical concentration in East Asian locations and highly variable strategies of in-house production and outsourcing pursued by top six to seven global lead firms in all four major segments (see more on these firm-specific strategies in the next chapter). In semiconductors, only a few lead firms could maintain or grow their number of fabs and fab capacity during the 2010s. Many went "fab-lite" by engaging foundry service providers based primarily in East Asia. In ICT end products, while East Asia emerged as *the* main macroregion of final assembly, different lead firms sought a wide range of production options, from complete in-house production to a mix of or complete outsourcing to sustain their market positions. Overall, this complex and yet changing industrial-organizational geography of electronics production networks during the 2010s sets the crucial empirical baseline for this book's causal analysis of firm-specific global production networks in subsequent chapters.

### Semiconductors: All Applications

As Chapter 2 has elucidated, the interconnected worlds of semiconductors by the late 2010s had undergone profound changes far beyond the pre-2000 intense rivalries between the US and Japan well documented in most books on the industry (see also Chapter 1's subsection on the multinational worlds of innovation and production).[3] In particular, the rise of East Asia as the major center of production in ICT end products led to the concomitant emergence of very substantial semiconductor manufacturing located in different parts of East Asia. By the end of the 2010s, semiconductor production—from chip design to front-end wafer fabrication and back-end services in chip assembly, packaging, and testing—became much more integrated on a worldwide scale through globalized production networks, with the most significant wafer fabrication role occupied by only a few leading East Asian economies—Taiwan, South Korea, Japan, China, and Singapore.

Since Mathews and Cho's (2000) pioneering work on "tiger chips" in East Asia, two of their "tiger" economies of South Korea and Taiwan have evidently grown up to become ferocious leaders in the global semiconductor industry, with a third tiger, Singapore, limping along. Meanwhile, Japan's dominance prior to 2000—much feared by their US pioneers and European competitors—has been eclipsed by these East Asian tiger economies, while China moved forward rapidly (until the May 2020 export restrictions imposed by the former Trump administration). As was argued in Chapters 1 and 2, these changing fortunes in the worlds of semiconductors had much to do with state-sponsored sectoral industrial policy in East Asia and firm-specific initiatives, such as intrabusiness group cross-subsidization, aggressive investment in cutting-edge fabs, and strategic coupling with mostly US fabless chip design firms (see East Asian contexts in Table 1.2).[4] Even though some established US and European firms in integrated device manufacturing (IDM) have not leveraged well new areas of growth pertinent to innovative ICT products (e.g., logic chips for smartphones and data center servers), many remain dominant in specific industrial applications (e.g., Intel in microprocessors and Texas Instruments, NXP, and Infineon in analogue and microdevices for electronics and automotive applications). As were discussed in Chapter 2 (also Table 2.1), US fabless firms such as Broadcom, Qualcomm, AMD, Nvidia, and Apple (as a smartphone OEM lead firm) have partnered well with their foundry partners, mostly in East Asia, to emerge as dominant players in semiconductors.

This subsection analyzes such evolving geographies of chip production in relation to two key dimensions: (1) total semiconductor manufacturing worldwide in all industrial applications between 2000 and 2018, and (2) ICT-specific semiconductor manufacturing in 2015 and 2018. Table 4.1 illustrates important evolutionary dynamics among all semiconductor manufacturers (i.e., IDM firms and foundry providers) between 2000 and 2018.[5] These changes over the past two decades point to three interrelated shifts in the complex geographical configurations of semiconductor production networks:

(1)    a geographical shift in wafer fabrication toward far greater concentration in East Asia,

(2)    an industrial-organizational shift from IDM firms worldwide to foundry service providers mostly based in East Asia, and

(3)    an end-market shift in product technology and industrial applications toward rapidly growing ICT segments (e.g., wireless communications and data centers).

The first major change in the geographical reconfiguration of semiconductor manufacturing since 2000 is fairly obvious. In 2000, there were 325 fabs globally, and most of them were located in Japan, the US, and Europe.

TABLE 4.1. World's total semiconductor manufacturers by fab location, product applications, and capacity, 2000, 2010, and 2018 (foreign-owned in parentheses; capacity in thousands of 8-inch equivalent wafer starts per month)

| Fab location | 2000 Fab # | 2000 Capacity | 2010 Fab # | 2010 Capacity | 2018 Fab # | 2018 Capacity |
|---|---|---|---|---|---|---|
| **US** | | | | | | |
| Analog | 26 (7) | 358 (77.6) | 18 (3) | 351 (39.9) | 13 (2) | 325 (10.5) |
| Discrete | 12 (2) | 223 (49.5) | 9 (2) | 251 (49.5) | 6 (2) | 157 (51.6) |
| Logic | 14 (2) | 311 (85.5) | 11 (3) | 589 (309) | 4 (3) | 433 (370) |
| Memory | 6 (3) | 251 (134) | 5 (1) | 319 (36.0) | 4 (0) | 244 (0) |
| Microcomponent | 6 (2) | 77.9 (20.8) | 9 (2) | 240 (20.8) | 9 (1) | 325 (10.0) |
| Foundry | 4 (2) | 90.6 (39.3) | 5 (3) | 125 (73.8) | 8 (4) | 285 (105) |
| Total | 68 (18) | 1,310 (407) | 57 (14) | 1,875 (529) | 44 (12) | 1,770 (547) |
| **Japan** | | | | | | |
| Analog | 23 (2) | 333 (73.5) | 22 (4) | 351 (124) | 12 (3) | 203 (114) |
| Discrete | 26 (1) | 268 (10.0) | 25 (3) | 294 (32.3) | 12 (0) | 213 (0) |
| Logic | 43 (6) | 509 (121) | 47 (6) | 696 (125) | 25 (0) | 481 (0) |
| Memory | 14 (0) | 359 (0) | 13 (0) | 1,035 (0) | 14 (2) | 1,658 (281) |
| Microcomponent | 23 (0) | 197 (0) | 20 (0) | 232 (0) | 13 (0) | 168 (0) |
| Foundry | 3 (1) | 57.9 (38.3) | 4 (1) | 58.1 (25.7) | 10 (3) | 242 (76) |
| Total | 132 (10) | 1,724 (243) | 131 (14) | 2,667 (307) | 87 (8) | 2,965 (471) |
| **South Korea** | | | | | | |
| Analog | 2 (0) | 53.4 (0) | 0 (0) | 0 (0) | 0 (0) | 0 (0) |
| Discrete | 3 (3) | 107 (107) | 2 (2) | 74.4 (74.4) | 2 (2) | 50.8 (50.8) |
| Logic | 9 (0) | 314 (0) | 10 (0) | 772 (0) | 10 (0) | 722 (0) |
| Memory | 7 (0) | 555 (0) | 9 (0) | 2,000 (0) | 13 (0) | 2,579 (0) |
| Microcomponent | 0 (0) | 0 (0) | 0 (0) | 0 (0) | 0 (0) | 0 (0) |
| Foundry | 1 (0) | 28.6 (0) | 2 (0) | 92.3 (0) | 3 (0) | 211 (0) |
| Total | 22 (3) | 1,058 (107) | 23 (2) | 2,939 (74.4) | 28 (2) | 3,563 (50.8) |
| **Taiwan** | | | | | | |
| Analog | 0 (0) | 0 (0) | 0 (0) | 0 (0) | 0 (0) | 0 (0) |
| Discrete | 1 (1) | 1.7 (1.7) | 1 (1) | 1.7 (1.7) | 1 (1) | 1.7 (1.7) |
| Logic | 2 (0) | 54.7 (0) | 4 (0) | 144 (0) | 5 (0) | 238 (0) |

| Fab location | 2000 Fab # | 2000 Capacity | 2010 Fab # | 2010 Capacity | 2018 Fab # | 2018 Capacity |
|---|---|---|---|---|---|---|
| Memory | 6 (0) | 154 (0) | 13 (0) | 830 (0) | 10 (3) | 831 (393) |
| Microcomponent | 0 (0) | 0 (0) | 0 (0) | 0 (0) | 0 (0) | 0 (0) |
| Foundry | 17 (0) | 514 (0) | 24 (0) | 1,630 (0) | 27 (0) | 2,947 (0) |
| Total | 26 (1) | 724 (1.7) | 42 (1) | 2,606 (1.7) | 43 (4) | 4,017 (395) |
| **China** | | | | | | |
| Analog | 1 (1) | 5.6 (5.6) | 2 (2) | 28.1 (28.1) | 3 (3) | 76.1 (76.1) |
| Discrete | 2 (2) | 6.8 (6.8) | 2 (2) | 6.8 (6.8) | 3 (3) | 9.0 (9.0) |
| Logic | 1 (0) | 7.2 (7.2) | 1 (0) | 8.1 (8.1) | 1 (0) | 12.9 (0) |
| Memory | 0 (0) | 0 (0) | 3 (3) | 189 (189) | 5 (1) | 728 (3.4) |
| Microcomponent | 0 (0) | 0 (0) | 0 (0) | 0 (0) | 0 (0) | 0 (0) |
| Foundry | 4 (0) | 64.8 (0) | 19 (2) | 681 (92.2) | 25 (4) | 1,364 (264) |
| Total | 8 (3) | 84.3 (19.5) | 27 (9) | 913 (232) | 37 (11) | 2,189 (353) |
| **Europe** | | | | | | |
| Analog | 18 (12) | 223 (113) | 13 (9) | 216 (106) | 10 (6) | 194 (94.6) |
| Discrete | 17 (10) | 204 (134) | 9 (7) | 134 (44.1) | 9 (6) | 155 (83.1) |
| Logic | 9 (3) | 164 (58.0) | 6 (1) | 167 (36.0) | 4 (0) | 134 (0) |
| Memory | 5 (2) | 136 (59.6) | 4 (2) | 116 (55.0) | 2 (0) | 65.0 (0) |
| Microcomponent | 3 (2) | 71.9 (46.9) | 3 (2) | 104 (79.1) | 4 (3) | 212 (188) |
| Foundry | 3 (1) | 47.3 (25.5) | 7 (4) | 150 (121) | 8 (4) | 259 (193) |
| Total | 55 (30) | 845 (437) | 42 (25) | 889 (441) | 37 (19) | 1,019 (559) |
| **Singapore** | 8 (3) | 167 (14.6) | 14 (14) | 702 (702) | 12 (12) | 1,042 (1,042) |
| **Israel/Malaysia** | 6 (5) | 77.8 (68.8) | 8 (2) | 290 (228) | 8 (2) | 431 (373) |
| Total | 325 | 5,991 | 344 | 12,879 | 296 | 16,997 |

Source: Based on individual fab-level data from IHS Markit/Informa Tech Custom Research for GPN@NUS Centre, July–October 2016 and 2019.

As Chapters 1 and 2 have contextualized, the 1980s witnessed intense and often nationalistic rivalries between US/European IDM firms and their Japanese competitors. While chip production became more internationalized in the 1990s, much of this capacity growth took place within the domestic and foreign fabs of these IDM firms from the "Triad" regions. With 132 fabs (122 domestic-owned), Japan led the world with over 40 percent of total number of fabs and 29 percent of the world's fab capacity in 2000. The US and Europe followed with 123 fabs in total, but 48 of these were owned by foreign firms (e.g., Germany's Infineon in the US and Texas Instruments in Scotland since the 1960s). With "only" 22 fabs (3 by US-origin ON Semiconductor[6]), South Korean IDM firms already had a massive capacity of just over 1 million wafers per month, more than 0.85 million in all 55 fabs in Europe combined. Taiwan's wafer fab capacity was also quite significant, at 0.72 million.[7] China was still an insignificant player, with fab capacity accounted for by three small domestic foundry providers (China Resources, Huada, and HuaHong Grace).

This late-1990s geography of Triad-dominated semiconductor fabrication began to change dramatically during the 2000s, with massive growth in the number of new fabs in China, Taiwan, and Singapore, and in total fab capacity in South Korea, Taiwan, and China. By 2010, the strong position of these East Asian economies in semiconductor manufacturing became apparent. As was noted in Chapter 2's discussion of lead firms in semiconductors, South Korean IDM firms became dominant in memory chips and Taiwan's TSMC and UMC in pureplay foundry services. With marginal growth in new fabs but almost tripling of total capacity to 3 million wafers per month, South Korea became the world's largest location for semiconductor manufacturing in 2010. Japan came second in total capacity and yet had the most number of fabs. With 16 more fabs established since 2000, Taiwan now had the third largest fab capacity at 2.61 million, slightly less than Japan's 2.67 million. Meanwhile, the US and Europe experienced decreasing number of fabs and modest growth in fab capacity during the 2000s—some of these fabs and capacity owned by Micron (US) and STMicroelectronics (France/Italy) were shifted to Singapore that saw almost doubling in fab numbers and a four times increase in fab capacity. With three times more fabs than in 2000, China's total capacity also grew over tenfold to 0.91 million and exceeded that of all 42 fabs in Europe combined. Taken together, East Asia, including Japan and

Singapore, had 237 fabs and total capacity of 9.83 million (76 percent of world total) in 2010.

Throughout the 2010s, this locational shift in wafer fab capacity toward East Asia continued unabated. By 2018, the world's semiconductor manufacturing became even more concentrated in East Asia. As a whole, the macroregion had 207 fabs (70 percent of all fabs) and a total capacity of 13.8 million wafers per month (81 percent of world total). Within East Asia, there were important shifts as well. Japanese IDM firms experienced very substantial consolidation, leading to a drastic reduction in total number of fabs from 131 in 2010 to 87 in 2018. While Japan still led the world in terms of fab numbers, Taiwan's total fab capacity of 4 million became the largest in the world, followed closely by South Korea (3.56 million), Japan (3 million), and China (2.2 million). Singapore's entirely foreign-owned fab capacity of 1.04 million slightly exceeded that of all 37 fabs in Europe combined, whereas the US experienced slight decline in both fab numbers and fab capacity throughout the 2010s. During the recent 2019–2021 period, China's fab capacity continued to grow rapidly by 14 percent in 2019, 21 percent in 2020, and an estimated 17 percent in 2021 to reach 3.5 million and third largest after Taiwan and South Korea in 2021.[8]

Underpinning this important geographical shift is the second major change much more intensified since the 1990s—an industrial-organizational shift toward foundry production in semiconductors (see also Chapter 2's discussion of industrial origin and key firms). In 2000, there were only 38 foundry providers, such as IDM firms (e.g., Samsung from South Korea and IBM Microelectronics division) and pureplay firms (e.g., TSMC from Taiwan), with a modest total capacity of 0.88 million wafers per month or 14.7 percent of world total semiconductor capacity at 6 million in Table 4.1.[9] By 2010, pureplay foundry production led by TSMC became an innovative mainstream form of organizing semiconductor production networks, supporting hundreds of mostly US fabless chip design firms (e.g., the largest being Broadcom, Qualcomm, AMD, Marvell, MediaTek, and Nvidia in Table 2.3). The total capacity of 72 foundry fabs, primarily located in Taiwan, China, and Singapore, had grown to 3.2 million (25 percent of world total in all semiconductors). None of the Big Three—South Korea, Japan, the US—had any prominent role in foundry production.

The 2010s, however, was the golden era of this fabless-pureplay foundry production model due to both leading fabless firms' highly innovative designs in logic chips for wireless communications underpinning the market shift to notebook PCs and the "smartphone revolution" (see Table 2.1) *and* their pureplay foundry providers' significant capital investment and collaborative ecosystem development with highly specialized global suppliers of equipment, materials, and software, as was described in Chapter 2. Theorized in Chapter 3's first section on geographical configurations, this is known as the "inside-out" form of international trade in industrial goods through which East Asian foundry providers fabricate chipsets designed by fabless customers and export to the OEM customers of these fabless firms for assembly into final products (still mostly located in East Asia). Together, these fabless firms and their foundry providers are strategically coupled with the wider global production networks of OEM lead firms in all sorts of ICT end products.

In 2018/2020, five of the world's top 15 semiconductor firms in Table 2.2 were fabless: Broadcom, Qualcomm, Nvidia, MediaTek, and AMD. Supporting their massive growth and success were the top foundry service providers from Taiwan (TSMC and UMC) and elsewhere (e.g., Global-Foundries, SMIC, and Samsung foundry). By 2018 there were 90 foundry fabs worldwide, and their total capacity at 5.8 million wafers per month accounted for 34 percent of all semiconductor fab capacity (see Table 4.1). Almost 90 percent of this huge foundry capacity in 2018 was located in East Asia, consolidating the macroregion's "inside-out" form of geographical network configuration. Doubling its foundry capacity from 1.6 million in 2010 to 3.0 million in 2018, Taiwan alone accounted for over 50 percent of global foundry capacity. But if we include all Taiwan-owned foundry fabs in China (TSMC and UMC), Singapore (SSMC-TSMC and UMC), and the US (TMSC)—described in Chapter 3 as another "inside-out" foreign investment form of network configuration—Taiwan's share would reach 57 percent. China's foundry capacity also doubled between 2010 and 2018, mostly through new domestic-owned fabs (e.g., SMIC). This tremendous capacity growth in foundry production during the 2010s represents the most significant contributor to the geographical shift in semiconductor manufacturing centered in East Asia.

To a large extent, this industrial-organizational shift toward the foundry model of semiconductor production is directly related to the third important shift in end-markets for semiconductor products during the 2010s—much greater demand for logic (and memory) chips. As Chapter 2 has already noted but will be detailed in the following three subsections, global electronics during the 2010s was defined by the dominance of mobile computing technologies and wireless communications, most commonly found in notebook PCs, tablets, smartphones, and other wireless ICT products (e.g., Internet of Things devices) and services (e.g., 5G networks, cloud computing, and data servers) depicted in Figure 2.1. Between 2008 and 2018, semiconductors for computer and data storage and wireless communications experienced enormous growth from their relatively high baselines, whereas semiconductors for consumer electronics suffered from an absolute decline in total revenue (though revitalized since the COVID-19 pandemic in 2020/2021) (see Table 2.5). Forecast data show that by 2021, all three industrial applications will likely reach new historical peaks.

These critical end-market shifts and their corresponding impact on the changing geography of semiconductor production are clearly visible in Table 4.1. In 2000, Triad-based fabs in the US, Japan, and Europe were generally strong in analog, discrete, logic, and microcomponent products, whereas Japan and South Korea were leaders in memory products. As was discussed in Chapter 2, this pattern of country-level specialization in different semiconductor devices, i.e., the US in digital chips (logic and microdevices), Western Europe in discrete and analog devices, and Japan in memory, has had its origin since the era of integrated circuits during the 1960s (see also Table 2.1). By 2018, however, IDM firms in Japan had suffered significant decline in fab numbers and capacity in analog, discrete, logic, and microcomponent products, whereas similar decline among IDM firms in the US and Europe had also taken place in analog, discrete, and logic products.[10] And yet none of the Big Three East Asian economies in semiconductors—Taiwan, South Korea, and China—had gained much in these semiconductor product applications. In fact, South Korea and Taiwan had no IDM fabs at all in analog and microcomponent products and were weak in discrete products.

Despite its aggressive sectoral industrial policy since the 2000s (see Table 1.2), China's position in these product categories was also weak. Its small number of fabs in analog and discrete were all foreign owned (e.g., Texas Instruments from the US and Rhom from Japan), and no microcomponent IDM fab was located in China. Despite its dominant role in the final assembly of ICT end products (shown in later subsections), China's 26 domestic fabs (see Table 4.1) produced only about 6 percent of the domestic semiconductor market of $131 billion in 2019 and $143 billion in 2020. This share increased marginally to 16 percent even if large capacity foreign-owned fabs by SK Hynix, Samsung, Intel, TSMC, and UMC were included. At this pace, it will be far short of China government's goal of 70 percent self-sufficiency for semiconductor production in the "Made in China 2025" initiative unveiled on May 19, 2015. As of 2020, China's giant semiconductor market remained heavily reliant on imported chips manufactured elsewhere in East Asia (and some in the US and Europe). Since 2018, China has been importing annually over $300 billion worth of chips—reaching $380 billion in 2020 and $163 billion in the first five months of 2021. About half of these imported chips went into ICT final products for domestic sales and exports.[11]

To examine further these evolving geographical configurations of semiconductor manufacturing during the 2010s, I compile detailed fab-level data for 2015 and 2018 in Table 4.2 that covers all fabs worldwide producing chips—microprocessors, logic and memory chips, image sensors—for ICT-specific devices, such as PCs, smartphones, and tablets (see full table in Appendix C Table C5). The most significant finding is that there is a strong geographical concentration of fabs and fab capacity in East Asia in both years, and forecast data point to further growth taking place primarily in East Asia for the 2020–2022 period. In 2018, East Asia-based fab capacity reached 6.5 million wafer starts per month or 83 percent of the 7.8 million total worldwide fab capacity for all chips in ICT devices (or 38 percent of world's total fab capacity of 17 million in Table 4.1). Due to the home fabs of market leaders Samsung and SK Hynix, South Korea had the largest total fab capacity of about 2.8 million in 2018 (36 percent of total fab capacity worldwide). There were also some fabs located in the US and other non–East Asia locations because of the dominant role of two US IDM firms—Intel in microprocessors (fabs in the US, Israel, and Ireland) and Micron in memory devices (smaller fabs in the US). Meanwhile, foundry fabs were much more geographically concentrated in Taiwan because of the enormous market dominance of TSMC and its much smaller sibling UMC. Their combined capacity was 1.4 million or 54 percent of total foundry fab capacity at 2.5 million in 2018. China followed with 0.64 million in 2018, and fabs in Germany, Japan, and the US had much less capacity in foundry.

This geographical concentration in fabs and fab capacity for semiconductors to be assembled into ICT devices also reflects the peculiar industrial-organizational and end-market shifts in these ICT products

TABLE 4.2. World's top 7 manufacturers of semiconductors for ICT devices by fab location, process technology, customers, and capacity, 2015–2022 (in thousands of 8-inch equivalent wafer starts per month)

| Firm | Location | 2015 Fab name | Process (nm) | Customer[1] | Capacity | 2018 Fab name | Process (nm) | Customer[1] | Capacity | 2020–2022 Fab name[2] | Most adv process (nm) | Capacity |
|------|----------|---------------|--------------|-------------|----------|---------------|--------------|-------------|----------|------------------------|------------------------|----------|
| **IDM** | | | | | | | | | | | | |
| Intel | US | F12/32 | 14–32 | Intel | 113 | F12/32 | 14/22 | Intel/TH | 124 | F42 | 7 | 90 |
| | US | D1X | 14 | Intel | 90 | D1D/X | 10–22 | Intel/TH | 121 | D1X | 10 | 90 |
| | Ireland | F24 | 14 | Intel | 90 | F14/24 | 14/22 | Intel/TH | 188 | F24 | 14 | 188 |
| | Israel | F28 | 22 | Intel | 90 | F28 | 14–45 | Intel | 113 | F28 | 10 | 113 |
| Samsung | Korea | L11–17 | 20/35 | Samsung | 1,990 | L11–17 | 14–45 | Samsung | 1,386 | S3; S4/V1 | 7/5 | 180/225 |
| | Korea | S1 | 14–28 | AP/QU | 146 | S1/1B; L6–8 | 10–45 | AP/QU/SM | 298 | - | - | - |
| | Korea | - | - | - | - | L18N | 16/20 | Samsung | 180 | LX | 5/3 | - |
| | US | S2 | 14/28 | QU/SM | 124 | S2-I/II | 14/28 | AP/QU/SM | 270 | - | - | - |
| SK Hynix | China | HC2 | 27 | Hynix | 338 | HC2 | 17/25 | Hynix | 338 | - | - | - |
| | Korea | M10/14 | 27 | Hynix | 788 | M10/14 | 17/25 | Hynix | 788 | - | - | - |
| | Korea | - | - | - | - | M8 | 90/110 | Hynix | 150 | - | - | - |
| Micron | US | F6D | 20/25 | Micron | 101 | F6D | 20 | Micron | 101 | - | - | - |
| | Japan | E300 | 20/25 | Micron | 225 | E300-1/2 | 15–20 | Micron | 270 | - | - | - |
| | Taiwan | R1 | 20/25 | Micron | 191 | R1 | 15/25 | Micron | 191 | - | - | - |

(continued)

TABLE 4.2. (*continued*)

| Firm | Location | 2015 Fab name | Process (nm) | Customer[1] | Capacity | 2018 Fab name | Process (nm) | Customer[1] | Capacity | 2020–2022 Fab name[2] | Most adv process (nm) | Capacity |
|---|---|---|---|---|---|---|---|---|---|---|---|---|
| **Foundry** | | | | | | | | | | | | |
| TSMC | Taiwan | F12 | 16–90 | Many | 405 | F12 P1-7 | 7–90 | Many | 429 | F12 | 7 | 405 |
|  | Taiwan | F15 | 28 | Many | 270 | F15 P1-7 | 7/28 | Many | 648 | F15 | 7 | 270 |
|  | Taiwan | F14 | 20 | Many | 450 | F14 P1-7 | 12–90 | Many | 590 | F18 P1-6 | 5/3 | 450 |
|  | China | - | - | - | - | F16 P1-2 | 16 | Many | 41 | F16 P1-2 | 16 | 90 |
| Global-Foundries | Germany | M1/2 | 28/45 | AMD/BR | 135 | M1/2/AX | 22/45 | Many | 248 | - | - | - |
|  | Singapore | F7 | 45 | MT | 158 | - | - | - | - | - | - | - |
|  | US | F8 | 14 | AMD | 113 | F8 | 12/14 | Many | 135 | - | - | - |
| UMC | Taiwan | F12A | 28 | Many | 113 | F12/12A | 14–28 | Many | 225 | - | - | - |
|  | Singapore | F12i | 45 | Many | 113 | - | - | - | - | - | - | - |
|  | China | - | - | - | - | F12X | 28/40 | Many | 113 | - | - | - |
| **Total** | China only | 4 | - | - | 518 | 7 | - | - | 981 | - | - | - |
|  | East Asia | 26 | - | - | 5,747 | 35 | - | - | 6,509 | - | - | - |
|  | **Worldwide** | **37** | - | - | **6,643** | **49** | - | - | **7,809** | - | - | - |

Note: See full table and notes in Appendix C Table C5.

[1] AP = Apple; BR = Broadcom; MT = MediaTek; QU = Qualcomm; SM = Samsung; and TH = Tsinghua (Unisoc)

[2] Only most advanced fabs shown, based on existing data and public announcements as of end June 2021.

Source: Data from IHS Markit/Informa Tech Custom Research for GPN@NUS Centre, July–October 2016 and 2019.

that will be discussed in the next three subsections, in particular the over-whelming role of East Asian locations in the final assembly of notebook and desktop PCs, mobile handsets, and TVs. As was discussed in Chapter 2's industry contexts, the heightened global competition by the late 2010s in PCs and mobile handsets not only led to far greater market concentration among top OEM lead firms (see Table 1.1) but also demanded chip production using the most advanced process technology nodes (7 nanometer [nm] in 2018, 5 nm in 2020, and 3 nm by mid-2022) that could pack billions of transistors into very small processor chips.[12] In 2015, the most advanced node in semiconductor manufacturing was at 14 nm, and several foreign fabs outside the home locations of IDM firms in Table 4.2 had this process technology, e.g., Intel's F24 in Leixlip, Ireland, and Samsung's S2 in Austin, Texas (serving Qualcomm). At 16 nm, TSMC's most advanced F12 in Hsinchu was still trailing behind GlobalFoundries' 14 nm F8 in Malta, New York (serving AMD).

By 2018, this most advanced process technology (7–10 nm) was only available in the home locations of top chip makers and thus singularly determined the fab and locational choice of their key customers, i.e., fabless chip design firms and OEM lead firms in ICT end products. The changing fortunes of these semiconductor firms were closely intertwined with not only process innovation in their own fabs but also technological and product innovations of their most important customers—OEM lead firms in ICT devices for IDM firms (e.g., Intel and Samsung) and fabless design firms for pureplay foundry providers (e.g., TSMC and GlobalFoundries). The top three foundry providers of TSMC, Samsung, and GlobalFoundries dedicated their advanced fabs to serve their most important fabless customers, such as Apple (by far the largest customer for TSMC), Qualcomm, and HiSilicon in application processors, Broadcom and Qualcomm in wireless networking chips, and Nvidia and AMD in graphics chips.

Evolving from the early internationalization during the 1990s and the 2000s described in Chapter 2, market leadership among top semiconductor firms during the second half of the 2010s remained quite globalized, as evident in Table 1.1. But the competition for technological leadership in wafer fabrication or chip making became much more intensified and yet confined only to three technology leaders—Intel, TSMC, and Samsung. According to industry sources, Intel's 10 nm node in 2018 was closer in density and comparable to TSMC's 7 nm node. Similarly, its much delayed 7 nm and 5 nm process to be launched in Fab 42 in Chandler, Arizona, in

2022 and thereafter will be closer to TSMC's 5 nm and 3 nm nodes in its Tainan Fab 18 entering into mass production respectively from mid-2020 and 2022 onward.[13] Meanwhile, Samsung's 7 nm process in Hwaseong's Fab S3 first entered into mass production in early 2019, after TSMC had started its 7 nm mass production in Hsinchu's Fab 12 and Taichung's Fab 15 in 2018. Its 5 nm process in two fabs in Hwaseong and Pyeongtaek, however, would catch up with TSMC's Fab 18 and commence mass production in the second half of 2020 and 2021.[14]

By 2020/2021, this intense technological competition among the world's top three chip makers, Intel, Samsung, and TSMC, was emblematic of the broader interconnected worlds of global electronics underpinned by sophisticated and cross-regional production networks. As stylized in Figure 4.2, these globalized production networks of semiconductor manufacturing in the most advanced fabs of TSMC (Hsinchu and Tainan in Taiwan) and Samsung (Giheung and Pyeongtaek in South Korea) necessarily bring together not only highly complex ecosystems of chip design (e.g., Qualcomm) and specialized suppliers in electronic design automation software, chip-making devices and equipment, and silicon materials and chemicals from the US, the Netherlands, and Japan, but also diverse ICT end product vendors that locate their final assembly facilities in China and other East Asian economies to serve end markets worldwide. While the next two chapters will explain the firm-specific strategies and causal drivers behind these rather complicated production network configurations, the following three subsections unpack further the industrial-organizational geography in three leading ICT end products—PCs, mobile handsets, and TVs—that rely critically on semiconductors.

### Personal Computers: Notebooks and Desktops

In 2018, personal computers (PCs) were the second largest segment in global electronics, after mobile handsets. As indicated in Figure 2.3, the PC segment had 14,280 firms with $1.4 trillion in combined revenue or 32 percent of total revenue in global electronics. The global production of PCs has evolved dramatically since Dedrick and Kraemer's (1998) comprehensive analysis of US-led production networks during the 1990s in their *Asia's Computer Challenge*.[15] While they predicted correctly the demise of IBM in PCs by the late 1990s and the emergence of a decentralized industrial structure based on global production networks, this "computer challenge" from Asia not only produced several top OEM competitors from

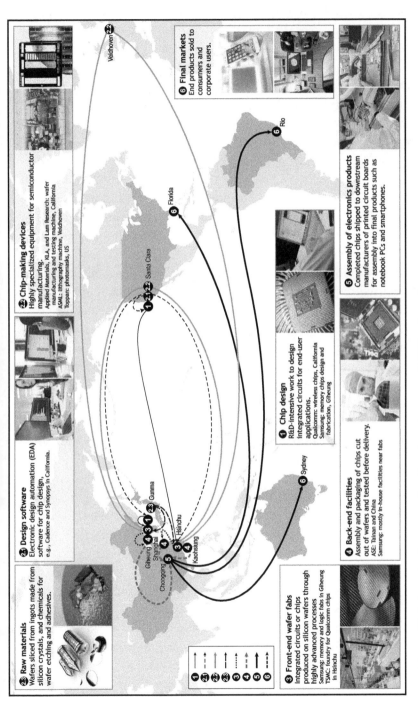

FIGURE 4.2. Global production networks of semiconductors and ICT end products.

Photo credits: with permission from flickr.com/Stratman[2]; pxhere.com/Alan Levine and 912827-2017; Pexels.com/ThisIsEngineering, Pok Rie, PhotoMIX Co, and Pixabay; ASML.com/43687, 48545, and 48546; iStock.com/coddy, FroggyFrogg, ranz12, and gorodenkoff; TSMC.com/ inc017_946 and waferc008_2536.

East Asia (China and Taiwan) to US PC lead firms by the 2010s but also shifted almost completely the center of global PC production to ODM and EMS providers from these East Asian economies. As contextualized in Table 1.2, these East Asian firms emerged from domestic market liberalization and financial deregulation during the 2000s that created strong "windows of opportunity" for their strategic coupling with OEM lead firms in global production networks. Through far more intensified outsourcing of design and final assembly to these East Asian ODM/EMS providers (primarily from Taiwan), much of the world's PC production is now located in their assembly factories in China and a few sites in Southeast Asia, South Asia, Eastern Europe, and Latin America. Yet, this spatial concentration in China and its subnational regions is much more pronounced in notebook PCs. In desktop PCs, a more diversified geographical configuration beyond China is evident.

As noted in Table 1.1, the global revenue of notebook and desktop PC sales decreased respectively from $116 billion and $47 billion in 2015 to $109 billion and $37 billion in 2018, and total shipment has been declining from its historical peak of 364 million units in 2011. Chapter 2 has already elaborated on the changing industry contexts of PCs since the mid-2000s toward greater market concentration among top six OEM lead firms, the dramatic market shift toward notebook PCs, and the critical role of Taiwan's ODM firms as the manufacturing partners for these PC vendors (also Table 2.1). Chapter 3's stylized discussion of notebook PC manufacturing by Hewlett-Packard and its ODM partners from Taiwan has also offered an example of how this strategic coupling between an OEM lead firm and its ODM partner in its global production network can help integrate different national worlds of electronics production (also Figure 3.1). The following empirical analysis examines more fully three main trends in the evolving industrial-organizational geography of PC production during the 2015–2018 period (and thereafter):

(1)    China as the predominant center for the final assembly of notebook PCs by ODM firms from Taiwan,

(2)    limited outsourcing by East Asian notebook PC vendors and the high concentration of production in East Asian locations among all top six notebook PC vendors, and

(3)    the more diversified and globalized geography of final assembly in desktop PCs.

Table 4.3 reports the shipment units by final assembly among the world's top six notebook PC OEM firms in both 2015 and 2018. First, China serves as the primary location for notebook PC assembly due to the dominance of Taiwanese ODM firms in this segment—top three of Compal, Quanta, and Wistron, together with Pegatron, Inventec, and Foxconn (the top EMS provider). Theorized in Chapter 3 as an "inside-out" process of geographical configuration driven by foreign investment, all of these Taiwanese firms have invested in assembly factories in China, with multiple locations in Eastern regions, such as Kunshan/Suzhou (Compal, Quanta, Wistron, and Pegatron), and Shanghai (Quanta), and Western China, such as Chongqing (all) and Chengdu (Compal and Foxconn)—full data on these factory locations are in Appendix C (Table C6). The proportion of notebook PCs assembled in these locations within China grew substantially from an already very high level of 83 percent of the total worldwide shipment in 2015 to 91 percent in 2018.

Within China, major geographical shifts in ODM factory output occurred between 2015 and 2018, from those located in Western China back to Eastern China. Despite the earlier success of Western China's Chongqing[16] (and Chengdu) in attracting the location of Taiwanese ODM assembly activities since the late 2000s, its total notebook PC assembly output was reduced from 93.3 million units in 2015 to 76.7 million units in 2018. Its share in China's total output was also reduced from 63 percent in 2015 to 51 percent in 2018. Much of this locational shift within China was accounted for by shift in orders from Compal's top three OEM customers in notebook PCs—Hewlett-Packard, Lenovo, and Dell. Dell's relocation of assembly share in Compal's Chongqing factory (12.9 million units in 2015) to its Kunshan factory (13.7 million units in 2018) was the most significant.

This substantial growth in the share of China from 83 percent in 2015 to 91 percent in 2018 came on the back of the dwindling worldwide shipment of notebook PCs from 178 million units in 2015 to 163 million units in 2018 (much less than its peak of 212 million units in 2012). Interestingly, China's growing share is due to the dramatic decline in shipment from locations outside China, such as Pegatron and Foxconn factories located in Brazil (São Paulo), Mexico (Juarez), Turkey, and Czech Republic. All these changes indicate a clear pattern of the geographical consolidation of global notebook PC production into assembly factories in China for worldwide shipment. Meanwhile, only Taiwan experienced some growth in notebook PC shipment between 2015 and 2018. This was prompted

TABLE 4.3. World's top 6 notebook PC OEM firms by shipments and location of final assembly, 2015 and 2018 (in millions of units)

| ODM | Location | HP 2015 | HP 2018 | Lenovo 2015 | Lenovo 2018 | Dell 2015 | Dell 2018 | Asus 2015 | Asus 2018 | Acer 2015 | Acer 2018 | Apple 2015 | Apple 2018 | Total (all firms) 2015 | Total (all firms) 2018 |
|---|---|---|---|---|---|---|---|---|---|---|---|---|---|---|---|
| Compal | Taiwan | - | 0.3 | - | - | - | - | - | - | - | - | - | - | - | 0.3 |
| | China | 2.5 | 11.7 | 9.6 | 5.6 | 12.9 | 19.6 | 4.0 | - | 4.7 | 3.6 | - | - | 34.9 | 41.0 |
| Quanta | China | 12.5 | 14.7 | 7.0 | 1.6 | 3.8 | 0.3 | 2.8 | 5.6 | 4.1 | 5.8 | 14.5 | 7.7 | 46.5 | 37.1 |
| Wistron | Chongqing, China | 3.0 | 3.7 | 5.5 | 3.6 | 4.2 | 6.9 | 1.9 | - | 3.6 | 1.3 | - | - | 19.4 | 15.8 |
| Inventec | Taiwan | - | 0.5 | - | - | - | - | - | - | - | - | - | - | - | 0.5 |
| | China | 7.5 | 9.3 | - | - | - | - | - | - | - | - | - | - | 12.3 | 10.1 |
| Pegatron | China | 1.8 | - | 1.5 | - | - | - | 6.8 | 7.1 | 1.2 | 1.1 | - | - | 12.9 | 8.6 |
| | Mexico | 2.8 | - | - | - | - | - | - | - | - | - | - | - | 2.8 | - |
| Hon Hai/ Foxconn | China | 1.6 | - | - | - | 1.0 | - | - | - | - | - | 3.4 | 2.7 | 6.0 | 3.0 |
| | Mexico/Brazil | 1.9 | - | - | - | - | - | - | - | - | - | - | - | 1.9 | - |
| | Turkey/Czech Rep | 1.4 | - | - | - | - | - | - | - | - | - | - | - | 1.4 | - |
| In-House | China | - | - | 13.4 | 20.7 | - | - | - | - | - | - | - | - | 13.4 | 24.6 |
| Total | China—West | 24.9 | 31.3 | 15.3 | 4.6 | 18.1 | 13.0 | 15.4 | 12.7 | 9.0 | 8.9 | - | 2.7 | 93.3 | 76.7 |
| | China—East | 4.0 | 8.1 | 16.0 | 6.2 | 3.8 | 13.7 | - | - | 4.7 | 2.9 | 14.5 | 7.7 | 45.5 | 41.5 |
| | China—total | 28.9 | 39.4 | 37.0 | 36.5 | 21.9 | 26.7 | 15.4 | 13.6 | 13.7 | 12.0 | 17.9 | 10.4 | 148.0 | 149.0 |
| | **Worldwide** | **35.0** | **40.3** | **37.0** | **36.5** | **21.9** | **26.7** | **15.4** | **13.6** | **13.7** | **12.0** | **17.9** | **10.4** | **178.1** | **163.4** |

Note: See full table and location details in Appendix C Table C6.
Source: Data from IHS Markit/Informa Tech Custom Research for GPN@NUS Centre, July–October 2016 and 2019.

by the reshoring of Taiwanese ODM firms at the request of their lead firm customers, particularly those of US-origin such as Hewlett-Packard and Dell, in order to serve the US market due to uncertain geopolitical constraints under the former Trump administration (2017–2021) and in anticipation of the US-China trade war since March 2018. Shipments from these ODM factories in home location (Taiwan) increased quite massively from a negligible size in 2015 to 6.7 million units in 2018.

Second, the geographical shifts in notebook PC assembly point to the highly differentiated outsourcing and partnership patterns among the top ten OEM vendors—see further explanations of firm-level strategies in the next chapter. In both 2015 and 2018, all PC OEM firms from the US (Hewlett-Packard, Dell, and Apple) and Taiwan (Asus and Acer) outsourced 100 percent of their final assembly to ODM providers from Taiwan.[17] The geography of their output thus matches closely the locations of factories by these ODM firms. However, Lenovo, Samsung, and all three Japanese OEM firms (Fujitsu, NEC, and Toshiba) had substantial in-house assembly production in 2018, ranging from 100 percent (Samsung's 2.7 million units in Suzhou, China; NEC's 1.2 million units in Japan; and Toshiba's 0.4 million units in Hangzhou, China) to 57 percent for Lenovo (major factories in Hefei[18] and Shenzhen) and 72 percent for Fujitsu (1.4 million units in Torine, Japan).[19] Among the top six notebook PC lead firms, Asus and Apple had the fewest ODM partners, and their production locations were the most concentrated in 2018—Asus in Chongqing (by Quanta and Pegatron) and Apple in Shanghai (by Quanta) and, to a lesser extent, Chengdu (by Foxconn). Among all Taiwanese ODM factories in China, only Quanta's Shanghai factory and Inventec's Chongqing factory were dedicated to their respective OEM customers—Apple and Hewlett-Packard. In 2018, each of these two customers accounted for 92–93 percent of the shipment output of 8.4 million and 10.1 million units from either factory.

Third, the geography of final assembly of desktop PCs by ODM firms and EMS providers in Table 4.4 is relatively more diversified and globalized in comparison with notebook PCs. While China's role as the location for final assembly was still important in both 2015 and 2018, its locational share hovered around 47 percent of the respective worldwide shipment of 94 million units and 87.5 million units. This represents just about half of its geographical share in notebook PC assembly due to several logistical and marketing reasons.[20] A notebook PC's light weight means that it

TABLE 4.4. World's top 6 desktop PC OEM firms by shipments and location of final assembly, 2015 and 2018 (in millions of units)

| ODM/EMS | Location | Lenovo | | HP | | Dell | | Acer | | Asus | | Apple | | Total (all firms) | |
|---|---|---|---|---|---|---|---|---|---|---|---|---|---|---|---|
| | | 2015 | 2018 | 2015 | 2018 | 2015 | 2018 | 2015 | 2018 | 2015 | 2018 | 2015 | 2018 | 2015 | 2018 |
| Hon Hai/ | Longhua, China | – | – | – | – | – | – | – | – | – | – | 2.0 | 1.0 | 2.0 | 1.0 |
| Foxconn | Wuhan, China | – | – | 5.0 | 4.9 | 10.2 | 3.4 | – | – | – | – | – | – | 15.2 | 8.3 |
| | São Paulo, Brazil | – | – | – | – | – | – | – | – | – | – | – | 0.2 | – | 0.2 |
| | Juarez, Mexico | – | – | 2.0 | 1.3 | – | 2.7 | – | – | – | – | – | – | 2.0 | 4.1 |
| | Pardubice, Czech Rep | – | – | 1.9 | 1.9 | – | – | – | – | – | – | – | – | 1.9 | 1.9 |
| | Çorlu, Turkey | – | – | 1.1 | 1.1 | – | – | – | – | – | – | – | – | 1.1 | 1.1 |
| | Pantnagar & Bengalaru, India | – | – | 0.5 | 0.5 | – | – | – | – | – | – | – | – | 0.5 | 0.5 |
| Compal | Chengdu, China | – | 9.2 | – | – | – | – | 1.6 | 1.8 | – | 0.8 | – | – | 1.6 | 11.8 |
| | Chongqing, China | – | – | – | – | – | 4.8 | – | – | – | – | – | – | – | 4.8 |
| Pegatron | Kunshan, China | – | – | – | – | – | – | 0.4 | 0.5 | 1.5 | 1.3 | – | – | 2.3 | 1.8 |
| | Juarez, Mexico | – | – | 8.4 | 9.5 | – | – | – | – | – | – | – | – | 8.4 | 9.5 |
| Quanta | Kunshan, China | – | – | – | – | – | – | 1.4 | 1.5 | – | 0.3 | – | – | 1.4 | 1.8 |
| Wistron | Zhongshan, China | – | – | – | – | – | – | 1.2 | 1.2 | – | 0.3 | – | – | 1.2 | 1.4 |

| | | | | | | | | | | | | | | |
|---|---|---|---|---|---|---|---|---|---|---|---|---|---|---|
| **Flex** | Zhuhai, China | – | – | – | – | 6.2 | 0.7 | – | – | – | – | – | – | 6.2 | 0.7 |
| | Austin, TX, US | – | – | – | – | – | – | – | – | – | – | 1.9 | 0.9 | 1.9 | 0.9 |
| **In-House** | Beijing, China | 9.0 | 7.0 | – | – | – | – | – | – | – | – | – | – | 9.0 | 7.0 |
| | Chengdu, China | 6.0 | 2.5 | – | – | 3.9 | – | – | – | – | – | – | – | 6.0 | 6.4 |
| | Huizhou, China | 2.0 | 1.2 | – | – | – | – | – | – | – | – | – | – | 2.0 | 1.2 |
| | Xiamen, China | – | – | – | – | 0.9 | – | – | – | – | – | – | – | – | 0.9 |
| | Hortolandia, Brazil | – | – | – | – | 0.4 | – | – | – | – | – | – | – | – | 0.4 |
| | Sriperumbudur (Chennai), India | – | – | – | – | 0.4 | – | – | – | – | – | – | – | – | 0.4 |
| | Cork, Ireland | – | – | – | – | – | – | – | – | – | – | 1.3 | 0.5 | 1.3 | 0.5 |
| | Legnica SEZ, Poland | 1.0 | 1.2 | – | – | – | – | – | – | – | – | – | – | 1.0 | 1.2 |
| **Total** | China only | 17.0 | 19.8 | 5.0 | 4.9 | 16.4 | 13.7 | 4.6 | 5.1 | 1.5 | 2.6 | 2.0 | 1.0 | 46.9 | 47.1 |
| | **Worldwide** | **18.0** | **21.0** | **18.9** | **19.3** | **16.4** | **17.1** | **4.6** | **5.1** | **1.5** | **2.6** | **4.3** | **2.6** | **94.1** | **87.5** |

Source: Data from IHS Markit/Informa Tech Custom Research for GPN@NUS Centre, July–October 2016 and 2019.

can be shipped worldwide by air from major production hubs in China. Desktop PCs are far heavier and uneconomical to ship via air freight. The inventory costs associated with desktop PCs in transshipment by rail and/ or sea taking up to one week or more are simply too high. Chapters 5 and 6 will explain in depth these different supply chain strategies of lead firms and their implications for inventory costs and market reach in the geographical configuration of PC production. For example, having final configuration centers for desktop PCs near major macroregional markets in the Americas, Europe, and Asia can speed up time-to-market and fulfil better customization of desktop PC products. Some host markets may also have stringent government policies regulating the public procurement of desktop PCs (e.g., security-related concerns) and local content preferences (e.g., in developing countries).

In 2018, the top three EMS/ODM firms, Foxconn, Compal, and Pegatron, assembled worldwide a total of 45 million units of desktop PCs, just over half of total desktop PC shipments. This was a significant increase from their combined total of 35 million units or 37 percent share of total shipment in 2015. Within China, two locations were the most significant among these top three assembly providers—Wuhan in Central China (Foxconn for Hewlett-Packard and Dell) and Chengdu in Western China (Compal for Lenovo and others). Meanwhile, three PC OEM lead firms, Lenovo, Dell, and Apple, remained committed to in-house assembly of desktop PCs in their facilities in China and elsewhere worldwide that served specific national and macroregional market needs. Through an "outside-in" process of geographical configuration (Chapter 3) during the 2010s, these US lead firms established in-house assembly facilities in several Asian locations that facilitated the embedding of strategic partners and domestic suppliers into their global production networks.

Of all top six PC OEM firms, only the second large vendor, Hewlett-Packard, had a much more diversified location of final assembly covering five countries—China, Czech Republic, India, Mexico, and Turkey, a clear indication of its globalization of desktop PC assembly to serve all major markets worldwide. In fact, Hewlett-Packard's largest location for final assembly in 2018 was in Juarez, Mexico, by Foxconn (serving both Hewlett-Packard and Dell) and Pegatron (dedicated factory). The combined output of 10.8 million units for Hewlett-Packard from these two ODM/EMS-owned factories in Mexico more than doubled the 4.9 million units of Hewlett-Packard desktop PCs assembled in Foxconn's Wuhan factory in China. In short, the Americas remains as the primary market for Hewlett-Packard's desktop PCs, followed by Asia and Europe.[21] Like Hewlett-Packard, another US OEM lead firm, Apple, was geographically quite diversified in its desktop assembly in 2018, with outsourced and in-house facility located in major macroregions of North and South America, Europe, and Asia. In comparison, the top three US PC vendor Dell focused much more on the East Asian market, with four assembly locations in China (two by ODM firms and two in-house) producing over 80 percent of its worldwide desktop shipment.

All in all, the above global production maps of notebook and desktop PCs during the 2015–2018 period demonstrate an overwhelming significance of China as the location for final assembly in notebook PCs and the significance of two main regions within China (western and eastern) for the location of assembly factories owned by leading ODM and EMS providers from Taiwan. In desktop PCs, the geographical configurations of final assembly were relatively more globalized such that top OEM vendors could better serve specific national and macroregional markets worldwide. This global presence in final assembly was particularly evident among all three US-origin vendors (Hewlett-Packard, Dell, and Apple), a reflection of their global market appeal and penetration. In both product categories, substantial in-house production took place among OEM lead firms from East Asia—Lenovo from China, Samsung from South Korea, and Fujitsu, NEC, and Toshiba from Japan. By the late 2010s, PC production clearly became more consolidated in terms of geographical configurations and industrial organization. Such geographical configurations of production were also evident in other computing products, such as servers and tablets.[22]

## Mobile Handsets: Smartphones

In 2018, mobile handsets were the largest segment in global electronics, with 33,775 firms and $2.1 trillion in combined revenue worldwide in Figure 2.3. In many ways, one would expect the geography of mobile handset production to resemble closely that of tablets and notebook PCs (also known as "mobile PCs" in the ICT sector).[23] Among the top ten mobile handset vendors in 2018 (Table 1.1), eight were from East Asia—two from South Korea (Samsung and LG) and six from China (Huawei, Xiaomi, Oppo, Vivo, Lenovo-Motorola, and TCL-Alcatel). Apple and Microsoft-Nokia from the US were the only top ten vendors from outside South

Korea and China. Chapter 2 has already examined the evolutionary dynamics of these lead firms within the mobile handset segment since the "smartphone revolution" (see also Table 2.1). Unlike semiconductors and PCs, the geographical configuration of mobile handset assembly is actually quite diversified *within Asia*—comprising Northeast Asia (primarily China), Southeast Asia (Vietnam), and South Asia (India)—with extended presence in South America (Brazil). These top ten OEM firms have little or no assembly facilities in North America, Europe, the Middle East, and Africa.

Table 4.5 demonstrates this Asia-centered geography of final assembly among the world's top seven smartphone OEM firms in 2015 and 2018. Several interesting observations can be made in relation to

(1)    a diversified geography of final assembly in East and South Asia,

(2)    an organizational mix of EMS/ODM providers and the role of dedicated factories, and

(3)    the continual significance of in-house production.

First, the importance of China as the preferred location for final assembly is reduced over time, from a substantial share of 62 percent in 2015 to slightly less than half or 49 percent in 2018. This decreasing share of China in final assembly took place on the back of increasing total worldwide shipment of smartphones from 1.38 billion units in 2015 to a historical peak at 1.41 billion units in 2018 (but reduced to 1.37 billion in 2019 and 1.25 billion in 2020; see Table 2.9).[24] Much of this increase in shipment output up to 2018 came from India (tripling from 102 million units in 2015 to 294 million units in 2018) and Vietnam (from 59 million units in 2015 to a whopping 161 million units in 2018) that more than compensated for the corresponding reduction in China's output from 856 million units in 2015 to 688 million units in 2018. In the midst of the COVID-19 pandemic though, China's share in total smartphone production actually increased to 68 percent in 2020, whereas India's share decreased to 15 percent.[25] Chapters 5 and 6 will explain how and why such geographical diversification in smartphone production networks from China to Vietnam and India can be explained by organizational innovation in firm strategies and specific causal dynamics, such as cost differential, logistical capability, and localized ecosystems of suppliers.

TABLE 4.5. World's top 7 smartphone OEM firms by shipments and location of final assembly, 2015 and 2018 (in millions of units)

| EMS | Location | Samsung | | Huawei | | Apple | | Xiaomi | | Oppo | | Vivo | | LG | | Total (all firms) | |
|---|---|---|---|---|---|---|---|---|---|---|---|---|---|---|---|---|---|
| | | 2015 | 2018 | 2015 | 2018 | 2015 | 2018 | 2015 | 2018 | 2015 | 2018 | 2015 | 2018 | 2015 | 2018 | 2015 | 2018 |
| Hon Hai / | China | – | – | 20.1 | 51.5 | 146 | 132 | 47.3 | 32.1 | 22.8 | 34.6 | 24.9 | 57.2 | – | – | 302 | 330 |
| Foxconn | Brazil | – | – | 0.3 | 3.1 | 17.0 | 11.5 | 0.5 | 2.4 | – | – | – | – | – | – | 17.8 | 16.9 |
| | India | – | – | – | – | 3.1 | – | 12.5 | 47.5 | – | – | – | – | – | – | 15.6 | 51.4 |
| Flex | India | – | – | 36.5 | 94.8 | – | – | – | – | – | – | – | – | – | – | 36.5 | 95.1 |
| Pegatron | China | – | – | – | – | 60.2 | 52.6 | – | – | – | – | – | – | – | – | 60.2 | 52.6 |
| Inventec | China | – | – | – | – | – | – | 8.9 | 23.7 | – | – | – | – | – | – | 8.9 | 23.7 |
| Wistron | China | – | – | – | – | 5.7 | 8.2 | – | – | – | – | – | – | – | – | 7.4 | 8.2 |
| | India | – | – | – | – | – | 0.6 | – | 7.2 | – | – | – | – | – | – | 0 | 7.8 |
| BYD | China | – | – | 19.0 | 28.8 | – | – | – | – | – | – | – | – | – | – | 19.0 | 28.8 |
| In-House | China | 156 | 31.3 | 24.7 | 27.8 | – | – | 4.0 | 5.9 | 23.0 | 34.6 | 15.9 | 26.0 | 36.5 | 23.4 | 387 | 193 |
| | Brazil | 21.5 | 10.7 | – | – | – | – | – | – | – | – | – | – | 5.8 | 2.0 | 40.5 | 14.4 |
| | India | 41.6 | 60.3 | 2.8 | – | – | – | – | – | – | 40.3 | 4.4 | 20.8 | 0.6 | 1.1 | 50.3 | 140 |
| | Indonesia | – | 6.4 | – | – | – | – | – | – | – | 5.8 | – | – | – | – | 0 | 12.1 |
| | South Korea | 40.8 | 33.3 | – | – | – | – | – | – | – | – | – | – | 5.4 | 4.4 | 46.2 | 37.8 |
| | Vietnam | 50.9 | 148 | – | – | – | – | – | – | – | – | – | – | 8.3 | 13.3 | 59.2 | 161 |
| Total | China only | 155 | 31.3 | 69.4 | 108 | 212 | 193 | 55.6 | 61.9 | 45.7 | 69.2 | 40.8 | 83.2 | 36.5 | 20.8 | 856 | 688 |
| | Outsourced | 0 | 0 | 81.5 | 178 | 232 | 205 | 69.2 | 113 | 22.8 | 34.6 | 24.9 | 57.2 | 3.1 | 0 | 587 | 793 |
| | Worldwide | 320 | 290 | 109 | 206 | 232 | 205 | 73.2 | 119 | 45.7 | 115 | 45.2 | 104 | 59.8 | 44.2 | 1,377 | 1,410 |

Note: See full table and location details in Appendix C Table C7.
Source: Data from IHS Markit/Informa Tech Custom Research for GPN@NUS Centre, July–October 2016 and 2019.

During the same period, final assembly outputs from Brazil, South Korea, and other locations (both outsourced and in-house) were reduced, indicating a segment-wide consolidation of final assembly into only three major locations in East and South Asia—China, India, and Vietnam. Within China, EMS/ODM firms from Taiwan have engaged in an "inside-out" process of foreign investment since the mid-2000s to establish assembly facilities in different subnational regions. Foxconn's four locations in China collectively assembled 330 million units, representing almost 48 percent of China's total output in 2018 and a substantial increase from its share of 35 percent in 2015. Another major cluster in Eastern China—comprising three Taiwanese ODM firms of Pegatron, Inventec, and Wistron in Nanjing, Kunshan, Shanghai, and Suzhou—contributed to another 84.5 million units in 2018 (or 12 percent of China's total output).

Second, the outsourcing of smartphone final assembly by OEM lead firms, with the exceptions of South Korea's Samsung and LG, is supported by a diverse organizational mix of EMS and ODM providers (see also Chapter 2's discussion of industry context in relation to the "OS war" and the demise of Nokia). Apart from the leading EMS provider, Foxconn, and three Taiwanese ODM firms, two major EMS providers from the US (Flex[26]) and China (BYD) have also established dedicated factories in India (Flex in Chennai) and China (BYD in Huizhou and Longgang) to serve Huawei's outsourced smartphone assembly. Among this group of EMS/ODM providers, only Foxconn's factories in China, Brazil, and India, and Wistron's factories in China and India served two or more smartphone OEM customers (see location details in Appendix C Table C7). With an output of 196 million in 2018, Foxconn's megafactory in China's Guanlan was the largest among all smartphone assembly factories worldwide and served the largest number of OEM customers.[27] Foxconn was also the only EMS provider offering global production services through its multiple assembly factories in China, Brazil, and India.

Among the largest smartphone OEM lead firms, Apple and Xiaomi relied almost exclusively on these EMS/ODM providers to assemble their smartphones in 2018. As will be explained in greater detail in Chapter 5, both of them developed extensive outsourcing relationships with Foxconn and supplemented these with smaller assembly volumes by Pegatron (Apple), Inventec (Xiaomi), and Wistron (Apple and Xiaomi). To strengthen their partnership with these two major OEM lead firms, all four EMS/ODM providers offered dedicated factories in China in 2018 to serve Apple (e.g., Foxconn in Zhengzhou) or Xiaomi (e.g., Inventec in Nanjing and Shanghai). This organizational phenomenon of offering exclusive or dedicated factories to serve specific OEM customers is unique to the mobile handset segment; it does not occur in the PC or TV segments. The geography of the final assembly of products by these smartphone vendors can therefore be mapped directly onto the locations of their dedicated EMS/ODM factories.

Third and again unlike in the PC segment, in-house production remains very significant in mobile handsets, led by the market leader Samsung and followed in a hybrid way by others such as Huawei, Oppo, Vivo, LG, and so on. Samsung is clearly distinctive here, in relation to the domination of fewer but more powerful chaebol in post-2000 South Korea (see summary in Table 1.2) and its intrachaebol organization of mobile handset production network discussed in Chapter 2's industry context, As the top vendor with 290 million units shipped in 2018, its complete internalization of smartphone manufacturing is astonishing and contrasts sharply with complete outsourcing by Apple and Xiaomi—a key topic for further explanations in the next two chapters. To serve its global market, Samsung has engaged in an extensive "inside-out" process of establishing its in-house production network in mobile handsets, with large final assembly facilities in China, Brazil, India, South Korea, and Vietnam. The other three top vendors from China (Huawei, Oppo, and Vivo) do not have such extensive in-house global production networks and, instead, consolidate their in-house assembly facilities into China and India. Similarly, most other East Asian smartphone vendors retain home country production for their domestic markets, e.g., Samsung/LG in South Korea and Fujitsu and Kyocera in Japan. Overall, the geography of smartphone production is much more diversified and globalized than PCs, due to a relatively long "tail" of mostly smaller OEM firms in developing countries (e.g., China's Transsion in Africa and South Asia and Newsan in Latin America).[28]

### Consumer Electronics: Televisions

Unlike its early heydays in microelectronics before the "PC revolution" in the 1980s and the "smartphone revolution" in the late 2000s (Table 2.1), consumer electronics is no longer the most important segment in today's global electronics.[29] In 2018, this segment reached $320 billion in total revenue, with about 3,076 firms in Figure 2.3. These figures are far lower than mobile handsets and PCs. Within consumer electronics, televisions (TVs) are *the* dominant high-tech product, and their production by leading OEM firms is often organized through cross-border production networks centered in East Asia with the following key attributes during the 2010s:

(1)    the dominant role of East Asian lead firms, but fairly globalized geography of final assembly,

(2)    a mix of in-house production and outsourced final assembly, and

(3)    the critical role of semiconductors, particularly flat panel displays fabricated entirely in East Asia.

Similar to PCs and mobile handsets, the TV segment intersects closely with optical semiconductors and integrated circuits (e.g., display drivers and digital display processors) that constitute the core components of flat panel displays. Despite early inventions in the US (e.g., RCA and IBM),[30] flat panel displays are now primarily manufactured by dominant technology leaders and suppliers from East Asia, such as South Korea's Samsung and LG, Taiwan's Innolux and AUO, Japan's Sharp and JDI, and China's BOE. Not surprisingly, many TV OEM lead firms are also major players in the mobile handset segment, such as four of the top seven TV OEM firms (Samsung, LG, TCL, and Xiaomi). But unlike in PCs and mobile handsets, the TV segment is almost entirely controlled by lead firms from East Asia: South Korea, China, and Japan (see national contexts in Table 1.2). No US or European OEM firms are ranked among the top fifteen. Two former world leaders in analogue TVs from Germany and the US—Grundig (now Turkish-owned) and RCA (now French-owned)—had respectively only 0.3 percent and 0.1 percent of the global market share in 2018.

First and as evident in Table 4.6, the geography of the final assembly of TVs is fairly globalized. While there is a high concentration of assembly in China among Chinese OEM lead firms (all four in the top seven), three market leaders from outside China, such as Samsung, LG, and Sony, are much less dependent on China as production sites (and markets). Indeed, Samsung and LG had only 15–16 percent of their TV units assembled in China in 2018. To reach better their worldwide markets in the Americas, Europe, Africa and the Middle East, and other parts in Asia, these two top OEM firms from South Korea assembled TVs mostly through an "inside-out" geographical configuration of in-house facilities located in Eastern Europe,[31] Latin America, Africa and the Middle East, South Asia, and Southeast Asia.[32] Three Chinese OEM firms of TCL, Hisense, and

TABLE 4.6. World's top 7 TV OEM firms by shipments and location of final assembly, 2015 and 2018 (in millions of units)

| EMS | Location | Samsung 2015 | Samsung 2018 | LG 2015 | LG 2018 | TCL 2015 | TCL 2018 | Hisense 2015 | Hisense 2018 | Sony 2015 | Sony 2018 | Xiaomi 2015 | Xiaomi 2018 | Skyworth 2015 | Skyworth 2018 | Total[1] 2015 | Total[1] 2018 |
|---|---|---|---|---|---|---|---|---|---|---|---|---|---|---|---|---|---|
| BOE | China | - | 2.1 | - | 2.1 | - | 0.4 | - | - | - | - | - | 0.2 | - | 0.2 | - | 10.8 |
| TCL | China | - | - | - | - | - | - | - | - | - | - | - | 4.1 | - | - | - | 11.5 |
| TP Vision | China | - | - | - | 1.4 | - | - | - | 0.2 | - | 0.4 | - | - | - | 0.2 | 7.9 | 7.7 |
| Amtran | China | - | 0.3 | 6.2 | - | - | - | - | - | - | - | - | 2.4 | - | - | 8.8 | 3.5 |
| Foxconn | India, Mexico, Slovakia | - | - | - | - | - | - | - | - | 13.2 | 5.8 | - | - | - | - | 22.3 | 6.5 |
| Others | China, Eastern Europe, and Latin America | - | 3.4 | - | 0.6 | - | 1.0 | - | - | - | 1.1 | - | 2.7 | - | - | 60.0 | 77.5 |
| **In-House** | China | - | 0.9 | - | - | - | 12.6 | - | 11.4 | - | 3.0 | - | - | - | 8.2 | | |
| | South Korea | - | - | - | 4.7 | - | - | - | - | - | - | - | - | - | - | - | - |
| | Japan | - | - | - | - | - | - | - | - | - | 0.7 | - | - | - | - | - | - |
| | Middle East and Africa | - | 3.5 | - | - | - | - | - | - | - | - | - | - | - | 0.2 | - | - |
| | Eastern Europe | - | 11.7 | - | 5.1 | - | 1.0 | - | - | - | - | - | - | - | - | - | - |
| | Latin America | - | 12.7 | - | 12.5 | - | 1.6 | - | 4.3 | - | - | - | - | - | - | - | - |
| | Southeast Asia | - | 6.9 | - | 4.8 | - | 1.1 | - | - | - | 0.7 | - | - | - | 0.4 | - | - |
| **Total** | China only | - | 6.7 | - | 4.1 | - | 12.6 | - | 11.6 | 13.2 | 4.5 | - | 9.4 | - | 8.6 | - | - |
| | Outsourced | 0 | 5.8 | 6.2 | 4.1 | 0 | 1.4 | 0 | 0.2 | - | 7.3 | - | 9.4 | 0 | 0.4 | 99 | 118 |
| | **Worldwide** | 55.0 | 41.4 | 30.8 | 27.1 | 16.2 | 17.7 | 16.0 | 15.9 | 13.2 | 11.7 | - | 9.4 | 14.3 | 9.2 | 249 | 257 |

[1] Production shipment values are greater than market sales in Table 1.1 due to unsold inventories.
Source: Data from IHS Markit/Informa Tech Custom Research for GPN@NUS Centre, July–October 2016 and 2019.

Skyworth have also followed this "inside-out" process of network configuration and globalized their production facilities to locations outside China, such as Eastern Europe, Latin America, Southeast Asia, and South Africa.

Second, the extent of limited outsourcing in TVs is similar to the mobile handset segment, hovering around 40–45 percent during the 2015–2018 period. While there is a high degree of insourcing among the top four OEM firms, even the largest TV OEM firms (e.g., Samsung, LG, and TCL) outsourced some assembly units to EMS providers—Chapter 5 will follow up on this intrafirm strategy of mixed insourcing/outsourcing of final assembly. Among these EMS providers, Taiwan's Foxconn is "only" a relatively small player, offering EMS services in India, Mexico, and Slovakia to OEM firms such as Sony and others to reach their worldwide markets. Together with Taiwan's Amtran, three EMS providers from China—BOE (display panel maker), TCL, and TP Vision (formerly Philips TV)—are far larger than Foxconn and serve two or more OEM lead firms through their China-based assembly facilities. Meanwhile, other top OEM firms such as Sony and Xiaomi are highly dependent on outsourcing. This high degree of outsourcing also applies to other smaller OEM firms. In the "Others" category of OEM firms (not shown in Table 4.6), some 89 million units or 71 percent were outsourced from a total shipment volume of 125 million units in 2018. Similar to the mobile handset segment, this large Others category (48 percent of total worldwide shipment) indicates the presence of a relatively large group of small and less known domestic firms in many different countries and macroregions worldwide.

Third and to understand further the geography of TV assembly, I now examine Table 4.7's fab-level production data between 2000 and 2018 on flat panel displays—the most important component of TVs and one of the most important modules for PCs and mobile handsets (see Chapter 5's analysis of their top components).[33] In 2000, South Korea's Samsung Display and LG Display already dominated the world of flat panel display fabrication, producing some 43 percent of the world's total capacity of 3.4 millions of m². Japan and Taiwan followed with respectively 27 percent and 22 percent of capacity share. China was relatively small at just 8 percent. By 2010, the industry's total capacity reached 172 millions of m², having expanded over fifty times its output in 2000! Table 4.7 shows the global location of all display panel fabrication throughout the 2010s. By 2018, the total capacity grew further to 305 millions of m². But the growth rate

TABLE 4.7. World's top flat panel display manufacturers by fab location and area capacity, 2010, 2015, and 2018 (in millions of m²)

| Manufacturer | Region and city[1] | 2010 Fab # | 2010 Capacity | 2015 Fab # | 2015 Capacity | 2018 Fab # | 2018 Capacity |
|---|---|---|---|---|---|---|---|
| **China** | | | | | | | |
| BOE | BJ, CD, CQ, FZ, HF, OD | 3 | 2.2 | 8 | 24.4 | 9 | 48.3 |
| China Star (CSOT) | Shenzhen | - | - | 3 | 11.8 | 4 | 21.4 |
| LG Display | Guangzhou | - | - | 1 | 6.1 | 2 | 13.9 |
| CEC Panda | Chengdu, Nanjing | - | - | 2 | 3.9 | 3 | 9.8 |
| Samsung Display | Suzhou | - | - | 1 | 4.3 | 1 | 8.3 |
| HKC Display | Chongqing | - | - | - | - | 1 | 4.9 |
| Tianma | CD, SH, WH, XM | 4 | 1.5 | 6 | 2.9 | 7 | 4.2 |
| CHOT | Xianyang | - | - | - | - | 1 | 3.8 |
| InfoVision | Kunshan | 1 | 2.1 | 1 | 2.0 | 1 | 1.9 |
| Foxconn | Shenzhen | 1 | 0.9 | 1 | 1.7 | 1 | 1.7 |
| Others | FZ, HZ, KS, SH, SZ | 6 | 0.3 | 4 | 0.3 | 9 | 3.0 |
| Total | | 15 | 7.0 | 27 | 57.4 | 39 | 121.0 |
| **South Korea** | | | | | | | |
| LG Display | Kumi, Paju | 11 | 38.1 | 10 | 47.8 | 8 | 42.2 |
| Samsung Display | Asan, CheonAn | 11 | 41.5 | 11 | 49.8 | 8 | 41.6 |
| Hydis | Ichon | 3 | 0.5 | - | - | - | - |
| Total | | 25 | 80.1 | 21 | 97.7 | 16 | 83.8 |

(continued)

TABLE 4.7. (*continued*)

| Manufacturer | Region and city[1] | 2010 Fab # | 2010 Capacity | 2015 Fab # | 2015 Capacity | 2018 Fab # | 2018 Capacity |
|---|---|---|---|---|---|---|---|
| **Taiwan** | | | | | | | |
| Innolux Corp. | Jhunan, Kaohsiung, Tainan | 14 | 28.8 | 12 | 37.7 | 14 | 41.6 |
| AUO | Hsinchu, Taipei, Tainan, Taoyuan | 15 | 26.0 | 14 | 31.1 | 13 | 33.1 |
| CPT | Taoyuan | 3 | 4.8 | 3 | 3.3 | 2 | 3.8 |
| HannStar | Tainan | 1 | 2.5 | 1 | 2.5 | 1 | 2.4 |
| Others | Hsinchu, Taoyuan | 6 | 1.1 | 4 | 0.7 | 3 | 0.5 |
| Total | | 39 | 63.2 | 34 | 75.4 | 33 | 81.4 |
| **Japan** | | | | | | | |
| Sharp | Mie, Nara, Osaka, Tottori | 7 | 14.6 | 9 | 14.8 | 8 | 13.9 |
| Japan Display (JDI) | Aichi, Chiba, Ishikawa, Saitama, Tottori | 11 | 2.2 | 9 | 3.8 | 5 | 3.4 |
| Panasonic LCD | Hyogo | 2 | 4.4 | 1 | 3.2 | 1 | 1.0 |
| Others | Akita, Kochi, Shisui, Yasu | 8 | 0.5 | 6 | 0.4 | 6 | 0.4 |
| Total | | 28 | 21.7 | 25 | 22.2 | 20 | 18.7 |
| **Singapore** | | | | | | | |
| AUO (Taiwan) | | 1 | 0.3 | 1 | 0.3 | 1 | 0.3 |
| **Total** | | 108 | 172.3 | 108 | 253.0 | 109 | 305.1 |

[1] BJ = Beijing; CD = Chengdu; CQ = Chongqing; FZ = Fuzhou; GZ = Guangzhou; HF = Hefei; HZ = Huizhou; KS = Kunshan; NJ = Nanjing; OD = Ordos; SH = Shanghai; SZ = Shenzhen; WH = Wuhan; XM = Xiamen
Source: Based on individual fab-level data from IHS Markit/Informa Tech Custom Research for GPN@NUS Centre, July–October 2016 and 2019.

clearly slowed down during this decade, pointing to a maturing phase of the industry's consolidation centered in East Asia in support of production networks in ICT and other industries.

While outputs from these display makers can be used in a wide range of electronics products (e.g., TVs, PCs, and mobile handsets) and nonelectronics products (e.g., automotive, aerospace, industrial and health-care equipment, etc.), TV OEM firms represent a major group of end users for flat panel displays.[34] As documented in Table 4.7, global panel display manufacturing capacity during the 2010s was clearly centered in East Asia, primarily in China, Taiwan, and South Korea, and much less in Japan and Singapore. With an area capacity of 121 millions of m$^2$, China alone accounted for about 40 percent of the worldwide total capacity in 2018, almost doubled its 22 percent share in 2015 and sixfold of a mere 6.5 percent share in 2010. Much of this new capacity in China added to the entire industry's growth during the same period. This reflects the entry of many new domestic and foreign display makers (from 15 fabs in 2010 to 39 fabs in 2018) and the enormous growth in the capacity of TV production in China since 2010. Within China, LG Display and Samsung Display from South Korea have engaged in an "outside-in" configuration of their display fabs and are now ranked among the top five panel display makers. Adding their China outputs to home-based outputs (an "inside-out" configuration of exporting intermediate goods; see Chapter 3), LG Display and Samsung Display clearly remain as the world's top two largest display panel makers, followed closely by China's BOE and Taiwan's Innolux and AUO.

Moreover, market concentration is very high in flat panel displays. LG Display and Samsung Display, together with BOE, Innolux, and AUO, supply much of the display requirement of the top seven TV OEM firms in Table 4.6.[35] While the geography of TV assembly is quite globalized, TV OEM firms remain constrained by the East Asia–specific locations of panel display fabrication by their top suppliers. In notebook PCs, this spatial logic of colocation is much more pronounced. The four largest flat panel display suppliers in 2018 were BOE, AUO, Innolux, and LG Display. While AUO and Innolux supplied from their Taiwan fabs to about 25–33 percent of display units for each top five notebook PC customer in Table 4.3, BOE specifically established large display fabs in Chongqing (B8) to supply to ODM firms assembling Hewlett-Packard, Dell, Asus, and Acer notebook PCs, and in Hefei (B3) to cater primarily to Lenovo's PC factory and Apple's ODM provider Quanta. Chapter 5 will offer a more detailed analysis of the intra- and interfirm strategies between these display suppliers and their lead firm customers in PCs and mobile handsets. Summing up, the industrial-organizational geography of TV production points to variegated global production networks comprising fairly globalized TV assembly and highly concentrated panel display fabrication centered in East Asia.

## Firm-Level Geographical Configurations of Global Production Networks

As summarized in Table 4.8, the above section has described the broader geographical shift in global electronics production toward East Asia by the late 2010s in semiconductors, PCs, mobile handsets, and TVs. This coevolutionary shift is underpinned by cross-border interfirm production networks spearheaded by global lead firms as well as their intrafirm corporate networks. This section examines this internal geographical organization of production networks within specific lead firms, with a particular focus on their activities in East Asia. It focuses on 41 out of the 44 firms interviewed in my 2017–2018 study and listed in Appendix B (Table B1) and describes the geographical divisions of labor within each firm when data are available.[36] As noted in Figure 2.3, some 36 of these 44 firms are among the top 15–25 global lead firms in the above four major segments of global electronics. This fairly representative analysis is therefore about each lead firm operating as a transnational corporation with its worldwide subsidiaries and affiliates. These intrafirm activities include corporate control functions, manufacturing, research and product development, sales and marketing, and distribution. Mapped directly onto Chapter 3's theory of firm strategies in global production networks, the next chapter will explain this intrafirm coordination by lead firms and their interfirm control/partnership relationships with strategic partners and key customers and suppliers.

### Corporate Control: Headquarters and Regional Headquarters

Of the forty-one firms with available data, corporate headquarters in home locations continue to control most key functions, particularly in strategic planning and decisions, finance, R&D, supply chain, and operations. In some cases of lead firms from South Korea, Japan, and European countries, the master factories remain located in the home countries and are often very close to their main R&D facilities (e.g., Samsung's mobile

TABLE 4.8. Geographical configurations of production in key segments of global electronics during the 2010s

| Key segments | Geographical configurations | Industrial and market organization |
|---|---|---|
| **Semiconductors** | - Shift in wafer fabrication toward much greater concentration in East Asia<br>- Consolidation of IDM fabs worldwide and new foundry fabs mostly located in East Asia<br>- More dispersed R&D facilities in Triad regions | - High market concentration<br>- Product technology and industrial applications toward rapidly growing ICT segments (e.g., data storage and wireless communications) |
| **Personal computers** | - China as the predominant center for the final assembly of notebook PCs<br>- Higher concentration of production locations in East Asia among all top six notebook PC vendors<br>- More diversified and globalized geography of final assembly in desktop PCs | - Very high market concentration<br>- Limited outsourcing by notebook PC vendors from East Asia<br>- Some in-house production by desktop PC vendors from the US |
| **Mobile handsets: smartphones** | - Consolidation of worldwide final assembly in Asia, but more diversified locations within East and South Asia<br>- Decreasing role of China in final assembly<br>- Continual significance of home-country production among vendors from East Asia | - Very high market concentration<br>- A good mix of EMS and ODM providers from East Asia: some with dedicated factories to serve lead firm customers<br>- Substantial to complete in-house production by vendors from East Asia |
| **Televisions (and flat panel displays)** | - Fairly globalized locations of TV final assembly<br>- High concentration of TV assembly in China due to several Chinese OEM firms<br>- Predominant role of East Asia in production of flat panel displays | - A mix of in-house production and outsourced assembly of TVs<br>- Significant role of China-based EMS providers and facilities in outsourced assembly of TVs<br>- Critical role of flat panel display makers (some also TV OEM firms) |
| **Overall: global electronics** | - Much greater geographical "stretch" or distancing of global production networks<br>- Very high degree of geographical consolidation in production locations within East Asia (Taiwan, South Korea, Japan, and China in semiconductors; China and Vietnam in assembly) and South Asia (India in assembly)<br>- Concentration of R&D facilities in Triad regions | - Far higher market concentration, but a mix of in-house and outsourced production<br>- Market access critical to production of some product categories outside Asia |

handset division in Suwon's Samsung Digital City and its semiconductor division in Hwaseong's Samsung Nano City).

To manage their operations in the Asia Pacific, most of these forty-one firms have established regional headquarters in major gateway cities in Northeast Asia (Hong Kong and Shanghai) and Southeast Asia (Singapore). But there is a significant difference in the geographical coverage of regional headquarters between Asia-origin and US/EU-origin lead firms. Asia-origin lead firms, such as Samsung (South Korea), Hitachi (Japan), Lenovo (China), and Acer (Taiwan), tend to locate their regional headquarters in Singapore to take charge mainly of their Southeast Asia operations. Sometimes, these regional headquarters in Singapore may also manage operations in South Asia (India), Australasia, and Oceania. In Northeast Asia, the headquarters of these lead firms deal directly with customers within the macroregion. In specific Northeast Asian economies (e.g., China or Greater China, South Korea, or Japan), Asia-origin lead firms tend to manage their country operations as separate entities by establishing key offices in each of these Asian economies. This geographical configuration of corporate control applies particularly to lead firms from South Korea or Japan.

For those lead firms from the US and European countries, a large number have chosen Singapore to locate their regional headquarters in order to manage their entire Asia Pacific and Japan operations. Prominent examples are Cisco, Dell, and Hewlett-Packard from the US and Nokia and Ericsson from Nordic countries. Very few of them have located regional headquarters in Hong Kong, though some have based their Greater China operations in Beijing, Shanghai, or Hong Kong (e.g., Dell and Hewlett-Packard). More specifically, the regional headquarters of these lead firms in Singapore have gained substantial control and managerial functions covering all aspects of business operations, including production and procurement.

The next two subsections examine the geographical distribution of the manufacturing, product development, and sales and marketing operations of these lead firms, based on detailed interview data and further research of corporate reports and websites. I count each corporate entity in actual operation as one facility or office, but I am unable to account for their nature and scale of operations (e.g., large versus small manufacturing factories or advanced versus applied R&D offices) due to data unavailability at the level of individual factory or office. Among the 41 firms with locational data on their facilities or offices in 2018, I have identified a worldwide aggregate total of 455 manufacturing facilities, 378 R&D facilities, and 2,083 sales and marketing offices.

The overall picture is clear. There is an obvious presence of Northeast Asia and, to a much lesser extent, Southeast Asia as key sites in global electronics manufacturing among the thirty-five manufacturing firms in all four segments. This finding still stands if the five biggest firms (Big 5) or the twelve semiconductors firms are excluded. However, there is much less dominance of Northeast and Southeast Asia in R&D and sales/marketing locations—the shares of Europe and US/Canada are also quite significant, followed by South Asia and Commonwealth of Independent States.

## Manufacturing Facilities

In manufacturing and as examined in the earlier section, the general trend among US and European lead firms is to engage in extensive outsourcing to their manufacturing partners in East Asia, whereas Asia-origin lead firms prefer more to establish their own in-house production facilities. My sample of 35 manufacturing firms interviewed includes 17 OEM lead firms from the US, Nordic countries, and East Asia; 2 ODM firms from Taiwan; 4 large specialized suppliers; and 12 semiconductors firms in IDM, foundry, or assembly, packaging, and testing services (known as "back-end services" in Figure 4.2). Nine other firms interviewed either have no manufacturing facilities (8 firms) or information is unavailable (1 firm). This observation at the intrafirm level is broadly consistent with the detailed segment-level analysis of IHS Markit/Informa Tech datasets in the previous section. Figure 4.3 illustrates all 455 manufacturing facilities worldwide among 35 firms—pattern-shaded territories correspond to percentage-shares of data in pie charts. For a clearer understanding and less distortion by the largest outlier lead firms, the data are further segmented by removing the Big 5 lead firms (each having 29 to 43 manufacturing facilities). A separate analysis is also conducted for the manufacturing facilities of 12 semiconductors firms that might exhibit different geographical patterns from their end-product OEM lead firms in PCs, mobile handsets, and TVs.

Three key findings in the late 2010s can be observed, and they reinforce those in the earlier segment-specific analysis summarized in Table 4.8:

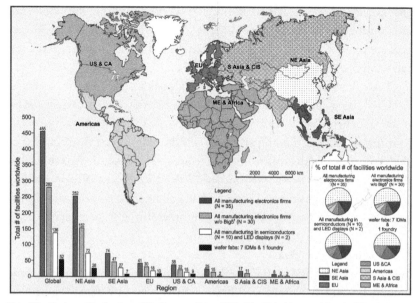

Note: NE = Northeast; SE = Southeast; EU = European Union; US & CA = United States and Canada; CIS = Commonwealth of Independent States; ME = Middle East
[1] Big 5: defined as each lead firm having 29 to 43 manufacturing facilities. All are from South Korea and Japan.

FIGURE 4.3. Worldwide manufacturing locations among 35 firms interviewed, 2017–2018 (including 12 semiconductor firms).

Source: Data from interviews and corporate reports/websites.

(1)     a high geographical concentration of manufacturing production in Northeast Asia, particularly China,

(2)     the quite significant role of Southeast Asia in manufacturing, and

(3)     a strong presence of East Asia in semiconductor fabrication, but also continual significance of wafer fabs in the US and Europe.

First, there is a high concentration of all electronics manufacturing facilities in Northeast Asia, hovering around at least 54 percent of all facilities with or without the Big 5 (all from Japan or South Korea)—see Figure 4.3's two upper pie charts (light-dotted shade). As shown in Figure 4.4, China alone accounts for around 30–32 percent of all manufacturing facilities of these 35 firms. Interestingly, Taiwan and Japan retain a significant share of manufacturing facilities at about 11 to 14 percent. This is due to the substantial home facilities of top firms from Taiwan (e.g., in

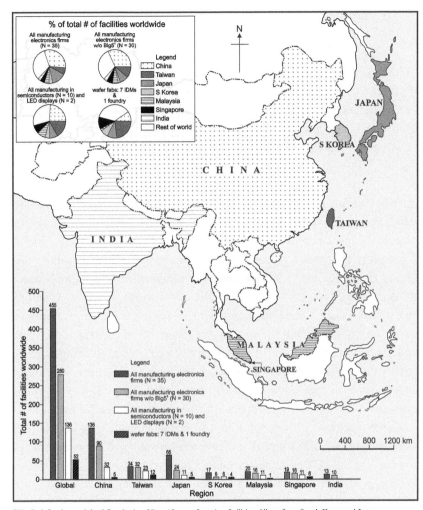

FIGURE 4.4. Manufacturing locations in Asia among 35 firms interviewed, 2017–2018.

Source: Data from interviews and corporate reports/websites.

semiconductor foundry and PCs) or Japan (e.g., in all categories of ICT products). The significance of China in global electronics manufacturing is clearly linked to its importance as *the* global supply base. There are thus major location advantages arising from its supplier ecosystem and other factors (e.g., factory automation and tax incentives). As was pointed out by the senior vice president in charge of procurement and supply chain for top five PC OEM-22,[37]

Everybody knows it, and I think everybody asks the question, "What's the next China?," and the answer they always get is "The next China is China." The reason is because they have such a good ecosystem of components. When you consider the cost of moving those components from China to Vietnam or Indonesia or the Philippines, it breaks the business case every time. The labor benefit you get out of moving away from China is always offset by the cost of moving all the components outside of China.

His view is echoed by the vice president for supply chain operations in Asia Pacific and Japan from top US OEM-16 in mobile handsets and telecom equipment. This US OEM lead firm has attempted to move its manufacturing facilities to the lowest-cost location. But one of the crucial aspects of lowest cost is the supply base, and China remains the most logical choice for such a supply base. The senior director for supply chain of top three ODM-26 from Taiwan also has a similar concern. When its Brazil factory had a material quality issue in 2017, it took over a month to fix because of the time taken for the new or improved material to be ready and made available locally. In China, he claimed, the same issue could be fixed within a day, perhaps at even lower prices, since there were many suppliers within 200 km and competition among them was huge.[38] However, this high geographical concentration of all manufacturing facilities in China does lead to some concerns among lead firms with geopolitical issues related to difficulties of exporting to some countries that are wary of mission-critical ICT products made in China (e.g., government procurement and high-end servers) and the need for corporate diversification of assembly facilities to reduce dependency on China-based manufacturing. Chapters 5 and 6 will examine further these critical issues of regulatory and geopolitical risks and their causal impact on firm strategies and production network configurations.

Second, Southeast Asia remains as a significant macroregion for global electronics manufacturing, attracting the location of more than 16 percent (with or without the Big 5) or 74 of all 455 facilities shown in Figure 4.3 (black-shaded). But as shown in Figure 4.4, these manufacturing facilities are heavily concentrated in Malaysia and Singapore (39 facilities or 53 percent of the total in Southeast Asia). Interestingly and consistent with earlier research,[39] India is not a significant destination for electronics manufacturing by my sample firms, attracting only a very small share of about 3 percent of global total facilities among these 35 firms. At 10 percent of total number of facilities, the combined share of all other developing macroregions outside Asia remains modest.

Third and consistent with findings in the earlier subsection on semi-conductors, the geographical concentration of global manufacturing facil-ities is even more obvious in semiconductors. Figure 4.3's lower right pie chart illustrates the data on about 52 wafer fabs—highest value and capital-intensive manufacturing facilities in semiconductors—from seven IDM lead firms and one foundry provider. These remain highly concentrated in Northeast Asia (50 percent) and Southeast Asia (14 percent). Unlike the final assembly facilities in PCs, mobile handsets, and TVs examined in the earlier subsections, the shares of Europe (19 percent) and the US (17 percent) in wafer fabs are rather significant. But consistent with findings in Table 4.1, there is a complete absence of wafer fabs in any macroregion and national economy outside this Triad of East Asia (Northeast and South-east), Western Europe, and the US.

Not surprising in Figure 4.4's lower right pie chart, Taiwan (in dark grey shade) is the most important location for wafer fabs worldwide (23 percent), followed by Europe (19 percent), the US (17 percent), and Sin-gapore (12 percent). As the vice president for Asia Pacific from top ten European IDM-41 noted,

> When I say "You cannot ignore Taiwan," this statement can be under-stood in many different ways. In the semiconductor industry, you have thousands of jobs in R&D, chip design, manufacturing, or testing in a firm. If you are in the semiconductor industry, you cannot avoid Tai-wan because at some point, they will have something better than you, but cheaper than you and faster than you.

Interestingly, at 9.6 percent each, both China and Japan are "only" ranked joint-third in Asia, suggesting their relatively weaker position in wafer fabs—the most capital- and technology-intensive segment of global electronics manufacturing (see also Table 4.1).

If we include all other facilities in semiconductors (from fabs for flat panel displays to back-end services), we can identify some 136 manufac-turing facilities (including 52 wafer fabs), shown in Figure 4.3's lower left pie chart. The locational share of Northeast and Southeast Asia grows slightly, and there is a corresponding decline of shares in Europe and the US, reflecting cost advantage in the more labor-intensive activities in semiconductors manufacturing (e.g., back-end services in chip assembly and testing). As shown in Figure 4.4's lower left pie chart, China now has the largest share at 24 percent, followed by Taiwan at 17 percent. Even with these labor-intensive activities, however, there is still an almost completely insignificant role of South Asia (e.g., India) and other developing macroregions outside Asia (e.g., Central/South Americas and the Middle East and Africa) among the twelve semiconductor firms represented in the interviews.

### R&D, Product Development, and Sales and Marketing Operations

On R&D and sales/marketing locations, I have information on 41 out of the 44 firms represented in the interviews. Figure 4.5 shows that these 41 firms have 378 R&D facilities worldwide. Unsurprisingly, this number is smaller than the total number of manufacturing facilities (455) by the

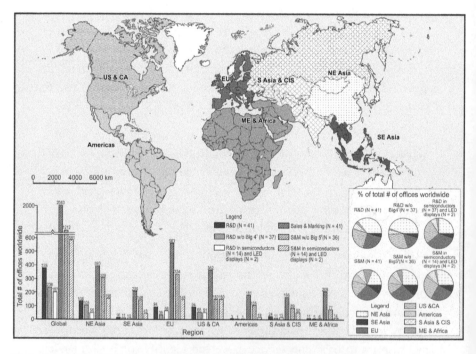

[1] Big 4: defined as each lead firm having 28 to 44 R&D facilities; mostly in semiconductors.
[2] Big 5: defined as each lead firm having 122 to 226 sales and marketing operations; all in telecommunications equipment.

FIGURE 4.5. Worldwide R&D and sales and marketing locations among 41 firms interviewed, 2017–2018.

Source: Data from interviews and corporate reports/websites.

same 35 firms within this group. Still, two interesting geographical patterns stand out on these 378 R&D facilities (see also summary Table 4.8). First, the influence of semiconductor R&D in the overall picture is vital. With 16 lead firms, the semiconductor segment alone contributes to 197 or 52 percent of the total 378 R&D facilities worldwide. Four IDM lead firms (Big 4) have a large number of R&D facilities, ranging between 28 and 44 facilities each.

Geographically, North America (the US in particular) and Europe (France, Germany, Italy, and the Netherlands) remain as the most significant locations for semiconductor R&D facilities (upper right pie chart), a reflection of the continual dominance of US semiconductor firms in fabless- and IDM-led R&D activities and European IDM firms. Despite a strong presence of R&D facilities by US and European IDM firms (e.g., Micron, Infineon, NXP, and STMicroelectronics) in Northeast Asia, it lags slightly behind North America. This globally dispersed pattern of R&D facilities in semiconductors differs quite substantially from semiconductor manufacturing facilities (e.g., wafer fabs and back-end services) that are much more concentrated in East Asia (see also Table 4.1).

Second, as in all segments of global electronics, there is a clear concentration of R&D locations in Northeast Asia, Western Europe, and North America (the US and Canada). These Triad macroregions account respectively for 36 percent, 25 percent, and 25 percent of the total 378 R&D facilities worldwide (Figure 4.5, upper left pie chart). Only the remaining 14 percent are located elsewhere in other developing macroregions. If we exclude the Big 4 (all IDM lead firms in semiconductors) from these 41 firms in the upper middle pie chart, Northeast Asia's share increases much further to 45 percent of the global total, making it by far the most prominent macroregion for R&D in global electronics in the PC, mobile handset, and TV segments in which many top OEM lead firms from East Asia are dominant. Compared to semiconductors, there seems to be a stronger relationship between R&D locations and manufacturing sites in Northeast Asia in these three segments of global electronics, consistent with findings in the earlier three subsections (also in Table 4.8). Meanwhile, other developing macroregions have a limited role to play in global electronics R&D. Even South Asia and Commonwealth of Independent States (e.g., India) and Southeast Asia (e.g., Singapore) each accounts for only 5–6 percent of global total R&D facilities. In the Americas, the Middle East, and Africa, the presence of R&D facilities is generally rather limited.

These findings on R&D facilities are consistent with earlier work on global innovation networks in the ICT sector.[40] Through an "outside-in" geographical configuration of R&D facilities theorized in Chapter 3, more US and European firms consider East Asia (outside Japan) as an important location for their R&D activities. Based on a survey of 178 ICT transnational corporations, De Prato and Nepelski (2013) found that in 2009, US and European firms had respectively 16 percent and 18 percent of their R&D centers located in East Asia. These US and EU firms also owned 29 percent and 22 percent of R&D centers in East Asia. These facilities in East Asia attracted substantial R&D expenditure by European semiconductor firms (16 percent, as compared to 9 percent in their US facilities) and US semiconductor firms (12 percent, as compared to only 4 percent in their European facilities and 1 percent in their Japan centers). Their follow-up study of almost 4,500 R&D centers by about 210 global lead firms in 2011 and 2015 pointed to the strong network effect of R&D internationalization in the ICT sector such that "countries establish R&D relationships with countries that they are already connected with. This type of clustering reveals that there are strong 'local' linkages."[41]

In sales and marketing, the offices of these 41 firms are more evenly distributed globally. As evident in Figure 4.5 (lower pie charts), these firms have 2,083 sales and marketing offices worldwide, significantly more than their manufacturing and R&D facilities combined (833 facilities). In general, there is still a visible concentration of these offices in Triad macroregions, but it is less significant than in R&D facilities. There are more sales and marketing offices distributed in other developing macroregions for obvious market access reasons. There is also no significant difference after the Big 5 lead firms are removed. These Big 5 are all in telecommunications equipment from the three Triad macroregions; they alone account for 871 or 42 percent of total sales and marketing offices worldwide among all 41 firms interviewed! Even in semiconductors (lower right pie chart), the data in Figure 4.5 show less geographical concentration of sales and marketing offices in East Asia (Northeast and Southeast) due to the market reach necessary in Europe and the US and other developing macroregions. As the senior vice president and chief technology officer of top ten European IDM-36 argued, market proximity "is very critical. Some of the customers don't even engage with you unless you have some local presence and local support. We are basically talking about major market segments—China, the US, and Europe." These macroregions outside Asia all have higher shares of sales and marketing offices among the 41 firms relative to their shares of offices in the semiconductors segment (all facilities or only wafer fabs). This reflects the highly globalized market reach in the different segments of global electronics today.

## Conclusion

The geographical configurations of production in the global electronics industry shifted further in favor of East Asia during the 2010s. More complex and intensified than the earlier decades of internationalization since the early 1990s examined in Chapters 1 and 2, this coevolutionary shift occurred at both the industry level through different interfirm production networks and at the intrafirm level within specific global lead firms. This empirical chapter has analyzed the emergence and dominance of East Asia in this significant reconfiguration of production in the four major segments of global electronics—semiconductors, personal computers, mobile handsets, and televisions (with flat panel displays). In each of these segments, virtually all top ten lead firms have engaged their manufacturing partners, mostly from East Asia (Taiwan, Singapore, South Korea, and China), to fabricate their semiconductor chips or to assemble their ICT end products.

Table 4.8 has summarized the key trends in these major segments during the 2010s, and they should be understood in relation to the evolving national-institutional contexts in Table 1.2 and industry contexts in Table 2.1. In semiconductors, the geographical shift toward East Asia, particularly Northeast Asia comprising South Korea, Taiwan, China, and Japan, has been most apparent. During the 2010s, this capital- and technology-intensive segment witnessed a much higher degree of outsourcing by fabless and "fab-lite" semiconductor firms to cutting-edge foundry providers based in East Asian economies. In all three end-product segments, while China emerged as the leading destination for the location of final assembly sites, its overwhelming significance was most evident only in notebook PCs. In desktop PCs, mobile handsets, and TVs, the shares of final assembly by other macroregions outside East Asia were also quite substantial, reflecting the global reach of OEM firms in these ICT products and their desire for final assembly in close proximity to end markets. This highly differentiated role of China in the different segments of ICT global production networks offers a more nuanced mapping and understanding than the China-centric analysis of ICT exports and production in the recent literature on global value chains.[42]

Among the forty-four firms represented in my study interviews during the 2017–2018 period, such geographical configurations of production centered in East Asia are also evident. East Asia, particularly Northeast Asia, has served as the most significant macroregion in electronics manufacturing for forty-one firms. This East Asia–centered configuration of manufacturing facilities is less evident in their R&D activities. In semiconductors, the US and Europe have remained as the critical sites for R&D activities among leading IDM and fabless firms from these macroregions. In sales and marketing, a more evenly distributed geographical pattern is also evident in their worldwide offices located in different macroregions.

By the late 2010s, these complex cross-regional production networks in the various segments of global electronics had connected diverse worlds of electronics through global integration between and within firms. Theorized in Chapter 3, this industrial-organizational process of strategic coupling in turn brought together OEM lead firms in the Triad macroregions of North America, Western Europe, and East Asia, and their East Asian manufacturing partners to constitute a globalized mosaic of interconnected worlds in electronics production (see also Figures 3.1 and 4.2). Mapping closely onto Chapter 3's GPN 2.0 theory, the next two empirical chapters will explicitly explain the "how" (firm strategies) and the "why" (causal dynamics) of these complex geographical configurations of global production networks during the 2010s.

## CHAPTER 5

# Firm Strategies and Organizational Innovations in Production Networks

THE GEOGRAPHICAL CONSOLIDATION OF semiconductor production and final assembly of end products in the information and communications technology (ICT) sector into East Asian locations by the late 2010s took place through an industrial-organizational innovation that is perhaps *the* most critical phenomenon in the twenty-first-century global economy—the emergence of multiple and complex global production networks that crisscross different macroregions and national economies. In these networks operating at different geographical scales, global lead firms cooperate with their strategic partners and key suppliers to compete against other lead firms in the same industrial segment. Put in its historical contexts specified in Chapters 1 and 2 (see also summary Tables 1.2 and 2.1), this organizational innovation might not appear to be entirely new, as some of the trends in the internationalization of production were already observed in the 1980s and the 1990s.[1] Indeed, Saxenian's (1991, 1994) early analysis of Silicon Valley-based high-tech production in the United States during the late 1980s has identified interfirm partnership as "new supplier relationships"—the key factor for Silicon Valley's resurgence vis-à-vis the continual decline of Massachusetts's Route 128 in the US electronics industry. Her pioneering study found that lead firms in Silicon Valley sought local suppliers nearby as their network partners so that they could be "drawn into the design and development of new systems and components at a very early stage; and they are typically more closely integrated into the customer's organization in this process."[2]

While these localized production networks largely benefitted from agglomeration economies in high-tech clusters such as Silicon Valley,[3] their industrial organization on much larger geographical scales—from the macroregional to the global—in the form of global production networks entails different and more diverse firm strategies. As Chapter 3's GPN 2.0 theory has conceptualized (also Figure 3.2), firm-specific strategies of intrafirm coordination, interfirm control and partnership, and extrafirm bargaining can help us understand better how global lead firms respond effectively to different causal dynamics and risk conditions by reconfiguring their increasingly globalized production networks. These organizational innovations in global production networks pursued through different firm-level strategies in turn explain the evolving geographical configurations of global electronics production that became much more centered in East Asia by the late 2010s—an empirical phenomenon having already been mapped out fully in Chapter 4 (see Table 4.8 for a summary).

Focusing on the innovative organization of electronics global production networks during the late 2010s, this empirical chapter maps directly onto my earlier conceptualization of firm strategies and organizational innovations in Chapter 3's penultimate section. Here, I examine intrafirm coordination in sourcing and production by lead firms and interfirm control and partnership relationships between lead firm customers and their suppliers in the four major segments of global electronics analyzed in the previous chapter: semiconductors, personal computers (PCs), mobile handsets, and consumer electronics (i.e., TVs). Less attention is paid to the strategy of extrafirm bargaining due to the lack of data at the firm level, but the issue will be brought to the fore where relevant (e.g., US sanctions on China's Huawei since 2019). Still, this chapter's production network–level analysis of firm strategies in different segments is set within the evolving "extrafirm" national and industry contexts and the semiconductor segment's unique characteristics described in Chapters 1 and 2.

With these caveats, I argue that understanding firm strategies is a necessary step in the causal explanation of the complex geographical configurations of electronics production networks centered in East Asia by the late 2010s. Nevertheless, this chapter's analysis of firm strategies (i.e., "how" in the GPN 2.0 theory) needs to be read together with next chapter's analysis of causal dynamics (i.e., "why") to form a complete explanation of such evolving configurations of global production networks. The chapter has two main sections that analyze these organizational specificities in intra- and interfirm production networks governed by different firm strategies. Here, it is important to reiterate Chapter 3's argument that firms in the same networks may adopt different strategies and/or they may exercise multiple strategies in different networks. For each firm, the precise combination of its strategies can only be ascertained through detailed empirical analysis, as in the following sections. Whenever possible and consistent with the earlier chapters, the same sequence of product segments—starting with semiconductors before ICT end products such as PCs and mobile handsets—will be followed within each subsection.

To begin, the next section explains the intrafirm coordination in sourcing and production among lead firms that may also engage in some outsourcing by developing interfirm relationships. The second section examines in detail how, through these interfirm relationships, lead firms interact with key suppliers and manufacturers in semiconductors, PCs, mobile handsets, and TVs. As major customers, some lead firms exercise strong control in their interfirm relationships, whereas other lead firms develop strategic partnership with key suppliers in East Asia and elsewhere. In the concluding section, these main findings on firm strategies and organizational dynamics are linked back, in a summary table, to Chapter 4's key observations on the changing geographical configurations of electronics global production networks during the 2010s.

## Intrafirm Coordination: Internalization and Outsourcing by Lead Firms

To determine how lead firms in global electronics organize their production networks during the 2010s, it is necessary to unpack these networks and examine the organizational relationships within and among firms theorized in Chapter 3 (see also Table 3.3). The following subsection outlines such production networks in semiconductors and ICT end products before offering some quantitative data on the firm-specific sourcing of key components. Using custom data covering 2015 and 2018 from IHS Markit/Informa Tech (see Appendix A), I analyze these intricate organizational relationships between highly specialized firms in core components (e.g., semiconductor chipsets and panel displays) and their lead firm customers, i.e., original equipment manufacturing (OEM) lead firms in PCs and mobile handsets. In the second subsection, I draw on qualitative data from 64 interviews with senior executives from 44 firms (see Appendix B) to elaborate on three strategic considerations in sourcing that are critical to lead firms in their intrafirm coordination (insourcing) and interfirm relationships (outsourcing).[4]

### Insourcing versus Outsourcing in Different Product Segments

Figure 5.1 illustrates the codominance of integrated device manufacturing (IDM) and fabless/foundry firms in the actual organization of global production networks in semiconductors as of the late 2010s. As was described earlier in Chapter 2's industry context, intrafirm coordination through vertical integration has been highly significant among the world's leading IDM firms from the early days of integrated circuits during the 1960s. Since then, IDM firms have not only internationalized their labor-intensive chip

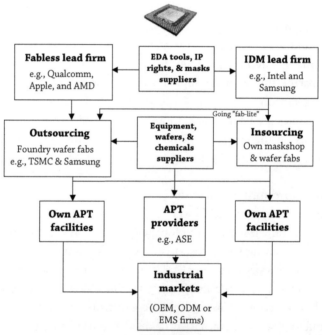

Note: APT = assembly, packaging, and testing; EDA = electronic design automation; EMS = electronics manufacturing services; IDM = integrated device manufacturing; IP = intellectual property; ODM = original design manufacturing; OEM = original equipment manufacturing

FIGURE 5.1. Lead firms and their organization of semiconductor production networks.

Source: Interviews with senior executives of semiconductor IDM, fabless, and APT firms.

assembly and testing facilities, but more importantly also their capital- and technology-intensive wafer fabs (see 2015–2022 firm-specific fab locations in Table 4.2). Intrafirm coordination remains as the most significant strategy for IDM firms to organize their global production networks and represents a lead firm-centric form of organizing production networks theorized in Chapter 3 (see Table 3.4 and Figure 3.3a).

With the maturing and increasing codominance of the fabless-foundry model of wafer fabrication or "chip" production during the 2010s (see Table 2.1 summary), however, semiconductor production networks have become much more complex. The market and technology leadership of IDM or fabless firms depends not only on their firm-specific capabilities but also a great deal on a small group of highly specialized and yet powerful suppliers of chip design tools, fab equipment and materials, and foundry service providers. As indicated in Figure 5.1, even IDM lead firms must develop sophisticated interfirm relationships with these specialized suppliers. In Chapter 2, this small group of suppliers includes US-based chip design and implementation software firms, such as Cadence, Synopsys, and Mentor Graphics, and vendors of intellectual property libraries, such as ARM and Synopsys. For fabless chip design firms, these intellectual property vendors offer a royalty model backed by top foundry providers such that fabless firms can get access to intellectual property in standard cell libraries, memories, and microprocessors and pay for them through their foundry service providers, such as TSMC or GlobalFoundries. The royalty paid to these intellectual property suppliers is based on wafer sales and thus can be built into wafer pricing quoted by the foundry provider.[5] As will be exemplified in the next section on interfirm relationships, the sourcing relationship between semiconductor fabs (owned by IDM firms and foundry providers) and specialized equipment suppliers is also very intimate. This intermediate market is dominated by several US firms (e.g., Applied Materials, KLA, and Lam Research) and European/Japanese firms (e.g., ASML, Tokyo Electron, and Nikon).

This innovative intrafirm coordination and interfirm organization of complex global production networks in semiconductors are further mapped out in Figure 5.2 (extending the simpler Figure 4.2). Intrafirm coordination takes place among IDM firms (e.g., Intel, Samsung, and Micron) that locate their chip-design functions in major research and development (R&D) centers near to corporate headquarters or in-house fabs (see earlier analysis in Chapter 4's penultimate section). In the classic case of the world's top IDM firm, Intel epitomizes this close integration of R&D and manufacturing that has been fundamental to its core competitive advantage. Gordon Moore, arguably the most famous among Intel's cofounders due to his "Moore's Law" of annual doubling of chip density, recalled that

> when we set up Intel, we decided we would avoid that split between R&D and manufacturing. We would be willing to accept somewhat less efficient manufacturing for a more efficient technology transfer process. In order to avoid the difficulties of internal technology transfer, we made the R&D people actually do their development work right in the production facility, and we have continued that (with some variation) ever since.[6]

Over time, though, in-house chip production among IDM firms has become much more internationalized through new fabs in foreign locations, e.g., Intel in Ireland and Israel, Micron in Singapore, and Samsung in the US and China (see fab details in Table 4.2). Their back-end facilities in chip assembly, packing, and testing services are also located close to in-house fabs worldwide. Taken together, this intrafirm sourcing strategy among IDM firms exists alongside increasingly sophisticated interfirm relationships with their highly specialized suppliers of software, intellectual property rights, materials, and equipment from a small number of advanced countries, such as the US, Japan, Germany, and the Netherlands. During the 2010s, some suppliers of these equipment and materials also emerged in the East Asian economies of South Korea, Taiwan, and China due to growing domestic ecosystems supported by proactive industrial policy (see their changing national-institutional contexts in Table 1.2).

In ICT end products, Chapter 4 has already analyzed in depth the geography of final assembly by global lead firms that rely on a mix of in-house facilities and external suppliers known as original design manufacturing (ODM) firms or providers of electronics manufacturing services (EMS). Figure 5.3 outlines these production networks of global lead firms and their key suppliers and production partners. As Chapter 4's analysis has noted, OEM lead firms interact differently with their ODM firms and EMS providers. In notebook PCs, OEM lead firms have developed and maintained very close relationship with their ODM partners that provide design and R&D work in Taiwan and final assembly primarily in China.

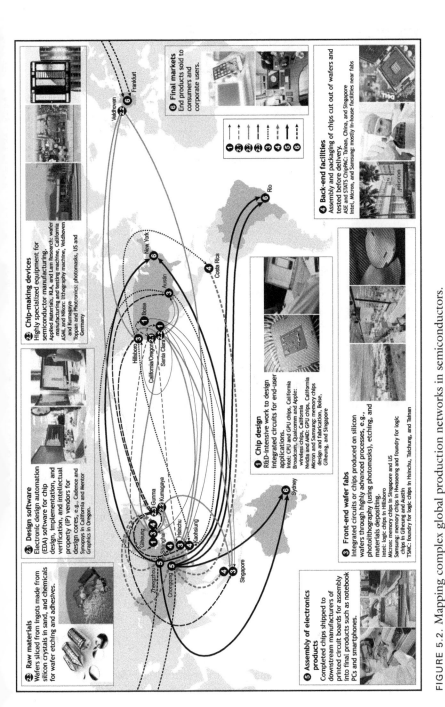

FIGURE 5.2. Mapping complex global production networks in semiconductors.

Photo credits: with permission from flickr.com/Stratman²; pxhere.com/Alan Levine and 912827–2017; Pexels.com/ThisIsEngineering, Pok Rie, PhotoMIX Co, and Pixabay; ASML.com/43687, 48545, and 48546; iStock.com/coddy, knowlesgallery, FroggyFrogg, ranz12, and gorodenkoff; TSMC.com/inc017_946 and waferc008_2536; and Micron.com.

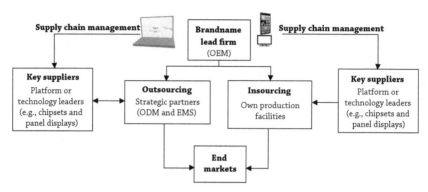

FIGURE 5.3. OEM lead firms and their production networks in ICT end products.
Source: Interviews with senior executives of OEM lead firms.

In desktop PCs, mobile handsets, and TVs, lead firms typically exercise more arm's-length relationships with their outsourcing partners. On the right-hand side of Figure 5.3, some top OEM lead firms in these segments also procure a mix portion of their desktop PCs, mobile handsets, and TVs from in-house facilities and EMS providers in different locations worldwide. Intrafirm coordination in final assembly tends to be more prevalent in these segments than in notebook PCs (see also Table 3.4).

A complete production network analysis of these ICT end products, however, must examine diverse types of firm actors theorized in Chapter 3 (Table 3.3) and go beyond mapping the intra- and interfirm organization of final assembly only. As illustrated in Figure 5.3, it entails a close examination of the sourcing of key components by OEM lead firms that relate to the critical role of specialized suppliers in different production network configurations (see also Figure 3.3). Tables 5.1–5.3 present proprietary data on the procurement unit share of key suppliers among the top six OEM lead firms in PCs and mobile handsets in four to five major components in 2015 and 2018. A thorough analysis of these data reveals three important findings on the sourcing strategies of OEM lead firms in their organization of global production networks:

(1)     the prevalence of both intrafirm coordination (insourcing) and interfirm outsourcing,

(2)     the dominant role of platform and technology leaders in several core components critical to ICT end products, and

(3)     the different supply chain practices among dominant suppliers.

First, while production networks are conceptualized as lead firm–centric in Chapter 3 (Figure 3.3) and Figures 5.1 and 5.3, this can take the organizational forms of both intrafirm coordination and interfirm outsourcing. Indeed, the majority of top OEM lead firms in PCs and mobile handsets have sourced core components from technology leaders and outsourced substantially production of their final products. Key suppliers of these core components in semiconductors and panel displays are often lead firms in their own right or, in some specific cases, platform leaders (e.g., Intel and Qualcomm in processor chips respectively for PCs and mobile handsets). In production, most OEM lead firms have engaged design work from ODM firms and final assembly services from these ODM firms and/or other EMS providers. As was detailed in Chapter 4, most of these ODM/EMS providers are from Taiwan, but their assembly facilities are located primarily in China and elsewhere (e.g., India and Mexico).

There are important exceptions to this interfirm outsourcing, though, mostly among East Asia–based OEM lead firms due to substantial corporate investment over two decades that was facilitated by more patient domestic financial systems, family- or state-linked ownership, and supportive home government policies within their evolving national-institutional and industry contexts (summarized in Tables 1.2 and 2.1). In notebook PCs (Table 5.1), top OEM firms from the US (Hewlett-Packard, Dell, and Apple) and Taiwan (Asus and Acer) outsource virtually all components and production to third-party firms. Only Lenovo (China) produces some 53 to 57 percent of their notebook PCs in in-house facilities. But all top six lead firms source key components from external platform/technology leaders. This sourcing pattern is also replicated among the top six desktop PC OEM firms, except that even two US OEM firms, Dell and Apple, engage some in-house production facilities for the final assembly of a significant portion of their desktop PCs (see Table 5.2). In mobile handsets (Table 5.3), the extent of intrafirm sourcing is much more pronounced among the top three market leaders of Samsung, Huawei (China), and Apple. Here, all three OEM firms procure in-house a significant share of their application processors, the core chip designed to support applications in the mobile operating systems of their smartphones. For example, Apple has been sourcing all of its A-series application processors for iPhones from internal silicon design, though the fabrication of the different generations of these A-series chips has been completely outsourced to foundry providers such as Samsung before 2016 and, thereafter, TSMC (Taiwan)—see a full case

TABLE 5.1. World's top 6 notebook PC OEM firms by procurement unit share of key component suppliers, 2015 and 2018 (in percent and US$)

| Key components and suppliers | HP | | Lenovo | | Dell | | Asus | | Acer | | Apple | |
|---|---|---|---|---|---|---|---|---|---|---|---|---|
| | 2015 | 2018 | 2015 | 2018 | 2015 | 2018 | 2015 | 2018 | 2015 | 2018 | 2015 | 2018 |
| **1. Processors (CPU)** | | | | | | | | | | | | |
| Intel (%) | 81.2 | 89.1 | 81.2 | 89.1 | 81.2 | 89.1 | 100.0 | 89.1 | 81.2 | 89.1 | 100 | 100 |
| AMD (%) | 18.8 | 5.1 | 18.8 | 5.1 | 18.8 | 5.1 | - | 5.1 | 18.8 | 5.1 | - | - |
| ASP ($)[1] | 85.0 | 135 | 85.0 | 135 | 85.0 | 135 | 85.0 | 135 | 85.0 | 135 | 85.0 | 135 |
| **2. Wireless chips** | | | | | | | | | | | | |
| Broadcom (%) | 36.7 | 46.6 | 36.7 | 46.6 | 36.7 | 46.6 | 36.7 | 46.6 | 36.7 | 46.6 | 36.7 | 46.6 |
| Qualcomm (%) | 31.8 | 29.2 | 31.8 | 29.2 | 31.8 | 29.2 | 31.8 | 29.2 | 31.8 | 29.2 | 31.8 | 29.2 |
| Intel (%) | 23.5 | 8.1 | 23.5 | 8.1 | 23.5 | 8.1 | 23.5 | 8.1 | 23.5 | 8.1 | 23.5 | 8.1 |
| ASP ($) | 3.6 | 0.57 | 3.8 | 0.57 | 3.8 | 0.57 | 4.2 | 0.59 | 3.7 | 0.59 | 4.5 | 0.59 |
| **3. DRAM memory** | | | | | | | | | | | | |
| Samsung (%) | 20.7 | 44.8 | 55.2 | 44.8 | 8.0 | 44.8 | 67.6 | 44.8 | - | 44.8 | - | 44.8 |
| SK Hynix (%) | 34.0 | 31.0 | 44.8 | 31.0 | 34.7 | 31.0 | 26.2 | 31.0 | 53.2 | 31.0 | 31.8 | 31.0 |
| Micron (%) | 45.4 | 24.2 | - | 24.2 | 57.2 | 24.2 | 6.3 | 24.2 | 46.8 | 24.2 | 68.2 | 24.2 |
| ASP ($) | 32.1 | 125 | 24.0 | 125 | 29.0 | 125 | 23.6 | 131 | 25.2 | 131 | 29.7 | 131 |

## 4. Display

| | | | | | | | | | | | |
|---|---|---|---|---|---|---|---|---|---|---|---|
| AUO (%) | 23.2 | 32.9 | 26.4 | 24.9 | 27.7 | 0.3 | 26.2 | 31.4 | 38.2 | 2.1 | - |
| BOE (%) | 7.4 | 31.2 | 32.2 | 19.8 | 32.2 | 3.9 | 30.0 | 4.3 | 22.9 | - | 22.3 |
| Innolux (%) | 24.0 | 25.4 | 28.5 | 12.9 | 18.7 | 40.0 | 35.2 | 39.2 | 31.2 | - | - |
| LG Display (%) | 21.5 | 6.8 | 10.8 | 28.1 | 12.1 | 19.3 | 6.4 | 25.0 | 6.0 | 46.0 | 72.6 |
| ASP ($) | 80.2 | 42.0 | 41.3 | 46.6 | 42.4 | 48.6 | 41.6 | 46.0 | 38.1 | 40.6 | 83.9 |
| **Production** | | | | | | | | | | | |
| In-house (%) | 2.1 | - | 57.0 | - | - | - | - | - | - | - | - |
| Compal (%) | 9.5 | 53.1 | 15.3 | 59.0 | 73.3 | 26.0 | - | 34.2 | 29.7 | - | - |
| Quanta (%) | 27.5 | 30.0 | 4.4 | 17.3 | 1.0 | 18.1 | 41.2 | 30.2 | 48.3 | 74.9 | 74.0 |
| Wistron (%) | 26.7 | 9.2 | 9.9 | 19.1 | 25.7 | 12.1 | - | 26.6 | 10.8 | - | - |
| Top 3 ODM (%) | 80.8 | 90.8 | 29.6 | 95.4 | 100 | 88.3 | 100 | 91.0 | 88.9 | 100 | 100 |
| **Total units (mil)** | **35.0** | **40.3** | **37.0** | **21.9** | **26.7** | **15.4** | **13.6** | **13.7** | **12.0** | **17.9** | **10.4** |
| Market share (%) | 19.7 | 24.7 | 20.8 | 12.3 | 16.3 | 8.6 | 8.3 | 7.7 | 7.3 | 10.1 | 6.4 |

[1] Average selling price (ASP) refers to the largest supplier, based on data provider's best estimate of supplier pricing along with insights from industry-wide conversations.

Source: Data from IHS Markit/Informa Tech Custom Research for GPN@NUS Centre, July–October 2016 and 2019.

TABLE 5.2. World's top 5 desktop PC OEM firms by procurement unit share of key component suppliers, 2015 and 2018 (in percent and US$)

| Key components and suppliers | Lenovo | | HP | | Dell | | Acer | | Asus | | Apple | |
|---|---|---|---|---|---|---|---|---|---|---|---|---|
| | 2015 | 2018 | 2015 | 2018 | 2015 | 2018 | 2015 | 2018 | 2015 | 2018 | 2015 | 2018 |
| **1. Processors (CPU)** | | | | | | | | | | | | |
| Intel (%) | 81.0 | 89.1 | 81.0 | 89.1 | 81.0 | 89.1 | 81.0 | 89.1 | 100 | 89.1 | 100 | 100 |
| AMD (%) | 19.0 | 5.1 | 19.0 | 5.1 | 19.0 | 5.1 | 19.0 | 5.1 | - | 5.1 | - | - |
| ASP ($)[1] | 73.0 | 106 | 73.0 | 106 | 73.0 | 106 | 73.0 | 106 | 73.0 | 106 | 73.0 | 106 |
| **2. Wireless chips** | | | | | | | | | | | | |
| Broadcom (%) | 40.0 | 46.6 | 40.0 | 46.6 | 40.0 | 46.6 | 40.0 | 46.6 | 40.0 | 46.6 | 40.0 | 46.6 |
| Qualcomm (%) | 30.0 | 29.2 | 30.0 | 29.2 | 30.0 | 29.2 | 30.0 | 29.2 | 30.0 | 29.2 | 30.0 | 29.2 |
| Intel (%) | 20.0 | 8.1 | 20.0 | 8.1 | 20.0 | 8.1 | 20.0 | 8.1 | 20.0 | 8.1 | 20.0 | 8.1 |
| ASP ($) | 4.1 | 0.57 | 4.3 | 0.57 | 4.5 | 0.57 | 4.1 | 0.59 | 4.4 | 0.59 | 4.5 | 0.59 |
| **3. DRAM memory** | | | | | | | | | | | | |
| Samsung (%) | 40.0 | 44.8 | 40.0 | 44.8 | 40.0 | 44.8 | 40.0 | 44.8 | 40.0 | 44.8 | 40.0 | 44.8 |
| SK Hynix (%) | 35.0 | 31.0 | 35.0 | 31.0 | 35.0 | 31.0 | 35.0 | 31.0 | 35.0 | 31.0 | 35.0 | 31.0 |
| Micron (%) | 25.0 | 24.2 | 25.0 | 24.2 | 25.0 | 24.2 | 25.0 | 24.2 | 25.0 | 24.2 | 25.0 | 24.2 |
| ASP ($) | 31.7 | 53.5 | 37.7 | 53.5 | 35.3 | 53.5 | 30.3 | 55.2 | 29.3 | 55.7 | 37.6 | 55.7 |

## 4. Display

| | | | | | | | | | | | | |
|---|---|---|---|---|---|---|---|---|---|---|---|---|
| AUO (%) | 20.0 | 8.8 | 23.2 | 10.2 | 24.9 | 13.6 | 31.4 | 43.0 | 28.7 | 46.3 | 2.1 | - |
| BOE (%) | 10.6 | 35.1 | 7.4 | 22.9 | 19.8 | 32.3 | 4.3 | - | 3.9 | - | - | - |
| Innolux (%) | 24.0 | 31.4 | 24.0 | 11.9 | 12.9 | 13.7 | 39.2 | 36.0 | 40.0 | 37.3 | - | - |
| LG Display (%) | 25.5 | 21.2 | 21.5 | 37.7 | 28.1 | 35.5 | 25.0 | 21.0 | 19.3 | 16.4 | 46.0 | 100 |
| ASP ($) | 44.8 | 49.7 | 80.2 | 53.6 | 46.6 | 58.1 | 46.0 | 51.9 | 48.6 | 56.8 | 40.6 | 82.9 |
| **Production** | | | | | | | | | | | | |
| In-house (%) | 100 | 56.2 | - | - | - | 32.5 | - | - | - | - | 11.5 | 18.0 |
| Foxconn (%) | - | - | 55.5 | 50.7 | 62.2 | 35.9 | - | - | - | - | 45.6 | 45.8 |
| Compal (%) | - | 43.8 | - | - | - | 27.8 | 34.2 | 36.3 | - | 30.0 | - | - |
| Pegatron (%) | - | - | 44.5 | 49.3 | - | - | 9.4 | 10.2 | 100 | 50.0 | - | - |
| Top 3 (%) | 0.0 | 43.8 | 100 | 100 | 100 | 67.5 | 90.6 | 89.8 | 100 | 90.0 | 88.5 | 82.0 |
| **Total units (mil)** | **18.0** | **21.0** | **18.9** | **19.3** | **16.4** | **17.1** | **4.6** | **5.0** | **1.5** | **2.6** | **4.3** | **2.6** |
| Market share (%) | 19.1 | 23.6 | 20.0 | 21.7 | 17.4 | 19.2 | 4.9 | 5.7 | 1.6 | 2.9 | 4.6 | 2.9 |

[1] Average selling price (ASP) refers to the largest supplier, based on data provider's best estimate of supplier pricing along with insights from industry-wide conversations.

Source: Data from IHS Markit/Informa Tech Custom Research for GPN@NUS Centre, July–October 2016 and 2019.

TABLE 5.3. World's top 6 smartphone OEM firms by procurement unit share of key component suppliers, 2015 and 2018 (in percent and US$)

| Key components and suppliers | Samsung | | Huawei | | Apple | | Xiaomi | | Oppo | | Vivo | |
|---|---|---|---|---|---|---|---|---|---|---|---|---|
| | 2015 | 2018 | 2015 | 2018 | 2015 | 2018 | 2015 | 2018 | 2015 | 2018 | 2015 | 2018 |
| **1. Processors (AP)** | | | | | | | | | | | | |
| Qualcomm (%) | 55.8 | 30.9 | 32.3 | 19.0 | 50.0 | - | 44.7 | 66.0 | 69.4 | 65.0 | 37.6 | 58.0 |
| MediaTek (%) | - | 10.2 | 25.7 | 5.0 | - | - | 36.5 | 34.0 | 30.6 | 35.0 | 62.4 | 42.0 |
| In-house (%) | 33.0 | 55.4 | 39.8 | 76.0 | 43.5 | 100 | - | - | - | - | - | - |
| APU ASP ($)[1] | 16.2 | 17.6 | 16.8 | 21.6 | 25.7 | 20.7 | 21.1 | 12.1 | 11.8 | 12.2 | 10.9 | 12.3 |
| **2. Wireless chips** | | | | | | | | | | | | |
| Broadcom (%) | 66.6 | 50.0 | 100 | 38.0 | 100 | 100 | 20.0 | 8.0 | - | - | - | - |
| Qualcomm (%) | 33.0 | 38.0 | - | 20.0 | - | - | 43.5 | 49.0 | 69.0 | 62.0 | 38.0 | 46.0 |
| MediaTek (%) | - | - | - | - | - | - | 36.5 | 39.0 | 31.0 | 38.0 | 62.0 | 54.0 |
| ASP ($) | 2.8 | 3.3 | 2.9 | 3.1 | 2.6 | 3.3 | 2.4 | 2.5 | 2.3 | 2.5 | 1.5 | 2.4 |
| **3. Memory** | | | | | | | | | | | | |
| Samsung (%) | 90.0 | 84.0 | 20.8 | 43.0 | 28.6 | 14.0 | 26.7 | 56.0 | 25.2 | 89.0 | 50.0 | 78.0 |
| SK Hynix (%) | 6.7 | - | 8.3 | 23.0 | 64.4 | 22.0 | 26.7 | 33.0 | 49.6 | 11.0 | 50.0 | 22.0 |
| Micron (%) | 3.3 | 5.0 | 50.0 | 7.0 | - | 29.0 | 46.6 | 4.0 | 25.2 | - | - | - |
| ASP ($) | 17.5 | 27.4 | 10.5 | 21.6 | 21.7 | 31.2 | 17.1 | 26.3 | 6.6 | 24.6 | 18.1 | 21.9 |

## 4. Display

| | | | | | | | | | | | | |
|---|---|---|---|---|---|---|---|---|---|---|---|---|
| BOE (%) | 27.1 | 29.4 | 26.0 | 26.1 | - | - | 6.4 | 17.6 | 1.7 | 23.4 | 1.2 | 33.6 |
| Innolux (%) | - | - | 16.9 | 1.9 | 37.0 | - | - | - | - | 9.8 | - | - |
| Japan Display (%) | 1.4 | 0.4 | 31.4 | 5.3 | 36.4 | 26.9 | 17.5 | 3.1 | 14.4 | 17.0 | - | - |
| Samsung DSP (%) | 61.0 | 64.2 | 4.5 | 6.3 | 26.7 | 31.4 | - | 7.7 | 23.0 | 30.4 | 25.3 | 32.2 |
| ASP ($) | 10.5 | 36.5 | 16.3 | 17.8 | 9.4 | 40.6 | 12.7 | 17.9 | 17.0 | 28.0 | 17.0 | 25.5 |

## 5. Rear image sensor

| | | | | | | | | | | | | |
|---|---|---|---|---|---|---|---|---|---|---|---|---|
| Omnivision (%) | 26.6 | - | 20.3 | 45.0 | - | - | 40.0 | 18.0 | 6.5 | 8.0 | 18.8 | - |
| Samsung (%) | 46.8 | 72.0 | - | - | - | - | 23.1 | 42.0 | - | 25.0 | 26.5 | 50.0 |
| Sony (%) | 26.6 | 28.0 | 39.1 | 55.0 | 100 | 100 | 36.9 | 40.0 | 93.5 | 67.0 | 54.7 | 50.0 |
| ASP ($) | 4.4 | 4.8 | 7.0 | 5.9 | 7.0 | 7.3 | 2.2 | 4.2 | 7.0 | 4.6 | 7.0 | 3.0 |
| **Total units (mil)** | **320** | **290** | **109** | **206** | **232** | **205** | **73.1** | **119** | **45.7** | **115** | **45.2** | **104** |
| Market share (%) | 23.2 | 20.6 | 7.9 | 14.6 | 16.8 | 14.5 | 5.3 | 8.4 | 3.3 | 8.2 | 3.3 | 7.4 |

[1] Average selling price (ASP) refers to the largest supplier, based on data provider's best estimate of supplier pricing along with insights from industry-wide conversations.

Source: Data from IHS Markit/Informa Tech Custom Research for GPN@NUS Centre, July–October 2016 and 2019.

study of evolving relationships among these three industry leaders in the next section (subsection on sharing risks).

With its own semiconductor division, Samsung has been sourcing a mix of its application processors from in-house Exynos-series and technology leader Qualcomm (Snapdragon-series) and MediaTek (Helio- and MT-series), but the share of its in-house sourcing in Table 5.3 grew substantially from 33 percent in 2015 to 55 percent in 2018. Huawei is following a similar practice, and its in-house sourcing of application processors from HiSilicon (Kirin-series), its wholly owned fabless chip design subsidiary, also increased rapidly from 40 percent in 2015 to 76 percent in 2018. Among all OEM lead firms in mobile handsets, only Samsung has sufficient internal capabilities in semiconductor fabrication to provide a greater share of in-house supply in key semiconductor components over time, e.g., up to 55 percent of application processors, 84 percent of memory chips, 64 percent of panel displays, and 72 percent of imaging sensors (for cameras) in 2018. As was discussed in the previous chapter (Table 4.5), Samsung also assembled all of its 290 million smartphones in in-house manufacturing facilities in Vietnam and other locations worldwide in 2018. In short, Samsung's smartphone production network best resembles the lead firm-centric control model in Figure 3.3(a).

Second, while most studies in the literature tend to privilege OEM lead firms as the most powerful actor in global production networks,[7] Tables 5.1–5.3 and Figure 5.3 show a clear but small group of dominant platform and technology leaders as key suppliers in several core semiconductor components critical to end products, such as PCs (e.g., notebooks, desktops, and tablets) and mobile handsets.[8] Here, stable and enduring relationships between these dominant suppliers and their OEM lead firm customers have been developed and reproduced over time due to their leadership in technology (e.g., processor chips in PCs and mobile handsets and panel displays in premium smartphones) and scale economies coupled with strong process technology (e.g., memory chips). As platform or technology leaders, these dominant suppliers charge higher average selling prices (ASPs) in general.[9] In notebook PCs (Table 5.1), for example, the ASP increase in DRAM chips supplied by Samsung was most significant, from the range of $24–$25 in 2015 to well over $125–$133 in 2018—approaching the cost of main processor chips ($135)![10] As was noted in Chapter 2's discussion of its home country institutional support (also Table 1.2), Samsung's technological and cost leadership in this core component has been strong ever since the late 1990s. Its two main competitors, SK Hynix (South Korea) and Micron (US), had lower market shares and higher ASPs in 2018, respectively at the range of $130–$139 and $133–$142—a reflection of the escalated worldwide demand for ICT products with ever more memory storage (see Table 2.5).

Among all these dominant suppliers, the most significant platform leader is Intel, which has enjoyed an almost monopoly position in the PC market for central processing unit (CPU) chips ever since inventing the first microprocessor Intel 4004 in 1971 (see Chapter 2; also Figure 2.1). In both notebook and desktop PCs (Tables 5.1 and 5.2), Intel's commanding market share of 81 percent in 2015 was increased further to 89 percent in 2018 among all PC OEM firms (and 100 percent in ASUS and Apple PCs). The ASP of its CPU chips in both categories also increased significantly from $73 in desktops and $85 in notebooks in 2015 to respectively $106 and $135 in 2018. Moreover, Intel's market power was so enormous that it did not lower its ASP even for the world's largest PC OEM firms. Intel's ASP for processors in 2015 and 2018 was the same among all top PC OEM firms, unlike market leaders in wireless communication chips (Broadcom) and DRAM chips (Samsung) that offered lower ASP for Hewlett-Packard, Lenovo, and Dell—the top three OEM lead firms in both notebook and desktop PCs.

To sustain this almost monopolistic market power, Intel exercised strong intrafirm coordination by relying completely on in-house chip design and fabrication in its facilities located in the US, Ireland, and Israel (see Table 4.2). As was indicated in Chapter 2, Intel's proprietary technological knowhow and vast suites of patents in microprocessors remained as its core competitive advantage. Through vertical integration in this part of PC global production networks, Intel was able to carve out an unparallel position even among the largest PC OEM firms. In comparison, Intel's fabless CPU competitor, AMD, could only compete by achieving lower cost through outsourcing wafer fabrication to its former spin-off foundry provider, GlobalFoundries' fab in Malta, New York (see Chapter 4). In 2018, the ASP of its CPU chips were $96 in desktops and $122 in notebooks, on average $10–$13 lower than Intel's chips. But as will be noted in Chapters 6 and 7, the global market and technology competition for microprocessors has since become more intensified after AMD switched to TSMC's cutting-edge process node for its latest CPU chips in 2019 and

Apple decided to replace Intel CPU chips with its own M-series chips fabricated by TSMC for its Macintosh PCs from 2020 onward.

In mobile handsets (Table 5.3), OEM lead firms are also subject to the strong bargaining power of technology leaders, such as Broadcom and Qualcomm in application processors and wireless networking chips and Samsung in memory and panel displays. But these OEM firms operate different sourcing preferences in comparison with their PC counterparts. Most rely on *fewer* key suppliers for components in semiconductors and panel displays. Having developed its own application processors for all iPhones, even Apple has to source all wireless chips from Broadcom and image sensors from Sony, whereas Xiaomi, Oppo, and Vivo have mostly two major suppliers: application processors and wireless chips from Qualcomm and MediaTek (Taiwan) and memory chips from Samsung and SK Hynix. Some lead firms have also developed in-house suppliers in application processors (e.g., Huawei and Samsung) and other core components (e.g., Samsung in memory, display, and image sensor). Overall, technology leaders are relatively less powerful in the mobile handset segment in which OEM lead firms have internalized some of the core components or engaged in a dual-sourcing strategy to avoid lock-ins to specific suppliers.

Third, the sourcing strategies of OEM lead firms in these ICT end products are further complicated by the different supply chain practices of dominant suppliers in semiconductors. To optimize the efficiency of their production networks, lead firms must take into account this additional complexity associated with the insourcing/outsourcing practices of their chip suppliers. For example, top fabless firms in Table 2.2—Broadcom, Qualcomm, Nvidia, MediaTek, and AMD—are now major suppliers to OEM lead firms in PCs and mobile handsets. But as was discussed in Chapter 4, their foundry providers are based primarily in East Asia (Taiwan, South Korea, Singapore, and China). As will be examined further in the next subsection, the complex organizational relationships between these fabless firms and their foundry providers and back-end chip assembly, packaging, and testing service providers are crucial to the strategic considerations of OEM lead firms in ICT end products due to their concerns with supply capacity, timely delivery, and risk mitigation. One might think that these supply chain issues are less troubling for IDM firms with their own fabs, such as Intel, Samsung, SK Hynix, and Micron. With the exception of Intel, the high geographical concentration of these fabs in specific locations—Samsung and SK Hynix in South Korea and Micron in the US and Singapore—also poses a major organizational challenge to OEM lead firms' geographical configuration of global production networks centered in East Asia. This geographical risk is also increasingly apparent in the case of flat panel display supply that, as documented in Table 4.7, has shifted massively toward China since the late 2010s.

### Strategic Considerations in Firm-Specific Sourcing

The above network analysis of intrafirm coordination and interfirm sourcing practices during the late 2010s has revealed significant differences even among lead firms in the same product segment (e.g., Intel vs. Qualcomm in semiconductors and Samsung vs. Apple in mobile handsets). To explain these innovative organizational dynamics that are consistent with Chapter 4's findings on their geographical configurations centered in East Asia, a more firm-specific analysis of sourcing motivations and strategies is necessary. The following examination of qualitative data from 64 interviews with senior executives from 44 firms in my study points to three strategic considerations in their sourcing decisions:

(1)    insourcing to speed up innovation and time-to-market,
(2)    in-house manufacturing important to risk mitigation, and
(3)    outsourcing to focus on technology development and to leverage partner's scale economies.

Clearly, these strategic considerations are related to the causal dynamics of optimizing cost-capability ratios, sustaining market development, and managing risks in the GPN 2.0 theory (Chapter 3; also Table 3.4). The market imperative and risks conceptualized in Table 3.4 are related to the above strategic considerations (1) and (2), and a lead firm is more likely to adopt the intrafirm coordination strategy when competitive pressures from these two causal dynamics are relatively high. While generally less critical to intrafirm coordination, cost-capability ratios can be reduced through capability building (innovation and technology development) and leveraging partner's cost advantage in both strategic considerations (1) and (3). The full explanation of these causal dynamics in relation to firm-specific strategies and geographical configurations, however, will be offered in the next chapter that completes the analytical circle and specifies the causal mechanisms of global production networks.

Among all forty-four firms represented in interviews[11] and as summarized in Table 4.8, insourcing or in-house manufacturing tends to be more prevalent among IDM firms in semiconductors and OEM lead firms from East Asia: Japan (e.g., Sharp and Toshiba), South Korea (e.g., Samsung and LG), and China (e.g., Lenovo and Huawei). Many of these East Asian lead firms were founded as manufacturers of electronics products. Among US and European lead firms, in-house manufacturing is more common if the lead firm is concerned with system integration with proprietary software and solutions and testing for quality and other reasons (e.g., customer requirements). Among some IDM and OEM lead firms, this intrafirm coordination of manufacturing activities is driven by their strategic concerns with innovation for faster time-to-market and risk mitigation through securing in-house production quality and supplier capacity.

First, OEM lead firms from East Asia in PCs, mobile handsets, and TVs rely particularly on the closer integration of R&D and manufacturing to speed up innovation and time-to-market. In these ICT end product segments, this strategy of intrafirm coordination can respond effectively to the immense pressure of market imperative theorized in Chapter 3 (Table 3.4). Apart from facilitating innovation, in-house manufacturing can speed up time-to-market, a key competitive advantage in today's fast-moving global electronics markets. The vice president for corporate innovation of top three consumer electronics OEM-3 from East Asia explained:

> We have to be advanced in terms of speed and technology. As we are doing so, we may cost a little extra, but the market itself is growing. So, we can do it that way. We can save additional costs associated with vertical integration because that was the time saved when we innovated in that sense. There are a lot of outsourcing manufacturers out there. But we couldn't tolerate in terms of their [slower] speed.

Samsung, for example, famously takes on average one year or less to launch new mobile handsets and TVs, whereas Sharp needs up to three years.

Second, insourcing can serve a lead firm by allowing it to mitigate supply risk by avoiding capacity problems at key suppliers and, sometimes, to benchmark internal factories against outsourced partners. As noted in Table 3.4, this supply risk condition is highly relevant for pursuing intrafirm coordination of production networks. In semiconductors, in-house fabs can be critical to managing supply capacity. The head of Asia Pacific marketing of top 10 European IDM-41 noted that there is clearly advantage in keeping the full vertical control of technology and manufacturing because it's yours. You don't have any strong dependency factor based on what is going to be the arbitration made by the suppliers [foundry]. At some point these guys also have limited capacity, and they may decide to do some arbitration there—to arbitrate between this or that customer. Ultimately down the line, there will be a trickle-down effect on your end customers because they will be impacted. So, what's the best thing here to do? It's probably a mix.

This sourcing mix refers to an intrafirm strategy of in-house fabs for high-mix low-volume chip products and outsourcing for high-volume low-mix products. As will be discussed in the next section, such high-mix products require tight technology and product design integration due to their small-batch and/or highly customized production (e.g., for OEM customers in automotive).

In ICT end products (PCs, smartphones, and TVs), this intrafirm coordination of production networks and "head-to-head" benchmarking against outsourced partners in interfirm production networks also takes place in both final assembly and the manufacturing of core components. As the market leader in mobile handsets, for example, Samsung has insourced most of its core components for smartphones, from semiconductor chips to glass covers and batteries, and assembled them in its own facilities in Vietnam, India, South Korea, China, and worldwide (see Tables 4.5, 4.7, and 5.3). And yet Samsung has taken external benchmarking seriously in order to push its intragroup suppliers to strive for greater technological improvement and efficiency gains. The vice president for chip design in top fifteen US Fabless-42 described how it became an external supplier for Samsung and served as a benchmark for its internal suppliers of smartphone panels and display drivers:

> Even though the panel makers have their own internal supply chain, usually the pricing is not as good. Once you have just one supply chain, one supplier for a long period of time, then that supplier will become very lazy. Samsung's mobile division, as a company, cannot rely on a single supplier. Even though they have their own internal supplier, they would also from time to time want to invite external suppliers to try. But for us, these are very difficult to judge because sometimes you succeed and sometimes you fail. As an external supplier, we also judge on

a case by case to decide whether we want to engage or not. We need to make sure Samsung is indeed serious in looking for a second source.

His observation on Samsung is also confirmed by the managing director of semiconductor IDM-31's Southeast Asian manufacturing, who noted: "Why Samsung needs others to supply them? This is risk management and the competition they want to maintain because they are leading in the industry. . . . Samsung makes this strategy to keep competition. They want to collect up-to-date market and technology information, because today if they buy from in-house, in-house can charge them higher or they always have internal arguments."

Third, my interviews with many senior executives of OEM lead firms show that over time, more of them prefer production outsourcing, particularly in final assembly, to focus on technology development and to leverage outsourced partners' economies of scale—both can contribute to lower cost-capability ratios that are much more significant for interfirm relationships (see Table 3.4). In semiconductors, a few IDM firms, such as STMicroelectronics (France/Italy), Infineon (Germany), and Texas Instruments (the US), have gone "fab-lite" and sourced technologically advanced wafers from Taiwan's foundry providers, such as TSMC and UMC.[12] As was explained by the vice president of a leading semiconductor firm SE-43 from Taiwan, these IDM firms do not have the most advanced process because "they are all doing fab-lite or R&D-lite now. So they just sell their products and do their unique ones [in-house]. Like Infineon and STM, they may still be making display, power, and auto chips." This production outsourcing also occurs in the more labor-intensive segment of semiconductors—back-end services in assembly, packaging, and testing (APT). A significant number of top IDM firms have outsourced partially or completely these services to leading APT providers, such as ASE (Taiwan), Amkor (the US), and STATS ChipPAC (Singapore), in order to leverage their enormous scale and expertise. Explaining why it entered into a joint venture with a top APT service provider by selling 60 percent of its China facility to this provider, the senior vice president and chief technology officer of another top ten European IDM-36 said:

> I think it's an extremely smart move on our part. We can still continue to enjoy the internal factory's cost while having the flexibility in the same factory. . . . If you have any spillover in demand, naturally it

doesn't require any kind of requalification on anything. It just increases the order, just that you have to pay a little bit more to your partner— so, increase of flexibility that way. I think more importantly it's because we can leverage our partner's manufacturing management expertise.

As outsourced partners, these lead providers of APT services can identify specific products or modules to negotiate for collaboration even with the world's largest IDM lead firms (e.g., Intel, Micron, and Samsung). While having their own in-house APT facilities (see Figure 5.2), these top IDM lead firms may have a relatively smaller market share and thus production volumes in specific semiconductor products or modules (e.g., Intel in baseband chips for smartphones and Samsung in CMOS sensors). While insourcing APT services in fabricating microprocessors (Intel) and memory chips (Micron and Samsung), these IDM firms cannot match the same scale economies and operational efficiency enjoyed by leading APT providers. To the chief operating officer of top Asian semiconductor firm SE-30, this is how his firm can leverage its market share in specific product segments to capture substantial outsourcing business from IDM firms, such as Intel, Micron, Samsung, Infineon, NXP, and others. To him, SE-30 has turned its growing market share into what he terms "market entitlement," i.e., leverage in specific semiconductor product categories.

As was discussed in Chapter 4 (see also Tables 4.3–4.6), this tendency toward outsourcing also takes place in ICT end products when OEM lead firms from the US, Europe, and increasingly East Asia, work with ODM firms and EMS providers to design and/or assemble their products. Situated within the national-institutional and industry contexts described in Chapters 1 and 2, this coevolutionary move in favor of international outsourcing started in the late 1980s (see also summary Tables 1.2 and 2.1). But significant shifts in firm strategy toward interfirm control and partnership emerged in the next two decades in tandem with more geographically distanced and organizationally sophisticated global production networks. In my study focusing on the 2010s, more OEM lead firms want to focus on technology development rather than manufacturing. This strategy can be achieved when they divest existing production facilities to ODM firms or EMS providers, which then become their external suppliers. How then do these outsourced partners manage their interfirm relationships with key customers who became more powerful in governing increasingly global-ized production networks by the late 2010s?

## "Customer Is King": Interfirm Control and Partnership Relationships

In my study, there is strong evidence that the geographical configurations of electronics production networks pivoting toward East Asia in the 2010s are shaped by supplier firms' relationships with major customers. To ac-count for these trends in the interconnected worlds of global electronics summarized in Table 4.8, we need to specify empirically complex inter-firm relationships in these production networks. As Chapter 3's GPN 2.0 theory has already conceptualized (also Table 3.4), customer-supplier re-lationships are shaped by several causal drivers that will be examined fully in the next chapter. Suffice to say here that the need for customer orienta-tion represents a key market imperative in shaping production network configurations. As was discussed in the earlier subsection, production outsourcing is also critical to optimizing cost-capability ratios—another important causal driver of interfirm relationships. Similarly, risk conditions are significant in driving firms to share risks through interfirm partnership.

Overall then, interfirm relationships in electronics global production networks exhibit different degrees of control and partnership, depending on the relative significance of these different competitive dynamics and risk conditions (summarized in Table 3.4). The following detailed em-pirical analysis is based on qualitative material from 64 interviews with se-nior executives of 44 firms comprising 36 global lead firms and 8 foundry, ODM, and key component suppliers (see Appendix B). Since many of these lead firms and their ODM/foundry partners and suppliers are in the same production networks, their information and claims can be cross-examined and treated with circumspection. Specifically, I analyze four ways in which lead firms govern interfirm production networks—(1) and (2) in semiconductors and (3) and (4) in ICT end products:

(1)    developing deep relationships with long-term customers in industrial markets,

(2)    sharing risks with internal and external customers in semicon-ductors,

(3)    optimizing total cost of ownership through supply chain con-trol, and

(4)    serving as strategic partners through customization and dedicated facilities.

### Developing Long-Term Relationships in Industrial Markets

Some lead firms have successfully developed long-term interfirm partnership relationships with their key customers who have become influential
in their locational choice of R&D and production facilities. This market
imperative occurs particularly in intermediate goods or industrial markets,
such as semiconductors and their automotive customers, where semiconductor lead firms supply key modules or components to OEM firms in
other industries on the basis of long-term contracts. In these industrial
markets, interfirm cooperative relationships can take ten or more years to
establish and nurture. Chapter 4 has analyzed the globally dispersed geography of R&D in semiconductors and East Asia-centered chip production
(see also Table 4.8). In East Asia, some semiconductor lead firms have
established production facilities in Japan and China specifically to cater to
their long-term customers in automotive and industrial machinery. In automotive, product design and qualification of semiconductor suppliers can
take two to three years. As the vice president of top ten European IDM-32
described, "The partnership with the customer in automotive is very long
term. But the good thing is that once you are in, it's very difficult to go
out. The qualification of a new supplier for them is very expensive."

To sustain such long-term relationships, IDM-32 has set up design centers near its major automotive OEM customers in different East Asian
economies. These OEM customers in the automotive industry also offer
very long-term contracts up to twenty years to their most preferred suppliers (semiconductor lead firms), because of the wide-ranging application
of key components in the different models of automotive end-products.
The senior vice president and chief technology officer of another top ten
European IDM-36 pointed to this observation on its key customers:

> In automotive, our customers are very sticky because the risk involved
> is extremely high. Let's just say qualifying. Imagine I have a power
> transistor that can be used in a battery control system in automotive.
> In order to use that transistor, they have to qualify first in the module.
> And that module is applied to many models and then you apply to
> [top European auto OEM-A]. [OEM-A] has a series of car models as
> well. And you then have to qualify all of that. The qualification cost is

astronomically high. So, once it's qualified, you basically lock in for the lifetime of that model. And we usually have to sign a fifteen- or even twenty-year supplier agreement. That means we are going to continue supplying. Technology doesn't even matter, because you could be a little bit more advanced, but reliability and quality are always the No.1 consideration.

This concern with the reliability of its microcontrollers and power management chips for OEM customers in the automotive industry explains why IDM-36 still keeps seven not-so-advanced "legacy" fabs in the US, Europe, China, and Singapore—as noted in Chapter 4 (endnote 14) and Table 4.8, despite its overall strategy of going "fab-lite" by sourcing from TSMC advanced logic chips and microcontrollers (with embedded memory) that utilize TSMC's leading-edge process nodes at 28 nm or lower.[13] Working closely with its major automotive customers and their first-tier suppliers of electronics modules in these macroregions, IDM-36 can achieve strong competitive advantage in high-performance mixed-signal analogue products through its stringent qualification processes, high functionality and reliability design architecture, extensive design-in timeframes, and long product life cycles.

The key to IDM-36's successful products for automotive is the tight coupling of its product design with greater functionalities within the very stringent reliability and quality parameters of its automotive OEM customers. This requirement for close interfirm integration at the product level gives IDM-36 more advantage over its competitors—US fabless design firms that rely on Taiwan's foundry providers for chip production. Without their own fabs, these fabless firms can only design their analogue products based on the chip fabrication platforms developed by their foundry providers located in East Asia. This weaker integration between analogue product designs by fabless firms and outsourced fabrication platforms allows IDM-36 to win over its automotive OEM customers who are much more concerned with the functionalities, reliability, and secured long-term supply of microcontrollers and power chips in their end products. As will be discussed in Chapter 7, this secured supply of qualified chips became extremely critical in ensuring the continuous mass production of vehicles by automotive firms during the global chip shortage in late 2020 and throughout 2021.

In short, semiconductor lead firms have built tightly coordinated design and road map relationships with key customers. In some cases, semiconductor lead firms may give up some control of their own design process to enable "design-in" and roadmap alignment with their key OEM customers. Through this process of "design-in," the products of some lead firms are selected as strategic components in systems and key platforms for automotive OEM lead firms. In automotive, large first-tier suppliers to OEM assemblers (i.e., car makers) can also become powerful "customers" of semiconductor lead firms. Coming from different macroregions, these first-tier suppliers, such as Denso, Bosch, and Continental, serve top automotive OEM lead firms (e.g., BMW, Mercedes, Toyota, Volkswagen, and so on). These "mega-suppliers" have become powerful customers of IDM lead firms because their relationships with automotive OEM firms are no longer one-way in favor of OEM lead firms.[14] The vice president of top ten European IDM-32 reflected on this:

> This is where the power play comes in and actually this is also a very delicate situation for us, and we have to manage these with extreme care. Tier one big boys have a lot more power against the OEMs because they are huge. They can walk in and say "I don't want your business." I know they also walk away from business with OEMs because if they find it not profitable, they don't want to do it. When we handle them together with OEMs, we have to be very careful. We cannot just go in and tell [top T1 supplier-A] that "[top European auto OEM-A] says this." It will be a complete disaster.

Even within semiconductors as an industrial market, customer-supplier relationships are often strategic and long term throughout different parts of the chip production network—from specialized equipment for cutting-edge fabs to front-end wafer fabrication and back-end chip assembly, packaging, and testing (see illustration in Figures 5.1 and 5.2). In semiconductor fab equipment dominated by a small number of highly specialized equipment suppliers, such as Applied Materials and Lam Research from the US and ASML from the Netherlands, the relationship between customers (IDM firms and foundry providers with fabs) and equipment suppliers can be very intimate. To maintain its leadership in process technology, for example, TSMC invested over $1.3 billion in 2018 in the industry's most advanced extreme ultraviolet (EUV) lithography equipment for chip making from ASML of the Netherlands—the only supplier of EUV machines indispensable to cutting-edge fabs operating advanced process technology nodes at 10 nanometer (nm) or lower. In volume production since mid-2020, TSMC's Fab 18 in Tainan alone required more than 50 EUV sets, but ASML produced about 31 sets in 2020 and estimated 48 sets in 2021 and up to 55 sets in 2022. Priced per set at over US$100 million in 2018 and €200 million in 2021, ASML had 75 percent of global market share in advanced lithography equipment in 2018 and coinvested in EUV technology development with all top three semiconductor firms—Intel, Samsung, and TSMC.[15]

The senior vice president of top ten IDM-39 from East Asia explained this critical importance of mutual lock-ins with their long-term equipment suppliers such as ASML:

> We have early joint development agreements with equipment suppliers. But I think at the end of the day, it is an open competition. Because there are fewer suppliers, the buyer cannot do without the suppliers. If the suppliers having struggled relation, you can't say "Forget with what I said today. Oh, next generation it will be this process node. I am going to work with Nikon instead of ASML." It's just not possible. The buyer has to work with ASML.

His view is supported by the vice president and chief supply chain officer of another top ten non-Asian IDM-34. While IDM-34 has invested in its own proprietary test technology and automated testing equipment, it has developed very long-term and intimate relationships with two leading US-based equipment suppliers—Applied Materials and Lam Research:

> Our strategy is not to become a photolithography company or whatever. But it is our relationship that starts very early back end and pathfinding part of research all the way through technology development. We spent a lot of time growing our relationship [with equipment suppliers] that is a part of life cycle. And the value to Lam Research and Applied Materials is to be with us all the way through. We do believe that there is some value in that, and we have North America–based research and design. We try to leverage that as the supply base as much as we can. As you well know, semiconductor is an electrical-chemical process. So there is a lot of secret sauce that all of us try to get. But I think it's like how do you take a highly capable Lam Research tool

for example and match it with your know-how? And you need Applied Materials. But we definitely try not to do one-offs. Then you have no head-to-head. I cannot take a Lam and have it compete with Applied Materials.

In wafer fabrication, the relationship between fabless technology leaders and their foundry providers is also highly strategic precisely because of this "secret sauce" in the electrical-chemical process of wafer fabrication, indicated in the above quote by IDM-34, the very sophisticated manufacturing process (600+ steps in most advanced nodes; many debugs and long engagement), and enormous complexity in capacity allocation based on demand forecast and negotiation three to four months ago or even earlier.[16] As will be discussed at length in the Apple-Samsung-TSMC case in the next subsection, it is very difficult to switch foundry providers due to different foundry designs (device libraries) and very short product life cycles that will be over after the switch of foundry providers. The senior manager of top five Fabless-33 further noted:

> This kind of relationship must be strategic. The foundry gets involved from the beginning. Because once the design is set, it defines the product. You must know which process meets the most confident performance request and can have a best-cost structure. So, we must involve foundry from the beginning. And if you want to design, you must get the device library fundamentals from them. The device library is the whole. You must compare one by one and choose one.

Because of its strategic relationship with its preferred foundry provider, another top five fabless firm from the US, Fabless-29, can achieve some flexibility in wafer production and negotiations. Due to its low-volume orders, other leading foundry providers are unwilling to offer such production flexibility. To do so, Fabless-29 puts its process engineers on site at its foundry provider to ensure smooth transition in process technology toward cutting-edge nodes. This flexibility in turn enables it to develop a strong relationship with its end customers—OEM lead firms in PCs. As its corporate vice president explained,

> Because of the relationship between us and [foundry-A], we are able to do some very specific types of wafers and some very specific projects. I think we get a little more of their attention than from [top foundry-B or foundry-C—both market leaders], and we've been very successful.

If I get [top PC OEM-A] to do a certain architecture, a certain product family and we need to reduce cost whatever, we can pick up the
phone and call [foundry-A]: "Hey, gives us a deal there," whereas we
couldn't imagine doing that unless it was a much bigger scale with [top
foundry-B or foundry-C].

Even in semiconductor back-end services discussed in the previous section, long-term partnerships can be developed between IDM firms and
their outsourced providers of assembly, packaging, and testing services.
Despite its top three market position in a key category of semiconductor
devices, non-Asian IDM-34 has decided to work closely with Taiwan's ASE
in these back-end services because of the latter's enormous scale and technical strength in good manufacturing practices and unique understanding
in the materials science and advanced packaging of semiconductor dies. To
the vice president and chief supply chain officer of top ten IDM-34,

the relationship [with ASE] is more than just a cost optimization. It's
more than a purchasing relationship. It's definitely a strategy. It also
goes towards our supplier quality, and we try to integrate the supplier
quality, their quality management systems, so that we have one face
to our customer. . . . We do a lot of new product introduction and as-
sessments, a lot of design of engineering experience, and a lot of DoEs
[design of experiments] with them. They see a lot of different people's
dies. They see a lot of people's products. And of course, then you have
the risk of they see yours too. So, I think there is a shared learning that
goes beyond the transaction.

### Sharing Risks with Customers in Semiconductors

In semiconductors, some lead firms have engaged in interfirm partnership to share risks through dual-purpose technology development for
both internal and external customers. Cutting-edge process development
and production facilities for new-generation integrated circuits can be extremely costly to build, to the tune of several billion dollars in the 2010s
and tens of billions in the 2020s (see more on this causal driver of financial
discipline in Chapter 6). An IDM lead firm can sometimes better justify
such massive investment in new production facilities if it has secured an
end product customer within the same business group (intrafirm network)
and its new facilities can possibly serve as a foundry to external fabless or

fab-lite customers in the same or different industries (interfirm networks). In East Asia and as contextualized in Table 1.2, such business groups and family-owned enterprises are highly influential in the domestic economies. Indeed, some East Asian IDM firms are part of larger business groups that produce end products in ICT and other industries (e.g., Samsung from South Korea and Sharp and Toshiba from Japan). As the senior vice president of top ten IDM-39 from East Asia further elaborated,

> By having our sister company's product and being able to do that very early on is a higher risk. But knowing there is not guaranteed but at least a good chance if you deliver a proper product to the sister company you can be selected for mass volume, you can take more risks. So, we can start process activity early. In one way, this is the path paved for the rest of the foundry customers [external OEM firms]. And it's a win-win situation—to pave the path, you pay the cost and you can get in early. Or you can come in later with less risk and still enjoy the results that will come later.

As was introduced in my earlier discussion of semiconductors in Chapters 2 and 4, one such prominent example involves two powerful technology leaders in wafer fabrication by the late 2010s—Samsung and TSMC—and their interfirm cooperative relationships with top fabless chip design firms and key OEM customers in mobile handsets. The evolving and yet competing leadership between Samsung and TSMC in process technology among their top foundry fabs in East Asia listed in Table 4.2 has profound implications for the industrial-organizational geography of semiconductor and smartphone production networks examined in Chapter 4 (see summary in Table 4.8).

The following detailed case study illustrates how Samsung and, later, TSMC provide exclusive foundry services to Apple by fabricating its different generations of application processors powering iPhones, iPads, and other Apple wireless devices, and how their evolving interfirm partnership relationship since 2007 has been underpinned or even undermined by this strategy of risk sharing with customers. After the mid-2010s, the switch from Samsung to TSMC as Apple's exclusive chip foundry supplier has stimulated the massive growth in foundry fab capacity and technological leadership centered in East Asia.

The story begins with Samsung fabricating application processor chips for Apple's iPhones since its launch in June 2007 and benefiting from sharing the risk of costly investment in its dual-purpose fabs with such major external customers.[17] Their interfirm partnership, however, did not last long when Apple asked for dedicated fab facilities from Samsung in the mid-2010s. To sustain its strategic pursuit of dual-purpose fabs for both internal Samsung and external fabless customers, Samsung refused Apple's demand for dedicated fabs and ended its new process development for Apple's application processor chips. Since 2016, TSMC has taken over this challenging foundry chip supply deal from Apple and invested heavily in new cutting-edge fab facilities dedicated to Apple's in-house designed chips—A10-series onward and, from 2020, M-series for Mac PCs and iPads. Interestingly though, this TSMC-Apple partnership has heralded a new era of global technological leadership in semiconductor manufacturing centered in Taiwan (TSMC) and South Korea (Samsung) since the late 2010s.

Back in 2007, Samsung's System LSI and foundry facilities in Austin (US) and, later in 2009, Giheung (South Korea) fabricated chips for both its internal customer—application processors in Samsung's mobile handsets—and external customers, e.g., Samsung-designed application processors for iPhones (first generation to 3GS) and Apple-designed A4–A7 and A9 application processors for iPhone 4 to iPhone 6S (see fab details in Table 4.2). Its Austin fab in the US was first built in the early 1990s to make memory devices for OEM customers in PCs, such as Dell (also in Austin), and to overcome political pressure against foreign dumping lobbied by Micron and other US semiconductor firms, as was noted in Chapter 1's discussion of US protectionist trade policy then.

When Samsung secured Apple's first order for the core application processor (Samsung S5L8900, an ARM-based RISC SoC) in its newly launched iPhone in 2007, it did not build a dedicated fab and instead used its Austin fab to serve Apple's order. Apple's own forecast for the first generation iPhones was rather low, and it secured supply of its application processor from Samsung, which was aggressively building up its external customers and took on Apple's order.[18] Later in around 2009–2010, Samsung successfully converted within ten months its Austin fab S2's 32 nm process from making memory chips to foundry for logic chips in order to fabricate Apple-designed application processors for its new iPhones and iPads—from the A4 series for iPhone 4 and first iPad in 2010 to eventually up to the A9 series in 2015–2018. Meanwhile, its S1 fab in Giheung was opened in 2009 to serve both internal Exynos series and external foundry customers such as Apple. This dual-purpose logic worked well for Samsung and justified its heavy investment in new process technology (from 32 nm to 14 nm for Apple's A4–A9 chips) and capacity in foundry fabs in Austin and Giheung, resulting in significant foundry capacity growth in South Korea and the US during the 2010s in Table 4.1.

By 2016, however, Apple switched completely to Taiwan's TSMC for its A10 chips using then TSMC's latest 16 nm process technology, because its demand for dedicated fabs from Samsung could not be met by the latter's dual-purpose fab strategy for risk sharing with internal demand and external customers. To secure this exclusive "trophy" order from Apple, TSMC offered custom processes and dedicated facilities within its Fab 12 and Fab 15, respectively located in Taiwan's Hsinchu and Taichung (Table 4.2), to fabricate Apple's application processor chips—from 16 nm in 2016 to 10 nm in 2017 and 7 nm in 2018–2019. In mid-2020, its latest 5 nm Fab 18 in Tainan entered into mass production and counted Apple as its earliest and most important customer. Between 2016 and 2021, Apple's share of TSMC's rapidly growing total revenue in Table 2.4 increased from 17 percent to 25 percent.[19] Daniel Nenni, a senior industry specialist at SemiWiki .com, observed that TSMC was able to win over Apple's chip business due to not only its cutting-edge process technology but also its exclusive interfirm partnership that demands dedicated fab facilities: "Apple essentially leases the TSMC fabs. Apple gets most favored nation status with custom processes that only Apple has access to. It really is a unique and very profitable relationship that has evolved over 10+ years."[20] To entice Apple, TSMC even freezes the leading process node in the last quarter of each year for Apple so that it can have high volume production of A-series chips for newly launched iPhones (and iPads), and the same practice will repeat after next fall's launch of these new devices.

Meanwhile, this case illustrates Samsung's determination in pursuing dual-purpose foundry fabs in its organization of semiconductor production network. Samsung gave up the opportunity to make Apple's application processors from the A10 series onward primarily because of Apple's demand for dedicated fabs. Samsung perceived the investment required for new process technology transition in these dedicated facilities would be enormous, risky, and likely unprofitable. For example, a 12-inch fab at 40 nm would need about $90–$110 million of capital expenditure in specialized equipment. By 2020, this expenditure would rise rapidly to over $2 billion for 28 nm and exponentially to $13 billion for 14–16 nm and $15 billion for 10 nm, $18 billion for 7 nm, $20 billion for 5 nm, and over $25 billion for 3 nm.[21] Giving up a very large external customer (i.e., Apple) led to a drop in Samsung's foundry revenue between 2015 and 2018 (see Table 2.4) when all top three foundry providers had revenue increase. It also resulted in delay in Samsung's investment in new cutting-edge foundry fabs. In comparison to TSMC's 7 nm process entering in mass production by 2018 in its Hsinchu Fab 12 and Taichung Fab 15, Samsung's 7 nm process in Hwaseong's Fab S3 first entered into mass production only in early 2019. By 2020, Samsung foundry was able to recover from the loss of Apple's order and to grow substantially its foundry business after it had gained many more orders from AMD, Nvidia, and Qualcomm. In Table 2.4, its revenue of $14.5 billion in 2020 not only quadrupled its 2018 revenue but also enabled it to leapfrog GlobalFoundries and UMC to be by far the second largest foundry provider after TSMC.

Indeed, the cutting-edge application processors for mobile devices with 5G and artificial intelligence functions in the early 2020s require the most advanced process technology in chip manufacturing. In August 2018, GlobalFoundries, then second largest foundry provider after TSMC, decided to give up transition to the latest technology node at 7 nm or below, effectively ruling out its role in making cutting-edge chips for wireless communications. It chose instead to focus on improving its existing 12–14 nm process technology in its Malta F8 (see Table 4.2), mostly for fabricating AMD's microprocessors. Experiencing delay in mass production at its 10 nm Fab D1X in Hillsboro (Oregon) and Fab 28 in Kiryat (Israel) in 2019, Intel continued to invest in its 7 nm Fab 42 in Chandler, Arizona, that will only be ready in 2021 or later. Meanwhile, TSMC and Samsung have started volume production of their 5 nm process in 2020, and will transit toward 3 nm process in 2022 and beyond (see Chapter 4 endnotes 12–13). The next chapter will discuss briefly their investment plans in the 2020s.

The extremely high investment cost of cutting-edge fabs since the mid-2010s explains why risk sharing with internal and external customers was critical in Samsung's decision not to support Apple's demand for exclusive fab capacity at 16 nm or below. At these latest technology nodes (7 nm in 2018, 5 nm in 2020, and 3 nm in 2022), TSMC essentially has to dedicate a fab's process node initially to Apple that demands exclusive access and custom process for its application processors used in latest iPhones and iPads. At the beginning of each technology frontier (16/10/7/5/3 nm), a fab's yield tends to be low, as any of the few hundred to a thousand steps in the fabrication process can go wrong. New but very expensive manufacturing and test equipment from ASML, Applied Materials, and so on also needs to be calibrated and optimized for volume production. Diagnosing and fixing bugs and problems in the entire wafer fabrication process is mostly done through trial and error, delicate recalibrations, and accumulated past learning and experience. This is the so-called secret sauce or tacit knowledge in semiconductor manufacturing that explains why by the late 2010s, existing top IDM firms (e.g., Intel) or foundry providers (e.g., Global-Foundries) could not catch up with TSMC's recursive learning-by-doing at the cutting-edge nodes and strong support from the wider ecosystem of top customers (e.g., Apple, HiSilicon, and Qualcomm) and highly specialized suppliers of equipment and software services.

At the interfirm organizational level, due to its agreement on the exclusive supply of custom process to Apple, a top foundry provider (i.e., Samsung or TSMC) normally cannot sign on new external customers until the fab's yield improves over time and mass production is achieved through ramping-up. This is where the yield-demand paradox might occur—low yield during high demand and high yield when demand drops. Apple's chip volume is typically high at the beginning of its latest product launch (often in the fall), when the foundry fab's custom process yield at the latest node is likely the lowest. But as the foundry fab's yield gets stabilized and capacity increases within three to six months, the demand from Apple for the same process node might be reduced due to the maturing product cycle and its pending new processor for the next-generation iPhones and iPads (i.e., demanding new custom process at even more advanced node). In 2016, Samsung's internal demand for the latest technology node (10 nm) in fabricating its Exynos 9000-series application processors for premium Galaxy S-series smartphones simply could not fill up the rest of its fab capacity when Apple's chip demand dropped. In absolute unit terms, Samsung's demand for the latest technology node was much smaller than Apple.

Unlike Apple's strategy of having only a very limited range of iPhone models utilizing the latest process nodes, Samsung has multiple series of premium and mass-market Galaxy smartphones. In 2018, its in-house Exynos 5000- and 7000-series application processors for mass market smartphones used less advanced technology nodes at 14–28 nm and were fabricated in older fabs, such as S2 in Austin.[22] But as indicated in Table

4.2, Apple's A12 chips in 2018 were already fabricated with TSMC's 7 nm process node in its Fab 12 in Hsinchu and Fab 15 in Taichung. This paradox of mismatch in chip demand and fab yield/capacity and risk sharing with intrafirm customers is also evident in TSMC's exclusive order from Apple. For example, TSMC lost out in the 20 nm node after supporting Apple's initial A9 chip business in 2015–2016 because the node was not used by other mobile handset customers then. While its 7 nm Fab 12 and Fab 15 were first dedicated to making Apple's A12 chips in 2018, it only began to make application processor chips for the next customer, Huawei, via a foundry contract with Huawei-owned fabless design firm HiSilicon in the second half of 2019.

As TSMC's second largest customer in 2019 and 2020 (after Apple), HiSilicon ironically posed a significant demand risk for TSMC's latest technology node due to unexpected restrictions imposed by the US government in May 2019 and 2020.[23] Huawei's ramp-up demand for its 7 nm Kirin 980 chips in 2019 had much to do with extrafirm bargaining relationships due to heightened geopolitical tensions in the Taiwan Strait and US-China relations since the mid- to late 2010s. As a top three smartphone vendor by 2015 (see Table 2.9), Huawei has actively reorganized its production network to mitigate extrafirm supply risk and to increase its network resilience. Apart from in-house chip development via its fabless subsidiary HiSilicon, it has also requested critical fabless chip suppliers, such as Qualcomm, Broadcom, and MediaTek, to source from foundry fabs in multiple locations outside Taiwan (e.g., Qualcomm sourcing from Samsung foundry in South Korea and SMIC in China and Broadcom and MediaTek from GlobalFoundries and UMC in Singapore). While this dual sourcing of key components on the basis of quality, supply stability and reliability, and pricing is possible, some cutting-edge chipsets are unique to fabs in specific locations due to peculiar process technology and production characteristics.

To Huawei, this critical extrafirm risk in chipset supply came to a head in mid-2020. Earlier on May 15, 2019, the former Trump administration had already imposed strict limits on US semiconductor firms supplying to Huawei by placing it on the US Commerce Department's "Entity List"—alternatively known as the "blacklist" for trade with the US. This executive move by then president Trump was widely seen as part of the worsening US-China trade war since March 2018. One year later on May 15, 2020, the US Commerce Department's Bureau of Industry and Security imposed further restrictions on the ability of Huawei and its fabless

HiSilicon to design and manufacture semiconductor products using US technology and software. This latest restriction on the export of US technology applies worldwide to Huawei's in-house semiconductor work and its key US fabless chip suppliers (e.g., Qualcomm) and East Asian foundry providers, such as Taiwan's TSMC (for HiSilicon, Qualcomm, and Broadcom), China's SMIC (for HiSilicon and Qualcomm), and South Korea's Samsung (for Qualcomm).

As noted at the beginning of this chapter (also Figures 5.1 and 5.2), all of these fabless firms use chip design software from top US electronic design automation firms, such as Cadence and Synopsys. The key foundry fabs of TSMC, Samsung, and SMIC are also fitted with chip production equipment from top vendors from the US, such as Applied Materials, KLA, and Lam Research. Even ASML from the Netherlands, the only supplier of extreme ultraviolet lithography machines for cutting-edge 3–7 nm foundry fabs of TSMC and Samsung, has sourced technology for its photolithography machines from such US suppliers as II-VI Inc and Lumentum Holdings that are subject to the same export restriction. These extrafirm US sanctions on Huawei and other Chinese semiconductor firms have led to significant reconfigurations of semiconductor and smartphone production networks since 2020.

In semiconductors, Huawei's supply chain was crippled. Losing Huawei's very substantial foundry business (via HiSilicon) also impacted on TSMC's revenue and the financial viability of its latest 5 nm fabs that entered into mass production in mid-2020. In 2019 and 2020, HiSilicon was TSMC's second largest customer (after Apple), accounting respectively for 15 percent and 13 percent of TSMC's total revenue.[24] In 2021, TSMC was expected to make up for the lost revenue from HiSilicon by increasing production for AMD and MediaTek that would become its second- and third-largest customers. In mobile handsets, Huawei responded in November 2020 by reorganizing its smartphone production networks. It decided to exit the low-to-medium-range smartphone market in China by selling its Honor unit to a consortium of thirty dealers backed by the Shenzhen government in China. After the divestment, Huawei's global smartphone share in 2021 is expected to be less than 4 percent or 45 million units in Table 2.9, a far cry from its peak market share of almost 20 percent and 240 million units in 2019.[25]

In summary, this extended case study of dramatically different interfirm strategies pursued by Apple, Samsung, and TSMC (and Huawei) in semiconductor and mobile handset production networks demonstrates how lead firms can compete and yet cooperate with each other through sharing risks with internal and external customers. In semiconductors, Apple and Samsung entered into interfirm partnership in wafer foundry services until Apple's complete switch to TSMC since 2016. OEM lead firms in mobile handsets are also capable of developing in-house processor chips to substitute for the need to source from external lead firms in semiconductors. To fend off this potential "competition" from their customers, top fabless firms such as Qualcomm and MediaTek have built extensive ecosystems or platforms around their chipsets by making it easy for other hardware and software firms to connect their products or services with their chipsets. In doing so, these fabless lead firms have also developed their own interfirm partnership through risk sharing with their key customers and ecosystem partners. In mobile handsets, Apple and Samsung (and Huawei) compete fiercely against each other by exercising strong control of their respective global production networks—Apple via interfirm control of its EMS providers (Foxconn and Pegatron) and Samsung via intrafirm coordination of its internal suppliers and in-house assembly facilities. In the next two subsections, I examine how such strategies of interfirm control and partnership matter in the evolving production networks of these ICT end products.

### Optimizing Total Cost of Ownership through Supply Chain Control

In PCs and mobile handsets, supply chain practices in interfirm relationships are more variegated and diverse than in semiconductors. Through my interviews with senior executives of twenty-one OEM lead firms and six ODM firms and key component suppliers, I have identified three models of supply chain management practiced by lead firms in these end products: supplier- or vendor-managed inventories (VMI), assigned-vendor assigned-price (AVAP), and lead firm buy-sell or "clean sheeting." The degree of interfirm control by lead firms in their global production networks, as was theorized in Chapter 3, increases from VMI to AVAP and finally to "clean sheeting." This in turn relates to a lead firm's management and technological capabilities. In VMI, OEM customers provide information on the products they outsource to ODM firms or EMS providers that typically take over the control and management of supply chains for these products. These ODM/EMS providers or "vendors" are therefore responsible for the timely availability of parts and components that go into their OEM customers' products. They negotiate directly with suppliers of parts and components for pricing, manage contract terms, and place order and hold the inventories, and therefore assume the cost of these inventories until they are assembled into finished products and shipped to their OEM customers.

In AVAP, the OEM lead firm determines the price and supplier allocation for each component, but the ODM firm or EMS provider decides on the timing, quantity, and supply capacity for the component. The lead firm has sourcing personnel who take charge of negotiations with suppliers on prices as well as allocation of total available market (e.g., share by each vendor) and turn-around maintenance (e.g., payment and cash flow processes). The lead firm's own resources (i.e., its own-badged personnel) may also be stationed with component vendors to "assign" supplies and inventories in order to control and manage parts indirectly. This is crucial to the OEM lead firm due to cost allocation and implications for cash flow. The inventory becomes a lead firm's cost once a finished product with the component(s) leaves the factory of its ODM/EMS vendor.

In the most aggressive form of interfirm control, an OEM lead firm engages directly in a buy-sell model or "clean sheeting" in its negotiation and outsourcing arrangement with ODM/EMS providers. This supply chain control model operates like a sheet of paper on which all factor costs, from raw materials to labor wages and productivity drivers, are individually itemized and added up to form the overall base-cost structure. This "shift-cost modeling" becomes part of the OEM firm's intellectual property and capability. Also known as "zero-base pricing," the OEM lead firm takes over the entire supply chain if its ODM or EMS provider is unable to get better pricing from parts suppliers. The lead firm negotiates all the terms and costs, actually buys the components, and sells them to its ODM/EMS providers. This model can be applied to parts or components that are more sensitive to cost and market fluctuations. But to exercise this supply chain control well, the OEM lead firm must have sophisticated capability to understand component costs, all the way down to raw materials.

Figure 5.3 earlier has outlined the production networks of global lead firms and their suppliers in PCs, mobile handsets, and TVs. Among twenty-one OEM lead firms in all segments of global electronics, the VMI model is most commonly practiced in the PC segment because of its simplicity for and ease of use by OEM customers. Very few lead firms adopt the clean sheeting model—the most explicit strategy of interfirm control. Those doing so, such as Dell since about 2010, are able to control as much as up to 75 percent of material costs. Ultimately, a lead firm is concerned with managing the total cost of ownership where supplier capability can make a major difference. As was described by the vice president of top five PC OEM-22, this total cost includes bill materials costs, transformation costs (e.g., overhead, shipping, and transport), and after-sales costs (e.g., warranty and quality assurance).

Exercising strong interfirm control of supply chains can also be costly such that few OEM lead firms can afford. Apple, for example, spent an enormous sum of capital expenditure on equipment to be placed with its key EMS providers in order to control supply by "owning" these factories (e.g., Foxconn and Pegatron). Between 2007 and 2013, Apple spent close to $30 billion in machinery for its iPhone production in its key EMS providers and parts suppliers. Through its equipment in these supplier factories, Apple is able to enjoy exclusivity in terms of not only its own original equipment manufacturing in these factories, but also access to the suppliers' specialty technologies and materials.[26]

Interestingly and as was evident in Chapter 4's empirical analysis, OEM lead firms interact differently with their ODM firms and EMS providers. In notebook PCs, OEM lead firms have developed and maintained very close relationships with their ODM partners that provide design and R&D work in Taiwan and final assembly primarily in China. This has created more difficulties for EMS newcomers in notebook PCs due to their lack of experience and intellectual property, supply chain problems (securing 200–300 different parts), and weaker partnerships with platform or technology leaders (e.g., Intel, Microsoft, Nvidia, and AMD). These leaders typically do not have, or want to invest in, extra resources to support newcomers, such as large EMS providers of the likes of Foxconn and Flex, that only have a small market share of notebook PCs in Table 4.3. In desktop PCs and mobile handsets, lead firms typically exercise more arm's-length relationships with their outsourcing partners. This crucial difference in interfirm organizational relationships explains why EMS providers such as Foxconn and Flex have only secured much greater share in the final assembly of desktop PCs and smartphones (see Tables 4.4 and 4.5). In both segments, OEM lead firms tend to procure a mixed portion of their end products from in-house facilities and these EMS providers in different locations worldwide, as summarized in Table 4.8.

## Serving as Strategic Partners through Customization and Dedicated Facilities

An outsourced partner's strategic role in production networks can be substantially influenced by its extent of customization and joint development with major OEM customers. In ICT end products, my interviews with senior executives of both top OEM lead firms (customers) and their ODM partners (suppliers) show good consistency in how this strategic partnership can be developed through mutual efforts. In notebook PCs, major ODM firms want to become the strategic partners of OEM lead firms by being deeply involved in these customers' future roadmaps—an interfirm partnership form of organizing production networks theorized in Chapter 3 (also Figure 3.3b). Some of them even have staff stationed near to the headquarters of OEM lead firms outside East Asia, e.g., Dell in Austin, Texas, and Hewlett-Packard in Palo Alto, California. Internally, these ODM firms have organized dedicated groups to provide one-stop product and market solutions for their largest OEM customers described in Chapter 4 (Table 4.3). The chief technology officer of top three ODM-27 explained:

> You have to be their partner. Otherwise, you won't survive. It's more like the longevity of the partnership, that's definitely one indicator. We are already a business partner. If they shop around frequently, then that's not partnership. That's more transactional. So, some customers are transactional in nature, but the likes of Dell and Lenovo are very relationship-based. Most of the big customers are very relationship-oriented; they really treat you as a partner. Some customers trust us and allow us into that process, for example [top OEM-A]. [Top OEM-A] definitely trusts us a lot. Very deep. We know what they are thinking, one year and two years ahead. We exchange opinions, even at the [PC] architecture level.

In what is dubbed "ODM 2.0" depicted on the right-hand side of Figure 5.4, ODM firms no longer compete on the basis of operationally optimized and cost-effective factories, as they did in the 2000s (ODM 1.0). During the 2010s, their OEM customers became much more demanding due to severe competitive pressures in declining end markets (see Table

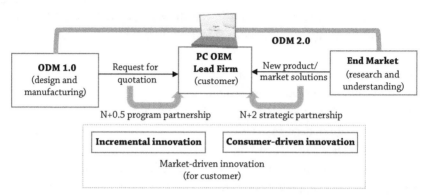

FIGURE 5.4. ODM 2.0: Strategic partnership with notebook PC OEM lead firms.

Source: Interviews with senior executives of PC OEM and ODM firms.

2.7). Most importantly, these OEM lead firms in notebook PCs required one-stop new product and market solutions from their preferred ODM partners. In this "N+2" form of strategic partnership (ODM 2.0), ODM firms must develop two new capabilities—understanding both consumer-driven innovation and end markets indicated in Figure 5.4—to design in and advise their OEM customers with one-stop solutions. To the senior vice president of another top three ODM-26,

> we want to talk the same language as the brand companies [OEM firms]. We start from understanding the entire consumer behavior and the dynamic megatrends of the entire global economy, and it starts from there. Identifying potential need and insights from the voices of consumers, we come up with a few solutions and then we start from there. We talk about needs and then we come to solutions. . . . We are not just a factory, but we hope ourselves to be a world-class design consultant plus product solutions and one-stop solutions and, of course, a very effective and efficient factory.

My interviews with their customers, i.e., top five PC OEM lead firms, show that these OEM firms appreciate the "N+2" efforts by their preferred ODM partners. Describing how it has codeveloped over four generations of premium notebook PC products with one leading ODM partner from Taiwan, the senior vice president for worldwide procurement and supply chain of top five PC OEM-22 explained how this strategic partnership works in its global production network:

When myself and my team build our notebook strategy, we are looking at sourcing the product [from ODM-26]. We are looking at some of their design services and using some of their manufacturing services. We built a strategy that's multiyear with key partners around that. They can be disposed of, but we see them as strategic partners in the sense that we are going to partner with them over multiple years. We are going to have to align our objectives. So they have a CRM [customer relationship management] plan that tries to grow revenue, improve profitability and what have you. We have a SRM [supplier relationship management] plan that we are trying to drive cost reduction, innovation, and capability building. We'll sit down and align those. And actually, every year we kick off the plan—it didn't change a whole lot, only in focused areas. And then both sides will invest in resources to look after what we are trying to be doing.

From its earlier model of complete in-house design within OEM-22 and outsourcing only final assembly to contract manufacturers such as Flextronics and Foxconn in the early 2000s, this OEM-22's relationship with ODM-26 has evolved into a codevelopment and strategic partnership model of global production network since the mid-2010s. The close working relationships between its R&D engineers and those at its key ODM partner are particularly necessary for commercial notebook PCs that have higher complexity and engineering demands because of the stricter requirements, cycle time, and quality demand by corporate customers. In this product category, OEM-22 has worked *only* with ODM-26 for over ten years because switching its ODM partner can be highly time consuming due to the familiarity of stringent requirements by ODM-26's engineering team and highly costly because of product-specific investment in equipment and intangibles. This strategic partnership also makes it less practical for OEM-22 to engage in dual or second sourcing for each notebook PC model because the cost of manufacturing will double—the volume for each ODM partner will be much reduced and yet the cost for parallel engineering and sourcing of components will increase substantially.

In mobile handsets, such strategic partnership is equally crucial to achieving the lower cost and faster time-to-market advantage. To the vice president in charge of supply chain in top five mobile handset OEM-14 from East Asia, strategic partners are those that OEM-14 offers "first look, last look"—"first look" when OEM-14 shares future technology roadmaps and demand forecasts with its partners, and "last look" when OEM-14 shows its bottom line as the last chance for its partners to improve pricing. These "first look" opportunities are critical for improving both lead time in production and capacity planning through realistic forecast. This kind of strategic partnership between an OEM customer and its key suppliers clearly goes beyond a typical buyer-seller transactional relationship of "Party A" and "Party B." He further explained:

> When you [a strategic partner] have new ideas, the first person you think of is me. Then we begin to work it out and finally we may be successful. Or after a period of time, because of your internal management or some other reasons, you cannot reach my standards like price or capacity, does it mean it is not a strategic supplier? No. When you cannot do it and before I decide not to cooperate with you, I will show you the last look of my bottom line such as 60 cents in USD. If you can do it, then you do it. If you cannot do it, then this project no longer belongs to you. But the next project we are still willing to work with you, because I've shown you the last look. This is our relationship.

Indeed, this top five mobile handset OEM-14 works mostly with first-tier megasuppliers in chipsets, camera lens, and memory devices as strategic partners. It has an almost 90 percent overlap in its choice of premium suppliers of major components vis-à-vis top market leaders in Table 5.3. Due to its strategic relationship with these first-class suppliers, OEM-14 is able to negotiate for better (or "second-class") prices since these partners have top engineers and thus design optimization, best-in-class factories and/or higher production volumes, and lower operating cost for financials and utilities. Its flagship smartphones with similar core components are often priced at less than half of those by top market leaders. In return, OEM-14 offers its preferred suppliers large and stable long-term orders for its different models to optimize its strategic partner's utilization of engineering resources and expected margins.

To secure long-term partnership with key OEM customers in notebook PCs and mobile handsets, some ODM and EMS firms from East Asia have offered dedicated facilities and separate quality assurance lines or locations in East Asia for different OEM customers so that the latter would find it harder to switch outsourcing suppliers. In notebook PCs, this is a common practice. ODM firms routinely place their dedicated factories in specific locations to serve their OEM customers (see summary in Table

4.8). For example, Chapter 4 has already showcased how Quanta dedicates its Shanghai factory to serve exclusively Apple's notebook PC assembly, whereas Inventec's Chongqing factory assembles primarily Hewlett-Packard's notebook PCs (see Table 4.3). From an OEM customer's point of view, these dedicated factories are convenient because they are simpler to audit and provide one-stop service. When an OEM customer conducts audit and inspection, the entire factory has only its own brand-name products, and it is easier to audit if the ODM firm has followed the customer lead firm's specification and standards. For example, top three ODM-26 has dedicated factories in China's Chengdu for OEM-A, Chongqing for OEM-B, and Kunshan for OEMs-C to E. In mobile handsets, all four major EMS/ODM providers (Foxconn, Inventec, Pegatron, and Wistron) have dedicated factories in China to serve only specific global lead firms (see earlier analysis in Chapter 4 and Table 4.5).

Even specialized component suppliers may offer dedicated R&D teams and factories for key OEM customers in PCs and mobile handsets. According to the vice president for sales and R&D of top component Supplier-28, having dedicated factories in China for each OEM customer has enabled it to achieve mutual trust and strategic partnership with premium OEM lead firm customers and, therefore, direct deals and higher margins. Supplier-28 has ten to twenty dedicated R&D staff for each OEM customer, and they participate closely in the customer's product roadmap and work directly with the design and product development teams of customer lead firms in their corporate headquarters in the US and East Asia. As a major producer of a key and expensive component for notebook PCs and premium smartphones, Supplier-28's R&D staff have to be involved very early on in different OEM lead firms' new product development, often well before those concepts come to the chosen ODM providers of these OEM lead firms. This process of both R&D teams working together has led to joint patents held by Supplier-28 with some of its OEM lead firms in process and materials technology. It also gives Supplier-28 a better grasp of the entire end market because of its privileged access ("first look") to confidential future product roadmaps of major OEM lead firms in those segments.

## Conclusion

This chapter's in-depth empirical analysis of firm-specific strategies in global electronics has demonstrated the highly differentiated and yet innovative organization of cross-regional production networks spear-headed by lead firms, together with their intrafirm affiliates and interfirm partners and suppliers. These increasingly globalized production networks are far more complex organizationally and difficult to manage than those localized production networks in Silicon Valley during the late 1980s described at the beginning of this chapter. Revisiting my theoretical framing in Chapter 3 (also Figure 3.3), these organizational innovations entail both lead firm-centric and strategic partnership models of organizing global production networks. Table 5.4 summarizes this chapter's main findings on firm strategies and organizational dynamics since the late 2010s and maps them onto Chapter 4's findings on changing geographical configurations during 2010s (see Table 4.8). Among lead firms in semiconductors, PCs, smartphones, and TVs, a mix of in-house production and outsourcing remains as the most commonly adopted organizational form necessary to sustain their competitive advantage during the 2010s. The former model of more insourcing is driven by greater intrafirm coordination by lead firms and thus represents a lead firm–centric control model. Those lead firms engaging in substantial or complete outsourcing tend to take a strategic partnership approach to organizing their production networks on the basis of cooperative interfirm relationships.

In the top four to five core components for PCs and smartphones, my empirical analysis of the 2015 and 2018 data shows that the global production networks of most top OEM lead firms are premised on enduring interfirm relationships with a very small number of dominant platform and technology leaders (e.g., Intel, Broadcom, Qualcomm, and Samsung), together with their preferred manufacturing partners (i.e., ODM firms and/or EMS providers). As noted in Table 5.4, while OEM lead firms from East Asia tend to engage more in intrafirm coordination by internalizing some core components (e.g., Samsung and Huawei insourcing application processors for their smartphones) and final assembly activities, their counterparts from the US are much more reliant on outsourced partners, most of which are also located in East Asia. Collectively, these organizationally differentiated strategies implemented by lead firms in their global production networks during the 2010s have co-constituted the interconnected worlds of electronics production by binding highly specialized suppliers from advanced countries, such as the US, Germany, the Netherlands, and Japan, with their East Asian manufacturing partners and OEM customers. Meanwhile, lead firms from these advanced countries in the US, Japan,

TABLE 5.4. Firm strategies, organizational dynamics, and geographical configurations in electronics global production networks, 2018–2021

| Firm strategy | Organizational dynamics | Geographical configurations | Segment examples |
|---|---|---|---|
| Intrafirm coordination | - Insourcing to speed up innovation and time-to-market<br>- In-house manufacturing important to risk mitigation<br>- Outsourcing to focus on technology development and to leverage partner's scale economies | - Strong concentration of wafer fabs in East Asia<br>- Worldwide distribution of final assembly facilities, but more concentrated in East Asia and South Asia | - Tight integration of chip design and production through in-house fabs in semiconductors<br>- Substantial to complete in-house production by East Asian OEM firms in PCs, mobile handsets, and TVs |
| Interfirm control | - Optimizing total cost of ownership through supply chain control | - High concentration of notebook PC production in China | - OEM lead firms (e.g., Dell) and ODM partners in PCs |
| Interfirm partnership | - Developing deep relationships with long-term customers in industrial markets<br>- Sharing risks with internal and external customers<br>- Serving as strategic partners through customization and dedicated facilities | - Globally dispersed geography of R&D in semiconductors<br>- Heavy concentration of wafer fabs in East Asia<br>- Strong concentration of final assembly facilities in East Asia and South Asia | - IDM firms and OEM customers in automotive<br>- Semiconductor foundry (TSMC and Samsung), fabless firms (Apple, Qualcomm, and HiSilicon), and lead firms in mobile handsets (Apple, Samsung, and Huawei)<br>- OEM lead firms and partners in notebook PCs and mobile handsets |
| Extrafirm bargaining | - Supply risks in semiconductors due to government regulation<br>- Reorganization of production network through divestment<br>- Pressures from host market governments | - Dual sourcing from fabs in multiple locations in East Asia<br>- Strong presence of Chinese smartphone OEM firms<br>- New locations for ODM and EMS assembly | - Geopolitical tensions and US sanctions: Huawei's sale of its Honor business unit in mobile handsets<br>- Apple's partners setting up new assembly operations in India |

and Western Europe have become more deeply coupled with specialized suppliers in semiconductors and panel displays based in East Asia and engaged in cross-regional production facilitated by their chosen ODM firms and/or EMS providers in East Asia.

To organize and manage successfully their global production networks centered in East Asia—as summarized in Table 5.4, many lead firms in my study have engaged in in-house production to facilitate technological innovation, time-to-market, and risk mitigation. These lead firms in semiconductors and ICT end products have also outsourced a significant portion of their manufacturing activities to strategic partners such as foundry and ODM/EMS providers. From the perspective of these "suppliers," developing and sustaining long-term relationships with lead firm customers are paramount to continual strategic coupling with lead firms' production networks. In organizational terms, this strategic partnership can be accomplished through "deep dive" commitments, such as risk sharing, equity joint ventures, technological collaboration through customization and roadmap sharing, and provision of dedicated facilities (e.g., exclusive fab facilities in Taiwan and assembly factories in China and elsewhere). Managing these complicated interfirm relationships is no easy task. While there are different models of supply chain management, supplier- or vendor-managed inventories is the most commonly practiced model among lead firms in ICT end products.

Through these organizational innovations in intrafirm coordination and interfirm control and partnership, lead firms in global electronics have developed extensive production networks centered in East Asian economies within their evolving national-institutional contexts, summarized in Table 1.2. Having unpacked these geographical configurations of production networks in Chapter 4 and their organizational processes driven by firm-specific strategies in this chapter, the remaining task of my GPN 2.0 theory–inspired analysis is to explain *why* these different geographical and network configurations have emerged even among global lead firms in the same product segment (e.g., semiconductors, PCs, mobile handsets, and TVs) and from similar geographical origin (e.g., the US, South Korea, and China). As will be evident in the next empirical chapter, there are specific causal dynamics at work that drive such differentiated outcomes in organizing global production networks.

# CHAPTER 6

# Explaining Production Networks: Causal Drivers and Competitive Dynamics

THE DETAILED EMPIRICAL ANALYSIS in the previous two chapters has examined the complex and yet changing geography and organization of global production networks coordinated by lead firms in the information and communications technology (ICT) sector during the 2010s. We now have a clearer sense of where and how an innovative organizational mix of insourcing and global outsourcing is deployed by these lead firms originating mostly from the United States and East Asia, where and how they work with key customers worldwide to engage in joint product development and develop long-term relationships, and how they manage key suppliers and even nurture some of them to become strategic partners in their globalized production networks centered in East Asia.

Here, it is useful to summarize briefly the key "where" and "how" trends during the 2010s in the four industry segments examined in Chapters 4 and 5 before explaining them empirically in relation to the causal drivers and competitive dynamics conceptualized in Chapter 3's GPN 2.0 theory (see also summary Tables 4.8 and 5.4). In semiconductors— arguably the most critical intermediate good for ICT end products, the 2010s witnessed growing total revenue that peaked at \$485 billion in 2018 but declined to \$466 billion in 2020 due to geopolitical tensions and the COVID-19 pandemic. With more fabless firms over time, market concentration among top ten firms also increased substantially from 48 percent of total revenue in 2010 to 55 percent in 2020 (Table 2.2). During this decade, very strong investment in new fabs and capacity growth took place in East Asia in relation to:

(1)    the continual dominant role of East Asian integrated device manufacturing (IDM) firms in memory chips,

(2)    the dominance of cutting-edge foundry providers from East Asia preferred by fabless or fab-lite firms from the US and Europe for wafer fabrication in logic, microprocessor, and other integrated circuits or "chips", and

(3)    the much greater concentration of chip demand for computer and data storage devices and wireless ICT products mostly assembled in East and South Asia for worldwide end markets.

In terms of firm-specific strategies, even lead firm competitors in the same product category and from the same home economy can operate drastically different models of intrafirm and interfirm production networks. Intel's complete insourcing of its microprocessor chips contrasts sharply with its "lesser" competitor in microprocessors, AMD, which relies on GlobalFoundries' Fab 8 in Malta, New York, and since 2019, TSMC's leading fabs in Taiwan. Intel's fabless competitors in graphics processors and wireless logic chips, such as AMD, Nvidia, Broadcom, and Qualcomm, also rely completely on their foundry providers' cutting-edge fabs located in Taiwan (TSMC and UMC), South Korea (Samsung), Singapore (GlobalFoundries and UMC), and China (SMIC and UMC). As both a top IDM firm in semiconductors and a dominant original equipment manufacturing (OEM) lead firm in mobile handsets and consumer electronics, Samsung's partial intrafirm sourcing of mobile chips and memory devices from in-house fabs in South Korea and the US (Austin) is rather different from market leader Qualcomm and Broadcom's complete outsourcing to East Asian foundry providers.

In personal computers (PCs)—a highly concentrated end market with 85 percent of total shipment in 2018 by top ten OEM firms (see Table 1.1), global lead firms from the US remain dominant among the top six lead firms, such as Hewlett-Packard, Dell, and Apple, but the rest of the top ten are all from East Asia, such as Lenovo (China), Asus and Acer (Taiwan), and Samsung (South Korea), and Fujitsu and NEC (Japan). Still, these US OEM firms outsource the production of *all* of their notebook PCs to East Asian partners, known as original design manufacturing (ODM) firms. In notebook PC production networks, Taiwan's ODM firms are most significant in the design and assembly roles of the organizationally fragmented divisions of labor centered in the US, Taiwan, and China. And yet China's Lenovo has retained substantial in-house production of over half of its notebook PCs, and China has become the predominant center for the final assembly of notebook PCs. But in desktop PCs, such out-sourcing of final assembly is organizationally less significant and geograph-ically much more globalized. With the exception of microprocessors by Intel and AMD produced mostly in US-based in-house facilities (Intel) or foundry fabs (GlobalFoundries), all major components for notebook and desktop PCs, such as wireless connectivity and memory chips, flat panel displays, and metal chassis, are supplied by technology leaders from the US and East Asia and manufactured in East Asian locations.

In mobile handsets—a rapidly growing and highly concentrated end market with top ten firms accounting for over 80 percent of the record shipment in 2018 (Table 1.1), Apple remains as the only top nine OEM lead firm from outside East Asia in a market dominated by lead firms from South Korea and China. While there is a high degree of geographical con-solidation of worldwide final assembly by electronics manufacturing ser-vices (EMS) providers in Asia, China's role as a dominant location has been reduced due to the emergence of more diversified locations in Southeast Asia (Vietnam and Indonesia) and South Asia (India). The market leader Samsung not only assembles everything in-house in several Asian locations but also relies on its own supply of many critical components and mod-ules for its mobile handsets and other ICT products. In contrast, Apple outsources virtually everything in its iPhones—from components to final assembly (by Taiwan's Foxconn and Pegatron in China), but it does retain the most critical design of its core application processors (A-series chips manufactured by TSMC in its leading fabs at home) and operating system (iOS) in Silicon Valley. Other OEM lead firms from China, such as Hua-wei, Oppo, and Vivo, rely almost entirely on technology leaders for core components and yet retain a significant portion of final assembly in their in-house facilities in China and India.

In consumer electronics (i.e., TVs), East Asian lead firms are domi-nant in both TVs and flat panel displays (the core component for TVs, notebook PCs, and high-end smartphones), with an organizational mix of insourcing and outsourcing of final assembly. Research and development (R&D) design for TVs and panel display production facilities are heavily concentrated in the home countries of OEM lead firms from South Korea,

China, Japan, and in nearby Taiwan where major ODM firms and EMS providers for the PC and mobile handset markets are headquartered. Similar to desktop PCs, though, the final assembly of TVs is fairly globalized in order to be cost-effective and nearer to end markets.

By the end of the 2010s and just before the unprecedented global disruptions unleashed by the COVID-19 pandemic in 2020 and thereafter, these diverse and coevolutionary industrial-organizational configurations of electronics global production networks had brought together advanced design and R&D locations in the US, Western Europe, and East Asia with production sites throughout East Asia and elsewhere (e.g., the US and Germany) to constitute the interconnected worlds of global electronics. As Chapter 3 has theorized, a full account of these evolving geographical configurations and firm-specific organizational innovations must offer comprehensive explanations that answer the *why* question by probing into the causal drivers of these complex configurations of global production networks. Chapter 3's GPN 2.0 theory has already conceptualized four causal drivers and competitive dynamics—optimizing cost-capability ratios, sustaining market development, working with financial discipline, and managing risks. Mapping directly onto this theory (see also Table 3.4), the following four sections elaborate empirically on each causal dynamic operating in the major segments of global electronics—starting with semiconductors before ICT end products, whereas the concluding section summarizes these causal explanations in a table and evaluates their relative significance in these different segments.

## Cost-Capability Ratios

As was argued in Chapter 3, most existing explanations of global outsourcing focus on reduction in wage and transport costs as the key driver of OEM lead firms while overlooking the equally important role of firm-specific capability at the receiving end of their offshoring (of in-house production) and/or outsourcing (to foundry providers, strategic partners, and/or key suppliers). In manufacturing, we often hear that lower cost is the main selection criterion determining where a lead firm locates its in-house production activity or outsources its manufacturing work. In Chapters 4 and 5, I have demonstrated the fact that even lead firms in the same product category (e.g., processor chips, notebook PCs, or mobile handsets) have chosen diverse locations for their worldwide production and/or adopted different firm-specific strategies for insourcing and/or outsourcing. These major variations in their organization of global pro-duction networks point to the need to understand better the nuanced nature of cost in relation to firm-specific capability.

In my study of forty-four firms in the late 2010s, lead firms in both semiconductors (as intermediate goods) and ICT end products are clearly more concerned with managing the total cost of ownership in which sup-plier capability and the nature of the supply ecosystem can be very crucial. Lead firm customers may get involved in ramping up the technological and/or production capability of their strategic partners in order to reduce this total cost. In short, it is not just the nominal cost, such as labor wages, of a supplier that matters. Rather, this cost has to be measured against the capability of the partner/supplier for an outsourcing deal to be economi-cal. As was theorized in Chapter 3 (and Table 3.1), this dynamic concept of optimizing cost-capability ratios in the GPN 2.0 theory is critical in explaining where and how production networks in global electronics are configured, but its applicability varies from relatively less significance in semiconductors to high significance in all ICT end product segments.

In semiconductors, cost-capability ratio in wafer fabrication is directly linked with equipment/materials costs, timely delivery, and quality/yield of fabs. Labor cost is relatively less significant due to extensive automation in each fab. As Chapter 5 has noted, the cost of building and running a new cutting-edge fab that will depreciate rapidly within five years has been exceedingly high since the mid-2010s. In 2013, new 14 nanometer (nm) fabs at the planning stages for Intel and GlobalFoundries would cost up to $10 billion each. TSMC's new 3 nm fab to be opened for volume produc-tion in mid-2022 would cost $20–$23 billion! This high capital investment in cutting-edge wafer fabrication means that cost-capability ratios are strongly skewed toward the capability-side of the equation—the timely delivery and quality/yield of foundry providers for their fab-lite IDM firms and fabless customers. This in turn explains why the most advanced fabs of top foundry providers (see Table 4.2), such as TSMC (7 nm) and Samsung (10 nm) in 2018, are located in their home bases of Hsinchu/Taichung in Taiwan (TSMC) and Giheung in South Korea (Samsung). As Chapter 4 has discussed, their most advanced nodes at 5 nm in 2020 and 3 nm in 2022 are also located in their new fabs in Taiwan's Tainan (TSMC) and, for Samsung, Hwaseong and Pyeongtaek in South Korea.[1] Their fab capability is also embedded in an extensive and collaborative ecosystem of leading equipment and materials suppliers from the US, Europe, and

Japan, discussed in Chapters 2 and 5 (see an illustration in Figure 5.2). For their fab-lite or fabless customers worldwide that require access to these latest technology nodes to support their most advanced logic chips, high foundry production capability and process technology are of paramount importance. But these determinants are heavily influenced by the competitive dynamics of financial discipline that impinge much more significantly on the production networks of leading semiconductor firms—a key causal driver to be examined in the third section.

While fab capacity in China grew very rapidly during the 2010s (see Table 4.1), its labor cost advantage was not the decisive driver, because Taiwan's fab capacity increased even more significantly during the same period (2010–2018) and became the largest in the world in 2018. The three high-cost countries of South Korea, Japan, and the US combined also had four times more fab capacity than China in 2018. Still, semiconductor manufacturing and fab capacity have clearly moved to East Asia during this period. Within the semiconductor manufacturing process, there is one subset that can be quite labor intensive—back-end services in the assembly, packaging, and testing of chip products, as illustrated in Figures 5.1 and 5.2. Here, all but one of the world's top ten independent back-end service providers are based in East Asia—mostly in Taiwan and a few in China. They provide competitive outsourced back-end services to major IDM firms (e.g., Samsung, Micron, NXP, and so on) and foundry firms (e.g., TSMC and GlobalFoundries). As several interviewees in Chapter 5's discussion of intrafirm considerations in semiconductor outsourcing have noted, these independent providers of back-end services enjoy significant advantage in their lower cost-capability ratios vis-à-vis even in-house back-end facilities of leading semiconductor firms located in the same macro-region and thus the same cost environment (e.g., Samsung and Renesas within East Asia), making outsourcing of back-end services a viable strategy even for East Asian IDM or foundry firms.

Despite this major shift of both the front end and back end of the semiconductor manufacturing process to East Asia, semiconductor design and ecosystem (e.g., design software providers, intellectual property libraries vendors, and capital equipment suppliers) remain primarily US-based due to the dense technology and venture capital networks, specialized skills, and end markets in Silicon Valley and elsewhere within the US. The overseas design centers of US fabless and IDM firms are also established in Western Europe and Japan to access specialized skills, e.g., consumer multimedia in the United Kingdom and wireless network technology in Nordic countries. Chip design is therefore not driven by low cost per se or even fab locations, but by the availability of specialized skills and agglomeration economies. India's case is instructive here. As argued by Brown and Linden (2011, 169), despite its success in capturing much global software outsourcing from the US, India failed to entice a single wafer fab to be built between 1995 and 2008. A decade later in 2018, India remained "fabless," as indicated in Table 4.1, and a minor player in the global semiconductor industry. In March 2021, the Indian government even offered $1 billion in cash to any semiconductor firm setting up wafer fabrication in India.[2] Most importantly, though, chip design needs to be closely in tune with end user product and market development (e.g., OEM firms in the ICT and automotive sectors), and this critical market imperative will be examined later in the second section.

In comparison with semiconductors, optimizing cost-capability ratios in the production of ICT end products represents a very significant causal driver in explaining the changing geographical and organizational configurations of global production networks throughout 2010s. Framed in the GPN 2.0 theory in Figure 3.2, this causal dynamic of cost-capability optimization has driven lead firms' strategy of intrafirm coordination and/or interfirm relationships, resulting in more East Asia–centered geographical configurations of their production networks during the decade. Let me start with the cost side of the ratio. Figure 6.1 illustrates the changing manufacturing labor cost in Asia between 2010 and 2018. In 2010, the average monthly base salary of manufacturing workers in China was $303, only slightly higher than India, Malaysia, and Thailand, but much more than other Southeast Asian developing countries. Set within its changing national-institutional context toward industrial upgrading and the restructuring of state-owned enterprises (see Table 1.2), China engaged in significant labor market reform in the late 2000s.[3] By 2016, China's average worker salary had increased by over 41 percent to reach $428 and become much higher than India and Southeast Asian countries (less than $350). From a high base in 2016, it increased further by over 15 percent to reach $493 in 2018, making China by far the highest labor cost among all developing economies in East and South Asia. During the same period of 2016–2018, Vietnam's average worker salary increased only slightly from $204 to $227, whereas the average salaries in Indonesia and the Philippines actually decreased respectively to $296 and $220.

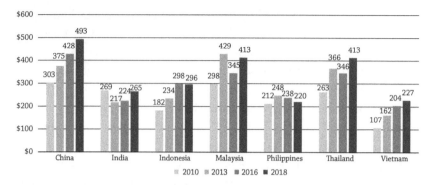

Note: Average salaries are based on JETRO surveys of Japanese companies in respective countries. The number of responding firms in the 2018 survey ranges from 52 in the Philippines to 245 in Thailand, 325 in Vietnam, and 344 in China.

FIGURE 6.1. Average monthly base salaries of manufacturing workers in Asia, 2010–2018 (in US$).

Source: Data from JETRO (2010, 51; 2013, 53; 2016, 62; 2018, 73).

Ironically, this rapidly increasing labor cost in China during the 2010s had not driven much labor-intensive final assembly work in global electronics out of China by the late 2010s. In notebook PCs (Table 4.3), China's share in final assembly actually increased from 83 percent in 2015 to 91 percent in 2018, and its total shipment remained the same at just below 150 million units, despite the rising labor cost in China and declining overall shipment units (i.e., reduction in production elsewhere in Brazil, the Czech Republic, Mexico, and Turkey). The same observation also applies to desktop PCs. The clustering of a large number of suppliers in China's eastern region (Kunshan and Shanghai) and western region (Chongqing and Chengdu) indeed enabled Taiwanese ODM firms to enjoy lower logistics cost and thereby to secure an overwhelming share of the notebook PC assembly outsourced from all top six OEM lead firms (except Lenovo's majority in-house assembly in Hefei and Shenzhen). In Chapter 5's analysis of interfirm strategic partnerships (e.g., Quanta-Apple in Shanghai and Inventec-Hewlett-Packard in Chongqing), providing dedicated factory lines in China for their major OEM customers also strengthened the tighter coupling of these ODM firms' design-manufacturing capabilities with their customer's R&D and marketing activities located in their China headquarters (Shanghai), regional headquarters (e.g., Singapore and Hong Kong), or global headquarters (the US). In short and throughout the 2010s, these ODM firms from Taiwan continued to strengthen their firm-specific capabilities and optimize their cost-capability ratios in the codesign and assembly work for most top PC OEM firms that had outsourced all notebook PC production to ODM partners' assembly facilities in China.

On the locational choices of new in-house production facilities by OEM lead firms (e.g., Lenovo in PCs and Samsung and Oppo/Vivo in mobile handsets), the nominal cost (e.g., wages, utilities, land) can be counterbalanced by the capability of the supplier ecosystem (e.g., logistics cost, timeliness of delivery, and availability of local suppliers). Geographical shift may take place when the cost-capability ratio in the new location becomes lower than the existing in-house facility elsewhere. In the following case of Samsung's intrafirm production network in mobile handsets, the rising wage cost of its smartphone assembly factories in China's Huizhou and Tianjin during the 2010s was compensated for by the availability of sophisticated local supplier networks in China. The cost-capability ratios of these two sites in China were therefore quite well optimized up to the mid-2010s. As indicated in Table 4.5, these two factories in China were still assembling almost half of Samsung's historic peak of 320 million units of smartphones shipped in 2015. Samsung's Huizhou operation grew out of a joint venture signed with the Huizhou city government on August 24, 1992, four days before the official establishment of diplomatic relations between China and South Korea. In operation since 1993, the Huizhou factory was assembling Samsung's latest and most popular consumer electronics, from audio systems in the 1990s and MP3 players in the early 2000s to feature phones and smartphones since 2007. By the mid-2010s, the Huizhou factory was supported by over one hundred local suppliers, such as Hong Kong–invested Bern Optical for glass covers and Shenzhen-listed Janus for precision components, before its eventual closure in October 2019.[4]

Meanwhile in 2015, Samsung's in-house facilities in Vietnam assembled "only" about 51 million units or 16 percent of its total shipment of 320 million units (see Table 4.5), having started operation in 2009. While labor cost in Vietnam was about one-third of China in 2010 and less than half of China in 2016 (Figure 6.1), the lack of capable supplier networks for mobile handsets and local logistics support for Samsung in Vietnam meant that the cost-capability ratio was much higher in these Vietnamese facilities. To improve its internal cost-capability ratio in Vietnam, Samsung encouraged its intrachaebol affiliates, such as Samsung SDI (20 percent owned), Samsung Electro-Mechanics (24 percent owned), and Samsung Display (85 percent owned), to set up in-house supplier networks in Vietnam's Thai Nguyen and Bac Ninh provinces so that the entire smartphone production system could be established in northern Vietnam by the late 2010s.[5]

Samsung SDI, a world leader in smartphone batteries, started operation in Bac Ninh province's Que Vo industrial park in 2010. In 2016, it sought approval to double its investment by another $120 million and to increase substantially production capacity in light of limited domestic supplier capability. Samsung Display, the world's leading producer of flat panel displays (see Table 4.7), also received approval in February 2017 to invest another $2.5 billion in its operation in the nearby Yen Phong Industrial Zone. By 2018, the cost-capability ratios between its in-house facilities in China and Vietnam shifted in favor of the latter. The senior vice president of top three PC OEM-22 pointed out that Samsung's capability in building up and coordinating its in-house supplier ecosystem in Vietnam was instrumental in its geographical reconfiguration of smartphone production from China to its Vietnam facilities. But this would be harder to achieve in PCs and other larger ICT products:

> The question is "Is it possible to build up that ecosystem somewhere else"? I would argue it is possible. If you look at Samsung smartphones, they have been able to do that in Vietnam. So they have built an ecosystem there, with very high control. But when you start thinking about some of these other ICT categories, it's much more difficult. First of all, the product starts to get bigger in size, which means it costs more to move it around the world. And then there is a lot of capital equipment and capital that would be required to bring up local business.

With lower wage cost and capable intragroup supplier networks, Samsung Electronics Vietnam took charge of over 50 percent of all 290 million Samsung smartphones assembled worldwide in 2018, almost three times the production volume in 2015 (see Table 4.5). Much of this massive increase came from the dramatic reduction in its two Chinese factories in Huizhou (from 95.9 million units in 2015 to 27.5 million units in 2018) and Tianjin (from 59.6 million units to 3.8 million units). By October 2019, Samsung closed its last smartphone assembly factory in Huizhou, having ended its Tianjin factory earlier in December 2018 (first in operation in the mid-2000s).

In (re-)configuring its intrafirm production network, Samsung focused on three key factors influencing its cost-capability ratios: cost structures, profit margins, and technology and product maturity. Unlike most OEM lead firms in global electronics (e.g., Apple, Dell, Huawei, and Lenovo), Samsung has a large range of ICT products, from PCs and mobile handsets to consumer electronics (e.g., TVs, cameras, and household appliances). Each of these products at its initial introduction entails a different cost structure, profit margin, and product maturity—a premium Galaxy S-series smartphone retailed at $800–$1,000 is very different from a low-end feature phone at $50. The same consideration applies to a large-format 55/65-inch QLED TV and a low-end small 28-inch LCD TV. To categorize their different cost structures, profit margins, and product maturity, Samsung has 4 to 5 levels for mobile handsets and 7 to 8 levels for TVs. Premium products at the highest levels are viewed as profit and technology drivers because profit margins are better and technological requirements for production are much higher. They are often manufactured in "master factories" back in South Korea where higher wages of manufacturing workers are compensated for by more mature technological and production capability in quality and yield (i.e., higher cost but higher capability). For products that move to or start at lower levels of margins and product maturity, the sensitivity to labor cost is higher and the demand for in-house or supplier capability is lower. They can be manufactured in facilities located outside South Korea, such as those developing countries in Figure 6.1, with lower labor cost but likely lower capability.

In all of these cases of PCs, mobile handsets, and other ICT end products, the causal driver of production network configurations is cost-capability ratios—the lower the better. As conceptualized in Table 3.1, such low ratios can be achieved by both a lead firm (LF1) and a partner/supplier (PS1) through an optimal combination of lower cost and higher capability. Optimizing these ratios is critical to OEM lead firms' strategy of intrafirm coordination (insourcing via in-house production) and/or outsourcing through developing interfirm relationships. But measuring these ratios can be quite complex and challenging. To the chief technology officer of top three PC ODM-27, this ratio is measured "in terms of yield rates as well as it's in the overall picture of productivity—revenue contribution per number of manpower." In my study, two major nonmaterial costs come to the forefront—labor and logistics. First, labor cost remains a significant component of cost-capability ratios and is particularly substantial in final assembly facilities for ICT end products (PC OEM-24 and Supplier-5). As shown in earlier examples, however, higher wages and labor costs can be compensated for if labor productivity and/or supplier capability is high. The share of labor cost in the total cost of ownership can be reduced through higher management capability, better work experience and efficiency, process design (e.g., more automation), and development of soft capability (e.g., focus on skill upgrading and worker productivity).

Second, logistics cost can be much more significant than sheer labor cost or government incentives in the total cost of ownership and, thereby, in driving a lead firm's configuration of its global production network. Logistics cost is primarily related to transport (e.g., road conditions and accessibility), traffic and port facilities, capability of logistics service providers, and custom clearance for imports (intermediate goods) and exports (finished goods). In semiconductors, logistics cost contributes to at least 10 percent of each chipset's value, similar to design costs.[6] In PCs, lead firms may incur 30 to 40 percent of total supply chain cost from logistics. Supply chain sourcing and inventory management are very critical to optimizing cost-capability ratios. As Chapter 5's section on interfirm relationships has examined, most OEM firms in PCs rely on the supplier- or vendor-managed inventories model of supply chain management. The capability of ODM firms exercising this model can make much difference to the total cost of their OEM customers because the cost of all parts and components will be transferred to the OEM customer once they are assembled into a PC and shipped out of the ODM factory.

Meanwhile, faster time-to-market may entail greater inventories (assembled stocks) and higher total cost. This may not be conducive to hyper–cost competition in certain product segments, such as desktop PCs and mass market TVs. But it is more amenable in notebook PCs with an efficient build-to-order configuration of production networks supported by highly capable ODM partners. The head of supply demand planning in top three PC OEM-23 argued that

> from the supply chain perspective, actually to stock the right product is very difficult and having that process to stock a product needs not necessarily be an advantage to the company. In fact, it can be a burden. Because with so many configurations we have in the market, it's no point to build [a notebook PC] in advance. You need to build to the

demand, and we call it "build-to-order." So, when your order comes and we build, and I don't have the burden of having to rework existing stocks to reconfigure the product.

To manage effectively such inventory cost, OEM-23 follows Dell's strategy and outsources completely its notebook PC assembly to Taiwan's ODM firms. Instead of final assembly, it focuses on R&D and sales and marketing of its PCs. But unlike Dell, which practices the "clean sheeting" model of interfirm control in supply chain management described in Chapter 5 and directly controls up to 75 percent of materials costs, OEM-23 works very closely with its ODM partners on a vendor-managed inventories model to plan for highly differentiated market demand and to ensure adequate supply of its PCs to end market customers. The capability of its ODM partners in supply chain management thus becomes critical to OEM-23's ability to supply to its demand forecast with competitive cost-capability ratios.

Taken together, lower labor costs in East Asian locations are often measured against supplier/supply chain capabilities. Locations with optimized cost-capability ratios have lower total cost of ownership for lead firms and can attract investment in new production facilities by these lead firms for in-house manufacturing (e.g., Lenovo PCs in China's Hefei and Samsung smartphones in northern Vietnam) or by ODM/EMS providers for their outsourcing business (e.g., notebook PCs and smartphones in China's eastern and western regions). In Chapters 3 and 4, this is referred to as an "inside-out" process of geographical (re-)configuration of global production networks. Many lead firms have also spent much effort in managing their logistics costs through developing stronger in-house capability (e.g., procurement and supply chain knowhow) and/or supplier capability to meet the highly challenging market demand to be examined next.

## Market Imperative

While cost-capability considerations can directly determine the make-or-buy and capital investment choices of global lead firms, the need to sustain market development—the so-called market imperative in Chapter 3's GPN 2.0 theory—can also exert quite significant influence on their geographical and organizational configurations of production networks. In some cases, growing market share has become more important than maximizing short-term return on invested capital in a lead firm's choices of organizational strategy and geographical configurations. Focusing on the firm- and network-level analysis, Chapter 5's section on "customer is king" and interfirm relationships has examined the importance of proximity to customers and markets as a key strategy in lead firms' innovative organization of production networks. Using data at the more aggregate level of world markets by major macroregions and countries, this section explains why new market growth dynamics in the Asia Pacific during the 2010s became the critical market imperative driving lead firms and their partners/suppliers in different industrial and end markets.

In semiconductors, the market imperative is highly segmented by worldwide industrial applications in different intermediate "user" markets. This user demand through intersectoral linkages, such as military procurement, consumer electronics, and computers, has always been critical in the development of the semiconductor industry (see Chapter 2's historical context). In Table 6.1, this market segmentation by major macroregions and countries between 2013 and 2023 is clearly evident. In the Americas, the largest demand comes from automotive, computing and data storage, and industrial electronics. Industrial users in the US are the most significant in each of these three applications that are expected to double in demand between 2013 and 2023. The strong demand for semiconductors in advanced automotive and autonomous systems in the US, for example, comes from such developers as Tesla, Google, and the Big Three (Ford, General Motors, and Chrysler).[7]

The massive growth of the global digital economy before and after the COVID-19 pandemic and the continual US leadership in platform-based services dominated by the FAANGs (Facebook, Amazon, Apple, Netflix, and Google) and others (e.g., Amazon, Microsoft, IBM, and Apple in cloud computing) have also created unprecedented demand for data centers and corporate storage facilities located in the US and elsewhere (e.g., the Asia Pacific).[8] In 2018, over 68 percent of the $22.4 billion worth of semiconductor shipment in computing and data storage for the Americas (see Table 6.1) went just to DRAM memory for data center servers ($3.8 billion) and other corporate storage ($11.5 billion)![9] Despite the COVID-19 pandemic in 2020/2021, strong demand for logic (processors) and memory chips has come from these data centers and 5G communications infrastructure sectors that support remote work and online learning/access during and after the pandemic. In Table 2.5, the world demand for logic and memory chips in 2021 has been forecast to grow substantially

TABLE 6.1. World semiconductor shipment revenue by macroregions and industrial applications, 2013–2023 (in US$ billions)

| Region | 2013 | 2014 | 2015 | 2016 | 2017 | 2018 | 2019[E] | 2020[E] | 2021[E] | 2022[E] | 2023[E] |
|---|---|---|---|---|---|---|---|---|---|---|---|
| **Americas** | | | | | | | | | | | |
| Automotive | 5.2 | 5.7 | 5.6 | 6.2 | 7.3 | 8.0 | 7.9 | 8.4 | 9.1 | 10.1 | 10.9 |
| Comp & DS[1] | 8.7 | 12.1 | 11.5 | 11.7 | 16.5 | 22.4 | 16.7 | 17.5 | 19.7 | 19.4 | 18.9 |
| Consumer elec.[1] | 2.4 | 2.3 | 2.1 | 1.8 | 1.9 | 2.1 | 2.0 | 1.9 | 1.8 | 1.8 | 1.9 |
| Industrial elec. | 12.9 | 14.2 | 14.0 | 14.5 | 16.1 | 17.0 | 16.9 | 17.9 | 19.2 | 20.4 | 21.8 |
| Wired comm.[1] | 4.0 | 3.9 | 3.6 | 4.2 | 4.4 | 4.4 | 4.8 | 5.2 | 5.0 | 5.3 | 5.8 |
| Wireless comm. | 1.6 | 2.0 | 2.4 | 2.7 | 3.2 | 2.9 | 2.5 | 2.8 | 3.2 | 3.3 | 3.1 |
| Total | 34.8 | 40.2 | 39.2 | 41.1 | 49.4 | 56.8 | 50.8 | 53.7 | 58.0 | 60.3 | 62.4 |
| **EMEA[2]** | | | | | | | | | | | |
| Automotive | 7.1 | 8.1 | 8.0 | 8.9 | 10.4 | 11.3 | 11.3 | 12.1 | 13.2 | 14.6 | 15.8 |
| Comp & DS | 5.5 | 6.1 | 6.3 | 6.3 | 7.8 | 9.7 | 7.9 | 8.1 | 8.6 | 8.8 | 9.1 |
| Consumer elec. | 3.5 | 3.3 | 3.1 | 2.5 | 2.8 | 3.2 | 2.9 | 2.8 | 2.6 | 2.6 | 2.7 |
| Industrial elec. | 10.4 | 11.5 | 11.4 | 11.8 | 13.4 | 14.4 | 14.3 | 15.3 | 16.4 | 17.6 | 18.8 |
| Wired comm. | 3.3 | 3.5 | 3.4 | 3.7 | 4.3 | 4.4 | 4.6 | 4.8 | 4.8 | 5.0 | 5.5 |
| Wireless comm. | 4.5 | 5.7 | 5.8 | 5.9 | 6.0 | 6.2 | 5.1 | 5.9 | 6.3 | 6.1 | 5.4 |
| Total | 34.3 | 38.2 | 38.0 | 39.1 | 44.7 | 49.2 | 46.1 | 49.0 | 51.9 | 54.7 | 57.3 |
| **Japan** | | | | | | | | | | | |
| Automotive | 4.4 | 4.8 | 4.7 | 5.0 | 5.7 | 6.1 | 5.9 | 6.1 | 6.7 | 7.4 | 8.0 |
| Comp & DS | 5.4 | 6.1 | 6.4 | 7.3 | 10.8 | 13.8 | 9.0 | 10.3 | 13.1 | 14.5 | 12.3 |

(*continued*)

TABLE 6.1. (*continued*)

| Region | 2013 | 2014 | 2015 | 2016 | 2017 | 2018 | 2019[F] | 2020[F] | 2021[F] | 2022[F] | 2023[F] |
|---|---|---|---|---|---|---|---|---|---|---|---|
| Consumer elec. | 6.5 | 5.0 | 4.4 | 4.2 | 4.8 | 4.8 | 4.7 | 4.6 | 4.9 | 5.1 | 5.2 |
| Industrial elec. | 3.8 | 3.9 | 3.4 | 3.3 | 3.3 | 3.3 | 3.0 | 2.9 | 3.1 | 3.3 | 3.6 |
| Wired comm. | 2.4 | 2.4 | 2.4 | 2.4 | 2.9 | 3.0 | 3.0 | 3.1 | 3.2 | 3.3 | 3.6 |
| Wireless comm. | 5.7 | 5.5 | 5.2 | 4.4 | 4.6 | 4.3 | 3.3 | 3.4 | 3.7 | 3.5 | 3.2 |
| Total | 28.2 | 27.7 | 26.5 | 26.6 | 32.1 | 35.3 | 28.9 | 30.4 | 34.7 | 37.1 | 35.9 |
| Asia Pacific | | | | | | | | | | | |
| Automotive | 9.7 | 10.5 | 10.8 | 12.1 | 14.4 | 16.2 | 16.4 | 18.1 | 19.7 | 21.2 | 22.6 |
| Comp & DS | 83.6 | 92.7 | 87.2 | 89.7 | 114 | 131 | 112 | 118 | 124 | 129 | 127 |
| Consumer elec. | 32.0 | 31.5 | 28.1 | 26.4 | 30.4 | 31.6 | 30.3 | 30.7 | 33.4 | 33.8 | 34.6 |
| Industrial elec. | 11.0 | 12.6 | 12.8 | 13.8 | 15.9 | 17.4 | 17.9 | 19.6 | 21.1 | 22.5 | 24.1 |
| Wired comm. | 10.2 | 11.4 | 10.4 | 11.8 | 13.3 | 14.6 | 32.3 | 15.3 | 16.5 | 17.4 | 18.2 |
| Wireless comm. | 83.3 | 89.8 | 92.9 | 94.1 | 117 | 133 | 106 | 113 | 131 | 137 | 129 |
| Total | 230 | 249 | 242 | 248 | 306 | 344 | 315 | 315 | 345 | 361 | 355 |
| **Grand total** | **327** | **355** | **346** | **355** | **432** | **485** | **441** | **448** | **490** | **513** | **511** |

Note: 2019–2023 data are forecast data at the end of second quarter 2019. Actual numbers in 2021–2023 will likely be much higher due to the post-COVID-19 pandemic recovery and greater demand for semiconductors. Data from World Semiconductor Trade Statistics (https://www.wsts.org, released on June 8, 2021) forecast the Americas to almost double to $106 billion in 2021 and $116 billion in 2022 and the worldwide semiconductor market at $527 billion 2021 and $573 billion in 2022.

[1] Comp & DS = computing & data storage; elec. = electronics; comm. = communication

[2] EMEA refers to Europe, the Middle East, and Africa.

Source: Based on device- and component-level data from IHS Markit/Informa Tech Custom Research for GPN@NUS Centre, July–October 2019.

from lower levels in 2019, accounting for 55.8 percent of the total world-wide semiconductor market at $527 billion in 2021. In comparison, the growth in demand for other chip categories will be relatively modest.

As shown in Table 6.1, the Asia Pacific has been by far the largest market and accounted for over 70 percent of the global semiconductor shipment since 2013, more than *all* other macroregions combined. As Chapter 4 has discussed, five economies in the Asia Pacific—Taiwan, South Korea, Japan, China, and Singapore—also form the largest bloc of semiconductor producers, contributing to more than 70 percent of all wafer fabs worldwide and 81 percent of global fabrication capacity in 2018 (see Table 4.1). Much of this semiconductor production and shipment goes into two major industrial applications—computing and data storage (PCs, tablets, and servers) and wireless communications (mobile handsets and telecommunications equipment). In 2018, shipment in microprocessors ($38.9 billion) and memory devices ($61.3 billion in flash NAND and DRAM) for the final assembly of PCs, tablets, and servers in China and other East Asian locations contributed to over 76 percent of total semiconductor shipment in the computing and data storage category ($131 billion). In wireless communications, the final assembly of the vast majority of mobile handsets in East and South Asia by the late 2010s also created an enormous demand for application-specific integrated circuits, such as logic and processor chips ($50.4 billion), memory devices ($33.1 billion), analogue devices ($12.9 billion), and image sensors ($12.2 billion) in 2018. Together, these semiconductor devices for mobile handsets made up 82 percent of the total Asia Pacific semiconductor market in wireless communications at $133 billion in 2018.

Similar to the role of end user demand (i.e., consumers in China, India, and other Asia Pacific economies) in driving the geographical configuration of final assembly of ICT end products—to be analyzed later in this section, market proximity is evident in the colocation of semiconductor producers and their OEM customers, i.e., in-house facilities and/or ODM/EMS partners, within the Asia Pacific (see also a stylized illustration in Figure 4.2). This intermediate market demand comes from much of the final assembly in China in all three product categories and India and Vietnam in the case of mobile handsets.[10] Put in the GPN 2.0 theory in Figure 3.2, this important causal dynamic of the market imperative has compelled IDM and fabless firms in semiconductors to pursue strategies of intrafirm coordination and/or interfirm partnership in their global production networks that led to substantial geographical reconfigurations through new fabs and capacity growth centered in East Asia during the 2010s (see also summary Tables 4.8 and 5.4).

While market proximity to the final assembly of ICT devices and TVs and end user consumers in the Asia Pacific, particularly China, is important to semiconductor production and shipment, it is necessary to point out that a significant number of top OEM and semiconductor IDM firms and most leading fabless firms originate from and are based in the US. Component-level data and analysis in Chapter 5 and Table 5.1 to 5.3 have already confirmed the dominance of US semiconductor firms in microprocessors and application-specific logic chips for PCs and mobile handsets, whereas semiconductor firms from South Korea, Taiwan, China, and Japan are particularly dominant in memory devices, flat panel displays, and image sensors.

This visible market segmentation in components and devices in the global semiconductor industry requires most lead firms to organize their production networks in ways that connect them closely to the design and R&D centers of these US-origin OEM and semiconductor firms located in Silicon Valley and Texas and selected sites in Western Europe (e.g., Intel in Leixlip, Ireland, and GlobalFoundries in Dresden, Germany) and their in-house or ODM/EMS/foundry partners' production and final assembly locations throughout East Asia. In short, the former set of US-oriented market and technology connections matters much in the "deep dive" and technology roadmap alignment of strategic partners and key suppliers with OEM and/or fabless customers in their US headquarters, as was analyzed in Chapter 5 on interfirm relationships. The latter set of Asia-based network relationships contributes much to the execution and implementation of these US-oriented market connections at the production and final assembly levels, as was mapped out in Chapter 4. Together, these two sets of interconnections in semiconductor global production networks are driven by a significant market imperative in which China and the Asia Pacific have become increasingly indispensable to any lead firm's global ambition.

Take a new Dell notebook PC as an example of these intertwined market dynamics and production networks that integrate different localities in the interconnected worlds of global electronics (see earlier illustrations in Figures 4.2 and 5.3). As were noted by my interviewees involved as senior management in Dell's global production network,[11] its in-house design centers in Round Rock (Texas) and Taipei (Taiwan) work closely with its chosen ODM partner for the new model—Compal or Wistron from Taiwan. The initial architecture of the new model comes from its R&D team before it is handed over to the ODM partner for more wiring up and implementation. The final design and architecture resemble a joint development model analyzed in Chapter 5's section on strategic partnership. During this entire design and development process, Dell and the ODM firm keep very close working relationships with the core suppliers of semiconductors,[12] such as Intel (microprocessor made in its fabs in the US, Ireland, or Israel), Broadcom (connectivity chip made by foundry providers in East Asia), Samsung (memory made in South Korea), and BOE and AU Optronics (flat panel displays made in China and Taiwan). There are many other local suppliers clustering around the site of final assembly in China's Chengdu or Kunshan that collectively constitute this complex production network of a Dell notebook PC. Conceptualized in Figure 3.3, all of these firms—be they Dell, other lead firms, platform or technology leaders, strategic partners or local suppliers—are embedded and influenced by the same market imperative logic and therefore place a high value on their geographical and relational proximity to key customers and end markets.

Despite East Asia's overwhelming role in electronics manufacturing, many semiconductor lead firms from the US and Western Europe retain or even strengthen their R&D centers and wafer fabs in their home macroregions. As was mapped out in Chapter 4's section on intrafirm geographical configurations (Figure 4.5) and analyzed in Chapter 5's section on long-term interfirm relationships, this continual importance of the US or Europe in their organization of production networks is primarily driven by the need for intimacy with end customers whose corporate R&D functions are headquartered there. This customer intimacy remains particularly critical in automotive and industrial electronics, two major industrial applications for semiconductors in the Americas and Europe in Table 6.1. The senior vice president and chief technology officer of top ten European IDM-36 explained why over 75 percent of its R&D engineers worldwide are still located in the US and Europe (about half in each macroregion):

Customer intimacy is very critical. You really understand what the customer wants and then build this trusting relationship with their engineers. If I have some issues, I will tell you "I can solve this way." All of a sudden, a solution comes out and the business will be generated. So

I think that's the main reason. Otherwise, you know from cost perspective, then everybody just builds everything in India. Even it doesn't make any sense to build anything in China nowadays.

In ICT end products, the market imperative is also quite significant in shaping the network strategy and configurations pursued by different OEM lead firms. For products that require geographical proximity to customers and end markets, locating production networks—from R&D to manufacturing and sales and market functions—in the respective East Asian economies becomes necessary. Meanwhile, products requiring component assembly can go to locations that are cost effective in labor-intensive production. Chapter 4 has mapped in detail how China has emerged to be the dominant center for global electronics manufacturing—from key components, such as panel displays, printed circuit boards, and mechanical chassis, to final assembly (see summary Table 4.8). But its dominance as "the world factory" in global production networks is increasingly explained by its growth market dynamics, not just its low-cost advantage. Xing's (2021, 121) recent study has shown that the share of foreign firms in China's total exports was reduced from its peak at 58 percent in 2006 to 42 percent in 2018 due to the shift in their focus from exports to serving the rapidly growing domestic market in China. A former board director of the world's top three OEM-3 in consumer electronics thus argued:

> The more sophisticated manufacturing becomes, the closer you have to be to the market. This is because there is no differentiation in cost anymore. . . . Nobody invests in China anymore to do low-cost manufacturing. You invest in China to reach the market. That's what you do.

His sentiment on proximity to China as an important "domestic" market for foreign lead firms was also shared by the vice president for supply chain in top three mobile handset OEM-13:

> We were just not looking for cheaper labor cost. But we have all that strategic vision, and we want to have China as a "domestic" market growth. So, it's a part of the localization of manufacturing for China as well. Because we anticipated that there will be a lot of domestic brands that will grow, we wanted to be under the same competitive situation as other global players.

In PCs/tablets and TVs, Table 6.2 presents some trends in the world market between 2014 and the second quarter of 2019, based on custom data on 25 leading OEM firms in PCs/tablets and 36 OEM firms in TVs. While overall shipments declined in all three end products during this period, the drop was particularly drastic for tablets, at almost 50 percent, in a market dominated by Apple (31 percent share in 2018) and Samsung (17 percent). Within this context of declining world markets even before the US-China trade war since March 2018 and the COVID-19 pandemic in 2020/2021, China remained as a major and steady market for notebook PCs (almost as large as Western Europe) and TVs (the largest market).

Together with Japan and the Asia Pacific, China formed a formidable market bloc during the second half of the 2010s (see subtotals in Table 6.2), rivalling North America in PC and tablet shipment and doubling North America and trebling Western Europe in TV shipment. China's share in TV revenue, however, was less than its share in shipment units, an indication of its smaller domestic market in premium TVs. But its revenue share in notebook PCs and tablets was similar to North America and Western Europe. Overall and since the mid-2010s, China and developing economies in the Asia Pacific region are no longer only "cheap" sites for labor-intensive manufacturing as commonly understood in the existing literature on electronics production in the Global South; they have also become very important new markets for OEM lead firms from the US and East Asia (home macroregion).[13]

To examine the relative importance of China and the Asia Pacific for global lead firms, Table 6.3 focuses specifically on the top three OEM lead firms in these three end products and their world markets in 2015 and 2018. Here, the causal dynamic of home market influence is particularly visible in notebook PCs such that the US and North America accounted for around 40 percent share of Hewlett-Packard's shipment and 45–48 percent of Dell in 2015 and 2018. The corresponding home market share (China) in Lenovo's shipment was smaller at 25–33 percent. While virtually all notebook PCs by these three lead firms were assembled in China (see Table 4.3), Lenovo was able to supply to its domestic market by sourcing entirely from its in-house facilities in Hefei and Shenzhen.

In TVs, the same causal dynamic of home market influence applies to the top three lead firm—China's TCL, which assembled in its China facilities more than 70 percent of its total shipment in 2018 (Table 4.6). The huge share of its domestic market becomes the overriding driver in its

TABLE 6.2. World market for notebook PCs, tablets, and TVs, 2014–2019 Q2 by shipment and revenue (in millions of units and US$ billions)

| Product category | 2014 units | 2016 units | 2018 units | 2019 Q2 units | 2014 $b | 2016 $b | 2018 $b | 2019 Q2 $b |
|---|---|---|---|---|---|---|---|---|
| **Notebook PCs** | | | | | | | | |
| North America | 56.0 | 55.8 | 55.0 | 28.2 | 37.2 | 40.1 | 37.5 | 18.3 |
| Western Europe | 36.8 | 32.5 | 31.8 | 14.7 | 23.3 | 23.3 | 21.0 | 9.6 |
| Eastern Europe | 13.9 | 10.8 | 10.2 | 4.8 | 8.0 | 7.0 | 6.5 | 3.0 |
| Latin America | 11.3 | 10.2 | 10.2 | 4.2 | 6.0 | 5.5 | 5.9 | 2.4 |
| Middle East and Africa | 9.3 | 5.6 | 4.4 | 2.0 | 5.7 | 4.2 | 2.7 | 1.2 |
| China | 28.7 | 29.6 | 27.1 | 11.8 | 17.9 | 20.4 | 18.8 | 8.7 |
| Japan | 10.3 | 8.4 | 8.5 | 5.3 | 7.8 | 6.6 | 5.9 | 3.9 |
| Asia Pacific | 19.7 | 15.7 | 16.2 | 9.2 | 10.9 | 9.7 | 10.3 | 5.7 |
| Subtotal | 58.7 | 53.7 | 51.8 | 26.3 | 36.6 | 36.7 | 35.0 | 18.3 |
| **Total** | **186** | **169** | **163** | **80.2** | **117** | **117** | **109** | **52.6** |
| **Tablets** | | | | | | | | |
| North America | 61.1 | 44.1 | 39.0 | 16.7 | 20.7 | 15.6 | 12.9 | 6.6 |
| Western Europe | 44.1 | 33.3 | 31.7 | 12.3 | 14.9 | 11.3 | 9.0 | 4.3 |
| Eastern Europe | 15.6 | 9.7 | 7.6 | 2.8 | 4.9 | 2.8 | 1.8 | 0.8 |
| Latin America | 20.3 | 12.2 | 5.5 | 2.3 | 5.0 | 2.6 | 1.2 | 0.5 |
| Middle East and Africa | 7.2 | 9.6 | 7.2 | 2.1 | 2.2 | 2.6 | 1.5 | 0.6 |
| China | 51.0 | 40.2 | 24.8 | 10.8 | 13.9 | 12.5 | 8.3 | 4.4 |
| Japan | 10.4 | 9.2 | 8.3 | 3.7 | 4.1 | 3.8 | 3.1 | 1.8 |
| Asia Pacific | 40.4 | 30.3 | 16.6 | 6.5 | 10.2 | 6.7 | 4.6 | 2.2 |
| Subtotal | 102 | 79.7 | 49.7 | 21.0 | 28.2 | 23.0 | 16.0 | 8.4 |
| **Total** | **250** | **189** | **141** | **57.2** | **75.8** | **57.9** | **42.3** | **21.2** |
| **TVs** | | | | | | | | |
| North America | 43.5 | 43.5 | 43.9 | 18.5 | 21.1 | 19.6 | 22.5 | 9.3 |
| Western Europe | 32.1 | 29.9 | 29.1 | 13.4 | 14.7 | 12.2 | 20.6 | 8.4 |
| Eastern Europe | 20.5 | 14.6 | 15.5 | 7.0 | 8.1 | 4.8 | 7.9 | 3.4 |

|  | 2014 | 2016 | 2018 | 2019 Q2 | 2014 | 2016 | 2018 | 2019 Q2 |
| Product category | units | units | units | units | $b | $b | $b | $b |
|---|---|---|---|---|---|---|---|---|
| Latin America | 29.3 | 22.2 | 24.2 | 11.9 | 10.2 | 6.6 | 14.5 | 6.1 |
| Middle East and Africa | 16.7 | 14.0 | 12.2 | 6.3 | 6.3 | 4.3 | 5.6 | 2.6 |
| China | 54.0 | 59.8 | 54.5 | 22.5 | 26.9 | 25.9 | 22.6 | 9.2 |
| Japan | 5.7 | 5.0 | 5.2 | 2.6 | 2.1 | 1.5 | 3.8 | 1.8 |
| Asia Pacific | 33.2 | 33.6 | 36.7 | 17.3 | 9.9 | 9.0 | 18.0 | 7.4 |
| Subtotal | 92.9 | 98.4 | 96.4 | 42.4 | 38.9 | 36.4 | 44.4 | 18.4 |
| **Total** | **235** | **223** | **221** | **99.5** | **99.2** | **83.9** | **116** | **48.4** |

Source: Data from IHS Markit/Informa Tech Custom Research for GPN@NUS Centre, July–October 2016 and 2019.

geographical configuration of intrafirm production network. Meanwhile, South Korea's Samsung and LG have only limited production capacity of about 15–16 percent in China because of their lesser share in this world's largest market dominated by domestic Chinese OEM firms, such as TCL, Hisense, Xiaomi, and Skyworth. LG serves its small market share in China and nearby economies in the Asia Pacific by outsourcing TV assembly to its Chinese EMS partners (BOE and TP Vision). To serve their major markets in the Americas and Europe and to outperform their OEM competitors from China, Samsung and LG have engaged in significant intrafirm coordination of their TV global production networks and established in-house facilities in Latin America (Brazil and Mexico) and Eastern Europe (Samsung in Hungary, Slovakia, and Russia, and LG in Poland). Samsung has also established an assembly facility in Egypt to serve the Middle East and Africa market.

In mobile handsets—by far the largest segment in global electronics in 2018 (Figure 2.3) due to very high growth since the "smartphone revolution" (Table 2.1), the market significance of China and Asia has been much more pronounced since the mid-2010s. The product dominance of smartphones, as opposed to feature phones, is evident in its rapidly growing share in mobile handsets from a modest 29 percent of total demand in 2010 to 85 percent in 2018 and 95 percent in 2023 (projected). As indicated in Tables 6.4 and 6.5, China alone has been a gigantic market for

TABLE 6.3. World market for top 3 OEM firms in notebook PCs, tablets, and TVs, 2015 and 2018, by shipment (in millions of units)

| Product category | 2015 | 2018 | 2015 | 2018 | 2015 | 2018 |
|---|---|---|---|---|---|---|
| **Notebook PCs** | **HP** | **HP** | **Lenovo** | **Lenovo** | **Dell** | **Dell** |
| North America | 13.5 | 16.3 | 6.7 | 8.6 | 9.7 | 12.9 |
| Western Europe | 7.3 | 8.9 | 9.5 | 8.4 | 2.6 | 3.6 |
| Eastern Europe | 3.2 | 2.8 | 2.3 | 3.0 | 1.5 | 1.3 |
| China | 3.3 | 4.2 | 11.8 | 9.4 | 3.3 | 3.4 |
| Japan | 0.9 | 2.1 | 1.0 | 0.8 | 0.4 | 0.7 |
| Asia Pacific | 2.0 | 2.2 | 2.1 | 3.3 | 2.6 | 2.3 |
| Latin America | 3.3 | 2.7 | 2.1 | 2.3 | 1.4 | 1.9 |
| Middle East and Africa | 1.4 | 1.2 | 0.8 | 0.8 | 0.5 | 0.8 |
| **Total** | **34.9** | **40.4** | **36.3** | **36.6** | **22.0** | **26.9** |
| **Tablets** | **Apple** | **Apple** | **Samsung** | **Samsung** | **Huawei** | **Huawei** |
| North America | 13.8 | 13.0 | 7.3 | 6.5 | 0.0 | 0.1 |
| Western Europe | 9.3 | 7.9 | 7.9 | 6.0 | 1.2 | 2.0 |
| Eastern Europe | 1.5 | 1.3 | 3.2 | 1.7 | 0.4 | 1.8 |
| China | 14.7 | 10.7 | 1.2 | 0.5 | 2.9 | 6.4 |
| Japan | 2.9 | 2.8 | 0.1 | 0.0 | 1.0 | 1.8 |
| Asia Pacific | 5.4 | 5.2 | 8.7 | 5.2 | 0.8 | 0.9 |
| Latin America | 1.2 | 1.1 | 2.8 | 1.8 | 0.2 | 0.5 |
| Middle East and Africa | 0.8 | 1.3 | 3.7 | 2.7 | 1.1 | 1.0 |
| **Total** | **49.6** | **43.3** | **34.9** | **24.4** | **7.6** | **14.5** |
| **TVs** | **Samsung** | **Samsung** | **LG** | **LG** | **TCL** | **TCL** |
| North America | 11.1 | 10.5 | 4.5 | 5.8 | 0.4 | 5.6 |
| Western Europe | 10.1 | 7.3 | 4.5 | 4.4 | 1.1 | 0.8 |
| Eastern Europe | 6.8 | 4.4 | 5.9 | 3.8 | 0.1 | 0.2 |
| China | 2.8 | 0.9 | 0.9 | 0.3 | 8.5 | 7.1 |
| Japan | 0.0 | 0.0 | 0.2 | 0.1 | 0.0 | 0.1 |
| Asia Pacific | 7.2 | 6.9 | 6.1 | 4.8 | 1.2 | 1.8 |
| Latin America | 7.9 | 7.9 | 7.7 | 5.5 | 0.5 | 1.7 |
| Middle East and Africa | 7.0 | 3.5 | 4.3 | 2.3 | 0.4 | 0.5 |
| **Total** | **52.9** | **41.4** | **34.1** | **27.0** | **12.2** | **17.8** |

Note: TV data for 2015 refer to 2014.

Source: Data from IHS Markit/Informa Tech Custom Research for GPN@NUS Centre, July–October 2016 and 2019.

TABLE 6.4. World market for new mobile handset purchases, 2010–2023 (in millions of units)

| Region/Country | 2010 | 2013 | 2014 | 2015 | 2016 | 2017 | 2018 | 2019ᶠ | 2020ᶠ | 2021ᶠ | 2022ᶠ | 2023ᶠ |
|---|---|---|---|---|---|---|---|---|---|---|---|---|
| North America | 15.9 | 14.1 | 14.9 | 10.3 | 12.8 | 12.5 | 13.3 | 12.9 | 11.5 | 11.4 | 8.7 | 8.2 |
| Latin America | 84.7 | 32.1 | 22.2 | 18.1 | 14.2 | 12.5 | 14.1 | 15.1 | 13.8 | 11.5 | 10.2 | 5.1 |
| West Europe | 50.0 | 8.4 | 7.0 | 5.1 | 5.0 | 5.0 | 4.5 | 5.2 | 5.2 | 4.9 | 4.5 | 4.0 |
| East Europe | 38.9 | 1.3 | 0.9 | 0.0 | 0.2 | 0.4 | 1.1 | 1.0 | 0.9 | 0.9 | 0.8 | 0.8 |
| China | 89.2 | 110 | 89.4 | 34.5 | 37.4 | 40.1 | 41.5 | 142 | 120 | 80.5 | 59.6 | 50.1 |
| Japan | 6.4 | 7.4 | 8.5 | 9.4 | 6.3 | 5.1 | 6.3 | 6.7 | 2.4 | 1.4 | 1.0 | 0.5 |
| South Korea | 1.7 | 2.3 | 3.2 | 4.0 | 2.6 | 2.7 | 2.9 | 1.5 | 1.3 | 1.1 | 0.7 | 0.5 |
| Asia, Others | 320 | 284 | 95.1 | 64.5 | 92.4 | 107 | 133 | 151 | 162 | 155 | 135 | 112 |
| Others | 49.4 | 63.6 | 50.3 | 25.6 | 38.1 | 48.1 | 56.9 | 76.4 | 76.9 | 67.2 | 55.5 | 48.1 |
| **Total** | **657** | **523** | **292** | **172** | **209** | **234** | **273** | **412** | **394** | **334** | **276** | **229** |

Note: 2019–2023 data based on forecast at the end of second quarter 2019. Actual numbers in 2020–2023 are/will be likely lower due to the COVID-19 pandemic in 2020/2021.

Source: Data from IHS Markit/Informa Tech Custom Research for GPN@NUS Centre, July–October 2016 and 2019.

TABLE 6.5. World market for mobile handset replacement, 2010–2023 (in millions of units)

| Region/Country | 2010 | 2013 | 2014 | 2015 | 2016 | 2017 | 2018 | 2019F | 2020F | 2021F | 2022F | 2023F |
|---|---|---|---|---|---|---|---|---|---|---|---|---|
| North America | 106 | 105 | 110 | 111 | 108 | 112 | 110 | 105 | 111 | 110 | 111 | 113 |
| Latin America | 74 | 128 | 143 | 152 | 158 | 156 | 153 | 151 | 154 | 157 | 159 | 160 |
| West Europe | 117 | 108 | 110 | 112 | 112 | 112 | 112 | 105 | 109 | 110 | 111 | 112 |
| East Europe | 58 | 81 | 81 | 81 | 79 | 79 | 77 | 77 | 76 | 76 | 76 | 76 |
| China | 167 | 272 | 336 | 393 | 391 | 395 | 367 | 261 | 281 | 326 | 343 | 356 |
| Japan | 34 | 32 | 30 | 26 | 28 | 30 | 29 | 28 | 33 | 31 | 32 | 32 |
| South Korea | 21 | 21 | 22 | 20 | 22 | 23 | 23 | 24 | 25 | 25 | 25 | 25 |
| Asia, Others | 164 | 377 | 601 | 637 | 595 | 576 | 525 | 484 | 454 | 472 | 503 | 517 |
| Others | 122 | 155 | 179 | 214 | 213 | 221 | 216 | 181 | 171 | 180 | 208 | 215 |
| **Total** | **864** | **1,279** | **1,610** | **1,746** | **1,708** | **1,704** | **1,612** | **1,416** | **1,413** | **1,486** | **1,568** | **1,606** |

Note: 2019–2023 data based on forecast at the end of second quarter 2019. Actual numbers in 2020–2023 are/will be likely much lower due to the COVID-19 pandemic in 2020/2021. Data from Trendforce (https://www.trendforce.com, released on January 5 and May 10, 2021) and Canalys (https://www.canalys.com, released on June 14, 2021) show global smartphone production and shipments at 1.25–1.27 billion units in 2020 and forecast at 1.36–1.42 billion units in 2021 and 1.48 billion units in 2022.
Source: Data from IHS Markit/Informa Tech Custom Research for GPN@NUS Centre, July–October 2016 and 2019.

new mobile handset purchases and replacement, accounting for 15–34 percent between 2010 and 2018 and 20–30 percent in 2019–2023 (projected). Other Asian economies, from India to large Southeast Asian countries such as Indonesia, the Philippines, and Vietnam, form an even bigger market bloc for both new handset purchases and replacement during this period. Together, China and Asia (Others) now account for 50–60 percent of the global market for new purchases and replacement in mobile handsets. This massive Asian home market explains why Samsung has established its largest in-house mobile handset assembly operations in high-growth Asian countries, such as Vietnam and India (see Table 4.5).

Within East Asia, this home market influence remains significant for mobile handset lead firms from South Korea, China, and Japan, which often use home markets as a test bed for new products before rolling out for worldwide markets.[14] This in turn explains why their core R&D functions and "master factories" remain located in home countries, e.g., Samsung and LG in South Korea and Fujitsu and Kyocera in Japan. All major mobile handset OEM firms from China, such as Huawei, Xiaomi, Oppo, and Vivo, also have massive assembly operations in India that are either in-house (Oppo and Vivo) or outsourced to Flex (Huawei) and Foxconn (Xiaomi). The causal role of market presence in driving their assembly production networks is clearly quite significant, once these lead firms have overcome the thorny issue of optimizing cost-capability ratios in their production sites outside China.

### Financial Discipline

Financial consideration is often one of the most important explanations for how some lead firms organize their production networks, whether it is about outsourcing to strategic partners, capital investment to support existing or new customers, or joint product development with key suppliers. Among many of the lead firms interviewed, important financial indicators are return on invested capital, cash cycles, and cost ratios. All of these can significantly influence a lead firm's shareholder value that may in turn impact on its stock price if a lead firm is publicly listed, particularly those on the NYSE or Nasdaq in New York. Delivering higher shareholder value through the optimal geographical and organizational configurations of their production networks has become an overarching goal of lead firms in general, as was theorized in Chapter 3's causal driver of financialization—a process understood as financial market dynamics driving an OEM lead firm's (re-)allocation of value propositions and its productive and intangible assets.

In semiconductors, financial discipline is clearly much more imposing than in ICT end products. Its segment-specific causal dynamics in terms of high financial market pressure and high capital expenditure and sunk costs in new fabs merit more detailed analysis below. First and as explained by the vice president and chief supply chain officer of top ten IDM-34 from outside East Asia, the role of financial market pressure through quarterly reports or what he terms "the sunshine test of ninety days" can be huge, but it does compel IDM-34 to move faster and configure its production network efficiently. IDM-34 used to be a "book value" company, i.e., market value equivalent to the net value of its balance sheet. To improve its cash flow and the financial performance of its newly acquired wafer fabs since the mid-2010s, IDM-34 invested heavily in improving the operational efficiency and process innovation of its worldwide fabs even before the arrival of new customer orders—a significant financial risk in the boom-and-bust business cycles of semiconductors. After a good period of delivering predictable earnings per share (EPS), its market value went up multiple times of its book value, and that helped improve its cash flow for further capital expenditure and better debt management. On this immense quarterly pressure from financial markets, he noted:

> Well, in one sense, it's actually good because the transparency around the financial data across areas of the company is phenomenal. . . . But we know that we have to continue to get the EPS to be multiple. And multiple is everything because if we get market capital through that, we then have different opportunities. So, I think I actually like being in the sunshine test of ninety days—the business I came in, the quality of the discussion, and the urgency to make decisions is much better. I don't know for any better making it, but the pressure is very good.

Second, investment in new fabs since the mid-2010s has become very costly due to high capital spending, rapid depreciation, and frequent process technology upgrades. The cost of building new fabs easily exceeds $10–$15 billion per fab and capital expenditure is often very large for leading semiconductor firms. As of 2021, the ten-year cost of a leading-edge foundry fab, from initial expenditure to annual operating costs, can reach $40 billion.[15] In foundry services, this enormous pressure from financial discipline on the broader semiconductor industry has ironically favored only a few foundry providers from Taiwan (TSMC), South Korea (Samsung foundry), and China (SMIC) that invested aggressively in new fabs and capital equipment during the 2010s. As was noted in Chapter 1's national and institutional contexts (see summary Table 1.2), more "patient capital" is available in the East Asian business systems through longer-term capital markets, intra–business group cross-subsidization, family or state ownership and control, and supportive sectoral industrial policy.[16]

China's SMIC, for example, counts the state-backed China Integrated Circuit Industry Investment Fund—also known as the National IC Fund—among its major shareholders and is a major beneficiary of the socialist state's Made in China 2025 plan in 2015 to channel $150 billion over ten years through the fund to boost China's domestic semiconductor production. Despite US sanctions on its import of US chip-making equipment and technology, SMIC remained committed to establishing new fabs to cater to applications in automotive and consumer electronics. On March 18, 2021, it announced a new $2.4 billion 28 nm fab to be built by 2022 in the southern city of Shenzhen, with 23 percent stake owned by the Shenzhen government.[17] This new fab adds to the planned $7.7 billion new fab in Beijing to be ready by 2024.

On the contrary and with very few exceptions (i.e., Intel and Micron), capital markets in the US do not favor IDM firms that incur high capital expenditure. In Silicon Valley, venture capital prefers to invest in high-value and potentially high-return chip design work by US semiconductor firms that remain fabless or fab-lite and yet strong in proprietary technology and intellectual property.[18] Throughout the 2010s, the preferred model for Silicon Valley-based semiconductor firms was to focus on software and custom chip designs and to outsource wafer manufacturing to foundry providers (e.g., TSMC, GlobalFoundries, and Samsung foundry) and their back-end service partners (e.g., ASE) in chip assembly, packaging, and testing, as illustrated in Figure 5.2.

As technology leaders in semiconductor manufacturing, two very large East Asian foundry firms—TSMC and Samsung's foundry division—were able to raise capital domestically in Taiwan and South Korea to fund their massive investments in new and existing fabs during the 2010s (see Tables 4.1 and 4.2). As was discussed in the Apple-Samsung/TSMC case in Chapter 5 and the earlier section in this chapter, the cost associated with the most advanced nodes can be enormous (e.g., TSMC's new 3 nm fab in mid-2022 costing at least $20 billion). To put in perspective this high capital spending, cutting-edge technology nodes at 5 to 7 nm are currently needed in fabricating the most powerful logic chips (e.g., application processors for smartphones) or microprocessors from Intel, AMD, or Nvidia for new advanced applications (e.g., artificial intelligence, cloud computing, 5G communications, and autonomous systems).[19] Chapter 5 has already mentioned GlobalFoundries' premature ending of planned transition to 7 nm process node in August 2018 because its $10–$15 billion price tag could not be justified on financial grounds. Since its spin-off from AMD (then an IDM firm) in 2009, GlobalFoundries has entered into a long-term and renewable wafer supply agreement with AMD. But its termination of transition to cutting-edge process technology in late 2018 has compelled now fabless AMD to find new foundry partners to sustain its continuous innovation in chip design.

Since 2019, AMD has switched to TSMC's 7 nm node to fabricate its most advanced microprocessors so that it can compete against Intel in the PC and gaming markets. The same competitive logic applies to the graphics processors market led by AMD, Nvidia, and then Intel. By moving into semicustom chips for game consoles by Sony (PlayStation) and Microsoft (Xbox) and graphics chips for PC lead firms, AMD has tried since 2019 to keep up with Intel's challenge (having its own 10 nm fabs) by combining in-house design capabilities with TSMC's proven 7 nm process technology. Meanwhile, another leading fabless firm from the US, Nvidia, also relies on TSMC 7–10 nm fabs to fabricate its market-leading graphics processor chips.[20] In his comparison of the foundry fabs of GlobalFoundries and TSMC, the corporate vice president of top US Fabless-29 confirmed:

> TSMC has basically done all the graphics chips for Nvidia, and they've got a lot of specialized technology for GPUs [graphics processing units]. So they've been sort of the de facto standard. GlobalFoundries didn't start doing graphics until AMD moved over because it had a wafer agreement. TSMC was the sole manufacturer for all of AMD's GPUs. . . . It's very clear that the expertise that TSMC has is still benefitting AMD—just cheaper and much higher yield, frequent technology updates, less delays, and less problems. TSMC's is a much more mature process for GPUs.

How significant then are the financial commitments of TSMC, Samsung, Intel, and a few others in their new fab investment during the 2010s

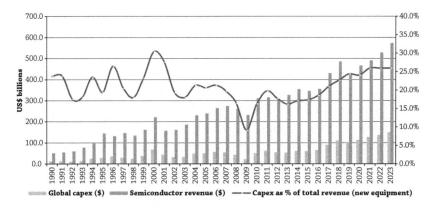

Note: 1990–2020 data are actual and 2021–2023 are forecast.

FIGURE 6.2. Capital expenditure to revenue ratios in the global semiconductor industry, 1990–2023 (in US$ billions and percent).

Sources: 1990–2023 data from IHS Markit/Informa Tech Custom Research for GPN@ NUS Centre, July–October 2019; 2019–2023 data updated from Downey (2021), IC Insights (https://www.icinsights.com, released on March 16, 2021), and World Semiconductor Trade Statistics Forecast (https://www.wsts.org, released on June 8, 2021).

in order to support their in-house needs (Samsung and Intel) and foundry demand from fabless or fab-lite customers (TSMC and Samsung)? Figure 6.2 offers an overview of the capital expenditure (capex) in the global semiconductor industry from 1990 to 2023.[21] In an industrial context of growing revenue that peaked in 2018, global capex has been gradually increasing to its first peak at $67 billion in 2000 due to new demand from the Y2K problem and the dot.com rush. But this increase in global capex began to taper off to $40–$50 billion annually during the 2000s and $50–60 billion annually up to the mid-2010s. In 2018, global capex exceeded $100 billion for the first time and will likely increase much further to over $140 billion in 2021. Viewed as a percentage of total industry revenue, however, capex in new equipment shows very significant variations, from the peak of 30–35 percent in 2000 to 9 percent in 2009 during the global financial crisis and 22–26 percent in the 2017–2021 period.

Meanwhile, the semiconductor manufacturing equipment used in the most advanced process nodes at the technological frontiers has become much more costly to develop. Only a few top IDM and foundry firms can afford them in their new fabs. In this heavily consolidated segment, there are often only one to two dominant suppliers for certain equipment. In 2018, the top five equipment suppliers ranked by revenue—Applied Materials (US), Tokyo Electron (Japan), Lam Research (US), ASML (the Netherlands), and KLA-Tencor (US)—accounted for over 74 percent of the $64.5 billion market. Each of them is dominant in a specific equipment segment: chemical vapor deposition (50 percent by Applied Materials, then Lam Research and Tokyo Electron), photolithography (75 percent by ASML, then Canon and Nikon from Japan), etch (60 percent by Lam Research, then Tokyo Electron and Applied Materials), and quality and process control (55 percent by KLA-Tencor). By 2020, this worldwide market for semiconductor manufacturing equipment increased further to a historical peak at $71 billion, though the top five share decreased to 61 percent. The SEMI forecast in July 2021 indicates massive market growth to $95 billion in 2021 and over $100 billion in 2022.[22] ASML, for example, is the only supplier for the most advanced photolithography equipment, priced at over $100 million each in 2018, for chip production based on its proprietary extreme ultraviolet lithography (EUV) technology indispensable for cutting-edge wafer fabrication at 7 nm node or below.[23] As was lamented by the senior vice president and chief technology officer of top ten European IDM-36 that had gone fab-lite in lieu of spending billions of dollars in capex per year,

> We have 300 to 400 steps in every process, and anything can go wrong. If one thing goes wrong, the entire thing will be wiped out. So it's not worth the risk of engaging with nonstandard or unproven equipment. That is the reason why for equipment vendors, the entry barrier is extremely high because the cost of ownership goes way beyond the machine itself. Machine itself is almost nothing. So that's why ASML is selling this equipment for $100 million per piece. But you have to go with it.

The vice president of another leading Asian semiconductor firm SE-43 also echoed this: "Some suppliers are competing against each other. But some suppliers don't have competitors. There is nothing we can do. Like ASML doesn't have competitors actually. There is Tokyo Electron, but it cannot compare with them. ASML's quality is definitely much better."

Between 2005 and 2018 in Figure 6.2, the total industry revenue doubled from $240 billion to the historical peak at $485 billion. But global capex only managed to catch up with this doubling of industry revenue by 2017 and 2018, indicating a divergent trend of relatively higher revenue generated by *more* leading IDM and fabless firms, and modest capex by *fewer* top IDM and foundry firms. To probe further this divergence in semiconductor revenue (by more large firms) and capex (by only a few large investing firms), Table 6.6 examines firm-specific capital spending by IDM firms and foundry providers between 2000 and 2021. Several important observations stand out. First, the share of top ten semiconductor firms (IDM and foundry) in global capex almost doubled between 2005 (45 percent) and 2020 (86 percent), but their share in industry revenue increased only slightly from 48 percent to 55 percent, pointing to a much greater concentration in spending power among these top ten firms. In short, only the highest revenue–generating semiconductor firms can invest heavily in new fabs or process upgrades in the late 2010s and beyond.

Second, the mix of these top ten semiconductor firms in capex has changed drastically over this period. In 2000, two foundry providers TSMC and UMC were among the top ten, together with a diverse mix of IDM firms from the US, Western Europe, Japan, and South Korea. By 2018, this list of top ten capex spenders changed dramatically in favor of East Asian firms—only Intel and Micron from the US remained in the top list. The rest were Samsung and SK Hynix from South Korea, TSMC from Taiwan, Toshiba (renamed to Kioxia in 2019) from Japan, and three newcomers in memory chips from China (Yangtze River, Changxin Memory, and Fujian Jinhua).[24]

Third and similar to its increasing share over time in semiconductor product categories (34 percent in 2018 in Table 2.5), the share of memory chips in global capex increased massively during this period, from 39 percent in 2005 to peak at 60 percent in 2018. Except Micron from the US, this segment of semiconductors has long been a strong foothold of IDM firms from East Asia since the heydays of Japanese memory chip production in the 1980s (see Chapter 2). Fourth, the share of foundry providers in global capex has grown from 9.7 percent in 2000 to peak at 29 percent in 2016, but since then, decreased to only 14 percent in 2018 and will likely exceed 29 percent in 2021. As the only pureplay foundry provider going against this downward trend in overall capex share, TSMC has been a formidable market leader. Between 2000 and 2021, its capex was consistently among the top three globally—below Samsung but above Intel in some years.

TABLE 6.6. Global semiconductor capital spending by top IDM and foundry firms, 2000–2021 (in US$ billions)

| | 2000 | 2005 | 2010 | 2012 | 2015 | 2016 | 2017 | 2018 | 2019 | 2020 | 2021[F] |
|---|---|---|---|---|---|---|---|---|---|---|---|
| **IDM** | | | | | | | | | | | |
| Samsung | 4.1 | 7.0 | 9.7 | 13.1 | 12.8 | 11.3 | 24.2 | 26.9 | 20.0 | 28.1 | 28.0 |
| Intel | 6.7 | 5.8 | 5.2 | 11.0 | 7.3 | 9.6 | 11.8 | 15.2 | 16.2 | 14.3 | 19.5 |
| SK Hynix | 1.6 | 1.8 | 3.0 | 3.7 | 6.0 | 5.1 | 8.1 | 14.5 | 8.3 | 8.9 | 9.5 |
| Micron | 1.5 | 1.2 | 1.1 | 1.6 | 4.4 | 6.1 | 5.9 | 9.1 | 9.0 | 7.9 | 9.0 |
| Kioxia (Toshiba) | 1.4 | 1.8 | 2.7 | 1.6 | 2.5 | 4.1 | 4.7 | 6.0 | 5.5 | 4.5 | 5.5 |
| Yangtze River | 0.0 | 0.0 | 0.0 | 0.0 | 0.0 | 0.0 | 2.5 | 3.0 | 2.7 | 4.5 | 5.5 |
| Changxin Memory | 0.0 | 0.0 | 0.0 | 0.0 | 0.0 | 0.0 | 0.5 | 3.6 | 2.2 | 2.0 | 2.0 |
| Fujian Jinhua | 0.0 | 0.0 | 0.0 | 0.0 | 0.0 | 0.0 | 1.0 | 2.3 | 0.5 | 0.3 | – |
| Infineon | 1.7 | 1.6 | 0.5 | 0.8 | 0.8 | 0.9 | 1.1 | 1.5 | 1.7 | 1.1 | 1.9 |
| Sony | 0.8 | 1.4 | 0.8 | 1.4 | 1.8 | 1.2 | 0.9 | 1.4 | 0.8 | 2.5 | 2.2 |
| Texas Instruments | 2.8 | 1.3 | 1.2 | 0.5 | 0.6 | 0.5 | 0.7 | 1.1 | 0.9 | 0.7 | 1.0 |
| STMicroelectronics | 3.3 | 1.4 | 1.0 | 0.5 | 0.5 | 0.6 | 1.3 | 1.3 | 1.2 | 1.3 | 2.0 |
| NXP (Freescale) | 1.5 | 0.4 | 0.3 | 0.3 | 0.3 | 0.4 | 0.6 | 0.6 | 0.5 | 0.4 | – |
| JP IDM firms[1] | 9.0 | 4.3 | 1.7 | 0.7 | 0.9 | 1.1 | 1.1 | 0.6 | 0.5 | 0.5 | – |
| US IDM firms[1] | 4.4 | 1.4 | 1.0 | 0.6 | 0.2 | 0.0 | 0.0 | 0.0 | 0.0 | 0.0 | – |

**Foundry**

| | | | | | | | | | | | |
|---|---|---|---|---|---|---|---|---|---|---|---|
| TSMC | 2.5 | 2.5 | 6.1 | 8.2 | 7.9 | 10.1 | 10.9 | 10.5 | 14.9 | 17.2 | 30.0 |
| GlobalFoundries | 0.0 | 0.0 | 2.9 | 3.8 | 4.4 | 2.7 | 2.8 | 1.9 | 0.7 | 0.7 | 1.4 |
| SMIC | 0.0 | 0.8 | 0.7 | 0.5 | 1.6 | 2.7 | 2.5 | 1.8 | 2.1 | 6.7 | 4.3 |
| UMC | 2.6 | 0.7 | 1.9 | 1.8 | 1.9 | 2.9 | 1.5 | 0.7 | 0.6 | 1.0 | 1.5 |
| **Total capex** | | | | | | | | | | | |
| Global capex (A) | 67.0 | 49.5 | 50.7 | 54.5 | 60.0 | 65.6 | 90.2 | 109.9 | 103 | 113 | 127 |
| Memory capex | - | 19.4 | 19.3 | 13.6 | 23.8 | 27.7 | 47.5 | 66.1 | 49.9 | 56.2 | 59.5 |
| Memory % of (A) | - | 39.3 | 38.2 | 25.0 | 39.7 | 42.2 | 52.7 | 60.1 | 48.5 | 50.2 | 46.9 |
| Foundry capex | 6.5 | 6.0 | 12.2 | 14.8 | 16.1 | 19.1 | 18.2 | 15.4 | 18.7 | 26.0 | 37.6 |
| Foundry % of (A) | 9.7 | 12.1 | 24.0 | 27.2 | 26.9 | 29.1 | 20.2 | 14.1 | 18.2 | 23.2 | 29.6 |
| Top 10 capex | 20.6 | 22.3 | 29.6 | 40.1 | 50.5 | 55.9 | 74.8 | 92.8 | 81.7 | 96.6 | 116 |
| Top 10 of (A) | 31.0 | 45.0 | 58.5 | 73.7 | 84.1 | 85.1 | 83.1 | 84.4 | 79.3 | 86.3 | 91.3 |
| Global revenue (B) | 221 | 240 | 312 | 308 | 346 | 353 | 430 | 485 | 422 | 466 | 527 |
| (A) % of (B) | 30.3 | 20.6 | 16.3 | 17.7 | 17.3 | 18.6 | 21.0 | 22.7 | 24.4 | 24.0 | 24.1 |
| Top 10 revenue | 98.9 | 115 | 147 | 152 | 183 | 191 | 251 | 291 | 232 | 257 | - |
| Top 10 of (B) | 44.8 | 48.1 | 47.3 | 49.3 | 53.0 | 54.2 | 58.5 | 60.3 | 55.0 | 55.2 | - |

[1] Japan IDM firms: Fujitsu, Hitachi, Mitsubishi, NEC, Panasonic, Renesas, and SCEI (Sony); US IDM firms: IBM and Motorola (Freescale).

Sources: 2000–2019 data from IHS Markit/Informa Tech Custom Research for GPN@NUS Centre, July–October 2019; 2019–2021 (forecast) capex data updated from various company reports, Downey (2021), and IC Insights (https://www.icinsights.com, released on March 16, 2021); 2019–2021 (forecast) data on global revenue from Gartner (http://www.gartner.com, released on April 12, 2021) and World Semiconductor Trade Statistics Forecast (https://www.wsts.org, released on June 8, 2021).

From the above trends on capital expenditure in semiconductor fabs, it is clear that by the late 2010s, only a few IDM firms and TSMC could afford the truly massive capital investment required in building or transiting toward the latest technological nodes in wafer fabrication. At $27 billion in 2018, Samsung's capex more than doubled TSMC's spending and was just below the next two IDM firms combined—Intel and SK Hynix. But given Intel and SK Hynix's exclusive focus on one key product category each—Intel in microprocessor chips and SK Hynix in memory, only Samsung covers several product categories, from its market-leading position in memory to its logic and foundry fabs. In memory chips, the demand for the latest technology node is relatively less than in logic chips (microprocessors for PCs, servers, and mobile handsets).

By end of 2021 and in 2022, TSMC will exceed Samsung's $28–$32 billion capital expenditure, as both lead firms had announced eye-popping fab investment plans—TSMC's $100 billion plan for 2022–2025 announced on April 1, 2021, and Samsung's $151 billion plan in nonmemory chips through to 2030 announced on May 13, 2021.[25] To reduce its technology and market gaps with TSMC and Samsung, Intel announced a $20 billion plan in March 2021 to build two advanced foundry fabs next to its Fab 42 in Chandler, Arizona. These foundry fabs will operate under its new independent business unit, Intel Foundry Services, and might count on Qualcomm, Amazon, Cisco, and Microsoft as its early customers.[26] With all these enormous fab projects, Semiconductor Equipment and Materials International (SEMI) forecasted that the industry would break ground on nineteen new high-volume fabs in 2021 and ten in 2022, pushing capital expenditure on equipment in these fabs to over $140 billion in two years.[27]

As was mapped out in Chapter 4 and elaborated further in Chapter 5, in this technologically most demanding market for logic chips, the top four firms in 2018 were all from the US, and three of them were fabless—Broadcom, Qualcomm, and Nvidia, together with Intel. Another fabless firm, MediaTek from Taiwan, was ranked fifth. All four fabless firms depend on top foundry providers, led by TSMC and Samsung, for their wafer fabrication. But MediaTek was catching up quickly and indeed eclipsed Qualcomm as the top smartphone chipset vendor in 2020 (and most likely in 2021). Unlike Qualcomm using both TSMC and Samsung to leverage pricing for its high-volume chips, MediaTek worked primarily with TSMC and thus benefited from access to its latest process technologies in semiconductor fabrication. In 2021, MediaTek would become TSMC's third largest customer with 8.2 percent share, after Apple (25 percent) and AMD (9.2) but before Broadcom (8.1 percent) and Qualcomm (7.6 percent).[28] The top three OEM lead firms in mobile handsets—Samsung, Apple, and Huawei (up to 2020)—also rely on a mix of application processor chips designed by in-house teams (100 percent in Apple's case) and external suppliers such as Qualcomm and MediaTek. But even these in-house-designed chips require the cutting-edge foundry production—Apple and Huawei chips by TSMC and Samsung by its foundry division.

In a nutshell, the fast-moving financial pressure of Wall Street and venture capitalists in Silicon Valley favors investment in the design of high-value and high-return logic chips by these fabless firms that go into all ICT products.[29] Neither Intel nor Micron was able to keep up with the capital spending by TSMC and Samsung in the cutting-edge nodes at 5 nm and 3 nm entering mass production respectively in 2020 and 2022 that could support these fabless firms and Samsung's internal demand through to the mid-2020s. Financial discipline has therefore driven most major IDM and fabless firms to reconfigure geographically and organizationally their production networks toward East Asia–based fabs since the mid-2010s. In response to increasing geopolitical tensions and the ongoing US-China trade war since March 2018—a causal driver to be discussed later in the final section on risks, TSMC announced on May 15, 2020, that it would invest up to $12 billion over nine years between 2021 and 2029 to build a 5 nm fab in Arizona, the US. But by the time this relatively small fab goes into actual operation in 2024, it would not be at the cutting edge because TSMC's $20+ billion 3 nm fab in Taiwan is expected to start volume production in the second half of 2022. This Arizona fab's proposed capex of $12 billion over nine years is also rather modest compared to TSMC that spent $17.2 billion in 2020 alone and a whopping $30 billion in 2021 (Table 6.6) and expected $44 billion in 2022! Some of TSMC's spending might go into its future US plan for up to six new fabs at the Arizona site over a ten- to fifteen-year time period.[30]

In ICT end products, financial discipline is relatively less significant as a causal driver than in semiconductors and impacts on production network configurations in more indirect ways. Still, many lead firms in my study have conceded that shareholder pressure comes primarily from meeting market forecasts rather than stock price per se. The senior vice president for Asia Pacific and Japan of European top OEM-12 in mobile handsets and telecommunications noted that his firm is very concerned with meeting its market forecasts:

> We like to make a forecast of the market in terms of where the market is going to be and where the profitability and share price etc. we want to be. . . . and that we absolutely want to take as something which we have to at the minimum deliver. We don't want to surprise the market either negatively or too far positively as well. . . . So to be clear, shareholder value is important but to keep to our forecast is absolutely critical.

All top US-origin OEM lead firms in my study, such as those in PCs (Dell, Hewlett-Packard, and Apple), mobile handsets (Apple), and telecommunications equipment (Cisco), are subject to immense financial market pressures to meet or exceed market forecasts on revenue and profit margins. This financial discipline from Wall Street has prompted them to find innovative ways to organize and reconfigure their production networks. As were analyzed in Chapter 4 (also Tables 4.3 and 4.4), all three US PC lead firms, for example, have divested as much as possible their final assembly operations to stay "asset-lite" and outsourced production activities to their preferred ODM and/or EMS partners from Taiwan. In notebook PCs, they have also developed very close working relationships with ODM partners and leveraged their design and production capabilities and R&D resources to codevelop new generation products, as were discussed in Chapter 5's section on strategic partnership.[31] Since the mid-2010s, these strategic partners from Taiwan have developed a new ODM 2.0 model that can provide greater value services, such as product innovation and market solutions, to their OEM customers. In their notebook PC business, these US lead firms are able to economize on their ODM partner's product design knowhow and manufacturing excellence and capture more value from branding and marketing expertise through this asset-lite or "factory-less" approach to financial management. In mobile handsets, Apple is well known for its complete outsourcing of all iPhone assembly to EMS providers from Taiwan, such as Foxconn, Pegatron, and Wistron in Table 4.5.[32]

Only in desktop PCs do these lead firms retain some control over final assembly by having their own in-house configuration facilities in Ireland (Apple) and China, Brazil, and India (Dell). One of the key financial drivers for retaining these in-house assembly facilities in their global production networks is cash cycles. For example, top three PC OEM-22 has a punishing cash cycle of eleven to thirteen days from payables of acquiring inventory (parts and components) to receivables based on the actual sale of its PCs. It prefers ODM partners for notebook PC assembly because of "longer" supply chains arising from the greater complexity and more components and parts involved in producing a notebook PC. By outsourcing completely to ODM partners and yet maintaining strong supply chain control, PC OEM-22 can optimize its inventory costs such that 70–80 percent are borne by these partners until its notebook PCs reach end customers (corporate or consumers). For long-distance markets in the Americas and Europe, shipment by air is used to optimize inventory cost while products are in transit.

But for OEM-22's desktop PCs, fewer parts and production complexity are involved, and the supply chain can be shorter and more localized near to end markets. It makes no financial sense to assemble a desktop PC in China and ship it to the Americas or Europe via sea freight that may take six to eight weeks. The inventory cost of these desktop PCs in transit will be high and stretched well beyond its short cash cycle (<14 days). From this financial perspective, it becomes more viable for OEM-22 to source by air freight the "barebone" (chassis and motherboard) subassembly of a desktop PC from East Asian locations and to complete the labor-intensive final assembly process in its in-house configuration centers that serve as regional hubs for delivering to major end markets outside the Asia Pacific.

**Risk Mitigation**

As global electronics production has evolved from the earlier decades of internationalization to become even more centered in East Asia during the 2010s, the risk driver in configuring production networks is also becoming more apparent. Chapter 3's GPN 2.0 theory has identified different types of risks during the 2010s and the relevant examples in global electronics in Table 3.2. In my study, two major risks have been recognized by lead firms, and I will explain them in detail here—environment and regulatory risks. To begin, environmental risks are very significant in semiconductors due to the extremely high-precision production equipment in fabs that can be vulnerable to unexpected environmental disturbances arising from strong vibration and/or sudden disruption in electricity and water supply. Much less of direct significance to the production of ICT end products, this environment-induced risk of supply shortage due to wafer fabs out of operation can apply to both IDM lead firms and fabless lead firms working with their strategic foundry providers. In fact, the 2011 Tōhoku earthquake and tsunami in Japan significantly affected many OEM customers of Japanese IDM firms (e.g., Renesas and Denso). Some of these OEM firms, particularly in automotive and industrial machinery, had to reduce their dependence on Japanese IDM firms and/or dual-source much more from US and European firms. The vice president of top ten non-Asian IDM-32 recalled:

> The tsunami many years ago created a lot of opportunities for us because from that experience, a lot of Japanese companies realize that actually they rely too much on Renesas. They don't have other semiconductors and no other backup points. . . . The only thing the customer brought up was during the natural disasters, they said, "What is your strategy in terms of business continuity? Do you have a dual fab strategy?" . . . Because once you qualify a certain fab, you cannot change that fab. For automotive, this is very critical. That's why you want, at the early stage, to qualify the fab.[33]

To most IDM firms, having a geographically distributed network of qualified in-house wafer fabs and back-end chip assembly and packaging facilities is good for risk mitigation, particularly in semiconductor applications that require developing long-term relationships in industrial markets such as automotive (see also Chapter 5's discussion of such relationships). Through its intrafirm coordination strategy, another top ten non-Asian IDM-34 has spread its risk through not only having multiple fabs in the US and Asia, but also setting up back-end facilities worldwide to minimize supply disruption. As was reflected by its vice president and chief supply chain officer,

> now our attention is turned to what you do with the very distributed global network, but the strategy has served us extremely well. We now have scale to compete. And we also have, quite honestly, risk mitigation through the distributed network versus all being as geographically centric as some people are [its key competitors in Asia].

This preference for minimizing environmental risks also applies to fabless lead firms because they may be beholden to the chosen process technology only available in the specific fabs of their foundry providers. While the cutting-edge process technology and lower cost-capability ratios of

Taiwan's world-leading foundry providers are very attractive to their out-sourcing choice, some fabless lead firms prefer the geographical diversi-fication of wafer fabs due to the possibility of natural hazards in Taiwan. In early 2016, a severe earthquake adversely affected wafer manufacturing operations at UMC's 12-inch Fab 12A in Taiwan's Tainan. Describing risk mitigation pressure from its OEM customers in ICT end products, the vice president of chip design from top fifteen US Fabless-42 explained:

> In terms of risk management, because Taiwan is on this earthquake zone, our customers care, and we care. If a foundry has one factory outside Taiwan and one factory in Taiwan and both factories can do the same process, that will be a tough choice. But then those occasions are very minimum. Usually even in foundry, they only have certain fabs that can do the process we choose. That's a luxury to us now. But we prefer multiple geographical locations due to the risk of manufacturing in Taiwan particularly.

Indeed, such risk mitigation and business continuity considerations were paramount when UMC, Taiwan's second and the world's third larg-est foundry provider, decided in December 2000 to establish a new 12-inch fab in Singapore to serve its IDM and fabless customers specializing in industrial and automotive electronics, such as Infineon and Texas Instru-ments. It entered into a joint venture with Infineon, the world's leading IDM firm in power semiconductors for automotive and industrial elec-tronics, and the Singapore government's investment agency, Economic Development Board Investment. Robert Tsao, its then chairman, was drawn by Singapore's international reach and the absence of earthquakes or typhoons. This UMC Fab 12i entered into full production in March 2004 and was designated as a Specialty Technology Center of Excellence in May 2013.[34]

Apart from environmental risks, lead firms in my study have also faced significant regulatory and geopolitical risks in relation to unfavorable government policies, such as local content and production requirements, complicated taxation, and restrictions on imports or exports. Many lead firms pointed to the (geo-)politically motivated practice of local content and production expectations in many countries throughout the world, and these were not limited to Asia only. In China, India, Indonesia, Brazil, Venezuela, and even the US, preferential government procurement con-tracts for selected ICT products are often given to "domestic" firms. This regulatory risk prompted at least six or more lead firms to set up production facilities in these countries in order to bid for government contracts. In more recent years since the mid-2010s, geopolitical tensions between the major powers of the US and China have led to intense trade wars and export restrictions that are meant to curb China's high-tech ambition. All these government-related risks have impacted significantly on lead firms in global electronics that respond by engaging in a mix of intra-/interfirm strategies and/or even extrafirm bargaining in order to ensure the resilience and efficiency of their global production networks. Chapter 5's subsection on risk sharing in interfirm relationships has already examined Huawei's unsuccessful extrafirm bargaining in 2019–2020 and its eventual decision to divest its Honor brand of mass market mobile handsets in November 2020.

The following analysis examines in more depth why such regulatory and/or geopolitical risks are causally significant for understanding firm-specific strategies and subsequent production network (re-)configurations. In semiconductors, such risks can be very significant in terms of (1) local production requirement and (2) restrictions on foreign investment and technology exports. First, some lead firms in my study noted that certain East Asian governments, including China, require the wafer fabrication and even back-end assembly, packaging, and testing services of chips for the final assembly of ICT products in their countries to be located locally, i.e., "domestic" production of chips. Imported chips may be subject to extra inspection and other nontariff barriers. Top five US Fabless-37 pointed out that its chip products experienced "random customs checks" that might be "politically motivated" to compel it (and other foreign semiconductor firms) to locate their wafer sourcing or production in these East Asian countries, such as China.

In Chapter 4's discussion of fab capacity growth during the 2010s, China's wafer fabs—both domestic and foreign owned—together produced only up to 16 percent of the $131–$143 billion domestic chip market during the 2019–2020 period. Since 2018, over half of China's annual $300–$380 billion imported chips has gone into the final assembly of ICT end products for domestic and foreign markets. The political pressure for much more "Made in China" chips was very significant. The vice president of a leading Asian semiconductor firm SE-30 in Shanghai pointed out that under the former Trump administration (2017–2021), the US-China trade war makes people [outside China] realize more that some of the ICs [integrated circuits] need to be done locally or some of the ICs need to be controlled, not to be exported to China. I can see more and more requests by the Chinese government that the foundry and the assembly and test process need to be done locally. Of course, if they decide to ask these big players in the US to be done locally, they will also suggest them to use local OSAT [outsourced semiconductor assembly and test services]. But so far, the decision is still in our customers' hands. People are worried about that. People cannot describe what the impact is. But I know the Chinese government is trying to make sure there is more local sourcing [of "Made in China" chips].

Second, some lead firms have experienced unfavorable home government restrictions on technology exports that might also be (geo-)politically motivated. The best-known examples are regulatory restrictions imposed by the US and Taiwan on semiconductor products and production facilities for/in China and semiconductor-related technology used in these products or fabs. Even before the May 2020 US export restrictions on US technology used in semiconductors for China, some US lead firms had already (re-)organized carefully their production networks, both in-house fabs and/or outsourced foundry partners, to ensure that their high-end chip products were neither made in China nor exported to China.

Within East Asia, geopolitical tensions between China and Taiwan led to the Taiwanese government's restriction on the cross-Strait investment by its domestic IDM and foundry firms. In place since August 2002 through its "N-1 strategy," the Taiwanese government requires these domestic semiconductor firms to have more advanced wafer fabs established in Taiwan *before* building less advanced fabs in China (e.g., TSMC's 8-inch fab in Shanghai in 2004 and 12-inch fab in Nanjing in 2018 and UMC's 12-inch fab in Xiamen in 2016).[35] To invest in new markets emerging from the dominance of China in the final assembly of most ICT end products, as was explained in the earlier section, UMC had to acquire the 8-inch fab of China's HeJian Technology in Suzhou in March 2013 because it was not allowed by the home government in Taiwan to build a 12-inch fab in China. Although its new 12-inch fab in China's Xiamen started construction in March 2015 and entered into volume production in November 2016, UMC only received the home government's approval to move its 28 nm technology into this new 12-inch F12X fab after it had begun shipping 14 nm technology products in its Tainan Fab 12 in February 2017 (see fab details in Table 4.2).[36]

Throughout the 2010s, these regulatory risks and geopolitical concerns compelled leading IDM firms and foundry providers to diversify their facilities geographically. This in turn explains why despite its small size as a city-state and its high cost of manufacturing, Singapore has been preferred as a geopolitically "neutral" key site for global semiconductor fabrication by IDM firms (e.g., Micron and STMicroelectronics) and foundry providers (e.g., GlobalFoundries, SSMC by TSMC-NXP, and UMC). As shown in Table 4.1, all 12 fabs in Singapore in 2018 were foreign owned, but the total capacity of these Singapore-based fabs was already about 60 percent of all 44 fabs in the US and larger than the total output by all 37 fabs in all of Europe![37] Still, this risk mitigation through the geographical diversification of fabs only works to a certain extent because some fabs specialize in certain products and process technologies that cannot be easily replaced. For logic chips in wireless communications at the cutting-edge technology nodes (e.g., 7 nm or 10 nm in 2018 and 5 nm from 2020 onwards), only two foundry providers in their home fabs—TSMC in Taiwan (Hsinchu, Taichung, and Tainan) and Samsung in South Korea (Giheung and Hwaseong)—have the requisite process nodes to engage in volume production. The practice of multiple sourcing from more than one foundry provider, though at much higher total costs for the customer, is only feasible for large-volume orders of, say, more than three thousand wafers per month. Only a small number of top fabless firms can afford such large orders (e.g., Qualcomm and Nvidia sourcing from both TSMC and Samsung).

The ongoing US-China trade war since March 2018 has also led to tremendous pressure on US fabless firms to outsource their chip production to a small number of existing trailing-edge foundry fabs located in the US. As mentioned earlier and in a telling sign to reconcile this geopolitical tension with the regulatory pressure confronting its leading US customers such as Apple, Qualcomm, Broadcom, and Nvidia, TSMC announced on May 15, 2020, that it would build a 5 nm fab in Arizona, with committed support from both the Arizona state and the federal governments. Chandler, Arizona, is already hosting Intel's next cutting-edge Fab 42 at 7 nm to be launched in 2022 (much delayed since 2019!) and at 5 nm thereafter. While TSMC's fab construction in Arizona started in

2021, actual production will only begin in 2024 and eventually reach a modest full capacity of 20,000 wafers per month. However, this Arizona fab capacity pales in comparison with TSMC's cutting-edge home fabs: 270,000–405,000 wafers per month in two 7 nm fabs (Fab 12 and 15) as of 2020 and 120,000 wafers per month in the 5 nm fab (Fab 18) when it reaches full capacity as early as in 2022. This raises a potentially serious issue of the Arizona fab lacking economies of scale and thus likely higher pricing per wafer for its US end customers. In short, the reconfigurations of production networks in response to causal dynamics driven by regulatory and geopolitical pressures will likely result in suboptimal competitive outcomes. The concluding chapter will consider some of these implications for business and policy in the postpandemic and post-Trump 2020s.

In ICT end products, regulatory and geopolitical risks are generally less severe, and their causal impact can be mitigated via different strategies of intrafirm coordination and interfirm partnership. Some developing countries use import licensing to restrict foreign lead firms that reluctantly respond by establishing domestically oriented factories. In some developed countries, government may engage in trade restrictions through import controls (e.g., end products for government procurement cannot be made in certain countries) or export controls (e.g., domestic lead firms cannot export their most sophisticated products to certain "black-listed" countries). The senior vice president for procurement and supply chain of top three PC OEM-22 lamented:

> You know, for China customers, nationalism is definitely in play, and the more you can become local for the China market the better off you are, although we deal with some big Chinese competitors. But having presence there is very strategic on the kind of market side. India, you know, there are things that pop up. Right now, there are some questions on what [Prime Minister] Modi is actually going to accomplish, but at the same time there are government purchases, preferred market access requirements, things like that, that we pay attention to. And then the US, it's federal government, and we are basically complying with the trade agreement act requirements. And so those products for the federal government, we don't build in China.[38]

In another case, top five East Asian OEM-13 decided in the late 2000s that putting all of its intrafirm production facilities in China would be too risky due to changing geopolitical relations between its home country and

China. It planned secretly to reconfigure its production network toward new assembly sites in Southeast Asia, even though the total cost of ownership in Southeast Asia was not lower than China at that time (see 2010 wage cost comparison in Figure 6.1). This intrafirm diversification strategy was meant to mitigate the geopolitical risk of putting all production facilities in China. As was noted by its vice president for corporate business innovation:

> We wanted diversification because we knew the relationship [in China]. We tried and we knew what it would be like. We knew the growth strategy for China. We've been very consistent in the sense we don't put all the eggs in a basket. So when the dependency on China manufacturing got heavier, we were thinking of alternatives because we didn't want to put all the eggs in one China basket. It was a very secretive decision at that time. Now we are looking back. I mean if we were the major ones, then we could have stayed. But you know the entire manufacturing is becoming a dependency, and global dependency on China is higher. And then China would start using that as a weapon against other countries.

Not all countries in Southeast Asia, however, are fully supportive of foreign investors such as OEM-13. Some Southeast Asian countries can pose significant regulatory risks due to government restrictions on imports of ICT products. In Southeast Asia, one country was specifically mentioned by several lead firms as a prime example of regulatory risk. The same OEM-13's vice president for Southeast Asia marketing further pointed out:

> Actually the [Southeast Asian country A] government requires that in all sectors, if you want to sell high-end products, you need to have a manufacturing facility. So we built up the facility and we complied with the government. Still the market is huge, and we cannot afford to miss their market. We need to come up with a way to grow out of those kinds of challenges applied by the government.

Last but not least, several OEM lead firms have been confronted with complex taxation issues arising from host government regulation, e.g., higher duty, customs taxes, and value-added taxes for nonlocal products in Brazil and India. Revisiting the earlier causal analysis of cost-capability ratios, these regulatory issues highlight the vital role of government taxes and policy interventions in shaping firm-specific costs and local supplier capabilities that are critical in the total cost of ownership approach to understanding factory locations and production network configurations. Tapping into their interfirm partnership to overcome some of these complicated regulations, some OEM lead firms have outsourced more production to their existing ODM or EMS partners that have already set up manufacturing facilities in these countries. For example, top three ODM-27 established two factories in India to assemble mobile handsets for their lead firm customers "because they raised the import tax for phones. So that's forcing everyone to consider local manufacturing or assembling." Similarly, another top three ODM-26 established factories in Brazil and India to assemble end products for lead firm customers aiming at the large domestic markets. Its senior director for supply chain explained that host government taxes and policy interventions could be a significant driver in its total cost approach to configuring the location of factories for final assembly:

> We think about total cost. Whether we will put the factory in Brazil or India, we consider our total cost. The reason why we put the factory in Brazil is the duty and custom tax. So if US government imposes a higher tax on notebooks, of course, there is no choice but you have to go.

## Conclusion

Complementing my detailed empirical analysis of the geographical configurations and organizational processes of electronics global production networks in the previous two chapters, this final empirical chapter has provided causal explanations for these variegated geographical and organizational configurations summarized in Tables 4.8 and 5.4. In conceptual terms, this chapter has completed the analytical circle of Chapter 3's GPN 2.0 theory and specified the causal mechanisms of global production networks underpinning the interconnected worlds of global electronics in the late 2010s. More specifically, I have examined empirically the differentiated role of four causal drivers—cost-capability ratios, market imperative, financial discipline, and risk mitigation—in explaining the variegated configurations of production networks in semiconductors and key ICT end products (i.e., PCs, mobile handsets, and TVs). I now draw some concluding remarks on their relative importance, as summarized in Table 6.7.

TABLE 6.7. Causal dynamics and key geographical and organizational configurations of production networks in global electronics, 2010–2021

| Segment in global electronics | Causal drivers and competitive dynamics | | | | Key geographical and organizational configurations |
|---|---|---|---|---|---|
| | Cost-capability ratio | Market imperative | Financial discipline | Risks | |
| Semiconductors | **Less significant** ✓<br>- total cost of ownership, fab technology, and ecosystem capability matter more than labor cost<br>- lower cost ratios more relevant in back-end services | **Quite significant** ✓✓<br>- segmented markets among OEM users<br>- Asia Pacific as largest market<br>- customer intimacy via fab proximity | **Very significant** ✓✓✓<br>- high capital spending and depreciation<br>- only few top firms can finance new fabs; reliance of fabless on foundry fabs<br>- more patient capital in East Asia | **Very significant** ✓✓✓<br>- high supply risks due to supply chain vulnerability and geopolitical tensions<br>- mitigating risk via intrafirm networks and extrafirm bargaining | Strong investment in and geographical diversification of new fabs and capacity growth in East Asia:<br>(1) greater role of East Asian IDM firms;<br>(2) dominance of cutting-edge foundry providers from East Asia preferred by fabless or fab-lite firms from the US and Europe; and (3) high market concentration in computer & data storage and wireless ICT end products assembled in East and South Asia |
| Personal computers | ✓✓✓<br>- importance of logistics and supplier ecosystem<br>- optimizing ratios via intrafirm networks and interfirm partnership | ✓✓<br>- segmented but revitalized worldwide market due to COVID-19 pandemic<br>- home market influence on top OEM lead firms | ✓✓<br>- US lead firms more pressured to go "asset-lite" via interfirm partnership | ✓<br>- security concerns in mission critical and institutional or government procurement | Very significant role of US and East Asian lead firms; extensive outsourcing of production to ODM firms in East Asia (China in notebook PCs); key components by platform and technology leaders from the US, South Korea, and Japan; and outsourcing of final assembly in desktop PCs less significant and more globalized |

| | Mobile handsets | TVs (and flat panel displays) |
|---|---|---|
| ✓✓✓ | - importance of logistics and supplier ecosystem<br>- optimizing ratios via intrafirm networks and interfirm partnership | - importance of transport and logistics costs<br>- optimizing ratios via intrafirm networks |
| ✓✓ | - very strong demand in Asia Pacific<br>- value capture via intrafirm networks in home markets | - strong demand in Asia Pacific<br>- value capture via intrafirm networks in home and host markets |
| ✓ | - much more pressure on US lead firms<br>- more patient capital in East Asia | - less capital pressures from state, family, or intra-group ownership in East Asia |
| ✓ | - host country regulation in local content and taxation<br>- US sanctions on chip design and production technology | - host country regulation in local content and taxation |
| | Dominant role of East Asian lead firms, except Apple; dominance of US platform and technology leaders in core components, but some insourcing by East Asian lead firms; and a mix pattern in final assembly—from complete outsourcing to EMS providers in East Asia to full in-house production in East and South Asia | Dominance of East Asian lead firms in both TVs and flat panel displays, with a mix pattern of insourcing and outsourcing of final assembly; panel display production entirely based in East Asia, but location of TV final assembly near end markets worldwide |

In semiconductors, the mix of causal drivers from the perspective of the GPN 2.0 theory is rather different from ICT end products. In this unique segment of intermediate goods highly critical to electronics production networks, cost-capability ratios matter in terms of the production efficiency of IDM and foundry fabs and their in-house or increasingly outsourced back-end services. But the most significant causal driver of semiconductor production networks is financial discipline because of the enormous capital spending on and rapid depreciation of new fabs affordable only by a small number of top IDM and foundry firms since the late 2010s—they lead in cutting-edge process technology that in turn enables innovations in chip design and new industrial applications (e.g., 5G communications, autonomous systems, artificial intelligence, and high performance computing, see Figure 2.1).

At the frontier of semiconductor technologies, however, the market imperative of "customer intimacy" also becomes quite significant because more chip designs are becoming custom or semicustom and "designed-in" due to application-specific demands by key customers in the electronics, computing and data storage, automotive, and other high-tech industries. Meanwhile, as the fabless-foundry model of semiconductor production networks has become even more prominent since the mid-2010s (discussed in Chapters 2 and 5), the environmental and/or regulatory risks associated with supply chain disruptions assume much greater significance, driving the strategic (re-)configuration of their production networks. Many semiconductor firms have attempted to mitigate such risks through the geographical diversification of chip sourcing and/or wafer fabrication. A very telling recent example of such a fabless-foundry model subject to unexpected regulatory risk is the export restrictions on May 15, 2020, imposed by the US government on China's Huawei and its fabless subsidiary HiSilicon that source from foundry providers equipped with US technology, such as TSMC (Taiwan) and SMIC (China). Even other Chinese OEM lead firms are now vulnerable to such risks in their production networks that source semiconductor products using US technology and software, e.g., Xiaomi's "blacklisting" by the US Department of Defense in January 2021 (though quickly revoked in May 2021).

In PCs, it is clear that optimizing cost-capabilities ratios serves as the overriding causal driver explaining why OEM lead firms from the US, China, and Taiwan have chosen to work with certain ODM partners and configured their production networks through a combination of in-house and outsourced production. Among the top six PC vendors, only China's Lenovo leverages the cost-capability advantage of its in-house domestic facilities in China to assemble over half of its PCs. This outsourcing consideration is also related to the quite significant financial discipline imposed on OEM lead firms, particularly those from the US, such as Hewlett-Packard, Dell, and Apple, that inevitably outsource almost their entire PC production to East Asian partners in order to achieve "asset-lite" and good capital market valuations. While declining end markets and regulatory risks are important to the overall business performance of most PC OEM firms, these causal drivers are less directly significant in explaining how lead firms organize production networks, except in desktop PCs for proximity to end markets outside East Asia.

In mobile handsets and TVs, the same very high importance of optimizing cost-capabilities ratios applies, but these segments are relatively less driven by financial discipline and risk mitigation. In mobile handsets, US-origin lead firms (e.g., Apple) have been outsourcing much more than their East Asian-origin competitors. These mobile handset OEM lead firms from South Korea (Samsung and LG) and China (Oppo and Vivo) have developed substantial intrafirm production networks to take advantage of their lower cost-capability ratios and, in the cases of Samsung and LG, capable in-house suppliers of key components and modules, such as chipsets and panel displays. Even though they follow Apple's model of outsourcing to EMS providers (e.g., Foxconn), China's Huawei and Xiaomi still keep small in-house assembly facilities respectively in Shenzhen/Dongguan and Beijing as "master factories" for test-bedding their latest innovations driven by the causal dynamics of high market growth, in particular very strong demand within the Asia Pacific, that has become more significant in mobile handsets and TVs than in PCs.

In TVs, this importance of the market imperative is also evident in the tendency of TV production to be located near end markets because of high transport costs (similar to the case of desktop PCs). In-house production is also more prevalent in TV production networks where demand in the Asia Pacific has been most significant. Supported by strong in-house supply or domestic suppliers of panel displays, TV OEM lead firms from South Korea (Samsung and LG) and China (TCL and Hisense) enjoy relatively lower cost-capability ratios and favorable market access through their intrafirm production networks.

In these highly interconnected worlds of global electronics, production networks are not only geographically dispersed in relation to firm-specific causal drivers and industry-level competitive dynamics, but also highly differentiated through intra- and interfirm organizational processes premised on a mix of insourcing, outsourcing, and offshoring. These complex geographical and organizational dynamics in global electronics point to major issues and challenges in the developmental trajectories of macroregions, national economies, and localities that are integrated through these diverse production networks spanning the global economy. Our understanding of these phenomena has critical implications for the business and policy-making communities and future academic research, particularly in the context of the devastating COVID-19 pandemic, severe disruptions in global production networks, the ensuring economic crisis/recovery, and escalated geopolitical tensions in 2020 and thereafter. In the next and concluding chapter, I will examine these thorny issues and implications for the 2020s and beyond, in relation to the key findings of this study on globalized electronics production centered in East Asia in the late 2010s.

## CHAPTER 7

# Whither (De-)Globalized Electronics Production in the 2020s? Current Trajectories and Future Agendas

THIS BOOK BEGAN WITH SILICON VALLEY'S predicament in the early 1990s and went on to demonstrate how its weakness in the mass production of innovative high-tech electronics products was overcome in the next two decades by expanding global production networks integrating the cutting-edge technologies of Silicon Valley firms and the manufacturing excellence of their strategic partners and key suppliers located in East Asia. By the late 2010s, Silicon Valley had not only become the indisputable global capital of the newly emerged digital platform economy[1] but also maintained its strong technological leadership in semiconductors, personal computers, and mobile handsets—the three most important hardware segments of global electronics today, measured by their role in leading or inducing major technological innovations (Figure 2.1) and by their largest shares in the sector's overall firm number and revenue (Figure 2.3). For every Google, Facebook, Airbnb, and Uber in digital platform services, there are industry-leading Silicon Valley firms in semiconductors (Intel, AMD, Qualcomm, and Nvidia), personal computers (Hewlett-Packard and Apple), and mobile handsets (Apple). Their industrial might is also joined by other US siblings in nearby states—Dell and Texas Instruments in Texas, and Micron in Idaho.

As was detailed throughout this book, all of these leading US electronics firms have worked closely with their manufacturing partners and key suppliers in East Asia to compete against newly emerged industry leaders from East Asia in the same industrial segments: semiconductors (Samsung, SK Hynix, and TSMC), personal computers (Lenovo, Acer, and Asus), and mobile handsets (Samsung, Huawei, Xiaomi, Oppo, Vivo, and so on). Apple's famous back-of-device imprint "Designed by Apple in California Assembled in China" epitomizes very well this innovative way of organizing its global production networks for many generations of Macintosh computers, iPhones, iPads, and many other digital devices. In some cases, US lead firms have also established in-house manufacturing facilities in East Asian locations to enjoy cost benefits in production and to serve better their industrial customers and end-user markets. To a large extent, their European and Japanese counterparts have taken on a similar approach to working with leading East Asian partners from Taiwan, China, and Singapore.

Evolving from the earlier decades of international production since the 1990s, these complex interdependencies within and between lead firms in organizationally complex and geographically dispersed production networks constitute today's interconnected worlds of globalized electronics production spanning the Triad macroregions of North America, Western Europe, and East Asia. Describing and explaining these geographical and organizational configurations of global production networks centered in East Asia during the 2010s was the core empirical focus of this book. Indeed, earlier academic studies of the global electronics industry and the broader information and communications technology (ICT) sector have provided critical insights on these interdependencies and their implications for trade, innovation, and, more broadly, economic development. In their *Revolution in Miniature*—a tour de force on the incredible era of microelectronics then yet to come in the 1980s and beyond, Braun and MacDonald (1982, 215; my emphasis) concluded that

> the economic role of microelectronics will become even greater in its influence upon world trading success. This certainly does not mean that the fabrication of microelectronic circuits will become the entry fee to the club of advanced countries, but that the use of microelectronic circuits in products and production technology will be indispensable. The picture so far seems fairly clear, if not especially comforting; what makes matters rather more confused is the role of *transnational corporations*. Their ability and tendency to switch resources from one

country to another at the drop of a hat adds considerable uncertainty to the role of microelectronics in the future of North-South trade.

What they did not anticipate in this rather nationally centric view of world trade—then prevalent in the 1980s, as was discussed in chapter 1—was the intricate organizational fragmentation of electronics production through vertical specialization coordinated by different lead firms and the subsequent emergence of global production networks through which then developing economies in the Global South and, in particular, East Asia could play an increasingly significant role. Also missing in their conclusion was the critical understanding that transnational corporations, or "global lead firms" in my terminology, could adopt the twin strategies of vertical disintegration (outsourcing) and in-house production globalization (offshoring), leading to the rise of their strategic partners, specialized suppliers, and other firms in organizationally much more complex and geographically much more distanced *global* production networks.

More recently, the social science studies of electronics global production networks and global value chains (GVCs) have focused on their immense possibility for technological innovation and industrial upgrading in latecomer economies eager to catch up with advanced industrialized countries.[2] And yet in his recent *The Art of Economic Catch-Up*, Keun Lee (2019, xvii) argued for

> a GVC-related detour, in which an economy should initially learn by participating at the GVC but should later reduce its reliance on these chains at a certain point by building increased domestic value chains in sequential entries into high-end segments. Otherwise, the latecomers would remain at low value-added segments, which is a middle income trap (MIT) symptom.

This useful caution for "upgraders" in innovation and technology studies points to the critical issues of value capture and developmental benefits arising from the strategic coupling of domestic firms with global production networks and its central importance for understanding national and firm-specific competitiveness.[3] As Chapter 1 has introduced, this incessant concern with national competitiveness underpinned much of the nationalist sentiments in the United States and Western Europe during the 1980s (and again in the US since the late 2010s!). Further documented in my empirical chapters, national economies do not directly compete against each other, but lead firms and their strategic partners in different global production networks do.[4] The competitive success and much greater market dominance of top ten lead firms in the different segments of global electronics today provides the prima facie evidence for why their innovative organization of production networks matters so much to our nuanced understanding of global competition and its uneven geographical outcomes worldwide.

Taking a theory-led and yet empirically oriented analytical approach, this book has developed and substantiated the above arguments. I moved systematically from the national worlds of the electronics industry in Chapter 1 to the industry-firm nexus of global electronics in Chapter 2 (see summary Table 2.1), and, most importantly, the firm-production network optic in empirical Chapters 4 to 6. As summarized respectively in Tables 4.8, 5.4, and 6.7, my detailed empirical analysis of the "where," "how," and "why" of these complex production networks in global electronics centered in East Asia by the late 2010s was guided by the theory of global production networks (GPN 2.0) that explained the emergence of these interconnected worlds in Chapter 3 (see Figure 3.2 and Table 3.4). In the following three sections of this concluding chapter, I offer some further remarks in relation to the book's key observations on the coevolutionary trajectories of global electronics up to the late 2010s. While some of these trends were established ahead of the 2010s, their intensity and significance became more apparent throughout the 2010s. I then examine their most significant implications for business and public policy in the postpandemic and post-Trump 2020s and, finally, end with a brief reflection on several theoretical and methodological lessons from this book's GPN 2.0 analysis and a discussion of the relevant future research agendas for the academic studies of global production networks and global value chains.

## Key Observations on Globalized Electronics Production by the Late 2010s

Based on comprehensive proprietary datasets and qualitative interviews, this book has focused on how global production networks were actually organized in semiconductors, personal computers (PCs), mobile handsets, and consumer electronics (i.e., TVs) up to 2018/2019—a historical peak period in the global markets for these intermediate and end products just before the devastating impacts arising from the US-China trade war since mid-2018 and the COVID-19 pandemic since 2020. While the concluding sections of empirical Chapters 4 to 6 and Tables 4.8, 5.4, and 6.7 have provided specific summaries of key findings on these main segments of global electronics, I now discuss four key observations that tie together these empirical findings and add to the previous major works in the literature:[5]

(1)    the variegated geographical configurations of global production networks centered in East Asia,

(2)    the significant role of intrafirm coordination and interfirm partnership strategies in production network configurations,

(3)    new end market dynamics in East Asia, and

(4)    major challenges from radical technological change and new product development.

First, the actually existing geographical configurations of production networks in global electronics by the late 2010s were quite mixed, ranging from high spatial concentration in one national economy (e.g., advanced logic chips in Taiwan, memory chips in South Korea and Japan, and notebook PCs in China) to fairly globalized production (e.g., desktop PCs and TVs). Balancing this mix of spatial concentration and dispersal remained a tricky act for most lead firms in my study because of the differential costs, market opportunities, and risks associated with diverse East Asian locations and the internal capabilities of these firms. While Chapter 4 has shown that China was the dominant global center for manufacturing facilities and, in particular, labor-intensive assembly operations, other locations in Southeast Asia, South Asia, Eastern Europe, and Latin America were also quite significant in certain segments of global electronics production primarily because of logistical and market access considerations. The final assembly of desktop PCs, mobile handsets, and TVs in the late 2010s clearly reflects this empirical reality.

To a large extent, these geographically variegated configurations of global electronics could be explained by firm-specific strategic considerations and preferences. Some lead firms preferred more dispersed production networks in order to be responsive and adaptable to geographical differences in costs, markets, and risk. This spatial dispersion logic applied particularly to the R&D and sales and marketing functions of lead firms, and, to a lesser extent, to their manufacturing activities inside and outside East Asia. Other lead firms favored more geographically concentrated configurations of production networks to increase its "deep dive" and "stickiness" with customers in specific industrial markets for intermediate products, such as semiconductors and flat panel displays. Only a small number of lead firms exclusively positioned their manufacturing facilities in very few East Asian locations (e.g., Toshiba/Kioxia fabs only in Japan and iPhones and notebook PCs primarily assembled in China).

Second, the organizational locus of intrafirm coordination and inter-firm partnership in global production networks was critical to lead firms' competitive strategy. As Chapter 5 has examined fully, semiconductor lead firms in integrated device manufacturing (IDM) with their own fabs and fabless-foundry lead firms coexisted and competed against each other in the most technologically demanding segment of global electronics, e.g., the production of microprocessor, memory, and wireless and communi-cations chips for PCs, mobile handsets, and other computer and storage devices. In other major end product segments, the organizational pattern of internalization versus outsourcing was also a mixed one. The make-or-buy decision confronting most lead firms engaging in original equipment manufacturing (OEM) remained dynamic and could not be easily reduced to one or the other. In PCs, some OEM lead firms such as Lenovo, Dell, and Apple retained limited in-house production facilities for desktops, while outsourcing over half to all of their notebook PCs to strategic part-ners from Taiwan and elsewhere (e.g., Singapore) that provided worldwide support through their original design manufacturing (ODM) services or electronics manufacturing services (EMS). In mobile handsets (and TVs), a number of OEM lead firms such as Samsung and LG relied exclusively on in-house facilities to manufacture their end products, in contrast to "factory-less" lead firm such as Apple and Xiaomi (China).

In all of these cases, the degree of interfirm control and partnership strat-egy within respective global production networks significantly influenced where and how a lead firm's production network was organized. As Chap-ter 6 has explained at length, these firm-specific strategies were driven by a differential combination of causal dynamics in relation to cost-capability ratios, market imperative, financial discipline, and risk mitigation (see also Table 6.7). In semiconductors, we observed tightly coupled production networks comprising IDM/foundry lead firms and their back-end service providers, such as assembly, packaging, and testing facilities, in specific East Asian locations (e.g., Taiwan and South Korea, as illustrated in Figure 5.2). While many OEM lead firms in PCs and mobile handsets outsourced most, if not all, of their end product assembly to East Asian ODM firms and/ or EMS providers, some of them still retained substantial control—via specific supply chain practices such as assigned-vendor assigned-price and "clean sheeting"—over the choice of key suppliers for parts and modules and even the location of dedicated facilities by their ODM/EMS providers. This interfirm control strategy practiced by lead firm customers in turn influenced the location of key suppliers wanting to be closer to these ODM/EMS facilities throughout East and South Asia.

Third, the global electronics market in the late 2010s remained volatile and yet highly dynamic. While most lead firms in my study were already market leaders in their own right (see Table 1.1), they nevertheless pursued relentlessly new market opportunities as their strategic imperative. As was documented in Chapter 6's causal explanations grounded in the GPN 2.0 theory, East Asia had emerged by the early to the mid-2010s as the dominant market for intermediate products supporting final assembly facilities throughout the macroregion *and* an enormous end market for finished products in all segments of the broader ICT sector. For those OEM lead firms in end-user markets (e.g., PCs, mobile handsets, and consumer electronics), their market success worldwide depended a great deal on their supply chain capability (managing efficiently optimal cost-capability ratios) and production capacity (responding effectively to changing market demand and forecast).

This market success among OEM lead firms in turn depended on the network support from their strategic manufacturing partners (e.g., ODM firms and EMS providers) and key component suppliers from the Triad macroregions (e.g., semiconductors and flat panel displays). These worldwide strategic partners and key suppliers thrived in such industrial or intermediate markets by working closely with their long-term OEM customers and even participating in the joint product development spearheaded by these lead firm customers. The cooperative interfirm relationships in these production networks and, thereby, their eventual market success were premised on the mutual trust and strategic alignment of interests among OEM lead firms, strategic partners, and key suppliers in the same global production networks.

Finally, while at least fourteen lead firms in my study were among the world's top five largest technology leaders in their respective market segments in 2018/2020 (Table 1.1), radical technological change and new product development presented the most significant challenge in their operating environment. In semiconductors, the continuous improvement in process technology supporting the most advanced chip manufacturing could only be attained with very heavy investment that barely a handful of top semiconductor firms could afford. As Chapters 4 and 6 have demonstrated, only those investing well in the range of $15–$30 billion in annual capital expenditure during the second half of the 2010s, such as TSMC, Samsung, and Intel, could retain their industrial leadership through cutting-edge process technology at the 7–10 nanometer node in 2018, 5–7 nm by late 2020, and 3–5 nm by 2022. During the decade, these top IDM firms and foundry providers, together with their fabless lead firm customers, helped drive the entire global electronics industry through their highly innovative semiconductor products and modules that went into the most sophisticated ICT end products (see also Figure 2.1). Some of their semiconductor products also contributed to great innovations in other major industries, such as automotive, aerospace, and medical equipment, and the broader digital economy. In automotive, for example, an average car had up to 1,400 chips in 2021, but this number would be going up with future autonomous cars having more electronics and electrical control functions. In 2018, semiconductor products had already contributed to at least 30 percent of the unit cost of high-end models with autonomous functions. This chip-to-total cost ratio is expected to increase to over 50 percent by 2023.[6]

To OEM lead firms in PCs and mobile handsets, new product and technology development became more evolutionary than revolutionary by the late 2010s. Similar to how the rapid ascendancy of notebook PCs had eclipsed the sales of desktop PCs by 2010, the "smartphone revolution" in 2007 and the subsequent dominance of the smartphone market quickened the decline in notebook PC sales in the second half of the 2010s (see Table 2.1 and data in Chapter 2). With the arrival of the Internet of Things, 5G communications, and artificial intelligence, many lead firms were attempting at developing new products beyond their core businesses in PCs and mobile handsets. During my main fieldwork period (2017–2018), these new efforts to incorporate innovative technologies were ongoing, but their payoffs were not quite apparent yet. Indeed, mobile handsets and PCs continued to be the largest contributors to the revenue and bottom line of these top OEM lead firms from the US, South Korea, China, and Japan in Table 1.1.

In this highly challenging environment of potentially new breakthrough ICT products obliterating existing devices and transforming end markets, top OEM lead firms relied extensively on the rapid technological advancement and production turnover of cutting-edge semiconductor chips and flat panel displays from their key suppliers in order to launch their new models of PCs and smartphones. As Chapters 5 and 6 have analyzed empirically, this accelerated cycle of product development prompted OEM lead firms to work even more closely with leading fabless chip suppliers in the US (e.g., Qualcomm, AMD, and Nvidia) and East Asia (e.g., MediaTek) and their dedicated foundry producers in East Asia (e.g., TSMC, Samsung, and UMC) and elsewhere (e.g., Samsung's foundry in the US and GlobalFoundries in the US and Germany). As dominant suppliers, a small number of major producers of memory devices and flat panel displays, mostly located in East Asia, became highly involved in the product differentiation of these new PCs and mobile handsets launched by OEM lead firms. The overwhelming presence of East Asia in the total number and capacity of semiconductor fabs by the late 2010s will likely reinforce the macroregion's central role in electronics global production networks during the 2020s.

## Implications for Business and Public Policy in the Postpandemic and Post-Trump 2020s

What might these observations on the trajectories of global electronics up to the late 2010s hold for firms and governments in the 2020s? As I have pointed out in the Preface, the unprecedented disruptions in the global economy since the late 2010s due to escalating geopolitical tensions (e.g., the US-China trade war since the former Trump administration) and the devastating COVID-19 pandemic in 2020–2021 have prompted some rethinking on the future of global production networks and the interdependent global economy. At the initial peak of the COVID-19 pandemic in March–May 2020, there was much discussion in then the Trump administration and the mainstream media in the US, the Europe Union, and Japan about the need to "break" global supply chains away from China and to "bring back" or "reshore" manufacturing production in what was known as "decoupling" and "deglobalization" initiatives.[7] Driven by geopolitical concerns and the "decoupling" imperative, the US government took further high-profile action against specific firms from China, such as tightened export controls on Huawei and its chip design subsidiary HiSilicon in May 2020 and China's leading foundry provider SMIC in September 2020. On June 8, 2021, the new Biden administration gained strong bipartisan support to pass the sweeping US Innovation and Competition

Act of 2021 to counter and compete with China. Worth over $250 billion, the act earmarked $52 billion specifically to support US semiconductor manufacturing, design, and research under the Creating Helpful Incentives to Produce Semiconductors (CHIPS) for America Act passed in late 2020.[8] In Europe, the European Union announced in March 2021 an ambitious $150 billion program with the goal of doubling its share of global semiconductor production to at least 20 percent by 2030.[9]

Meanwhile in its May 2020 report on COVID-19 risks outlook, the World Economic Forum ranked prolonged recession of the global economy (68 percent), surge in bankruptcies and industry consolidation (57 percent), and failed recovery of industries and sectors in some countries (56 percent) as the top three most likely fallout risks for the world economy up to end 2021.[10] Impacting greatly on both intermediate and end markets worldwide, these economic risks were ranked much higher than the protracted disruption of global supply chains (42 percent) associated with manufacturing and logistics issues—ranked last among the seven most likely fallout risks highlighted. Premised on my empirical analysis in earlier chapters, I now consider some key implications of this study of global electronics for business and public policy in the 2020s beyond the current COVID-19 pandemic and the former Trump administration (replaced in January 2021 by the more trade-friendly and multilateralist Biden administration).

### Business Strategy in the 2020s

There are at least three implications for decision makers in business:

(1)    the greater significance of East Asia as a major end market, geographical proximity to East Asia, and the continual importance of China in global electronics manufacturing,

(2)    more attention to capability development and supply ecosystems in the total cost of ownership approach to industrial competition, and

(3)    strategic partnership through global production networks as the organizational key to resilience building.

The first implication from my study is fairly self-evident—no major electronics lead firm can afford to underestimate East Asia's role as the dominant manufacturing center and, more significantly, a major end market in global electronics. Within the Asia Pacific, East Asia (Northeast and

Southeast) has already become the key center of global electronics manufacturing. But the importance of the entire Asia Pacific macroregion as an end market for all ICT products will only grow over time and become even more significant in the 2020s, as was evident in the 2013–2023 forecast data presented in Chapter 6. This end market-orientation for firms and business in global electronics will be more critical in the postpandemic world economy in which prolonged recession, bankruptcies, and industry consolidation will impact more negatively on end markets in the US, the Europe Union, and Japan due to their uneven recovery from the pandemic as of mid-2021.

From their respective historical peaks of $485 billion and 1.41 billion units in 2018, global semiconductor sales and smartphone shipment declined to $466 billion and 1.25 billion units in 2020, following an earlier year of decline in 2019 (see Tables 2.2 and 2.9). Global trade volumes also decreased significantly by 7.4 percent to $17.6 trillion in 2020 before a projected 8 percent rise in 2021 (though will still remain below the 2018 peak of $19.5 trillion). Sectors with more complex global production networks, such as automotive, experienced a steeper fall in trade in 2020. Still, Asia's merchandise trade in 2020 was mixed: 0.3 percent for exports but -1.3 percent for imports—by far the best performer among all other macroregions suffering -8 percent or higher declines due to production disruptions and constrained consumption arising from the more deadly waves of COVID-19 in the second half of 2020 and the first half of 2021.[11]

In the midst of the pandemic, foreign direct investment (FDI) also declined by the largest amount of 35 percent, from $1.5 trillion in 2019 to $1 trillion in 2020—a figure almost 20 percent below the 2009 trough right after the global financial crisis. This massive decline in global investment was most significant among developed countries, where FDI fell by 58 percent. Nevertheless, FDI inflows to Asia actually grew by 4 percent to $535 billion in 2020—China by 6 percent to $149 billion and India by 27 percent to $64 billion (due to major ICT-related acquisitions). In terms of GDP growth among the G20 countries, only China and Turkey grew respectively at 2.3 and 1.8 percent in 2020, whereas the US, the Euro zone and the UK, and Japan contracted between -1 percent (South Korea) to -10 percent (Argentina, Spain, and the UK), and the wider global economy at -3.5 percent.[12]

To tap into both the manufacturing capability and the expanding end market in East and South Asia within the broader Asia Pacific macroregion in the 2020s, lead firms from the US and Europe need to be geographically closer to, and develop innovative ways to work with, their strategic partners and key suppliers in Asia. From my interviews, it is clear that developing and nurturing trust through geographical proximity is one of the indispensable network mechanisms in such relationship building. Some US lead firms have gone much further than their competitors by letting their key manufacturing partners work in close proximity to their major R&D centers and align with their own technology and product road maps to achieve mutual gains in their interfirm cooperative relationships. Other OEM lead firms have developed strong supply chain capability together with their ODM partners and EMS providers and benefited from the latter's optimized cost-capability ratios through locating production facilities in East Asia and elsewhere. Such strong interfirm partnership in expanding production networks will remain as the most powerful competitive strategy in the 2020s.

Within East Asia, reducing dependency on China as *the* dominant manufacturing center via the "China+N" strategy of geographical diversification has already taken place even before the COVID-19 pandemic, for example, in the case of Samsung's complete shift of mobile handset manufacturing from China to Vietnam by 2019.[13] Since mid-2019 and in response to escalating US-China trade tensions, US lead firms in PCs and mobile handsets have increasingly asked their ODM firms and EMS providers from Taiwan to relocate *some* China-based final assembly capacity back to Taiwan or to new locations in Southeast Asia (e.g., Vietnam and Indonesia), South Asia (India), Latin America (e.g., Mexico and Brazil), and Eastern Europe (e.g., the Czech Republic and Poland). But to those US OEM lead firms that have moved some in-house assembly capacity to Southeast Asia, India, Latin America, and/or Eastern Europe, China has remained as the central node in their global production networks procuring the vast majority of core materials and critical components through its well-established ecosystems for electronics production.

For example, Taiwan's Hon Hai Precision Industry, also known as Foxconn and by far the world's largest EMS provider, announced in August 2020 that it was gradually adding more assembly capacity outside of China, its main production base for assembling desktop PCs, mobile handsets, and other electronics devices for decades (see Tables 4.3–4.5). But this geographical diversification has not been easy due to its strong embeddedness in China's electronics production ecosystems. Between

June 2019 and August 2020—a period of intense US-China trade conflicts and the COVID-19 pandemic, the proportion of Foxconn's manufacturing outside China increased by only 5 percent, from 25 percent to 30 percent.[14] Meanwhile, more firms in China are moving some capacity to member states of the Association of Southeast Asian Nations (ASEAN) to fulfil their "China+ASEAN" strategy: China-origin firms now account for 40 percent of manufacturing FDI in Southeast Asia, up from about 10 percent before the pandemic.[15]

Despite the above attempt by lead firms and their strategic partners to implement the "China+N" strategy, no US lead firms in my study have succeeded in moving final assembly back to the US (i.e., reshoring). Clearly, even a partial reshoring of manufacturing back to the US among these US lead firms will be futile as the labor cost can be very high, and the dedicated supplier ecosystem is mostly absent in the US. More importantly, the import of many crucial intermediate goods from production sites in China necessary for the final assembly of PCs, mobile handsets, and other ICT devices in the US will likely be subject to the same punitive tariffs as part of the US-China trade war, making the reshoring option all but infeasible. This was a key point lamented by top five PC OEM-22's senior vice president for worldwide procurement.[16] OEM-22 has modest manufacturing capacity in the US, but moving the final assembly of PCs to its US facility simply does not make good economic sense. In this regard, the late Steve Jobs's candid reply to then US president Barack Obama in 2012 about bringing iPhone production back to the US will still ring true even a decade later—"Those jobs aren't coming back"![17]

Reshoring and decoupling from China would be very costly for both US lead firms and their end customers in the US. Data from late 2020 through to mid-2021 clearly point to the limited effects of such decoupling initiatives.[18] Even in the midst of the COVID-19 pandemic in March 2020, 70 percent of respondents to a member survey by the American Chamber of Commerce in Shanghai, China, said they were not thinking of moving their operations out of China because of its enormous market size and its world-class manufacturing and logistics base. Released in March 2021, another annual survey by the same organization covering October–November 2020 showed that 83 percent of the 345 US member firms surveyed would maintain their existing manufacturing and sourcing in China in 2021, with a mere 2 percent considering reshoring back to the US. The US-China Business Council and the European Union

Chamber of Commerce in China also noted some diversification away from China, but certainly no wholesale rush for exits. In the Economist Intelligence Unit's report released on June 16, 2021, most firms and investors remained deterred by North America's lack of competitiveness vis-à-vis East Asian economies. Despite the Biden administration's June 8, 2021, announcement of establishing the Supply Chain Disruptions Task Force to strengthen US production, its lingering protectionism and cross-border tensions within the US-Mexico-Canada Agreement would prevent the macroregion serving as a realistic production substitute for East Asia at least through the medium term.

A recent comparison of Apple's supplier list for 2017 and 2020 further shows that nearly one-third of the 52 newly shortlisted suppliers were from China and 80 percent of its 200 suppliers in 2020 had at least one production site in China, highlighting the continual importance of China in global electronics. As noted earlier, China's FDI inflows in 2020 actually experienced a 6 percent growth, despite the massive decline of 35 percent in global FDI flows. In the first quarter of 2021, a total of 10,263 new foreign firms were established in China, marking respectively 48 percent and 7 percent growth compared to 2020 and 2019. FDI inflows in nonfinancial sectors surged by almost 44 percent year-on-year to $46 billion, representing the highest quarterly growth rate since 2008 and a 25 percent increase from the same quarter in prepandemic 2019. Between June 2020 and May 2021, China's exports also experienced 11 consecutive months of year-on-year growth and would likely remain strong throughout 2021.

This brings me to the second major implication for firms in global industries such as electronics: the total cost of ownership matters a great deal in competitive production networks and business success. It goes far beyond simply labor cost or other material input costs because it incorporates crucial logistics and other supply chain costs. The incessant drive to lower production cost has led many firms and analysts to focus on direct costs, such as labor, materials, and parts costs. As many examples throughout this book have illustrated, these direct costs neither truly reflect the total cost of ownership nor incorporate the importance of supplier and ecosystem capability.[19] In short, they do not fully constitute the cost-capability ratios, conceptualized in Chapter 3's GPN 2.0 theory, that ultimately drive firm-specific strategies and production network configurations analyzed in Chapters 5 and 6. To lower such ratios, lead firms in the

2020s should focus their attention on not only cutting direct costs, but perhaps more importantly, also enhancing the capability of their suppliers and supply ecosystems, when making outsourcing and locational choices.

Moreover, it becomes quite evident that global lead firms in my study are successful not only because of their innovative products for end-user markets. Equally, if not more, critical are their supply chain capabilities. These firm-specific capabilities, ranging from in-house procurement and supply chain knowhow to sustainable long-term relationships with strategic partners, have greatly enhanced their competitive advantage in global electronics. This possibly explains why the World Economic Forum (2020) survey ranked protracted disruption of global supply chains the lowest among seven most likely fallout risks for the world economy in the 2020–2021 period. As their supply chain capabilities grow, these lead firms in global electronics can achieve greater operational efficiency via their well-coordinated organization of production networks that can lead to lower cost-capability ratios and higher/faster market reach. In the postpandemic world economy, strengthening geographical proximity to key customers and suppliers will likely enable such development and enhancement of supply chain capabilities and network resilience. This approach to network resilience has been recognized in the 2021 *World Investment Report* that recommends network restructuring through production (re-)location decisions and supply chain management solutions via planning, forecasting, buffers, and flexibility.[20]

Third, strategic partnership through global production networks will remain as the organizational key to future competition and resilience building in the global electronics industry. Whether a lead firm prefers internalizing or outsourcing manufacturing as its competitive strategy, it simply cannot do it all alone. In semiconductors, a number of US fabless lead firms (e.g., Qualcomm, AMD, and Nvidia) have partnered with technologically advanced foundry providers based in East Asia and led the world with cutting-edge semiconductor products. The top three lead firms in mobile handsets—Samsung, Apple, and Huawei (position replaced by Xiaomi in 2021)—also depend on these most advanced foundry fabs for their application processor chips. As this book has evidently explained (see also Table 2.3), the rise of TSMC (Taiwan) and Samsung foundry (South Korea) as the world's leading semiconductor manufacturers overtaking Intel's fab technology by the late 2010s also had much to do with their firm-specific success in codeveloping strong and collaborative ecosystems with leading software, equipment, and materials suppliers from the US, Europe, and Japan (see discussion in Chapter 6).

Geopolitical tensions and trade wars since the late 2010s will likely favor these top foundry providers from Taiwan and South Korea and their fabs throughout East Asia. The former Trump administration's export controls imposed on China's leading foundry, SMIC, on September 15, 2020, has already led to a significant reduction in its planned 2020 capital spending by 12 percent, which SMIC Chairman Zixue Zhou blamed on the "uncertainty of certain equipment deliveries from U.S. suppliers due to export restrictions" and logistics-related delays for moving equipment into its fabs.[21] Lacking access to semiconductor ecosystems dominated by US software and equipment firms, SMIC's technology gap with TSMC and Samsung will be widened further in the early 2020s, and its non-China customers such as Qualcomm will likely shift their existing orders to these top East Asian foundry partners.[22]

Into the 2020s, TSMC and Samsung foundry will likely become even more important strategic partners of all leading fabless firm and even Intel, a longstanding vanguard of in-house semiconductor manufacturing epitomizing the technology prowess of Silicon Valley. In mid-2020, Apple announced its shift from Intel microprocessors to in-house designed microprocessor (M-series) chips manufactured in TSMC's 5 nm fabs in Taiwan for its new Macintosh computers, ending a fifteen-year partnership with Intel. Since early 2021, Intel has also started sourcing its new high-end graphics processors from TSMC's 7 nm fabs due to substantial delay in its own Arizona Fab 42's transition to 7 nm (by 2022) and its key competitors (AMD and Nvidia) already benefitting from TSMC and Samsung's cutting-edge fab technologies (see Chapter 6's section on financial discipline).[23] Even though Intel has long been sourcing less advanced chips from TSMC, this outsourcing of its top graphics chips (DG2) for 2022 release represents the end of its "do it all alone" approach to semiconductor manufacturing enshrined as its founding principle since 1968 (see discussion of Intel fabs in Chapters 4 and 5). The strengthening of Intel's strategic partnership with TSMC is estimated to lead eventually to some 20 percent of its flagship microprocessor chips to be sourced from TSMC for release in 2023, although TSMC needs to invest as much as $10 billion in its Tainan F18 fab capacity just for making Intel's chips.[24]

In PCs and mobile handsets, such strategic partnership has already worked out very well for many top lead firms that engage their partners in "design-in," customization, and joint product development. Several OEM lead firms in PCs and mobile handsets have worked closely with their respective ODM firms and EMS providers in East Asia to produce different generations of market-leading products for end-user markets worldwide. Their interfirm partnership will likely strengthen in the 2020s as industrial concentration in both end product segments gets even higher among top ten OEM lead firms and top five ODM/EMS firms (see Tables 1.1 and 2.8). While China's OEM lead firms in PCs and mobile handsets will likely benefit from continual domestic market growth, their competitive future remains highly dependent on sourcing and importing key semiconductor components fabricated in East Asia and the US by IDM and fabless firms that are mostly from the US (microprocessors and logic chips) and South Korea (memory). Huawei's crippled chip supply chains in late 2020 demonstrates the extremely high fragility of this dependency of China's OEM lead firms on core components from US firms and/or made with US technology. Even Xiaomi, a top five smartphone vendor, was threatened by the US Department of Defense's blacklisting on January 14, 2021, (revoked on May 12, 2021, after Xiaomi's lawsuit against the US government).

Taken together, global electronics production in the 2020s will likely remain highly globalized and less subject to pressures from (geo-)politically motivated "decoupling" and "deglobalization" initiatives. While China's domestic semiconductor firms and some lead firms in end products (e.g., Huawei and ZTE) may be decoupled from production networks and technological platforms led by US firms, China will remain as the major center for global electronics manufacturing and a huge end market for ICT products in the 2020s. Other East Asian economies will likely gain from this partial decoupling—their semiconductor firms will take over the additional demand for fab capacity, and their lead firms in PCs and smartphones will capture more market shares from Chinese OEM lead firms. The future of global competition in electronics is likely about how global lead firms find new and innovative ways to diversify their supply dependency by developing new international partnerships and how these different partnerships in global production networks compete against each other. The clear message for business is that developing and pursuing strong strategic partnership will be an indispensable strategy to future success in the interconnected worlds of global electronics.

### Public Policy in the 2020s

In the public policy arena, my empirical analysis also points to three major implications for steering economic development in the postpandemic world economy.

(1)    industrial development as nurturing specialized niches in the complex geographical divisions of labor in electronics production networks,

(2)    a pro-ecosystem approach to capability development and market access, and

(3)    defensive and protectionist interventions as ineffective and compromised policy instruments.

First and foremost, there are clear benefits from the participation of national economies and subnational regions in East Asia in the expanding macroregional divisions of labor underpinned by electronics global production networks. This book has shown that a number of East Asian economies have played a major role in global electronics, and their domestic firms and workers have benefitted from such an opportunity of "plugging in" different electronics production networks. In some cases, such as Japan, South Korea, China, and Taiwan, their national economies have also nurtured successfully, within their evolving institutional contexts summarized in Table 1.2, a substantial number of global lead firms in the respective segments of global electronics.

What then can other national governments in Asia and developing countries in the Global South do to engage in such a form of strategic coupling, i.e., ensuring domestic firms and related industries can strategically couple or work with lead firms in different global production networks?[25] The restructuring of global production networks in response to geopolitical tensions and supply chain disruptions during and after the COVID-19 pandemic in 2020–2021 will likely open up new opportunities for such firm-specific coupling, irrespective of whether production networks will be more "decoupled" from China or even East Asia and become more internally organized within the macroregions of the Americas, Europe, Asia and the Pacific, and Africa.[26] McKinsey Global Institute's (2020, 7) report on risk and resilience in the postpandemic world economy further considered value chains in semiconductors, computers and electronics, and communication equipment as "the most sought after by countries . . . These value chains have the further distinction of being high value and relatively concentrated, underscoring potential risks for the global economy." At the general level of economic development, there are several key challenges identified in Table 7.1 for policy and practice among national and subnational governments.

In the above-discussed changing context for industrial development during the 2020s, there is an urgent need for a better recognition in the public policy domain of the importance and complexity of global production networks as a form of geographical divisions of labor in which certain localities and subnational regions specialize in the specific segments and/or functions of global electronics. Unlike the nationalist thinking in the 1980s and earlier—as was discussed in Chapter 1, it is necessary for policy makers to move away from viewing electronics as a "national" industry that needs to be completely "onshore" or domestic for dubious reasons associated with economic nationalism prevalent in the "decoupling" and "deglobalization" rhetoric. Instead, rational policy makers in both advanced and developing economies should conceive industrial development as nurturing specialized niches in electronics production networks. This "niche thinking" entails the dire need for detailed knowledge and analysis of national and subnational regional prospects in the different segments of electronics production networks.

If well planned and executed, this niche approach to industrial development will enable governments and policy makers to take advantage of new opportunities arising from the likely reconfigurations of production networks in the postpandemic era, e.g., the "China+N" strategy pursued by some or most lead firms in the early 2020s. Touted as the world's largest free-trade agreement and signed on November 15, 2020, the recently concluded Regional Comprehensive Economic Partnership (RCEP) among fifteen national economies within the Asia Pacific will consolidate and strengthen such intraregional divisions of labor in electronics production networks within the Asia Pacific by lowering production costs through preferential or no tariffs and speeding up custom clearance through a single rule of origin. When in force by early 2022 after national ratification—China first ratified on March 8, 2021, these advantages will likely benefit lead firms, strategic partners, and suppliers in any of these fifteen member states when they engage in cross-border intrafirm and interfirm sourcing within the RCEP.

TABLE 7.1. Policy framework for economic development in a postpandemic world of global production networks (GPNs)

| Key elements[1] | Principal policy actions at the national level[1] | Strategic coupling: policy and practice at the subnational level |
|---|---|---|
| Embedding GPNs in development strategy | - Incorporating GPNs in industrial development policies<br>- Setting policy objectives along GPN development paths<br>- Seeking international economic partnership | - Understanding current regional capabilities and positions in global industries<br>- Aligning regional endowments with targeted global industries: be realistic of achievable strategic coupling<br>- Mindful of "race to bottom" kind of strategic coupling<br>- A network and partnership approach to industrial development in regional economies |
| Enabling participation in GPNs | - Creating and maintaining a conducive environment for trade and investment<br>- Putting in place the infrastructural and logistical prerequisites for GPN participation | - Regional policies facilitating international trade and investment<br>- National policy incentives for regional coupling in GPNs, e.g., special tax regimes or financial grants<br>- Importance of regional ties and transnational communities |
| Building domestic productive capacity | - Supporting enterprise development and enhancing the bargaining power of firms<br>- National institutional support for resilience and capability development of firms<br>- Strengthening skills of the workforce | - Regional institutional support for resilience and capability development of local firms: e.g., technological transfer and equity investment<br>- Regional clustering and linkage development to enhance strategic coupling<br>- Upgrading of skills and knowledge: from industrial to services and managerial skills |
| Providing a strong environmental, social, and governance framework | - Minimizing risks associated with GPN participation through regulation, and public and private standards<br>- Supporting local enterprise in complying with international standards (e.g., certification) | - Effective regulation, social dialogue, and an active civil society in the region<br>- Deployment of voluntary and regulatory standards, e.g., corporate social responsibility programs<br>- Assistance to domestic firms in their adoption of sector-specific international standards |

| Key elements[1] | Principal policy actions at the national level[1] | Strategic coupling: policy and practice at the subnational level |
|---|---|---|
| Synergizing trade and investment policies and institutions | - Ensuring coherence between trade and investment policies<br>- Synergizing trade and investment promotion and facilitation (e.g., RCEP in the Asia Pacific and Europe-China investment agreement in late 2020)<br>- Creating "international industrial development compacts" | - Credibility and consistency in regional policy and practice<br>- Establishing regional institutions promoting strategic coupling in GPNs, e.g., industry groups, intermediaries, and public-private consortiums<br>- Developing cross-regional linkages and GPN couplings |

[1] Adapted from UNCTAD (2013, Table IV.11; 176).

Take semiconductors and mobile handsets as examples. In semiconductors, the vast majority of chip design and fabrication in the entire Asia Pacific macroregion in 2018 was located in just five East Asian economies—Taiwan, South Korea, Japan, China, and Singapore (see Table 4.1). My empirical analysis in Chapter 6 has already shown that developing a strong niche in semiconductor global production networks (illustrated in Figure 5.2) can be very costly due to heavy capital spending and high risks in both environmental and regulatory terms. Long-term thinking and strong policy support for building domestic capabilities in semiconductors are crucial to any existing players or newcomers. China's "Made in China 2025" ambition in building its domestic semiconductor firms and production networks will be stepped up in light of recent geopolitical tensions and US export controls that will likely remain in place under the Biden administration in the early 2020s. Meanwhile, the Biden administration has also strengthened its federal policy support for new and/or reshored semiconductor manufacturing. All of these major policy changes in China and the US will create new niches and partnership opportunities for leading players or ambitious newcomers in East Asia and the wider Asia Pacific that can take advantage of optimized cost-capability ratios and better market access within the RCEP provisions. Some of these cross-border opportunities are in inputs to front-end chip production (e.g., production and supply of materials and specialized equipment) and in back-end services such as chip assembly, packaging, and testing.

Similarly, in mobile handsets, not all Asian economies are actively involved in the regionally organized production of smartphones. In fact,
the top five OEM lead firms in 2018 tended to concentrate their in-house
production or outsourced assembly operations only in China, Vietnam,
and India, whereas a small number of other locations in Asia (e.g., Japan,
Taiwan, South Korea, China, and Singapore) were involved in manufacturing the critical parts and modules that went into each smartphone. In
this regard, India's opting out of the November 2020 RCEP may reduce
its role as a regional production center within the Asia Pacific, though its
large domestic market will still be attractive to the final assembly of smartphones for local sales.[27] The RCEP thus opens up new opportunities for
other Asia Pacific economies to couple with these global production networks in mobile handsets. For these Asia Pacific and developing countries,
public policy needs to be attuned to the specific needs and conditions
in favor of attracting niche functions and segments in global electronics.
Since the mid-2000s, for example, Vietnam has been quite successful in
plugging into Samsung's global production network in mobile handsets.
Even though its industrial development of local supplier capability and/
or domestic lead firms remains limited, Vietnam will benefit further from
the RCEP, and more foreign lead firms in global electronics will shift parts
of their production networks to Vietnam (and nearby ASEAN countries).

Second, the book's empirical analysis has made it abundantly clear that
firm-specific capability is one crucial determinant of how national firms
and their home economies can play a major role in global electronics.
While Table 7.1 recommends a stronger policy focus on capability development and market access, I do not suggest an exclusive policy focus on
domestic firms only (i.e., a return to nationalist thinking). In fact, public
policy oriented toward improving firm capability at the level of the entire
industrial ecosystem within a national economy and its subregions will
be much more effective in supporting strategic coupling with global lead
firms in electronics production networks. These policies can be oriented
toward trade facilitation in production inputs and intermediate goods and
services (e.g., RCEP in November 2020), investment promotion through
market access provisions (e.g., Europe's Comprehensive Agreement on
Investment with China signed on December 30, 2020),[28] better provision
of infrastructure, logistics, and tax regimes, and skill development through
education, apprenticeship, and entrepreneurship training.

WHITHER (DE-)GLOBALIZED ELECTRONICS PRODUCTION    295

This pro-ecosystem approach to firm-specific capability development will be most helpful in promoting new domestic capacity and/or foreign investment in the higher value-adding functions of electronics production networks and in developing a global supply base through a strategic combination of local and foreign firms. If domestic supplier capability remains weak, explicit industrial policy for supplier development programs will be necessary (e.g., supplier certification and OEM customers-matching programs). Even in such national programs, the role of foreign firms, particularly global lead firms, is vital because they can be leveraged to provide access to skills, technology, and international markets.

Third, my empirical analysis in Chapter 6 has already shown that defensive policy interventions, such as local content expectations and irregular customs tax regulation, can be ineffective and counterproductive to strategic coupling with global production networks. In some Asian countries such as India and Indonesia, lead firms in my study had to establish local assembly operations through in-house facilities or outsourced partners just to meet such protectionist requirements from the host country governments. But their local production was inevitably only meant for the domestic market, albeit large in size and potential, and these locally assembled products were often inferior in quality and unsuitable for exports to other major markets. These products were also heavily dependent on core components and materials sourced from other East Asian economies, particularly China.[29] To a limited extent then, such unfavorable policy interventions could only achieve short-term objectives (e.g., more locally assembled products by foreign lead firms), but not long-term industrial development due to these lead firms' lack of strategic imperative in providing access to skills, technology, and markets. When implemented in 2022, such protectionist policies within the Asia Pacific will be unacceptable under the RCEP.

In this context of policy failures in developing countries, the recent geopolitical drive in the US toward reshoring global manufacturing may take at least five to ten years to see some tangible results, and yet may not yield overwhelmingly positive outcomes. To be fair, many US high-tech lead firms and industry associations in the US knew precisely the fallacy of this kind of highly politicized decision during the former Trump administration in the 2019–2020 period and lobbied hard against the federal government's excessive policy interventions in the US-China trade in electronics intermediate goods and services (e.g., semiconductors, design software, and capital equipment) and ICT final products (e.g., PCs and smartphones). They argued that the national need to reduce import dependency in critical health-care and medical supplies during the COVID-19 pandemic in 2020 should not be used as an excuse to force protectionist measures onto other technology-intensive sectors characterized by highly extensive and efficient global production networks, such as electronics.

Two brief examples in global electronics are indicative of this tendency toward highly compromised outcomes arising from defensive policy interventions in the US. In the first case, Taiwan's Foxconn Technology, the world's largest EMS provider and the parent company of the largest flat panel display makers from Taiwan (Innolux) and Japan (Sharp) (see Table 4.7), announced in July 2017 that it would invest $10 billion by 2023 to build a very large panel display plant in Wisconsin, the US, that could employ up to 13,000 US workers and receive up to $3 billion in subsidies from the Wisconsin state government. Foxconn's pledge was immediately touted by then the newly inaugurated president Trump as a big win for his "Made in the USA" drive. When in initial production by end 2020, the Wisconsin plant would supply panel displays for computers, TVs, and automotive dashboards made in the US.[30]

Despite the plant's celebrated ground breaking by President Trump and Foxconn chairman Terry Guo on June 28, 2018, progress in plant construction and investment was slow. As of December 2019, construction had yet to begin. By early 2020, Foxconn had invested only $372 million at the Mount Pleasant site and scaled down the project from a cutting-edge large-panel Generation 10.5 gigafactory in the initial plan to a much smaller and older Generation 6 factory[31] producing small panels for education, medicine, entertainment, and the military, making it unattractive for key suppliers to invest and develop the local ecosystem in Wisconsin. On April 20, 2021, Foxconn negotiated further with the State of Wisconsin and scaled down this deal to "only" $672 million in investment and 1,454 jobs by 2025. This U-turn in Foxconn's investment commitment is not surprising, given the supply overcapacity in the global flat panel display industry and the exclusive geographical concentration of panel production in five East Asian economies (see Table 4.7). The lack of scale economies among potential end customers and the absence of PC, mobile handset, and TV manufacturing in the US further disadvantaged Foxconn's original big plan for the Wisconsin plant that will not be well coupled with major electronics global production networks in these end products.

In the second and more recent case alluded to briefly in Chapter 6, Taiwan's world leading semiconductor foundry provider, TSMC, announced a plan on May 15, 2020, to invest up to $12 billion between 2021 and 2029 to build a 5 nm fab in Arizona. While this investment apparently represents another policy "win" under the former Trump administration to wrestle semiconductor supply chains back to the US, it does make better sense than the compromised Foxconn project from this book's perspective. After all, the US and its leading fabless chip design firms—from Apple's in-house A- and M-series chips to Qualcomm and Broadcom's wireless chips and AMD and Nvidia's graphic processing chips—have been relying on TSMC as the preferred foundry partner (see Chapters 4–5). In short, the US and its fabless semiconductor firms have already been highly interdependent with TSMC's global production network.

But even in an optimistic scenario for a fab that started construction only in 2021, TSMC's Arizona fab will unlikely be serving many lead firm customers outside the US because of its lack of scale economies, modest technological edge, and insufficient engineering support for high operating efficiency—the same competitive issues confronting Foxconn's proposed panel display plant in Wisconsin. In his recent talk at a Taiwan forum in April 2021, TSMC's revered founder Morris Chang noted:

> The United States stood out for cheap land and electricity when TSMC looked for an overseas site but we had to try hard to scout out competent technicians and workers in Arizona because manufacturing jobs have not been popular among American people for decades.[32]

Indeed, by the time its 5 nm fab in Arizona produces the first batch of US-designed chips in 2024 at the earliest, TSMC's 5 nm home gigafab (Fab 18) in Taiwan would have well reached full capacity (since 2022), and its new and more advanced 3 nm gigafab in Taiwan should have already started volume production as early as in mid-2022. Even at full capacity of 20,000 wafers per month starting in 2024, this Arizona fab's output will be just about 5–10 percent of any of TSMC's four gigafabs back in Taiwan. Likely paying higher average prices for their chips fabricated in this less advanced TSMC fab in Arizona, the eventual end customers in the US will be in high-end defense and communications, such as artificial intelligence, 5G base stations, and F-35 fighter jets. For national security reasons, nevertheless, these end users might well be better served with TSMC's modest 5 nm fab in Arizona and, if all goes well in its future US plan, perhaps up to six new fabs at the Arizona site over a ten- to fifteen-year time period.

Ultimately, these ongoing cases of global production network reconfigurations compelled by host government pressures and geopolitical maneuvers—Foxconn in Wisconsin and TSMC in Arizona—demonstrate that it is necessary for all parties concerned (i.e., firms and policy communities) to recognize crucial international and intraindustry differences in the interconnected worlds of electronics global production networks. A nationalist approach (at the international scale) to seeking ownership control or even simple participation in these complex cross-macroregional production networks (at the intraindustry scale) is likely to be inefficient and costly for both domestic and international end users.[33] Successful development policy oriented toward benefiting from global production networks in both advanced countries and developing economies thus requires a careful calibration of policy instruments to appreciate and address these crucial differences, to minimize their negative impacts (e.g., protectionist trade regimes, supplier lock-ins, and "race to the bottom" outcomes), and to establish a competitive position through strategic coupling with global production networks. What then do all these mean for future academic research in the interdisciplinary field of global production networks and global value chains?

## Future Research Agendas

Much of the existing academic literature on global electronics has focused on the national scale of industrial competition and the role of innovation and technology in determining the success and failure of national competitiveness and firm performance in individual segments such as semiconductors and computers.[34] This book has gone beyond this vast literature by focusing on the organizational innovations underpinning diverse electronics global production networks centered in East Asia that enables a better understanding of the industrial and firm-specific dynamics in a rapidly changing world economy. The empirical coverage of the four major segments of global electronics—semiconductors, personal computers, mobile handsets, and consumer electronics—would not be possible without the comprehensive proprietary data and primary interview material covering up to the late 2010s. These empirical findings can serve as a definitive benchmark for future comparative studies of the likely massive global economic change throughout the 2020s.

Perhaps even more importantly, this book has demonstrated the analytical utility of the global production networks theory (GPN 2.0) in explaining the innovative organization of electronics production worldwide and the role of these intrafirm and interfirm production networks in co-constituting the interconnected worlds of global electronics. While the original GPN 2.0 theory in Coe and Yeung's (2015) *Global Production Networks* seeks to explain economic development and its uneven geographical outcomes,[35] this book has only deployed the first part of the theory that focuses on the industrial organization of global production networks in relation to causal dynamics and firm-specific strategies (see Figure 3.2). I believe my empirical focus has opened up the "black box" of electronics global production networks and laid the necessary groundwork for the next stage analysis of the causal links between these network dynamics and uneven development outcomes in future work. As I have argued elsewhere in Yeung (2019, 2021b), this two-stage analytical approach in the GPN 2.0 theory—first, unpacking the nature and logic of production networks in specific industries or sectors and, second, examining their unequal consequences for localities and national economies strategically coupled with these networks—can provide more robust answers to the confounding question in contemporary studies of economic development: "In what sense a GPN problem?"

Before I broaden out and raise several agendas for future academic research, let me reflect critically on several conceptual and methodological lessons from this book's "stress-testing" of the GPN 2.0 theory in one major industrial sector—global electronics. In terms of theory, the core elements of GPN 2.0 are generally applicable in my empirical analysis, though the relative importance of the four causal drivers and competitive dynamics in Chapters 3 and 6 is variable in different industrial segments and over time (see summary Table 6.7). This variability points to the necessity for a robust GPN analysis to be comparative (e.g., multiple segments and/or national economies) and dynamic (e.g., over a decade or longer) in order to reduce the "mechanistic" application of such causal theory and to contextualize better those segment- and/or country-specific dynamics.

This conceptual necessity and recent real-world events at the beginning of the 2020s bring me to the seemingly missing elements of the state and institutional contexts in this book, as my analytical focus was placed primarily at the network and firm level (see Chapters 1 and 2 and summary Tables 1.2 and 2.1). To begin, the GPN 2.0 theory conceptualizes the state as a constitutive part, but not necessarily the causal driver, of global production networks—global lead firms are indeed such coordinators, in conjunction with their strategic partners, key suppliers, and major customers in different national jurisdictions. While the state can influence lead firms and production networks through specific policy interventions, such as sectoral industrial policy or trade restrictions (examined as "regulatory risks" in Chapters 3 and 6), it does not directly "do" production networks such as involving in product development, manufacturing, and shipment logistics. In this sense, the state remains an "extrafirm" actor in global production networks.

There are exceptions, though, in a small number of cases of sovereign wealth funds (e.g., GlobalFoundries fully owned by Abu Dhabi's state Mubadala Investment Company until its successful listing as the largest semiconductor initial public offering on Nasdaq on October 28, 2021), state-linked enterprises (e.g., Italian-French state shareholding in STMicroelectronics and China's state funds as majority shareholders of SMIC), and private firms with alleged state links (e.g., Huawei and Xiaomi). But even in these cases involving the state, its direct influence in production networks remains ambiguous and quite hard to specify empirically. Bringing the state into a GPN 2.0 analysis requires specification of the state both as a political institution for collective action and national security *and* as an economic actor in its own right. It also necessitates an explicit examination of the ways in which the state is complicit in disrupting or reshaping the competitive logics of global production networks and its ramifications for network dynamics and development outcomes. As the case of US sanctions on Huawei in 2019–2021 has demonstrated (see details in Chapters 5 and 6), these questions of the state and international relations are really a "problem" of/for global production networks only when we can explicitly demonstrate how Huawei's production network dynamics matter in the origin and propagation of these political contestations and the consequences of different state policy interventions. In that sense, the state goes beyond its contextual role and becomes part of the "extrafirm bargaining" or a "GPN problem" in Huawei's global production network.

In terms of methodology, my empirical analysis has illustrated the substantive usefulness of a combination of quantitative datasets with detailed qualitative interview material. Still, there are operational difficulties in measuring some of the causal drivers in the GPN 2.0 theory. Cost-capability ratios and financial discipline, for example, are rather complex theoretical constructs beyond simple measurement. While costs are fairly direct and measurable, capability is less directly quantifiable. Chapter 6's analysis of cost-capability ratios has pointed to labor productivity—value added per employee—as a measure of firm-specific capability. But this simple measure does not take into account capability based on technologies (e.g., wafer fabs in semiconductors) and logistics (e.g., notebook PC production and supplier ecosystems). Future analysis should consider aggregating these different dynamic capabilities into a single measurement in order for the concept of cost-capability ratios to be better operationalized. Similarly, financial discipline is a causal driver that cannot be easily measured because its core element of financialization is not readily quantifiable. There are admittedly few empirical studies of electronics production networks that focus explicitly on the role of finance and investment returns.[36] In Chapter 6's analysis, I found strong empirical support for the role of financial discipline in semiconductors because of the high significance of capital spending and the availability of firm-specific data.

Looking forward, this book's GPN 2.0-inspired approach to analyzing the innovative organization of the global economy is only partial and unfinished, particularly in light of the dramatic transformations to be unleashed in the post-COVID-19 world economy during the 2020s. Grounded in the GPN 2.0 theory, three research agendas for future studies of global production networks and global value chains will be highly significant: (1) technology, (2) resilience, and (3) politics. As noted earlier, the role of the state is implicated in all of these agendas.

First, while not a causal driver in its own right, technology will fundamentally reshape the relevance of individual causal drivers in our future understanding of global production networks. Technological innovations will refigure competition among global lead firms and their strategic partners (changing cost-capability ratios) and industry-level opportunities (creating new market imperative). As an enabling factor, new technologies in 5G, artificial intelligence, 3D printing, and manufacturing platforms may seriously disrupt the existing organizational arrangements in global production networks, creating new opportunities for some firms and localities while making other firms and places obsolete or redundant.

In the existing literature on global production networks and global value chains,[37] there is currently far too little intellectual intersection with two strands of academic work most closely associated with the study of technological learning and capability and the digital platform economy.[38] The voluminous literature on technological learning can inform much on firm-specific capability building that will give more analytical strength to the key concepts of cost-capability ratios and firm-specific upgrading in future studies of global production networks. Much of the recent literature on global value chains tends to emphasize local upgrading through industry-level innovation systems or local clusters.[39] Future studies need to demonstrate much more explicitly how technological innovation and learning reshapes firm-level capability and their cost-capability ratios that drive the reorganization of global production networks in different industries and places.

On the other hand, recent theories of ecosystems and digital platforms have raised important questions for rethinking the nature of global production networks beyond hardware production in electronics and other manufacturing industries.[40] In their introduction to *Industry & Innovation*'s special issue on platforms, Kenney et al. (2019, 877) offered a critical agenda for studying future industrial change:

> What are the contours of industrial change? For example, the automobile industry is disrupted by autonomous vehicles, which will be dependent upon data capture and analysis; a firm with better software, more data, and superior analytics capability could displace or, as likely, relegate the automaker to a subordinate actor in the industry.

This discerning observation on the central role of data, algorithms, and analytics in digital platform ecosystems has huge implications for industrial lead firms in global production networks. Future studies can productively examine how lead firms in global electronics, for example, Samsung, Apple, Dell, Intel, TSMC, and Qualcomm, interact with platform ecosystems controlled by digital lead firms, such as Google, Amazon, and Microsoft, that are also outsourcing the production of their mobile devices and venturing into chip design for their in-house servers. Do these industrial lead firms serve as the "complementors" to platform owners in new kinds of industrial-digital global production networks? These interesting intersections between production-driven networks centered in East Asia and data-driven platforms (as multisided networks) strongly embedded in

Silicon Valley in the US (and China, in the cases of Tencent, Baidu, Byte-Dance, and Alibaba) will raise many challenging research questions on interfirm power relations, value capture trajectories, and strategic coupling possibilities.[41]

Second, future studies of global production networks must explicitly incorporate risk mitigation and resilience building into their analytical frameworks. Unlike much of the existing literature on global value chains,[42] this book has conceptualized risk as one of the four causal dynamics in the GPN 2.0 theory and examined empirically its importance in driving the geographical and organizational (re-)configurations of electronics production networks in Chapters 5 and 6. In the context of ongoing trade wars, tariffs on imports and disrupted supplies from affected countries can substantially raise the risk of supply chain vulnerability among customer firms and thus their much higher cost-capability ratios. Unexpected worldwide disruptions during the COVID-19 pandemic in 2020/2021 have also brought to the fore the critical importance of network resilience that enables firms in global production networks to foresee and adapt to such unpredictable systemic shocks. Still, my theoretical and empirical analysis remains quite limited on this highly pertinent issue of network resilience that will likely become more relevant for understanding global change in the postpandemic world economy during the 2020s.[43]

Massive worldwide disruptions to global production networks in many different industries took place throughout 2020 and up to mid-2021 due to travel and social restrictions imposed by national and local governments. The full effects of these disruptions will take some time to be fully ascertained. Suffice to say that in the global electronics industry, production network disruptions during the worst period of the pandemic in 2020 were seemingly less significant than in other sectors, such as essential health-care supplies, critical pharmaceutical and biomedical production, and agro-food distribution.[44] Major semiconductor producers in East Asia, such as Samsung and TSMC, did not report significant disruptions to their in-house fabs in 2020 and the first half of 2021. But other manufacturing activities in the final assembly stage of ICT products, such as smartphones and PCs, were more disrupted during the pandemic due to the large number of workers required in these labor-intensive facilities located throughout East Asia. In May 2021, India's deadly second wave caused severe disruption to the production of iPhones in several assembly factories in India that were owned by Taiwan's Foxconn and Wistron. A

Foxconn facility dedicated to iPhone assembly in the southern state of Tamil Nadu had its production cut by more than 50 percent. Compared to 2020, total smartphone production in India might decrease by 7.5 percent year-on-year. Earlier in December 2020, Wistron's dedicated iPhone assembly plant in southern Karnataka state was forced to shut down due to a rampage by thousands of its contract workers over payment delays.[45]

One major lesson in these examples for future studies of resilience in global production networks is the extent of digitalization and production automation, technological complexity, and supply chain capability among lead firms and their strategic partners and suppliers in different national and regional economies. Here, the role of global lead firms will likely be even *more* significant in building network resilience and risk mitigation by virtue of their geographically diversified sourcing and production activity and the continual adaptation and transformation of their cross-border value creation and capture in relation to new postpandemic realities. We also need better conceptualization of the key determinants of network resilience and its interaction with the causal effects of cost-capability ratios and risks in future theories of global production networks and global value chains. Whether in enhancing technology or resilience and in reshoring supply chains, however, the intervening role of the state in the future organization and governance of global production networks will likely be greater. While the existing literature on global value chains tends to focus on government policies in promoting industrial upgrading and technological catch-up, few have examined the politics and political contestation in such global production networks.[46] Recent events since 2018 ranging from highly politicized trade negotiations to the geopolitical challenges of (de-)coupling, however, have pointed clearly to the importance of network-level competitiveness as the key to understanding development in the postpandemic world economy.

As the third agenda for future academic research, many critical issues must be addressed in comprehending such politics of global production networks at both inter- and intrastate levels. These state-level politics will likely influence all causal drivers and competitive dynamics in the GPN 2.0 theory, from reshaping the cost-capability ratios of domestic firms to regulating differential access to end markets and financial resources and potentially escalating the risk environment. In the international political economy, different national states will likely intervene in their domestic economies to protect workers, firms, and industries vulnerable to the transformative global shift associated with the reorganization of production networks in the 2020s. Some of such protectionist politics will be framed in the form of firm-specific targeting and the broader industrial policy promoting industrial renaissance through various "Made in Home Country" initiatives.[47] Some hard questions have already been raised on the most recent $52 billion funding for the CHIPS for America Act 2020's effectiveness in reshoring semiconductor manufacturing: unjustified funding for domestic failure, unnecessary subsidies for foreign chip makers in the US, weak domestic semiconductor ecosystem and engineering pool, and, most critically, small in scale compared to the $100–$150 billion spending *each* announced by TSMC, Samsung, and SK Hynix, and the $150–$250 billion state funding by China and South Korea through to 2030.[48] While unlikely to be the only theatre of such interstate political maneuvers championing the nationalization of production networks in future, the US-China trade war since March 2018 represents a major flashpoint in the debilitating politics of international trade and its potentially devastating impact on global production networks in affected industries and sectors.

Meanwhile, domestic politics will impinge significantly on the reorganization of global production networks. The necessary understanding and nuanced appreciation of the policy dilemmas associated with strategic coupling with such networks, as the earlier section has indicated, will be crucial to productive domestic political debates and effective policy resolutions in both advanced industrialized countries and developing economies. A blanket demonization of global production networks as *the* source of all domestic economic malaises and/or shortages in essential healthcare and medical supplies during the COVID-19 pandemic in 2020 might seem politically expedient and feasible to some political elites and their unholy alliances in industry and business. But such a simplistic zero-sum reading conflating messy domestic politics and fractures with economic realities embedded in a highly complex and interdependent global economy is clearly untenable.

Having been examined with careful evidence throughout this book, global production networks are far more complex organizationally and entail much deeper linkages to geographically distanced actors elsewhere that defy easy political characterization and myth making. Future academic studies in the social sciences must theorize more robustly such inter- and intranational politics of global production networks and demonstrate empirically their consequential effects on people, places, and economies. As I have experienced well in writing this book on global electronics centered in East Asia, such an intellectual journey can be arduous and full of uncertainty, but ultimately fulfilling and even comforting in the interconnected worlds confronted by unprecedented once-in-a-generation challenges.

# IHS Markit/Informa Tech Custom Dataset, 2015 and 2018

TO CONDUCT A TRULY COMPREHENSIVE analysis of the dynamic changes in global electronics during the 2010s, the Global Production Networks Centre at the National University of Singapore (GPN@NUS Centre; https://fass.nus.edu.sg/gpn) purchased at substantial costs a very large and detailed set of proprietary data in June–October 2016 from IHS Markit, a leading global market information provider (https://ihsmarkit.com), and in July–October 2019 from Informa Tech (formerly IHS Markit until the exchange of its Technology research with Informa Plc to become Informa Tech division in July 2019 and Omdia in February 2020; https://www.informatech.com). Through multiple rounds of meetings and videoconferencing in 2016, we discussed our specific data requirements with a number of IHS Markit senior executives and analysts in charge of the different segments of global electronics (e.g., semiconductors, PCs and tablets, smartphones, and TVs).

We required custom data that show the specific suppliers, units, and pricing for the top five most significant components for each of the top ten global lead firms in three most important end product segments of global electronics, as well as details on their manufacturing outsourcing to providers of original design manufacturing (ODM) and/or electronics manufacturing services (EMS) by the geographical locations of production and factory outputs for each lead firm customer (known as original equipment manufacturing OEM firms). These components include semiconductor chips (processors and memory devices), panel displays, cameras, and so on. Some of these data were based on best estimates by the IHS Markit/Informa Tech's in-house research team comprising over three hundred staff and consultants worldwide who worked on the electronics industry. Half of these personnel were previously employed in the respective segments of global electronics. Their estimates were based on deep insights from industry-wide interviews and conversations, industry publications, and in-house secondary research. Insofar as possible and for the purpose of this book, I have triangulated these proprietary data with industry news, annual reports, and materials provided by my interviewees, particularly among those top lead firms, indicated in Appendix B.

Delivered over three phases up to three months in 2016 and 2019, these IHS Markit and Informa Tech custom data offer very detailed insights into the supply chain operations of specific OEM lead firms, their ODM/EMS providers, and key component suppliers. The dataset contains highly specific information at the firm, product, fab, and location level in all four segments of global electronics. In addition to this custom dataset for the respective years of 2015 and 2018, IHS Markit and Informa Tech also provided proprietary and detail historical datasets on semiconductors, computers, smartphones, TVs, panel displays, ODM-EMS providers, and global electronics manufacturing. Some of these data files date back to 2000 or earlier, whereas others contain very useful pivot data for further extraction and analysis. Since the custom data for 2015 and 2018 were obtained in two time periods in 2016 (IHS Markit) and in 2019 (Informa Tech), I use "IHS Markit/Informa Tech" as the named source for these custom and historical datasets throughout this book.

# APPENDIX B

# Methodology of the Study, 2016–2021

IN EXECUTING THIS COMPREHENSIVE study of global production networks in the electronics industry centered in East Asia, I adopted a two-pronged approach to collecting primary data and secondary data between 2016 and June 2021.

## Primary Data

In terms of primary data, we deployed the interview method. Instead of low responses from corporate surveys across many different countries or economies in which these firms were located, we believed interviews would yield the best qualitative data on the "how" and "why" questions in our study, whereas the IHS Markit/Informa Tech proprietary dataset could offer best answers to the "what" and "where" questions. We planned to conduct interviews with senior executives of global lead firms from any country of origin located in East Asia (Northeast and Southeast Asia) and their strategic partners and key suppliers in East Asia.

To ensure the representativeness and coverage of our lead firm sample, we developed a long list of global lead firms and their network members on the basis of proprietary data acquired from IHS Markit in June–October 2016 and further data extraction from Osiris and Orbis databases (www.bvdinfo.com) and various business directories. We then focused on the top twenty to thirty lead firms by their 2015 revenue in each of these four major segments of global electronics:

(1)    semiconductors,
(2)    personal computers (PCs),
(3)    mobile handsets (and telecommunications equipment), and
(4)    consumer electronics: televisions (TVs), wearables, and Internet of Things products.

Some of these firms were also in industrial hardware (e.g., automation and power electronics), ICT solutions (e.g., data storage), and commercial hardware (e.g. servers, terminals, and printers).

Starting in February 2017, we approached each of these top twenty to thirty firms through emails, letters, and phone calls. In general, we tried to interview the *most* senior or top executive based in East Asia and/or in charge of supply chain, manufacturing, or marketing. We identified these executives from corporate websites, LinkedIn listings, online databases, and other sources. Their positive responses to our interview requests were very encouraging and helpful!

From March 2017 to April 2018, we managed to conduct some 64 interviews with senior executives of 44 major electronics firms in various locations in East Asia—Singapore, Taiwan, South Korea, and China (see Table B1 for a full list of these firms). As the principal investigator of the GPN@NUS Centre, I conducted 52 of these interviews with senior executives of 42 lead firms in all four locations—all of these interviews (except one) were conducted face-to-face and recorded using a digital recorder after explicit consent had been given by interviewees in accordance with the requirements and approved procedures of the NUS Institutional Review Board. Most interviews lasted one to one and a half hours, and several were well over two hours. My postdoctoral fellow, Dr Carlo Inverardi-Ferri, conducted another 12 interviews with executives of 10 lead firms in Taiwan and China. Most of these interviews were face-to-face and recorded.

In terms of representativeness, the list in Table B1 offers clear evidence of our strong coverage of the top 20 firms. Some 37 of the 44 firms included are global lead firms across all segments of global electronics— they are typically among the top 20 lead firms in their market segment. Of the 16 lead firms in semiconductors, 7 are involved in integrated devices manufacturing (IDM), whereas another 5 are fabless design houses. The remaining four lead firms are in panel displays, foundry services, and assembly, packaging, and testing (APT) services, and they are the top three market leaders in these domains. Further 21 lead firms are engaged in

TABLE B1. List of all 44 electronics lead firms interviewed in East Asia, 2017–2018

| Number | Segment | Business | Lead firm | Cat A #[2] | Cat B #[2] | Total |
|---|---|---|---|---|---|---|
| 1 | Semiconductors | Fabless | AMD | 2 | - | 2 |
| 2 | Semiconductors | Fabless | MediaTek | - | 1 | 1 |
| 3 | Semiconductors | Fabless | Nvidia | - | 1 | 1 |
| 4 | Semiconductors | Fabless | Qualcomm CDMA Tech | - | 1 | 1 |
| 5 | Semiconductors | Fabless | Synaptics | 1 | - | 1 |
| 6 | Semiconductors | IDM | Infineon Technologies | 1 | - | 1 |
| 7 | Semiconductors | IDM | Micron Technology | 1 | - | 1 |
| 8 | Semiconductors | IDM | NXP Semiconductors | 1 | 1 | 2 |
| 9 | Semiconductors | IDM | Renesas Electronics | 1 | - | 1 |
| 10 | Semiconductors | IDM | Samsung Electronics | 1 | - | 1 |
| 11 | Semiconductors | IDM | STMicroelectronics | 2 | - | 2 |
| 12 | Semiconductors | IDM | Winbond | 1 | - | 1 |
| 13 | Semiconductors | Foundry | UMC | 1 | - | 1 |
| 14 | Semiconductors | APT[1] | ASE | 2 | - | 2 |
| 15 | Semiconductors | FPD IDM[1] | AU Optronics | 1 | - | 1 |
| 16 | Semiconductors | FPD IDM | Sharp Electronics | 1 | - | 1 |
| 17 | PC | OEM | Acer | 1 | - | 1 |
| 18 | PC | OEM | Asustek Computer | - | 1 | 1 |
| 19 | PC | OEM | Dell | 2 | 1 | 3 |
| 20 | PC | OEM | Hewlett-Packard Inc | 2 | 1 | 3 |
| 21 | PC | OEM | Lenovo | 1 | 2 | 3 |
| 22 | PC | OEM | Toshiba TEC | 1 | - | 1 |
| 23 | PC | ODM | Compal | 1 | 2 | 3 |
| 24 | PC | ODM | Wistron | 1 | - | 1 |
| 25 | PC | Components | Catcher Technology | 1 | - | 1 |
| 26 | Mobiles & telecom | OEM | Apple | - | 1 | 1 |
| 27 | Mobiles & telecom | OEM | Cisco Systems | 1 | 1 | 2 |
| 28 | Mobiles & telecom | OEM | Ericsson Telecom | 1 | - | 1 |

(continued)

TABLE B1. (*continued*)

| Number | Segment | Business | Lead firm | Cat A #[2] | Cat B #[2] | Total |
|---|---|---|---|---|---|---|
| 29 | Mobiles & telecom | OEM | Nokia | 1 | 1 | 2 |
| 30 | Mobiles & telecom | OEM | Samsung Electronics | 4 | - | 4 |
| 31 | Mobiles & telecom | OEM | Xiaomi | 1 | - | 1 |
| 32 | Mobiles & telecom | OEM | ZTE | 1 | - | 1 |
| 33 | Mobiles & telecom | Components | Merry Electronics | 1 | - | 1 |
| 34 | Mobiles & telecom | Components | Murata Electronics | 1 | - | 1 |
| 35 | Consumer elec. | OEM | LG Electronics | - | 1 | 1 |
| 36 | Consumer elec. | OEM | Omron | 1 | - | 1 |
| 37 | Consumer elec. | OEM | Pioneer | 1 | 1 | 2 |
| 38 | Consumer elec. | OEM | Samsung Electronics | 2 | - | 2 |
| 39 | Consumer elec. | OEM | Seiko Epson | 1 | - | 1 |
| 40 | Consumer elec. | Components | Bitron Electronics | - | 1 | 1 |
| 41 | ICT | OEM | Hewlett-Packard Enterprise | 1 | - | 1 |
| 42 | ICT | Systems | Hitachi Asia | 1 | - | 1 |
| 43 | ICT | OEM | Hitachi Vantara | 1 | 1 | 2 |
| 44 | ICT | OEM | Toshiba TMEIC Asia | 1 | - | 1 |
| **Total** | | | | **46** | **18** | **64** |

[1] APT: Assembly, packaging, and testing services; and FPD: flat panel displays.

[2] Category A interviewees: vice president, general manager, or higher (executive vice president, chief technology officer, chief supply chain officer, and chief operating officer); Category B interviewees: senior manager or director.

original equipment manufacturing (OEM) in PCs, mobile handsets (and telecommunications equipment), consumer electronics, and ICT devices. Apart from these 37 global lead firms, we have another 7 lead firms serving as specialized component suppliers and providers of original design manufacturing (ODM) or ICT solutions. Again, they are among the top three in their product categories.

As illustrated in Figure 2.3, the Osiris and Orbis databases contain details of all firms in each major segment of global electronics. The categorization of lead firms in these datasets is slightly different from Table B1 and thus the minor difference in total firm number in each segment. Still, our interviews achieved the highest coverage in semiconductors, with 11 out of top 21 lead firms interviewed. Their combined revenue contributed to 37 percent of the total revenue by these top 21 firms in 2018. In PCs, we interviewed at nine of the top 20 lead firms that accounted for 57 percent of the total revenue of top 20 firms in this segment in 2018. In mobile handsets (and telecommunications equipment), senior executives of 12 of the top 24 lead firms were interviewed. Their combined revenue was 54 percent of the total revenue by the top 24 firms in 2018. In consumer electronics, we spoke to senior executives at 4 of the top 15 lead firms, and their revenue was worth 51 percent of the total revenue of top 15 firms in this segment. From their corporate reports and interviews, the combined revenue of all these 44 firms in 2018 was $959 billion or $741 billion (without the largest lead firm). Some $233 billion was from all 14 semiconductor lead firms ($190 billion from 10 of them that had manufacturing facilities) and another $812 billion came from 35 manufacturing lead firms in PCs, mobile handsets, and consumer electronics.

In terms of interviewees, 46 of the 64 interviews were with top executives at the level of vice president and general manager or higher. In many cases, our interviewees were responsible for the Asia Pacific and Japan markets and/or operations. In several cases, we managed to interview the worldwide top executives for supply chain or manufacturing operations of lead firms headquartered in the US and Western Europe. These interviews took place when they visited their Singapore offices. In other cases, the unique nature of global electronics centered in East Asia means that such top executives from the headquarters outside Asia (i.e., US and European OEM firms) were based in East Asia. We interviewed several of these top executives in Singapore and Taiwan. For all those lead firms from within East Asia (e.g., South Korea, China, and Taiwan), we interviewed their senior/top executives in the corporate headquarters located in their home economies. Direct quotes from over 27 interviewees and 22 out of these 44 lead firms are used in the book's empirical Chapters 4–6.

In addition to this unique and high-level qualitative dataset based on full transcripts from interview recordings, our research team also conducted another fifteen interviews with senior executives of other lead firms and suppliers in China and four interviews with leaders of business associations in global electronics (e.g., Electronic Industry Citizenship Coalition) and China (e.g., China Quality Management Association for

Electronics Industry) during the 2017–2018 period. Some of this interview material is also used in this book's empirical analysis.

### Secondary Data

Apart from the above primary data, we collected extensive secondary data on global lead firms, strategic partners, and key suppliers in the electronic industry. First and as detailed in Appendix A, we purchased a very large and detailed set of proprietary data from IHS Markit, a leading global market information provider, in June–October 2016, and updated the dataset to 2018 with Informa Tech (formerly the Technology business of IHS Markit until July 2019) in July–October 2019. For the period from 2019 onwards, including forecast from 2021 to 2023, I updated the data presented in various tables based on the most recent data and press releases from seven reliable sources—Canalys, Gartner, IDC, IC Insights, Omdia, TrendForce, and World Semiconductor Trade Statistics:

(1)   semiconductors: Gartner (https://www.gartner.com, released on April 12, 2021); IDC (https://www.idc.com, released on May 6, 2021); IC Insights (https://www.icinsights.com, released on August 11, 2020; March 16, April 28, and May 4, 2021); TrendForce, (https://www.trendforce.com, released on March 25 and April 15, 2021); and World Semiconductor Trade Statistics Forecast (https://www.wsts.org, released on June 8, 2021),

(2)   PCs: Canalys (https://www.canalys.com, released on January 11 and May 4, 2021); Gartner (https://www.gartner.com, released on January 11, 2021); IDC (https://www.idc.com, released on March 10, 2021); and TrendForce (https://www.trendforce.com, released on January 6, 2021),

(3)   mobile handsets: Canalys (https://www.canalys.com, released on June 14, 2021); Gartner (https://www.gartner.com, released on June 7, 2021); and TrendForce (https://www.trendforce.com, released on January 5 and May 10, 2021), and

(4)   TVs: Omdia (https://omdia.tech.informa.com, released on February 17 and April 20, 2021) and TrendForce (https://www.trendforce.com, released on May 24, 2021).

Inevitably, some of these recent data and forecasts released by various sources differed from each other due to their different underlying methodology and assumptions used by the above commercial research consultancies and industry associations. In general, I tried to triangulate different sources of data. But if the data values varied too much across different sources, I tended to use the source(s) with *lower* values when updating the relevant tables.

Second, we used Orbis and Osiris databases published by the Bureau van Dijk (https://www.bvdinfo.com) to conduct empirical analysis and to augment the IHS Markit/Informa Tech datasets. The Orbis database contains records of close to 400 million firms worldwide, including over 70,000 public listed firms, in many industrial sectors such as electronics and automotive. We used standard NAICS SIC codes below to identify all firms with revenue data:

(1)    semiconductors: 3674 (Semiconductors and related devices),

(2)    PCs: 3571 (Electronic computers) and 3577 (Computer peripheral equipment),

(3)    mobile handsets: 3661 (Telephone and telegraph apparatus), 3669 (Communications equipment), and 3679 (Electronic components), and

(4)    consumer electronics: 3651 (Household audio and video equipment).

A few lead firms were moved to the most appropriate segment (e.g., SK Hynix, Infineon, and MediaTek to semiconductors, Dell to personal computers, and Philips and Hitachi to consumer electronics).

Third, we conducted extensive research into corporate reports, industry reports, media coverage, and online websites. This process has yielded additional detail and useful material for us to understand fully the production network activities at the level of individual lead firms and the industry as a whole.

# APPENDIX C

# Full Tables

TABLE C1. World's top 15 semiconductor firms by revenue and market share, 1972–2020 (in US$ billions and percent)

| 2018 rank | 1995 rank | 1980 rank | Firm | 1972 % | 1980 % | 1984 $ | 1990 % | 1995 $ | 1995 % | 2000 $ | 2000 % | 2005 $ | 2010 $ | 2010 % | 2015 $ | 2018 $ | 2018 % | 2019 $ | 2020 $ | 2020 % |
|---|---|---|---|---|---|---|---|---|---|---|---|---|---|---|---|---|---|---|---|---|
| | | | **IDM firms** | | | | | | | | | | | | | | | | | |
| 1 | 6 | - | Samsung Electronics | - | - | - | - | 8.3 | 5.7 | 8.9 | 4.0 | 17.7 | 28.4 | 9.1 | 38.7 | 74.6 | 15.4 | 52.4 | 57.7 | 12.4 |
| 2 | 1 | 8 | Intel | 1.3 | 4.1 | 1.2 | 7.0 | 13.2 | 9.1 | 30.2 | 13.7 | 35.5 | 40.4 | 13.0 | 51.4 | 69.9 | 14.4 | 67.8 | 72.8 | 15.6 |
| 3 | 10 | - | SK Hynix[1] | - | - | - | - | 4.1 | 2.8 | 5.1 | 2.3 | 5.6 | 10.4 | 3.3 | 16.5 | 36.3 | 7.5 | 22.3 | 25.8 | 5.5 |
| 4 | 12 | - | Micron Technology | - | - | - | - | 2.6 | 1.8 | 6.3 | 2.9 | 4.8 | 8.9 | 2.9 | 14.1 | 29.7 | 6.1 | 20.3 | 22.0 | 4.7 |
| 7 | 7 | 1 | Texas Instruments[2] | 11.8 | 11.2 | 2.4 | 6.0 | 7.8 | 5.4 | 9.2 | 4.2 | 10.8 | 13.0 | 4.2 | 12.3 | 15.4 | 3.2 | 13.4 | 13.6 | 2.9 |
| 8 | 3 | 7 | Kioxia (Toshiba)[3] | 4.2 | 4.5 | 1.5 | 7.0 | 10.1 | 7.0 | 10.4 | 4.7 | 9.1 | 13.0 | 4.2 | 8.8 | 11.4 | 2.4 | 7.8 | 10.4 | 2.2 |
| 10 | - | - | STMicroelectronics | 3.6 | 2.2 | - | - | - | - | 7.9 | 3.6 | 8.9 | 10.3 | 3.3 | 6.9 | 9.7 | 2.0 | 9.6 | 10.2 | 2.2 |
| 11 | - | 10 | Infineon (Siemens)[4] | 2.3 | 3.0 | 0.3 | - | - | - | 4.6 | 2.1 | 8.3 | 6.3 | 2.0 | 6.8 | 9.1 | 1.9 | 9.1 | 9.6 | 2.1 |
| 12 | 11 | 3 | NXP (Philips)[5] | 5.1 | 6.6 | 1.2 | 3.0 | 3.9 | 2.7 | 6.3 | 2.9 | 5.6 | 4.0 | 1.3 | 9.6 | 9.0 | 1.9 | 8.9 | 8.6 | 1.8 |
| 14 | 2 | 5 | Renesas Elec. (NEC)[6] | - | 5.4 | 2.0 | 8.0 | 11.3 | 7.8 | 8.2 | 3.7 | 8.1 | 11.9 | 3.8 | 5.7 | 6.7 | 1.4 | 6.5 | 6.5 | 1.4 |
| - | 4 | 6 | Elpida (Hitachi)[7] | 3.9 | 4.7 | 1.7 | 7.0 | 9.1 | 6.3 | 5.7 | 2.6 | 2.0 | 6.5 | 2.1 | - | - | - | - | - | - |
| - | 5 | 2 | Freescale (Motorola)[5] | 9.0 | 7.8 | 2.3 | 6.0 | 8.7 | 6.0 | 5.0 | 2.3 | 5.6 | 4.4 | 1.4 | - | - | - | - | - | - |
| - | 8 | - | Fujitsu | - | - | 0.8 | 5.0 | 5.5 | 3.8 | 5.0 | 2.3 | 2.6 | 3.1 | 1.0 | 1.1 | - | - | - | - | - |
| - | 9 | - | Mitsubishi | - | - | - | 4.0 | 5.3 | 3.7 | 5.8 | 2.6 | 1.0 | 1.6 | 0.5 | 1.4 | - | - | - | - | - |
| - | - | 4 | National Semi.[2] | 2.2 | 5.5 | 1.3 | 4.0 | - | - | - | - | 1.9 | 1.4 | 0.4 | - | - | - | - | - | - |
| - | - | 9 | Fairchild Semi.[2] | 4.8 | 4.0 | - | - | - | - | 1.4 | 0.6 | 1.4 | 1.6 | 0.5 | 0.4 | - | - | - | - | - |

**Fabless firms**

| | | | | | | | | | | | | | | | | | | | |
|---|---|---|---|---|---|---|---|---|---|---|---|---|---|---|---|---|---|---|---|
| 5 | Broadcom[8] | – | – | – | – | – | – | – | – | 1.1 | 2.7 | 6.7 | 2.2 | 8.4 | 17.5 | 3.6 | 15.3 | 15.8 | 3.4 |
| 6 | Qualcomm | – | – | – | – | – | – | – | – | 1.2 | 3.5 | 7.2 | 2.3 | 16.5 | 16.6 | 3.4 | 13.6 | 17.6 | 3.8 |
| 9 | Nvidia | – | – | – | – | – | – | – | – | 0.7 | 2.1 | 3.1 | 1.0 | 4.4 | 10.4 | 2.1 | 7.3 | 10.6 | 2.3 |
| 13 | MediaTek | – | – | – | – | – | – | – | – | 0.4 | 1.4 | 3.5 | 1.1 | 6.7 | 7.9 | 1.6 | 8.0 | 11.0 | 2.4 |
| 15 | AMD[9] | – | – | – | – | – | – | – | 3.8 | 1.7 | 3.9 | 6.4 | 2.1 | 3.9 | 6.0 | 1.2 | 6.7 | 9.8 | 2.1 |
| | Total fabless revenue | | | | | | | | 7.6 | 16.7 | 39.8 | 65.4 | 18.9 | 87.5 | 97.4 | 20.1 | 126 | 153 | 32.8 |
| | Top 10 firms | | 49.7 | 56.8 | 14.7 | 57.0 | 83.4 | 57.6 | 98.9 | 44.8 | 115 | 150 | 48.1 | 183 | 292 | 60.2 | 232 | 257 | 55.2 |
| | **Total market ($b)** | | | 3.5 | 10.0 | 26.0 | 50.5 | 144 | 221 | 240 | 312 | – | 346 | 485 | – | 422 | 466 | – |

[1] Hynix Semiconductor was formed in October 1999 after a merger of Hyundai Electronics with LG Semiconductor. In March 2012, SK Telecom became its largest shareholder and renamed it to SK Hynix.

[2] Texas Instruments acquired National Semiconductor in September 2011. Fairchild was sold to National Semiconductor in 1987 and then spun off in 1997 before its acquisition by ON Semiconductor in 2016.

[3] Toshiba's memory business was sold to a consortium led by Bain Capital in June 2018 and renamed to Kioxia in October 2019.

[4] Infineon Technologies was spun off from Siemens semiconductor division in 1999 and publicly listed in 2000.

[5] Philips semiconductor division was sold to private equity and renamed to NXP in 2006. Freescale was spun off from Motorola's semiconductor division in 2004, and NXP acquired Freescale in 2015.

[6] Renesas Electronics' data before 2010 refer to NEC that merged with Renesas Technology in April 2010 to create Renesas Electronics (a merged entity comprising Mitsubishi and Hitachi Semiconductors in November 2002).

[7] Elpida Memory was formed in 1999 through a merger of DRAM divisions of Hitachi and NEC. In 2003, it acquired Mitsubishi's DRAM division. In 2013, it was acquired by Micron Technologies.

[8] Singapore-incorporated Avago acquired Broadcom Corp for $37 billion in 2015 to become Broadcom Inc. Its 2015 revenue is incorporated into Broadcom.

[9] AMD became fabless after spinning off its wafer fabrication facilities to form GlobalFoundries in 2009.

Sources: 1972–1984 data from Malerba (1985, Tables 2.6 and 6.11; 22, 159); 1990 data from Brown and Linden (2011, Table 1.1; 18); 1995 data from Mathews and Cho (2000, Table 1.2; 37); 2000 data from Yeung (2016, Table 5.3; 135) based on Gartner Research (http://www.gartner.com) and IHS iSuppli Research (http://www.isuppli.com); 2005–2018 data are from IHS Markit/Informa Tech Custom Research for GPN@NUS Centre, July–October 2016 and 2019, and author's interviews; 2019–2020 data from Gartner (http://www.gartner.com, released on April 12, 2021) and IC Insights (https://www.icinsights.com, released on April 28 and May 4, 2021).

TABLE C2. World's total semiconductor market revenue by product categories and industrial applications, 2008–2021 (in US$ billions)

| | 2008 | 2010 | 2011 | 2012 | 2013 | 2014 | 2015 | 2016 | 2017 | 2018 | 2019 | 2020 | 2021ᶠ |
|---|---|---|---|---|---|---|---|---|---|---|---|---|---|
| **Revenue by product categories** | | | | | | | | | | | | | |
| **Integrated circuits (ICs)** | **218** | **258** | **257** | **248** | **266** | **290** | **286** | **293** | **362** | **413** | **333** | **361** | **436** |
| Logic ICs | 73.1 | 78.9 | 81.6 | 85.8 | 88.4 | 91.1 | 89.1 | 89.7 | 98.4 | 107 | 107 | 118 | 139 |
| General purpose logic | 12.5 | 12.9 | 12.5 | 12.4 | 12.2 | 13.0 | 11.9 | 11.5 | 13.0 | 14.2 | - | - | - |
| Standard logic | 1.8 | 1.7 | 1.7 | 1.7 | 1.5 | 1.5 | 1.5 | 1.3 | 1.5 | 1.5 | - | - | - |
| Display drivers | 7.0 | 6.5 | 6.1 | 6.3 | 6.2 | 6.5 | 6.1 | 5.7 | 6.4 | 6.9 | - | - | - |
| PLD | 3.7 | 4.8 | 4.8 | 4.5 | 4.5 | 5.0 | 4.4 | 4.6 | 5.0 | 5.8 | - | - | - |
| Logic ASICs | 60.6 | 65.9 | 69.1 | 73.4 | 76.2 | 78.1 | 77.3 | 78.2 | 85.5 | 93.0 | - | - | - |
| Memory ICs | 45.8 | 69.8 | 61.5 | 55.0 | 70.5 | 82.6 | 80.8 | 81.9 | 132 | 165 | 106 | 117 | 155 |
| DRAM | 23.7 | 39.7 | 29.6 | 26.4 | 35.0 | 46.3 | 45.1 | 41.5 | 73.5 | 98.9 | - | - | - |
| SRAM | 1.9 | 1.7 | 1.5 | 1.1 | 0.7 | 0.6 | 0.5 | 0.4 | 0.5 | 0.4 | - | - | - |
| Flash memory | 18.0 | 26.3 | 28.3 | 25.8 | 33.1 | 34.3 | 33.9 | 38.7 | 56.2 | 63.4 | - | - | - |
| NAND | 11.8 | 21.3 | 24.0 | 22.3 | 30.2 | 32.0 | 31.9 | 36.8 | 53.9 | 61.0 | - | - | - |
| NOR | 6.2 | 5.0 | 4.4 | 3.5 | 2.9 | 2.3 | 2.0 | 1.8 | 2.3 | 2.4 | - | - | - |
| Other memory | 2.3 | 2.1 | 2.1 | 1.7 | 1.6 | 1.5 | 1.3 | 1.3 | 1.7 | 1.8 | - | - | - |
| Microcomponent ICs | 55.6 | 61.0 | 66.0 | 61.5 | 60.5 | 65.7 | 63.1 | 67.7 | 73.3 | 80.1 | 66.4 | 70.0 | 75.3 |
| Microprocessor (MPU) | 34.3 | 39.6 | 45.1 | 43.1 | 42.4 | 46.8 | 44.7 | 48.8 | 52.0 | 58.0 | - | - | - |
| Microcontroller (MCU) | 15.5 | 15.8 | 15.9 | 14.9 | 15.5 | 16.2 | 15.8 | 16.1 | 18.3 | 19.0 | - | - | - |

| | | | | | | | | | | | | | |
|---|---|---|---|---|---|---|---|---|---|---|---|---|---|
| Digital signal processor | 5.8 | 5.7 | 5.0 | 3.4 | 2.6 | 2.6 | 2.6 | 2.9 | 3.1 | 3.1 | - | - | - |
| Analogue ICs | 43.9 | 47.7 | 48.2 | 46.1 | 46.8 | 51.0 | 52.3 | 53.1 | 58.3 | 61.0 | 53.9 | 55.7 | 67.7 |
| General purpose | 16.2 | 19.1 | 19.3 | 18.0 | 17.6 | 18.0 | 17.9 | 17.6 | 19.5 | 21.1 | - | - | - |
| Analogue ASICs | 27.8 | 28.7 | 28.9 | 28.1 | 29.2 | 33.1 | 34.4 | 35.5 | 38.7 | 39.8 | - | - | - |
| **Discretes** | **18.7** | **21.4** | **22.4** | **19.9** | **20.0** | **21.6** | **20.1** | **20.5** | **23.1** | **25.4** | **23.8** | **23.8** | **28.2** |
| Optical semiconductor | 19.2 | 27.3 | 29.2 | 32.1 | 33.5 | 34.5 | 33.6 | 32.5 | 35.5 | 36.9 | 41.6 | 40.4 | 44.4 |
| Sensors & actuators | 4.4 | 5.3 | 6.6 | 7.2 | 7.6 | 8.0 | 8.1 | 9.2 | 9.7 | 9.9 | 13.5 | 15.0 | 18.3 |
| **Total semiconductor[1]** | **261** | **311** | **316** | **308** | **355** | **355** | **346** | **355** | **430** | **485** | **412** | **440** | **527** |
| **Revenue by industrial applications** | | | | | | | | | | | | | |
| Computer & data storage | 94.2 | 111 | 105 | 97.9 | 103 | 117 | 111 | 116 | 150 | 177 | 136 | 160 | 173 |
| Wireless communications | 51.5 | 66.7 | 73.8 | 83.1 | 95.0 | 103 | 106 | 107 | 130 | 146 | 109 | 119 | 147 |
| Wired communications | 16.5 | 20.1 | 20.1 | 19.3 | 19.9 | 21.1 | 20.1 | 21.5 | 23.0 | 26.4 | - | - | - |
| Consumer electronics | 53.1 | 59.3 | 56.0 | 47.2 | 44.3 | 42.1 | 37.6 | 34.6 | 39.5 | 41.7 | 55.7 | 60.0 | 65.3 |
| Industrial electronics | 24.3 | 31.4 | 35.4 | 34.8 | 38.2 | 42.3 | 41.7 | 43.3 | 48.7 | 52.2 | - | - | - |
| Automotive electronics | 20.3 | 23.1 | 25.6 | 25.2 | 26.4 | 29.1 | 29.2 | 32.9 | 38.2 | 41.6 | 42.1 | 38.0 | 43.2 |
| **Total semiconductor[1]** | **261** | **311** | **316** | **308** | **355** | **355** | **346** | **355** | **430** | **485** | **419** | **464** | **522** |

[1] Revenue data for total semiconductor market in 2019–2021 (forecast) are slightly different from Tables 1.1 and 2.2 due to different data sources. Sources: 2008–2018 Data from IHS Markit/Informa Tech Custom Research for GPN@NUS Centre, July–October 2016 and 2019; and 2019–2021 (forecast) data from World Semiconductor Trade Statistics Forecast (https://www.wsts.org, released on June 8, 2021), IDC (https://www.idc.com, released on May 6, 2021), and IHS Markit (https://ihsmarkit.com, released on November 5, 2020).

TABLE C3. World's top 6 notebook ODMs from Taiwan by shipment and market share, 1999–2018 (in millions of units and percent)

| ODM | 1999 units | 2000 units | 2004 units | 2010 units | 2015 units | 2015 % | 2018 units | 2018 % | Largest client[1] | 2nd largest client | Next largest client(s) |
|---|---|---|---|---|---|---|---|---|---|---|---|
| Compal | 1.1 | 1.8 | 7.7 | 48.1 | 31.7 | 17.8 | 40.9 | 30.4 | Dell 20/13/11 | HP 12/NA/NA | Lenovo and Acer 5.6/5.5/NA and 3.6/4.7/18 |
| Quanta | 2.2 | 2.5 | 11.6 | 52.1 | 40.8 | 22.9 | 36.1 | 26.8 | HP 15/10/24 | Apple 7.7/13.4/5.5 | Acer and Lenovo 5.8/NA/NA and 1.6/5.2/6.0 |
| Wistron[2] | 1.5 | 1.8 | - | 27.5 | 24.4 | 13.7 | 17.3 | 12.9 | Dell 6.9/4.2/10 | HP 3.7/9.3/NA | Lenovo 3.6/4.2/7.0 |
| Inventec | 1.2 | - | - | 16.2 | 14.2 | 10.3 | 11.5 | 8.5 | HP 9.8/9.4/3.0 | Toshiba 0.0/4.0/12 | Others 1.7/0.8/NA |
| Pegatron | - | - | - | 15.5 | 11.7 | 8.5 | 8.4 | 6.5 | Asus 7.1/6.8/8.5 | Acer 1.1/1.2/NA | Lenovo 0.0/2.1/NA |
| Hon Hai | - | - | - | 10.0 | 8.1 | 5.9 | 2.7 | 2.0 | Apple 2.7/4.5/NA | HP 0.0/2.6/2.0 | Dell 0.0/1.0/3.0 |
| Others | - | 18.1 | 26.8 | 18.2 | 6.6 | 4.8 | 17.7 | 13.2 | - | - | - |
| **Total outsourced** | - | **24.2** | **46.1** | **187.6** | **137.5** | **100.0** | **134.5** | **100.0** | HP 40/35/NA | Dell 27/22/NA | Lenovo 16/17/NA |
| Taiwan share (%) | 39.0 | 52.0 | 72.0 | 95.0 | 95.2 | - | 86.8 | - | 100.0 | 100.0 | 100.0 |

[1] Figures refer to million units outsourced respectively in 2018/2015/2010. Ranking based on 2018 shipment.

[2] Wistron was spun off from Acer Inc in 2001 and listed in 2003.

Note: These figures include notebooks assembled in China by Taiwanese-owned production facilities.

Sources: 1999 data from Amsden and Chu (2003, Tables 2.6 and 2.7; 30, 33); 2000–2010 data from Yeung (2016, Table 4.3; 96) based on company annual reports and www.researchinchina.com, accessed October 1, 2014; and 2015–2018 data from IHS Markit/Informa Tech Custom Research for GPN@NUS Centre, July–October 2016 and 2019.

TABLE C4. World's top mobile handset OEM firms by shipment, market share, and outsourcing, 2008–2021 (in millions of units and percent)

| OEM firms | Samsung | Huawei | Apple | Xiaomi | Oppo | Vivo | LG | Lenovo-Motorola[1] | ZTE | Top 9 in 2018 | Worldwide Total | Nokia[2] | Blackberry | HTC | Sony (Ericsson) |
|---|---|---|---|---|---|---|---|---|---|---|---|---|---|---|---|
| 2008 shipment (m) | 5.3 | 0.0 | 13.7 | 0.0 | 0.0 | 0.0 | 0.0 | 9.2 | 0.0 | 28.2 | 161 | 60.5 | 22.6 | 12.7 | 5.2 |
| Market share (%) | 3.3 | - | 8.5 | - | - | - | - | 5.7 | - | 17.5 | 100.0 | 37.6 | 14.0 | 7.9 | 3.2 |
| 2010 shipment (m) | 11.8 | 0.0 | 38.8 | 0.0 | 0.0 | 0.0 | 1.8 | 15.8 | 0.0 | 68.2 | 320 | 128 | 56.6 | 23.2 | 9.0 |
| Market share (%) | 3.7 | - | 12.1 | - | - | - | 0.6 | 4.9 | - | 21.3 | 100.0 | 40.1 | 17.7 | 7.3 | 2.8 |
| 2015 shipment (m) | 320 | 109 | 232 | 73.1 | 45.7 | 45.2 | 59.7 | 73.9 | 59.8 | 1,018 | 1,377 | 27.3 | 3.9 | 15.9 | 29.4 |
| Market share (%) | 23.2 | 7.9 | 16.8 | 5.3 | 3.8 | 3.3 | 4.3 | 5.4 | 4.3 | 74.0 | 100.0 | 2.0 | 0.3 | 1.2 | 2.1 |
| 2018 shipment (m) | 290 | 206 | 205 | 119 | 115 | 104 | 44.2 | 41.8 | 15.0 | 1,140 | 1,410 | 15.1 | 1.1 | 2.2 | 8.1 |
| Market share (%) | 20.6 | 14.6 | 14.5 | 8.4 | 8.2 | 7.4 | 3.1 | 3.0 | 1.1 | 80.8 | 100.0 | 1.1 | 0.1 | 0.2 | 0.6 |
| 2020 shipment (m) | 263 | 170 | 199 | 146 | 144 | 110 | 23.0 | - | - | - | 1,250 | - | - | - | - |
| Market share (%) | 21.0 | 13.6 | 15.9 | 11.7 | 11.5 | 8.8 | 1.9 | - | - | - | 100.0 | - | - | - | - |
| 2021[F] shipment (m) | 267 | 45 | 229 | 198 | 185 | 145 | - | - | - | - | 1,360 | - | - | - | - |
| 2015 production[3] | | | | | | | | | | | | | | | |
| In-house (%) | 100 | 22.7 | 0.0 | 0.0 | 50.0 | 0.0 | 76.5 | 90.0 | 25.8 | 50.9 | 50.0 | 4.8 | 0.0 | 100 | 0.0 |
| Hon Hai (TW) | - | - | 71.5 | - | - | - | - | - | - | 16.3 | 15.9 | 95.2 | - | - | - |
| Foxconn Int'l (TW) | - | 19.8 | - | 80.0 | 50.0 | 100 | - | - | - | 14.5 | 14.2 | - | - | - | 76.2 |

(continued)

TABLE C4. (*continued*)

| OEM firms | Samsung | Huawei | Apple | Xiaomi | Oppo | Vivo | LG | Lenovo-Motorola[1] | ZTE | Top 9 in 2018 | World-wide Total | Nokia[2] | Black-berry | HTC | Sony (Ericsson) |
|---|---|---|---|---|---|---|---|---|---|---|---|---|---|---|---|
| Pegatron (TW) | - | - | 25.9 | - | - | - | - | - | - | 5.9 | 5.0 | - | - | - | - |
| Flex (SG) | - | 34.8 | - | - | - | - | 23.5 | 10.0 | - | 5.4 | 4.6 | - | 23.1 | - | - |
| Kaifa (CN) | - | 5.1 | - | - | - | - | - | - | 52.5 | 3.6 | 3.1 | - | - | - | - |
| Top 5 share (%) | - | 59.7 | 97.4 | 80.0 | 50.0 | 100 | 23.5 | 10.0 | 52.5 | 45.7 | 42.8 | 95.2 | 23.1 | - | 76.2 |
| **2018 production** | | | | | | | | | | | | | | | |
| In-house (%) | 100 | 13.5 | 0.0 | 5.0 | 70.0 | 44.9 | 100 | 61.5 | 59.3 | 46.5 | 43.7 | 0.0 | - | 100 | 50.0 |
| Hon Hai/Foxconn (TW) | - | 26.5 | 70.0 | 69.0 | 30.0 | 55.1 | - | - | - | 32.6 | 28.5 | 100 | - | - | 50.0 |
| Flex (SG) | - | 46.0 | - | - | - | - | - | 25.4 | - | 9.2 | 7.5 | - | - | - | - |
| Pegatron (TW) | - | - | 25.7 | - | - | - | - | - | - | 4.6 | 3.7 | - | - | - | - |
| BYD (CN) | - | 14.0 | - | - | - | - | - | - | - | 2.5 | 2.0 | - | - | - | - |
| Wistron (TW) | - | - | 4.3 | 6.1 | - | - | - | - | - | 1.4 | 1.1 | - | - | - | - |
| Top 5 share (%) | - | 86.5 | 100 | 75.1 | 30.0 | 55.1 | - | 25.4 | 0.0 | 50.4 | 42.8 | 100 | - | 0.0 | 50.0 |

[1] Lenovo acquired Motorola's handset business in 2014. Its data before 2014 belong to Motorola.

[2] Nokia's handset business was acquired by Microsoft in 2014.

[3] 2015 data refer to 1,205 million units with supplier information. Location refers to the headquarters of the EMS firm, not its actual manufacturing sites. TW = Taiwan; SG = Singapore; CN = China.

Sources: 2008–2018 data from IHS Markit/Informa Tech Custom Research for GPN@NUS Centre, July–October 2016 and 2019; and 2020–2021 (forecast) data from TrendForce (https://www.trendforce.com), released on January 5, 2021).

TABLE C5. World's top manufacturers of semiconductors for ICT devices by fab location, process technology, customers, and capacity, 2015–2022 (in thousands of 8-inch equivalent wafer starts per month)

| Semicon firm[1] | Location[2] | 2015 Fab name | Process (nm) | Semicon customer[1] | ICT device[3] | Capacity 8' equiv | 2018 Fab name | Process (nm) | Semicon customer[1] | ICT Device | Capacity 8' equiv | 2020– Most adv node 22 Fabs[4] | adv node (nm) | Capacity 8' equiv |
|---|---|---|---|---|---|---|---|---|---|---|---|---|---|---|
| **IDM** | | | | | | | | | | | | | | |
| SK Hynix | Wuxi, CN | HC2 | 27 | Hynix | M: all | 338 | HC2 | 17/25 | Hynix | M: all | 338 | - | - | - |
| | Icheon, SK | M10/14 | 27 | Hynix | M: all | 788 | M10/14 | 17/25 | Hynix | M: all | 788 | - | - | - |
| | Choengju, SK | - | - | - | - | - | M8 | 90/110 | Hynix | I: SP | 150 | - | - | - |
| Intel | Chandler, US | F12/32 | 14/22/32 | Intel | P/W: all-1 | 113 | F12/32 | 14/22 | Intel/TH | P/W: all | 124 | F42 | 7/5 | 90 |
| | Hillsboro, US | D1X | 14 | Intel | P: all-1 | 90 | D1D/X | 10–22 | Intel/TH | P/W: all | 121 | D1X | 10 | 90 |
| | Leixlip, IE | F24 | 14 | Intel | P: all-1 | 90 | F14/24 | 14/22 | Intel/TH | P/W: all | 188 | F24 | 14 | 188 |
| | Kiryat Gat, IL | F28 | 22 | Intel | P: all-1 | 90 | F28 | 14–45 | Intel | P/W: all | 113 | F28 | 10 | 113 |
| Micron | Manassas, US | F6D | 20/25 | Micron | M: all | 101 | F6D | 20 | Micron | M: all | 101 | - | - | - |
| | Hiroshima, JP | E300 | 20/25 | Micron | M: all | 225 | E300-1/2 | 15–20 | Micron | M: all | 270 | - | - | - |
| | Taichung, TW | R1 | 20/25 | Micron | M: all | 191 | R1 | 15/25 | Micron | M: all | 191 | - | - | - |
| Nanya | Taoyuan, TW | F3A | 20/25 | Nanya | M: TB | 135 | F3A/N | 20–42 | Nanya | M: TB | 248 | - | - | - |
| Samsung | Hwaseong, SK | L11-13/15-17 | 20/35 | Samsung | M: all | 1,990 | L11-13/15-17 | 14–45 | Samsung | M/I: all | 1,386 | S3 S4/V1 | 7 5 | 180 225 |
| | Giheung, SK | S1 | 14/20/28 | AP/QU | P: SP, TB | 146 | S1/1B; L6-8 | 10–45 | AP/QU/SM | P/W/I: all | 298 | - | - | - |

(continued)

TABLE C5. (*continued*)

| Semicon firm[1] | Location[2] | 2015 Fab name | Process (nm) | Semicon customer[1] | ICT device[3] | Capacity 8' equiv | 2018 Fab name | Process (nm) | Semicon customer[1] | ICT Device | Capacity 8' equiv | 2020– 22 Fabs[4] | Most adv node (nm) | Capacity 8' equiv |
|---|---|---|---|---|---|---|---|---|---|---|---|---|---|---|
| | Pyeongtaek, SK | - | - | - | - | - | L18N | 16/20 | Samsung | M: all | 180 | LX | 5/3 | - |
| | Austin, US | S2 | 14/28 | QU/SM | P: SP, TB | 124 | S2-I/II | 14/28 | AP/QU/SM | P/W: all | 270 | - | - | - |
| Winbond | Taichung, TW | F6 | 38 | Winbond | P: SP | 108 | - | - | - | - | - | - | - | - |
| **Foundry** | | | | | | | | | | | | | | |
| Dongbu | Eumseong, SK | - | - | - | - | - | F2 | 100 | Superpix | I: SP | 64 | - | - | - |
| Global- | Dresden, DE | M1/2 | 28/45 | AMD/BR/MT | P/W: all | 135 | M1/2/AX | 22/45 | Many | P/W: all | 248 | - | - | - |
| Foundries | Singapore | F7 | 45 | MT | W: SP | 158 | - | - | - | - | - | - | - | - |
| | Malta, US | F8 | 14 | AMD | P: DT/NB | 113 | F8 | 12/14 | Many | P/W: all | 135 | - | - | - |
| Huali | Shanghai, CN | F1 | 28 | MT | P: SP | 79 | F5 | 28 | MT | P/W: all | 79 | - | - | - |
| Huahong | Wuxi, CN | - | - | - | - | - | F7 | 55–90 | Cypress | W: all | 90 | - | - | - |
| SMIC | Beijing, CN | B1 | 40 | Leadcore | P: SP | 56 | B2 | 28 | QU | P: SP | 158 | - | - | - |
| | Shanghai, CN | F8 | 28 | Lead-core/QU | P: SP | 45 | F9 | 14/28 | QU | W: all | 158 | - | - | - |
| | Shenzhen, CN | - | - | - | - | - | - | - | - | - | - | JV | 28 | 40 |
| | Avezzano, IT | LF1 | 90 | ON Semicon | I: SP | 40 | - | - | - | - | - | - | - | - |

| | | 2016 | | | | | 2019 | | | | | 2021 (most advanced fabs) | | |
|---|---|---|---|---|---|---|---|---|---|---|---|---|---|---|
| | | Fab | nm | Customers | Components | Cap. | Fab | nm | Customers | Components | Cap. | Fab | nm | Cap. |
| Sony | Kyusyu/Oita/Naga/Yama, JP | F1/2/7/O | 65 | Sony/TB | I: SP | 137 | F1/2/7/O | 65 | Sony/TB | I: SP | 65 | – | – | – |
| TSMC | Hsinchu, TW | F12 | 16-90 | Many | P: SP/TB | 405 | F12 P1-7 | 7-90 | Many | All: all | 429 | F12 | 7 | 405 |
| | Taichung, TW | F15 | 28 | Many | P: SP/TB | 270 | F15 P1-7 | 7/28 | Many | P/W: all | 648 | F15 | 7 | 270 |
| | Tainan, TW | F14 | 20 | Many | P: SP/TB | 450 | F14 P1-7 | 12-90 | Many | P/W: all | 590 | F18 P1-6 | 5/3 | 450 |
| | Nanjing, CN | – | – | – | – | – | F16 P1-2 | 16 | Many | P/W: all | 41 | F16 P1-2 | 16 | 90 |
| UMC | Tainan, TW | F12A | 28 | Many | P: SP/TB | 113 | F12/12A | 14-28 | Many | W: all | 225 | – | – | – |
| | Singapore | F12i | 45 | Many | P/W: SP/TB | 113 | – | – | – | – | – | – | – | – |
| | Xiamen, CN | – | – | – | – | – | F12X | 28/40 | Many | W: all | 113 | – | – | – |
| **Total** | China only | 4 | – | – | – | 518 | 7 | – | – | – | 981 | – | – | – |
| | East Asia | 26 | – | – | – | 5,747 | 35 | – | – | – | 6,509 | – | – | – |
| | **Worldwide** | 37 | – | – | – | 6,643 | 49 | – | – | – | 7,809 | – | – | – |

[1] AP = Apple; BR = Broadcom; GF = GlobalFoundries; MT = MediaTek; QU=Qualcomm; SM = Samsung; TB = Toshiba; and TH = Tsinghua (Unisoc)

[2] CN = China; DE = Germany; IE = Ireland; IL = Israel; IT = Italy; JP = Japan; SK = South Korea; TW = Taiwan; and US = United States

[3] Components: M = memory; P = processor; I = imaging sensor; W = WLAN; all = M, P, I; Devices: DT = desktop PCs; NB = notebook PCs; SP = smartphones; TB = tablets; all = DT, NB, SP, and TB; and all-1 = DT, NB, and TB

[4] Only most advanced fabs shown, based on existing data and public announcements as of end June 2021.

Source: Data from IHS Markit/Informa Tech Custom Research for GPN@NUS Centre, July–October 2016 and 2019.

TABLE C6. World's top 6 notebook PC OEM firms by shipments and location of final assembly, 2015 and 2018 (in millions of units)

| ODM | Location | HP | | Lenovo | | Dell | | Asus | | Acer | | Apple | | Others | | Total | |
|---|---|---|---|---|---|---|---|---|---|---|---|---|---|---|---|---|---|
| | | 2015 | 2018 | 2015 | 2018 | 2015 | 2018 | 2015 | 2018 | 2015 | 2018 | 2015 | 2018 | 2015 | 2018 | 2015 | 2018 |
| Compal | Taiwan | - | 0.3 | - | - | - | - | - | - | - | - | - | - | - | - | - | 0.3 |
| | Chengdu, China | - | 3.6 | 9.6 | - | - | 5.9 | 4.0 | - | - | - | - | - | - | - | 13.6 | 9.5 |
| | Chongqing, China | 2.5 | - | - | - | 12.9 | - | - | - | - | 0.7 | - | - | 1.2 | 0.5 | 16.6 | 1.2 |
| | Kunshan/Suzhou, China | - | 8.1 | - | 5.6 | - | 13.7 | - | - | 4.7 | 2.9 | - | - | - | - | 4.7 | 30.3 |
| Quanta | Chongqing, China | 8.5 | 14.7 | - | 1.0 | - | 0.3 | 2.8 | 5.6 | 4.1 | 5.8 | - | - | 1.8 | 1.3 | 17.2 | 28.7 |
| | Kunshan, China | 4.0 | - | 7.0 | - | 3.8 | - | - | - | - | - | - | - | - | - | 14.8 | - |
| | Shanghai, China | - | - | - | 0.6 | - | - | - | - | - | - | 14.5 | 7.7 | - | - | 14.5 | 8.4 |
| Wistron | Chongqing, China | 3.0 | 3.7 | - | 3.6 | 4.2 | 6.9 | 1.9 | - | 3.6 | 1.3 | - | - | 1.2 | 0.4 | 13.9 | 15.8 |
| | Kunshan, China | - | - | 5.5 | - | - | - | - | - | - | - | - | - | - | - | 5.5 | - |
| Inventec | Taiwan | - | 0.5 | - | - | - | - | - | - | - | - | - | - | - | - | - | 0.5 |
| | Chongqing, China | 7.5 | 9.3 | - | - | - | - | - | - | - | - | - | - | 4.8 | 0.8 | 12.3 | 10.1 |
| Pegatron | Chongqing, China | 1.8 | - | - | - | - | - | 6.8 | 7.1 | 1.2 | 1.1 | - | - | 1.6 | 0.4 | 11.4 | 8.5 |
| | Kunshan/Suzhou, China | - | - | 1.5 | - | - | - | - | - | - | - | - | - | - | 0.1 | 1.5 | 0.1 |
| | Juarez, Mexico | 2.8 | - | - | - | - | - | - | - | - | - | - | - | - | - | 2.8 | - |
| Hon Hai/ Foxconn | Chengdu, China | - | - | - | - | - | - | - | - | - | - | - | 2.7 | - | 0.2 | - | 2.9 |
| | Chongqing/Wuhan, China | 1.6 | - | - | - | 1.0 | - | - | - | - | - | - | - | - | - | 2.6 | - |
| | Shenzhen/Longhua, China | - | - | - | - | - | - | - | - | - | - | 3.4 | - | - | 0.1 | 3.4 | 0.1 |

| | | | | | | | | | | | | | | | | |
|---|---|---|---|---|---|---|---|---|---|---|---|---|---|---|---|---|
| | Juarez, Mexico/Sau Paulo, Brazil | – | – | – | – | – | – | – | – | – | – | – | – | – | – | 1.9 | 1.9 |
| | Turkey/Czech Rep | – | – | – | – | – | – | – | – | – | – | – | – | – | – | 1.4 | 1.4 |
| Other | Taiwan | – | – | – | – | – | – | – | – | – | – | – | – | – | 5.9 | – | 5.9 |
| ODMs | Guangzhou/Shenzhen, China | – | – | – | 4.9 | – | – | – | – | – | 0.9 | – | 0.2 | – | 2.8 | – | 8.8 |
| | Other locations | – | – | – | – | – | – | – | – | – | – | – | – | 20.9 | 5.3 | 20.9 | 5.3 |
| In-House | Beijing, China | 5.7 | 5.7 | – | – | – | – | – | – | – | – | – | – | – | – | 5.7 | 5.7 |
| | Chengdu, China | – | – | 5.7 | 5.7 | – | – | – | – | – | – | – | – | – | – | 5.7 | 5.7 |
| | Hefei, China | – | – | – | – | – | 17.6 | – | – | – | – | – | – | – | – | – | 17.7 |
| | Shanghai, China | – | – | – | – | 2.0 | – | – | – | – | – | – | – | – | – | 2.0 | – |
| | Shenzhen/Longhua, China | – | – | – | – | – | – | – | 3.1 | – | 1.1 | – | – | – | – | – | 4.2 |
| | Suzhou/Kunshan, China | – | – | – | – | – | – | 2.6 | 2.7 | – | – | – | – | – | – | 2.6 | 2.7 |
| | Other locations | – | – | – | – | – | – | – | – | 3.1 | 2.4 | – | – | – | – | 3.1 | 2.4 |
| **Total** | Chengdu/Chongqing | 24.9 | 31.3 | 15.3 | 4.6 | 18.1 | 13.0 | 15.4 | 12.7 | 9.0 | 8.9 | – | 2.7 | 10.6 | 3.6 | 93.3 | 76.7 |
| | Kunshan/Shanghai/Suzhou | 4.0 | 8.1 | 16.0 | 6.2 | 3.8 | 13.7 | – | – | 4.7 | 2.9 | 14.5 | 7.7 | 2.6 | 2.8 | 45.5 | 41.5 |
| | **Worldwide** | 35.0 | 40.3 | 37.0 | 36.5 | 21.9 | 26.7 | 15.4 | 13.6 | 13.7 | 12.0 | 17.9 | 10.4 | 37.2 | 23.9 | 178.1 | 163.4 |

Source: Data from IHS Markit/Informa Tech Custom Research for GPN@NUS Centre, July–October 2016 and 2019.

TABLE C7. World's top 7 smartphone OEM firms by shipments and location of final assembly, 2015 and 2018 (in millions of units)

| EMS | Location | Samsung 2015 | Samsung 2018 | Huawei 2015 | Huawei 2018 | Apple 2015 | Apple 2018 | Xiaomi 2015 | Xiaomi 2018 | Oppo 2015 | Oppo 2018 | Vivo 2015 | Vivo 2018 | LG 2015 | LG 2018 | Others 2015 | Others 2018 | Total 2015 | Total 2018 |
|---|---|---|---|---|---|---|---|---|---|---|---|---|---|---|---|---|---|---|---|
| Hon Hai / Foxconn | Guanlan, China | – | – | 20.1 | 51.5 | 32.7 | 30.1 | – | – | 22.8 | 34.6 | 24.9 | 57.2 | – | – | 27.5 | 22.6 | 128 | 196 |
| | Lan Fang, China | | | – | – | – | – | 47.3 | 32.1 | | | | | | | – | – | 47.3 | 32.1 |
| | Tai Yuan, China | | | – | – | 25.7 | 25.6 | | | | | | | | | 13.5 | – | 39.2 | 25.6 |
| | Zhengzhou, China | | | – | – | 87.1 | 76.1 | | | | | | | | | | | 87.1 | 76.1 |
| | Sau Paulo, Brazil | | | 0.3 | 3.1 | 17.0 | 11.5 | 0.5 | 2.4 | | | | | | | | | 17.8 | 16.9 |
| | India (4 sites) | | | – | – | 3.1 | – | 12.5 | 47.5 | | | | | | | – | 3.9 | 15.6 | 51.4 |
| Flex | Chennai, India | | | 36.5 | 94.8 | – | – | | | | | | | | | – | 0.3 | 36.5 | 95.1 |
| Pegatron | Kunshan, China | | | – | – | 9.6 | 9.2 | | | | | | | | | | | 9.6 | 9.2 |
| | Shanghai, China | | | – | – | 46.1 | 38.9 | | | | | | | | | | | 46.1 | 38.9 |
| | Suzhou, China | | | – | – | 4.5 | 4.5 | | | | | | | | | | | 4.5 | 4.5 |
| Inventec | Nanjing, China | | | – | – | – | – | 2.4 | 15.4 | | | | | | | | | 2.4 | 15.4 |
| | Shanghai, China | | | – | – | – | – | 6.5 | 8.3 | | | | | | | | | 6.5 | 8.3 |
| Wistron | Kunshan, China | | | – | – | 5.7 | 8.2 | | | | | | | | | 1.7 | – | 7.4 | 8.2 |
| | India (2 sites) | | | – | – | – | 0.6 | – | 7.2 | | | | | | | | | 0 | 7.8 |
| BYD | Huizhou, China | | | 18.7 | 20.6 | – | – | | | | | | | | | | | 18.7 | 20.6 |
| | Longgang, China | | | 0.3 | 8.2 | – | – | | | | | | | | | | | 0.3 | 8.2 |
| Others | Other locations | | | 5.6 | – | | | | | | | | | 3.1 | – | 231 | 179 | 240 | 179 |

| In-House | | | | | | | | | | | | | | | |
|---|---|---|---|---|---|---|---|---|---|---|---|---|---|---|---|
| Beijing, China | – | – | – | – | – | 4.0 | – | – | – | – | – | 1.1 | 3.5 | 5.1 | 9.4 |
| Dongguan, China | – | – | 22.2 | 24.5 | – | 23.0 | 34.6 | 15.9 | 26.0 | – | – | 30.6 | 5.6 | 91.7 | 90.7 |
| Huizhou, China | 95.9 | 27.5 | – | – | – | – | – | – | – | – | – | 61.1 | 14.5 | 157 | 42.0 |
| Shandong, China | – | – | – | – | – | – | – | – | – | 36.5 | 23.4 | – | – | 36.5 | 23.4 |
| Shenzhen, China | – | – | 2.5 | 3.3 | – | – | – | – | – | – | – | 34.7 | 20.2 | 37.2 | 23.5 |
| Tianjin, China | 59.6 | 3.8 | – | – | – | – | – | – | – | – | – | – | – | 59.6 | 3.8 |
| Brazil | 21.5 | 10.7 | – | – | – | – | – | – | – | 2.0 | 5.8 | 13.2 | 1.7 | 40.5 | 14.4 |
| India | 41.6 | 60.3 | 2.8 | – | – | – | 40.3 | 4.4 | 20.8 | 1.1 | 0.6 | 0.9 | 17.5 | 50.3 | 140 |
| Indonesia | – | 6.4 | – | – | – | – | 5.8 | – | – | – | – | – | – | 0 | 12.1 |
| South Korea | 40.8 | 33.3 | – | – | – | – | – | – | – | 4.4 | 5.4 | – | – | 46.2 | 37.8 |
| Vietnam | 50.9 | 148 | – | – | – | – | – | – | – | 13.3 | 8.3 | – | – | 59.2 | 161 |
| Other locations | 10.2 | – | – | – | – | – | – | – | – | – | – | 76.7 | 58.2 | 86.9 | 58.2 |
| **Total** | | | | | | | | | | | | | | | |
| China only | 155 | 0 | 108 | 212 | 193 | 55.6 | 45.7 | 69.2 | 83.2 | 36.5 | 20.8 | 335 | 121 | 856 | 688 |
| Outsourced | 0 | 0 | 178 | 232 | 205 | 113 | 22.8 | 24.9 | 57.2 | 3.1 | 0 | 269 | 179 | 587 | 793 |
| **Worldwide** | **320** | **290** | **206** | **232** | **205** | **119** | **45.7** | **45.2** | **104** | **59.8** | **44.2** | **492** | **327** | **1377** | **1410** |

Source: Data from IHS Markit/Informa Tech Custom Research for GPN@NUS Centre, July–October 2016 and 2019.

# Notes

## Chapter 1

1. This motif of "world"/"worlds" draws upon Storper and Salais's (1997) *Worlds of Production* that examines the unique social relations, conventions, and institutions constitutive of such distinct "worlds" of innovation and technologically dynamic production systems in France, Italy, and the United States. See also Storper (1997) and my recent reconceptualization in Yeung (2021a).

2. Much has been written about the origin and success of Silicon Valley (e.g., Scott 1988; Saxenian 1994; Kenney 2000; Bresnahan and Gambardella 2004; O'Mara 2005, 2019; Storper et al. 2015) and the importance of the military-industrial complex in US high-tech industries (e.g., Borrus 1988; Markusen et al. 1991; Scott 1993; Angel 1994; Mazzucato 2013; Weiss 2014). In the early Cold War period, military contracts in favor of industrial dispersion were essential to the survival and future growth of small and new companies making high-tech electronic equipment and early computers (O'Mara 2005, 43). Over the decades, this spending in basic research and development (R&D) has led to tremendous innovation in general-purpose technologies that have been commercialized, particularly in the field of electronics products and digital services.

3. By the time US astronaut Neil Armstrong walked on the moon on July 21, 1969, California's Santa Clara Valley had already hosted almost 90 percent of all independent semiconductor firms in the US. In the late 1970s and the early 1980s, Santa Clara County had the highest defense spending per capita in the US, and one-fifth of its economic output still came from aerospace and defense (O'Mara

2019, 52; 249). See also Weiss (2014) for a critical analysis of the national security state in the US.

4. Florida and Kenney (1990b) offer a full discussion of this "breakthrough illusion" in Silicon Valley and the challenges of Japan in certain critical segments of the electronics industry during the 1980s, such as semiconductors (Borrus 1988) and computers (Anchordoguy 1989; Fransman 1995). See also useful firm- and national-scale analyses in Fransman (1990); Angel (1994); Curtis (1994); Dedrick and Kraemer (1998); and Campbell-Kelly and Garcia-Swartz (2015).

5. See Saxenian (1991; 1994).

6. Several earlier studies before 1990 have analyzed this internationalization of electronics production from Silicon Valley to Europe and Asia (e.g., Henderson and Scott 1987; Langlois et al. 1988; Scott and Angel 1988; Henderson 1989). In fact, some US semiconductor firms first expanded to East Asia by establishing chip assembly operations as early as in the 1960s. Borrus (1988, 88–89) estimated that in 1978, the top 9 US semiconductor manufacturers had 35 assembly facilities in ten economies throughout East Asia and Latin America. For work on international production between 1990 and up to the mid-2000s, see Dedrick and Kraemer (1998); Borrus, Ernst, and Haggard (2000); McKendrick, Doner, and Haggard (2000); Kenney and Florida (2003); Cassia (2010); and Brown and Linden (2011).

7. In the information and communications technology (ICT) equipment segment comprising personal computers, mobile handsets, and other digital devices, India (and South Asia) plays a relatively minor role as compared to East Asia, the focus of this book. In 2006, China's ICT hardware industry was already $579 billion in total revenue, as compared to India's $9.9 billion (Gregory, Nollen, and Tenev 2009, Table 9.3; 143). For a parallel phenomenon of the global shift in the production of ICT software services, see Saxenian (2006, ch. 7) and Gregory, Nollen, and Tenev (2009). The rapid development of India's software services industry and firms (e.g., TCS, Infosys, and Wipro) since the mid-1980s has been driven by tremendous R&D investment and outsourcing demand from US ICT firms (e.g., IBM, Hewlett-Packard, Texas Instruments, and Motorola) and non-ICT firms in all sectors.

8. Unless otherwise specified, quantitative data on global electronics in this book are based on the custom and proprietary datasets from IHS Markit/Informa Tech Custom Research that were commissioned by the Global Production Networks Centre of the National University of Singapore (GPN@NUS Centre) in July–October 2016 and July–October 2019. See Appendix A for a fuller description of these rich datasets that provide complete data up to 2019 Q2. These quantitative data are complemented by 64 personal interviews with senior executives of 44 leading electronics firms in various locations in East Asia—Singapore, Taiwan, South Korea, and China—and other secondary sources (see a full description of research methodology between 2016 and 2021 in Appendix B).

9. The Department of Commerce estimated that information technology industry shipments in the US alone would exceed $500 billion in 1998 (Dedrick and Kraemer 1998, 6). See Angel (1994); Dedrick and Kraemer (1998); and Chandler (2001) for earlier discussions of US firms in semiconductors and PCs during the 1990s. See Fransman (1995) for a similar analysis of Japanese firms in these two segments during the early 1990s.

10. IBM data from https://www.ibm.com/ibm/history/history/year_1990 .html.

11. Motorola data from https://www.motorolasolutions.com/en_us/about/ company-overview/history/annual-report-archive.html. From its historical high in 1990, Motorola's total revenue almost tripled to $27 billion in 1995, driven by a fourfold increase in revenue of general systems products (mainly cellular phones) from $2.6 billion in 1990 to $10.7 billion in 1995. First established in 1986, the general systems group designed and produced cellular phones and microcomputer boards and systems, and achieved $584 million in revenue.

12. Hobday (1995, 67) and Cyhn (2002, 263). As noted in Choi (1996, 206; Table 10.2), even Samsung semiconductor, its most technologically advanced division, was still very dependent on US and Japanese firms for core equipment (over 90 percent) and raw materials (75 percent) in 1991. It was then still very small in comparison to major semiconductor firms, such as NEC from Japan (four times bigger) and Motorola from the US (more than double in size). Meanwhile, Lucky-Goldstar Electronics was renamed to LG Electronics in 1995. The Daewoo group went bankrupt during the 1997 Asian economic crisis and was dissolved in 2000. Since then, Daewoo Electronics was acquired by different groups of creditors and investors.

13. Over three decades ago in their major study of the global electronics industry and its uneven development in the United Kingdom, Morgan and Sayer (1988, 41–42) already argued for the importance of examining separately these four major segments: "We have chosen to split the [electronics] industry up into four main sectors—semiconductors, consumer electronics, computer systems and telecommunications. While they do not totally exhaust the electronics industry, they dominate it and, although there are many interactions between these sectors, each also has a certain unity and distinctiveness which imparts different forms to their uneven development."

14. At the time of writing and final revisions up to July 2021, 2018 was the latest full year for which data are available in full detail at the individual lead firm level. The custom and proprietary datasets from IHS Markit/Informa Tech Custom Research contain such comprehensive data up to the second quarter of 2019. The year 2019 also experienced a relative decline in global electronics sales in almost all market segments due to geopolitical uncertainties and US-China trade wars since

March 2018. Compared to its historical peak at $485 billion in 2018 (Table 1.1), global semiconductor revenue declined significantly to only $422 billion in 2019, but rebounded to $466 billion in 2020. The IHS Markit and World Semiconductor Trade Statistics forecasted the segment's total revenue to grow over 12 percent to a new historical peak at $525 billion in 2021 (https://ihsmarkit.com, released on November 5, 2020; https://www.wsts.org, released on June 8, 2021). This massive growth is primarily due to the massive demand for chips in remote work/learning-related ICT products (e.g., notebook PCs and tablets), servers and data centers, automotive, and the adoption of new technologies (e.g., 5G communications and artificial intelligence) during and after the COVID-19 pandemic in 2020/2021. Excluding Chromebooks and tablets, global PC shipment also increased from 253 million units in 2018 to 275 million units in 2020 (Table 1.1). In IDC's projection (including Chromebooks and workstations), worldwide PC shipment would increase by 18 percent from 303 million units in 2020 to 357 million units in 2021 (https://www.idc.com, released on March 10, 2021). Meanwhile, global smartphone shipment declined from 1.41 billion units in 2018 to 1.37 billion units in 2019 and 1.25 billion in 2020 (Table 1.1). According to Canalys's forecast (https://www.canalys.com, released on June 14, 2021), total smartphone shipment in 2021 and 2022 would likely exceed the historical peak of 1.41 billion units set in 2018. In TVs, global shipments between 2019 and 2021 remained stable at 220–225 million units (https://www.trendforce.com, released on May 24, 2021).

15. In fact, Sharp and Toshiba, two of Chandler's (2001, 233) "Big Nine" Japanese firms in semiconductors, computers, and consumer electronics, had to be sold in the 2010s. Taiwan's Hon Hai Precision (parent company of Foxconn in China) acquired two-thirds of Sharp for $3.8 billion in May 2016, whereas Toshiba's PC business was sold to Sharp for $35 million in October 2018, and its highly profitable memory chip division was acquired by a consortium led by US private equity firm Bain Capital for $18 billion in June 2018 and renamed to Kioxia in October 2019 (https://www.kioxia-holdings.com). Earlier in the 2000s, the semiconductor divisions of three "Big Nine"—NEC, Hitachi, and Mitsubishi—were merged in 2002 and 2010 to form Renesas Electronics. Their memory chip business was merged to form Elpida Memory in 1999 and 2003 and acquired by Micron Technologies from the US in 2013.

16. New empirical material based on proprietary datasets on all these interfirm relationships in global production networks during the mid- to late 2010s will be examined in full detail in the empirical Chapters (4–6).

17. Using custom data from IHS Markit, Chapter 5 will provide a detailed analysis of the top five components in PCs and mobile handsets among these OEM lead firms in 2015 and 2018.

18. I have codeveloped a theory of global production networks in Coe and Yeung (2015). In Chapter 3, I will elaborate on this theory and expand on a concep-

tual framework for the empirical analysis of these interconnected worlds of global electronics in Chapters 4 to 6.

19. See Coe and Yeung (2015); Dicken (2015); Gereffi (2018); WTO (2019); McKinsey Global Institute (2020); and World Bank (2020) for more detailed analyses of these global production networks and global value chains. Kano, Tsang, and Yeung (2020) offer a comprehensive literature review.

20. See Evans, Hagiu, and Schmalensee's (2006) earlier business analysis of the role of different software platforms in product design and integration with upstream and downstream suppliers in PCs, mobile handsets, and other digital devices.

21. Unfortunately, I do not have any data on this link and the role of software in intra- and interfirm relationships. My custom data from IHS Markit/Informa Tech offer very detailed insights into only component-level supply chains and final assembly by manufacturing partners. This dataset on semiconductors, PCs, mobile handsets, and TVs does not contain any information on software vendors. Likewise, my interviews with senior executives of forty-four lead firms in these four segments also do not yield much information on the role of software. During these interviews, even top executives (from vice presidents to executive vice presidents and chief technology officers) in charge of supply chains and worldwide production in these leading OEM firms did not consider software services when we discussed their firm-specific production networks and supply chains. In all fairness, there is not much published material on the role of software in global production networks and global value chains. For example, Dedrick, Kraemer, and Linden's (2010) well-known work on value capture in iPods and notebook PCs only discusses Microsoft as the software vendor for PCs. But it does not go into detail *how* Microsoft interacts with these PC vendors to shape their actual production networks. Even in Gawer and Cusumano's (2002, ch. 5) classic study of platform leaders such as Microsoft, the empirical focus was on the strategy of its software development, not the global production networks of its Windows operating system and application-specific software (MS Office and so on). These empirical and data constraints in turn explain why software has received only minor discussion in key books on semiconductors (Mathews and Cho 2000; Brown and Linden 2011), PCs (Dedrick and Kraemer 1998; Campbell-Kelly and Garcia-Swartz 2015), and smartphones (Woyke 2014; Giachetti 2018).

22. See studies of the software industry in Mowery (1996); Campbell-Kelly (2003); Cusumano (2004); Evans, Hagiu, and Schmalensee (2006); and Ensmenger (2010), software-led industrial development in O'Riain (2004) and Breznitz (2007), and software in everyday life in Kitchin and Dodge (2011). This greater significance of software and digital ecosystems is also related to the broader rise of the so-called platform economy (see Kenney and Zysman 2016, 2020; de Reuver, Sørensen, and Basole 2018; Jacobides, Cemmano, and Gawer 2018; Van

Dijck, Poell, and de Waal 2018; Lan, Liu, and Dong 2019; Guillén 2021). Parker, Van Alstyne, and Choudary (2016) and McAfee and Brynjolfsson (2017) offer two accessible discussions of how this digital economy is reconstituted through artificial intelligence (machines), platforms, and the crowd (people).

23. For early studies of these electronics segments in the US and Western Europe, see Dosi (1984); Langlois et al. (1988); Morgan and Sayer (1988); Cawson et al. (1990); and Gandy (2013). Campbell-Kelly and Garcia-Swartz's (2015) work also examines the early history of US computer firms competing in an international industry.

24. See Scott (1988, chs. 6–7) for an analysis of such agglomerations of semiconductor and computer firms in Silicon Valley and Scientific City (south of Paris) and Morgan and Sayer (1988, ch. 11) for a similar analysis of ICL and many others along the M4 corridor in the UK. Scott (1993, chs. 5–7) offers a similar analysis of the aerospace and missile and space industries in Southern California (also Leslie 2000). O'Mara (2019) provides a compelling history of the complex interrelationships among innovations in Silicon Valley, techno-national defense spending, and the military-industrial complex in the US. Chu (2013, ch. 2) describes in depth the complex and multidimensional military applications of semiconductors in the US defense and security establishments and contractors.

25. Cassia (2010, 9).

26. See Braun and MacDonald (1982, ch. 11) and Malerba (1985, chs. 4–5) for the rise and decline of the semiconductor industry in Western Europe prior to the 1980s.

27. Langlois et al. (1988, 51, 171; original italics). See also Henderson's (1989, ch. 4) analysis of the regional divisions of labor among these wholly owned subsidiaries of US semiconductor firms in East Asia during the late 1980s.

28. Details on this challenge from leading Japanese firms will be discussed in Chapter 2 on semiconductors. See Zysman and Tyson (1983); Mowery (1983); and Borrus (1988) for early discussions of US policy responses to Japanese challenge in semiconductors and color TVs and Fransman (1990) for an analysis of cooperation and industrial policy in supporting Japan's computer industry. Tyson (1993) provides a comprehensive analysis of US trade conflicts with Japan and Europe in semiconductors, mobile phones, and consumer electronics. Chandler (2001, ch. 3) offers an excellent history of Japan's paths to global conquest in consumer electronics during the 1970s and the 1980s. For an update on the 1990s, see Macher and Mowery (2008).

29. See Johnson (1991) and Tyson (1993) for details on the 1986 Agreement and SEMATECH and Berlin (2005, ch. 12, 294) on the central role of Intel's cofounder Robert Noyce in lobbying for such a federal government–backed consortium.

30. See Langlois et al. (1988, 137–44) for a full case study of ESPRIT and Borrus (1988, ch. 8) on the strategic alliance initiatives among Western European semiconductor firms during the 1980s.

31. Morgan and Sayer (1988, 46).

32. Paprzycki (2005, 127–31). Ernst (2000a, 81) also notes that between 1991 and 1992, the affiliates of Japanese electronics firms in East Asia increased their sourcing from Japan from less than 40 percent to 47 percent.

33. See also Harman (1971, 19–22); Kelly (1987, 54–64); and Morgan and Sayer (1988, 88–90) on IBM's activities in Western Europe.

34. For details on these computer "national champions" in all four Western European countries, see Chandler (2001, 178–89) and Campbell-Kelly and Garcia-Swartz (2015, 88–98).

35. Data from Paprzycki (2005, 58–59).

36. Data from Hobday (1995, Table 2.4; 18–19).

37. Hobday (1995, 99–101).

38. See also Kim (2000) on Samsung in the 1990s.

39. See Pirie (2008); Gray (2011); and Yeung (2017) for details on the geopolitics of market deregulation and liberalization in South Korea and Taiwan during the 1990s.

40. See Wade (2003) and Weiss (2005) for a discussion of how the WTO made it difficult for developing countries to practice state-led industrial policy for technological catching-up and how advanced industrialized countries made use of this multilateral order to increase the scope for sponsoring their technology-intensive sectors critical to securing national prosperity.

41. As noted in Brown and Linden (2011); Kenney (2011); and Nenni and McLellan (2019), this opportunity for East Asian foundry providers to emerge in semiconductors has much to do with the extremely high cost of new semiconductor fabs in Silicon Valley and elsewhere in the US. Prompted by the preference of venture capital for investing in high-value and potentially high-return chip design work, more fabless semiconductor firms began to emerge in Silicon Valley since the late 1980s and outsource their wafer fabrication to then newly established providers of foundry and assembly, packaging, and testing services in East Asia.

42. Interview with a senior executive of TSMC in Taipei, July 2004, reported in Yeung (2016, 43).

43. See Langlois et al. (1988, ch. 5) for a full account of this foreign direct investment-based mode of industrial organization in semiconductors prior to 1990.

44. See details on these ODM and EMS providers in my earlier work on leading domestic firms from Taiwan and Singapore (Yeung 2016, chs. 3–4). For a general description of these different modes of global outsourcing in the electronics industry, see Cassia (2010) and Pawlicki (2016).

45. See Kawakami (2009, 111–15) for a detailed description of this ODM workflow process in the notebook computers segment of Taiwan's electronics industry in the early 2000s. Chapters 4–5 will offer an in-depth empirical analysis of these interfirm production networks during the 2015–2018 period.

46. For earlier in-depth studies of these learning and accumulation experiences among East Asian firms in the electronics industry, see Hobday (1995); Choi (1996); Borrus, Ernst, and Haggard (2000); Mathews and Cho (2000); Cyhn (2002); Amsden and Chu (2003); Khan (2004); Chang (2008); Ning (2009); K. Lee (2013, 2019); and Yap and Rasiah (2017). Other more recent studies at the industry level have pointed to the successful role of technological innovations in these East Asian economies (e.g., De Prato, Nepelski, and Simon 2013; Khan 2013, 2022; Nepelski and De Prato 2018; Breznitz 2021).

47. These transnational communities of technologists and entrepreneurs have been critical to firm-specific learning, access to global knowledge and technologies, and skilled human capital development since the 1990s and beyond. See Saxenian (2006); Zhou (2008); Malerba and Nelson (2012); and Fuller and Rubinstein (2013) for more in-depth studies.

48. For in-depth studies of the changing domestic institutional contexts and the less dominant role of the developmental state in East Asian industrial transformation since the 1990s, see Amsden and Chu (2003); Ning (2009); Wong (2011); K. Lee (2013, 2019); Yeung (2016); Sun and Grimes (2017); Ibata-Arens (2019); Whittaker et al. (2020); Doner, Noble, and Ravenhill (2021); Pempel (2021); and Y. Tan (2021). This recent literature builds on and extends beyond the earlier classic work on the strong state role in East Asian development in Johnson (1982); Amsden (1989); Haggard (1990); Wade (1990); Evans (1995); Woo-Cumings (1999); and Chang (2003)—see also reviews in Khan (2004); Fosu (2013); and Haggard (2018). For recent debates on industrial policy and state institutions, see Chang and Grabel (2014); Chang and Andreoni (2020); and Hamilton-Hart and Yeung's (2021a) special issue.

49. Building on the earlier theoretical perspectives on global production networks and global value chains between 1994 and 2005, this GPN 2.0 theory is fully developed in Coe and Yeung (2015). Chapter 3 will revisit this theory in relation to the organization and governance of production networks in the global electronics industry. It provides the necessary theoretical framing for my detailed empirical analysis in Chapters 4 to 6.

50. The unexpected turn in the global risk environment due to the US-China trade war since March 2018 and the COVID-19 pandemic in 2020/2021 will likely lead to another round of significant shifts in the contemporary worlds of electronics production. But these major disruptive effects will take some time to materialize and are far too early to be incorporated in this study. My comprehensive

empirical data end in 2019 Q2. New data on the post-COVID-19 world economy remain sketchy and speculative at the time of writing and revisions up to July 2021.

51. See Baldwin and Clark (2000) for modularity in product design rules, Langlois and Robertson (1992); Langlois (2002); and Sturgeon (2002) for the concept of modularization in flexible production systems, and Gawer and Cusumano (2002, 2014) and Gawer (2009) for firm- or industry-specific platforms. See also Jacobides, Cennamo, and Gawer (2018) for a recent theory of how modularity enables platform ecosystems and Lee and Gereffi (2021) for its application to the case of smartphones.

52. On the importance of systems integration to firm-specific capability building, see Hobday, Davies, and Prencipe (2005); Yeung (2007); and further elaboration in Yeung (2016, ch. 4).

53. See Yeung (2016, chs. 4–5) for details on these two mechanisms of strategic coupling—strategic partnership and industrial market specialization.

54. See Coe and Yeung (2019) and Kano, Tsang, and Yeung (2020) for the most recent comprehensive reviews of the vast empirical literature on global production networks and global value chains. For book-length studies of global production networks and global value chains, see Gibbon and Ponte (2005); Lane and Probert (2009); Neilson and Pritchard (2009); Selwyn (2012); Lüthje et al. (2013); Ouma (2015); Baldwin (2016); Nathan, Tewari, and Sarker (2016); Pickles and Smith (2016); Yeung (2016); Sun and Grimes (2017); Gereffi (2018); Liu (2020); Coe (2021); and Xing (2021). Other edited volumes are found in Gereffi and Korzeniewicz (1994); Borrus, Ernst, and Haggard (2000); Bair (2009); Cattaneo, Gereffi, and Staritz (2010); Kawagami and Sturgeon (2011); Dunaway (2013); Elms and Low (2013); Ferrarini and Hummels (2014); Neilson, Pritchard, and Yeung (2015); Drahokoupil, Andrijasevic, and Sacchetto (2016); De Marchi, Di Maria, and Gereffi (2018); and Ponte, Gereffi, and Raj-Reichert (2019). Most of these existing books, however, focus on industries and sectors other than electronics, e.g., agro-food (Daviron and Ponte 2005; Gibbon and Ponte 2005; Neilson and Pritchard 2009; Gibbon, Ponte, and Lazaro 2011; Ouma 2015; Barrientos 2019; Ponte 2019), apparel (Gibbon and Ponte 2005; Lane and Probert 2009; Pickles and Smith 2016; Mezzadri 2017; Liu 2020), steel (Wilson 2013), and automotive (Barnes 2018; Wong 2018; Liu 2020). Some books also address issues primarily related to labor (Posthuma and Nathan 2011; Selwyn 2012; Dunaway 2013; Lüthje et al. 2013; Newsome et al. 2015; Nathan, Tewari, and Sarkar 2016; Pickles and Smith 2016; Mezzadri 2017; Barnes 2018; Barrientos 2019), trade (Feenstra and Hamilton 2006; Gibbon, Ponte, and Lazaro 2011; Milberg and Winkler 2013; Ferrarini and Hummels 2014; Xing 2021), and standards and technology (Gibbon and Ponte 2005; Baldwin 2016).

55. These theoretical frameworks in the social science literature refer to Dicken et al. (2001); Henderson et al. (2002); and Coe et al. (2004) in analyzing the territorial organization of global production networks and their regional development outcomes, and Gereffi (1994); Humphrey and Schmitz (2002); and Gereffi, Humphrey, and Sturgeon (2005) in analyzing the governance of global value chains (GVC) and industrial upgrading. For the empirical literature utilizing these frameworks, see critical reviews in Coe and Yeung (2019) and Kano, Tsang, and Yeung (2020).

56. Several recent papers by Neilson et al. (2018); Vicol et al. (2019); and Lund and Steen (2020) have "tested" the efficacy of the GPN 2.0 theory.

57. See Yeung (2021b) for a recent clarification of this analytical procedure in GPN 2.0.

58. Some examples since the 1990s are Angel (1994); Curtis (1994); Chandler (2001); Gandy (2013); Campbell-Kelly and Garcia-Swartz (2015); and O'Mara (2019) on the US, Malerba (1985); Morgan and Sayer (1988); Cawson et al. (1990); and Gandy (2013) on several Western European countries, Anchordoguy (1989); Fransman (1995); and Paprzycki (2005) on Japan, and Hobday (1995); Choi (1996); Hong (1997); Lu (2000); Mathews and Cho (2000); Cyhn (2002); Pecht (2006); Peters (2006); Gregory, Nollen, and Tenev (2009); Ning (2009); Gabriele and Khan (2010); Chu (2013); Fosu (2013); Fu (2015); Sun and Grimes (2017); Yap and Rasiah (2017); and Xing (2021) on specific East Asian economies, such as China, South Korea, Taiwan, Singapore, and Malaysia.

59. While some earlier books have addressed the internationalization of production networks (e.g., Henderson 1989; Dedrick and Kraemer 1998; Borrus, Ernst, and Haggard 2000; McKendrick, Doner, and Haggard 2000; Tsang 2002; Kenney and Florida 2003), their theoretical framing pre-dates the recent conceptualization of global production networks and global value chains since the early 2000s. Their analytical focus is also placed on US-led international divisions of labor in the specific segments of global electronics, such as semiconductors (Henderson 1989), PCs (Dedrick and Kraemer 1998; Tsang 2002), and hard disk drives (McKendrick, Doner, and Haggard 2000). Some recent works have incorporated GVC or GPN thinking, but their unit of analysis has been confined primarily to the industry level, e.g., ICTs (Kawagami and Sturgeon 2011; De Prato, Nepelski, and Simon 2013; Nepelski and De Prato 2018; K. Lee 2019).

60. To my best knowledge, three edited books—Borrus, Ernst, and Haggard (2000); Kawagami and Sturgeon (2011); and Drahokoupil, Andrijasevic, and Sacchetto (2016)—are devoted to the analysis of electronics value chains and production networks in Asia and Eastern Europe, focusing respectively on the 1990s and the 2000s. Two recent books by Sun and Grimes (2017) and Xing (2021) have used custom trade data to examine ICT global value chains in China.

61. Prominent single-segment examples since the 1980s are Braun and Mac-Donald (1982); Malerba (1985); Angel (1994); Hong (1997); Mazurek (1999); Mathews and Cho (2000); Peters (2006); Brown and Linden (2011); Chu (2013); Yap and Rasiah (2017); and Nenni and McLellan (2019) on semiconductors; De-drick and Kraemer (1998); Lu (2000); Gandy (2013); Campbell-Kelly and Garcia-Swartz (2015); and Burgelman, McKinney, and Meza (2017) on PCs; McKendrick, Doner, and Haggard (2000) on hard disk drives; and Giachetti (2013, 2018); Woyke (2014); McNish and Silcoff (2015); and Doz and Wilson (2018) on mobile handsets. Only Chandler's (2001) epic history of the twentieth-century electronics industry has addressed three segments: consumer electronics and computers, and relatively light on semiconductors (122–31). Even Campbell-Kelly and Garcia-Swartz's (2015, 173–80) recent book on the international computer industry devotes only eight pages to smartphones, despite its title *From Mainframes to Smartphones*.

## Chapter 2

1. The recent literature on consumer electronics since the 2000s is also very limited. For the earlier history of consumer electronics, see Morgan and Sayer (1988, ch. 4) and Chandler (2001, chs. 2–3). The epic story of consumer electronics was rather simple. A world market dominated by national firms in the United States and Western European countries was decimated by the Japanese conquest within two decades during the 1970s and the 1980s. In turn, Japan's dominance was reversed by South Korean and Chinese firms since the 2000s. In digital TVs, a core subsegment of consumer electronics today, much of the value added comes from semiconductors ranging from display signal processors (logic chips) to flat panel displays (optical semiconductors). Chapters 5–6 will examine the global production networks of TVs, as an illustration of consumer electronics.

2. Authoritative data on international trade in intermediate and final goods in selected manufacturing sectors are available in the World Bank's World Integrated Trade Solutions (WITS)-GVC Database (https://wits.worldbank.org) that covers only electronics hardware, automotive, and textile/apparel/footwear industries. As of end June 2021, the database had complete data for all regions from 1989 to 2019. Due to ongoing trade tensions and the COVID-19 pandemic, world trade in 2019 and 2020 suffered from significant decline relative to its 2018 historical peak of $19.5 trillion. Data from UNCTADstat show that in 2019, the figure declined by 2.5 percent to $19.0 trillion, a likely outcome of increasing geopolitical tensions and trade wars since March 2018. Coupled with the COVID-19 pandemic and its worldwide disruptions, world merchandise trade in 2020 experienced an even more profound decline of 9.7 percent from its 2018 historical high to $17.6 trillion. The World Trade Organization forecasted a likely 8 percent rise in 2021 (https://www.wto.org/english/news_e/pres21_e/pr876_e.htm, accessed on

June 17, 2021). For this reason, I have chosen 2018 as the end point of my historical analysis.

3. These data are from Orbis, an extremely comprehensive database that contains records of close to 400 million firms worldwide, including over 70,000
public listed firms, in many industrial sectors, such as electronics and automotive
(https://www.bvdinfo.com/en-gb/our-products/data/international/orbis, accessed on June 26, 2021).

4. See Appendix B for interview methodology and the full list of 64 interviews
with senior executives of 44 major electronics firms in various locations in East
Asia.

5. Before World War II, European firms, particularly those from Germany (e.g.,
Siemens, Telefunken, and Bosch), the Netherlands (Philips), and Britain (GEC),
were at the technological frontiers of electronics, and their international competitiveness persisted during the transistor era in the late 1940s and the 1950s. Starting
in the 1960s, these European firms began to decline during the modern era of
integrated circuits and lag behind leading US semiconductor firms (see Malerba
1985, chs. 4–5).

6. Braun and MacDonald (1982, ch. 4) offer a fascinating account of their
invention process in Bell Labs. Dosi (1984, 28–38) discusses the enormous significance of Bell Labs in the early days of semiconductor innovations from 1950 to the
late 1960s.

7. Braun and MacDonald (1982) describe semiconductor electronics as a "revolution in miniature."

8. See Berlin (2005, 75–96) and O'Mara (2019, 39–42) for detailed accounts
of why and how these "Traitorous Eight" from Shockley Laboratories founded
Fairchild Semiconductor with Sherman Fairchild's funding based on his inheri-
tance of a massive amount of then IBM stock. Moore and Davis (2004) offer a
personal reflection on Gordon Moore's move in this group of eight from Shockley.
Meanwhile, Texas Instruments was also a major force to be reckoned with, holding
some one-third of the world's semiconductor market in early 1964 (Anchordoguy
1989, 28).

9. Data on 1966 share from Dosi (1984, Table 3.14; 168); Malerba (1985, Table
5.26; 132); and Chandler (2001, 124, 126). See also Borrus (1988, 73–79) for an
analysis of domestic competition between these IDM firms and large computer
systems houses, such as IBM.

10. According to Berlin's (2005, 164) biography of Robert Noyce, the name
Intel was abbreviated from "Integrated Electronics." See Berlin (2005, chs. 7–8)
for an intriguing history of the starting up and taking off of Intel during Robert
Noyce's tenure as its cofounder, first president (1968–1975), and chairman (1975–
1979) until his untimely death in 1990, and Moore and Davis (2004) for further

reflections on Intel's highly successful development since 1968. Half a century later in 2020, Intel remained as *the* world's top semiconductor firm in microprocessors and achieved a record revenue of $72.8 billion (see Table 1.1).

11. See details of these major innovations in Dosi (1984, Table 2.1; 30–31); Langlois et al. (1988, 8–13); Henderson (1989, 6, 32); and https://www.nobelprize.org/prizes/lists/all-nobel-prizes-in-physics for two Nobel prizes in physics given to the inventors of the transistor in 1956 and the integrated circuit in 2000.

12. Among these IDM firms, Intel remains faithful to its vertical integration strategy implemented ever since its founding in 1968. This close integration of R&D and manufacturing was essential to its competitive advantage. See Moore and Davis (2004, 21) for further elaboration on this strategy.

13. Data from Malerba (1985, Tables 4.2 and 5.1; 59, 101).

14. Data from Henderson (1989, Table 3.3; 37).

15. Data from Braun and MacDonald (1982, Table 10.1; 121).

16. Unless otherwise specified, data on semiconductor revenue by year and by firm in this section come from IHS Markit/Informa Tech Custom Research for GPN@NUS, July–October, 2016 and 2019. The IHS Markit historical data on semiconductors start in 1976. To maintain consistency, it will be used where possible throughout the book.

17. See Malerba (1985); Borrus (1988); Langlois et al. (1988); Henderson (1989); Angel (1994); Mazurek (1999); Brown and Linden (2011); and Yap and Rasiah (2017) for excellent studies of the restructuring of the global semiconductor industry that set the historical contexts for these challenges from East Asia during the 1980s and the 1990s.

18. Quote from Grove (1990, 159). See Gawer and Cusumano (2002, ch. 2) for an analysis of Intel's rise to platform leadership in PCs during the 1990s.

19. Data from Borrus (1988, 3); Brown and Linden (2011, 20); and Kim (2011, 310).

20. See similar arguments and findings in Langlois et al. (1988, ch. 6) and Fransman (1990, ch. 3), but Borrus (1988, chs. 5–6) for a contrasting view.

21. See full details on Samsung's foray into semiconductors in Choi (1996, chs. 5–8); Kim (1997, 149–70); Kim (2000, 145–48); Mathews and Cho (2000, 115–29); Cyhn (2002, ch. 3); Chang (2008, 34–35); and Yeung (2016, 147–51). Developing the world's first 1GB DRAM prototype in November 1996 (see Figure 2.1), Samsung closed the technology gap with its major competitors from Japan and the US (much weaker in memory chips) throughout the 1990s. By the mid-1990s, Samsung was able to transfer its 16MB synchronous DRAMs (SDRAMs) technology to Japan's Oki. This represents the first known case of South Korea–Japan technology transfer in semiconductors. In 2001, Samsung became the first DRAM maker in the world to use 300-millimeter or 12-inch wafer technology

for mass production, further widening the technological gap with its competitors from the US and Japan (Keller and Pauly 2003, 157; Shin 2017, 412).

22. See also Kenney (2011) for a similar perspective by venture capital in Silicon Valley. Nenni and McLellan (2019) offer the most comprehensive analysis of this fabless model of semiconductor manufacturing.

23. Data from Hof (1994) and Macher, Mowery, and Di Minin (2007, Table 1). See Mazurek (1999, 101–11, Table 3.2) and Brown and Linden (2011, 46–54) for an early history of fabless firms and foundry production in Silicon Valley and Texas during the 1980s and the 1990s.

24. This tremendous success and dominance of US fabless firms indeed goes against Borrus's (1988, 22) earlier prediction in the context of Japanese challenge in semiconductors that "given the strong linkages between process, manufacturing, and product, it appears that the U.S. industry cannot, on the basis of strengths in software and design, successfully hold product leadership in any category if it fails to maintain a leading position in process and manufacturing technology."

25. Qualcomm's success owes much to its dominance in the proprietary CDMA baseband processor chips (e.g., its Snapdragon series, see Figure 2.1) for smartphones since the late 2000s, whereas Broadcom dominates in wireless modem or Wi-Fi chips in the same market segments of smartphones and PCs. Prior to that, Texas Instruments used to be the dominant digital baseband chip supplier accounting for more than half of the global market share in all feature phones (also known as "cell phones"), including most of those in Nokia- and Ericsson-branded phones (Glimstedt, Bratt, and Karlsson 2010, 444–45; Brown and Linden 2011, 159). Chapters 4–6 will analyze their critical roles in electronics global production networks during the 2015–2018 period.

26. See also Mathews and Cho (2000, 177); Saxenian (2004, 209–12); Breznitz (2007, 98–99); and Hsu (2011, 2017) for the early evolution and political support of TSMC and UMC up to 2000, and Yeung (2016, 138–45) for an analysis of these foundry providers up to 2010.

27. The patent granted by the United States Patent and Trademark Office to top semiconductor firms from Taiwan (TSMC and UMC), South Korea (Samsung and Hyundai/Hynix), and Singapore (Chartered Semiconductor—later Global-Foundries) grew rapidly between 1997 and 2001. By 2001, these semiconductor firms had obtained far greater number of patents than the state-funded research institutes in their home economies, such as Taiwan's ITRI and South Korea's Electronic Technology Research Institute and Korea Institute of Science and Technology (Mathews 2007, Table 16.3; 323). See De Prato, Nepelski, and Simon (2013) and Yap and Rasiah (2017) for updated data up to 2010.

28. During the same time period, the outsourcing of chip assembly, packaging, and testing (APT) of many IDM and fabless firms to East Asia-based service providers, such as Taiwan's ASE and SPIL and Singapore's STATS ChipPac, was much

accelerated. By 2007, some 46 percent of all semiconductor APT was outsourced to these East Asian specialized service providers due to greater complexity and diversity of packages required (Brown and Linden 2011, Table 2.3; 45). Chapters 4–6 will analyze these interfirm networks in semiconductor production in the late 2010s.

29. See Yeung (2016, ch. 5) for an expanded explanation up to 2010 and Yap and Rasiah (2017) and Nenni and McLellan (2019) for an industry perspective.

30. See Fuller, Akinwande, and Sodini (2005, 80–81). This Berkeley transistor simulation model (BSIM) was formally adopted in 1994 over competing models as the standard for conveying process technology information between a fabless firm's foundry and its chip design teams using EDA software (Brown and Linden 2011, 46; Epicoco 2013).

31. See Nenni and McLellan (2019, ch. 6) for more on EDA software firms and Linden and Somaya (2003) on the importance of design cores.

32. In the same year, Texas Instruments was the world's third largest IDM firm and yet surprised the industry by announcing that it would not develop new in-house process technology after the 0.045 micron or 45 nanometer (nm) generation. Instead, it would rely on Taiwan's TSMC and UMC for process development beginning with the 32 nm generation (Brown and Linden 2011, 50). In this fab-lite strategy, IDM firms try to run their older fabs in full capacity while shifting excess demand to foundry providers. But they are unlikely able to develop new cutting-edge process technology and capability to compete in the most demanding categories of integrated circuits. See more details on this fab outsourcing during the late 2010s in Chapters 4–6.

33. In the calculation of total sales in the global semiconductor industry (e.g., Tables 2.2 and 2.4), the outputs and revenues of semiconductor foundry providers (e.g., TSMC and GlobalFoundries) are typically attributed to their customers, such as fabless firms (e.g., Qualcomm and Broadcom) (see Table 2.3) or fab-lite IDM firms (e.g., NXP and Texas Instruments) (see Table 2.2), as "cost of revenue." This is to avoid double-counting. Brown and Linden (2011, 49) estimate that foundry price is normally about one-third of the final chip value.

34. Forecast data from IHS Markit (https://ihsmarkit.com, released on November 5, 2020) and World Semiconductor Trade Statistics (https://www.wsts. org, released on June 8, 2021).

35. Data from Malerba (1985, 20).

36. Data from Mazurek (1999, 22).

37. Launching their first computer (Univac I) in 1951, Remington Rand was later merged with Sperry in 1955 to form Sperry Rand. See Harman (1971, 9–18); Gandy (2013, chs. 8–9); and Campbell-Kelly and Garcia-Swartz (2015, chs. 1 and 5) for the history of these BUNCH firms' foray into the mainframe computer market between the 1950s and the 1970s. See also Cortada (1993) for an early history of

these computer firms in producing data-processing machines before the mainframe computer era in the US and Bashe et al. (1986, chs. 1–2, 5) for a detailed history of IBM's inventions and technologies in punched cards and calculating machines during the 1930s and the 1940s and first-generation computers in the early 1950s (Type 701/702).

38. Data from Ensmenger (2010, 140).

39. Data from Stoneman (1976, 46); Anchordoguy (1989, 107); and Dedrick and Kraemer (1998, 31). Lamenting IBM's market dominance by the early 1970s, Stoneman (1976, 93) noted that "the major mainframe manufacturers cannot all go their own way, for the position of IBM in the market is so strong that if IBM announces a new product the other companies have to divert resources to match it. This would again limit any direct relationship between [their] R&D expenditure and innovation."

40. Data from Grove (1990, Figure 8; 155).

41. In 1985, for example, IBM produced $3 billion worth of integrated circuits in-house through its IBM Microelectronics division (representing 67 percent of all captive production and 20 percent of all chip production in the US) and bought another $630 million from IDM firms (e.g., Intel) in the open market. In Appendix C Table C1, IBM's in-house chip production value would rank it top in the 1984 list—higher than Texas Instruments' $2.4 billion. Moreover, IBM Microelectronics then was the only US "captive" firm (i.e., chip production for in-house use) that operated manufacturing facilities outside the US. It had chip production facilities in Sindelfingen, West Germany, and Corbeil-Essones, France, and pilot production in Japan (Harman 1971, 20–21; Langlois et al. 1988, 39–40, 168, Table 13). In 2015, IBM Microelectronics' remaining three fabs in the US were acquired by GlobalFoundries and incorporated into its foundry business, ending IBM's longstanding role in chip manufacturing.

42. In 1986, Burroughs merged with Univac of Sperry Rand to form Unisys in then the largest merger in the computer industry. With $10.5 billion combined revenue, Unisys became the second largest computer firm after IBM (Anchordoguy (1989, 107).

43. See also Chandler (2001, ch. 6) and Tsang (2002, ch. 2) for this story about the failure of Western European countries to commercialize IBM-compatible mainframes and then PC clones and Japan's relative success in doing so during the 1980s. At the turn of the 1990s, Japan's Fujitsu and NEC respectively acquired 80 percent of ICL in July 1990 (100 percent by 1998) and 4.7 percent of Groupe Bull in July 1991. Siemens only became a significant player after acquiring an independent firm Nixdorf Computer for $350 million to become Siemens-Nixdorf in 1990, but it was eventually sold to Fujitsu in October 1999.

44. See Anchordoguy (1989, chs. 1 and 5); Fransman (1990, 15–27; 1995, chs. 4 and 6); and Chandler (2001, 189–212) for more on how these three Japanese OEM

firms entered into "controlled competition" in mainframes through a cooperative relationship with NTT, a large domestic customer and user of equipment. Despite its rapid catching up in mainframes second only to IBM during the 1985–1995 period, Fujitsu's entrance into PCs was slow and unprofitable. The most paradoxical aspect of Japanese firms in computers was that by 1990, some 80 percent of the worldwide computer revenues of the Big Four—Fujitsu, NEC, Hitachi, and Toshiba—still came from the domestic market (Fransman 1995, 128). The highly proprietary computing environment in Japan (i.e., domestic demand structure) meant that these Japanese producers of customized software and PCs could not compete effectively in the global PC market dominated by IBM-compatible PCs.

45. Before 1981, what were known as "microcomputers" were mostly assembled and used by hobbyists and specialized users. The world's first "personal computer," as it was termed, was Altair in 1975, a microcomputer kit built by hobbyist Ed Roberts from MITS and featuring an Intel 8080 microprocessor (see Figure 2.1). When Apple Computer's two Steves (Wozniak and Jobs) launched Apple II in 1977, there were less than 50,000 personal computers in use. The PC business was merely about $100 million in sales in a much larger computer industry worth more than $22 billion and dominated by giant producers of mainframes and minicomputers (O'Mara 2019, 136, 146, 152). John Sculley, Apple's former CEO between 1983 and 1993, estimated about 200,000 PCs worldwide by the late 1970s (quoted in Steffens 1994, v).

46. See also the 1980 PC shipment data in Steffens (1994, 126–27). On NEC's venture in PCs, see Fransman (1995, 174–75, ch. 6). See Burgelman, McKinney, and Meza (2017) on Hewlett-Packard in both computing and PCs.

47. See Borrus and Zysman (1997) for an early analysis of "Wintelism," the codeword for the dominant role of Microsoft's Windows operating systems and Intel's microprocessors in setting the de facto product standards in the global PC industry since the 1980s. For more details on this early history of Microsoft and Intel in setting PC standards between 1981 and 1995, see Dedrick and Kraemer (1998, 50–58); Gawer and Cusumano (2002, chs. 2 and 5); and Campbell-Kelly and Garcia-Swartz (2015, 111–20). Casadesus-Masanell and Yoffie (2007) offer a contrarian view on the natural conflicts in pricing, timing of product release, and value capture in Wintelism.

48. Chandler (2001, 137–38).

49. Data from Fransman (1995, Table A4.1; 498). In the same year, DEC also suffered from a net loss of $2.1 billion from its $13.9 billion revenue.

50. Data from Dedrick and Kraemer (1998, 37–38, Table 2.2). See Saxenian (1994, 95–98) on DEC's success in minicomputers during the 1970s and the 1980s. Saxenian (1994, 98–104) further argued that the failure of Route 128 in Massachusetts, once the dominant center of minicomputer production in the late 1970s, to make the transition to smaller workstations and PCs during the 1980s led to its

demise as a locus of innovation and production in computers ever since. Suffering from major losses since the early 1990s, DEC was eventually acquired by a PC OEM firm, Compaq, in 1998.

51. Data from Steffens (1994, Table 7.1; 279).

52. Data from Angel and Engstrom (1995, 84–85).

53. Shipment data from IHS Markit/Informa Tech Custom Research for GPN@NUS Centre, July–October, 2016 and 2019.

54. 2021 forecast data from IDC and include Chromebooks and workstations (https://www.idc.com, released on March 10, 2021).

55. Interviews with top executives of Acer and two of its former spin-offs, BenQ and AU Optronics, in 2004, reported in Yeung (2016, 162–67). For fascinating case analyses of Acer from 1976 to 2000, see Ernst (2000b: 123–27); Mathews (2002, 55–92, 135–57); and Saxenian (2006, 153–62). See also Yu and Shih (2014) for an evolutionary analysis of Taiwan's PC makers and their capability development in relation to interactions with OEM lead firms.

56. Lenovo's former entity, known as Legend Computer, was established in China in 1970 by a group of engineers associated with the Chinese Academy of Sciences. In November 1984, the academy's Institute of Computing Technology established the New Technology Development Company and renamed it Beijing Legend in 1989. By 1996, Beijing Legend had emerged as the second largest PC vendor in China, with 7 percent of market share (Dedrick and Kraemer 1998, 201–2). In 1997, Legend Holdings was established. It went public in Hong Kong in June 2015, with the Chinese Academy of Sciences as its controlling shareholder (29 percent shares). Legend Holdings has a 30 percent controlling stake in Lenovo, the listed entity of its PC business (http://www.legendholdings.com.cn, accessed on September 5, 2019). See Lu (2000, chs. 1 and 3) for a brief history of computing R&D at the Institute of Computing Technology and the subsequent spin-off and development of the Legend group during the 1990s.

57. In their in-depth study of Asia's PC challenge to the US during the 1990s, Dedrick and Kraemer (1998, 85) singled out Toshiba as "Japan's only global PC competitor." In October 2018, Toshiba's PC business was sold to Sharp (majority-owned by Taiwan's Hon Hai Precision since May 2016), putting a formal end to Japan's substantial share in the global PC industry.

58. See Dedrick and Kraemer (1998) for an early in-depth study of Japan, South Korea, Taiwan, Hong Kong, and Singapore in the PC industry during the 1990s, and Lu (2000) for an early study of how China entered into the PC industry through the assembly work of ODM firms from Taiwan.

59. As the predecessor to today's notebook PCs, the portable PC was launched by US firm Osborne Computer in March 1981, just before the IBM 5150 desktop. In 1981, some 8,000 units of Osborne 1 were shipped in the US, and the total

revenue was $14 million. By 1986, the units shipped in the US reached 1.1 million, with a total revenue of just over $1 billion (Steffens 1994, Tables 5.6 and 5.11; 171–73, 189–92).

60. While the US firm RCA developed the first flat panel displays in 1968, it was Japan's NEC and Sharp that respectively produced the first large panel displays in 1990 and pioneered the mass production of an 8.4-inch flat panel displays for notebook computers in 1992 (Hu 2012, 541). In 1992, IBM's first ThinkPad notebooks had panel displays from Japan's Display Technologies (DTI), its joint venture with Toshiba established in 1988 (Eggers 2016, 1585).

61. As noted in Angel and Engstrom (1995, 87), US PC OEM firms generally lagged behind their Japanese competitors, such as NEC, Seiko-Epson, Sharp, Sony, and Toshiba, in adopting the automated assembly robotics and production design necessary in the high degree of miniaturization in notebook PCs. Up to the late 1980s, the notebook PCs of Apple and Compaq were assembled respectively by Japan's Sony and Citizen.

62. Interviews with senior vice presidents of Compal and Wistron, 2017–2018. See Appendix B for interview methodology.

63. See Gawer and Cusumano (2002, ch. 2) for an in-depth discussion of Intel's chipset strategy (the PCI architectural initiative between 1991 and 1993) and Tatsumoto, Ogawa, and Fujimoto (2009) and Yu and Shih (2014) for two studies of Intel's platform strategy in Taiwan during the 1990s and the 2000s.

64. Data from Hobday (1995, Table 5.3; 102).

65. Data from Dedrick and Kraemer (1998, Table 4.1; 118). As of 1995, for example, Apple's strategy was to produce its notebook and desktop PCs and monitors in its Singapore plant and outsource lower-end models to subcontractors in Taiwan and elsewhere. But after its major global market share decline in 1997, Apple cut back on its computer production in Singapore and outsourced most of it to emerging ODM firms from Taiwan.

66. Firm-specific outsourcing data from IHS Markit/Informa Tech Custom Research for GPN@NUS Centre, July–October, 2016 and 2019. Chapters 4 and 5 will analyze these insourcing and outsourcing strategies for the top six notebook OEM firms during the 2015–2018 period.

67. In 2012, Taiwan's semiconductor industry had 260 fabless firms, 11 wafer suppliers, 3 mask makers, 15 fabrications, and 37 packaging and testing service providers (Hwang and Choung 2014, 1248). This mutually reinforcing development of fabless design firms, foundry providers, testing and assembly services, and ODM-EMS providers in Taiwan's semiconductor ecosystem has been well acknowledged by Breznitz (2007, 126), who concluded that "the development of the IC design subsector thus enriches the Taiwanese IT industry with positive feedback, strengthening the Taiwanese position as midlevel supplier within the

global IT product networks. Each part of the Taiwanese IT hardware industry—OEM-ODMs, pureplay foundries, and IC design companies—strengthens and is in turn strengthened by the existence, outputs, and demands of the others."

68. Motorola's revenue from general systems products (mainly cellular phones) grew massively from $584 million in 1986 and $2.6 billion in 1990. Crossing $10.7 billion for the first time in 1995, its revenue from mobile devices peaked at $28.4 billion in 2006, the year before the launch of Apple's iPhone or the so-called smartphone revolution. In the same year 2006, Motorola's total revenue, including enterprise networks and home solutions, also peaked at $42.9 billion. Thereafter, its revenue in the mobile devices segment started to decrease rapidly to $7.1 billion in 2009 and thereafter, until its acquisition by Google in 2012 and Lenovo in 2014. Data from https://www.motorolasolutions.com, accessed on August 23, 2020. Motorola's semiconductors division was also spun off to become Freescale in 2004 before its acquisition by NXP in 2015.

69. Data from He, Lim, and Wong (2006, Table 1; 1148).

70. See Woyke (2014) for a fascinating history of the evolution of mobile phones and smartphones since Motorola's Martin Cooper demonstrated a workable prototype of the world's first handheld cellphone, the DynaTAC, in a press conference in Manhattan's Hilton Hotel on April 3, 1973. Interestingly, IBM perhaps created the world's first smartphone in 1992 and launched it with the Atlanta-based carrier BellSouth in August 1994. Named "Simon," it never took off in sales due to bad timing, weak IBM internal support, and its reliance on first-generation (1G) analogue technology.

71. Data from Richards (2004, 176) and Ornston (2018, 86). See also Richards (2004) and Glimstedt, Bratt, and Karlsson (2010) for two studies of the mobile handset business of Nokia and Ericsson up to the early 2000s. By then, Nokia had started to internationalize and develop its in-house production capacity in East Asia, in particular in China through its Xinwang Industrial Park in Beijing (see Yeung, Liu, and Dicken 2006).

72. Market share and revenue data from He, Lim, and Wong (2006, Table 1; 1148) and Giachetti (2018, 21). Samsung's foray into mobile phones did not start until launching its original Samsung Solstice in 1988. But due to poor quality and inferior products, its mobile phone business was not successful until at least the late 1990s. Hobday's (1995, 87) study of Samsung's telecommunications business concluded, "During the 1980s, Samsung sold large quantities of telecommunications equipment into the domestic market. However, it had little success in export markets and lagged behind European, Japanese and US leaders in high-end equipment."

73. Shipment and market share data from 2008 onward are from IHS Markit/Informa Tech Custom Research for GPN@NUS Centre, July–October, 2016 and

2019. For recent case studies of the competitive dynamics of OEM firms in the mobile handset segment of global electronics, see Giachetti (2013, 2018); Woyke (2014); McNish and Silcoff (2015); Giachetti and Marchi (2017); Sun and Grimes (2017); Doz and Wilson (2018); Lee and Gereffi (2021); and Xing (2021).

74. As discussed in Woyke (2014, 12–23), Nokia and Ericsson did launch their smartphones much earlier, respectively in 1996 (Nokia Communicator 9000) and 2000 (Ericsson R380). But both products were perhaps ahead of their time, and consumer adoption was limited to a couple hundred thousand units at most—see Doz and Wilson (2018) for Nokia's internal management problems and "collapse from within" just prior to the arrival of the iPhones. RIM launched its first smartphone BlackBerry 5810 in 2002 but achieved great market success only by 2009 when it accounted for 20 percent of the global smartphone market and more than 50 percent of the US smartphone market. By 2013, its market share in the US declined dramatically to only 1 percent (see McNish and Silcoff 2015).

75. See Evans, Hagiu, and Schmalensee (2006, ch. 7, 194) for a useful analysis of these earlier operating systems for mobile phones up to the mid-2000s. At its peak in 2003, Symbian had 66 percent of the market share. Some 12 million out of 22 million smartphones sold worldwide in 2004 used it as the operating system.

76. The following discussion of this competition in operating systems is based on Woyke (2014, 61–74); McAfee and Brynjolfsson (2017, 163–68); and Giachetti (2018, ch. 3 on Xiaomi). See also Basole and Karla (2011); Pon, Seppälä, and Kenney (2014); and Teece (2018) for discussion from a strategic management perspective.

77. Interview with its senior vice president, July 2017 (see Appendix B for interview methodology).

78. Data from https://www.idc.com/promo/smartphone-market-share/os, accessed on June 19, 2021.

79. A recent unexpected example is Huawei due to former US president Trump's executive order in May 2019 that banned US firms, including Google, from doing business with it. On August 9, 2019, Huawei rushed out its HarmonyOS in order to bypass this executive order and thus its dependence on Google's Android OS. In September 2020, it announced the complete switch from Android OS to its own HarmonyOS 2.0 for all of its smartphones beginning in 2021 (see Kharpal 2019; Chen 2020a; Chen and Haldane 2021).

80. According to McAfee and Brynjolfsson (2017, 166), Android's founder Andy Rubin had gone to South Korea to offer his little-known start-up to Samsung weeks before selling it to Google for $50 million in 2005!

81. See Sun and Grimes (2017, ch. 5) and Xing (2021, ch. 7) for two useful analyses of the rise of those four smartphone OEM lead firms from China since the mid-2010s. In April 2021, however, LG Electronics became the first major smartphone brand to withdraw completely from the smartphone market after suffering from

six consecutive years of losses totaling some $4.5 billion. Its smartphone division would be closed by end July (Lee and Yang 2021a).

82. Detailed firm-level data on key iPhone suppliers are from IHS Markit/Informa Tech Custom Research for GPN@NUS Centre, July–October, 2016 and 2019. See Giachetti (2018, 24–25) for a case study of Apple's exclusive partnership with AT&T, the largest US telecom carrier, during iPhone's first five years that gave Apple complete control over its iPhone's development, branding, and pricing. This arrangement between Apple and its telecom carrier "customer" was highly unusual because carriers normally used their networks as leverage to dictate the terms to their mobile phone vendors (or "suppliers") in such areas as design, features, interface, price, and network optimization. Apple also received about 10 percent share of revenue from AT&T's iPhone sales at its stores and monthly subscription fees. See also Woyke (2014, 83–86) for the significance of US telecom carriers in the smartphone industry's balance of power.

83. Quoted in Duhigg and Bradsher (2012); see also Pisano and Shih (2009, 2012); Duhigg and Barboza (2012); and Luk (2014).

84. For detailed case studies of Hon Hai/Foxconn, see Yeung (2016, 101–7) and van Liemt (2016). 2016–2020 financial data from https://www.honhai.com/en-us, accessed on June 19, 2021.

85. In Sturgeon's (2002, 460) pioneer study, all of the world's top five EMS providers in 1995 were based in North America. Ranked by their 2000 revenue, these were Solectron ($14.1 billion), Flextronics ($12.1 billion; acquired loss-making Solectron in 2007), Celestica ($9.8 billion; spun off from IBM Canada in 1996), Sanmina-SCI ($4.2 billion; acquired Apple's manufacturing facility in 1996), and Jabil Circuit ($3.6 billion). In comparison, Hon Hai's revenue was "only" $0.5 billion in 1995 and $2.8 billion in 2000 (see Yeung 2016, Table 4.4; 103). Saxenian (1991; 2000, 153–56) also offers an interesting case study of Flextronics's operations in its home base, Silicon Valley, during the 1980s.

86. See Kim's (2012) work on how the state and chaebol (business conglomerates) in South Korea worked together to challenge Qualcomm's dominance during the late 2000s. In 2016, the Korea Fair Trade Commission imposed a record fine of $873 million on Qualcomm for its unfair business practice in patent licensing and wireless chip sales. The High Court upheld the ruling in December 2019. See Yang (2019).

87. For useful case studies of Samsung's catching-up and success in mobile handsets, see Chang (2008); Whang and Hobday (2011); Park et al. (2014); Lee and Jung (2015); K. Lee (2016, 2019); and Yeung (2016, 168–72). Information is also based on my interviews with top executives of Samsung's IT & Mobile Communications division in Suwon in July 2017. Chapters 4–6 will present an updated analysis of Samsung's smartphone global production network in 2015 and 2018.

## Chapter 3

1. See World Bank in Cattaneo, Gereffi, and Staritz (2010); OECD (2011, 2015); WTO and IDE-JETRO (2011); WTO in Elms and Low (2013) and WTO (2019); OECD-WTO-UNCTAD (2013); UNCTAD (2013, 2020, 2021); World Bank (2013, 2020); and McKinsey Global Institute (2019, 2020). While the post-COVID-19 global economy during the early 2020s might look quite different, this long-term structural feature of the extensive presence of global production networks will not, and cannot, disappear easily within a short time frame of several years.

2. For some examples of such conceptual advancements in the social sciences, see Dicken et al. (2001); Henderson et al. (2002); Coe et al. (2004); Coe, Dicken, and Hess (2008); Yeung (2009, 2018, 2021a); Coe and Yeung (2015, 2019); and Yeung and Coe (2015) on global production networks, and Gereffi (1994, 1999, 2014, 2018); Humphrey (1995); Humphrey and Schmitz (2002); Sturgeon (2002); Gereffi, Humphrey, and Sturgeon (2005); Dallas, Ponte, and Sturgeon (2019); and Ponte, Gereffi, and Raj-Reichert (2019) on global value chains. See recent critical reviews of the GPN literature in Coe and Yeung (2019) and the GVC literature in Kano, Tsang, and Yeung (2020). There is another important strand of literature in international economics that examines production fragmentation, outsourcing and offshoring, and trading tasks in tradable goods (e.g., Feenstra 1998; Arndt and Kierzkowski 2001; Antràs and Helpman 2004; Grossman and Rossi-Hansberg 2008; Antràs and Chor 2013; Baldwin and Venables 2013; Koopman, Wang, and Wei 2014; Aichele and Heiland 2018; Chor 2019). These economic models attempt to modify or extend the conventional trade-in-finished-goods theory in international economics. Their explanatory emphasis is generally placed on decreasing communications and transport costs and trade-related transaction costs that in turn facilitate the trading of tasks across borders through international production fragmentation and outsourcing arrangements. Given my emphasis here on firm-specific strategies and organizational innovations in global production networks, I will not attempt to engage with this international economics literature (see Coe and Yeung 2015, ch.6).

3. This chapter draws extensively upon my recent conceptual work (Coe and Yeung, 2015, chs. 3–4; Yeung and Coe 2015, 34–52; Yeung 2018, 384–89; 2021a 997–1003) to provide a theory of interconnected worlds from the perspective of the GPN 2.0 theory. This GPN 2.0 theory was fully developed in Coe and Yeung's (2015) *Global Production Networks*. It emerged from our earlier theoretical work that had set up GPN 1.0 as an analytical framework in the early 2000s (Dicken et al. 2001; Henderson et al. 2002; Coe et al. 2004). While most book-length monographs on global value chains have strong empirical components (e.g., Lane and Probert 2009; Neilson and Pritchard 2009; Posthuma and Nathan 2011; Milberg and Winkler 2013; Pickles and Smith 2016; Sun and Grimes 2017; Gereffi 2018; Bar-

rientos 2019; Xing 2021), they do not have theory development as the central goal. See also Coe's (2021) advanced introduction to the global production networks approach and my recent critical reflections on its empirical application (Yeung 2021b).

4. See some prominent studies cited in Chapter 1's endnote 58.

5. While Gereffi, Humphrey, and Sturgeon's (2005) conceptualization of global value chain governance has addressed some of these interfirm relationships, their typology does not specify intrafirm and extrafirm organizational relationships. More importantly, their framework does not address geographical variations in organizing value chain governance and the competitive dynamics in multi-industry production networks. See Ponte, Gereffi, and Raj-Reichert (2019) and Kano, Tsang, and Yeung (2020) for this large literature on global value chain governance.

6. Given the book's focus on the industrial-organizational dynamics of electronics production networks centered in East Asia, my theoretical framing will focus less on the broader development issues, such as labor, industrial upgrading, environment, and the state/politics. See Coe and Yeung (2015, 2019) for more on such development outcomes. As I have argued elsewhere (Yeung 2021b), this focus on the "network box" and its underlying causal dynamics represents the necessary *first* step in a two-stage approach to GPN 2.0 and will be relevant for development scholars interested in the unequal and contentious consequences of the differential organization of global production networks.

7. Michael Porter's (1980, 1985) influential work on competitive strategy/advantage has pioneered this linear conception of the value chain.

8. Much of the current global value chain literature focuses on the key actors, particularly lead firms, that *govern* through interfirm relations in this complex process of value transformation and capture (Gereffi, Humphrey, and Sturgeon 2005; Bair 2009; Ponte and Sturgeon 2014; Gereffi 2018; Dallas, Ponte, and Sturgeon 2019; Ponte 2019; Ponte, Gereffi, and Raj-Reichert 2019; Strange and Humphrey 2019; cf. Benito, Peterson, and Welch 2019; Fortanier et al. 2020).

9. See the definitive work on platform leaders in Gawer and Cusumano (2002, 2014) and Gawer (2009) and recent collections in Tiwana (2014); Smedlund, Lindblom, and Mitronen (2018); and Guillén (2021). Much of this literature, however, is grounded in the management studies of complex product development (e.g., electronics and automotive), design rules (e.g., in-house component reuse), and innovation process and dynamics (e.g., Intel and Microsoft Windows in PCs). Focusing on product strategy, technological innovation, and production design, however, this fairly large literature in strategic management, industrial economics, and innovation studies pays less attention to how platforms are *geographically* organized across national and macroregional economies and how platforms interact with diverse global production networks spanning different national territories. In

short, it does not tell us much about how and why the interconnected worlds of production have come about.

10. Further to my caveat about software in global electronics in Chapter 1, it is important to note that software is hardly discussed in the enormous literature on global value chains. While software and business services are highly critical in value creation (making ICT products work) and value capture (almost monopolistic profit by platform leaders such as Microsoft and Google in operating systems), their actual influence in the organization and configurations of global value chains has yet to be theorized. Unlike intermediate goods and capital equipment, the "weightless" nature of software and services means that they can be delivered from centralized locations often hosted in the headquarters of these platform leaders. Their relationships with other firms, known as *complementors* in the digital platform literature, are also highly complex—often complementary, but sometimes also competitive or even predatory (see Kenney et al. 2019; Lan, Liu, and Dong 2019; Guillén 2021). In short, the explanatory difference that leading software and business service firms make to the organizational imperative of global lead firms in different industries, ranging from electronics and automotive to extractive sectors, apparel, pharmaceuticals, and agro-food, is often implicit in the existing theorization of global value chains. What is clear though is that software and business services are part of the critical enabling infrastructure that makes possible the globalization of production networks. See Jacobides, Cennamo, and Gawer (2018) for a recent theory of platform ecosystems and Teece (2018) for an analysis of value capture in the mobile handset ecosystem.

11. See further conceptual development in Coe et al. (2004); Yeung (2009, 2015, 2016); and Coe and Hess (2011). My 2016 *Strategic Coupling* provides the first book-length analysis of how strategic coupling with global lead firms can serve as a causal mechanism for industrial transformation in an interdependent world of global production networks (Yeung 2016). Liu's (2020) recent work puts this concept to its empirical context of industrial upgrading in China's Pearl River Delta.

12. This key question of firm-level strategies is left mostly unanswered in the existing conception of global value chain governance (e.g., Gereffi 1994, 1999; Gereffi, Humphrey, and Sturgeon 2005) and most economic models of global outsourcing (e.g., Grossman and Helpman 2002; Antràs and Helpman 2004; Grossman and Rossi-Hansberg 2008; Aichele and Heiland 2018).

13. This section is based on Yeung and Coe (2015, 34–42). While the existing literature has paid much attention to cost reduction rationalities in governing buyer-driven value chains and the importance of technological leadership in producer-driven value chains, few studies have brought together these two considerations and integrated them into a dynamic concept such as the cost-capability ratio. Even fewer studies in this literature have placed sufficient explanatory emphasis on market development and financial discipline in their analyses of global

production in different industries and sectors (for some exceptions, see Gibbon 2002; Milberg 2008; Hamilton, Petrovic, and Senauer 2011; Milberg and Winkler 2013; Hamilton and Kao 2018).

14. Neoclassical economic models of international outsourcing and global value chains tend to attribute causal effects to falling costs associated with improvements in communication and transportation technologies (e.g., Arndt and Kierzkowski 2001; Grossman and Rossi-Hansberg, 2008) and the specification of property rights (e.g., Antràs and Helpman 2004; Antràs 2005, 2016; Antràs and Chor 2013). In the GPN 2.0 theory, these cost improvements are conceptualized as enabling factors rather than causal conditions for the emergence of global production networks because as benefits of general-purpose technologies, they do not accrue only to particular firms and actors.

15. This is the phenomenon first identified as the new international division of labor in Fröbel, Heinrichs, and Kreye's (1980) seminal work that focused on the international relocation of German-owned textile and garment production over the 1960–1975 period, both within Europe and beyond to North Africa and Asia. See Henderson (1989) for a similar early study of the internationalization of chip assembly, packaging, and testing activities to East Asia by US semiconductor firms.

16. See conceptual development in Barney (1991, 2001); Birkinshaw and Hagström (2002); Gulati (2007); and Teece (2009). For a recent reconsideration, see Burt and Soda (2021).

17. There is a very large literature on how firms develop dynamic capability through learning processes embedded within specific national and/or sectoral innovation systems. See Lundvall (1992); Choi (1996); Lall (1996, 2003); Kim (1997); Cyhn (2002); Teece (2009); Gabriele and Khan (2010); Malerba and Nelson (2012); K. Lee (2013, 2019); Oqubay and Ohno (2019); and Khan (2022) for some extensive discussion of this literature.

18. See earlier examples in Yeung (2007, 2009, 2016); Appelbaum (2008); Sturgeon, Humphrey, and Gereffi (2011); Sun and Grimes (2017); Liu (2020); and Xing (2021).

19. The causal effects of this market imperative on the geographical configurations of global production are recognized in Gereffi's (1994, 1999) original formulation of buyer-driven global commodity chains in labor-intensive industries, such as apparel, footwear, and toys. In that formulation, market forces in advanced capitalist economies were embodied in the rise of large buyers—such as retailers, merchandisers, and their purchasing intermediaries—that in turn drove the internationalization of production and their overseas supplier networks.

20. See sociological theories of market constructions in Fligstein (2001); Caliskan and Callon (2010); and Fligstein and McAdam (2012). Hamilton and Kao (2018) offer a compelling empirical account of Taiwanese entrepreneurs in market making.

21. See Brown and Linden (2011, 77–94) for an analysis of how the shift from corporate to consumer markets in electronics products has impacted on the global semiconductor industry.

22. See recent work on the market importance of the Global South in Kaplinsky and Farooki (2011); Yang (2014); Ouma (2015); and Horner and Nadvi (2018).

23. See further elaboration in Krippner (2011) and Milberg and Winkler (2013).

24. The most recent manifestation of such significant regulatory risk is the US-China trade war originating on March 22, 2018, when former US president Donald Trump invoked Section 301 of the 1974 Trade Act and asked the US Trade Representative to investigate and consider applying tariffs on $50–60 billion worth of goods imported from China. This trade tension has subsequently led to tit-for-tat tariffs imposed on imported goods between the US and China worth several hundred billion dollars during the 2019–2020 period. In another context, the Japanese government announced on July 1, 2019, that it would impose export restrictions on three high-tech chemicals destined for South Korea's semiconductor and flat panel display manufacturing on the grounds of national security concerns (see report in Y. N. Lee 2019; Goodman, VerWey, and Kim 2019). Japanese firms dominate the world market in the production of these chemicals—90 percent of fluorinated polyimide and photoresists used in lithography or circuit printing on wafers, and 70 percent of hydrogen fluoride gases for dry etching on wafers. This official response from Japan was a protest against the October 2018 decision of the Supreme Court of South Korea on compensation by Japanese companies for the unfair treatment and exploitation of South Korean workers during the World War II period.

25. To cite two examples, a fire during equipment installation in SK Hynix's DRAM production plant in China's Wuxi on September 4, 2013, led to substantial disruption in the global supply of memory chips for electronics devices. Chip prices increased by 19 percent within days of the fire. With a third of the global market share in memory chips, SK Hynix from South Korea was and still is the world's second largest producer, after Samsung Electronics (see Table 1.1). Its Wuxi plant then produced about half of SK Hynix's total production (see Osawa 2013). In late 2020 and throughout 2021, producers of ICT end products and automotive assemblers worldwide faced severe shortages in specific semiconductors, such as Wi-Fi and Bluetooth chips and microcontrollers. Unexpectedly prolonged lockdowns and movement restrictions in Europe and Southeast Asia during the second half of 2020 impacted severely on the production capacity of chip fabrication and assembly factories in these locations. The just-in-time supply chain management and opaque demand planning practiced by automotive OEM lead firms, particularly those in the US, are also responsible for the shortage in capacity allocation by chip makers (see Jin, Busvine, and Kirton 2020; Reuters 2021).

26. This section is based on Yeung and Coe (2015, 43–52).

27. For example, Gereffi, Humphrey, and Sturgeon's (2005) typology of global value chain governance focuses on the entire value chain on the basis of discrete and dyadic (network) coordination relations between lead firms and their immediate (first tier) suppliers. The transactional characteristics and firm capabilities shaping these discrete governance relations are also assumed to be applicable to the entire value chain and, by inference, the industry.

28. For some key related works in international business studies, see Buckley (2009); Mudambi and Venzin (2010); Buckley and Strange (2015); Kano (2018); Mudambi et al. (2018); Benito, Petersen, and Welch (2019); Strange and Humphrey (2019); Fortanier et al. (2020); McWilliam et al. (2020); and Contractor (2021). See a critical review in Kano, Tsang, and Yeung (2020).

29. See Baldwin and Clark (2000) for modularity in design rules and Langlois and Robertson (1992); Langlois (2002); and Sturgeon (2002) for modularity in production networks. Jacobides, Cennamo, and Gawer (2018) offer a recent theory of how modularity enables platform ecosystems.

30. See empirical studies in Freidberg (2004); Barrientos and Dolan (2006); Barnett et al. (2011); Barrientos (2019); and Hughes, Morrison, and Rawanpura (2019).

31. See Levy (2008) for an early conceptualization of political contestation in global production networks and Yeung (2014, 2021b); Smith (2015); and Horner (2017) for changing state roles in global production networks. Recent studies have examined state politics and the changing organization of global production networks (e.g., Farrell and Newman 2014, 2019; Mayer and Phillips 2017; Dallas, Horner, and Li 2021; Gereffi, Lim, and Lee 2021).

32. See Johns and Wellhausen (2016).

33. See Baccini, Dür, and Elsig (2018); Eckhardt and Lee (2018); Osgood (2018); Kim et al. (2019); and Zeng, Sebold, and Lu (2020) for such domestic support for trade liberalization and trade agreements.

34. See Amsden and Chu (2003) and Breznitz (2007), but Yeung (2016); Hamilton and Kao (2018); and Hamilton-Hart and Yeung (2021b) offer a contrasting perspective. For the case of China, see Ning (2009); Fuller (2016); Sun and Grimes (2017); Liu (2020); and Xing (2021).

## Chapter 4

1. Complete region-to-region annual exports data on ICT intermediate and final goods between 1989 and 2019 are available on the World Bank's World Integrated Trade Solutions (WITS)-GVC Database, https://wits.worldbank.org/WITS/WITS/Restricted/Login.aspx, accessed on June 17, 2021. As was explained in Chapter 2's endnote 2, 2018 was chosen as an end point for this analysis due to the historical peak in world exports. Moreover, some of the WITS-GVC data cited in this section may not be presented in Figure 4.1.

2. See Appendixes A and B for details on these two main sources of original data deployed in this and the next two chapters. Unless otherwise specified, firm-specific information in this chapter is based on the proprietary datasets from IHS Markit/Informa Tech Custom Research.

3. See these earlier book-length analyses in Braun and MacDonald (1982); Malerba (1985); Angel (1994); Hong (1997); Mazurek (1999); Mathews and Cho (2000); Peters (2006); Brown and Linden (2011); and Chu (2013).

4. On the changing role of state in the East Asian semiconductor industry during the 2000s, see Breznitz (2007); Hsu (2011, 2017); Yeung (2016); and Yap and Rasiah (2017).

5. Proprietary data from IHS Markit/Informa Tech used in this table are at the individual fab level, with detailed information on each fab's company and fab name, location, product applications, process technology, wafer size, and quarterly capacity since 2000 through to 2023 (2019 Q3 to 2023 based on estimates).

6. These fabs were previously established by Fairchild Semiconductor from the US and specialized in power management solutions for portable applications. In 2016, ON semiconductor acquired Fairchild, and these fabs were transferred to ON Semiconductor, which remained the only foreign firm to own fabs in South Korea in 2010 and 2018. With a total revenue of $2.4 billion in 2018, ON Semiconductor was the second largest IDM firm in discrete components (after Infineon).

7. The only foreign fab in Taiwan in 2000 belonged to General Semiconductor, a spin-off of power semiconductors from New York–based General Instrument in 1997. In 2001, Vishay Intertechnology from the US acquired General Semiconductor and became the world's top manufacturer of rectifiers, glass diodes, and infrared components. Its fab in Taiwan remained operational in 2020.

8. Reported in Dieseldorff (2021). Much of this increase was in memory (95 percent), foundry (47 percent), and analog (29 percent).

9. These figures on foundry include those from TowerJazz's fab in Israel and five fabs by Chartered Semiconductor in Singapore (acquired by the controlling shareholder of AMD's spin-off GlobalFoundries in 2009).

10. Some of these semiconductor product markets became quite fragmented. The leading IDM firms producing analog products in 2018 ranked order were Texas Instruments, Analog Devices, and Qualcomm from the US; STMicroelectronics (France/Italy); and Skyworks Solutions (US). Together, they accounted for 44 percent of total market revenue in 2018. In discrete products, the top five ranked in 2018 were Infineon (Germany), ON Semiconductor (US), STMicroelectronics (France/Italy), and Mitsubishi and Toshiba from Japan. Similar to analog products, the global market for discrete products was also fragmented, with these top five accounting for only 41 percent of total revenue in 2018. In microcomponent products for computers and other numerical control devices, the market was dominated by the founder-giant Intel that still commanded 66 percent of market

share in 2018. The next four in ranked order—NXP (Netherlands), AMD (US), Texas Instruments (US), and Renesas (Japan)—followed at a considerable distance, with a combined market share of only 19 percent.

11. Data from Nenni (2020); Ye (2020, 2021a); IC Insights (2021); and https://www.bloomberg.com/news/articles/2021–02–02/china-stockpiles-chips-and-chip-making-machines-to-resist-u-s, accessed on February 3, 2021. See further discussion on China's institutional context for semiconductors in Fuller (2019); Ezell (2021); and Grimes and Du (2021).

12. As noted in Figure 2.1, this continuous improvement in cutting-edge process technology at smaller nanometer nodes per 8-inch (200 mm) or 12-inch (300 mm) wafer sustains the famous "Moore's law"—named after Intel's cofounder Gordon Moore who predicted in 1965 the doubling of the density of components in an integrated circuit or "chip" every year (revised to every two years in 1975). With more advanced nodes (i.e., smaller nanometers to shrink transistor dimensions), more transistors can be packed into the same chip, which results in higher chip density, faster processing performance, and lower power consumption. In July 2015, IBM teamed up with GlobalFoundries and Samsung to develop the world's first 7 nm test chip that packed more than 20 billion functioning transistors on a fingernail-size chip. In 2018, TSMC's 7 nm process could pack over 100 transistors per square millimeter and yield logic chips 1.6 times denser, 20 percent faster, and 40 percent less power consuming than chips fabricated via its 10 nm process. Entered in mass production since the first half of 2020, TSMC's 5 nm process offers about 20 percent speed improvement and 40 percent reduction in power consumption than its own 7 nm technology. By mid-2022, TSMC's 3 nm process will commence volume production and offer up to 15 percent speed improvement and 30 percent power reduction as compared with its 5 nm process (Khare 2019; TSMC, "Logic Technology," https://www.tsmc.com/english/dedicatedFoundry/technology/logic, accessed on June 19, 2021).

13. See Nenni and McLellan (2019, 65–66); Btarunr (2020); Hruska (2020); Jones (2021); and Maire (2021a). In 2017, Intel planned for its new Fab 42 in Chandler, Arizona, to operate at the 7 nm node by 2019 and, eventually, at the 5 nm node. But the implementation and equipping of this new cutting-edge fab was delayed due to internal management issues, the loss of very experienced engineers (since its workforce trimming by 11 percent in 2016), and the lack of sufficient demand for advanced technology from its own microprocessors and logic chips for PCs and other markets. Intel continued to support up to 10 nm in its existing Fab D1X in Oregon in 2018 and 2019 and, since late 2019, Fab 28 in Kiryat (Israel). But even in early 2021, Intel was still struggling with yield in its 10 nm process. Despite the "well publicized 7 nanometer stumbling" recognized by its CEO Patrick Gelsinger (2021), Intel's 7 nm process in Fab 42 would enter into volume production only in 2022 or later.

14. To put in perspective the global automotive chip shortage in late 2020 and throughout 2021 (Burkacky, Lingemann, and Pototzky 2021; further discussed in Chapter 7), the fabrication of automotive chips, such as power management units, microcontrollers, analog devices, and discretes, generally does not require leading-edge process nodes at 28 nm or lower. As Chapter 2 endnote 32 has indicated, leading IDM firms in automotive chips, such as Texas Instruments, Infineon, NXP, Renesas, and STMicroelectronics, have not invested in new in-house process technology below the 45 nm generation since the late 2000s. Taking this fab-lite approach, these IDM firms source automotive-related logic and processor chips requiring more technologically advanced process nodes at 28 nm or lower from top foundry providers such as TSMC, UMC, and GlobalFoundries. By 2020, the most advanced process nodes in the "legacy" fabs of these IDM firms remained at the trailing edge far behind the top foundry providers: Texas Instruments (130 nm), Infineon (90 nm), NXP (130 nm), Renesas (90 nm), and STMicroelectronics (90 nm). Only Renesas and STMicroelectronics have each invested in one 12-inch fab of modest capacity to produce logic chips: Renesas's Naka N3 fab (16,000 wafers per month at 40–65 nm) since 2009 and STMicroelectronics's Fab 2 in Crolles, France (20,000 wafers per month at 28–45 nm) since 2017. Both IDM firms continue to rely on leading foundry providers as their primary source for technologically advanced wafers: TSMC for Renesas and GlobalFoundries for ST-Microelectronics. Information based on fab-level data from IHS Markit/Informa Tech Custom Research for GPN@NUS Centre, July–October 2019.

15. See also earlier work on OEM PC firms by Lu (2000) on Lenovo; Mathews (2002) and Yeung (2016) on Acer; and Campbell-Kelly and Garcia-Swartz (2015) that ends in the late 2000s.

16. See earlier studies of the rise of Chongqing as China's premier location for notebook PC production by the mid-2010s in Gao et al. (2017, 2019) and Yang (2017).

17. Hewlett-Packard had a very small proportion of in-house production before 2018, e.g., 2 percent or 0.7 million units of 35.7 million units shipped in 2016 from its Akishima factory in Japan primarily serving the Japanese domestic market.

18. Lenovo's factory in Hefei was formerly a majority-owned joint venture with Compal, its exclusive ODM partner from Taiwan, to develop in-house design and manufacturing capability. But due to the high cost of such an exclusive arrangement, Lenovo subsequently decided to internalize the Hefei factory by buying out Compal's share in 2019 and engaging in multisourcing from both Compal and Quanta (since 2018). Information from interviews with senior executives of multiple PC lead firm and ODM firm leaders. See Appendix B for details on interview methodology, 2017–2018.

19. 2018 shipment figures for Samsung, Fujitsu, NEC, and Toshiba are in Table 2.7.

364 NOTES TO CHAPTER 4

20. Information from interviews with senior executives of all top five PC OEM customers and two top ODM firms, 2017–2018.

21. Foxconn's factory in Pardubice, Czech Republic, was first acquired from the former socialist state electronics firm, Tesla, in May 2000. It shipped 41,000 iMacs in 2000 and later also started assembly services for Compaq (acquired by Hewlett-Packard in 2002). Since 2004, it has become Foxconn's logistics center to serve the Europe, Middle East, and Africa (EMEA) macroregion (see Čaněk 2016, 97). In 2015 and 2018, it remained a major assembly site for Hewlett-Packard's desktop PCs for the EMEA market (see Table 4.4). See also Sacchetto and Andrijase (2016) for an analysis of Foxconn in Çorlu, Turkey that continued to assemble for Hewlett-Packard in 2015 and 2018.

22. I have not included servers and tablets in this book's empirical analysis because of their different market orientation and/or less significance in global electronics. Their combined revenue of $105 billion in 2018 was substantially smaller than PCs ($146 billion). The server market primarily catered to enterprises and government procurement. Compared to notebook PCs, it was also relatively small at about 10–11 million units between 2014 and 2018, with total market revenue between $46 billion in 2014 and $63 billion in 2018. The server market was dominated by entry-level and enterprise servers that accounted for $59.2 billion in 2018. Together with "white box" vendors such as Quanta, Wistron, and MiTAC from Taiwan (totaling 25 percent), three OEM firms, Dell-EMC, Hewlett-Packard Enterprise, and Inspur (China), took up 68 percent of the 2018 market. The geography of server assembly is quite similar to desktop PCs for the same reasons—weight, inventory, and regulatory constraints. In tablets that peaked in 2014 at 250 million units and $75.8 billion in total revenue, sales decreased rapidly to 140 million units and $42.3 billion in 2018. The top five vendors of Apple, Samsung, Huawei, Amazon, and Lenovo in 2018 followed broadly similar geographical configurations of final assembly as those of notebook PCs—all in China by Taiwanese EMS/ODM providers, except Samsung in South Korea.

23. Several earlier book-length analyses of smartphones in Giachetti (2013, 2018); Woyke (2014); McNish and Silcoff (2015); Doz and Wilson (2018); and Xing (2021) focus more on the rise and fall of individual OEM firms in mobile handsets rather than the changing geography of their production in Asia and elsewhere.

24. While mobile handsets include both smartphones and feature phones, smartphones have typically accounted for 75 percent of total shipment since the second half of the 2010s. Due to escalating trade tensions since 2018 and the COVID-19 pandemic in 2020/2021, the total smartphone shipment was reduced in 2019 and 2020. According to Canalys's forecast (https://www.canalys.com, released on June 14, 2021), total smartphone shipment in 2021 and 2022 will likely exceed the historical peak of 1.41 billion units set in 2018 due to the implementation of 5G technologies and the less government restrictions on individual mobility.

25. Data from Borak (2021).

26. While originating from Silicon Valley in California and listed in NASDAQ, Flex (renamed from Flextronics in July 2015) was a pioneer in electronics manufacturing outsourcing and offshoring during the 1980s and has its operational headquarters located in Singapore (https://flex.com, accessed on December 9, 2019). See Sturgeon (2002) for a discussion of Flextronics in its early decades and Yeung (2016, ch. 4) for an update to the early 2010s.

27. See earlier work by Lüthje et al. (2013) and van Liemt (2016) on Foxconn City in China's Shenzhen-Longhua that used to assemble most of Apple's iPhones in the early 2010s.

28. Entering the African market in 2008, Shenzhen-based Transsion overtook Samsung in 2017 to become Africa's top vendor for mobile phones, particularly in low-cost feature phones that accounted for 97 percent of all phones sold in Africa. By 2021, Transsion dominated Africa's market with a combined 44 percent share in both feature phones and smartphones (see Nyabiage 2021).

29. For a detail history of US consumer electronics in the 1950s and the 1960s and its decline due to formidable Japanese challenge in the 1970s and the 1980s, see Curtis (1994) and Chandler (2001). To my best knowledge, there is no recent book-length academic work focusing on consumer electronics.

30. Once the dominant player in the US during the 1950s and the 1960s, RCA developed the world's first flat panel display in 1968.

31. See Maciejewska (2016, 191) for a study of LG's operations in Poland's Mława (since 1999) and Biskupice Podgórne (since 2005). At one point in the early 2010s, these two facilities were assembling respectively 5 million and 8 million units of LG TVs. By 2018 (Table 4.6), their combined output (Eastern Europe) was much reduced to 5.1 million units.

32. While some of Samsung's TVs for the US market were assembled in China by its EMS providers (i.e., BOE from China and Amtran from Taiwan) in 2018, these EMS providers were moving or on the way to move their assembly facilities for Samsung from China to Vietnam from mid-2019 onward in order to avoid increasing tariffs on TV products destined for the US due to the ongoing US-China trade war. Amtran started to ramp up its TV set assembly in Vietnam for Samsung's US shipment from June 2019. BOE was requested by some OEM customers, including Samsung, to build TV set assembly capacity in Vietnam, and it was scheduled to ramp up from April 2020. Information from IHS Markit/Informa Tech Custom Research, October 2019.

33. See Murtha, Lenway, and Hart (2001) and Castellano (2005) for the earlier history of the plasma and TFT-LCD flat panel displays industry up to 2000. While both technologies were invented in the US—plasma display in 1964 at the University of Illinois and LCD display in 1968 by RCA—the industry's mass production and commercialization had been dominated by Japanese panel makers, such as

Hitachi, Sharp, and Toshiba, until 1995 when South Korean firms and, a couple of years later, Taiwanese firms entered into the rapidly growing industry. By the 2010s, they were joined by several major panel makers from China (Hu 2012; Chen and Ku 2014; Chen and Chen 2015; Lehmberg 2018; Yu, Liu, and Chen 2020).

34. Flat panel displays typically contribute to 40–50 percent of the total factory cost of large-size TVs and one-third of production costs in notebook PCs and high-end smartphones.

35. The following calculation of display supply to TV and PC OEM firms is based on the proprietary datasets from IHS Markit/Informa Tech Custom Research described in Appendix A.

36. Due to confidentiality and research consent with interviewees, this analysis does not present findings that identify directly a specific firm and/or interviewee. Instead, I anonymize the names of firms and individuals when quoting from interviewees. If appropriate, I indicate the segment (e.g., semiconductors or PCs) and nature (e.g., OEM or supplier) of the firm. The discussion here and in the next two empirical chapters draws extensively upon direct quotes from 27 interviewees in 22 out of the 44 firms in all segments of global electronics in my study (see Appendix B).

37. OEM-22 is anonymized and the firm number does not match #22 Toshiba TEC in Appendix B's Table B1. The same anonymity applies throughout this book.

38. This interviewee gave another example of a quick switch in its paint supplier for its notebook PC factory in Eastern China. Its existing paint supplier was shut down by the local government due to environmental concerns and had to buy new ventilation equipment to meet environmental requirements. But within 24 hours, ODM-26 was able to switch to another qualified paint supplier nearby. While this second source supplier initially quoted a higher price, ODM-26 managed to negotiate it down to the same level as the previous main supplier. To him, "that is the reason why people still prefer having the factory here in China. We can switch to different suppliers very fast. There is a lot of selection here. We moved to another supplier and negotiated for the same price."

39. See Saxenian (2006, ch.7) and Gregory, Nollen, and Tenev (2009) on the relatively insignificant role of India (and South Asia) in the manufacturing of ICT equipment but the rapid development of its ICT software services since the mid-1980s. Still and since 2018 in Table 4.5, India has emerged as a major destination for the final assembly of mobile handsets.

40. See De Prato, Nepelski, and Simon (2013) and Nepelski and De Prato (2018) for some recent studies at the industry level that elaborate on technological innovations in East Asia.

41. Nepelski and De Prato (2018, 960).

42. See examples in Sun and Grimes (2017) and Xing (2021).

## Chapter 5

1. See Borrus, Ernst, and Haggard (2000) for an early analysis of international production networks in the electronics industry during the 1990s.

2. Saxenian (1991, 428; 1994, 147).

3. There is a very large literature on this localized agglomeration of industrial activities in high-tech clusters. For a sample, see Storper (1997, 2013); Bresnahan and Gambardella (2004); Breschi and Malerba (2005); Asheim, Cooke, and Martin (2006); Tinguely (2013); Klepper (2015); and Fornahl and Hassink (2017); see a recent critical review in Harris (2021). For cluster studies from the perspective of global value chains and global production networks, see Pietrobelli and Rabellotti (2007); Kawagami and Sturgeon (2011); De Marchi, Di Maria, and Gereffi (2018); and Liu (2020).

4. Most existing book-length studies of global value chains rely either on case studies (lacking comprehensiveness) or industry-level analyses (lacking firm-specific details), e.g., Feenstra and Hamilton (2006); Lane and Probert (2009); Neilson and Pritchard (2009); Wilson (2013); Ferrarini and Hummels (2014); Ouma (2015); Pickles and Smith (2015); Sun and Grimes (2017); Barnes (2018); Hamilton and Kao (2018); Liu (2020); and Xing (2021). See Coe and Yeung (2019) and Kano, Tsang, and Yeung (2020) for recent reviews of these studies.

5. Details on how suppliers of intellectual property (IP) have become an important enabler of the fabless-foundry production model in semiconductors can be found in Nenni and McLellan (2019, ch. 7) who noted, "Once standard cell libraries, memories, and microprocessors were widely available to be licensed by anyone, it suddenly became possible, both from a business and a technology view, to design more complex chips that could then be manufactured at a pureplay foundry or within an IDM's own foundry" (251). The most successful IP supplier in design cores is the UK-based ARM, founded as Advanced RISC Machines in November 1990 through collaboration between UK's Acorn Computers and Apple and VLSI Technology from the US. ARM's design core is now in almost every processor of all electronic devices. In September 2016, Japan's Softbank acquired ARM for $32 billion. In 2018, ARM had more than 500 licensees that had collectively shipped over 130 billion cores, and the number was growing at 20 billion cores per year. In this highly concentrated IP business worth $4.6 billion in 2020, ARM remained dominant with 41 percent share and followed by two top chip design software firms—Synopsys (19 percent) and Cadence (6 percent): see Brown and Linden (2011, 68–72) and Esteve (2021). A top fabless firm, Nvidia, offered to acquire ARM for $40 billion on September 13, 2020 (https://nvidianews.nvidia.com, accessed on January 1, 2021), but the deal was still pending as of end June 2021 due to delays in regulatory approval.

6. Quotation from Moore and Davis (2004, 21). See also Berlin's (2005, 171–72) biographical discussion of this strategy of colocating development and manufacturing envisioned by Robert Noyce and Gordon Moore at their cofounding of

Intel in Mountain View, California, on July 18, 1968. Also from Fairchild Semiconductor, Andrew Grove (1996) joined Intel on its incorporation day.

7. Some recent examples are Kawagami and Sturgeon (2011); De Prato and Nepelski (2013); Sun and Grimes (2017); Gereffi (2018); and Xing (2021).

8. My custom data on different components from IHS Markit/Informa Tech focus on semiconductors and panel displays only and do not include other important and costly components, such as mechanical parts and camera modules. Based on separate IHS Markit/Informa Tech's teardown data in November 2017 on Apple's iPhone X (A1865), for example, one major mechanical part—rear enclosure with machined aluminum frame, glass cover, and stainless-steel plate—was the second most expensive part and cost up to $61 or 16 percent of iPhone X's total bill of material costs at $370. In comparison, iPhone X's advanced display module by Samsung was most expensive at $110, and camera modules another $35. Other chipsets ranked in material costs were $33 for memory, $28 for application processor (A11 Bionic), $18 for wireless communications, $17 for Wi-Fi and RF, and $14 for power management. Information from my interviews with senior executives of PC and mobile handset OEM lead firms shows that the major suppliers for metal casing in aluminum/magnesium alloy are from Taiwan (Casetek, Catcher, Foxconn, Silitech, and Waffer) and China (BYD and Juteng). These suppliers account for the overwhelming majority in the global metal casing supply in the notebook PC and mobile handset segments. Some of them are also directly linked to specific OEM firms (e.g., Casetek with Asus) and EMS providers (e.g., Foxconn). See Lee and Gereffi (2021) for a similar recent study of component suppliers for four top smartphone OEM firms.

9. The use of ASP requires a brief note. While the ASP for major components is given in Tables 5.1 to 5.3, it refers to the estimated average spend by an OME firm in a particular component, e.g., processor or memory chip. Invariably, each OEM firm has multiple models and products that use different chips or displays from the same supplier. Some chips are more powerful and efficient and cost more, whereas others from the same supplier are less cutting-edge in technology and performance and cost less. In November 2019 and for desktop PCs alone, for example, Intel had 8 different recommended prices for its 24 Pentium processors and some 45 different prices for its over 64 Core i3-i9 processors (https://www.intc.com/investor-relations/investor-education-and-news/cpu-price-list, accessed on December 23, 2019). The ASP refers to the average pricing of all components in the same category (e.g., processor) from the same supplier (e.g., Intel).

10. Some data on ASP presented here are not in Tables 5.1–5.3. They are based on the same custom dataset from IHS Markit/Informa Tech Custom Research for GPN@NUS Centre, July–October, 2016 and 2019.

11. Research protocols require full anonymity in all direct quotations from interviewees used in this book (see Appendix B for research methodology). When-

ever appropriate, I indicate the segment (e.g., semiconductors or PCs) and nature (e.g., OEM, fabless, or supplier) of the quoted interviewee's firm. In some instances, actual company names and cases are used when they are not directly linked to these quotations or specific interviewees.

12. As Chapter 2 endnote 32 has indicated, Texas Instruments went "fab-lite" as early as in 2007 when it decided to source wafers from the 32 nanometer (nm) generation onward from Taiwan's TSMC and UMC (Brown and Linden 2011, 50). In 2011, Texas Instruments outsourced about 20 percent of its wafers, with 70 percent of its logic chips from foundry providers. In 2019, TSMC's most advanced fabs already operated at the 7 nm node. But Texas Instruments still had 12 less advanced "legacy" fabs located in Texas (5) and Maine (1) in the US, Germany (1), Japan (4), and China (1). Data from IHS Markit/Informa Tech Custom Research (see Appendix A). See also Chapter 4 endnote 14 for fab-level data on the other top IDM firms in automotive chips, such as Infineon, NXP, Renesas, and STMicroelectronics.

13. In its 2021 Technology Symposium, TSMC described how its leading-edge process nodes from 5 nm to 28 nm could be deployed for fabricating high-performance SoC chips for automotive applications, e.g., power management, microcontroller functionality, image sensors, and 5G wireless communications in advanced driver-assistance systems and autonomous driving (see Dillinger 2021).

14. See Wong (2018) and Doner, Noble, and Ravenhill (2021) for recent book-length analyses of the greater importance of these megasuppliers in the global automotive industry during the 2010s.

15. Data from Nenni and McLellan (2019, 125); Goodman, VerWey, and Kim (2019, 8–9); Clark (2021); Nenni (2021); and Sterling (2021); see also earlier work on suppliers of lithography in Linden, Mowery, and Ziedonis (2000) and van de Kerkhof, Benschop, and Banine (2019). Lange, Müller-Seitz, and Windeler (2013) provide a detailed analysis of early coinvestment among SEMATECH, Intel, Samsung, and TSMC in ASML's extreme ultraviolet lithography technology during the 2000s.

16. See Nenni and McLellan (2019, ch. 3) for a well-known example of how the competitive success of two US fabless firms (Xilinx and Altera) between 1995 and 2018 was highly dependent on their Taiwan-based foundry providers' reliability in production yield and timeliness of implementing new process technology.

17. Information in this case study comes from interviews with senior executives of leading IDM firms in semiconductors and OEM firms in mobile handsets, 2017–2018. See also Nenni and McLellan (2019, 113–19) for a fascinating comparison of process technology in the foundry fabs of Samsung and TSMC, from 16 nm in 2015 to 5 nm in 2020, that rely on ASML's extreme ultraviolet lithography technology. See Müller-Seitz and Sydow (2012); Lange, Müller-Seitz, and Windeler (2013); Kapoor and McGrath (2014); and van de Kerkhof, Benschop, and Banine

(2019) for the development of extreme ultraviolet lithography technology since 1991 that has enabled sub-10-nm process nodes in wafer fabrication.

18. As was noted in Chapter 2, Apple launched its first iPhone in June 2007. But Samsung only entered into the emerging smartphone market and launched its Galaxy series smartphones in June 2009 when Nokia and RIM (Blackberry) were still the largest vendors in mobile phones, with a combined market share of over 57.8 percent in Table 2.9. But the incredible success of both iPhones and Galaxy subsequently launched the "smartphone revolution" at the beginning of the 2010s. The global market for mobile handsets began to shift away from Nokia and Blackberry from 2011 onward, culminating in their ultimate demise by the mid-2010s.

19. Apple's revenue share data from TSMC annual reports and Nenni (2021).

20. Quotation from https://semiwiki.com/forum/index.php?threads/after-switching-to-arm-expect-apple-to-buy-tsmc-too.12730/#post-43315; see also discussion in https://semiwiki.com/forum/index.php?threads/5nm-wafer-cost-very-high.13101/page-2#post-44161, accessed on December 30, 2020.

21. Data from Ezell (2021, 11).

22. In late 2020 and throughout 2021, this regular demand in mass-market ICT devices for chips fabricated with less advanced nodes at 14–28 nm overlapped with the surge in demand for advanced automotive chips utilizing the same process nodes at leading foundry providers, contributing to an unexpected and yet acute global chip shortage in the automotive industry (see further discussion in Chapter 7).

23. See Chapter 2 endnote 79. Huawei's case is based on reports in Kharpal (2019); King (2020); Bloomberg at https://www.bloomberg.com/news/articles/2020-06-07/huawei-troops-see-dire-threat-to-future-from-latest-trump-salvo, accessed on June 12, 2020; and Ezell (2021); and Department of Commerce's press release: https://2017-2021.commerce.gov/news/press-releases/2020/05/commerce-addresses-huaweis-efforts-undermine-entity-list-restricts.html, accessed on June 12, 2020.

24. Data from Nenni (2021).

25. See Chen (2020b).

26. See Woyke (2014, 112–19) for a discussion of Apple and Samsung's relationships with their key suppliers and Grimes and Sun (2016) and Xing (2021) for Apple's relationships with its iPhone suppliers based in China.

## Chapter 6

1. Data on Intel and GlobalFoundries from Nenni and McLellan (2019, 108) and TSMC and Samsung from Everington (2019) and Btarunr (2020). See also Chapter 4 endnotes 12–13.

2. See report in Phartiyal and Shah (2021). This is part of Prime Minister Narendra Modi's "Made in India" initiative launched on September 25, 2014. "Made in India" chips are deemed necessary to enhance its electronics supply chains for building a national assembly industry in smartphones and other ICT devices. In Chapter 4 and Table 4.5, India was already the second largest location for the assembly of smartphones in 2015. But the lack of supplier ecosystem and infrastructural support remains the key obstacle to attracting semiconductor manufacturing to locate in India.

3. Since its new labor contract law implemented at the beginning of 2008, China's labor cost has gone up steadily over time. By the mid-2010s, China was clearly no longer a "cheap labor" production site. See discussion in Périsse (2017); Song (2017); and Périsse and Séhier (2019).

4. See reports in Hu (2019) and Park (2019).

5. Information from my interviews with senior management at Samsung's IT & Mobile Communications division in Suwon in July 2017, other mobile handset OEM firms and semiconductor IDM firms, 2017–2018, and Vietnam investment news websites: https://www.vir.com.vn/1176-million-samsung-extension-to-support-vietnam-operations-40956.html and https://www.reuters.com/article/us-samsung-elec-vietnam-idUSKBN1631FL, accessed on January 2, 2020.

6. According to Brown and Linden's (2011, 70) extensive study of the semiconductor industry, design costs are typically about 10 percent of chip value.

7. This surge in demand for automotive chips precipitated a global chip shortage in late 2020 and throughout 2021 (see Burkacky, Lingemann, and Pototzky 2021; and further discussion in Chapter 7).

8. See Chapter 2's brief discussion of these software and digital ecosystems within the broader rise of the so-called "platform economy" (Kenney and Zysman 2016, 2020; Parker, Van Alstine, and Choudary 2016; McAfee and Brynjolfsson 2017; Guillén 2021).

9. Detailed breakdowns of semiconductor data in this section are derived from device- and component-level data from IHS Markit/Informa Tech Custom Research for GPN@NUS Centre, July–October 2019 (see more information on these datasets in Appendix A).

10. See Chu (2013, 188–92) for an earlier discussion of the importance of market proximity to the fab investment of some Taiwanese semiconductor firms in China during the 2000s, such as TSMC, UMC, and the rise of new foundry providers in China (e.g., SMIC, GMIC, and so on).

11. Information on Dell's case is based on multiple interviews with senior management at the level of senior vice president, chief technology officer, and vice president from the firms mentioned in this section—Dell, Compal, Wistron, AMD, Samsung, AU Optronics, and UMC (see Appendix B Table B1).

12. According to Perez (2020), an industry veteran directly responsible for eighteen chips ramped to mass production at Apple for iPhones and iPads, it is the outsourced partner (i.e., ODM firm) that interacts regularly with the semiconductor supplier (e.g., an IDM or a fabless firm), from the initial chipset to its mass production. Whenever there is a problem with the initial chipset, the ODM partner sends it back to the chip supplier's lab for failure analysis. The ODM partner also needs to discuss with the chip supplier other shipment details, such as the types of reels and part markings. Eventually, the ODM partner will submit purchase orders for mass production. Working closely with its outsourced partner(s), the OEM lead firm normally has many cross-functional teams that could be involved in the integration of this chipset into its final product.

13. See also recent studies examining the growing market importance of the Global South in Yang (2014) and Horner and Nadvi (2018).

14. See Whang and Hobday (2011) and Kim (2012) for earlier studies of how home production in South Korea served as an important test bed for Samsung to catch up with Apple and Qualcomm in smartphone technologies.

15. Data from Ezell (2021, 11–12).

16. For further elaboration on these characteristics of East Asian business systems, see Yeung (2004, 2016); Walter and Zhang (2012); Witt and Redding (2013); Hamilton and Kao (2018); Doner, Noble, and Ravenhill (2021); Hamilton-Hart and Yeung (2021b); and Xing (2021).

17. Reported in Pan (2021a) and the *Straits Times*, https://www.straitstimes.com/business/top-chinese-chipmaker-gets-govt-funding-for-3b-plant, accessed on June 21, 2021. See also Layton (2021). Ezell (2021, 17–19) argued that this channeling of state capital through investment funds to domestic semiconductor firms represents an institutional attempt to avoid charges of government subsidization. In SMIC, state ownership increased from 15 percent in 2014 to 45 percent in 2018—the National IC Fund (19 percent), state-owned Datang Telecom (19 percent) and Tsinghua Unigroup (7 percent). On May 13, 2021, the South Korean government also unveiled a national blueprint to spend $450 billion over ten years to strengthen its leadership in the global chipmaking race (Kim and Kim 2021).

18. See more analysis on this investment preference in Silicon Valley in Brown and Linden (2011); Kenney (2011); and Nenni and McLellan (2019). In Brown and Linden's (2011, ch. 7) study, US IDM and fabless firms were troubled by weak financial returns—low returns, high risks—during the 2000s. See also Nenni and McLellan (2019) on fab costs during the 2010s and most IDM firms' strategy of going fab-lite, leaving heavy investment in the most advanced nodes to TSMC, Samsung, and other foundry providers.

19. See Nenni and McLellan (2019, chs. 8) for these latest technology applications beyond 2020 and Wong (2018, ch. 7) in the context of autonomous driving and smart cars.

20. See Mayersen (2020) for a discussion of the competing demands of various top fabless firms for TSMC's 7 nm production capacity in 2020. TSMC's 5 nm fab (Fab 18) in Taiwan's Tainan started mass production in mid-2020, but its initial capacity was fully taken up by Apple's A14/A14X application processor chips and Huawei's Kirin 1000 network processor chips (https://www.tsmc.com/english/dedicatedFoundry/technology/5nm.htm, accessed on May 16, 2020). For the reported list of TSMC's 5 nm fab customers from 2020 to 2022, see Tyson (2020). Samsung's 5 nm foundry also started mass production by July 2020 and competed against TSMC for leading fabless customers, such as Nvidia and AMD (Btarunr 2020).

21. These capex data do not include capital spending by firms specializing in optical semiconductors for flat panel displays in Table 4.7. To stay ahead of intense technological change and market competition, these firms—all from East Asian economies—invest heavily in new-generation plants to manufacture flat panel displays in East Asia. From about $1 billion to build a fifth-generation (G5) plant— each new generation defined by larger glass panel size—the cost has escalated rapidly to $2 billion for G7 plants, $3.3 billion for G8 plants, and $11 billion for the latest and largest-size G10–G11 plants (Lee, Kim, and Lim 2011, 720; Chen and Chen 2015, 252; Wang and Seidle 2017, 172).

22. Data from Goodman, VerWey, and Kim (2019, 8–9) and Semiconductor Equipment and Materials International (SEMI) press releases on April 13 and July 13, 2021, https://www.semi.org/en/news-media-press/semi-press-releases/annual-global-semiconductor-equipment-sales, accessed on November 1, 2021.

23. In early 2021, the most advanced EUV photolithography systems from ASML cost €200 million and its CEO Peter Wennink has likened to €200 million "photocopiers" used by cutting-edge chipmakers such as TSMC, Samsung, and Intel (Sterling 2021). Still, these EUV systems were well oversubscribed in 2021. As was noted in Chapter 5, TSMC's 3 nm fab in Tainan's Fab 18 alone required more than 50 EUV sets, but ASML produced about 31 sets in 2020 and estimated 48 sets in 2021 and up to 55 sets in 2022 (Nenni 2021; also Clark 2021). While ASML's EUV production has a long and far-reaching supply chain, some key components such as Zeiss lenses are very finite in supply and very time consuming to expand production capacity. See also van de Kerkhof, Benschop, and Banine (2019) for reflections by three senior ASML executives responsible for developing its EUV systems. In another more extreme example reported in Alpeyev and Hirano (2020), a small and highly specialized supplier—Japan's Lasertec—has developed one-of-a-kind test equipment for inspecting internal flaws in photomasks used in the latest EUV-based 7/5/3 nm nodes. At $40 million or more per piece and taking up to two years to build, the Lasertec machine can be used to inspect both blank masks and masks printed with circuit designs. Each major logic chip manufacturer, such as TSMC, Samsung, and Intel, needs at least two such machines—one in the

photomask shop for inspecting the newly made mask and another in the wafer fab for monitoring the wear and tear to the mask due to the concentrated EUV light projecting through it repeatedly in the wafer fabrication process, illustrated in Figures 4.2 and 5.2.

24. The COVID-19 pandemic has severely dampened some of these massive fab ambitions in China. In November 2020, Yangtze River's state-backed parent holding company, the Tsinghua Unigroup, faced serious liquidity problems and defaulted the $200 million principal on a $450 million bond. The Tsinghua Unigroup had $31 billion in debt, half of which will mature by 2022. In another case of local state-funded investment in a planned $20 billion fab by Wuhan Hongxin, partial fab construction was stalled in July 2020 due to underfunding from its majority owner in Beijing, and there was no plan to resume work and production in 2021. See reports in Bray (2020); Ezell (2021); Horwitz (2021); and Zhang (2021).

25. See reports in Kim and Kim (2021); Lee and Yang (2021b); and Reuters, June 2, 2021, https://www.reuters.com/technology/tsmc-says-construction-has-started-arizona-chip-factory-2021-06-01, accessed on June 21, 2021. Slightly earlier on March 29, 2021, SK Hynix also announced a $106 billion project to build a new semiconductor fabrication complex with four fabs in South Korea's Yongin (south of Seoul), starting production in the first fab in 2025 (http://www.koreaherald.com/view.php?ud=20210329000989&A, accessed on June 21, 2021). This is in addition to its $97 billion commitment to expansion at existing facilities. Altogether, South Korea will spend $450 billion on nonmemory semiconductor manufacturing through 2030. Under a national blueprint by President Moon Jae-in announced on May 13, 2021, the massive investment will be funded by both private firms, such as Samsung and SK Hynix, and government tax credits.

26. See report in King (2021). Historically, Intel had a small foundry business with revenue above $100 million in 2006–2007 and 2014–2018 (IHS Markit/Informa Tech Custom Research for GPN@NUS Centre, July–October 2019).

27. Reported in Jewell (2021).

28. Data from Nenni (2021).

29. Empirical evidence seems to support such an investment preference by venture capital and Wall Street bankers. Shin, Kraemer, and Dedrick's (2017) work confirms that during the 2000–2010 period, fabless firms achieved higher profit margins and return on assets than IDM firms, after controlling for size, capital intensity, and R&D ratio (R&D/sales).

30. See TSMC's announcement on the Arizona fab: https://www.tsmc.com and https://www.eetimes.com/tsmc-to-build-5nm-fab-in-arizona, accessed on May 16, 2020. See also updates in Cheng and Li (2021) and Reuters, June 2, 2021, https://www.reuters.com/technology/tsmc-says-construction-has-started-arizona-chip-factory-2021-06-01, accessed on June 21, 2021.

31. Shin et al.'s (2012, 2013) studies show that ODM firms from Taiwan managed to achieve positive return on equity during the 2002–2009 period, despite negative return on equity for the global electronics industry as a whole during the 2000–2005 period. To Shin, Kraemer, and Dedrick (2012, 99), these results illustrate "how brutally competitive the electronics industry is."

32. Apple's business model of complete outsourcing to Taiwan's EMS providers in the context of financialization is instructive here. See Froud et al. (2012); Haslam et al. (2013); and Xing (2021, ch. 7) on how Apple's profitability is critically dependent on its exercise of lead firm power over its suppliers that in turn allows Apple to extract financial "point values" from its global production network. See Yeung (2016, 106–7) for the strategic relationship between Apple and Foxconn (Hon Hai Precision in Taiwan).

33. The same disruption to global automotive chip supply happened in 2021 because of the winter storm–induced shutdown of NXP fab in Austin (Texas) in February 2021 and Renesas's Naka (Japan) fab fire in March 2021.

34. Interviews with senior executives of semiconductor lead firms SE-32 and SE-43.

35. See Chu (2013, ch. 5) for a full discussion of this cross-Strait geopolitical issue during the 2000s. Into the 2020s, this geopolitical tension remains very significant. In mid-May 2021, the Chinese government's Xinhua News Agency had to publish an op-ed to warn against domestic "chip nationalism" in the context of the rising discontent on Chinese social media against TSMC's plan to invest $2.9 billion to double its Nanjing Fab 16 capacity. The plan had been approved earlier by TSMC's board of directors on April 23, 2021. Prominent critics in China claimed that TSMC was trying to "dump" its trailing-edge 16–28 nm chips on China to outcompete its Chinese rivals such as SMIC and Huali (Ye 2021b).

36. Information from interviews with senior executives of semiconductor lead firms SE-30 and SE-43. This Fab 12X in Xiamen was a three-way joint venture between UMC, Xiamen Municipal People's Government, and Fujian Electronics & Information Group, with $300 million initial investment from HeJian Technology and $450 million from UMC. The subsidy from Xiamen Government for Fab 12X was given on the condition that Fab 12X will offer lower prices to local Chinese fabless customers and use their photomask-making suppliers. By 2017, UMC increased its share of Fab 12X from the initial one-third to a controlling stake of 51 percent.

37. Coupled with Singapore's strong government support and ecosystem for semiconductor manufacturing, this geopolitical risk factor also explains why GlobalFoundries announced on June 22, 2021, that it will invest another $4 billion to expand its Singapore Fab 7 capacity by 0.45 million wafers per year by 2023. This new capital expenditure in Singapore will double its planned investment of

$1 billion each for its existing fabs in the US and Germany. See Choo (2021) and https://globalfoundries.com/press-release/globalfoundries-breaks-ground-new-fab-singapore, accessed on June 23, 2021.

38. In the early 2020s, this import control remained difficult for foreign firms in India. In May 2021, top OEM firms in PCs (Dell, HP, and Lenovo) and smartphones (Xiaomi, Oppo, and Vivo) had to delay their product launches in India due to the hold-up in the Communications Ministry's approvals for at least eighty pending applications for import of Wi-Fi modules from China since November 2020 or earlier. As Chapter 5 has examined, these wireless connectivity modules are core components in PCs and smartphones. This mandatory approval was implemented in March 2019 to replace the previous system of domestic and foreign firms self-declaring their import of wireless equipment. Industry lobby groups believed such regulatory delays underscored India's strategy for greater economic self-reliance and curbing Chinese imports (Phartiyal 2021a).

## Chapter 7

1. The rise of this "platform economy" has been closely associated with the greater significance of software and digital ecosystems mostly located in Silicon Valley and/or controlled by Silicon Valley firms (see Kenney and Zysman 2016, 2020; Parker, Van Alstyne, and Choudary 2016; McAfee and Brynjolfsson 2017; Guillén 2021). A few exceptions in the US are Amazon and Microsoft in Seattle and IBM in New York, whereas China now also hosts several major platform firms such as Alibaba, Baidu, ByteDance, and Tencent.

2. See also Kawagami and Sturgeon (2011); Lüthje et al. (2013); Drahokoupil, Andrijasevic, and Sacchetto (2016); Yap and Rasiah (2017); K. Lee (2019); Liu (2020); and Xing (2021).

3. See my earlier monograph *Strategic Coupling* (Yeung 2016) for a detail consideration of East Asian industrial transformation through the participation of domestic firms in global production networks. Liu (2020) offers a more recent work on the importance of strategic coupling for industrial upgrading in China's Pearl River delta.

4. As Krugman (1994, 31) famously argued sometime ago, "When we say that a corporation is uncompetitive, we mean that its market position is unsustainable—that unless it improves its performance, it will cease to exist. Countries, on the other hand, do not go out of business. They may be happy or unhappy with their economic performance, but they have no well-defined bottom line." See also Reich (1990, 1991).

5. See these works cited in Chapter 1 endnotes 58–61.

6. Information from interviews with senior executives of leading IDM and fabless firms supplying to automotive OEM firms (see firm list in Appendix B Table B1). In late 2020 and throughout 2021, however, the practice of just-in-

time production and opaque demand planning and sourcing in the automotive industry and the underinvestment in the mature nodes (40–180 nm) of legacy fabs among chip makers contributed to a severe global chip shortage that threatened car production worldwide. The industry would likely lose 7.7 million units or 10 percent of total production and at least $210 billion in sales in 2021. In April 2021, lead time for power management chips increased to 24 weeks and microcontrollers for another four weeks (Hu and Pan 2021; King and Wu 2021; Reuters 2021; Wayland 2021; Wu, Coppola, and Naughton 2021). This global chip shortage was also partly due to the understocking of logic chips outsourced by automotive chip suppliers to East Asian foundry providers, such as TSMC, whose existing capacity had already been taken up by the much larger demand from—and higher prices paid by—fabless firms for PC and smartphone chips during and after the COVID-19 pandemic. In early 2021, even the German economic minister had to ask his Taiwanese counterpart to seek additional capacity at TSMC for German automotive chip suppliers (Nienaber 2021). Meanwhile, Europe's second largest producer of automotive chips, STMicroelectronics, had to resort to price hike across product lines in June 2021 to address this unprecedented demand from automotive makers and the rising materials costs (Pan 2021b). Chapters 4 and 5 discussed such outsourcing of logic chips by Texas Instruments, Renesas, and top European automotive chip makers, such as Infineon, NXP, and STMicroelectronics. As Burkacky et al.'s (2021) McKinsey report noted, this automotive chip shortage cannot be resolved in the short term as capacity reallocation is difficult and capacity growth at foundry and/or IDM fabs will take several years. Solving this long-term problem requires a fundamental rethink of the existing sourcing and supply chain practices of automakers and their tiered-one suppliers (e.g., by moving to 6–12 months of upfront purchase order and volume commitments).

7. On April 7, 2020, Japan announced a $2.2 billion fund in its record $992 billion economic stimulus package to subsidize the cost of Japanese manufacturers shifting their production from China back to Japan (Reynolds and Urabe 2020). A small proportion of this fund, about 10 percent, was earmarked for those shifting from China to other countries, such as Southeast Asia where extensive Japanese production networks had been developed for decades (see Hatch and Yamamura 1996; Hatch 2010). While Larry Kudlow and Peter Navarro, respectively director of the National Economic Council and White House trade advisor in the former Trump administration, had been arguing for a similar approach to paying US manufacturing firms reshoring from China, the US has no formal corporate repatriation programs as of end May 2020 (Rapoza 2020). First discussed informally at the height of the pandemic in July 2020, the Supply Chain Resilience Initiative by Australia, India, and Japan was launched in April 2021 as a means of trade diversification to reduce their dependence on China (Tan and Wong 2021).

8. See Ezell (2021, 46–47); Fromer (2021); and Layton (2021). Chapter 6 has already noted that Intel planned to invest $20 billion in 2021 to build two advanced foundry fabs in its Chandler campus in Arizona. This initiative will likely be a beneficiary of the $52 billion funding for the CHIPS for America Act 2020.

9. Reported in Drozdiak (2021). In Chapter 4 and Table 4.1, I noted that Europe's share in total fab capacity was only about 6 percent in 2018, even slightly less than Singapore's capacity. The EU's new goal for 2030 therefore seems rather daunting.

10. Data from World Economic Forum (2020, Figure 0.1, 12). The report was based on a perception survey between April 1 and 13, 2020, of nearly 350 senior risk professionals in business, government, civil society, and academia who were asked to rank the top risks to the world and business up to the end of 2021. See also McKinsey Global Institute's (2020) report.

11. Data on trade from World Trade Organization's (2021) end March press release, https://www.wto.org/english/news_e/pres21_e/pr876_e.htm, accessed on June 21, 2021.

12. FDI data from UNCTAD (2021) and GDP data from OECD (2021).

13. As Chapter 6 has indicated, Samsung closed its last mobile handset factories in China's Tianjin in December 2018 and Huizhou in October 2019.

14. See Wu's (2020) report.

15. See Neumann's (2021) report. This realignment toward nearshoring or onshoring of supply chains and investments close to home in Asia was also noted in a poll of 800 business leaders from across the Asia Pacific region in the first quarter of 2021 by Baker McKenzie (reported in S. L. Tan 2021).

16. My follow-up interview in Singapore, August 2019.

17. Quoted in Duhigg and Bradsher (2012); see also Pisano and Shih (2009, 2012); Grimes and Sun (2016); and Xing (2021).

18. The following discussion is based on reports in Bermingham (2020); Goh (2020); Qu and Chen (2021); Mullen (2021); Shepherd (2021); and Wang (2021a, 2021b); and the White House press release on June 8, 2021, https://www.white house.gov/briefing-room/statements-releases/2021/06/08/fact-sheet-biden -harris-administration-announces-supply-chain-disruptions-task-force-to-address -short-term-supply-chain-discontinuities, accessed on June 23, 2021.

19. McKinsey Global Institute (2020, 59) found that only 13 percent of all traded goods in manufacturing industries were exported from low-wage to high-wage countries. Other competitive dynamics mattered more than labor-cost arbitrage, such as supplier ecosystems, proximity to major markets, access to skilled talent and resources, and supportive business environment.

20. UNCTAD (2021, ch. IV, 169–73); see also Contractor (2021) for an analysis of supply chain resilience in the postpandemic world and Burkacky, Lingemann, and Pototzky (2021) for a case study of the automotive industry.

21. Quoted in Cheng, Li, and Kawase (2020). See also Ezell (2021).

22. As was mentioned in Chapter 6 and Table C5 in Appendix C, SMIC's new $2.3 billion fab in Shenzhen operational by 2022 will focus on mature process technologies at 28 nm or above.

23. Intel CEO Patrick Gelsinger (2021) also noted recently that its first 7 nm CPU chip, Meteor Lake, would only be shipped in 2023.

24. See Apple's case in Haselton (2020) and Apple's press release, https://support.apple.com/en-sg/HT211814, accessed on January 13, 2021, and Intel and TSMC in Hille (2021); Nellis (2021); and Nellis and Bera (2021). Details on Intel and TSMC fabs in 2020–2022 are in Table 4.2.

25. For more details on this concept as a causal mechanism for industrial transformation and economic development, see Yeung (2016). Much has been written about how such strategic coupling or "plugging in" can be possible. See recent reviews of the literature in Yeung (2015, 2021a); McGrath (2018); Coe and Yeung (2019); Kano, Tsang, and Yeung (2020); and Coe (2021).

26. See also Narula (2020); UNCTAD (2020, ch. IV; 2021, ch. IV); Contractor (2021); Shepherd (2021); and Solingen (2021).

27. Borak (2021) and Phartiyal (2021b) reported that Apple's three EMS suppliers, Foxconn, Wistron, and Pegatron, have altogether committed $900 million through to 2025 to assemble iPhones in India, leveraging the country's $6.7 billion Production Linked Incentive scheme for boosting smartphone exports by hardware makers.

28. As of June 15, 2021, this landmark investment agreement faced political obstacles in the European Parliament due to member states' objection to China's sanctions imposed on European individuals and entities in March 2021. Any ratification of the agreement might not take place until at least 2023 (Lee 2021).

29. In India, for example, billionaire Mukesh Ambani's Reliance Industries recently entered into a deal with Google in July 2020 to develop an inexpensive Google-powered smartphone for the Indian market. But severe supply chain constraints in chipsets, displays, and other components from China caused delays from 2 to 6 months in 2021, forcing Reliance to lower its launch target in late 2021 to much less than the 200 millions units originally planned for 2022–2023 (Rai 2021).

30. See reports in Marley and Stein (2017); Zumbach (2020); and Bauerlein (2021).

31. See plant costs in Chapter 6 endnote 21: a G6 panel display plant would cost "only" about $1–$2 billion, as compared to $11 billion for a G10–11 plant.

32. Reported in Chen (2021).

33. See Ibata-Arens's (2019) *Beyond Technonationalism* for a similar argument in the context of innovation and entrepreneurship in the global biomedical industry in Asia and Breznitz's (2021) *Innovation in Real Places* for a contrarian take on the different routes to innovation and prosperity (see also Y. Tan 2021). Solingen's

(2021) collection reflects critically on the hidden costs of geopolitical shocks and trade wars in light of interdependent global supply chains.

34. See references cited in Chapter 1 endnotes 58 and 61. Recent examples are Campbell-Kelly and Garcia-Swartz (2015) and O'Mara (2019) on the US; Sun and Grimes (2017); Yap and Rasiah (2017); and Xing (2021) on China and East Asia; and Woyke (2014); McNish and Silcoff (2015); and Giachetti (2018) on smartphones.

35. See also Coe's (2021) advanced introductory text and recent GVC collections in De Marchi, Di Maria, and Gereffi (2018); Gereffi (2018); and Ponte, Gereffi, and Raj-Reichert (2019).

36. Some examples are Froud et al. (2012); Haslam et al. (2013); Lange et al. (2013); and Shin, Kraemer, and Dedrick (2017).

37. See references to this large literature cited in Chapter 1 endnote 54.

38. See K. Lee (2013, 2019) and Oqubay and Ohno (2019) for the recent literature on technological learning and capability, and Jacobides, Cennamo, and Gawer (2018); Teece (2018); Kenney and Zysman (2020); Guillén (2021); and Sturgeon (2021) for the recent work on the digital platform economy.

39. See examples in De Prato, Nepelski, and Simon (2013); De Marchi, Di Maria, and Gereffi (2018); Lema, Rabellotti, and Sampath (2018); Ponte, Gereffi, and Raj-Reichert (2019); and Buciuni and Pisano (2021).

40. See Jacobides, Cennamo, and Gawer (2018); Teece (2018); Kenney and Zysman (2020); and Guillén (2021).

41. See Lan, Liu, and Dong (2019); Grabher and van Tuijl (2020); Butollo (2021); and Sturgeon (2021) on power relations in industrial platforms and Coe and Yeung (2015) on value capture trajectories and strategic coupling possibilities.

42. While risk is quite well conceived in the supply chain management literature, very few publications on global value chains in the social sciences have explicitly examined risk. See Gereffi and Luo (2014) and Schwabe (2020) for some discussion of the different firm-level risk mitigation mechanisms in global value chains. Linton and Vakil (2020); McKinsey Global Institute (2020); Panwar (2020); Shih (2020); Contractor (2021); and Hitt, Holmes, and Arregle (2021) have examined risk and mitigation before and after the COVID-19 pandemic from the perspective of business policy.

43. See also Kano and Oh (2020); Strange (2020); Verbeke (2020); Contractor (2021); and Shepherd (2021).

44. In UNCTAD's (2020, Table I.2, 6) world investment report, the ICT sector reported one of the lowest average revisions to earning as of May 11, 2020. At -20 percent, it is much better than automotive (-50 percent), apparel (-49 percent), machinery (-39 percent), and the averages in manufacturing (-34 percent), primary (-65 percent), and services (-35 percent). Only medical supplies (-14 percent) and food (-15 percent) had slightly better averages.

45. Reported by Reuters, May 11, 2021, https://www.reuters.com/technology/exclusive-foxconn-iphone-india-output-drops-50-amid-covid-surge-sources-2021-05-11, accessed on June 21, 2021; and Borak (2021) and Phartiyal (2021b).

46. See Levy (2008) for an early conceptualization of political contestation in global production networks. Much of the later work in the global value chains literature has taken on this contestation in the form of corporate social responsibility, multistakeholder initiatives, and labor conflicts in lead firm-supplier relationships (see recent book-length examples in Pickles and Smith 2016; Bartley 2018; Ponte 2019; and Barrientos 2019). While few papers have conceptualized changing state roles in global production networks (Yeung 2014; Smith 2015; Horner 2017), some recent studies have examined state-level politics and mutual constraints in relation to the changing organization and governance of global production networks (e.g., Farrell and Newman 2014, 2019; Neilson, Pritchard, and Yeung 2014; Mayer and Phillips 2017; Kim and Spilker 2019; Narula 2020; Dallas, Horner, and Lee 2021; Gereffi, Lim, and Lee 2021; Hitt, Holmes, and Arregle 2021; Solingen 2021). See Yeung (2016) for a book-length analysis of the politics of industrial transformation through strategic coupling with global production networks in East Asia. More recent work can be found in Hamilton-Hart and Yeung's (2021a) special issue.

47. These nationalist initiatives range widely from Prime Minister Narendra Modi's "Made in India" launched on September 25, 2014, to Premier Li Keqiang's "Made in China 2025" plan unveiled on May 19, 2015, and former president Donald Trump's "Made in America" executive order signed on July 15, 2019.

48. See Maire (2021b) and Chapter 6 endnote 25 for details on these firm spending and state funding.

# References

Aichele, Rahel, and Inga Heiland. 2018. "Where Is the Value Added? Trade Liberalization and Production Networks." *Journal of International Economics* 115: 130–44.

Alpeyev, Pavel, and Kazu Hirano. 2020. "Japan's Hottest Stock Is Tiny Maker of $40 Million Machines." *Bloomberg*, May 26. https://www.bloomberg.com/news/articles/2020-05-25/japan-s-hottest-stock-is-tiny-maker-of-40-million-chip-machines, accessed on November 15, 2020.

Amsden, Alice H. 1989. *Asia's Next Giant: South Korea and Late Industrialization.* New York: Oxford University Press.

Amsden, Alice H., and Wan-Wen Chu. 2003. *Beyond Late Development: Taiwan's Upgrading Policies.* Cambridge, MA: MIT Press.

Anchordoguy, Marie. 1989. *Computers, Inc.: Japan's Challenge to IBM.* Cambridge, MA: Harvard University Press.

Angel, David P. 1994. *Restructuring for Innovation: The Remaking of the U.S. Semiconductor Industry.* New York: Guilford.

Angel, David P., and James Engstrom. 1995. "Manufacturing Systems and Technological Change: The U.S. Personal Computer Industry." *Economic Geography* 71 (1): 79–102.

Antràs, Pol. 2005. "Incomplete Contracts and the Product Cycle." *American Economic Review* 95 (4): 1054–73.

Antràs, Pol. 2016. *Global Production: Firms, Contracts, and Trade Structure*, Princeton, NJ: Princeton University Press.

Antràs, Pol, and Davin Chor. 2013. "Organizing the Global Value Chain." *Econometrica* 81 (6): 2127–204.

Antràs, Pol, and Elhanan Helpman. 2004. "Global Sourcing." *Journal of Political Economy* 112: 552–80.

Appelbaum, Richard P. 2008. "Giant Transnational Contractors in East Asia: Emergent Trends in Global Supply Chains." *Competition and Change* 12 (1): 69–87.

Arndt, Sven W., and Henryk Kierzkowski, eds. 2001. *Fragmentation: New Production Patterns in the World Economy.* Oxford: Oxford University Press.

Asheim, Bjørn T., Philip Cooke, and Ron Martin, eds. 2006. *Clusters and Regional Development.* London: Routledge.

Baccini, Leonardo, Andreas Dür, and Manfred Elsig. 2018. "Intra-industry Trade, Global Value Chains, and Preferential Tariff Liberalization." *International Studies Quarterly* 62 (2): 329–40.

Bair, Jennifer, ed. 2009. *Frontiers of Commodity Chain Research.* Stanford, CA: Stanford University Press.

Baldwin, Carliss Y. and Kim B. Clark. 2000. *Design Rules: The Power of Modularity.* Cambridge, MA: MIT Press.

Baldwin, Richard. 2016. *The Great Convergence: Information Technology and the New Globalization.* Cambridge, MA: Belknap Press of Harvard University Press.

Baldwin, Richard and Anthony J. Venables. 2013. "Spiders and Snakes: Offshoring and Agglomeration in the Global Economy." *Journal of International Economics* 90 (2): 245–54.

Barnes, Tom. 2018. *Making Cars in the New India: Industry, Precarity and Informality.* New Delhi: Cambridge University Press.

Barnett, Clive, Paul Cloke, Nick Clarke, and Alice Malpass. 2011. *Globalizing Responsibility: The Political Rationalities of Ethical Consumption.* Oxford: Wiley-Blackwell.

Barney, Jay B. 1991. "Firm Resources and Sustained Competitive Advantage." *Journal of Management* 17 (1):99–120.

Barney, Jay B. 2001. "Resource-Based Theories of Competitive Advantage: A Ten-Year Retrospective on the Resource-Based View." *Journal of Management* 27 (6): 643–50.

Barrientos, Stephanie. 2019. *Gender and Work in Global Value Chains: Capturing the Gains?* New Delhi: Cambridge University Press.

Barrientos, Stephanie, and Catherine Dolan, eds. 2006. *Ethical Sourcing in the Global Food System.* London: Earthscan.

Bartley, Tim. 2018. *Rules Without Rights: Land, Labor, and Private Authority in the Global Economy.* New York: Oxford University Press.

Bashe, Charles J., Lyle R. Johnson, John H. Palmer, and Emerson W. Pugh. 1986. *IBM's Early Computers: A Technical History.* Cambridge, MA: MIT Press.

Basole, Rahul C., and Jürgen Karla. 2011. "On the Evolution of Mobile Platform Ecosystem Structure and Strategy." *Business & Information Systems Engineering* 3 (5): 313–22.

Bauerlein, Valerie. 2021. "Foxconn Shrinks Plans for Wisconsin Plant." *Wall Street Journal,* April 20, https://www.wsj.com/articles/foxconn-shrinks-plans-for -wisconsin-plant-11618959964, accessed on July 1, 2021.

Benito, Gabriel R. G., Bent Petersen, and Lawrence S. Welch. 2019. "The Global Value Chain and Internalization Theory." *Journal of International Business Studies* 50 (8): 1414–23.

Berlin, Leslie. 2005. *The Man Behind the Microchip: Robert Noyce and the Invention of Silicon Valley.* New York: Oxford University Press.

Bermingham, Finbarr. 2020. "Trump Has Called on US Firms to Leave China, but No Mass Exodus among "Well-Rooted' Companies." *South China Morning Post,* September 9, https://www.scmp.com/economy/china-economy/ article/3100793/trump-has-called-us-firms-leave-china-no-mass-exodus- among, accessed on January 13, 2021.

Birkinshaw, Julian, and Peter Hagström. 2002. *The Flexible Firm: Capability Management in Network Organizations.* Oxford: Oxford University Press.

Borak, Masha. 2021. "Apple's Attempt to Diversify Manufacturing to India Is Being Stymied by New Delhi's Coronavirus Crisis." *South China Morning Post,* May 11, https://www.scmp.com/tech/big-tech/article/3132944/apples-at- tempt-diversify-manufacturing-india-being-stymied-new-delhis, accessed on June 21, 2021.

Borrus, Michael G. 1988. *Competing for Control: America's Stake in Microelectronics.* Cambridge, MA: Ballinger.

Borrus, Michael, Dieter Ernst, and Stephan Haggard, eds. 2000. *International Production Networks in Asia: Rivalry or Riches.* London: Routledge.

Borrus, Michael, and John Zysman. 1997. "Globalization with Borders: The Rise of Wintelism as the Future of Global Competition." *Industry and Innovation* 4 (2): 141–66.

Braun, Ernest, and Stuart MacDonald. 1982. *Revolution in Miniature: The History and Impact of Semiconductor Electronics,* 2nd ed. Cambridge: Cambridge University Press.

Bray, Chad. 2020. "China Chip Maker Tsinghua Unigroup to Default on US$450 Million Bond as Concerns Mount over Debt Levels on Mainland." *South China Morning Post,* December 10, https://www.scmp.com/business/ banking-finance/article/3113357/china-chip-maker-tsinghua-unigroup-default -us450-million, accessed on January 2, 2021.

Breschi, Stefano, and Franco Malerba, eds. 2005. *Clusters, Networks and Innovation*. Oxford: Oxford University Press.

Bresnahan, Timothy, and Alfonso Gambardella, eds. 2004. *Building High-Tech Clusters: Silicon Valley and Beyond*. Cambridge: Cambridge University Press.

Breznitz, Dan. 2007. *Innovation and the State: Political Choice and Strategies for Growth in Israel, Taiwan, and Ireland*. New Haven, CT: Yale University Press.

Breznitz, Dan. 2021. *Innovation in Real Places: Strategies for Prosperity in an Unforgiving World*. New York: Oxford University Press.

Brown, Clair, and Greg Linden. 2011. *Chips and Change: How Crisis Reshapes the Semiconductor Industry*. Cambridge, MA: MIT Press.

Btarunr. 2020. "Samsung Expands Its Foundry Capacity with a New Production Line in Pyeongtaek." *TechPowerUp*, May 21, https://www.techpowerup.com/267435/samsung-expands-its-foundry-capacity-with-a-new-production-line-in-pyeongtaek, accessed on June 12, 2020.

Buciuni, Giulio, and Gary Pisano. 2021. "Variety of Innovation in Global Value Chains." *Journal of World Business* 56 (2): 101167.

Buckley, Peter J. 2009. "The Impact of the Global Factory on Economic Development." *Journal of World Business* 44 (2): 131–43.

Buckley, Peter J., and Roger Strange. 2015. "The Governance of the Global Factory: Location and Control of World Economic Activity." *Academy of Management Perspectives* 29 (2): 237–49.

Burgelman, Robert A., Webb McKinney, and Philip E. Meza. 2017. *Becoming Hewlett Packard: Why Strategic Leadership Matters*. New York: Oxford University Press.

Burkacky, Ondrej, Stephanie Lingemann, and Klaus Pototzky. 2021. *Coping with the Auto-Semiconductor Shortage: Strategies for Success*. May, McKinsey & Company, https://www.mckinsey.com/industries/automotive-and-assembly/our-insights/coping-with-the-auto-semiconductor-shortage-strategies-for-success, accessed on June 25, 2021.

Burt, Ronald S., and Giuseppe Soda. 2021. "Network Capabilities: Brokerage as a Bridge between Network Theory and the Resource-Based View of the Firm." *Journal of Management* 47 (7): 1698–719.

Büthe, Tim, and Walter Mattli. 2011. *The New Global Rulers: The Privatization of Regulation in the World Economy*. Princeton, NJ: Princeton University Press.

Butollo, Florian. 2021. "Digitalization and the Geographies of Production: Towards Reshoring or Global Fragmentation?" *Competition and Change* 25 (2): 259–78.

Caliskan, Koray, and Michel Callon. 2010. "Economization, Part 2: A Research Programme for the Study of Markets." *Economy and Society* 38 (3): 369–98.

Campbell-Kelly, Martin. 2003. *A History of the Software Industry: From Airline Reservations to Sonic the Hedgehog*. Cambridge, MA: MIT Press.

Campbell-Kelly, Martin, and Daniel Garcia-Swartz. 2015. *From Mainframes to Smartphones: A History of the International Computer Industry*. Cambridge, MA: Harvard University Press.

Čaněk, Marek. 2016. "Building the European Centre in Czechia: Foxconn's Local Integration in Regional and Global Labour Markets." In *Flexible Workforces and Low Profit Margins: Electronics Assembly Between Europe and China*, edited by Jan Drahokoupil, Rutvica Andrijasevic and Devi Sacchetto, 95–112. Brussels: European Trade Union Institute.

Casadesus-Masanell, Ramon, and David B. Yoffie. 2007. "Wintel: Cooperation and Conflict." *Management Science* 53 (4): 584–98.

Cassia, Lucio. 2010. *Global Outsourcing Strategies: The Internationalisation of the Electronics Industry*. Cheltenham, UK: Edward Elgar.

Castellano, Joseph A. 2005. *Liquid Gold: The Story of Liquid Crystal Displays and the Creation of an Industry*. Singapore: World Scientific.

Cattaneo, Olivier, Gary Gereffi, and Cornelia Staritz, eds. 2010. *Global Value Chains in a Postcrisis World*. Washington, DC: World Bank.

Cawson, Alan, Kevin, Morgan, Douglas, Webber, Peter Holmes, and Anne Stevens. 1990. *Hostile Brothers: Competition and Closure in the European Electronics Industry*. Oxford: Clarendon Press.

Chandler, Alfred D. 2001. *Inventing the Electronic Century: The Epic Story of the Consumer Electronics and Computer Industries*. New York: Free Press.

Chang, Ha-Joon. 2003. *Globalisation, Economic Development, and the Role of the State*. London: Zed Books.

Chang, Ha-Joon, and Antonio Andreoni. 2020. "Industrial Policy in the 21st Century." *Development and Change* 51 (2): 324–51.

Chang, Ha-Joon, and Ilene Grabel. 2014. *Reclaiming Development: An Alternative Economic Policy Manual*. London: Zed.

Chang, Sea-jin. 2008. *Sony Versus Samsung: The Inside Story of Electronics Giants' Battle for Global Supremacy*. Singapore: Wiley.

Chen, Celia. 2020a. "Harmony OS: Everything You Need to Know about Huawei's Android Alternative." *South China Morning Post*, October 7, https://www.scmp.com/tech/gear/article/3104176/harmony-os-everything-you-need-know-about-huaweis-android-alternative, accessed on December 14, 2020.

Chen, Celia. 2020b. "Huawei's Former Budget Smartphone Unit Honor Sets Aggressive Targets for 2021, but Still Needs Greenlight from US." *South China Morning Post*, December 22, https://www.scmp.com/tech/big-tech/article/3114975/huaweis-former-budget-smartphone-unit-honor-sets-aggressive-targets, accessed on December 31, 2020.

Chen, Celia, and Matt Haldane. 2021. "Will Huawei's Harmony Operating System End the Global Duopoly of Google's Android and Apple's iOS?" *South

*China Morning Post,* June 4, https://www.scmp.com/tech/big-tech/article/3136017/will-huaweis-harmony-operating-system-end-global-duopoly-googles, accessed on June 23, 2021.

Chen, Frank. 2021. "TSMC Founder Doubts US Competence in Chip-Making." *Asia Times,* April 24, https://asiatimes.com/2021/04/tsmc-founder-doubts-us-competence-in-chip-making, accessed on June 24, 2021.

Chen, Jian-Hung, and Yijen Chen. 2015. "New Industry Creation in Less Developed Countries—The Case of the Taiwanese Flat Panel Display Industry." *Innovation* 17 (2): 250–65.

Chen, Tain-Jy, and Ying-Hua Ku. 2014. "Indigenous Innovation vs. Teng-Long Huan-Niao: Policy Conflicts in the Development of China's Flat Panel Industry." *Industrial and Corporate Change* 23 (6): 1445–67.

Cheng, Ting-Fang, Lauly Li, and Kenji Kawase. 2020. "China's Top Chipmaker SMIC Cuts Spending Due to US Export Curbs." *Nikkei Asia,* November 12, https://asia.nikkei.com/Economy/Trade-war/China-s-top-chipmaker-SMIC-cuts-spending-due-to-US-export-curbs, accessed on January 13, 2021.

Cheng, Ting-Fang, and Lauly Li. 2021. "TSMC Hikes Capex to Record $28bn as Chip Race Heats Up." *Nikkei Asia,* January 14, https://asia.nikkei.com/Business/Electronics/TSMC-hikes-capex-to-record-28bn-as-chip-race-heats-up, accessed on January 22, 2021.

Choi, Youngrak. 1996. *Dynamic Techno-Management Capability: The Case of Samsung Semiconductor in Korea.* Aldershot, UK: Ashgate.

Choo, Yun Ting. 2021. "Chip Giant GlobalFoundries to Build New $5.4 Billion Plant in S'pore, Add 1,000 High-Value Jobs." *Straits Times,* June 22, https://www.straitstimes.com/business/chips-giant-globalfoundries-to-increase-capacity-in-spore-add-1000-high-value-jobs, accessed on June 23, 2021.

Chor, Davin. 2019. "Modelling Global Value Chains: Approaches and Insights from Economics." In *Handbook of Global Value Chains,* edited by Stefano Ponte, Gary Gereffi, and Gale Raj-Reichert, 105–19. Cheltenham, UK: Edward Elgar.

Chu, Ming-chin Monique. 2013. *The East Asian Computer Chip War.* London: Routledge.

Clark, Don. 2021. "The Tech Cold War's "Most Complicated Machine' Is Out of China's Reach." *New York Times,* July 4, https://www.nytimes.com/2021/07/04/technology/tech-cold-war-chips.html?action=click&module=Top%20Stories&pgtype=Homepage, accessed on July 5, 2021.

Coe, Neil M. 2021. *Advanced Introduction to Global Production Networks.* Cheltenham, UK: Edward Elgar.

Coe, Neil M., Peter Dicken, and Martin Hess. 2008. "Global Production Networks: Realizing the Potential." *Journal of Economic Geography* 8 (3): 271–95.

Coe, Neil M., and Martin Hess. 2011. "Local and Regional Development: A Global Production Network Approach." In *Handbook of Local and Regional Development*, edited by Andy Pike, Andrés Rodríguez-Pose and John Tomaney, 128–38. London: Routledge.

Coe, Neil, Martin Hess, Henry Wai-chung Yeung, Peter Dicken, and Jeffrey Henderson. 2004. "'Globalizing' Regional Development: A Global Production Networks Perspective." *Transactions of the Institute of British Geographers* 29 (4): 468–84.

Coe, Neil M., and Henry Wai-chung Yeung. 2015. *Global Production Networks: Theorizing Economic Development in an Interconnected World*. Oxford: Oxford University Press.

Coe, Neil M., and Henry Wai-chung Yeung. 2019. "Global Production Networks: Mapping Recent Conceptual Developments." *Journal of Economic Geography* 19 (4): 775–801.

Contractor, Farok J. 2021. "The World Economy Will Need *Even More* Globalization in the Post-pandemic 2021 Decade." *Journal of International Business Studies*, advance online publication, https://link.springer.com/article/10.1057/s41267-020-00394-y

Cortada, James W. 1993. *Before the Computer: IBM, NCR, Burroughs, and Remington Rand and the Industry They Created, 1865–1956*. Princeton, NJ: Princeton University Press.

Curtis, Philip J. 1994. *The Fall of the US Consumer Electronics Industry: An American Trade Tragedy*. New York: Praeger.

Cusumano, Michael A. 2004. *The Business of Software*. New York: Free Press.

Cyhn, Jin W. 2002. *Technology Transfer and International Production: The Development of the Electronics Industry in Korea*. Cheltenham, UK: Edward Elgar.

Dallas, Mark P., Rory Horner, and Lantian Li. 2021. "The Mutual Constraints of States and Global Value Chains during COVID-19: The Case of Personal Protective Equipment." *World Development* 139: 105324.

Dallas, Mark, Stefano Ponte, and Tim Sturgeon. 2019. "Power in Global Value Chains." *Review of International Political Economy* 26 (4): 666–94.

Daviron, Benoît, and Stefano Ponte. 2005. *The Coffee Paradox: Global Markets, Commodity Trade and the Elusive Promise of Development*. London: Zed Books.

Davis, Gerald F. 2009. *Managed by the Markets: How Finance Reshaped America*. New York: Oxford University Press.

De Marchi, Valentina, Di Maria, Eleonora and Gereffi, Gary, eds. 2018. *Local Clusters in Global Value Chains: Linking Actors and Territories Through Manufacturing and Innovation*. London: Routledge.

De Prato, Giuditta and Daniel Nepelski. 2013. "Internationalization of ICT R&D: A Comparative Analysis of Asia, the EU, Japan, the U.S., and the

RoW." In *Asia in the Global ICT Innovation Network: Dancing with the Tigers*, edited by Giuditta De Prato, Daniel Nepelski and Jean Simon, 147–78. Oxford: Chandos.

De Prato, Giuditta, Daniel Nepelski, and Jean Simon, eds. 2013. *Asia in the Global ICT Innovation Network: Dancing with the Tigers*. Oxford: Chandos.

de Reuver, Mark, Carsten Sørensen, and Rahul C. Basole. 2018. "The Digital Platform: A Research Agenda." *Journal of Information Technology* 33 (2): 124–35.

Dedrick, Jason, and Kenneth Kraemer. 1998. *Asia's Computer Challenge: Threat or Opportunity for the United States and the World?* New York: Oxford University Press.

Dedrick, Jason, Kenneth L. Kraemer, and Greg Linden. 2010. "Who Profits from Innovation in Global Value Chains? A Study of the iPod and Notebook PCs." *Industrial and Corporate Change* 19 (1): 81–116.

Dicken, Peter. 2015. *Global Shift: Mapping the Changing Contours of the World Economy*, 7th ed. London: Sage.

Dicken, Peter, Philip Kelly, Kris Olds, and Henry Wai-chung Yeung. 2001. "Chains and Networks, Territories and Scales: Towards an Analytical Framework for the Global Economy." *Global Networks* 1 (2): 89–112.

Dieseldorff, Christian G. 2021. "China Surges Past Americas and Japan in IC capacity." *SEMI Blog*, January 25, https://www.semi.org/en/blogs/business-markets/china-surges-past-the-americas-and-japan-in-ic-capacity, accessed on June 21, 2021.

Dillinger, Tom. 2021. "Highlights of the TSMC Technology Symposium 2021—Automotive." *SemiWiki.com*, June 15, https://semiwiki.com/semiconductor-manufacturers/tsmc/299965-highlights-of-the-tsmc-technology-symposium-2021-automotive, accessed on June 24, 2021.

Doner, Richard F., Gregory W. Noble, and John Ravenhill. 2021. *The Political Economy of Automotive Industrialization in East Asia*. New York: Oxford University Press.

Dosi, Giovanni. 1984. *Technical Change and Industrial Transformation: The Theory and an Application to the Semiconductor Industry*. London: Macmillan.

Doz, Yves L., and Keeley Wilson. 2018. *Ringtone: Exploring the Rise and Fall of Nokia in Mobile Phones*. New York: Oxford University Press.

Drahokoupil, Jan, Rutvica Andrijasevic, and Devi Sacchetto, eds. 2016. *Flexible Workforces and Low Profit Margins: Electronics Assembly Between Europe and China*. Brussels: European Trade Union Institute.

Drozdiak, Natalia. 2021. "Europe Is Trying to Reclaim Its Lost Chipmaking Glory." *Bloomberg*, April 27, https://www.bloomberg.com/news/newsletters/2021-04-27/europe-is-trying-to-reclaim-its-lost-chipmaking-glory, accessed on June 21, 2021.

Duhigg, Charles, and David Barboza. 2012. "In China, Human Costs Are Built into an iPad." *New York Times*, January 25.

Duhigg, Charles, and Keith Bradsher. 2012. "How the U.S. Lost Out on iPhone Work." *New York Times*, January 21.

Dunaway, Wilma, ed. 2013. *Gendered Commodity Chains: Seeing Women and Households in 21st Century Global Production.* Stanford, CA: Stanford University Press.

Downey, Adrienne. 2021. "Semiconductor Capex to Grow 13.0% in 2021." March 23, https://semiengineering.com/semiconductor-capex-to-grow-13-0-in-2021, accessed on June 14, 2021.

Eggers, J. P. 2016. "Reversing Course: Competing Technologies, Mistakes, and Renewal in Flat Panel Displays." *Strategic Management Journal* 37 (8): 1578–96.

Eckhardt, Jappe, and Kelley Lee. 2018. "Global Value Chains, Firm Preferences and the Design of Preferential Trade Agreements." *Global Policy* 9 (S2): 58–66.

Elms, Deborah K., and Patrick Low, eds. 2013. *Global Value Chains in a Changing World.* Geneva: World Trade Organization.

Ensmenger, Nathan. 2010. *The Computer Boys Take Over: Computers. Programmers, and the Politics of Technical Expertise.* Cambridge, MA: The MIT Press.

Epicoco, Marianna. 2013. "Knowledge Patterns and Sources of Leadership: Mapping the Semiconductor Miniaturization Trajectory." *Research Policy* 42 (1): 180–95.

Ernst, Dieter. 2000a. "Evolutionary Aspects: The Asian Production Networks of Japanese Electronics Firms." In *International Production Networks in Asia: Rivalry or Riches,* edited by Michael Borrus, Dieter Ernst and Stephan Haggard, 79–107. London: Routledge.

Ernst, Dieter. 2000b. "What Permits David to Grow in the Shadow of Goliath? The Taiwanese Model in the Computer Industry." In *International Production Networks in Asia: Rivalry or Riches,* edited by Michael Borrus, Dieter Ernst and Stephan Haggard, 108–38. London: Routledge.

Esteve, Eric, 2021. "Design IP Sales Grew 16.7% in 2020, Best Growth Rate Ever!" *SemiWiki.com,* April 13, https://semiwiki.com/ip/297995-design-ip-sales-grew-16-7-in-2020-best-growth-rate-ever, accessed on June 24, 2021.

Evans, David S., Andrei Hagiu, and Richard Schmalensee. 2006. *Invisible Engines: How Software Platforms Drive Innovation and Transform Industries.* Cambridge, MA: MIT Press.

Evans, Peter. 1995. *Embedded Autonomy: States and Industrial Transformation.* Princeton, NJ: Princeton University Press.

Everington, Keoni. 2019. "TSMC Starts Work on US$19.6 Billion 3nm Fab in S. Taiwan." *Taiwan News,* October 28, https://www.taiwannews.com.tw/en/news/3805032, accessed on December 31, 2019.

Ezell, Stephen. 2021. *Moore's Law Under Attack: The Impact of China's Policies on Global Semiconductor Innovation*. Washington, DC: Information Technology & Innovation Foundation, https://itif.org/publications/2021/02/18/moores-law-under-attack-impact-chinas-policies-global-semiconductor, accessed on June 24, 2021.

Farrell, Henry, and Abraham L. Newman. 2014. "Domestic Institutions beyond the Nation-State: Charting the New Interdependence Approach." *World Politics* 66 (2): 331–63.

Farrell, Henry, and Abraham L. Newman. 2019. "Weaponized Interdependence: How Global Economic Networks Shape State Coercion." *International Security* 44 (1): 42–79.

Feenstra, Robert C. 1998. "Integration of Trade and Disintegration of Production in the Global Economy." *Journal of Economic Perspectives* 12 (4): 31–50.

Feenstra, Robert C., and Gary G. Hamilton. 2006. *Emergent Economies, Divergent Paths: Economic Organization and International Trade in South Korea and Taiwan*. New York: Cambridge University Press.

Ferrarini, Benno, and David Hummels, eds. 2014. *Asia and Global Production Networks Implications for Trade, Incomes and Economic Vulnerability*. Cheltenham, UK: Edward Elgar.

Fligstein, Neil. 2001. *The Architecture of Markets: An Economic Sociology of Twenty-First-Century Capitalist Societies*. Princeton, NJ: Princeton University Press.

Fligstein, Neil, and Doug McAdam. 2012. *A Theory of Fields*. New York: Oxford University Press.

Florida, Richard, and Martin Kenney. 1990a. "Silicon Valley and Route 128 Won't Save Us." *California Management Review* 33 (1): 68–88.

Florida, Richard, and Martin Kenney. 1990b. *The Breakthrough Illusion: Corporate America's Failure to Move from Innovation to Mass Production*. New York: Basic Books.

Fornahl, Dirk, and Robert Hassink, eds. 2017. *The Life Cycle of Clusters: A Policy Perspective*. Cheltenham, UK: Edward Elgar.

Fortanier, Fabienne, Guannan Miao, Ans Kolk, and Niccolò Pisani. 2020. "Accounting for Firm Heterogeneity in Global Value Chains." *Journal of International Business Studies* 51 (3): 432–53.

Fosu, Augustin K., ed. 2013. *Achieving Development Success: Strategies and Lessons From the Developing World*. Oxford: Oxford University Press.

Fransman, Martin. 1990. *The Market and Beyond: Cooperation and Competition in Information Technology in the Japanese System*. Cambridge: Cambridge University Press.

Fransman, Martin. 1995. *Japan's Computer and Communications Industry: The Evolution of Industrial Giants and Industrial Competitiveness*. Oxford: Oxford University Press.

Freidberg, Susanne. 2004. *French Beans and Food Scares: Culture and Commerce in an Anxious Age*. New York: Oxford University Press.

Fröbel, Folker, Jurgen Heinrichs, and Otto Kreye. 1980. *The New International Division of Labour*. Cambridge: Cambridge University Press.

Fromer, Jacob. 2021. "US Senate Passes Broad US\$250 Billion Legislation to Counter and Compete with China." *South China Morning Post*, June 9, https://www.scmp.com/news/china/diplomacy/article/3136563/us-senate-passes-broad-us250-billion-legislation-counter-and, accessed on June 21, 2021.

Froud, Julie, Sukhdev Johal, Adam Leaver, and Karel Williams. 2012. "Financialization across the Pacific: Manufacturing Cost Ratios, Supply Chains and Power." *Critical Perspectives on Accounting* 25 (1): 46–57.

Fu, Wenying. 2015. *Towards a Dynamic Regional Innovation System: Investigation into the Electronics Industry in the Pearl River Delta, China*. Berlin: Springer.

Fuller, Douglas B. 2016. *Paper Tigers, Hidden Dragons: Firms and the Political Economy of China's Technological Development*. Oxford: Oxford University Press.

Fuller, Douglas B. 2019. "Growth, Upgrading, and Limited Catch-Up in China's Semiconductor Industry." In *Policy, Regulation and Innovation in China's Electricity and Telecom Industries*, edited by Loren Brandt and Thomas G. Rawski, 262–303. Cambridge: Cambridge University Press.

Fuller, Douglas B., Akintunde I. Akinwande, and Charles G. Sodini. 2005. "Leading, Following, or Cooked Goose? Explaining Innovation Successes and Failures in Taiwan's Electronics Industry." In *Global Taiwan*, edited by Suzanne Berger and Richard K. Lester, 76–96. Armonk, NY: M. E. Sharpe.

Gabriele, Alberto, and Haider A. Khan. 2010. *Enhancing Technological Progress in a Market-Socialist Context: China's National Innovation System at the Crossroads*. Berlin: LAMBERT Academic Publishing.

Gandy, Anthony. 2013. *The Early Computer Industry: Limitations of Scale and Scope*. Houndmills, UK: Palgrave Macmillan.

Gao, Boyang, Mick Dunford, Glen Norcliffe, and Zhigao Liu. 2017. "Capturing Gains by Relocating Global Production Networks: The Rise of Chongqing's Notebook Computer Industry, 2008–2014." *Eurasian Geography and Economics* 58 (2): 231–57.

Gao, Boyang, Mick Dunford, Glen Norcliffe, and Weidong Liu. 2019. "Governance Capacity, State Policy and the Rise of the Chongqing Notebook Computer Cluster." *Area Development and Policy* 4 (3): 321–45.

Gawer, Annabelle, ed. 2009. *Platforms, Markets and Innovation*. Cheltenham, UK: Edward Elgar.

Gawer, Annabelle, and Michael Cusumano. 2002. *Platform Leadership: How Intel, Microsoft, and Cisco Drive Industry Innovation*. Cambridge, MA: Harvard Business School Press.

Gawer, Annabelle, and Michael Cusumano. 2014. "Industry Platforms and Eco-system Innovation." *Journal of Product Innovation Management* 31 (3): 417–33.

Gelsinger, Patrick. 2021. *Intel Corporation (INTC) CEO Pat Gelsinger Presents at JPMorgan 49th Annual Global Technology, Media and Communications Conference (Transcript).* May 24, https://seekingalpha.com/article/4430969-intel-corporation-intc-ceo-pat-gelsinger-presents-jpmorgan-49th-annual-global-technology, accessed on June 24, 2021.

Gereffi, Gary. 1994. "The Organization of Buyer-Driven Global Commodity Chains." In *Commodity Chains and Global Capitalism*, edited by Gary Gereffi and Miguel Korzeniewicz, 95–122. Westport, CT: Praeger.

Gereffi, Gary. 1999. "International Trade and Industrial Upgrading in the Apparel Commodity Chain." *Journal of International Economics* 48 (1): 37–70.

Gereffi, Gary. 2014. "Global Value Chains in a Post-Washington Consensus World." *Review of International Political Economy* 21 (1): 9–37.

Gereffi, Gary. 2018. *Global Value Chains and Development: Redefining the Contours of 21st Century Capitalism.* New Delhi: Cambridge University Press.

Gereffi, Gary, John Humphrey, and Timothy Sturgeon. 2005. "The Governance of Global Value Chains." *Review of International Political Economy* 12 (1): 78–104.

Gereffi, Gary, and Miguel Korzeniewicz, eds. 1994. *Commodity Chains and Global Capitalism.* Westport, CT: Praeger.

Gereffi, Gary, Hyun-Chin Lim, and Joonko Lee. 2021. "Trade Policies, Firm Strategies, and Adaptive Reconfigurations of Global Value Chains." *Journal of International Business Policy*, https://doi.org/10.1057/s42214-021-00102-z

Gereffi, Gary, and Xubei Luo. 2014. *Risk and Opportunities of Participation in Global Value Chains*, Background Paper to the 2014 World Development Report, Policy Research Working Paper 6847. Washington, DC: World Bank.

Giachetti, Claudio. 2013. *Competitive Dynamics in the Mobile Phone Industry.* Basingstoke, UK: Palgrave Macmillan.

Giachetti, Claudio. 2018. *Smartphone Start-ups: Navigating the iPhone Revolution.* Basingstoke, UK: Palgrave Macmillan.

Giachetti, Claudio, and Gianluca Marchi. 2017. "Changes in Industrial Leadership over the Life Cycle of the Worldwide Mobile Phone Industry." *Research Policy* 46 (2): 352–64.

Gibbon, Peter. 2002. "At the Cutting Edge? Financialisation and UK Clothing Retailers' Sourcing Patterns and Practices." *Competition and Change* 6 (3): 289–308.

Gibbon, Peter, and Stefano Ponte. 2005. *Trading Down: America, Value Chains and the Global Economy.* Philadelphia, PA: Temple University Press.

Gibbon, Peter, Stefano Ponte, and E. Lazaro, eds. 2011. *Global Agro-Food Trade and Standards: Challenges for Africa.* Basingstoke, UK: Palgrave Macmillan.

Glimstedt, Henrik, Donald Bratt, and Magnus P. Karlsson. 2010. "The Decision to Make or Buy a Critical Technology: Semiconductors at Ericsson, 1980–2010." *Industrial and Corporate Change* 19 (2): 431–64.

Goh, Sui Noi. 2020. "Breaking Up Is Hard to Do—Why China Is a Key Node in Supply Chains." *Straits Times*, May 19, https://www.straitstimes.com/opin ion/breaking-up-is-hard-to-do-why-china-is-a-key-node-in-supply-chains, accessed on January 13, 2021.

Goodman, Samuel, John VerWey, and Dan Kim. 2019. *The South Korea-Japan Trade Dispute in Context: Semiconductor Manufacturing, Chemicals, and Concentrated Supply Chains.* Office of Industries Working Paper ID-062, Washington, DC: US International Trade Commission.

Grabher, Gernot, and Erwin van Tuijl. 2020. "Uber-Production: From Global Networks to Digital Platforms." *Environment and Planning A: Economy and Space* 52 (5): 1005–16.

Gray, Kevin. 2011. "Taiwan and the Geopolitics of Late Development." *Pacific Review* 24 (5): 577–99.

Gregory, Neil, Stanley Nollen, and Stoyan Tenev. 2009. *New Industries From New Places: The Emergence of the Software and Hardware Industries in China and India.* Stanford, CA: Stanford University Press.

Grimes, Seamus, and Debin Du. 2021. "China's Emerging Role in the Global Semiconductor Value Chain." *Telecommunications Policy*, https://doi .org/10.1016/j.telpol.2020.101959

Grimes, Seamus, and Yutao Sun. 2016. "China's Evolving Role in Apple's Global Value Chain." *Area Development and Policy* 1 (1): 94–112.

Grossman, Gene, and Elhanan Helpman. 2002. "Integration versus Outsourcing in Industry Equilibrium." *Quarterly Journal of Economics* 117 (1): 85–120.

Grossman, Gene, and Esteban Rossi-Hansberg. 2008. "Trading Tasks: A Simple Theory of Offshoring." *American Economic Review* 98 (5): 1978–97.

Grove, Andrew S. 1990. "The Future of the Computer Industry." *California Management Review* 33 (1): 148–60.

Grove, Andrew S. 1996. *Only the Paranoid Survive: How to Identify and Exploit the Crisis Points that Challenge Every Business.* New York: Currency.

Guillén, Mauro F. 2021. *The Platform Paradox: How Digital Businesses Succeed in an Ever-Changing Global Marketplace.* Philadelphia, PA: Wharton School Press.

Gulati, Ranjay. 2007. *Managing Network Resources: Alliances, Affiliations, and Other Relational Assets.* Oxford: Oxford University Press.

Haggard, Stephan. 1990. *Pathways from the Periphery: The Politics of Growth in the Newly Industrializing Countries.* Ithaca, NY: Cornell University Press.

Haggard, Stephan. 2018. *Developmental States.* Cambridge Elements in the Politics of Development. Cambridge: Cambridge University Press.

Hamilton, Gary G., and Cheng-Shu Kao. 2018. *Making Money: How Taiwanese Industrialists Embraced the Global Economy.* Stanford, CA: Stanford University Press.

Hamilton, Gary G., Misha Petrovic, and Benjamin Senauer, eds. 2011. *The Market Makers: How Retailers Are Reshaping the Global Economy,* Oxford: Oxford University Press.

Hamilton-Hart, Natasha, and Henry Wai-chung Yeung, eds. 2021a. "Special Forum on "Institutions Under Pressure: The International Political Economy of States and Firms in East Asia." *Review of International Political Economy* 28 (1): 11–151.

Hamilton-Hart, Natasha, and Henry Wai-chung Yeung. 2021b. "Institutions under Pressure: East Asian States, Global Markets and National Firms." *Review of International Political Economy* 28 (1): 11–35.

Harman, Alvin J. 1971. *The International Computer Industry.* Cambridge, MA: Harvard University Press.

Harris, Jack Laurie. 2021. "Rethinking Cluster Evolution: Actors, Institutional Configurations, and New Path Development." *Progress in Human Geography* 45 (3): 436–54.

Haslam, Colin, Nick Tsitsianis, Tord Andersson, and Ya Ping Yin. 2013. "Apple's Financial Success: The Precariousness of Power Exercised in Global Value Chains." *Accounting Forum* 37 (4): 268–79.

Haselton, Todd. 2020. "Apple Will Stop Using Intel Chips in All Macs by 2021." *CNBC,* June 22, https://www.cnbc.com/2020/06/22/new-macbook-pro -and-imac-coming-with-arm-chips-instead-of-intel---kuo.html, accessed on January 13, 2021.

Hatch, Walter. 2010. *Asia's Flying Geese: How Regionalization Shapes Japan.* Ithaca, NY: Cornell University Press.

Hatch, Walter, and Kozo Yamamura. 1996. *Asia in Japan's Embrace: Building a Regional Production Alliance.* Cambridge: Cambridge University Press.

He, Zi-Lin, Kwanghui Lim, and Poh-Kam Wong. 2006. "Entry and Competitive Dynamics in the Mobile Telecommunications Market." *Research Policy* 35 (8): 1147–65.

Henderson, Jeffrey. 1989. *The Globalisation of High Technology Production.* London: Routledge.

Henderson, Jeffrey, Peter Dicken, Martin Hess, Neil Coe, and Henry Wai-chung Yeung. 2002. "Global Production Networks and the Analysis of Economic Development." *Review of International Political Economy* 9 (3): 436–64.

Henderson, Jeffrey, and Allen J. Scott. 1987. "The Growth and Internationalization of the American Semiconductor Industry." In *The Development of High Technology Industries: An International Survey,* edited by Michael Breheny and Ronald McQuaid, 37–79. London: Croom Helm.

Hille, Kathrin. 2021. "TSMC: How a Taiwanese Chipmaker Became a Linchpin of the Global Economy." *Financial Times*, March 24, https://www.ft.com/content/05206915-fd73-4a3a-92a5-6760ce965bd9, accessed on June 21, 2021.

Hitt, Michael A., R. Michael Holmes Jr., and Jean-Luc Arregle. 2021. "The (Covid-19) Pandemic and the New World (Dis)Order." *Journal of World Business* 56 (4): 101210.

Hobday, Michael. 1995. *Innovation in East Asia: The Challenge to Japan*. Cheltenham, UK: Edward Elgar.

Hobday, Michael, Andrew Davies, and Andrea Prencipe. 2005. "Systems Integration: A Core Capability of the Modern Corporation." *Industrial and Corporate Change* 14 (6): 1109–43.

Hof, Robert D. 1994. "Real Men Have Fabs." *Bloomberg*, April 11, 1994. https://www.bloomberg.com/news/articles/1994-04-10/real-men-have-fabs, accessed on October 4, 2019.

Hong, Sung Gul. 1997. *The Political Economy of Industrial Policy in East Asia: The Semiconductor Industry in Taiwan and South Korea*. Cheltenham, UK: Edward Elgar.

Horner, Rory. 2017. "Beyond Facilitator? State Roles in Global Value Chains and Global Production Networks." *Geography Compass* 11 (2): e12307. https://doi.org/10.1111/gec3.12307

Horner, Rory, and Khalid Nadvi. 2018. "Global Value Chains and the Rise of the Global South: Unpacking Twenty-First Century Polycentric Trade." *Global Networks* 18 (2): 207–37.

Horwitz, Josh. 2021. "China's Would-Be Chip Darling Tsinghua Unigroup Bedevilled by Debt and Bad Bets." *Reuters*, January 20, https://www.reuters.com/article/us-tsinghua-unigroup-strategy-analysis-idUKKBN29P0C2, accessed on January 21, 2021.

Hruska, Joel. 2020. "Intel Expects to Reach Process Parity with 7nm in 2021, Lead on 5nm." *ExtremeTech*, March 4, https://www.extremetech.com/computing/306978-intel-expects-to-reach-process-parity-with-7nm-in-2021-lead-on-5nm, accessed on May 25, 2020.

Hu, Huifeng. 2019. "Why Samsung's Last China Smartphone Factory Closed?" *South China Morning Post*, June 15, https://www.scmp.com/economy/china-economy/article/3014564/samsungs-last-china-smartphone-factory-closing-raising, accessed on January 2, 2020.

Hu, Minghe, and Che Pan. 2021. "Chip Shortage Restricts China's Car Production, Leaving Showrooms Empty, but Local Brands Are Faring Better." *South China Morning Post*, June 23, https://www.scmp.com/tech/tech-trends/article/3138438/chip-shortage-restricts-chinas-car-production-leaving-showrooms, accessed on June 23, 2021.

Hu, Mei-Chih. 2012. "Technological Innovation Capabilities in the Thin Film Transistor-Liquid Crystal Display Industries of Japan, Korea, and Taiwan." *Research Policy* 41 (3): 541–55.

Hughes, Alex, E. Morrison, and K. Ruwanpura. 2019. "Public Sector Procurement and Ethical Trade: Governance and Social Responsibility in Some Hidden Global Supply Chains." *Transactions of the Institute of British Geographers* 44 (2): 242–55.

Humphrey, John. 1995. "Industrial Reorganization in Developing Countries: From Models to Trajectories." *World Development* 23 (1): 149–62.

Humphrey, John, and Hubert Schmitz. 2002. "How Does Insertion in Global Value Chains Affect Upgrading in Industrial Clusters?." *Regional Studies* 36 (9): 1017–27.

Hsu, Jinn-yuh. 2011. "State Transformation and Regional Development in Taiwan: From Developmentalist Strategy to Populist Subsidy." *International Journal of Urban and Regional Research* 35 (3): 600–619.

Hsu, Jinn-yuh. 2017. "State Transformation and the Evolution of Economic Nationalism in the East Asian Developmental State: The Taiwanese Semiconductor Industry as Case Study." *Transactions of the Institute of British Geographers* 42 (2): 166–78.

Hwang, Hye-Ran, and Jae-Yong Choung. 2014. "The Co-evolution of Technology and Institutions in the Catch-Up Process." *Journal of Development Studies* 50 (9): 1240–260.

Ibata-Arens, Kathryn. 2019. *Beyond Technonationalism: Biomedical Innovation and Entrepreneurship in Asia.* Stanford, CA: Stanford University Press.

IC Insights. 2021. "China Forecast to Fall Far Short of Its 'Made in China 2025' Goals for ICs." *Research Bulletin*, January 6, https://www.icinsights.com/news/bulletins, accessed on January 11, 2021.

Jacobides, Michael G., Carmelo Cennamo, and Annabelle Gawer. 2018. "Towards a Theory of Ecosystems." *Strategic Management Journal* 39 (8): 2255–76.

Japan External Trade Organization (JETRO). 2010. *Survey of Japanese-Affiliated Companies in Asia and Oceania (FY2010 Survey.* Tokyo: JETRO. https://www.jetro.go.jp/en/reports/survey/biz, accessed on January 6, 2020.

Japan External Trade Organization (JETRO). 2013. *Survey of Japanese-Affiliated Companies in Asia and Oceania (FY2013 Survey.* Tokyo: JETRO. https://www.jetro.go.jp/en/reports/survey/biz, accessed on January 6, 2020.

Japan External Trade Organization (JETRO). 2016. *2016 JETRO Survey on Business Conditions of Japanese Companies in Asia and Oceania.* Tokyo: JETRO. https://www.jetro.go.jp/en/news/releases/2016/a7cc9235a41267aa.html, accessed on January 6, 2020.

Japan External Trade Organization (JETRO). 2018. *2018 JETRO Survey on Business Conditions of Japanese Companies in Asia and Oceania.* Tokyo: JETRO.

https://www.jetro.go.jp/en/news/releases/2019/6980a2e6ad84b745.html, accessed on January 6, 2020.

Jewell, Bill. 2021. "Semiconductor CapEx Strong in 2021." *SemiWiki.com*, June 23, https://semiwiki.com/semiconductor-services/300449-%ef%bb%bf-semi conductor-capex-strong-in-2021, accessed on June 27, 2021.

Jin, Hyunjoo, Douglas Busvine, and David Kirton. 2020. "Global Chip Shortage Threatens Production of Laptops, Smartphones and More." *Reuters*, December 17, https://in.reuters.com/article/us-chip-shortage -analysis/analysis-global-chip-shortage-threatens-production-of-laptops -smartphones-and-more-idINKBN28R0ZL, accessed on December 19, 2020.

Johns, Leslie, and Rachel Wellhausen. 2016. "Under One Roof: Supply Chains and the Protection of Foreign Investment." *American Political Science Review* 110 (1): 31–51.

Johnson, Bryan. 1991. *The US-Japan Semiconductor Agreement: Keeping up the Managed Trade Agenda*, Report Asia, The Heritage Foundation. https://www.heritage.org/node/21399, accessed on July 16, 2019.

Johnson, Chalmers. 1982. *MITI and the Japanese Economic Miracle: The Growth of Industrial Policy, 1925–1975*. Stanford, CA: Stanford University Press.

Jones, Scotten W. 2021. "ISS 2021 – Logic Leadership in the PPAC Era." *SemiWiki.com*, January 15, https://semiwiki.com/events/294639-iss-2021-scotten -w-jones-logic-leadership-in-the-ppac-era, accessed on June 21, 2021.

Kano, Liena. 2018. "Global Value Chain Governance: A Relational Perspective." *Journal of International Business Studies* 49 (6): 684–705.

Kano, Liena, and Chang Hoon Oh. 2020. "Global Value Chains in the PostÐCO-VID World: Governance for Reliability." *Journal of Management Studies* 57 (8): 1773–77.

Kano, Liena, Eric W. K. Tsang, and Henry Wai-chung Yeung. 2020. "Global Value Chains: A Review of a Multidisciplinary Literature." *Journal of International Business Studies* 51 (4): 577–622.

Kaplinsky, Raphael, and Masuma Farooki. 2011. "What Are the Implications for Global Value Chains When the Market Shifts from the North to the South?" *International Journal of Technological Learning, Innovation and Development* 4 (1–3): 13–38.

Kapoor, Rahul, and Patia J. McGrath. 2014. "Unmasking the Interplay between Technology Evolution and R&D Collaboration: Evidence from the Global Semiconductor Manufacturing Industry, 1990–2010." *Research Policy* 43 (3): 555–69.

Kawakami, Momoko. 2009. "Learning from Customers Growth of Taiwanese Notebook PC Manufacturers as Original Design Manufacturing Suppliers." *China Information* 23: 103–28.

Kawagami, Momoko, and Timothy J. Sturgeon, eds. 2011. *The Dynamics of Local Learning in Global Value Chains: Experiences from East Asia*. Basingstoke, UK: Palgrave Macmillan.

Keller, William W., and Louis W. Pauly. 2003. "Crisis and Adaptation in Taiwan and South Korea: The Political Economy of Semiconductors." In *Crisis and Innovation in Asian Technology*, edited by William W. Keller and Richard J. Samuels, 137–59. Cambridge: Cambridge University Press.

Kelly, Tim. 1987. *The British Computer Industry: Crisis and Development*. London: Croom Helm.

Kenney, Martin, ed. 2000. *Understanding Silicon Valley: The Anatomy of an Entrepreneurial Region*. Stanford, CA: Stanford University Press.

Kenney, Martin. 2011. "How Venture Capital Became a Component of the US National System of Innovation." *Industrial and Corporate Change* 20 (6): 1677–723.

Kenney, Martin, and Richard Florida, eds. 2003. *Locating Global Advantage: Industry Dynamics in the International Economy*. Stanford, CA: Stanford University Press.

Kenney, Martin, Petri Rouvinen, Timo Seppälä, and John Zysman. 2019. "Platforms and Industrial Change." *Industry and Innovation* 26 (8): 871–79.

Kenney, Martin, and John Zysman. 2016. "The Rise of the Platform Economy." *Issues in Science and Technology* 32 (3): 61–69.

Kenney, Martin, and John Zysman. 2020. "The Platform Economy: Restructuring the Space of Capitalist Accumulation', *Cambridge Journal of Regions, Economy and Space* 13 (1): 55–76.

Khan, Haider A. 2004. *Interpreting East Asian Growth and Innovation: The Future of Miracles*. New York: Palgrave Macmillan.

Khan, Haider A. 2013. "Development Strategies: Lessons from the Experiences of South Korea, Malaysia, Thailand, and Vietnam." In *Achieving Development Success: Strategies and Lessons From the Developing World*, edited by Augustin K. Fosu, 119–32. Oxford: Oxford University Press.

Khan, Haider A., ed. 2022. *Towards A New Theory of Innovation Systems for the Twenty First Century*. Oxford: Oxford University Press.

Kharpal, Arjun. 2019. "Huawei Launches New Operating System, Says It Can 'Immediately' Switch from Google Android If Needed." *CNBC*, August 9, https://www.cnbc.com/2019/08/09/huawei-launches-its-own-operating-system-hongmengos-or-harmonyos.html, accessed on December 21, 2019.

Khare, Mukesh. 2019. "How to Squeeze Billions of Transistors onto a Computer Chip." https://www.ibm.com/thought-leadership/innovation_explanations/article/mukesh_khare-on-smaller-transistors-analytics.html, accessed on June 4, 2020.

Kim, In Song, Helen V. Milner, Thomas Bernauer, Iain Osgood, Gabriele Spilker, and Dustin Tingley. 2019. "Firms and Global Value Chains: Identifying Firms' Multidimensional Trade Preferences." *International Studies Quarterly* 63 (1): 153–67.

Kim, Linsu. 1997. *Imitation to Innovation: The Dynamics of Korea's Technological Learning.* Boston: Harvard Business School Press.

Kim, Sohe, and Sam Kim. 2021. "Korea Unveils $450 Billion Push for Global Chipmaking Crown." *Bloomberg*, May 13, https://www.bloomberg.com/news/articles/2021-05-13/korea-unveils-450-billion-push-to-seize-global-chipmaking-crown, accessed on June 27, 2021.

Kim, Soo Yeon, and Gabriele Spilker. 2019. "Global Value Chains and the Political Economy of WTO Disputes." *Review of International Organizations* 14 (2): 239–60.

Kim, Sung-Young. 2012. "The Politics of Fast Followership in Korea: How Government and Business Challenged the Might of Qualcomm." *New Political Economy* 17 (3): 293–312.

Kim, Yongyul. 2011. "From Catch-Up to Overtaking: Competition and Innovation in the Semiconductor Industries of Korea and Japan." *Asian Journal of Technology Innovation* 19 (2): 297–311.

Kim, Youngsoo. 2000. "Technological Capabilities and the Samsung Electronics Network." In *International Production Networks in Asia: Rivalry or Riches*, edited by Michael Borrus, Dieter Ernst, and Stephan Haggard, 139–73. London: Routledge.

King, Ian. 2020. "Huawei Makes End-Run around U.S. Ban by Using Its Own Chips." *Bloomberg*, March 2, https://www.bloomberg.com/news/articles/2020-03-02/huawei-makes-end-run-around-u-s-ban-by-turning-to-its-own-chips, accessed on May 15, 2020.

King, Ian. 2021. "Intel Spending Billions to Revive Chip Manufacturing, Chase TSMC." *Bloomberg*, March 23, https://www.bloomberg.com/news/articles/2021-03-23/intel-to-spend-billions-on-manufacturing-revival-taking-on-tsmc, accessed on June 21, 2021.

King, Ian, and Debby Wu. 2021. "Chip Crisis in 'Danger Zone' as Wait Times Reach New Record." *Bloomberg*, May 19, https://www.bloomberg.com/news/articles/2021-05-18/wait-for-chip-deliveries-increased-in-sign-shortage-persists, accessed on June 23, 2021.

Kitchin, Rob, and Martin Dodge. 2011. *Code/Space: Software and Everyday Life.* Cambridge, MA: MIT Press.

Klepper, Steven. 2015. *Experimental Capitalism: The Nanoeconomics of American High-Tech Industries.* Princeton, NJ: Princeton University Press.

Koopman, Robert, Zhi Wang, and Shang-Jin Wei. 2014. "Tracing Value-Added and Double Counting in Gross Exports." *American Economic Review* 104 (2): 459–94.

Krippner, Greta R. 2011. *Capitalizing on Crisis: The Political Origins of the Rise of Finance*. Cambridge, MA: Harvard University Press.

Krugman, Paul R. 1994. "Competitiveness—A Dangerous Obsession." *Foreign Affairs* 73 (2): 28–44.

Lall, Sanjaya. 1996. *Learning from the Asian Tigers: Studies in Technology and Industrial Policy*. London: Macmillan.

Lall, Sanjaya. 2003. *Competitiveness, FDI and Technological Activity in East Asia*. Cheltenham. UK: Edward Elgar.

Lan, Sai, Kun Liu, and Yidi Dong. 2019. "Dancing with Wolves: How Value Creation and Value Capture Dynamics Affect Complementor Participation in Industry Platforms." *Industry and Innovation* 26 (8): 943–63.

Lane, Christel, and Jocelyn Probert. 2009. *National Capitalisms, Global Production Networks: Fashioning the Value Chain in the UK, US, and Germany*. Oxford: Oxford University Press.

Lange, Knut, Gordon Müller-Seitz, Jörg Sydow, and Arnold Windeler. 2013. "Financing Innovations in Uncertain Networks – Filling in Roadmap Gaps in the Semiconductor Industry." *Research Policy* 42 (3): 647–61.

Langlois, Richard N. 2002. "Modularity in Technology and Organization." *Journal of Economic Behavior and Organization* 49 (1): 19–37.

Langlois, Richard N., Thomas A. Pugel, Carmela S. Haklisch, Richard R. Nelson, and William G. Egelhoff. 1988. *Micro-Electronics: An Industry in Transition*. Boston: Unwin Hyman.

Langlois, Richard N., and Paul L. Robertson. 1992. "Networks and Innovation in a Modular System: Lessons from the Microcomputer and Stereo Component Industries." *Research Policy* 21 (4): 297–313.

Layton, Roslyn. 2021. "Will the US Let the Chips Fall on Semiconductor Policy?" *Forbes*, May 31, https://www.forbes.com/sites/roslynlayton/2021/05/31/will-the-us-let-the-chips-fall-on-semiconductor-policy, accessed on June 21, 2021.

Lee, Jeongsik, Byung-Cheol Kim, and Young-Mo Lim. 2011. "Dynamic Competition in Technological Investments: An Empirical Examination of the LCD Panel Industry." *International Journal of Industrial Organization* 29 (6): 718–28.

Lee, Joonkoo, and Gary Gereffi. 2021. "Innovation, Upgrading, and Governance in Cross-sectoral Global Value Chains: The Case of Smartphones." *Industrial and Corporate Change* 30 (1): 215–31.

Lee, Joyce, and Heekyong Yang. 2021a. "South Korea's LG Becomes First Major Smartphone Brand to Withdraw from Market." *Reuters*, April 5, https://www.reuters.com/article/us-lg-elec-smartphones-idUSKBN2BS032, accessed on June 23, 2021.

Lee, Joyce, and Heekyong Yang. 2021b. "Samsung Boosts Non-memory Chip Investment to $151 bln as S. Korea Offers Bigger Tax Breaks." *Reuters*, May 13, https://www.reuters.com/technology/samsung-raises-non-memory-chip-investment-target-skorea-announces-bigger-tax-2021-05-13, accessed on June 21, 2021.

Lee, Keun. 2013. *Schumpeterian Analysis of Economic Catch-up: Knowledge, Path-Creation, and the Middle-Income Trap.* Cambridge: Cambridge University Press.

Lee, Keun. 2016. *Economic Catch-Up and Technological Leapfrogging: The Path to Development and Macroeconomic Stability in Korea.* Cheltenham, UK: Edward Elgar.

Lee, Keun. 2019. *The Art of Economic Catch-Up: Barriers, Detours and Leapfrogging in Innovation Systems.* Cambridge: Cambridge University Press.

Lee, Keun, and Moosup Jung. 2015. "Overseas Factories, Domestic Employment, and Technological Hollowing Out: A Case Study of Samsung's Mobile Phone Business." *Review of World Economics* 15 (3): 461–75.

Lee, Keun, Chaisung Lim, and Wichin Song. 2005. "Emerging Digital Technology as a Window of Opportunity and Technological Leapfrogging: Catch-Up in Digital TV by the Korean Firms." *International Journal of Technology Management* 29 (1/2): 40–63.

Lee, Yen Nee. 2019. "The Japan-South Korea Dispute Could Push Up the Price of Your Next Smartphone." *CNBC Markets*, July 22, https://www.cnbc.com/2019/07/23/japan-south-korea-dispute-impact-on-semiconductor-supply-chain-prices.html, accessed on June 5, 2020.

Lee, Yen Nee. 2021. "EU-China Investment Deal Is Still Possible—but Not before 2023." *CNBC*, June 15, https://www.cnbc.com/2021/06/15/eu-china-investment-deal-still-possible-but-not-before-2023-analyst.html, accessed on June 23, 2021.

Lehmberg, Derek. 2018. "The Decline of the Japanese Flat Panel Display Industry." In *Japanese Management in Evolution: New Directions, Breaks, and Emerging Practices*, edited by Tsutomu Nakano, 87–106. London: Routledge.

Lema, Rasmus, Roberta Rabellotti, and Padmashree Gehl Sampath, eds. 2018. "Special Issue: Innovation Systems in the Era of Global Value Chains." *European Journal of Development Studies* 30 (3): 345–574.

Leslie, Stuart W. 2000. "The Biggest 'Angel' of Them All: The Military and the Making of Silicon Valley." In *Understanding Silicon Valley: The Anatomy of an Entrepreneurial Region*, edited by Martin Kenney, 48–67. Stanford, CA: Stanford University Press.

Levy, David L. 2008. "Political Contestation in Global Production Networks." *Academy of Management Review* 33 (4): 943–63.

Linden, Greg, David C. Mowery, and Rosemarie Ham Ziedonis, 2000. "National Technology Policy in Global Markets: Developing Next Generation Lithography in the Semiconductor Industry." *Business and Politics* 2 (2. 93–113.

Linden, Gre, and Deepak Somaya. 2003. "System-on-a-Chip Integration in the Semiconductor Industry: Industry Structure and Firm Strategies." *Industrial and Corporate Change* 12 (3): 545–76.

Linton, Tom, and Bindiya Vakil. 2020. "Coronavirus Is Proving We Need More Resilient Supply Chains." *Harvard Business Review*, March 5, https://hbr.org/2020/03/coronavirus-is-proving-that-we-need-more-resilient-supply-chains, accessed on January 13, 2021.

Liu, Yi. 2020. *Local Dynamics of Industrial Upgrading: The Case of the Pearl River Delta in China.* Singapore: Springer Nature.

Lu, Qiwen. 2000. *China's Leap into the Information Age: Innovation and Organization in the Computer Industry.* Oxford: Oxford University Press.

Luk, Lorraine. 2014. "Foxconn Struggles to Meet New iPhone Demand." *Wall Street Journal Digits*, September 17.

Lund, Henrik Brynthe and Markus Steen. 2020. "Make at Home or Abroad? Manufacturing Reshoring through a GPN Lens: A Norwegian Case Study." *Geoforum* 113: 154–64.

Lundvall, Bengt-Åke, ed. 1992. *National Systems of Innovation: Towards a Theory of Innovation and Interactive Learning.* London: Pinter.

Lüthje, Boy, Stefanie Hürtgen, Peter Pawlicki, and Martina Sproll. 2013. *From Silicon Valley to Shenzhen: Global Production and Work in the IT Industry.* Lanham, MD: Rowman & Littlefield.

Macher, Jeffrey T., and David C. Mowery, eds. 2008. *Innovation in Global Industries: U.S. Firms Competing in A New World.* Washington, DC: National Academies Press.

Macher, Jeffrey T., David C. Mowery, and Alberto Di Minin. 2007. "The 'Non Globalization' of Innovation in the Semiconductor Industry." *California Management Review* 50 (1): 217–42.

Maciejewska, Małgorzata. 2016. "'Union Busting Is Disgusting': Labour Conflicts at LG Corporation in Poland." In *Flexible Workforces and Low Profit Margins: Electronics Assembly Between Europe and China*, edited by Jan Drahokoupil, Rutvica Andrijasevic and Devi Sacchetto, 187–204. Brussels: European Trade Union Institute.

Maire, Robert. 2021a. "2020 Was a Mess for Intel." *SemiWiki.com*, January 13, https://semiwiki.com/semiconductor-services/294637-2020-was-a-mess-for-intel, accessed on January 20, 2021.

Maire, Robert. 2021b. "Chips for America Act—Funding Failures & Foreigners or Saving Semiconductors?" *SemiWiki.com*, June 6, https://semiwiki.com/

semiconductor-services/299777-chips-for-america-act-funding-failures-for-eigners-or-saving-semiconductors, accessed on June 24, 2021.

Malerba, Franco. 1985. *The Semiconductor Business: The Economics of Rapid Growth and Decline.* London: Pinter.

Malerba, Franco, and Richard Nelson, eds. 2012. *Innovation and Learning for Economic Development.* Cheltenham, UK: Edward Elgar.

Markusen, Ann, Peter Hall, Scott Campbell, and Sabina Deitrick. 1991. *The Rise of the Gunbelt: The Military Remapping of Industrial America.* New York: Oxford University Press.

Marley, Patrick, and Jason Stein. 2017. "Foxconn Announces $10 Billion Investment in Wisconsin and up to 13,000 Jobs." *Milwaukee Journal Sentinel,* July 26, https://www.jsonline.com/story/news/2017/07/26/scott-walker-heads-d-c-trump-prepares-wisconsin-foxconn-announcement/512077001, accessed on May 19, 2020.

Mathews, John A. 2002. *Dragon Multinational: A New Model for Global Growth.* Oxford: Oxford University Press.

Mathews, John A. 2007. "How Taiwan Built an Electronics Industry." In *Handbook of Research on Asian Business,* edited by Henry Wai-chung Yeung, 307–32. Cheltenham, UK: Edward Elgar.

Mathews, John A., and Dong-Sung Cho. 2000. *Tiger Technology: The Creation of A Semiconductor Industry in East Asia.* Cambridge: Cambridge University Press.

Mayer, Frederick W., and Nicola Phillips. 2017. "Outsourcing Governance: States and the Politics of a 'Global Value Chain World.'" *New Political Economy* 22 (2): 134–52.

Mayersen, Isaiah. 2020. "AMD Is Set to Become TSMC's Biggest 7nm Customer in 2020." *Techspot,* January 4, https://www.techspot.com/news/83400-amd-set-become-tsmc-biggest-7nm-customer-2020.html, accessed on January 6, 2020.

Mazurek, Jan. 1999. *Making Microchips: Policy, Globalization and Economic Restructuring in the Semiconductor Industry.* Cambridge, MA: MIT Press.

Mazzucato, Mariana. 2013. *The Entrepreneurial State: Debunking Public vs. Private Sector Myths in Innovation.* London: Anthem Press.

McAfee, Andrew, and Erik Brynjolfsson. 2017. *Machine, Platform, Crowd: Harnessing Our Digital Future.* New York: W. W. Norton.

McGrath, Siobhán. 2018. "Dis/articulations and the Interrogation of Development in GPN Research." *Progress in Human Geography* 42 (4) 509–28.

McKendrick, David G., Richard F. Doner, and Stephan Haggard. 2000. *From Silicon Valley to Singapore: Location and Competitive Advantage in the Hard Disk Drive Industry.* Stanford, CA: Stanford University Press.

McKinsey Global Institute. 2019. *Globalization in Transition: The Future of Trade and Value Chains.* McKinsey&Company.

McKinsey Global Institute. 2020. *Risk, Resilience, and Rebalancing in Global Value Chains,* August 6, https://www.mckinsey.com/business-functions/operations/our-insights/risk-resilience-and-rebalancing-in-global-value-chains, accessed on January 13, 2021.

McNish, Jacqui, and Sean Silcoff. 2015. *Losing the Signal: The Untold Story Behind the Extraordinary Rise and Spectacular Fall of BlackBerry.* New York: HarperCollins.

McWilliam, Sarah E., Jung Kwan Kim, Ram Mudambi, and Bo Bernhard Nielsen. 2020. "Global Value Chain Governance: Intersections with International Business." *Journal of World Business* 55 (4): 101067.

Mezzadri, Alessandra. 2017. *The Sweatshop Regime: Labouring Bodies, Exploitation, and Garments.* Cambridge: Cambridge University Press.

Milberg, William. 2008. "Shifting Sources and Uses of Profits: Sustaining US Financialization with Global Value Chains." *Economy and Society* 37 (3): 420–51.

Milberg, William, and Deborah Winkler. 2013. *Outsourcing Economics: Global Value Chains in Capitalist Development.* Cambridge: Cambridge University Press.

Moore, Gordon, and Kevin Davis. 2004. "Learning the Silicon Valley Way." In *Building High-Tech Clusters: Silicon Valley and Beyond,* edited by Timothy Bresnahan and Alfonso Gambardella, 7–39. Cambridge: Cambridge University Press.

Morgan, Kevin, and Andrew Sayer. 1988. *Microcircuits of Capital: 'Sunrise' Industry and Uneven Development.* Oxford: Westview. Republished in 2018 by Routledge.

Mowery, David C. 1983. "Innovation, Market Structure, and Government Policy in the American Semiconductor Electronics Industry." *Research Policy* 12 (4): 183–97.

Mowery, David C. 1996. *The International Computer Software Industry: A Comparative Study of Industry Evolution and Structure.* New York: Oxford University Press.

Mudambi, Ram, Lee Li, Xufei Ma, Shige Makino, Gongming Qian, and Ron Boschma. 2018. "Zoom in, Zoom out: Geographic Scale and Multinational Activity." *Journal of International Business Studies* 49 (8): 929–41.

Mudambi, Ram, and Markus Venzin. 2010. "The Strategic Nexus of Offshoring and Outsourcing Decisions." *Journal of Management Studies* 47 (8): 1510–33.

Mullen, Andrew. 2021. "US Optimism to Reshore Supply Chains from Asia 'Overblown,' with Region's Share of Global Exports Set to Rise." *South China Morning Post,* June 17, https://www.scmp.com/economy/china-economy/

article/3137485/us-optimism-reshore-supply-chains-asia-overblown-regions, accessed on January 23, 2021.

Müller-Seitz, Gordon, and Jörg Sydow. 2012. "Maneuvering between Networks to Lead—A Longitudinal Case Study in the Semiconductor Industry." *Long Range Planning* 45 (2–3): 105–35.

Murtha, Thomas P., Stefanie Ann Lenway, and Jeffrey A. Hart. 2001. *Managing New Industry Creation: Global Knowledge Formation and Entrepreneurship in High Technology.* Stanford, CA: Stanford University Press.

Narula, Rajneesh. 2020. "Policy Opportunities and Challenges from the CO-VID-19 Pandemic for Economies with Large Informal Sectors." *Journal of International Business Policy* 3 (3): 302–10.

Nathan, Dev, Meenu Tewari, and Sandip Sarkar. 2016. *Labour Conditions in Asian Value Chains.* New Dehli: Cambridge University Press.

Neilson, Jeff, and Bill Pritchard. 2009. *Value Chain Struggles: Institutions and Governance in the Plantation Districts of South India.* Oxford: Wiley-Blackwell.

Neilson, Jeff, Bill Pritchard, Niels Fold, and Angga Dwiartama. 2018. "Lead Firms in the Cocoa–Chocolate Global Production Network: An Assessment of the Deductive Capabilities of GPN 2.0." *Economic Geography* 94 (4): 400–24.

Neilson, Jeffrey, Bill Pritchard, and Henry Wai-chung Yeung. 2014. "Global Value Chains and Global Production Networks in the Changing International Political Economy." *Review of International Political Economy* 21 (1): 1–8.

Neilson, Jeffrey, Bill Pritchard, and Henry Wai-chung Yeung, eds. 2015. *Global Value Chains and Global Production Networks: Changes in the International Political Economy.* London: Routledge.

Nellis, Stephen. 2021. "Intel Graphics Chip Will Tap New Version of TSMC 7-Nanometer Process." *Reuters*, January 12, https://www.reuters.com/article/intel-tsmc/intel-graphics-chip-will-tap-new-version-of-tsmc-7-nanometer-process-sources-idUSL1N2JJ2Y4, accessed on January 13, 2021.

Nellis, Stephen, and Ayanti Bera. 2021. "Intel Avoids Outsourcing Embrace, Investigates Hack of Results." *Reuters*, January 22, https://www.reuters.com/article/us-intel-results/intel-avoids-outsourcing-embrace-investigates-hack-of-results-idUSKBN29Q2VD, accessed on January 23, 2021.

Nenni, Daniel. 2020. "Ten Chinese Semiconductor Start-Ups that Got a Leg Up from Their Founders' Foreign Experience." *SemiWiki.com*, December 27, https://semiwiki.com/forum/index.php?threads/ten-chinese-semiconductor-start-ups-that-got-a-leg-up-from-their-founders%E2%80%99-foreign-experience.13436, accessed on December 27, 2020.

Nenni, Daniel. 2021. "TSMC's Top Customers 2019–2021." *SemiWiki.com*, March 19, https://semiwiki.com/forum/index.php?threads/tsmcs-top-customers-2019-2021.13925, accessed on June 21, 2021.

Nenni, Daniel, and Paul McLellan. 2019. *Fabless: The Transformation of the Semiconductor Industry*. SemiWiki.com Project.

Nepelski, Daniel, and Giuditta De Prato. 2018. "The Structure and Evolution of ICT Global Innovation Network." *Industry and Innovation* 25 (10): 940–65.

Neumann, Frederic. 2021. "As Production Shifts from China to Asean, Asia's Supply Chains Remain Stronger than Ever." *South China Morning Post*, June 7, https://www.scmp.com/comment/opinion/article/3135941/production-shifts-china-asean-asias-supply-chains-remain-stronger, accessed on June 23, 2021.

Newsome, Kirsty, Phil Taylor, Jennifer Bair, and Al Rainnie, eds. 2015. *Putting Labour in its Place: Labour Process Analysis and Global Value Chains*. London: Palgrave.

Nienaber, Michael. 2021. "Germany Urges Taiwan to Help Ease Auto Chip shortage." *Reuters*, January 24, https://www.reuters.com/article/us-taiwan-autos-chips/germany-urges-taiwan-to-help-ease-auto-chip-shortage-idUSKBN29T04V, accessed on January 24, 2021.

Ning, Lutao. 2009. *China's Rise in the World ICT Industry: Industrial Strategies and the Catch-Up Development Model*. London: Routledge.

Nyabiage, Jevans. 2021. "Chinese Telecoms Firms Dial into Africa, the Last Big Growth Market for Phones." *South China Morning Post*, June 20, https://www.scmp.com/news/china/article/3138003/chinese-telecoms-firms-dial-africa-last-big-growth-market-phones, accessed on June 23, 2021.

OECD. 2011. *Global Value Chains: Preliminary Evidence And Policy Issues*. Paris: OECD, DSTI/IND(2011)3. http://www.oecd.org/dataoecd/18/43/47945400.pdf.

OECD. 2015. *Inclusive Global Value Chains: Policy Options in Trade and Complementary Areas For GVC Integration by Small And Medium Enterprises and Low-Income Developing Countries*. Paris: OECD.

OECD. 2021. *OECD Economic Outlook, 31 May 2021*. Paris: OECD. https://www.oecd.org/economic-outlook, accessed on June 21, 2021.

OECD-WTO-UNCTAD. 2013. *Implications of Global Value Chains for Trade, Investment, Development and Jobs*, Report Prepared for the G-20 Leaders Summit, September 2013, http://unctad.org/en/PublicationsLibrary/unctad_oecd_wto_2013d1_en.pdf.

O'Mara, Margaret. 2005. *Cities of Knowledge: Cold War Science and the Search for the Next Silicon Valley*. Princeton, NJ: Princeton University Press.

O'Mara, Margaret. 2019. *The Code: Silicon Valley and the Remaking of America*. New York: Penguin.

Oqubay, Arkebe, and Kenichi Ohno, eds. 2019. *How Nations Learn: Technological Learning, Industrial Policy, and Catch-up*. New York: Oxford University Press.

O'Riain, Sean. 2004. *The Politics of High-Tech Growth: Developmental Network States in the Global Economy*. Cambridge: Cambridge University Press.

Ornston, Darius. 2018. *Good Governance Gone Bad—How Nordic Adaptability Leads to Excess*. Ithaca, NY: Cornell University Press.

Osawa, Juro. 2013. "Chip Supply Concerns Linger after Hynix Factory Fire." *Wall Street Journal*, September 9.

Osgood, Iain. 2018. "Globalizing the Supply Chain: Firm and Industrial Support for US Trade Agreements." *International Organization* 72 (2): 455–84.

Ouma, Stefan. 2015. *Assembling Export Markets: The Making and Unmaking of Global Market Connections in West Africa*. Oxford: Wiley-Blackwell.

Pan, Che. 2021a. "China Semiconductors: SMIC Cements Its Role as Beijing's Best Hope in Chips Despite US Restrictions." *South China Morning Post*, April 1, https://scmp.com/tech/big-tech/article/3127971/china-semiconductors-smic-cements-its-role-beijings-best-hope-chips, accessed on June 21, 2021.

Pan, Che. 2021b. "Europe's No 2 Chip Maker STMicroelectronics Reportedly to Raise Prices from June 1, Citing Materials Shortages." *South China Morning Post*, May 18, https://scmp.com/tech/tech-trends/article/3133901/europes-no-2-chip-maker-stmicroelectronics-reportedly-raise-prices, accessed on June 21, 2021.

Panwar, Rajat. 2020. "It's Time to Develop Local Production and Supply Networks." *California Management Review*, https://cmr.berkeley.edu/2020/04/local-production-supply-networks, accessed on January 13, 2021.

Paprzycki, Ralph. 2005. *Interfirm Networks in the Japanese Electronics Industry*. London: RoutledgeCurzon.

Park, Ju-min. 2019. "Samsung Ends Mobile Phone Production in China." *Reuters*, October 2, https://www.reuters.com/article/us-samsung-elec-china/samsung-ends-mobile-phone-production-in-china-idUSKBN1WH0LR, accessed on January 2, 2020.

Park, S. C., Claes G. Alvstam, H. Dolles, and Patrick Ström. 2014. "Samsung Electronics: From "National Champion" to "Global Leader."" In *Asian Inward and Outward FDI: New Challenges in the Global Economy*, edited by C. G. Alvstam, H. Dolles, and P. Ström, 179–200. Basingstoke, UK: Palgrave Macmillan.

Parker, Geoffrey G., Marshall W. Van Alstyne, and Sangeet Paul Choudary. 2016. *Platform Revolution: How Networked Markets are Transforming the Economy and How to Make Them Work for You*. New York: W. W. Norton.

Pawlicki, Peter. 2016. "Re-focusing and Re-shifting – The Constant Restructuring of Global Production Networks in the Electronics Industry." In *Flexible Workforces and Low Profit Margins: Electronics Assembly Between Europe and China*, edited by Jan Drahokoupil, Rutvica Andrijasevic and Devi Sacchetto, 21–44. Brussels: European Trade Union Institute.

Pecht, Michael. 2006. *China's Electronics Industry: The Definitive Guide for Companies and Policy Makers with Interest in China.* Norwich, NY: William Andrew.

Pempel, T. J. 2021. *A Region of Regimes: Prosperity and Plunder in the Asia-Pacific.* Ithaca, NY: Cornell University Press.

Perez, Raul. 2020. "Managing Custom Silicon Projects with Transnational, Multi Company, and Cross Functional Teams." *SemiWiki.com*, December 30, https://semiwiki.com/semiconductor-services/custom-silicon/294329-man aging-custom-silicon-projects-with-trans-national-multi-company-and-cross -functional-teams, accessed on January 6, 2021.

Périsse, Muriel. 2017. "Labor Law in China: How Does It Contribute to the Economic Security of the Workforce? A Commonsian Reading." *Journal of Economic Issues* 51 (1): 1–26.

Périsse, Muriel, and Clément Séhier. 2019. "Analysing Wages and Labour Institutions in China: An Unfinished Transition." *Economic and Labour Relations Review* 30 (3): 400–421.

Peters, Stuart. 2006. *National Systems of Innovation: Creating High Technology Industries.* New York: Palgrave Macmillan.

Phartiyal, Sankalp. 2021a. "India Holds Up Wireless Approvals for China-Made Devices, Delaying Launches." *Reuters*, May 7, https://www.reuters.com/ business/media-telecom/exclusive-india-holds-up-wireless-approvals-china -made-devices-delaying-launches-2021-05-07, accessed on June 24, 2021.

Phartiyal, Sankalp. 2021b. "Wistron Shakes Up India Structure, Management after Factory Troubles." *Reuters*, April 15, https://www.reuters.com/world/ india/exclusive-wistron-shakes-up-india-structure-management-after-factory -troubles-2021-04-15, accessed on June 23, 2021.

Phartiyal, Sankalp, and Aditi Shah. 2021. "A Billion for Every Chip-Maker Who 'Makes in India.'" *Reuters*, March 31, https://www.reuters.com/article/ india-semiconductor-idUSKBN2BN12H, accessed on June 21, 2021.

Pietrobelli, Carlo, and Roberta Rabellotti, eds. 2007. *Upgrading to Compete: SMEs, Clusters and Value Chains in Latin America.* Cambridge, MA: Harvard University Press.

Pickles, John, and Adrian Smith. 2016. *Articulations of Capital: Global Production Networks and Regional Transformations.* Oxford: Wiley-Blackwell.

Pirie, Iain. 2008. *The Korean Developmental State: From Dirigisme to Neo-Liberalism.* London: Routledge.

Pisano, Gary P., and Willy C. Shih. 2009. "Restoring American Competitiveness." *Harvard Business Review*, July–August: 114–25.

Pisano, Gary P., and Willy C. Shih. 2012. "Does America Really Need Manufacturing?" *Harvard Business Review*, March: 94–102.

Pon, Bryan, Timo Seppälä, and Martin Kenney. 2014. "Android and the Demise of Operating System-Based Power: Firm Strategy and Platform Control in the Post-PC World." *Telecommunications Policy* 38 (11): 979–91.

Ponte, Stefano. 2019. *Business, Power and Sustainability in A World of Global Value Chains.* London: Zed Books.

Ponte, Stefano, Gary Gereffi, and Gale Raj-Reichert, eds. 2019. *Handbook on Global Value Chains.* Cheltenham, UK: Edward Elgar.

Ponte, Stefano, and Tim Sturgeon. 2014. "Explaining Governance in Global Value Chains: A Modular Theory-Building Effort." *Review of International Political Economy* 21 (1): 195–223.

Porter, Michael E. 1980. *Competitive Strategy: Techniques for Analyzing Industries and Competitors.* New York: Free Press.

Porter, Michael E. 1985. *Competitive Advantage: Creating and Sustaining Performance.* New York: Free Press.

Posthuma, Anne, and Dev Nathan. 2011. *Labour in Global Production Networks in India.* Oxford: Oxford University Press.

Qu, Tracy, and Celia Chen. 2021. "Apple Puts China Squarely at the Apex of Supplier List, Bucking Talk of Decoupling and Scrutiny of Its Vendors." *South China Morning Post*, June 1, https://www.scmp.com/tech/tech-war/ article/3135617/us-china-tech-war-apple-puts-china-squarely-apex-supplier -list, accessed on June 21, 2021.

Rai, Saritha. 2021. "Google Smartphone Tie-Up with Ambani Hits Supply Chain Snag." *Bloomberg*, June 16, https://www.bloomberg.com/news/ articles/2021-06-15/google-s-smartphone-tie-up-with-ambani-hits-a-supply -chain-snag, accessed on June 23, 2021.

Rapoza, Kenneth. 2020. "Kudlow: "Pay the Moving Costs' of American Companies Leaving China." *Forbes*, April 10, https://www.forbes.com/sites/ken rapoza/2020/04/10/kudlow-pay-the-moving-costs-of-american-companies -leaving-china/?sh=2818139113c6, accessed on January 13, 2021.

Reich, Robert B. 1990. "Who Is Us?" *Harvard Business Review* 68 (1): 53–64.

Reich, Robert B. 1991. *The Work of Nations: Preparing Ourselves for 21st Century Capitalism.* New York: Vintage Books.

Reuters. 2021. "TSMC says 2021 Output of Key Auto Chip component up 60% vs Last Year." May 21, https://www.reuters.com/article/us-tsmc-semiconductors -idUSKCN2D20A0, accessed on June 21, 2021.

Reynolds, Isabel, and Emi Urabe. 2020. "Japan to Fund Firms to Shift Production Out of China." *Bloomberg*, April 8, https://www.bloombergquint.com/ global-economics/japan-to-fund-firms-to-shift-production-out-of-china, accessed on January 13, 2021.

Richards, John E. 2004. "Clusters, Competition, and 'Global Players' in ICT Markets: The Case of Scandinavia." In *Building High-Tech Clusters: Silicon Valley and Beyond*, edited by Timothy Bresnahan and Alfonso Gambardella, 60–189. Cambridge: Cambridge University Press.

Sacchetto, Devi, and Rutvica Andrijase. 2016. "The Case of Foxconn in Turkey: Benefiting from Free Labour and Anti-union Policy." In *Flexible Workforces and Low Profit Margins: Electronics Assembly Between Europe and China*, edited by Jan Drahokoupil, Rutvica Andrijasevic and Devi Sacchetto, 113–30. Brussels: European Trade Union Institute.

Saxenian, Anne. 1991. "The Origins and Dynamics of Production Networks in Silicon Valley." *Research Policy* 20 (5): 423–37. Reproduced in Martin Kenney, ed. 2000. *Understanding Silicon Valley: The Anatomy of an Entrepreneurial Region*. Stanford, CA: Stanford University Press, 141–64.

Saxenian, AnnaLee. 1994. *Regional Advantage: Culture and Competition in Silicon Valley and Route 128*. Cambridge, MA: Harvard University Press.

Saxenian, Anne. 2004. "Taiwan's Hsinchu Region: Imitator and Partner for Silicon Valley." In *Building High-Tech Clusters: Silicon Valley and Beyond*, edited by Timothy Bresnahan and Alfonso Gambardella, 190–228. Cambridge: Cambridge University Press.

Saxenian, AnnaLee. 2006. *The New Argonauts: Regional Advantage in a Global Economy*. Cambridge, MA: Harvard University Press.

Schwabe, Julian 2020. "Risk and Counter-strategies: The Impact of Electric Mobility on German Automotive Suppliers." *Geoforum* 110: 157–67.

Scott, Allen J. 1988. *New Industrial Spaces: Flexible Production, Organisation and Regional Development in North America and Western Europe*. London: Pion.

Scott, Allen J. 1993. *Technopolis: High-Technology Industry and Regional Development in Southern California*. Berkeley: University of California Press.

Scott, Allen J., and David Angel. 1988. "The Global Assembly Operations of U.S. Semiconductor Firms: A Geographical Analysis." *Environment and Planning A* 20 (8): 1047–67.

Selwyn, Benjamin. 2012. *Workers, State and Development in Brazil: Powers of Labour, Chains of Value*. Manchester: Manchester University Press.

Shepherd, Ben. 2021. *The Post-Covid-19 Future for Global Value Chains*. Policy Brief, June 17, UNDP Regional Bureau for Asia and the Pacific, https://www.asia-pacific.undp.org/content/rbap/en/home/library/sustainable-development/the-post-covid-19-future-for-global-value-chains.html, accessed on June 25, 2021.

Shih, Willy C. 2020. "Global Supply Chains in a Post-pandemic World: Companies Need to Make Their Networks More Resilient; Here Is How." *Harvard Business Review* 98 (5): 82–89.

Shin, Jang-Sup. 2017. "A Dynamic Catch-Up Strategy in the Memory Industry and Changing Windows of Opportunity." *Research Policy* 46 (2): 404–16.

Shin, Namchul, Kenneth L. Kraemer, and Jason Dedrick. 2012. "Value Capture in the Global Electronics Industry: Empirical Evidence for the 'Smiling Curve' Concept." *Industry and Innovation* 19 (2): 89–107.

Shin, Namchul, Kenneth L. Kraemer, and Jason Dedrick. 2013. "Value Capture in Global Production Networks: Evidence from the Taiwanese Electronics Industry." *Journal of the Asia Pacific Economy* 19 (1): 74–88.

Shin, Namchul, Kenneth L. Kraemer, and Jason Dedrick. 2017. "R&D and Firm Performance in the Semiconductor Industry." *Industry and Innovation* 24 (3): 280–97.

Smedlund, Anssi, Arto Lindblom, and Lasse Mitronen, eds. 2018. *Collaborative Value Co-Creation in the Platform Economy*. Singapore: Springer.

Smith, Adrian. 2015. "The State, Institutional Frameworks and the Dynamics of Capital in Global Production Networks." *Progress in Human Geography* 39 (3): 290–315.

Solingen, Etel, ed. 2021. *Geopolitics, Supply Chains, and International Relations in East Asia*. Cambridge: Cambridge University Press.

Song, Yang. 2017. "Six Central Features of the Chinese Labour Market: A Literature Survey." *International Labour Review* 156 (2): 213–42.

Steffens, John. 1994. *Newgames: Strategic Competition in the PC Revolution*. Oxford: Pergamon.

Sterling, Toby. 2021. "ASML Exceeds Forecasts, Lifting Shares to Record High." *Reuters*, January 20, https://www.reuters.com/article/asml-holding-results-idCNL1N2JV0E9, accessed on January 23, 2021.

Stoneman, Paul. 1976. *Technological Diffusion and the Computer Revolution: The UK Experience*. Cambridge: Cambridge University Press.

Storper, Michael. 1997. *The Regional World: Territorial Development in a Global Economy*. New York: Guilford.

Storper, Michael. 2013. *Keys to the City: How Economics, Institutions, Social Interaction, and Politics Shape Development*. Princeton, NJ: Princeton University Press.

Storper, Michael, Thomas Kemeny, Naji Makarem, and Taner Osman. 2015. *The Rise and Decline of Great Urban Economies: Los Angeles and San Francisco Since 1970*. Stanford, CA: Stanford University Press.

Storper, Michael, and Robert Salais. 1997. *Worlds of Production: The Action Frameworks of the Economy*. Cambridge, MA: Harvard University Press.

Strange, Roger. 2020. "The 2020 COVID-19 Pandemic and Global Value Chains." *Journal of Industrial and Business Economics* 47: 455–65.

Strange, Roger, and John Humphrey. 2019. "What Lies between Market and Hierarchy? Insights from Internalization Theory and Global Value Chain Theory." *Journal of International Business Studies* 50 (8): 1401–13.

Sturgeon, Timothy J. 2002. "Modular Production Networks: A New American Model of Industrial Organization." *Industrial and Corporate Change* 11 (3): 451–96.

Sturgeon, Timothy J. 2021. "Upgrading Strategies for the Digital Economy." *Global Strategy Journal* 11 (1): 34–57.

Sturgeon, Timothy, John Humphrey, and Gary Gereffi. 2011. "Making the Global Supply Base." In *The Market Makers: How Retailers Are Reshaping the Global Economy*, edited by Gary G. Hamilton, Misha Petrovic and Benjamin Senauer, 231–54. Oxford: Oxford University Press.

Sun, Yutao, and Seamus Grimes. 2017. *China and Global Value Chains: Globalization and the Information and Communications Technology Sector*. London: Routledge.

Tan, Su-Lin. 2021. "Chinese Firms Outpace Regional Counterparts in 'De-risking' Supply Chains as Trend Grows in Asia-Pacific." *South China Morning Post*, May 14, https://www.scmp.com/economy/china-economy/article/3133388/chinese-firms-outpace-regional-counterparts-de-risking-supply, accessed on June 23, 2021.

Tan, Su-Lin, and Catherine Wong. 2021. "China Labels India, Australia, Japan Supply Chain Plan as 'Artificial' and 'Unfavourable' to Global Economy." *South China Morning Post*, April 28, https://www.scmp.com/print/economy/global-economy/article/3131449/china-labels-india-australia-japan-supply-chain-plan, accessed on June 23, 2021.

Tan, Yeling. 2021. *State Strategies Under Global Rules: Chinese Industrial Policy in the WTO Era*. Ithaca, NY: Cornell University Press.

Tatsumoto, Hirofum, Koichi Ogawa, and Takahiro Fujimoto. 2009. "The Effects of Technological Platforms on the International Division of Labor: A Case Study of Intel's Platform Business in the PC Industry." In *Platforms, Markets and Innovation*, edited by Annabelle Gawer, 345–67. Cheltenham, UK: Edward Elgar.

Teece, David J. 2009. *Dynamic Capabilities and Strategic Management: Organizing for Innovation and Growth*. Oxford: Oxford University Press.

Teece, David J. 2018. "Profiting from Innovation in the Digital Economy: Standards, Complementary Assets, and Business Models in the Wireless World." *Research Policy* 47 (8): 1367–87.

Tinguely, Xavier. 2013. *The New Geography of Innovation: Clusters, Competitiveness and Theory*. Basingstoke, UK: Palgrave Macmillan.

Tiwana, Amrit. 2014. *Platform Ecosystems: Aligning Architecture, Governance, and Strategy*. Amsterdam: Elsevier.

Tsang, Denise. 2002. *Business Strategy and National Culture: US and Asia Pacific Microcomputer Multinationals in Europe*. Cheltenham, UK: Edward Elgar.

Tyson, Laura D'Andrea. 1993. *Who's Bashing Whom? Trade Conflicts in High-Technology Industries*. Washington, DC: Institute for International Economics.

Tyson, Mark. 2020. "List of TSMC 5nm Customers and Their Orders Published." *HEXUS.net*, May 12, https://hexus.net/tech/news/industry/142480-list-tsmc-5nm-customers-orders-published, accessed on May 16, 2020.

UNCTAD. 2013. *World Investment Report 2013: Global Value Chains: Investment and Trade for Development*. New York: United Nations Conference on Trade and Development.

UNCTAD. 2020. *World Investment Report 2020: International Production Beyond the Pandemic*. New York: United Nations.

UNCTAD 2021. *World Investment Report 2021: Investing in Sustainable Recovery*. New York: United Nations.

van de Kerkhof, Mark, Jos P. Benschop, and Vadim Y. Banine. 2019. "Lithography for Now and the Future." *Solid-State Electronics* 155: 20–6.

Van Dijck, José, Thomas Poell, and Martijn de Waal. 2018. *The Platform Society: Public Values in a Connective World*. New York: Oxford University Press.

van Liemt, Gijsbert. 2016. "Hon Hai/Foxconn: Which Way Forward?" In *Flexible Workforces and Low Profit Margins: Electronics Assembly Between Europe and China*, edited by Jan Drahokoupil, Rutvica Andrijasevic and Devi Sacchetto, 45–66. Brussels: European Trade Union Institute.

Verbeke, Alan. 2020. "Will the COVID-19 Pandemic Really Change the Governance of Global Value Chains?" *British Journal of Management* 31 (3): 444–46.

Vicol, Mark, Niels Fold, Bill Pritchard, and Jeffrey Neilson. 2019. "Global Production Networks, Regional Development Trajectories and Smallholder Livelihoods in the Global South." *Journal of Economic Geography* 19 (4): 973–93.

Wade, Robert. 1990. *Governing the Market: Economic Theory and the Role of Government in East Asian Industrialization*. Princeton, NJ: Princeton University Press.

Wade, Robert. 2003. "What Strategies Are Viable for Developing Countries Today? The World Trade Organization and the Shrinking of 'Development Space.'" *Review of International Political Economy* 10 (4): 621–44.

Walter, Andrew, and Xiaoke Zhang, eds. 2012. *East Asian Capitalism: Diversity, Continuity, and Change*. Oxford: Oxford University Press.

Wang, I. Kim, and Russell Seidle. 2017. "The Degree of Technological Innovation: A Demand Heterogeneity Perspective." *Technological Forecasting & Social Change* 125: 166–77.

Wang, Orange. 2021a. "US-China Relations: Investment Environment Improving for American Firms, AmCham Survey Shows." *South China Morning Post*, March 9, https://www.scmp.com/economy/china-economy/

article/3124723/us-china-relations-investment-environment-improving-amer ican, accessed on June 24, 2021.

Wang, Orange. 2021b. "China's FDI Inflows Surge at Fastest Rate in 13 Years during First Quarter, Surpassing Pre-pandemic Level." *South China Morning Post*, April 15, https://www.scmp.com/economy/china-economy/article/3129713/ chinas-fdi-inflows-surge-fastest-rate-13-years-during-first, accessed on June 24, 2021.

Wayland, Michael. 2021. "Chip Shortage Expected to Cost Auto Industry \$210 billion in Revenue in 2021." *CNBC*, September 23, https://www.cnbc .com/2021/09/23/chip-shortage-expected-to-cost-auto-industry-210-billion -in-2021.html, accessed on November 1, 2021.

Weiss, Linda. 2005. "Global Governance, National Strategies: How Industrialized States Make Room to Move under the WTO." *Review of International Political Economy* 12 (5): 723–49.

Weiss, Linda. 2014. *America Inc.? Innovation and Enterprise in the National Security State.* Ithaca, NY: Cornell University Press.

Whang, Yun-kyung, and Michael Hobday. 2011. "Local 'Test Bed' Market Demand in the Transition to Leadership: The Case of the Korean Mobile Handset Industry." *World Development* 39 (8): 1358–71.

Whittaker, D. Hugh, Timothy Sturgeon, Toshie Okita, and Tianbiao Zhu. 2020. *Compressed Development: Time and Timing in Economic and Social Development.* Oxford: Oxford University Press.

Wilson, Jeffrey D. 2013. *Governing Global Production: Resource Networks in the Asia-Pacific Steel Industry.* New York: Palgrave.

Witt, Michael A., and Gordon Redding, eds. 2013. *The Oxford Handbook of Asian Business Systems.* Oxford: Oxford University Press.

Wong, Joseph. 2011. *Betting on Biotech: Innovation and the Limits of Asia's Development State.* Ithaca, NY: Cornell University Press.

Wong, Wilson Kia Onn. 2018. *Automotive Global Value Chain: The Rise of Mega Suppliers.* London: Routledge.

Woo-Cumings, Meredith, ed. 1999. *The Developmental State.* Ithaca, NY: Cornell University Press.

World Bank. 2013. *World Development Report 2014: Risk and Opportunity: Managing Risk for Development.* Washington, DC: World Bank.

World Bank. 2020. *World Development Report 2020: Trading for Development in the Age of Global Value Chains.* Washington, DC: World Bank.

World Economic Forum. 2020. *Covid-19 Risks Outlook: A Preliminary Mapping and Its Implications.* Geneva: World Economic Forum. https://www.wefo rum.org/reports/covid-19-risks-outlook-a-preliminary-mapping-and-its-im plications, accessed on May 20, 2020.

World Trade Organization. 2019. *Global Value Chain Development Report 2019*. Geneva: WTO.

World Trade Organization. 2021. *World Trade Primed For Strong But Uneven Recovery After COVID-19 Pandemic Shock*, Press Release #876 on March 31. Geneva: WTO.

WTO and IDE-JETRO. 2011. *Trade Patterns and Global Value Chains in East Asia: From Trade in Goods to Trade in Tasks*. Geneva and Tokyo: World Trade Organization and Institute of Developing Economies.

Woyke, Elizabeth. 2014. *The Smartphone: Anatomy of An Industry*. New York: New Press.

Wu, Debby 2020. "China's Days as World's Factory Are Over, iPhone Maker Says." *Bloomberg*, August 12, https://www.bloombergquint.com/business/hon-hai-beats-profit-estimates-after-pandemic-spurs-apple-demand, accessed on January 13, 2021.

Wu, Debby, Gabrielle Coppola, and Keith Naughton. 2021. "A Year of Poor Planning Led to Car Makers' Massive Chip Shortage." *Bloomberg*, January 19, https://www.bloomberg.com/news/articles/2021-01-19/a-year-of-poor-planning-led-to-carmakers-massive-chip-shortage, accessed on January 23, 2021.

Xing, Yuqing. 2021. *Decoding China's Export Miracle: A Global Value Chain Analysis*. Singapore: World Scientific.

Yang, Chun. 2014. "Market Rebalancing of Global Production Networks in the Post-Washington Consensus Globalizing Era: Transformation of Export-Oriented Development in China." *Review of International Political Economy* 21 (1): 130–56.

Yang, Chun. 2017. "The Rise of Strategic Partner Firms and Reconfiguration of Personal Computer Production Networks in China: Insights from the Emerging Laptop Cluster in Chongqing." *Geoforum* 84 (1): 21–31.

Yang, Heekyong. 2019. "Qualcomm to Appeal Record South Korean Anti-Trust Fine." *Reuters*, December 4, https://www.reuters.com/article/us-qualcomm-southkorea/qualcomm-to-appeal-record-south-korean-anti-trust-fine-idUSKBN1Y807J, accessed on December 22, 2019.

Yap, Xiao-Shan, and Rajah Rasiah. 2017. *Catching Up and Leapfrogging: The New Latecomers in the Integrated Circuits Industry*. New York: Routledge.

Ye, Josh. 2020. "China to Fall Short of Made in China 2025 Localisation Target for Integrated Circuits, says US Research Firm." *South China Morning Post*, May 22, https://www.scmp.com/print/tech/enterprises/article/3085656/china-fall-short-made-china-2025-localisation-target-integrated, accessed on June 12, 2020.

Ye, Josh. 2021a. "New Chinese Semiconductor Firms Have Tripled in 2021 as Beijing and Washington Jockey over Technological Supremacy." *South China Morning*

*Post*, June 9, https://www.scmp.com/tech/tech-war/article/3136660/new-chinese-semiconductor-firms-have-tripled-2021-beijing-and, accessed on June 23, 2021.

Ye, Josh 2021b. "Chinese State Media Pushes Back on Chip Nationalism after Social Media Vilifies TSMC's Nanjing Expansion." *South China Morning Post*, May 13, https://www.scmp.com/tech/tech-war/article/3133359/chinese-state-media-pushes-back-chip-nationalism-after-social-media, accessed on June 24, 2021.

Yeung, Henry Wai-chung. 2004. *Chinese Capitalism in a Global Era: Towards Hybrid Capitalism*. London: Routledge.

Yeung, Henry Wai-chung. 2007. "From Followers to Market Leaders: Asian Electronics Firms in the Global Economy." *Asia Pacific Viewpoint* 48 (1): 1–25.

Yeung, Henry Wai-chung. 2009. "Regional Development and the Competitive Dynamics of Global Production Networks: An East Asian Perspective." *Regional Studies* 43 (3): 325–51.

Yeung, Henry Wai-chung. 2014. "Governing the Market in a Globalizing Era: Developmental States, Global Production Networks, and Inter-firm Dynamics in East Asia." *Review of International Political Economy* 21 (1): 70–101.

Yeung, Henry Wai-chung. 2015. "Regional Development in the Global Economy: A Dynamic Perspective of Strategic Coupling in Global Production Networks." *Regional Science Policy & Practice* 7 (1): 1–23.

Yeung, Henry Wai-chung. 2016. *Strategic Coupling: East Asian Industrial Transformation in the New Global Economy*, Cornell Studies in Political Economy Series. Ithaca, NY: Cornell University Press.

Yeung, Henry Wai-chung. 2017. "Rethinking the East Asian Developmental State in Its Historical Context: Finance, Geopolitics, and Bureaucracy." *Area Development and Policy* 2 (1): 1–23.

Yeung, Henry Wai-chung. 2018. "The Logic of Production Networks." In *The New Oxford Handbook of Economic Geography*, edited by Gordon L. Clark, Maryann P. Feldman, Meric S. Gertler, and Dariusz Wójcik, 382–406. Oxford: Oxford University Press.

Yeung, Henry Wai-chung. 2019. "Rethinking Mechanism and Process in the Geographical Analysis of Uneven Development." *Dialogues in Human Geography* 9 (3): 226–55.

Yeung, Henry Wai-chung. 2021a. "Regional Worlds: From Related Variety in Regional Diversification to Strategic Coupling in Global Production Networks." *Regional Studies* 55 (6): 989–1010.

Yeung, Henry Wai-chung. 2021b. "The Trouble with Global Production Networks." *Environment and Planning A: Economy and Space* 53 (2): 428–38.

Yeung, Henry Wai-chung and Coe, Neil M. 2015. "Toward a Dynamic Theory of Global Production Networks." *Economic Geography* 91 (1): 29–58.

Yeung, Henry Wai-chung, Weidong Liu, and Peter Dicken. 2006. "Transnational Corporations and Network Effects of a Local Manufacturing Cluster in Mobile Telecommunications Equipment in China." *World Development* 34 (3): 520–40.

Yu, Howard, H., and Willy C. Shih. 2014. "Taiwan's PC Industry, 1976–2010: The Evolution of Organizational Capabilities." *Business History Review* 88 (2): 329–57.

Yu, Jiang, Rui Liu, and Feng Chen. 2020. "Linking Institutional Environment with Technological Change: The Rise of China's Flat Panel Display Industry." *Technological Forecasting and Social Change* 151: 119852.

Zeng, Ka, Karen Sebold, and Yue Lu. 2020. "Global Value Chains and Corporate Lobbying for Trade Liberalization." *Review of International Organizations* 15 (2): 409–43.

Zhang, Jane. 2021. "China's Semiconductors: How Wuhan's Challenger to Chinese Chip Champion SMIC Turned from Dream to Nightmare." *South China Morning Post*, March 20, https://www.scmp.com/tech/tech-trends/article/3126124/chinas-semiconductors-how-wuhans-challenger-chinese-chip-champion, accessed on June 21, 2021.

Zhou, Yu. 2008. *The Inside Story of China's High-Tech Industry*. Lanham, MA: Rowman and Littlefield.

Zumbach, Lauren. 2020. "Foxconn's Wisconsin Factory Isn't What It Initially Promised. Can It Still Turn Mount Pleasant into a High-Tech Hub?" *Chicago Tribune*, February 28, https://www.chicagotribune.com/business/ct-biz-foxconn-wisconsin-changing-plans-20200228-hn6wzt4fyzenpdeznicyw642qu-story.html, accessed on May 19, 2020.

Zysman, John, and Abraham Newman. 2006. "The State in the Digital Economy." In *The State After Statism: New State Activities in the Age of Liberalization*, edited by Jonah D. Levy, 271–300. Cambridge, MA: Harvard University Press.

Zysman, John, and Laura Tyson, eds. 1983. *American Industry in International Competition: Government Policies and Corporate Strategies*. Ithaca, NY: Cornell University Press.

# Index

Note: *f* denotes figure; *t* denotes table.

181; production networks in, 223; relationships in production of, 180; shift to notebooks from, 68, 69, 81, 134; world's top 5 desktop PC OEM firms by procurement unit share of key component suppliers, 2015 and 2018, 184–85*t*; world's top 6 desktop PC OEM firms by shipment and location of final assembly, 2015 and 2018, 146–47*t*

Device Solutions (Samsung), 80

Di Minin, Alberto, 50

domestic economic liberalization, 118–19

dominant suppliers, 73, 180, 188–89, 190–91, 252, 281

Dongbu HiTek, 54*t*

DRAM (dynamic random-access memory), 45, 47, 48–49, 58, 234

DRAM chips, 188, 189

dual-purpose foundry fabs, 204–5

dual sourcing, 190, 208

DynaTAC 8000x, 73

Eagle, 65

East Asia: causal dynamics and key geographical and organizational configurations of production networks in global electronics, 2010–2021, 268–69*t*; competitive success of, 9; countries in, 2; development of firm-specific capabilities of to serve as "system integrators," 27; as dominant macroregion for production and consumption of ITC goods, 125; evolving national and institutional contexts of industry development in selected economies of, 1980–2021, 24–25*t*; firm strategies, organizational dynamics, and geographical configurations in electronics global production networks, 2018–2021, 219*t*; geographical configurations

of global electronics centered in, 123–72; geographical configurations of production in during 2010s, 161*t*; growth and development in technological and production capabilities of domestic electronics firms in, 20; as having extensive interfirm relationships with US lead firms, 5; as leading producer of intermediate and final goods, 125; as major market for intermediate and final goods, 125; shift in electronic manufacturing production networks toward, 4–5; shift of PC production toward, 68; strong presence of in semiconductor fabrication, 164, 167

Economic Development Board Investment (Singapore), 261

economic liberalization, 17, 118–19

Economic Planning Board (South Korea), 26

economic risk, 104*t*

electronic design automation (EDA), 56

electronics manufacturing services (EMS), 21, 29, 78–79, 117, 178

electronics production: coevolution in worlds of, 80; complex and globalized worlds of, 2; current trajectories and future agendas, 273–306; global integration in, 90; global market for before early 1990s, 14; integrating national worlds of, 88*f*; shift to global production networks spearheaded by US firms focusing largely on East Asia, 3–5, 9

Electronic Technology Research Institute (South Korea), 22

emerging worlds, as one of three historical periods of coevolution in complexity and interconnectedness, 13, 17–26

end market dynamics, 277

Lightning Source UK Ltd.
Milton Keynes UK
UKHW041054070722
405507UK00006B/192